User Behavior in Ubiquitous Online Environments

Jean-Eric Pelet
IDRAC International School of Management, Nantes University, KMCMS, France

Panagiota Papadopoulou
University of Athens, Greece

A volume in the Advances in Human and
Social Aspects of Technology (AHSAT)
Book Series

An Imprint of IGI Global

Managing Director:	Lindsay Johnston
Production Manager:	Jennifer Yoder
Publishing Systems Analyst:	Adrienne Freeland
Development Editor:	Austin DeMarco
Acquisitions Editor:	Kayla Wolfe
Typesetter:	Christina Barkanic
Cover Design:	Jason Mull

Published in the United States of America by
Information Science Reference (an imprint of IGI Global)
701 E. Chocolate Avenue
Hershey PA 17033
Tel: 717-533-8845
Fax: 717-533-8661
E-mail: cust@igi-global.com
Web site: http://www.igi-global.com

Library of Congress Cataloging-in-Publication Data

User behavior in ubiquitous online environments / Jean-Eric Pelet and
Panagiota Papadopoulou, editors.
     pages cm
  Includes bibliographical references and index.
    ISBN 978-1-4666-4566-0 (hardcover) -- ISBN 978-1-4666-4567-7 (ebook) --
ISBN 978-1-4666-4568-4 (print & perpetual access) 1. Telematics. 2. Human-
computer interaction. 3. Ubiquitous computing. 4. Mobile computing. I.
Pelet, Jean-Eric, 1976- II. Papadopoulou, Panagiota, 1975-
  TK5105.6.U74 2014
  004.01'9--dc23
                                    2013027722

This book is published in the IGI Global book series Advances in Human and Social Aspects of Technology (AHSAT)
(ISSN: 2328-1316; eISSN: 2328-1324)

British Cataloguing in Publication Data
A Cataloguing in Publication record for this book is available from the British Library.

All work contributed to this book is new, previously-unpublished material. The views expressed in this book are those of the authors, but not necessarily of the publisher.

Advances in Human and Social Aspects of Technology (AHSAT) Book Series

Ashish Dwivedi
The University of Hull, UK

ISSN: 2328-1316
EISSN: 2328-1324

MISSION

In recent years, the societal impact of technology has been noted as we become increasingly more connected and are presented with more digital tools and devices. With the popularity of digital devices such as cell phones and tablets, it is crucial to consider the implications of our digital dependence and the presence of technology in our everyday lives.

The **Advances in Human and Social Aspects of Technology (AHSAT) Book Series** seeks to explore the ways in which society and human beings have been affected by technology and how the technological revolution has changed the way we conduct our lives as well as our behavior. The AHSAT book series aims to publish the most cutting-edge research on human behavior and interaction with technology and the ways in which the digital age is changing society.

COVERAGE

- Activism & ICTs
- Computer-Mediated Communication
- Cultural Influence of ICTs
- Cyber Behavior
- End-User Computing
- Gender & Technology
- Human-Computer Interaction
- Information Ethics
- Public Access to ICTs
- Technoself

IGI Global is currently accepting manuscripts for publication within this series. To submit a proposal for a volume in this series, please contact our Acquisition Editors at Acquisitions@igi-global.com or visit: http://www.igi-global.com/publish/.

Titles in this Series

For a list of additional titles in this series, please visit: www.igi-global.com

User Behavior in Ubiquitous Online Environments
Jean-Eric Pelet (IDRAC International School of Management, LEMNA, IAE-IEMN – Nantes University, France) and Panagiota Papadopoulou (University of Athens, Greece)
Information Science Reference • copyright 2014 • 310pp • H/C (ISBN: 9781466645660) • US $175.00 (our price)

Innovative Methods and Technologies for Electronic Discourse Analysis
Hwee Ling Lim (The Petroleum Institute-Abu Dhabi, UAE) and Fay Sudweeks (Murdoch University, Australia)
Information Science Reference • copyright 2014 • 546pp • H/C (ISBN: 9781466644267) • US $175.00 (our price)

New Media Influence on Social and Political Change in Africa
Anthony A. Olorunnisola (Pennsylvania State University, USA) and Aziz Douai (University of Ontario Institute of Technology, Canada)
Information Science Reference • copyright 2013 • 373pp • H/C (ISBN: 9781466641976) • US $175.00 (our price)

Cases on Usability Engineering Design and Development of Digital Products
Miguel A. Garcia-Ruiz (Algoma University, Canada)
Information Science Reference • copyright 2013 • 470pp • H/C (ISBN: 9781466640467) • US $175.00 (our price)

Human Rights and Information Communication Technologies Trends and Consequences of Use
John Lannon (University of Limerick, Ireland) and Edward Halpin (Leeds Metropolitan University, UK)
Information Science Reference • copyright 2013 • 324pp • H/C (ISBN: 9781466619180) • US $175.00 (our price)

Collaboration and the Semantic Web Social Networks, Knowledge Networks, and Knowledge Resources
Stefan Brüggemann (Astrium Space Transportation, Germany) and Claudia d'Amato (University of Bari, Italy)
Information Science Reference • copyright 2012 • 387pp • H/C (ISBN: 9781466608948) • US $175.00 (our price)

Human Rights and Risks in the Digital Era Globalization and the Effects of Information Technologies
Christina M. Akrivopoulou (Democritus University of Thrace, Greece) and Nicolaos Garipidis (Aristotle University of Thessaloniki, Greece)
Information Science Reference • copyright 2012 • 363pp • H/C (ISBN: 9781466608917) • US $180.00 (our price)

Technology for Creativity and Innovation Tools, Techniques and Applications
Anabela Mesquita (ISCAP/IPP and Algoritmi Centre, University of Minho, Portugal)
Information Science Reference • copyright 2011 • 426pp • H/C (ISBN: 9781609605193) • US $180.00 (our price)

www.igi-global.com

701 E. Chocolate Ave., Hershey, PA 17033
Order online at www.igi-global.com or call 717-533-8845 x100
To place a standing order for titles released in this series, contact: cust@igi-global.com
Mon-Fri 8:00 am - 5:00 pm (est) or fax 24 hours a day 717-533-8661

Table of Contents

Detailed Table of Contents

Chapter 1

  Yuuki Kato, Sagami Women's University, Japan
  Shogo Kato, Tokyo Woman's Christian University, Japan
  Kunihiro Chida, Toei Animation Co., Ltd., Japan

This study investigates the timing of replies to mobile phone text messages focusing especially on the timing of replies from the perspective of the "recipient" of the message. In a previous study, the authors evaluated the timing of replies and the emotional strategies associated with such timing from the perspective of the "sender" and found they employed an emotional strategy whereby they "waited" before responding to mobile text messages in order to continue positive communication. In the present study, they examine if the same strategy is as effective from the perspective of recipients of the messages. Specifically, study participants were asked by questionnaire to rate what emotions they would feel and to what degree when the other party waited before replying to the mobile text messages the participants had sent, where the message sent had conveyed one of four emotions: happiness, sadness, anger, or guilt. These four emotional scenarios are the same as used in the previous study to allow for comparative analysis of the two studies. Additionally, participants in the present study were asked to provide freeform responses for scenarios where they felt it was desirable to wait before replying themselves. The results show differences between the emotional strategic intent of senders for waiting before replying, as determined in the previous study, and how this is perceived by the recipients. The results suggest that there are gaps in perception between senders and recipients regarding the intentional manipulation of reply timing (especially waiting before replying). One suggested gap is that senders that intentionally manipulate the timing of replies for negative or hostile emotions, such as sadness, anger, or guilt, run the risk of making the recipient feel the opposite of the sender's intended outcome.

Chapter 2

This chapter examines how local residents were informed and rallied by the Internet and mobile phone messages for an unprecedented protest against the construction of a hazardous chemical plant in Xiamen, China, and how the municipal government responded by encouraging public participation in environmental decision making via the same communicational platforms. Using combined research methods including interviews and secondary data analysis, this research investigates the role of the Internet and cell phone message in mobilizing the general public to participate in the environmental protection movement in China. The role of Word Of Mouth (WOM) in the environmental movement is discovered for the first time. The unique mechanism of cellular telephones and the Internet in public participation involving multiple stakeholders in China's environmental policy-making process is also discussed.

Chapter 3

This chapter analyses the evolution of the Internet, shifting from a decentralized architecture designed around the end-to-end principle with powerful mainframe/personal computers at each end, to a more centralized network designed according to the mainframe model, with increasingly weaker user's devices that no longer have the ability to run a server nor to process any consistent amount of data or information. The advantages of ubiquitous computing (allowing data to become available from anywhere and at any time regardless of the device) should thus be counterbalanced with the costs it entails (loss of users' autonomy, concerns as regards privacy, and freedom of expression, etc.).

Chapter 4

In this chapter, the authors present the project "WITE 2.0." This project is at the crossroads of various issues related to mobility (Urry, 2007) and use of Information and Communication Technologies. WITE 2.0 is a part of the designing process of a collaborative communication tool: "a virtualized and unified platform." The authors define scenarios of teleworking practices, "equipped" by ICTs, and use these scenarios to better specify the platform. The project started at the end of 2010 and continued for a period of 18 months. The analysis is based on several complementary methodologies: a qualitative study (47 semi-structured interviews) and an experimentation of the platform. They present the main results of the interview survey through the following themes: remote management, skills, articulation of private and professional spheres, and the maturity of technologies. The authors also describe how these elements help the understanding of the evolution of workers' practices.

Chapter 5

Shang Gao, Zhongnan University of Economics and Law, China

Little research has been done to explore the adoption of mobile information services from a cultural perspective. This research is designed to study mobile information services adoption from a cultural perspective. Based on the two cultural dimensions (individualism/collectivism, uncertainty avoidance), two research hypotheses are presented. To examine these hypotheses, an exploratory study is carried out with a mobile information service called Mobile Tourist Service Recommender (MTSR) system with both respondents from developed countries and China. According to the results, one research hypothesis is supported, while the other research hypothesis (H1) is not supported in this exploratory study. The findings indicate that the cultural dimensions play important roles in how mobile information services are used and adopted in two different cultural settings: culture in developed countries and the Chinese culture. The results also highlight the relevance of the cultural dimensions (individualism/collectivism, uncertainty avoidance) as the factors affecting the adoption of mobile information services.

Chapter 6

Anna Kasimati, University of Piraeus, Athens
Sofia Mysirlaki, University of Piraeus, Athens
Hara Bouta, University of Piraeus, Athens
Fotini Paraskeva, University of Piraeus, Athens

The rise of mobile broadband devices and services has significantly changed the role of mobile devices in people's daily lives by enabling the provision of innovative applications and services anywhere, anytime. Despite the fact that new ideas and innovation mainly occur within Higher Education Institutions (HEIs), the adoption of mobile and ubiquitous technologies by HEIs is still in its early stages. This chapter attempts to provide a framework to support Higher Education Institutions towards implementing mobile and ubiquitous, game-based learning activities. Aligned with the objective of this book, this chapter presents some examples and best practices of implementing this framework towards achieving the learning goals of future professionals in the fields of electronic and ubiquitous commerce.

Chapter 7

Latifa Chaari, Higher Institute of Management of Tunis, Tunisia

This chapter aims at better understanding the behavior of the Internet user. It suggests studying the role of communication on the trust of Internet users towards commercial Websites. In order to realize this research, the authors mobilized the Communicative Action Theory of Jürgen Habermas (1987). Therefore, they have brought a new perspective in understanding online trust following action theory. For Habermas, communication is an action that depends on contextual, cultural, and human factors, which cannot be reduced to deterministic mechanisms. He deals with three types of action, which an actor might pursue following his interests, which can be instrumental, strategic, or emancipatory. The instrumental and strategic are purposive-rational actions, which aim at achieving success and at developing a calculated trust based on calculation of the advantages and the costs of the relation, whereas, the communicative action is coordinated by mutual understanding that allows the development of a relational trust based on social interactions. In communicative action, mutual understanding through language allows the social integration of actors and the coordination of their plans and their different interests. In this case, trust is based on a common definition of the situation and the resolution of conflicts of interests between actors. Internet is a medium of communication that can support the three kinds of action. The instrumental and strategic actions allow the development of calculated trust, whereas the communicative action allows the development of relational trust based on social interaction and mutual comprehension.

Chapter 8

There are growing concerns over the user friendliness and other usability issues of South African Universities' Web Portal Interfaces (UWPIs), which obviously will negate the user acceptance of the UWPIs. The main goal of this study is to develop a framework that could be used to evaluate and provide additional guidelines to improve the Usability and User Acceptance of South African UWPIs. The study applies a triangulation of Ubiquitous computing Evaluation Areas (UEAs) and the Technology Acceptance Model (TAM) as theoretical foundations to derive the research model. Multiple regression and stepwise regression analyses are used. The results suggest that Interaction and Invisibility of UWPIs are the most important measures that have a huge impact on user acceptance and usability, respectively. The results of the study provide guidelines for the design and development of South Africa UWPIs to meet their usability and user acceptance.

Chapter 9

Flow theory, as a basis to facilitate the development of compelling experiences, has received growing attention over the past two decades. Facing this plethora of interest, it is obvious that telepresence and flow in human-computer interactions are important issues. The objectives of this chapter is to review and empirically analyze the relationships among flow theory, the telepresence concept, and online behaviour. Particularly, this research investigates the impact of telepresence and flow on Websites visitors' visit time, perceived visit time, and number of visited pages. An online survey was conducted. The findings indicate that telepresence has a positive effect on the flow state, as measured by concentration and enjoyment. The consumers' level of concentration positively influenced their visit time, perceived visit time, and number of visited pages. Enjoyment has a positive effect on perceived visit time, but no significant effect on actual visit time and number of visited pages. Discussion and implications of these results are exhibited. Suggestions concerning future research are also presented.

Madhavi M. Chakrabarty, Verizon Wireless, USA

Organizations constantly strive to improve the richness and reach of their knowledge resources to ensure optimal performance of their employees in their job functions. Some of the techniques that organizations have used in the past have included state-of-the-art search engines, creating a directed navigation by mapping content to employee transactions, and incorporating user experience design heuristics. Search engine improvement is reputed to be the most used technique, even though its effectiveness in organizational knowledge management systems has not been confirmed. With more and more organizations now having a mobile employee base, there is now a need to provide employees access to organizational resources anytime and anywhere. This chapter provides insight into some of the challenges in organizational knowledge management systems and the implications of designing a mobile system. It proposes some heuristics on designing a knowledge management system for mobile systems and proposes a framework to validate it against available user acceptance models.

Marie Haikel-Elsabeh, University Paris X, France

What are the drivers for Brand engagement and implication on Facebook? In order to explore the impact of motivations on content and information sharing on Facebook brand pages, this study proposes an analysis focused on a reduced number of motivations and a proposal of a statistical model attempting to link the frequency of posting and liking on Facebook in general and Brand engagement to motivations. The aim of the study is to assess the impact of motivations on brand implication and frequency of posting on Facebook. The authors use the concept of brand implication measure a deep interest toward brands on Facebook. The concept of frequency of posting and liking focuses on the tendency to post or like frequently each time the user connects to Facebook. The motivations the authors introduced are based on the literature for sharing on social networks.

Foreword

Online communication is not a new phenomenon. However, the ubiquity of online communication is new. Furthermore, the rapid development of ubiquitous online environments caught Internet observers off guard. There was no way to anticipate how the advent of smart cellular telephones and computer tablets would lead to users living online 24/7. Today, individuals and organizations maintain an ongoing online presence as a matter of practice and a lived reality of modern life. Virtual life as a parallel and omnipresent reality has captured the interest of users in both developed and developing countries, of men and women, adults and children, the educated and the learning, the wealthy and the poor. Food, clothing, shelter, and cell phones have become the necessities of modern life.

Indeed, checking online messages (email, Websites, blogs, social media, and so forth) has become ubiquitous in every way. Almost every person on the planet who can financially afford one (and many people who cannot) possess a smart telephone. Users carry their devises with them at all times and sleep with them at their bedsides. These devises are omnipresent; they are out and in use in business meetings, government hearings, courtrooms, classrooms, restaurants, and family dinners. The propensity of users to simultaneously live online and off-line raises a number of questions concerning user behavior that simply could not be observed or studied until the manifestation of the phenomenon itself—in other words until now. The book you hold in your hand is among the first to address questions relevant to this new ubiquity.

The purpose of this book is to examine how ubiquity (a) influences user behavior and, as a result, ultimately (b) influences the mechanisms designed to facilitate user behavior. As with any first effort, the book covers a wide range of relevant topics. Examined issues of ubiquity range from users' motivations to engage with Facebook to the evolution of workers' online practices, from managing mobile employee databases to texting practices on cell phones. By carefully curating examinations of such diverse contexts and issues, the editors allow the reader's focus to remain on the overriding concern of discerning patterns in user behavior in ubiquitous online environments.

The chapter authors appear to achieve the impossible: They provide appropriate theoretical perspectives, employ sound analytic and research methodologies, as well as translate their results into practical advice. Therefore, the book will prove useful for scholars, users, and practitioners who desire to understand the influence of ubiquity on user behavior in private and commercial ventures.

The most impressive feature of this book is its scope. Chapter authors employed multiple sound methodologies (i.e., historical analysis, interviews, online surveys, freeform responses to scenarios, and experimental platforms) to collect data in multiple countries (i.e., China, France, Japan, South Africa, Tunisia, United States of America). The researchers examined many important objects of study:

- Evolution of the Internet.
- Websites including commercial Websites and retailer Websites.
- Web management tools such as corporate knowledge management systems, university Web portals, and collaborative research tools.
- Trends in user behavior such as adoption of mobile information, brand engagement, and the timing of texts.

The book's most impressive scholarly achievement, however, is the examination of a long list of variables containing some classic concerns in studies of online behavior (i.e., telepresence, usability, relational trust, privacy, user-friendliness, uncertainty avoidance) as well as some relative newcomers (e.g., flow, motivations for posting, frequency of posting, sender versus receiver perspectives) in studies that yielded interesting results in the new worldwide ubiquity of online behavior.

Taking the book's body of work as a whole, researchers appear to be moving from assessing individual users' perspectives and behaviors to assessing the interactions (a) between users as well as (b) between users and platforms—an appropriate evolution in assessment, given the tendency in ubiquitous online environments for users to conduct both personal and professional business online. It is important to note that such an observation (the above-described shift in the focus of assessment) could only be achieved by examining a collection such as this—a well selected, edited, and curated collection of original research on user behavior in ubiquitous online environments.

The book contained herein is necessarily limited, given that user behavior in ubiquitous online environments is a relatively new phenomenon and given that the research examining the phenomenon is in its infancy. Nonetheless, this book fills an important scholarly niche by beginning conversations about how to study and adapt to user behavior in ubiquitous online environments. All explorations must begin somewhere, and this book provides a particularly good beginning.

I laud the book editors for beginning the exploration of user behavior in ubiquitous online environments on a multi-national level and with such an impressive collection of research reports. The book captures the current state of knowledge on user behavior in ubiquitous online environments, as each chapter begins with a review of past and relevant research. Equally important, the book "pushes the envelope" of our knowledge and research methods by featuring new and exciting studies of previously unexplored phenomena—research at the heart of this bedeviling, new ubiquity.

In short, this wonderful collection makes an important contribution to both research and practice on the new, exciting subject of user behavior in ubiquitous online environments. This book represents a necessary and appropriate beginning to the scholarly conversation on user behavior in ubiquitous online environments. The editors did a masterful job of beginning to answer important questions about the phenomenon. They did so by collecting, editing, and curating multiple perspectives from multiple countries that speak eloquently to the innovations in user behavior in ubiquitous online environments. Congratulations to Jean-Eric Pelet and Peggy Papadopoulou on an important collection.

Lynne M. Webb
Florida International University, USA

Lynne M. Webb *(PhD, University of Oregon, 1980) is Professor of Communication Arts, Florida International University, and J. William Fulbright Master Researcher, University of Arkansas. She has published two scholarly readers, including Computer Mediated Communication in Personal Relationships, and over 70 essays including multiple theories, research reports, and pedagogical essays.*

Preface

Let's imagine that we are swimming at the swimming pool (see Figure 1), wearing our "Arena Glasses," different than the "Google Glasses" since they can be used beneath the surface of the water, in a zone where WIFI, RFID, Bluetooth, and other wireless communication technologies cannot work. Rather than counting the number of lengths at the pool, the Arena goggles enable me to shop thanks to the virtual reality application, which is used by my preferred brand for shopping food. I can fly in the shelves of the shop like I used to fly in World of Warcraft or Second Life in order to find the best parmesan to accommodate it with my pasta, my dinner of the day. I will then easily find the tomato sauce, since this u-commerce store allows customers to find all they need for a special dish at once, without having to run from one corner of the store to the other one in order to complete the dinner based on pasta, parmesan, and tomato sauce…. This is what could be possible very soon, if technology keeps on progressing this way.

Felix Baumgartner (see Figure 2) was able to send a SMS a few seconds before jumping from the space capsule attached to a giant helium balloon above the so-called "Armstrong Line." There is no phone line in space, but he was able anyway to send SMSs…as he could also do some shopping during these last very intensive minutes before jumping. All this should be possible in a foreseeable future where connectivity will provide broadband Internet access to individuals, even if customers are swimming or trekking in the desert.

This is not a dream, it's a prevision based on the speed of propagation of wireless technologies as well as the progression of the mobile devices we use every day. Progression in terms of energy savings, in terms of performance, in terms of ease of use and usability as well as accessibility, and progression in their capacity to find Internet signals in order to be connected at anytime, almost anywhere…

Figure 1. Swimmer

Figure 2. Felix Baumgartner jumps from the space capsule after sending an SMS and doing some shopping on his mobile

This is the theme of this book, dedicated to the next step of the shopping era where after exchanges made from outskirts to centers of town, as explained by Braudel (2008), about the history of capitalism which can be traced back to early forms of merchant capitalism practiced in Western Europe during the Middle Ages, we can now do shopping in our favorite swimming pool in parallel to maintaining our body as healthy as possible.

Ubiquitous is an adjective originated since mid 19th century, from modern Latin ubiquitas (from Latin ubique 'everywhere', from ubi 'where') which means present, appearing, or found everywhere especially at the same time, according to the Oxford dictionary. Applied to commerce, it can mean that people are able to do shopping anytime, anywhere. This seems difficult to see this in practice since shopping malls and in-store commerce exist in proper places, with no possibilities for consumers to modify the latter, but once it is in relation to the electronic commerce, this assumption becomes possible. Indeed, the progression of technology now enables each of us to conduct transactions with a device which is diversely affordable depending on the region of the world it is sold, according to the exigency of the owner or future owner in terms of design, technical, or network capabilities, but which enables anyone to buy, sell, share, give, steal sometimes, somehow easily. This raises plenty of questions that this book strives to pose as well as to answer. In order to offer the most up to date content to our readers, we conducted a speed process of edition by asking academic authors to provide a chapter on the following topic: "User Behavior in Ubiquitous Online Environments."

Based on 11 chapters written by 15 authors from 8 countries (Japan, France, China, Greece, South, Africa, Tunisia, USA), during a period of 7 months after release of the call for chapters, this book was written following a usual double (sometimes triple) blind review process, during 3 waves of submissions. In order to keep anonymity for both authors and reviewers, the reviewers have not been apprised of the authors' names or institutions in the submitted chapters. The aim of the book was to introduce a concept that is still quite new in 2013, which originated from a conversation we had last year with a philosopher about the possibilities of shopping, learning, communicating, and so on in a near future. His answers referred to ubiquity with almost no constraints, enabling consumers with seamless, personalized solutions across the full buying process to shop the way they want, even away from wifi or 3G/4G zones. Indeed, as consumers demand greater access to information, offers, and payment functionality anytime, anywhere, the lines between offline and online shopping, between in-store commerce, e-commerce, and mobile commerce are blurring. This gives the opportunity to evoke ubiquity, in particular to an academic audience, issued from several fields of study such as marketing, information systems, business and management, media and communication, law, social and economic sciences, computer sciences and knowledge management, and even art. The interested reader is advised to read Kato, Kato, and Chida (2013) for more information on this topic.

The onset of electronic/mobile commerce, electronic/mobile learning, and knowledge management technologies, on screens from desktops and laptops, but also on devices such as smartphones, tablets, watches or glasses, combined with other technologies has an impact on organizations and their relationships within/outside their boundaries. This impact plays in favor of social changes in our western and eastern societies, progressively transforming human beings into ubiquitous human beings.

This edited book intends to assess the impact of u-commerce, u-learning, and u-knowledge management technologies on different organizations, such as online stores, higher education institutions, multinational corporations, health providers, and others. It also integrates multiple theoretical perspectives where they are needed and make industry specific comparisons of e-m-commerce, e-m-learning, and knowledge management technologies and their practices.

Current scholarship on ubiquitous technologies and their impact on user behavior is rather scarce. As ubiquitous online applications are increasingly used in various contexts, new models of user activity emerge. The behavior of users is changed in unprecedented ways that are yet to be explored, as our knowledge with respect to the ubiquitous user is still limited. There is an emerging need for researchers and practitioners to fully understand the potential of ubiquitous environments for successful commercial, educational, entertainment, or any other type of activity, and the changes they impose to existing to user behavior. This book intends to fill this gap, providing a systematic synthesis of the latest research findings and professional experience on ubiquitous online environments and user behavior.

This book aims to provide relevant theoretical frameworks and the latest empirical research findings regarding ubiquitous computing and ubiquitous online environments. It will be valuable to academics and practitioners who want to improve their understanding of the strategic impact of ubiquitous technologies in a wide range of applications and organizations in sectors such as business, commerce, marketing, knowledge management, learning, entertainment, human-computer interaction, and social media. The book aspires to bring together the latest academic research and professional practice, covering all aspects of ubiquitous user activity and behavior in diverse contexts. It thus offers concentrated knowledge and a much needed structured roadmap for studying, planning, and implementing ubiquitous technology strategies for all types of organizations.

The target audience of this book can be composed of researchers and professionals working in the field of marketing, information systems, IT-enabled change, and change management in various disciplines, including library, information, and communication sciences; administrative sciences and management; education; adult education; sociology; computer science; and information technology. Moreover, the book provides insights and support to executives concerned with the management of e- and m-commerce, e- and m-learning, and knowledge management applications, as well as enable the assessment of the organizational impact of such applications in different environments.

The book points to a gradual move from engineering-driven to socioeconomic-focused research about u-commerce. It aims at providing a glimpse into the questions on m-commerce researchers' minds today. Research on mobile and tablets commerce is attracting the interest of e-commerce scholars ever since mobile and portable devices become a widespread and effective means of commercial transactions and business practices. However, it also allows us to investigate what lies ahead in the future of m-commerce research as we move toward the more social-minded, hyperconnected world of tomorrow's social commerce (s-commerce) while entering the still unknown u-commerce era.

Kato, Kato, and Chida have investigated the timing of replies to mobile phone text messages focusing especially on the timing of replies from the perspective of the "recipient" of the message. In a previous study, they evaluated the timing of replies and the emotional strategies associated with such timing from the perspective of the "sender" and found they employed an emotional strategy whereby they "waited" before responding to mobile text messages in order to continue positive communication." In the present study, "Reply Timing as Emotional Strategy in Mobile Text Communications of Japanese Young People: Focusing on Perceptual Gaps between Senders and Recipients," the authors examined if the same strategy was as effective from the perspective of recipients of the messages. Specifically, study participants were asked by questionnaire to rate what emotions they would feel and to what degree when the other party waited before replying to the mobile text messages the participants had sent, where the message sent had conveyed one of four emotions: happiness, sadness, anger, or guilt. These four emotional scenarios are the same as used in a previous study, to allow for comparative analysis of the two studies. Additionally, participants in the present study were asked to provide freeform responses for scenarios where they felt it was desirable to wait before replying themselves. The results showed differences between the emotional strategic intent of senders for waiting before replying, as determined in the previous study, and how this was actually perceived by the recipients. The results suggest that there are gaps in perception between senders and recipients regarding the intentional manipulation of reply timing (especially waiting before replying). One suggested gap is that senders that intentionally manipulate the timing of replies for negative or hostile emotions such as sadness, anger, or guilt, actually run the risk of making the recipient feel the opposite of the sender's intended outcome.

In her chapter, "Texted Environmental Campaign in China: A Case Study of New Media Communication," Wang explains that mass media have been a central public arena for disseminating environmental issues and contesting claims, arguments, and opinions about our use and protection of the environment (Hansen, 2010). Media products, together with perceptions of the products by their audiences, make an impact upon political decision-makers regarding a wide scope of issues related to environmental protection issues. Over the past decade, there has been a clear transition in the environment communication domain: The scope for the concept of the environment has been expanded from natural phenomenon to an anthropocentric abstraction form representing the totality of nature (Walker, 2005). Communication scholars therefore need to examine the environmental issues from racial, socio-economic, political (Hansen, 2010), and cultural perspectives (Deluca, 1999; Gibbs, 1993). In other words, mass media need to approach environmental movements and organizations as a "collection of agencies making social problems claims" (Yearley, 1991, p. 52). Communication is the central means for the general public to understand the environmental issues, and mass media has been the major platform to shape the public opinion. Mass media also influence the pattern of their users' information-seeking behaviors. On the other hand, the drastically worsening natural environment in China has been routinely underrepresented or ignored in traditional media, due to its sensitive nature and potential threaten to "social stability." The environmental protection awareness among Chinese people is relatively low, and civic engagement in environmental policy-making is not encouraged by the government. Therefore, there is a need for readers to understand the strength and weakness of new media in environmental decision-making process in a special social and political context such as China.

This chapter aims to draw a dynamic map about how the environmental message was initiated and disseminated using Web-based communicational channels, and how the message tailor-made based on the natures of the Internet and cell phone mobilized the public participation in environmental protection events. To be specific, this study addresses mechanisms of mobile phone and the Internet as powerful communication channels to call for public attention on environmental issues and organize environmental protection events. The Web-based technology makes it possible for people with different social and economic backgrounds (especially marginalized grassroots) in China to communicate effectively while dealing with environmental problems and engaging in policy-making process. Besides the analysis based on mass communication frameworks, the Word Of Mouth (WOM) communication at interpersonal level is also investigated in this study. Drawing on the personal experience by witnesses and participants in Xiamen PX protest, this chapter addresses the roles of the Internet and mobile phone in China's environmental decision-making process by analyzing the delivery channels of the environmental decision, most circulated messages in the Internet and mobile phone during the street protest period, as well as documents related to the case. Data used in this chapter was retrieved from survey, in-depth interviews, and secondary data in December 2010. A triangulation of quantitative (regression analysis) and qualitative (content analysis) methods are employed to identify the key issues of China's environmental movement using Web-based technology and patterns of messages used in the new media sphere. The outcome of the regression analysis provides an opportunity for the author to have a primary look at the relationship among the variables included in the model, and identify the possible factors that have an impact upon people's willingness to participate environmental protection events. The statistical outputs show that a positive and strong association between age and people's willingness to join environmental protection movements, a negative and strong association between the reception of PX text message and the willingness of environmental participation, and a weak and positive relationship between the number of people whom respondents relayed text message to and the dependent variable. The examination of the most quoted environmental and protest messages from the Internet and mobile phone indicates that messages are carefully designed and disseminated through various channels (opinion leaders, platforms on the Internet, mobile phones, and WOM) to reach its target audience to the greatest extent. Given that all the literature made a distinguishable focus on persuasive effects of mobile phone text and online message, it is surprising to find that over than half of the respondents reported that they first learned about the PX project through friends, relatives, or other interpersonal channels. A graph mapping the dynamic flow of the environmental information in PX protest is also provided to illustrate how the information regarding the polluting PX project was initiated by the opinion leader(s), processed and delivered by the online media, and finally reached the general public. The information simultaneously reached the interest group and environmental group via online platforms from opinion leaders. But the two parties delivered messages through different communicational channels to its audience, the Internet and WOM used by the environmental group and mobile text message by interest group. Future research could be conducted on whether and how the Internet and mobile phone could facilitate cooperative activities in environmental campaigns across the globe, and how the pressure group's message could be tailor-made to address the trend of globalization in dealing with environmental issues and compete for mainstream media attention to the greatest extent. The study on how opinion leaders utilize new technology in environmental protection events could be furthered to their capability of influencing or shaping grassroots' opinion, and their perception of the effectiveness of the completed environmental campaign. The scarcity of scholarly work in media and environmental issues in oriental culture suggests a meta-analysis of literature over public opinion towards environmental issues across eastern countries, as well as the factors contributing to the fickleness of the public opinion over time in one country or region could be worthy inquiry for future research. Last but not the least, it would be important for researchers to examine the magnitude of impacts by different medium forms (television, newspaper, Internet, mobile phone, etc.) in participatory events, and how to utilize multiple propagation tools to mobilize the population with different demographic backgrounds (children, seniors, etc.) to take part in the environmental protection campaign which benefits every single living being on this beautiful planet.

De Filippi analyzes in her chapter, "Ubiquitous Computing in the Cloud: User Empowerment vs. User Obsequity," the evolution of the Internet, shifting from a decentralized architecture designed around the end-to-end principle with powerful mainframe/personal computers at each end, to a more central-ized network designed according to the mainframe model, with increasingly weaker user's devices that no longer have the ability to run a server nor to process any consistent amount of data or information. The advantages of ubiquitous computing (allowing data to become available from anywhere and at any time, regardless of the device) should thus be counterbalanced with the costs it entails (loss of users' autonomy, concerns as regards privacy and freedom of expression, etc).

The advent of Internet and digital technology has drastically changed the way people act and in-teract both at work and at home. People's personal lives and professional lives are being increasingly intertwined. The office does not longer consist exclusively of a place for work, but is increasingly used by people dealing with personal matters, such as e-mails and social media. Conversely, professional activities extend throughout the day – either at home or at office during lunch break, while traveling, or in the evening after a long day of work, people do not hesitate to check their e-mails and, if necessary, to complete their work.

In most developed countries, the Internet has become a necessity. People need to be able to access the Internet at anytime and from anywhere. This obviously implies that they must be able to access all their personal or professional files without having direct access to their computer. Hence, mobile phones are turned into "smart phones" – intelligent devices able to provide all the necessary services to satisfy all the emerging needs of users in terms of connectivity. Thanks to the Internet, any device can potentially provide access to a world of information that was previously only available to a limited number of people connected to a given network. Over the past 20 years, users have become more and more demanding. They constantly expect new services and innovative applications that cannot be easily provided on the limited architecture of most mobile devices. Most of these applications are thus provided on remote servers accessible through the Net. As opposed to the traditional architecture of the Internet based on the end-to-end principle, with intelligent terminals that communicate with each other through the network, we are nowadays moving towards a system of increasingly less sophisticated terminals communicating through centralized online applications. The intelligence is progressively moving from the terminals to the core of the network: from personal computers, to laptops, tablets, smart-phones or any other device whose sole function is to access a particular online application. Nowadays, in order to communicate on the Internet, users increasingly rely more on technological platforms provided by third parties. The result is that, today, most of the means of production (in terms of hardware resources, software, content or data) are concentrated in the hands of large Internet services providers.

Hence, perhaps ironically, the ubiquity of the Internet is promoting a species of "user impotence." With more reliance on centralized architecture, user devices become less powerful, less generative, and less capable of interacting with anything but the central server to which it is tethered. Similarly, the control over possible applications remains centralized. A wide choice of consumer applications does mask the reality that consumers increasingly take rather than generate.

This impotence relates to content as well. As resources move away from users to increasingly centralized architectures with large processing power and virtually unlimited storage capacity, users gradually lose control not only over the means of communication, but on the contents of their communications as well. With the advent of cloud computing, more and more hardware, software, and informational resources are exported into the "cloud" – where they are often controlled by large corporations mainly interested in the maximization of profits.

Despite the new opportunities provided by mobile applications, the growing centralization of these applications is likely to significantly impinge upon the freedom of users. Indeed, while ubiquitous computing definitely provides users with a greater degree of quality and comfort, the underlying architecture of these applications, however, plays an important role in shaping the way communications are regulated on the Internet. To the extent that technology determines how people can communicate with each other, users' freedom may potentially be limited by the constraints imposed (either voluntarily or not) at the level of the user interface. Hence, the higher is the level of centralization, the smaller is the number of alternatives that users can choose from, and the stronger is the degree of control that Internet service providers can exert over the content of communications. Ubiquity breeds impotence.

After an initial period of euphoria on the part of the users, who enjoy the benefits of ubiquitous access to a growing number of online services, the dangers of ubiquitous computing and mobile applications are becoming more apparent. Users have become increasingly aware that more and more online applications are governed by centralized entities controlled by private companies and governments, and the most savvy of them are developing alternative platforms based on decentralized architectures. Such is the case of Eben Moglen's "Freedom Box" – a small user's device that uses free software and peer-to-peer technologies in order to allow users to communicate freely and independently on the Internet. Unlike smartphones, tablets, or other mobile devices specifically designed to control and monitor user activities and communications, the majority of these decentralized alternatives are intended to allow users to bypass censorship and control by re-appropriating the resources that had been previously exported onto the Cloud.

Most of these decentralized systems are generally difficult to use and are often not as comfortable as many cloud-based services. Yet, they nonetheless play an important role to the extent that they can be regarded as a "counter-power" against potential abuses by large cloud operators. While they do not have to be as big, nor as good, as most of the cloud services they compete with, their mere existence constitutes a safeguard for users who—were the cloud to become too "foggy" or nefarious"—would preserve the ability to shift towards more decentralized alternatives, as a last resort. Certainly, there will always be a role for persons versed in the technology—the so-called hackers and geeks—to test limits, probe technologies, and otherwise serve as technological "watchdogs" in the cloud space. One might also envisage a number of collective responses posed by the twin challenges of ubiquity and impotence. Governments, public institutions (such as quangos, public research institutions, or universities), and community organizations might respond by providing their own cloud-based solutions, setting up their own clouds and providing services to certain communities, segments of the population, or indeed the population at large. Such responses would enable users to interact on the cloud, taking advantage of its ubiquity, without giving up their autonomy. As is the case for the user-driven responses identified above, these solutions need not be as comprehensive as the cloud solutions offered by the private sector; they merely have to be a viable alternative that stands in effect as an insurance policy against the concentration of cloud power in the hands of a few.

Fernandez and Marrauld evocate in their chapter, "How to Design a Virtualized Platform? A Socio-Technical Study about the Current Practices of Teleworking," the WITE 2.0 (Work IT Easy) project. It is a research and innovation program supported by public funds. It is a multi-partner project (academic and industrial actors). The aim of this project is to create a virtualized platform. This platform represents a unified work environment, based on virtualization, instant communication and interoperability of systems, and it allows the individuals to work anywhere (and possibly anytime). The platform is a software solution that centralizes the access to a set of functionalities, originally offered by several applications: it is the principle of unified communications. Unified Communications (UC) is the integration of real-time communication services such as instant messaging (chat), presence information, telephony (including IP telephony), video conferencing, data sharing (including Web connected electronic whiteboards aka IWBs or Interactive White Boards), call control, and speech recognition with non-real-time communication services such as unified messaging (integrated voicemail, e-mail, SMS, and fax). This platform is accessible from any connected terminal, either fixed or mobile (desktop, laptop, tablet, Smartphone, etc.). The WITE 2.0 platform will provide a wide range of communication tools that can be activated on demand in different situations, and depending on users' needs (VoIP, discussion groups, instant messaging, email, etc.). The project has four main stages, divided into several subsections each. It is supported by a socio-technical analysis. Telecom ParisTech has assumed leadership in the scientific study of the needs and uses by administrating semi-structured interviews with individuals regularly working "remotely." They wanted to better characterize these work situations: at home, on the premises of the employer but in geographically dispersed locations: in telecentres/co-working spaces/business center, with geo-distributed teams working. Mobility at work is spreading in the context of the mobility paradigm's evolution. The project WITE 2.0 intends to address the urgent need for solutions in the field of remote collaborative work. These needs include ways to collaborate, communicate and socialize, but also to access these features regardless of the location, and from any workstation. It will provide a unified interface integrating all the features, and having a wide range of communication tools selectable on demand.

The project WITE2.0 is divided into four major phases. The first one concerns the study of employees' needs and uses, for remote collaborative work. In order to capture the needs and uses, the researchers conducted two surveys: first, a qualitative study based on 47 semi-structured interviews, and second, an online quantitative survey with 553 individuals. The object of this phase is to highlight the kinds of remote collaboration in order to make recommendations related to the design of the platform. The results are published in the report "Work, Socialize, and Collaborate Remotely." The main preliminary results of this report focus on how to socialize in a context of teleworking, the question of remote management, and of the technical skills needed for the use of ICT. The recommendations focus on the access to digital resources, the business information systems, and on issues related to security. The second phase of the project focuses on the technology. It is divided into two parts. The first part consists of the writing of functional and technical specifications of the platform WITE2.0. This document contains descriptions of service needs, and a comparison of various existing virtualization solutions. The authors notice that, since the launching of the project WITE 2.0, some other virtualization solutions have appeared on the market (Citrix, etc.). Through the comparison of different solutions, they highlight the distinguishing features and the technological services of the platform WITE 2.0. The second part of the phase 2 includes the implementation of all the technical elements necessary for the platform WITE2.0. These technical elements include the virtualization, the development of a socialization software solution, the services integration, the development of a unified software, and a beta testing of the platform. In the third phase, the project partners have introduced new technological elements for the components and voice applications, the mobile profiles, and the SIP recorder.

The major technical element of this platform is based on the virtualization of Information Systems (IS). The workstation virtualization solution that the authors are interested in is also called the "PC on demand." The virtual workstation displays a virtual image on the user workstation that is executed on a remote server (not virtualized). This technology has several advantages (centralizing logical components, checking the lifecycle of workstation, access to an individual virtual PC guaranteeing better mobility management of the employee). Virtual workstations will address a number of challenges compared to "ordinary" workstations (especially at the administrative, security, and deployment of machines levels). Virtual machines, for example, can decrease functional costs (maintenance, etc.), and technical problems such as obsolescence of the workstation. With VDI architecture, the ISD has no longer constraints related to maintenance and administration of its fleet of workstations. The user is no longer dependent on a single physical computer and can connect to his "own PC" from different physical devices, even from terminals like thin clients. Hence, virtualization is an already existing technology. The value of the WITE 2.0 platform is to combine this existing technology with a collaborative tool (unified communication). The aim is actually double: in one hand, to reduce (or eliminate) the problems due to data security, and on the other hand, to improve the level of collaboration between employees. In a context of managerial culture based on "face to face," the new paradigm of mobile work does not seem to establish in French companies. Some forms of work organization are deeply rooted. Some managers and IT system directors still reluctant to introduce new developed technologies because of the security of the data circulation. The researchers' bias is to say that the paradigm shift can take place now if they take into account the issues of teleworking in "sociological" and "technical" terms: hence, the importance of analyzing the practices of work organization and use of ICT, and also the experimentation of the virtual platform. In their analysis, the authors are interested in a key notion: the concept of "teleworking" that the authors have considered in its most classic form (the homework), but also in the most diverse realities that it could be today: either, all forms of "remote working," i.e., forms of organization and/or performing work outside the classical unity of time and place. Indeed, many studies emphasize that the unity of time and place that characterized the traditional organization of work, would tend to disappear. Thus, the definition of teleworking that they have selected is based on: 1) The fixed place of work or alternating between several workplaces, provided they are removed from the hierarchy and/or colleagues; 2) The relationship to the employer and colleagues, remotely and by electronic links, thus justifying the name of teleworking. The first results that they will present in this chapter are based on a qualitative analysis approach. The authors have particularly studied the practices of coordination and cooperation in various configurations of remote work, more specifically in management practices supported by different communication technologies (fixed or mobile). They believe this kind of qualitative study is the most relevant because the authors make a statement about teleworkers' practices. As the virtualized and unified platform technology is designing, they realized that they actually had little knowledge about the current technologies' practices' realities. The classic typology of the four kinds of teleworkers—homeworkers, mobile workers, telecenter worker, virtual team worker—should really be evolved. They have decided to question the realities of the teleworkers' practices to understand the evolution of the work organization and to link the technology to specific uses (or link uses to specific technology). Hence, they have thought that the most equipped teleworker will be the most graduated (with the most responsibilities). They have discovered that the uses of mobile ICTs evolved in a very paradoxical way.

In his chapter, "Explaining Mobile Services Adoption between China and Developed Countries from a Cultural Perspective," Gao shows that little research has been done to explore the adoption of mobile information services from a cultural perspective. This research is designed to study mobile information services adoption from a cultural perspective. Based on the two cultural dimensions (individualism/collectivism, uncertainty avoidance), two research hypotheses are presented. To examine these hypotheses, an exploratory study is carried out with a mobile information service called Mobile Tourist Service Recommender system (MTSR) with both respondents from developed countries and China. According to the results, one research hypothesis was supported, while the other research hypothesis (H1) was not supported in this exploratory study. The findings indicate that the cultural dimensions play important roles in how mobile information services are used and adopted in two different cultural settings: culture in developed countries and the Chinese culture. The results also highlight the relevance of the cultural dimensions (individualism/collectivism, uncertainty avoidance) as the factors affecting the adoption of mobile information services.

The rapid growth of mobile communication and usage of mobile devices in recent years has provided a great opportunity for creating a variety of mobile services. The advanced mobile devices enable users to try out new mobile services, but the adoption of many advanced mobile services has been slower than expected. On one hand, unlike some old technology-based products (e.g., landline phones), some users are not aware of some of the mobile services which mobile devices are able to offer. On the other hand, some users are afraid to use some mobile services because of the lack of technological knowledge. Therefore, it is necessary to consider non-technical factors, which might impact mobile services diffusion. As cultural characteristics have a fundamental effect on how users perceive mobile services, the appropriateness of a mobile service for one culture may not be appropriate for others. Little research has been done to explore the adoption of mobile information services from a cultural perspective. The objective of this chapter is to investigate how the different cultural dimensions influence users' adoption of mobile services. In order to address this, the authors carry out an experiment to examine the adoption of some advanced mobile services with people from both China and developed countries from a cultural perspective.

Culture has been defined in a number of ways because of its multi-dimensional characteristics. Hofstede defined culture as mental programming (Hofstede, 1980), which refers to patterns of thinking, feeling, and potential acting, which were learned throughout people's lifetimes. Hofstede's study with a survey of IBM employees in 40 different countries found that the values of employees differed more based on their nationality, age, and education than their membership in organizations (Hofstede, 1980). From the study (Hofstede, 1980), four dimensions have been identified to distinguish among different cultures: uncertainty avoidance, power distance, individualism-collectivism, and masculinity-femininity. Hofstede and Bond (1988) subsequently added the fifth dimension: long-term versus short-term orientation. Schwartz and Sagiv (1995) identified two fundamental dimensions of cultural variables: openness to change (includes self-direction and stimulation value types) versus conservation (includes security, conformity, and traditional value types), and self-enhancement (includes hedonism, power, and achievement value types) versus self-transcendence (includes universalism and benevolence value types). Moreover, Bond's Chinese Culture Connection (CCC) study revealed four factors derived from the Chinese culture: integration, Confucian work dynamism, human-heartedness, and moral discipline (Bond, 1988). The most commonly cited cultural dimensions are summarized in this chapter. An overview of the existing technology acceptance models and theories is also given in this chapter.

In addition, related work on the influence of cultural characteristics on mobile services adoption is searched. Harris, Rettie, and Kwan (2005) compared mobile commerce usage in the UK and Hong Kong. They found significant differences between the UK and Hong Kong in attitudes to mobile commerce services. They attributed these differences to the levels of collectivism and power distance in the cultures and to structural differences between the two markets. Marcus and Gould (2000) found that cultural elements are embedded in user interfaces as a set of contextual and social cues that enable effective use by applying the cultural dimensions proposed by Hofstede (1980) to Website design. Lee, Choi, Kim, and Hong (2007) constructed and verified a research model, based on interaction theory and the cultural lens model, that focuses on the relationship between users' cultural profiles and post-adoption beliefs in the context of the mobile Internet.

Based on the two cultural dimensions (individualism/collectivism, uncertainty avoidance), the following two research hypotheses are presented: H1) People from high individualism cultures will be more likely to adopt mobile information services than people from low individualism cultures; H2) People from high uncertainty avoidance cultures will be less likely to adopt mobile information services than people from low uncertainty avoidance cultures. To examine these hypotheses, an exploratory study is carried out with a mobile information service called Mobile Tourist Service Recommender system (MTSR) with both respondents from developed countries and China. China and the Developed countries represent two distinct cultures. The developed countries can be seen as a representation of western culture while China represents the epitome of eastern culture. The cultural values are meant to be different in the developed countries and China. These facts provide us with a good basis to analyze mobile information services adoption between these two distinct cultures. The MTSR system is a mobile service, which was developed at a Norwegian university. The MTSR system is intended to help tourists find Points Of Interest (POI) such as hotels and restaurants in order to let them schedule their time more efficiently and increase the probability that they will visit places that they will actually enjoy. By taking location, among other things, into the consideration, the system aims to provide better information to users. The validated instrument measure from previous research is used as the foundation to create survey items for this study. The authors recruited the experiment subjects by posting announcements to a number of student mailing lists. Students from several departments, studying for an undergraduate program or a graduate program, were invited to participate in the experiment of using the MTSR running on an Android mobile device. As a result, 46 testers participated in the experiment.

According to the results, one research hypothesis (H2) was supported, while the other research hypothesis (H1) was not supported in this exploratory study. The authors believe that some possible reasons exist for this finding. Firstly, the sample size of this pilot study was quite small. Most participants were experienced users of mobile devices and mobile services. They might expect to experience different kinds of new mobile services. In addition, oversea students from China might be influenced by western culture. As a result, it leads them to be the first one to try new services. Furthermore, some Chinese participants are well-educated in IT. They might be addicted to advanced mobile services. The findings indicate that the cultural dimensions play important roles in how mobile information services are used and adopted in two different cultural settings: culture in developed countries and the Chinese culture. On one hand, from an academic perspective, this study contributes to the literature on mobile services adoption and diffusion by examining the importance of the cultural dimensions to mobile information services adoption. On the other hand, from a business perspective, the results also provided some implications for practitioners. The results also highlight the relevance of the cultural dimensions (individualism/collectivism, uncertainty avoidance) as the factors affecting the adoption of mobile information services.

In their chapter, "Ubiquitous Game-Based Learning in Higher Education: A framework towards the Effective Integration of Game-Based Learning in Higher Education using Emerging Ubiquitous Technologies" Kasimati et al. show that the rise of mobile broadband devices and services has significantly changed the role of mobile devices in people's daily lives by enabling the provision of innovative applications and services anywhere, anytime. Despite the fact that new ideas and innovation mainly occur within HEIs (Higher Education Institutions), the adoption of mobile and ubiquitous technologies by HEIs is still in early stages. This chapter attempts to provide a framework to support the latter towards implementing mobile and ubiquitous, game-based-learning activities. Aligned with the objective of this book, this chapter presents some examples and best practices of implementing this framework towards achieving the learning goals of future professionals in the fields of electronic and ubiquitous commerce.

This chapter presents a methodological framework towards the effective implementation of Game-Based Learning (GBL) in Higher Education Institutions using ubiquitous and mobile devices. The proliferation of digital games along with the effectiveness of game play on cognitive development has sparked a fascination with its integration in learning process and educational curriculums at an international level. A great number of research efforts and applications have been carried out, mainly focusing on the integration of GBL at early educational levels, specifically K-12 education. However, taking into consideration that the population of gamers is continuously increasing and was about 70 million people in 2011, 40% of which are aged between 20 and 34 years old, and the fact that all 21st century learners have grown up in a world where digital games have always been an important part of their lives (Johnson, Adams, & Cummins, 2012), it is a great opportunity and a need for Higher Education Institutions to focus on GBL towards achieving their goals with regards to their students' collaboration, problem solving, critical thinking, creativity and digital literacy skills. Based on current literature, games, when carefully included in learning processes, have been proven to raise student's motivation and engagement in a wide variety of activities that can support the development of many valuable skills (Kasimati & Zamani, 2012). Additionally, they are highly effective in interdisciplinary areas where students are required to combine knowledge from different fields and apply critical thinking and problem solving skills towards achieving their learning goals (Shabalina, Vorobkalov, Kataev, & Tarasenko, 2008). Game play, game design and production require research, collaboration, teamwork, creativity, problem solving and communication skills and critical thinking ability, all listed among the 21st century skills. Getting students through a well-supported game-based learning process (game play or game design and production) helps them improve their skills while simultaneously enhancing their knowledge; thus provides them with increased potential to succeed in the current innovation-driven economies at a global level. Equally important, the participation in such activities using innovative IT tools increases students digital literacy, their ability to effectively use and manage information technology, also considered as a skill for the 21st century citizens (Simões, Redondo & Vilas, 2012). As a result, the integration of GBL principles and digital games in tertiary education can significantly improve the quality of learning process and empower future professionals with improved high-order thinking skills.

Despite the fact that a great number of Higher Education Institutions include in their curriculums courses for game design and development, only few of them apply basic gaming principles in order to enhance their educational services. GBL practices and methodologies can provide Higher Education Institutions with new forms of learning content, interaction and collaboration, while providing potential for constant evaluation and provision of direct feedback (Derryberry, 2012). Equally important, the proliferation of mobile devices (smartphones and tablets) can further support Higher Education Institutions towards adopting GBL practices. Specifically, student's (always increasing) use of ubiquitous online applications, when investigated within a learning-centered context, provides Higher Education Institutions with a unique opportunity to easily engage students into game-based learning activities using their mobile devices as an educational tool. In conclusion, the adoption of game-based learning by Higher Education Institutions is just two to three years away (Johnson, Adams, & Cummins, 2012). However, in order for digital games to be effectively integrated in Higher Education, proper methodology and instructional design should be followed during the preparation, the delivery and the evaluation phase of GBL activities. To this end, this chapter aims to provide a robust literature review and combine GBL principles and methodologies into a framework for their proper integration in Higher Education Institutions and their alignment with technological specifications of mobile and ubiquitous technologies.

The chapter is organized in two parts where Part A investigates the basic principles towards the effective implementation of GBL (focusing on digital games) in HEIs; it further delineates the way mobile and ubiquitous technologies can support the smoothest integration of GBL in those specific organisations and its fastest adoption by relevant stakeholders (teaching staff, administrative staff, middle-level management employees, students). Part B presents implementation scenarios of the proposed mobile GBL framework in Higher Education. The provision of such implementation scenarios on specific relevant activities using mobile devices can guide academics and instructors realize the impact of these innovative educational practices thus leading to their fastest and smoothest adoption in HEIs' curricula.

The proliferation of mobile technologies and GBL practices provides a unique opportunity for the Higher Educational Institutions. Usual problems encountered by academics and which concern student's engagement and motivation can be effectively tackled with the proper integration of GBL in their curriculums. Additionally, 21st century learners and citizens are familiar with mobile devices and services, and are used to being always connected (any time, any place) even when they are on the move. This fact provides multiple opportunities for the provision of learning activities on mobile devices, thus providing a more learner-centered learning process. As a result, Higher Education Institutions are given the opportunity to combine two equally popular and effective learning practices (GBL and mobile) and properly integrate it into their curriculum in order to enhance student's motivation and engagement, and also achieve demanding learning goals. Last but not least, the adoption of such practices by Higher Education Institutions can provide them with a competitive advantage against other globally or nationally recognized ones due to the provision of innovative and high-quality learning services to their students.

The proposed chapter can enhance Higher Education Institutions ability to adopt and apply such practices, providing significant insight and guidance throughout all development phases (design, development, implementation, evaluation). Moreover, the provision of best practices and examples on the use of specific GBL activities using mobile devices will help academics and instructors into realizing the real impact of these innovative educational practices thus leading to their quickest and smoothest adoption in Higher Education Institution's curriculum.

Chaari's chapter, "The Role of Communication in Online Trust: The Communicative Action Theory Contribution," aims at better understanding the behavior of the Internet user. It suggests studying the role of communication on the trust of Internet users towards commercial Websites. In order to realize this research, the author has mobilized the Communicative Action Theory of Jürgen Habermas (1987). Therefore, she has brought a new perspective in understanding online trust following action theory. The literature on information systems, marketing and e-commerce highlights the critical role of trust in success of Business/Consumer relationships (Gefen et al. 2003; Chouk and Perrien, 2003, 2004, 2006; McKnight et al. 2002; Hoffman et al. 1999). According to several researchers, the lack of trust is the main reason of Internet users' reluctance towards online shopping. Kearney has concluded that 82% of online shoppers abandon shopping from the early stages of their visits to the Websites (Hausman and Siekpe, 2009). Quelch and Klein argue that "trust is a critical factor in stimulating purchases over the Internet" (Corbitt et al. 2003, p.1). Online, the consumer cannot verify the quality of the offered products/services, and he cannot control the security of his personal and financial information. Thereby, he feels that his private life is totally dominated by Internet technology which exploits his vulnerability and protects the interest of the economic system (Salter, 2005). The opportunistic behavior of firms and the colonization of the consumer's life world by the Website explain his rejection and his resistance to buying online.

Considering the prominent place of trust in Business/Consumer relationships, researches have focused on studying the determining factors of this phenomenon. One stream of search is characterized by a technological determinism highlighting the role of Websites' technical characteristics as perceived by Internet users (Gefen et al, 2003). Another stream deals with individual variables related to the Internet user like psychological antecedents (Lundgren and Walczuch, 2004) and familiarity with an Internet vendor (Gefen, 2000; Bhattacherjee, 2002). Another research avenue was interested in the variables related to the merchant like organizational reputation (McKnight et al. 2002) and perceived size of the organization (Jarvenpaa et al. 2000). Some researchers were concerned with the pivotal role of communication in the development of online trust. Morgan and Hunt (1994) highlight that communication is a very important factor for trust development. These authors have defined communication as the formal and informal sharing of relevant, secure, and real time information between a consumer and a vendor. Chouk and Perrien (2004) have shown the role of third parties in influencing user's attitude and trust development towards an E-merchant. However, most researchers were focused on technical and persuasive aspects of online communication and neglect to conceive it as an action that implies all participants (users and merchant) in a social interaction. According to Shih (2004), the purchase of an online product implies intense information communication, and an interactive behavior between firms and Internet users.

Following an instrumental rationality, the positivist approach of communication conceives the commercial Web site as a technology that supports the egocentric needs and the utilitarian interests of the parties (Firms and Internet users), protecting the capitalism ideology as the dominant class (Salter, 2005). It is a medium used by the firms to colonize the Internet users' world and to directly change their attitudes and behaviors. Along those lines, most commercial Websites conceive of communication as one-way directed by the firm towards the Internet user where the technical features of the Website are used as a means to manipulate the Internet users' behavior. Kozinets (2002), assumes that the market has for a long time dominated the consumer's identity who is considered passive and devoid of expression. With the theory of communicative action of Jürgen Habermas (1987), there has been a major paradigm shift. The conviction that technology directly influences the users' behavior gives place to a new conception according to which the Internet user is considered as an actor who can accept, refuse and even criticize the received message from the commercial Website. Indeed, the interactivity which characterizes commercial Websites support new forms of communication in two directions, exceeding the traditional and the determinist forms of communication between the firms and Internet users. Among these new communication forms, the authors mention e-mailing, discussion forums, and chat rooms which are open for all users and which make the Website a place of exchange of rational and ethical discussions as it is promoted by the democratic project of Jürgen Habermas (1987). For Habermas, communication is an action which depends on contextual, cultural and human factors, which cannot be reduced to deterministic mechanisms. He deals with two types of action which an actor might pursue following his interests that can be instrumental, strategic or emancipatory. The instrumental and strategic are purposive-rational actions which aim at achieving success and at developing a calculated trust based on calculation of the advantages and the costs of the relation, whereas, the communicative action is coordinated by mutual understanding that allows the development of a relational trust based on social interactions. In communicative action, mutual understanding through language allows the social integration of actors and the coordination of their plans and their different interests. In this case, trust is based on common definition of the situation and the resolution of conflicts of interests between actors. Technology Internet is a medium of communication that can support the three kinds of action. The instrumental and strategic actions allow the development of calculated trust based on the control of the situation and the egocentric calculation of the outcomes of the exchange relationship. Whereas the communicative action, allows the development of relational trust based on social interaction and mutual comprehension. The instrumental and strategic conception of Website is very reductionist; it neglects the interactional aspect of communication which enables the development of relational or affective trust. Communication on the Website is also an interaction that helps build relationships among participants.

According to Habermas, the economic system is guided by an instrumental (technical) rationality. On the other hand, life world is a cultural resource guided by communicative action which enables common construction of sense and providing a communicative rationality. The lack of communicative activity is explained by the colonization of the life world by instrumental and strategic rationality (Habermas, 1987; Salter, 2005). The colonization aspects of Website, as a technology that support the interests of economic sphere, are at the origin of lack of online trust and their resistance from buying online. The emancipatory interests of consumer can only be achieved through open an equal discourse that guarantees the participation of all actors.

The objective of this chapter is to study the role of communicative activity in the development of consumer online trust. Trust based on social interaction, not on the calculus of utilitarian interests of the relation. Hence, the authors suggest studying the role of communication on the trust of Internet users towards commercial Websites from a new perspective to highlight the importance of discourse and mutual understanding in establishing collaboration and resolving conflicts, and then the development of mutual trust based on social interaction and the knowledge of the other. From this point of view, communication is not conceptualized as a linear process oriented toward a purpose, rather, it's an action oriented towards mutual understanding and coordination of action between participants. From this perspective, shopping online is no longer seen as a passive action, it becomes an autonomous action where consumers participate actively in the process of communication and establish a relation with the other. Commercial Web sites are useful not only for control but also for effective communication between actors in a democratic manner.

According to the chapter "Evaluation of South African Universities Web Portal Interfaces using a Triangulation of Ubiquitous Computing Evaluation Areas and Technology Acceptance Model" of Booi and Ditsa (2013), there are growing concerns over the user friendliness and other usability issues of South African Universities Web Portal Interfaces (UWPIs), which obviously will negate the user acceptance of the UWPIs. The main goal of this study is to develop a framework which could be used to evaluate and provide additional guidelines to improve the Usability and User Acceptance of South African UWPIs. The study applied a triangulation of Ubiquitous computing Evaluation Areas (UEAs) and Technology Acceptance Model (TAM) as theoretical foundations to derive the research model for this study. Multiple regression and stepwise regression analysis were used. The results suggest that Interaction and Invisibility of UWPIs are the most important measures that have a huge impact on user acceptance and usability respectively. The results of the study will provide guidelines for the design and development of South Africa UWPIs to meet their usability and user acceptance.

This study is about the usability and user acceptance of Web Portal Interfaces in South African universities. Usability and user acceptance problems of Computer System Websites and Interfaces attracted many researchers from different domains such as psychology, human factors, human computer interaction and management because of the occurrences of problems and the growing concerns associated with them. Human Computer Interaction (HCI) standards have three goals that must be met when designing interfaces (Battleson, 2000): (a) provide support to enable users to achieve their goals and to meet their needs; (b) provide the ease of use with minimal errors; and (c) provide a pleasant interface design. Even though Websites or Web Portal Interfaces may be highly usable and may be considered as such, there are no guarantees that they will be acceptable to the users (Davis, 1989). Battleson (2000) further argues that HCI research concentrate on usability as if it is a prerequisite of acceptance and overlooked some concepts of acceptability of new technologies. Two major methodologies for usability testing, which are laboratory studies (user participation) and field studies were identified in the work of Zhang and Adipat (2005). Interface design process involves user participation, and it has been considered as the best practice in the HCI domain, and it was used in this study. Introduction Computer System Websites and Interfaces can only add value to institutions or individuals if the systems are usable and acceptable. In his work Nielson (2001) defines usability as a quality characteristic that measures how easy the user interfaces are for the user to use. The Higher Education Sector in South Africa consists of 23 universities, which are categories as follows: 11 traditional universities; 6 comprehensive universities (merger between Traditional universities and Technikons); and 6 universities of technology (merger between Technikons). All these universities have one major goal, which is to provide quality information and knowledge to students, staff and the general public to sustain competitive advantage locally and globally. Web portals are provided as means of making sure that the universities achieve this goal. Research Problem Web portal interfaces suffer from a number of weaknesses such as technical difficulties, user unfriendliness and other usability issues. There are increasing alarms over the technical difficulties, user friendliness and other usability issues of South African UWPIs. Some of these issues raised the question whether these Web portal interfaces are evaluated for their usability and user acceptance. These usability issues will obviously have a negative impact on the user acceptance of the UWPIs. University Web portals and their interfaces being ubiquitous computing applications, the research problem that this study therefore sought to provide answers to is: what ubiquitous criteria should be used in evaluating South African Universities Web Portal Interfaces for their usability and user acceptance? Following from the purpose of the study and research problem, the main objective addressed in this study is to select and use appropriate usability and user acceptance criteria to evaluate South African UWPIs for their Usability and User Acceptance and to suggest an improvement on them.

The study applied a triangulation of the Ubiquitous computing Evaluation Areas (UEAs) framework and the Technology Acceptance Model (TAM) as theoretical foundations to derive the research model for this study. Based on the research model hypotheses were formulated and tested. Data Collections and Results A total number of 200 questionnaires were distributed and 180 returned. Of the total 180 returned, 118 questionnaires were suitable for analysis. The data collected was analysed using SPSS. In order to identify the variables that were relatively important in determining Usability leading to User Acceptance of UWPIs, Multiple Regression analysis was performed. In this study's analysis, a variable was not entered into regression model unless the p-value for that variable was less than or equal to 0.05. The same level was also set for removal of variables. A stepwise regression was used by allowing addition and removal of variables at various steps in progressively building the regression model. The results of the Pearsonel's Product-moment correlations indicated that the majority of correlations were statistically significant. The highest correlation reported was between Invisibility of the UWPIs and usability of UWPIs (H4, r = 0.720). The research questions which were addressed using multiple regression analysis and the stepwise regression analysis showed that Appeal, Application Robustness and Invisibility constructs from the UEAs have no significant contribution towards User Acceptance. The results also suggest that invisibility and interaction of South African UWPIs have a great impact on user usability and acceptance respectively. The results of the study will provide guidelines for the development of South African UWPIs to meet usability and user acceptance. Based on the findings presented, the overall conclusion that can be drawn for this study is that: Interaction, Appeal, Application Robustness and Invisibility measures represent important variables that explain how the UWPIs are evaluated as well as the criteria which users use for evaluating UWPIs. Their importance from the most influential to the least influential is Invisibility, Interaction, Appeal and Application Robustness. The results of the study will provide guidelines for the development of South African UWPIs to meet their usability and user acceptance. Theoretically, the study is significant in providing a framework for research into UWPIs usability and user acceptance. Practically, the results of this study will provide guidelines for designers/developers, particularly in South Africa.

In his chapter, "Telepresence, Flow, and Behaviour in Virtual Retail Environment," Ettis explains that mediated Communication Technology has undergone significant development over the past decades. They tend to utilise multiple media and richer graphical interfaces to excite and engage the user. Recently, new forms of communication and technology are emerging such as virtual reality display function, 3D graphics, video, interface avatars, online chat, and recommendation tools (Zhao & Dholakia, 2009). One key advantage of these Web 2.0 interactive technologies is that they provide users with a higher level of telepresence (or presence) within their virtual environment (Siriaraya & Ang, 2012). This heightened level of telepresence could potentially result in a more satisfying and immersive experience. This experience allows users to perceive an augmented sense of flow; a state of total concentration and enjoyment (Jahn, Drengner, & Furchheim, 2013; Koufaris, 2002; Novak, Hoffman & Yung, 2000; Wang, Baker, Wagner, & Wakfield, 2007). Practitioners and academics alike have recognised telepresence and flow as a key attribute of the user interaction experience with new media (Mollen & Wilson, 2010; Tikkanen, Hietanen, Henttonen, & Rokka, 2009; Wang, Yang, & Hsu, 2013), making these environments valuable as tools for use in purposes such as educational, entertainment, and e-commerce activity. Despite the growing importance of these new media and their adoption, the special characteristics of virtual worlds and their impact on user behaviour needs to be further explored (Domina, Lee, & MaGillivray, 2012; Kober & Neuper, 2013; Rose, Clark, Samouel, & Hair, 2012; Tikkanen et al., 2009). The objective of this chapter is to review the flow theory, the telepresence concept and their interrelationship with the online behaviour. The study applies this framework to Web stores. Hence, this research empirically investigates the impact of telepresence and flow state experienced during online shopping, on e-commerce Websites visitor's behaviour.

Understanding factors that influence use of a virtual world for shopping will help e-retailers create compelling virtual environments and develop better marketing strategies to enhance the consumer shopping experience in the virtual stores, while positively influencing purchase and return intentions. In this study, based on the flow theory, telepresence is considered to predict Websites visitor's experience of flow as measured by concentration and enjoyment. Flow is assumed to influence e-consumer behaviour in terms of number of visited pages, actual visit time, and perceived visit time. Among eight hypotheses, this research finds support for four. It has showed that telepresence is an important determinant of flow. The concentration dimension of flow is crucial to enhance consumer's number of visited pages and visit time. Consequently, this research gives evidence that the flow theory and the telepresence concept are valuable in the context of online shopping. A self-administered online survey was conducted to test the hypothesised relationships. The data were collected from a fictitious consumer electronics online retailer. The Website was created for the purpose of this research. The retailer Website was carefully created by experts with a Web content and design similar to others e-commerce Website in the net. This was to prevent the e-store from being confounded by an unnatural or strange design that is not well suited to the consumer's expectations. The homepage include the most common interactive functions and graphical interfaces. The Website was uploaded to the Internet. In this method, the content was viewed in its actual form and in a realistic setting.

The findings of the study show that telepresence could enhance the flow sate. The more the Website visitors are immersed and feel present in the mediated virtual environment, the more they will tend to be concentrated and enjoyed, and then experience flow. In the same way, findings from this study seem to empirically validate the relationship between the constructs of telepresence and concentration. The findings can affirm that in a computer-mediated environment, telepresence is an essential factor for enabling the person to remain concentrated on the computer-based task. The results of the study also confirmed some prior research on the theoretically elaborated relationship between flow and consumer behaviour. Interestingly, it is found that e-consumers in flow state might visit more pages and extent their Website visit duration. This effect is mainly produced by concentration. Based on these collective findings, it appears that telepresence plays an important role in influencing flow. Flow in turn influences e-consumer behaviour in the context of the Internet shopping. These results have a number of theoretical, methodological, and managerial implications. For more rigorous and practical implications, further research is needed to empirically investigate the role of telepresence in enhancing the other components of flow mentioned by Csikszentmihalyi (1997). Moreover, we know relatively little about the vividness and interactivity characteristics of Websites that encourage telepresence and flow. For instance, it would be appreciated to elucidate the role played by the collaborative Web 2.0 interactive technologies such as wiki, podcast, geographic mapping, and social sharing. Further research is needed, thus designers will be given clearer guidance as to what aspects they can alter to increase the chances of the user having an optimal experience. In addition, it would be valuable to monitor individual antecedents of telepresence and flow experience. In e-marketing, there have been studies on a variety of individual characteristics such as motivation, knowledge, need for cognition, shopping familiarity, and innovation. In addition, it is important to examine the role of socio-demographic characteristics (gender, age, education…), situational factors (product and Internet involvement, shopping goals...), and cultural settings. Such investigations will be valuable for our understanding of the universal phenomenon. Further recommendation for future research is that researchers extend the scope of the e-consumer behaviours to get a more profound understanding of telepresence and flow outcomes in e-shopping. It might be valuable to test the effects of cognitive and affective dependent variables such as satisfaction, impulse buying, recall, loyalty, and brand image change. Besides, it will be worthwhile to use clickstream data to assess the role played by telepresence and flow in user's decision to continue browsing the site or to exit and how long a user views each page during a site visit. Finally, future research could analyze several other interesting issues that remain unresolved. Future studies will be required to investigate telepresence and flow experience in other device such as smartphones, handheld computers, and PDA. It will be interesting to assess the extent to which a tiny screen may hinder telepresence and flow experiences. This chapter may stimulate more research in this field identified as still being under-explored. The research area is potentially fruitful. Many issues remain unresolved and many questions unanswered. The literature on telepresence and flow is extensive, but there are many challenges that need to be resolved. These challenges are mostly methodological. Studies involving flow measurement assessment demonstrate that some potentially serious difficulties exist, and researchers need to think carefully about the direction of causality between flow constructs and the measurement approaches (Hoffman & Novak, 2009; Koufaris, 2002; Siekpe, 2005).

Chakrabarty evokes in her chapter, "'From Clicks to Taps and Swipes': Translating User Needs to a Mobile Knowledge Management Experience," that knowledge management systems can be defined as systems that support creation, transfer and application of knowledge in organizations. A good knowledge management system helps to maintain the tacit and explicit knowledge of its users and the success of an organizational knowledge management system depends on how effectively it can be used by its user base at the time of need. To make a knowledge management system effective, it has to be easy to access, and provide accurate information in a timely manner. Organizations constantly strive to make their knowledge management systems more effective by improving the richness of the systems and increasing the reach of the knowledge resources to help employees in their job functions. Some of the techniques recommended by experts to improve access to knowledge resources include providing a search feature so that employees can access information from large knowledge resources. Inclusion of search is the most recommended and advocated technique in most organizations though there are not many studies to confirm it. Other ways to improve access and usability of organizational knowledge sources include improving the user interface of the systems and creating a directed navigation where the system is designed to mimic the transactions that users are expected to perform. Even as knowledge management systems are becoming more efficient and robust, the organizational landscapes are also evolving. One noticeable change that impacts the design and development of knowledge management systems is that more and more organizations now have a mobile employee base. The inclusion of mobile employees has created the need to provide access to organizational information anytime and anywhere. As a result, organizations are seeking a solution that serves the need of a mobility agnostic solution for a knowledge management system. Current techniques of usability and user feedback techniques to gather requirements have shown that overwhelmingly, the users perceive the inclusion of a "Google" search engine implemented at an organizational level to be the best solution. However, in technical terms, the limitation or drawback of just mobilizing the existing knowledge resources is not necessarily the result of an underperforming search engine. An Internet search engine like Google works better in chaotic data because chaotic data accounts for ambiguity of search terms, different vocabularies, and user description of the problem used by the users. An organizational knowledge management system on the other hand is very structured and consistent when it comes to using terms and definitions. When employees look for information based on user queries, their language may not always reflect the language used by the subject matter experts of the organization. As a result, the performance of the search engines like Google is not always the optimal solution.

With the mobilization of organizations, the employees and the workplace, there is a need to mobilize the learning and reference content for the employees. This helps the employees to keep up with the organizations' needs and helps them to complete their job responsibilities more effectively. The challenge for the knowledge managers is to enable mobile organizational knowledge resources to its employees at any time or at any place. Currently, many organizations were willing to invest in new technologies and infrastructure to support the growing needs of the business and its employees. The need to mobilize the systems have come as a boon to the knowledge managers who see this new requirement as a chance to revamp the existing knowledge management systems from scratch rather than go for a iterative update or facelift on an existing system. Understanding the specific needs of a new knowledge management system can be derived from investigations that go beyond user feedback. This chapter provides the insight into some of the challenges in organizational knowledge management systems and the implications of designing a mobile system. When user feedback techniques like focus groups and surveys do not yield any actionable items for the knowledge managers to formalize their requirements for a new system, it becomes necessary to find alternate mechanisms to understand user behavior in the existing systems and how the behavior would be impacted when the system is mobilized. In other words, the challenge is to understand what the users need and not what the users want. For mobile systems, it also translates into understanding what resources need to be included in the system and how it can be accessed in the system. This chapter presents one approach to answer the "what" and the "how." The "what" is answered using a combination of available log files and interactive sessions like card-sorting. The "how" is answered by understanding the system characteristics that can or cannot be used on the mobile device. System log files, page view information, and navigation information like start point and end point helps to understand the user's choice of path in the existing systems. This is called content footprint.

Understanding when the users choose one type of content over the other and how users navigate through the content helps to identify the different content types, the relative importance and usage frequency. Search logs from the knowledge management systems can help understand the specific pieces of information that users look for in the organization. It can also provide an insight into the vocabulary of the employees and the customers being served by the employees. Since the employees search the knowledge base in response to a customer's query, most often they repeat the same words or phrase in the search engine. Analyzing and normalizing the search logs help to identify and remove language ambiguity and wording inconsistencies. The navigation elements of the system including the taxonomy and metadata can be designed based on the results of card-sorting exercise where system users can categorize and rank different chunks of information based on how they are used. Card sorting exercise can be repeated with different user groups with various job responsibilities to understand how content was perceived and used differently by different user groups. Once the navigation elements are decided, the next step is to answer how to place these navigational elements on the mobile interface. The navigation of the system can be designed as a function of the surface area of the mobile device to facilitate the use of muscle memory of the user. Specific areas on the surface can be assigned to different content types to facilitate the use of the users muscle memory. The choice of location and content type needs to be predefined and fixed. A layout configuration that supports the user's cognitive load and helps them navigate the system with the same ease as a television remote control or a car's dashboard needs to be decided. A few configurations are presented in the chapter to help users select the most suitable layout. Changing the location of the navigation elements without proper thought can lead to poor user experience."

Finally, Haikel-Elsabeh in the chapter, "Understanding Brand Implication and Engagement on Facebook," shows that marketers are increasingly interested by social network and virtual community analysis. Firms want to understand their Facebook, Twitter, Pinterest fans in order to create and develop new relations with them. Yet, researchers want to understand why individuals post online by studying the context of professional virtual communities for instance (Wasko and Faraj, 2005). Also, why do they adopt certain types of behaviors online as in travel related Websites for example (Yoo & Gretzel, 2008)? The authors are also interested by their relations to virtual communities (Dholakia et al., 2004). Indeed, researchers have employed various theories regarding social network analysis, motivational theory (Bagozzi & Dholakia, 2002), and brand engagement (Sprott, Czellar & Spangenberg, 2009). They chose the social network Facebook because brands are increasingly developing their strategy to target their fans on their brand pages. Yet brands want to understand why their consumers are increasingly interested by their pages on social networks like Facebook. Thus they want to comprehend their users' behavior in order to develop their brand equity and marketing strategies.

What are the drivers for Brand engagement and implication on Facebook? In order to explore the impact of motivations on content and information sharing on Facebook brand pages, this study proposes an analysis focused on a reduced number of motivations and a proposal of a statistical model attempting to link the frequency of posting and liking on Facebook in general, and Brand engagement to motivations. The aim of the study is to assess the impact of motivations on brand engagement and frequency of posting and liking on Facebook. The authors used the concept of brand engagement measure a deep interest toward brands on Facebook. The concept of frequency of posting and liking was focused on the tendency to post or like frequently each time the user connects to Facebook. The motivations they introduced were based on the literature for sharing on social networks. Overall, the objective is to open the path to new studies using the authors' scale on specific brand pages on Facebook and to the cross comparisons between those different brands. In order to understand the drivers behind brand implication it is important to go beyond the existing scales on Facebook. Facebook is a real opportunity for marketers. There are 18 million users in France and 10 million spend 55 minutes per day on the plateform . The aim of the study conducted by a communication Web agency called DDB is to understand why brand fans in France like their favorite brands on Facebook . The majority of users that answered the survey were women (55%) the average age was 31 years old. The fans that are heavy likers are called "Hard core users" they connect to Facebook several times a day. They use the plateform to have fun (49%), talk to their families and friends (32%), and to search for new information (16%). Why Facebook users become brand fans? For 75% of users they liked a brand because they received an invitation or email. They also liked a brand because of the Word of Mouth of their friends on Facebook (59%). The other reason why they liked a brand is because they conducted an active search on Facebook to find a specific brand or product (49%). Fans have specific expectations toward their favorite brands: they want to gain the attention of their favorite brands when they become fans (53%). When they are attached to the brand, they become ambassadors (48%) and recommend the brand to their friends. Fans want the brands to have on their pages: promotions (41%), news regarding the brand (35%). Yet, not all fans are ready to comment or like: only 50% of the fans are ready to contribute on the brand page. Nonetheless, 76% have already liked a brand post on a brand page. Being a fan impacts the intentions of buying the brands' products and services (36%). Brand fans are also 92% to recommend the brand to their friends. The hard users give a very high grade (between 8 and 10) to their favorite brands on Facebook. Nonetheless, brand fans can be quick to unlike a brand on Facebook, specifically when the brand posts too much information (82%). This phenomenon should be carefully studied and taken into account by both researchers and marketers alike. What are Brand pages users on Facebook interested by? According to the study, Facebook users tend to be interested by media (55%), important causes (51%), and fashion and luxury brands (46%).

The DDB study was focused on a reduced number of users. Yet when we go on Social bakers Website we can clearly see the favorite brands worldwide on Facebook with regards to the total number of likes. If we look at the top ten, 7 out of 10 brands provide food and/or beverages to the masses: Coca cola, Red Bull, Starbucks, Oreo, McDonald's, Wal Mart. Thus food related brand appear to dominated worldwide on Facebook. Thus it is essential to study the literature on Brand communities to comprehend more deeply why users engage in brand engagement behavior and why do users contribute to brand communities on Facebook. Brand communities are defined by Muniz and O'Guinn (2001) as a "specialized, non-geographically bound community, based on a structured set of social relations among admirers of a brand." The members of brand community share in common their interest for a brand but also consume the brand's products or services. These individuals share knowledge about the brand's news, share information about their interest for the brand. According to McAlexander et al. (2002) brand communities enable the "creation and negotiation of meaning." The social structure and the exchange of information foster brand engagement and loyalty Muniz and O'Guinn (2001). Indeed, according to Dholakia et al. (2004) there are individual as well as group motivations for participating in brand communities in social networks. The individual drivers are that social network users that engage in virtual communities seek to share and learn information and to engage in social relations in the community.

The aim of this chapter is to propose a new scale of motivations for online posting on brand Facebook pages. Its objective is to assess whether the motivations for posting and liking on a brand page on Facebook have an impact on brand interest behavior (brand engagement) with regards to the general frequency of posting on Facebook. Three axis were explored to comprehend the drivers for brand engagement on Facebook. First, the authors studied the literature on the eWOM on Facebook to comprehend why users recommend and like to share information about brands with others. Second the motivations for brand engagement behavior are studied: what are users motivations to contribute to brand communities. Third, the authors analyzed the literature on brand implication in order to explain the phenomenon of brand interest on Facebook.

Jean-Eric Pelet
IDRAC International School of Management, Nantes University, KMCMS, France

Panagiota Papadopoulou
University of Athens

REFERENCES

Bagozzi, R. P., & Dholakia, U. M. (2002). Intentional social action in virtual communities. *Journal of Interactive Marketing, 16*(2), 2–21. doi:10.1002/dir.10006.

Battleson, B., Booth, A., & Weintrop, J. (2000). Usability testing for an academic library web site: A case study. *Journal of Librarianship, 27*(3), 188–198.

Bhattacherjee, A. (2002). Individual trust in online firms: Scale development and initial test. *Journal of Management Information Systems, 19*(1), 211–241.

Bond, M. H. (1988). Finding universal dimensions of individual variation in multicultural studies of values: The rokeach and Chinese value surveys. *Journal of Personality and Social Psychology, 55*(6), 1009. doi:10.1037/0022-3514.55.6.1009.

Booi, V. M., & Ditsa, G. E. (2012). Evaluating South African universities web portal interfaces for usability and user acceptance: Preliminary study. In Proceedings of IASTED International Conference on Human Computer Interaction 2012. IASTED.

Braudel, F. (2008). La dynamique du capitalisme. Flammarion: Champs Histoire.

Chouk, I., & Perrien, J. (2003). *Les déterminants de la confiance du consommateur lors d'un achat sur un site marchand: Proposition d'un cadre de recherche préliminaire. Centre de recherche DMSP. Cahier n° 318.* Université Paris-Dauphine.

Chouk, I., & Perrien, J. (2004). Les facteurs expliquant la confiance du consommateur lors d'un achat sur un site marchand: Une étude exploratoire. Décisions Marketing, 75-86.

Chouk, I., & Perrien, J. (2006). Déterminants de la confiance du consommateur vis-vis d'un site marchand internet non familier: Une approche par le rôle des tiers. In Actes du XXII Congrès AFM – 11 et 12 Mai.

Corbitt, B., & Thanasankit, T., & Yi. (2003). Trust and e-commerce: A study of consumer perceptions. *Electronic Commerce Research and Applications, 2,* 203–215. doi:10.1016/S1567-4223(03)00024-3.

Csikszentmihalyi, M. (1997). *Finding flow: The psychology of engagement with everyday life.* New York: Basic Books.

Davis, F. D. (1989). Perceived usefulness, perceived ease of use, and user acceptance. *Management Information Systems Quarterly, 3*(3), 319–340. doi:10.2307/249008.

DeLuca, K. (1999). *Image politics: The new rhetoric of environmental activism.* New York: Guilford.

Dholakia, U. M., Bagozzi, R. P., & Pearo, L. K. (2004). A social influence model of consumer participation in network- and small-group-based virtual communities. *International Journal of Research in Marketing, 21*(3), 241–263. doi:10.1016/j.ijresmar.2003.12.004.

Domina, T., Lee, S. E., & MacGillivray, M. (2012). Understanding factors affecting consumer intention to shop in a virtual world. *Journal of Retailing and Consumer Services, 19,* 613–620. doi:10.1016/j.jretconser.2012.08.001.

Gefen, D. (2000). E-commerce: The role of familiarity and trust. *The International Journal of Management Science, 28,* 725–737.

Gefen, D., Karahanna, E., & Straub, D. (2003). Trust and TAM in online shopping: An integrated model. *Management Information Systems Quarterly, 27*(1), 51–90.

Gibbs, L. (1993). Celebrating ten years of triumph. *Everyone's Backyard, 11*(1), 2–3.

Habermas, J. (1987). *Théorie de l'agir communicationnel: Pour une critique de la raison fonctionnaliste (Vol. 2).* (Schlegel, J.-L., Trans.). Paris, France: Fayard.

Hansen, A. (2010). *Environment, media and communication.* New York: Routledge.

Harris, P., Rettie, R., & Kwan, C. C. (2005). Adoption and usage of m-commerce: A cross-cultural comparison of Hong Kong and United Kingdom. *Journal of Electronic Commerce Research, 6*(3), 210–224.

Hausman, A. V., & Siekpe, J. S. (2009). The effect of web interface features on consumer online purchase. *Journal of Business Research, 62,* 5–13. doi:10.1016/j.jbusres.2008.01.018.

Hoffman, D., & Novak, T. P. (2009). Flow online: Lessons learned and future prospects. *Journal of Interactive Marketing, 23*(1), 23–34. doi:10.1016/j.intmar.2008.10.003.

Hoffman, D. L., Novak, T. P., & Peralta, M. (1999). Building consumer trust online. *Communications of the ACM, 42*(4). doi:10.1145/299157.299175 PMID:11543550.

Hofstede, G., & Bond, M. H. (1988). The Confucius connection: From cultural roots to economic growth. *Organizational Dynamics, 16*(4), 5–21. doi:10.1016/0090-2616(88)90009-5.

Hofstede, G. H. (1980). *Culture's consequences: International differences in work-related values.* Beverly Hills, CA: Sage Publications, Inc..

Jahn, S., Drengner, J., & Furchheim, P. (2013). Flow revisited process conceptualization and extension to reactive consumption experiences. In Proceedings of the AMA Winter Educators' Conference. Las Vegas, NV: AMA.

Jarvenpaa, S. L., Tranctinsky, N., & Vitale, M. (2000). Consumer trust in an internet store. *Information Technology Management, 1,* 45–71. doi:10.1023/A:1019104520776.

Johnson, L., Adams, S., & Cummins, M. (2012). The NMC horizon report: 2012 higher education ed. Austin, TX: The New Media Consortium.

Kato, Y., Kato, S., & Chida, K. (2012). Reply timing and emotional strategy in mobile text communications of Japanese young people: Replies to messages conveying four different emotions. In Long, S. D. (Ed.), *Virtual Work and Human Interaction Research* (pp. 99–114). Hershey, PA: IGI Global. doi:10.4018/978-1-4666-0963-1.ch006.

Kober, S. E., & Neuper, C. (2013). Personality and presence in virtual reality: Does their relationship depend on the used presence measure? *International Journal of Human-Computer Interaction, 29*(1), 13–25. doi:10.1080/10447318.2012.668131.

Koufaris, M. (2002). Applying the technology acceptance model and flow theory to online consumer behavior. *Information Systems Research, 13*(2), 205–223. doi:10.1287/isre.13.2.205.83.

Kozinets, R. V. (2002). Can consumer escape the market? Emancipatory illumination from burning man. *The Journal of Consumer Research, 29.*

Lee, I., Choi, B., Kim, J., & Hong, S.-J. (2007). Culture-technology fit: Effects of cultural characteristics on the post-adoption beliefs of mobile Internet users. *International Journal of Electronic Commerce, 11*(4), 11–51. doi:10.2753/JEC1086-4415110401.

Lundgren, H., & Walczuch, R. (2004). Psychological antecedents of institution-based trust in e-retailing. *Information & Management, 42,* 159–177. doi:10.1016/j.im.2003.12.009.

Marcus, A., & Gould, E. W. (2000). Crosscurrents: Cultural dimensions and global web user-interface design. *Interaction, 7*(4), 32–46. doi:10.1145/345190.345238.

McAlexander, J. H., Schouten, J. W., & Koenig, H. F. (2002). Building brand community. *Journal of Marketing, 66*(1), 38–54. doi:10.1509/jmkg.66.1.38.18451.

McKnight, H., Choudhury, V., & Kacmar, C. (2002). The impact of initial trust on intentions to transact with a web site: A trust building model. *The Journal of Strategic Information Systems, 11,* 297–323. doi:10.1016/S0963-8687(02)00020-3.

Mollen, A., & Wilson, H. (2010). Engagement, telepresence and interactivity in online consumer experience: Reconciling scholastic and managerial perspectives. *Journal of Business Research, 63,* 919–925. doi:10.1016/j.jbusres.2009.05.014.

Morgan, R. M., & Hunt, S. D. (1994). The commitment-trust theory of relationship marketing. *Journal of Marketing, 58*(3), 20–38. doi:10.2307/1252308.

Muniz, A., & O'Guinn, T. (2001). Brand community. *The Journal of Consumer Research, 27,* 412–432. doi:10.1086/319618.

Nielson, J. (2001). How to conduct heuristic evaluation. Retrieved May 7, 2010, from www.usit.com/papers/heuristic/

Novak, T. P., Hoffman, D. L., & Yung, Y. F. (2000). Measuring the flow construct in online environments: A structural modeling approach. *Marketing Science, 19*(1), 22–42. doi:10.1287/mksc.19.1.22.15184.

Rose, S., Clark, M., Samouel, P., & Hair, N. (2012). Online customer experience in e-retailing: An empirical model of antecedents and outcomes. *Journal of Retailing, 88*(2), 308–322. doi:10.1016/j.jretai.2012.03.001.

Salter, L. (2005). Colonization tendencies in the development of the world wide web. *New Media & Society, 7*(3), 291–309. doi:10.1177/1461444805050762.

Schwartz, S., & Sagiv, L. (1995). Identifying culture-specifics in the content and structure of values. *Journal of Cross-Cultural Psychology, 26*(1), 92–116. doi:10.1177/0022022195261007.

Shih, H. P. (2004). An empirical study on predicting user acceptance of e-shopping on the web. *Information & Management, 41.*

Siekpe, J. S. (2005). An examination of the multidimensionality of flow construct in a computer-mediated environment. Journal of Electronic Commerce Research, 6(1). Retrieved February 06, 2012, from www.csulb.edu/web/journals/jecr/issues/20051/paper2.pdf

Siriaraya, P., & Ang, C. S. (2012). Age differences in the perception of social presence in the use of 3D virtual world for social interaction. *Interacting with Computers, 24,* 280–291. doi:10.1016/j.intcom.2012.03.003.

Sprott, D., Czellar, S., & Spangenberg, E. (2009). The importance of a general measure of brand engagement on market behavior: Development and validation of a scale. *JMR, Journal of Marketing Research, 46*(1), 92–104. doi:10.1509/jmkr.46.1.92.

Tikkanen, H., Hietanen, J., Henttonen, T., & Rokka, J. (2009). Exploring virtual worlds: Success factors in virtual world marketing. *Management Decision, 47*(8), 1357–1381. doi:10.1108/00251740910984596.

Walker, G. (2005). Sociological theory and the natural environment. *History of the Human Sciences, 18*(1), 77–106. doi:10.1177/0952695105051127.

Wang, C. C., Yang, Y. H., & Hsu, M. C. (2013). The recent development of flow theory research: A bibliometric study. Paper presented at the 2013 International Conference on e-CASE & e-Tech. Kitakyushu, Japan.

Wang, L. C., Baker, J., & Wagner, J., & Wakefield, K. (2007). Can a retail web site be social? *Journal of Marketing*, *71*, 143–157. doi:10.1509/jmkg.71.3.143.

Wasko, M. M., & Faraj, S. (2005). Why should I share? Examining social capital and knowledge contribution in electronic networks of practice. *Management Information Systems Quarterly*, *29*, 35–57.

Yearley, S. (1991). *The green case*. London: Harper Collins.

Yoo, K.-H., & Gretzel, U. (2011). Influence of personality on travel-related consumer-generated media creation. *Computers in Human Behavior*, *27*(2), 609–621. doi:10.1016/j.chb.2010.05.002.

Zhang, D., & Adipat, B. (2005). Challenges, methodologies, and issue in usability testing of mobile applications. *International Journal of Human-Computer Interaction*, *18*(3). doi:10.1207/s15327590ijhc1803_3.

Zhao, M., & Dholakia, R. R. (2009). A multi-attribute model of website interactivity and customer satisfaction: An application of the Kano model. *Managing Service Quality*, *19*(3), 286–307. doi:10.1108/09604520910955311.

ENDNOTES

1. Arena is a brand of competitive swimwear, one of the most famous brands of swim glasses.
2. World of Warcraft (WoW) is a massively multiplayer online role-playing game (MMORPG) by Blizzard Entertainment.
3. Second Life is an online virtual world developed by Linden Lab. It was launched on June 23, 2003.
4. Felix Baumgartner, 42-year-old, jumped out of a space capsule from an altitude of approximately 71,580 feet as the Red Bull Stratos Project, 15th of March 2013.

Chapter 1
Reply Timing as Emotional Strategy in Mobile Text Communications of Japanese Young People:
Focusing on Perceptual Gaps between Senders and Recipients

Yuuki Kato
Sagami Women's University, Japan

Shogo Kato
Tokyo Woman's Christian University, Japan

Kunihiro Chida
Toei Animation Co., Ltd., Japan

ABSTRACT

This study investigates the timing of replies to mobile phone text messages focusing especially on the timing of replies from the perspective of the "recipient" of the message. In a previous study, the authors evaluated the timing of replies and the emotional strategies associated with such timing from the perspective of the "sender" and found they employed an emotional strategy whereby they "waited" before responding to mobile text messages in order to continue positive communication. In the present study, they examine if the same strategy is as effective from the perspective of recipients of the messages. Specifically, study participants were asked by questionnaire to rate what emotions they would feel and to what degree when the other party waited before replying to the mobile text messages the participants had sent, where the message sent had conveyed one of four emotions: happiness, sadness, anger, or guilt. These four emotional scenarios are the same as used in the previous study to allow for comparative analysis of the two studies. Additionally, participants in the present study were asked to provide freeform responses for scenarios where they felt it was desirable to wait before replying themselves. The results show differences between the emotional strategic intent of senders for waiting before replying,

DOI: 10.4018/978-1-4666-4566-0.ch001

as determined in the previous study, and how this is perceived by the recipients. The results suggest that there are gaps in perception between senders and recipients regarding the intentional manipulation of reply timing (especially waiting before replying). One suggested gap is that senders that intentionally manipulate the timing of replies for negative or hostile emotions, such as sadness, anger, or guilt, run the risk of making the recipient feel the opposite of the sender's intended outcome.

INTRODUCTION

The importance of supporting the emotional perspective of learners has been highlighted in the area of e-learning in recent years. For example, sense of community theory (Brook & Oliver, 2003) and social presence theory (Garrison & Anderson, 2003) frequently appear in research related to e-learning. A specialized way of thinking about emotional presence from the perspective of emotion has also been reported in e-learning research (Kang, Kim, & Park, 2007). With frequent reports from various organizations on increasing student dropouts with the shift from the e-learning implementation stage to the operation stage, there is an ever-increasing focus being placed on providing emotional support to students. However, nearly all studies conducted thus far have involved distance learning, such as e-learning, and have focused mainly on cognitive issues such as acquisition and understanding of knowledge, making it difficult to avoid the impression that any consideration of the emotional aspect is of secondary importance at best.

It is thought that communication both within and outside the e-learning environment is important for supporting the emotions of learners and guiding them toward continual learning activities. Learners' emotions are influenced in e-learning environments by their communications with instructors, mentors or other students attending the same course, and are influenced outside of the e-learning environment by their communications with family members, company colleagues, or friends who support them as they pursue education through e-learning. Through these various types of communication, learners will likely have increased desire toward learning if they experience happiness or interest, and will have decreased desire toward learning if they experience antipathy, anger, or sadness. In other words, we believe that the emotions of learners are more strongly influenced by the various communications that surrounds them than by the instructional materials or contents of the courses themselves.

In modern life, much of our communication is text-based communication. Of course, text-based communication in the form of, for example, letters or facsimiles have existed for a long time. However, it cannot really be said that these were the primary forms of communication means of the time. However, with many households now accessing the Internet, text-based communications such as electronic mail and electronic bulletin boards have spread into our daily lives. In recent years, blogs, tweets, and social networking have also become extremely popular. It goes without saying that communication in e-learning has also come to be commonly conducted by text communication. The different types of text communication have become second nature to us because we can use them not only from personal computers but also from mobile phones and smart phones.

We believe, therefore, that by examining the emotional aspect of text communication especially, clues will be discovered that will effectively support the emotional aspect of e-learning students, and will form a basis for continued research. Our recent research, including this study, therefore focuses on investigating the emotional aspects of text communication.

Emotional Aspects of Text Communication

We paid attention to emotional aspects of communication in our previous studies (e.g., Kato, Kato, & Akahori, 2006; Kato, Kato, & Scott, 2007) continuously. Many of our daily interactions take place either face-to-face (F2FC) or synchronously. Within such contexts, we are highly effective at judging people's characteristics, such as familiarity, gender, emotions, and temperament (Cheng, O'Toole, & Abdi, 2001). To make general judgments about others—a process which is a significant aspect of human interpersonal communications—we employ all of the information available to us. Some F2FC research has indicated that both nonverbal and verbal cues affect the process of judgment (Krauss & Fussell, 1996; Kraut, 1978; Patterson, 1994). Computer-Mediated Communication (CMC) such as email is now commonplace in most areas of our daily lives (Joinson, 2003), and most types of CMC are text-based communications that lack important nonverbal information. Therefore, during CMC people must make do with limited cues to help them estimate the emotional state, disposition, and reactions of others to their written messages (Gill, Oberlander, & Elizabeth, 2006; Marttunen & Laurinen, 2001; Rooksby, 2002). This is especially true when CMC users cannot see each other or the CMC environment is otherwise restricted in terms of the nonverbal cues available (Sproull & Kiesler, 1991; Shklovski, Kiesler, & Kraut, 2006).

As the feelings of one's communication partner cannot be easily interpreted or easily transmitted in CMC, emotional misunderstanding can often result (Hancock, 2007; Kato & Akahori, 2004, 2006). Through our own experiences and on the basis of previous research it is not hard to imagine that such emotional misunderstandings during CMC could develop into serious human-relation problems (e.g. Dyer, Green, Pitts, & Millward, 1995; Lea, O'Shea, Fung, & Spears, 1992; Morahan-Martin, 2007; Siegel, Dubrovsky, Kiesler, & McGuire, 1986; Thompsen & Foulger, 1996). Recently, the use of CMC has increased not only in the workplace and at home, but also in educational environments (e.g. Ben-Ami & Mioduser, 2004; Berge & Collins, 1995; Garrison & Anderson, 2003; Gunawardena & Zittle, 1997). For CMC used in educational settings, if one student experiences emotional misunderstanding with other students, it may interfere with his or her achievement of educational targets. In some cases it may also lead to Internet bullying, which has become a growing problem as more young people communicate online (McKenna & Seidman, 2006).

News reports of Internet and email bullying, stabbing incidents, or suicides involving children and juveniles that result from the problems generated through use of CMC are becoming more frequent. As examples, the fatal stabbing of a sixth-grader by a classmate in Sasebo-city, Nagasaki, Japan in June 2004 was due to the victim allegedly posting detrimental comments about her attacker on the Internet. This case caused shock waves not only in educational circles but across society as a whole. Moreover, in March 2008, a third-year student in junior high school in Katagami City, Akita, Japan committed suicide after being reprimanded by her homeroom teacher over a malicious text message she sent to a schoolmate the day before. CMC-related problems are now recognized as a serious social issue rather than an educational issue and, as such, should be urgently tackled by researchers in the field of social informatics. To promote effective CMC, we believe it necessary to focus on the potential problems encountered in such communication, such as emotional misunderstandings, so as to eventually develop strategies to reduce or eliminate them.

With the goal of gaining educational insight into how to avoid these kinds of problems in text communication, we have focused our previous research on the daily experience of users of text communication to consider these problems. For example, our work on message content (Kato,

Sugimura, & Akahori, 2002) and writing style (Kato, Kato, & Akahori, 2006a) has shown that posing questions to the recipient or using emoticons are effective strategies for invoking happiness or positive emotion in the recipient. Moreover, in examining the perspective of different parties in email conversation, we considered the impact on reader emotion of text written by persons with a different perspective (Kato, Kato, & Akahori, 2006b). The results suggested that familiar expressions in an email from a classmate, or an honest and serious writing style for an email received from a person of seniority such as an instructor, can invoke positive emotions in student readers. In addition, in our studies on the transmission of emotion, we investigated which emotional states of a writer would be incorrectly interpreted by the reader (Kato, Kato, & Akahori, 2007; Kato, Kato, & Scott, 2007) and found that, compared to positive emotions which were correctly conveyed, emotions such as sadness or anger were difficult to convey and were easily misunderstood. Moreover, we found that mistakes in interpreting emotion were more likely for the use of emoticons that convey negative emotions than for the use of those that convey positive emotions (Kato, Kato, & Scott, 2009).

As can be seen, many studies examining the emotional aspects of CMC and other forms of text communication have considered the difficulty of interpreting the emotions of another party due to the limited clues available. We have also considered various scenarios within this framework. However, in recent years, we have begun to discover and focus on the possibility that text communication users express their own emotions by intentionally changing them, "taking advantage" of the fact that clues are limited. We refer to this phenomenon as "emotional strategy."

Emotional Strategy

We explained emotional strategy in our previous study (Kato, Kato, & Chida, 2012) as follows. We focused on the use of emotional strategy

in text communications, taking the Emotional Intelligence (EI) model (Salovey & Mayer 1990; Mayer 2000) as a theoretical background. The EI model emphasizes "internal emotional aspects" and addresses "how to deal with emotions that should be suppressed." We apply this model to the communication process (Kato, Kato, Scott, & Sato, 2008) and use the term "emotional strategy" to refer to the act of manipulating the interaction between "emotional aspects of self and those of another party (Kato, Kato, & Chida, 2012)." When we communicate, we sometimes do not directly convey the emotions we are feeling in order to manipulate the emotions of the other person(Kato, Kato, & Chida, 2012). In other words, it seems that sometimes we "only correctly convey those emotions that we consider ideal (Sato, Kato, & Kato, 2008)."

Before we had conducted some of our most recent previous studies (discussed below), for example, those regarding communication between A and B, the authors had debated the accuracy of emotional transmission with "A's actual emotional state" and "B's interpretation of A's emotional state," and as an extension, the goodness of that interaction. These studies focused on how well the emotion produced by mediated-communication users is conveyed to their partner. One barrier to this process is the possible disconnect between the sender's intended emotion and the actual message they compose (Kato, Kato, Scott, & Sato, 2010; Kato, Scott, & Kato, 2011a). That is, the sender may be angry, but does not want to project that emotion too strongly or directly to the receiver. In studies related to the expression of emotions in facial expressions, these traits we found to be particularly common among Japanese people. Japanese language and culture place an emphasis on toning down or suppressing one's true feelings to avoid complicating or damaging interpersonal relations (Matsumoto, 1996; Matsumoto & Kudoh, 1993). We have now come to believe that it is important to consider the ways in which individuals intentionally convey emotions different from they actually feel in order to manipulate the emotions of others, and to consider whether their attempts result in the other person's emotions being manipulated as planned.

As one example of our previous research on the existence of emotional strategies when conveying emotions during communication, a mobile text user relies on various strategies for manipulating his or her own emotions and the emotions of the other person. These are specific strategies, such as to what degree to use emotional expressions, whether to use emoticons, which medium to use, or whether to change the medium (e.g. responding to a mobile text message with a phone call instead of a text message) (Kato, Kato, Scott, & Sato, 2008; Sato, Kato, & Kato, 2008; Kato, Kato, Scott, & Sato, 2010; Kato, Scott, & Kato, 2011b). It should be noted that to our knowledge, the only previous studies—both inside and outside of Japan—related to communication by texting that focus on emotional strategies are the authors' own. Therefore, most studies investigate Japanese people in Japan, and there is currently only one published study that compares emotional strategies of Americans and Japanese, also part of our previous research (Kato, Scott, & Kato, 2011b). This study showed that emotional strategies exist in both countries, and compared to the Japanese, who try more frequently to convey positive emotions such as happiness, Americans tend to convey feelings of anger (not just anger at the other person, but also anger about a situation or something in the discussion). In other words, emotional strategies are thought to be employed both in Japan and overseas, but because there are likely cultural differences in their expression, it is necessary to collect and carefully review additional research data.

From the many strategy-related comments we have collected in our research to date, it appears that people employ a tactic of "waiting before replying" to messages with emotional content. We investigated this aspect of delaying a response (versus replying immediately) (Kato, Kato, & Chida, 2012) and we compare our findings with those of the present study in this report.

Previous Study on Reply Timing in Mobile Text Communications

Our previous study, the findings of which we will use in the comparative analysis, investigated the timing of replies of 224 Japanese university students to senders of mobile text messages (Kato, Kato, & Chida, 2012). Study participants were asked to rate on a 6-point scale whether they would wait before replying to mobile text messages from senders conveying each of four emotions: happiness, sadness, anger, and guilt. They were also asked to give a freeform answer as to why they would respond in such way. The results showed that for each of the four emotional settings, participants adjusted the timing of their message replies in order to manipulate the emotions of others or their own emotions, according to the situation. Individual differences were also observed in participant's thoughts about adjusting reply timing and manipulating emotions.

This previous study focused on the actions of "senders" as they delay replying to mobile text messages. The findings highlighted the possibility that senders use the act of delaying their reply as an emotional strategy. However, it was not clear whether the sender's emotional strategy actually has the desired effect on the recipient. Therefore, the focus of the present study is shifted to the "receiver" of the mobile text messages and we investigate here how the emotions of the recipients are affected by senders' waiting to reply.

Study Objectives

This study focuses on the timing of replies to messages from the perspective of the "recipient" of mobile text messages and makes a comparative analysis with the results of our previous study on the timing of received mobile text messages and emotional strategies from the perspective of the "sender" (Kato, Kato, & Chida, 2012). Our previous study found that mobile text senders 'waited' before responding in order to continue positive communication. We aimed here, by employing the same experimental methods, to determine whether the abovementioned strategy is as effective maintaining positive communication from the perspective of recipients of the messages as it is for the senders.

METHOD

Participants

The participants were 168 first- and second-year university students (81 males, 87 females; mean age 19.38 years [SD 0.96], range 18-24 years) majoring in arts/humanities who used mobile text messaging on a daily basis. It should be noted here that these are completely different participants from those who took part in our previous study (Kato, Kato, & Chida, 2012).

Four Emotions Selected for This Study

The many emotions we convey in everyday life can, according to some, be sorted into basic emotional categories. For example, Ekman (1992) proposed six basic emotions of happiness, sadness, anger, surprise, fear, and disgust. In our previous studies on computer- and mobile phone-based communications (Kato, Kato, Sugimura, & Akahori, 2008; Kato, Sugimura, & Akahori, 2002; Scott, Coursaris, Kato, & Kato 2009), we used Izard, Libero, Putnam, & Haynes's DES-IV: Interest, enjoyment, surprise, sadness, anger, disgust, contempt, fear, guilt, shame, shyness, and inward hostility (Izard, Libero, Putnam, & Haynes 1993). In these studies, we had performed a factor analysis on the ratings on the DES-IV. As the results of the factor analysis, the twelve emotions were classified into the following three categories: Positive emotions (Interest, Joy, Surprise, Willingness), Hostile emotions (Anger, Disgust, Contempt) and Negative emotions (Sadness, Anxiety, Guilt,

Shyness, Inward Hostility). We decided to focus on the basic emotions of happiness, sadness, and anger for this study as they correspond to positive, negative, and hostile emotion, respectively, as well as the emotion of guilt as it is closely related to apologizing and could help avoid emotional misunderstandings. These four emotions are the same emotions used in our previous study (Kato, Kato, & Chida, 2012).

In this study, scenarios were set where participants were asked to imagine messages conveying each of these four types of emotions arriving by mobile text message, and to respond to the questions shown below. The examples of scenarios by the following items were provided to help participants imagine specific cases of messages including the four types of emotions.

Happiness: You send a happy message to a friend, saying, 'I studied the right things and passed the test with flying colors.'

Sadness: You send a sad message to a friend, saying, 'I studied the wrong things and failed the test.'

Anger: Your send an angry message to a friend, saying, 'I failed the test because you taught me completely the wrong things.'

Guilt: You send an apology to a friend, in response to this message: 'My friend failed the test because you taught him completely the wrong things that were not on the test.'

Questionnaire

The questionnaire used in this study is comprised of 3 main sections. First, in order to investigate whether participants as message recipients had experience with sensing that a communication partner waited before replying, they were asked "Have you ever felt that someone to whom you have sent a message intentionally did not immediately reply (intentionally waited before replying), even though you feel that he or she received the mail quickly?" They answered on a 6-point scale: (1: Never, 2: Almost never, 3: Infrequently, 4: Sometimes, 5: Frequently, 6: Extremely frequently). Next, participants were asked for each of the four emotions, "When you send a mobile text message conveying 'happiness,' ('sadness,' 'anger,' 'guilt') and imagining a scenario in which the recipient does not immediately reply (intentionally waits before replying), even though you believe he or she immediately read the message, how do you feel about the following 4 items?" for the following items: "To what degree do you feel 'happiness?'" "To what degree do you feel 'sadness?'" "To what degree do you feel 'anger?'" "To what degree do you feel 'guilt?'" For each of these, participants were asked to respond on a 6-point scale: (1: Not at all, 2: Almost none, 3: Not very much, 4: Somewhat, 5: Quite a bit, 6: Extremely). Finally, participants were asked to answer in a freeform response in what situations they felt it would be "desirable not to reply immediately (wait before replying), even though the message recipient is thought to have immediately read the message."

Additionally, in responding to this questionnaire, for all questions, participants were instructed to imagine a friend as the other party in the mobile text message exchange.

RESULTS AND DISCUSSION

Frequency in Which It Was Felt That the Recipient Intentionally Waited Before Responding

Figure 1 shows the number of participants responding to each of the 6-point scales for the questionnaire item: "Have you ever felt that someone to whom you have sent a message intentionally did

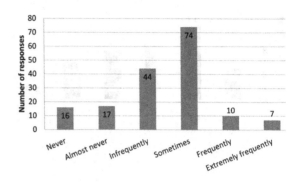

Figure 1. Frequency of experience as a recipient of a feeling of having been intentionally kept waiting before receiving a reply

not immediately reply (intentionally waited before replying), even though you feel that he or she had immediately read the mail?" The response "Sometimes" was by far the most frequent, followed by "Infrequently." In other words, most participants had experienced another party intentionally waiting before replying during a mobile text message exchange.

Considering the phenomenon of waiting before responding from the sender's point of view, we previously asked senders to what degree they waited before responding (Kato, Kato, & Chida, 2012). Comparing those results with the results of the present study, we see that recipients more frequently feel that recipients are waiting before responding. This suggests that recipients may be incorrectly presuming that senders are "intentionally" not responding immediately, even when senders have some other "reason for not immediately responding." Or, recipients may be perceive that they are being kept waiting, even for only short time periods. In any case, there appears to be a gap between the senders and recipients in their perception of the frequency of "intentionally waiting before responding" (see Figure 2).

Figure 2. Frequency of sender intentionally waiting before responding (from Kato, Kato, & Chida, 2012)

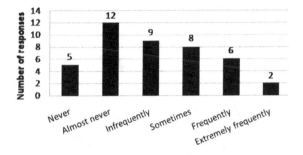

Frequency of the Four Types of Emotions for Each Scenario

Comparison between 4 Emotion Types for Each Scenario

Figure 3 shows the results for the items about what degree the recipients felt each of the four types of emotions, for each of the four situations, when they thought their message partner had immediately read the message but delayed replying. Also, Figure 3 shows a comparison of the occurrences of the four types of emotions for each scenario when sending mobile text messages conveying each of the four types of emotions. A one-way repeated measures ANOVA performed for all scenarios showed a significant difference for the four emotions for all four scenarios: Happiness scenario, $F(501, 3)=43.57$, $p<0.01$; Sad-ness scenario, $F(501, 3)=108.69$, $p<0.01$; Anger scenario, $F(501, 3)=81.30$, $p<0.01$; and Guilt scenario: $F(501, 3)=196.95$, $p<0.01$.

Figure 4 shows the results of multiple comparisons with Bonferroni method to determine any significant differences between emotions for each scenario. The values shown for each emotion are mean values of the 6-point scale (values in parentheses are standard deviations).

From the results shown in Figures 3 and 4, we see a greater incidence in all scenarios for the sadness emotion. In other words, it is thought that the recipient is more likely to feel sadness when it is perceived that the other party is intentionally waiting before replying. Similarly for the anger scenario, there is a greater incidence of anger when it is perceived that the other party is intentionally waiting before replying. Furthermore, for the guilt scenario, there is greater incidence of both sadness and guilt. From these results, we surmise the following: When the recipient believes that the reply was intentionally delayed, this does not help to increase the recipient's feelings of happiness for any emotional scenario. In other words, from these results, the sender's act of waiting before replying does not appear to have a positive emotional effect on the recipient. Waiting to reply to messages that contain the emotion of anger in particular seems to increase the recipient's feelings of anger, and waiting to reply to messages that contain the emotion of guilt seems to increase the recipient's feelings of guilt.

Figure 3. Comparison between the four emotion types for each scenario

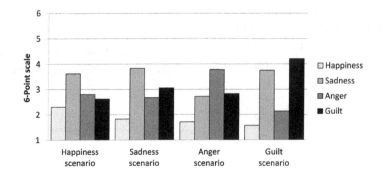

Figure 4. Results of multiple comparisons of the four emotion types for each scenario. Note: ** p<0.01, * p<0.05

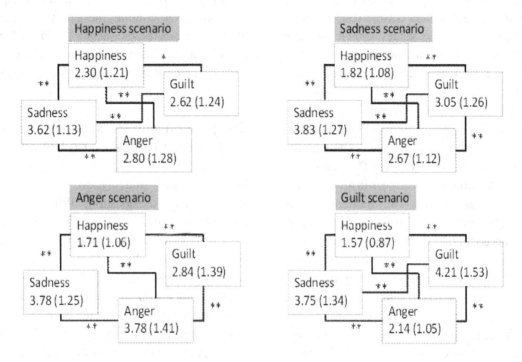

Comparison between Scenario Types for Each of the Four Emotions

Figure 5 shows the results for the items about what degree the recipient felt the four types of emotions for the four scenarios when they thought the message partner immediately read the message but delayed replying. In other words, this section compares the scenarios for each emotion, rather than comparing emotions for each of the scenarios as above. A one-way repeated measures analysis of variance performed for each emotion showed a significant difference between the four scenarios for all emotions: Happiness, $F(501, 3)=35.57$, $p<0.01$; Sadness, $F(501, 3)=49.76$, $p<0.01$; Anger, $F(501, 3)=84.25$, $p<0.01$; and Guilt, $F(501, 3)=73.38$, $p<0.01$.

Figure 5. Comparison between scenario types for the four emotions

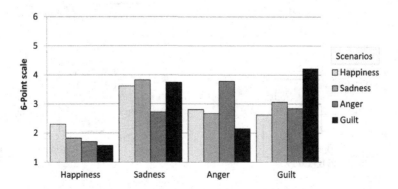

Figure 6 shows the results of multiple comparisons with Bonferroni method to determine any significant differences between the scenarios for each emotion. The values shown for each scenario are mean values on the 6-point scale (values in parentheses are standard deviation values).

From Figures 5 and 6, we can see that for the emotion of happiness, although there is a significant difference between the scenarios, the rating for all scenarios is low. The score was higher for the emotion of sadness in all scenarios except the anger scenario. The emotion of anger scored highest in the anger scenario. The emotion of guilt scored highest in the guilt scenario. From these results, for all four scenario types in this study, intentionally waiting before replying cannot be said to cause the recipients to feel happiness. Meanwhile, the emotion of sadness was highest for the three scenarios excluding anger, although it was also increased to some degree in the anger scenario. So, we can generally state that recipients are more likely to feel sadness when they believe that a sender has intentionally waited before reply-

ing. As was also mentioned above, this comparison more clearly shows that waiting to reply to messages that contain the emotion of anger likely increases the recipient's feelings of anger, and waiting to reply to messages that contain the emotion of guilt likely increases the recipient's feelings of guilt.

Comparison with Results Obtained in the Previous Research on Senders

In our previous study (Kato, Kato, & Chida, 2012), we asked the question: "When you receive a mobile text from a friend conveying each of the four types of emotions (4 scenarios), do you wait before responding?" Participants answered on a 6-point scale (1: Never; 2: Almost never; 3: Not frequently; 4: Occasionally; 5: Frequently; 6: Every time). Figure 7 shows the distribution of the results for each of the emotion scenarios. As can be seen, there is a large variance in ratings for all emotional scenarios, and the effect of how each individual perceives the reply timing is greater than the effect due to the emotional scenario types,

Figure 6. Results of multiple comparisons of each scenario for the four emotion types. Note: ** p<0.01

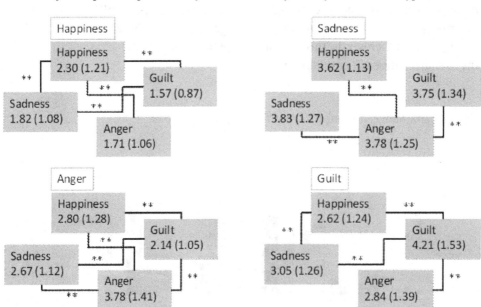

Figure 7. Frequency of intentionally waiting before replying as the sender for each scenario (revised from Kato, Kato, & Chida, 2012)

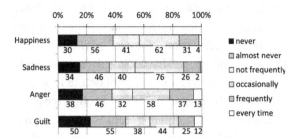

Table 1. Reasons given by senders for intentionally waiting before replying as an emotional strategy (revised from Kato, Kato, & Chida, 2012)

Reason for Waiting Before Replying in Happiness Scenario
• To stretch out the happiness.
-Reason for waiting before replying in Sadness scenario.
• To provide encouragement.
• To wait until the sadness fades.
-Reason for waiting before replying in Anger scenario.
• To wait for the anger to die down.
• Replying quickly would make things worse.
• To convey a sense of reflection.
-Reason for waiting before replying in Guilt scenario.
• To make the other person think about it more.
• Because I'm angry.
• To put the other person at ease.
• It doesn't really bother me.

suggesting the likelihood of individual variations (Kato, Kato, & Chida, 2012). In other words, our previous study showed that the action of waiting before replying does not necessarily cause any difference to each emotion scenario, but that in all scenarios approximately the same number of senders wait before replying. Also, for each scenario, we asked participants who said they waited before replying to mobile text messages to answer in freeform why they intentionally waited (Kato, Kato, & Chida, 2012). Table 1 summarizes for each emotional scenario the reasons given by senders for intentionally waiting before replying "as an emotional strategy."

Let us now discuss the results obtained in the present study on recipients while referring to the findings of our previous study on senders shown in Table 1. First, it is difficult to say that the expected outcome was obtained for the reason given in the happiness scenario of "to stretch out the happiness." It is also difficult to say that the reasons given for waiting before replying for the sadness scenario, namely, "to provide encouragement" and "to wait until the sadness fades," were as expected. In other words, it is possible that delayed replies actually result in greater sadness for the recipient. For the anger scenario, the results were not as expected for the sender's reasons for delaying replies, namely, "to wait for the anger to die down," "replying quickly would make things worse," and "to convey as sense of reflection."

From these results, we cannot deny the possibility that waiting recipients could grow even angrier and that relationships could be worsened. Finally, for the guilt scenario, the reasons given by the sender for waiting before replying, namely, "to make the other person think about it more" and "because I'm angry," can be said to have been effective because, by waiting before replying, recipients did feel an increased sense of guilt. On the other hand, the present study suggests the opposite outcome for the recipient for the sender's reasons of "to put the other person at ease" and "it doesn't really bother me."

Scenarios as the Receiver where the Sender Intentionally Waiting before Replying is Desirable

Finally, the following items shows a summary of responses given by participants who were asked what situations they felt it would be desirable not to receive reply immediately even though the message recipient was thought to have immediately read the message. To analyze the freeform responses, all responses were categorized according to their meaning and content. This categorization task was performed jointly by the three researchers, who confirmed their agreement for all responses.

- When I am busy. (62 responses)
- When the other party sent me a message that makes me think deeply. (20 responses)
- When sending a message to help me work through my problems. (17 responses)
- When making a declaration of love. (13 responses)
- When I know the other party is busy. (6 responses)
- When it is late at night. (6 responses)
- When I sent a message by accident. (5 responses)
- When sending a monologue or musing message. (4 responses)
- When sending an "all business," administrative contact message. (3 responses)
- When sending a message with very serious content. (3 responses)
- When the interest in the subject matter has died off (grown bored with the subject.) (3 responses)
- When declining an invitation by the other party. (2 responses)
- When sending a lengthy message. (2 responses)
- When sending a message only as a polite greeting. (1 response)
- When afraid of the other party's reaction. (1 response)
- When expecting a message with photo attachment. (1 response)

The most common response was "when I am busy." In other words, it seems that they hoped for a delayed reply because they were busy and would be unable to continue to read the other party's reply and then again reply in turn. Also, it seems that they wished for a delayed reply in

cases that would require time to write the reply message, such as "when the other party sent a message that makes me think deeply" and "when sending a message that helps me work through my problems." Furthermore, for the reason of "when making a declaration of love," participants are thought to have hoped for a delayed response while the other party carefully thought before replying. Lastly, for the reason of "when I sent a message by accident," participants seem to want enough time to send a message to correct their mistake.

Looking at these results in total, it appears that the participants hoped for quick replies as a general rule, but were comfortable with late replies in cases where it would take time for the other party to write the reply. In other words, in cases where the recipients wanted the other party to take time to write the reply, they might doubt the other party's sincerity when the reply was immediate.

There may also be a generational difference in response timing. The participants of this study and those of our previous study (Kato, Kato, & Chida, 2012) are members of the younger generation, so-called "digital natives." There exist some symbolic episodes that represent this generational gap (Kato, Kato, & Chida, 2012).

A university professor was working until late at night preparing for class and sent an advance email to students with various details about the lecture. However, a student complained about this professor. The student complained that: "I lose sleep because since this professor sends emails late at night and I need to reply to them."

The university professor in this episode probably sent the message to the student's personal computer email address (provided by the university). However, the student might have configured his computer email to forward to his mobile phone. For a typical modern-day student, a mobile phone is a very personal communication form that is kept nearby, even when sleeping. The student probably felt compelled to reply immediately when the professor's email arrived. This is not surprising from the perspective of the student. The professor however, views email as an asynchronous form of communication. Furthermore, for digital natives, mobile phones are all-purpose tools that are used synchronously not just for mobile phone email but also for other forms of communication, such as Twitter or social networking. Members of the professor's generation have a strong tendency to regard mobile phones as devices for making telephone calls. This kind of mobile phone messaging generational gap, and as an extension of the mobile phone generational awareness gap, demands further consideration regarding the timing of replying to messages.

This study used a questionnaire to investigate reply timing, but measuring actual reply times is only one possibility. Another possible method could be to send mobile text messages to participants containing the four types of emotional content shown in Table 1, and measure the time until a reply is received from the participant. However, the authors feel that it would be difficult to experimentally measure reply time, due to problems with writing messages and gathering content in an experiment as well as problems measuring the reaction to the message. It would be necessary to control various factors such as the message delivery timing and time (such as whether it is morning or night or summer vacation), the precise relationship with the other person, and the lifestyles of the other person in addition to the participant (e.g. class schedules, working hours, or club activities if they are students). All of these would limit the results that could be obtained. For these reasons, rather than measuring the time until replying, the method chosen for this study was to ask participants whether they "intentionally" waited before replying. In other words, even when there are differences in the time

passed before replying, the aim of this study was to ask whether the delay was intentional and to consider the underlying reasons.

Finally, let us consider the impact that the present results could have for e-learning. In e-learning, text messages are shared in a variety of situations such as to distribute class materials or make administrative notifications, or to communicate with faculty, mentors, or with other students. In this study, we cannot make any specific reference to the potential impact of efficient timing of distributions of class materials or administrative notices; however, the findings of this study may prove useful in developing effective strategies for faculty and mentors to communicate with students. When faculty or mentors send messages to students or students send messages to faculty or mentors, it is not unusual in actual e-learning environments for such communications to expand beyond communications about study content into counseling about study-related problems or concerns. It is also probably common for students to forward e-learning-related messages to their mobile telephones. When faculty or mentors communicate with students, it is difficult for them to synchronously reply to the first message that they receive from a student. However, when responding, faculty and mentors should make an effort to wait for a while to see whether there is another message from the student. Of course, the meaning of this is not to continue in a synchronous conversation from that point, but to understand what sort of timing the other party uses to respond. In other words, faculty and mentors can use what is known about the timing tendencies of students sending messages to provide better direction to that student. Students expect that faculty and mentors understand that students will (intentionally or mistakenly) perceive messages sent with the same timing to be of similar importance.

CONCLUSION

This study focused on mobile text messages, which are considered to be a form of synchronous communication, whereas conventional computer-based email is an asynchronous communication form in which delays between sending and replying s are common. For this reason, some people are happy to wait several days for an email reply before perceiving that a reply is late. However, even in cases in which the reply takes a long time, rather than have an emotional awareness as seen experimentally in this study, in most cases recipients begin to self-question whether they have done something wrong. In other words, personal computer email and mobile phone email communications are seen as very different despite both being forms of email communication. For this reason, there is merit in this study considering the response timing for communication via mobile text messages. The findings indicate that the reply timing for mobile text messages serves as an emotional clue in the interaction between senders and receivers of these communications.

This study focused on how recipients felt with regard to the timing of replies to mobile text messages, especially toward the act of senders who intentionally waiting before replying. A comparison with the results of our previous study on how senders feel in this instance (Kato, Kato, & Chida, 2012), especially the mindset of senders that wait before responding, revealed differences between the emotional strategic intent of senders for waiting before replying (Kato, Kato, & Chida, 2012) and how they were actually perceived by the recipients. Based on this, there is thought to be a perpetual gap between senders and recipients in the intentional manipulation of reply timing (especially waiting before replying). Senders who intentionally manipulate the timing for negative or hostile emotions such as sadness, anger or guilt

actually run the risk of creating the opposite feelings in the recipient. Specifically, when the sender intentionally delays replying with the intent of lessening these negative or hostile feelings, this may actually increase the recipient's feelings of these emotions.

The participants of this survey were Japanese people in Japan. Therefore, surveys should be administered in other countries and intercultural comparative studies should be performed. Obtaining quantitative trends in reply timing could be useful in the educational arena, such as choosing the most effective time in e-learning to send messages. There is therefore merit in working on an experimental design to measure actual reply timing.

REFERENCES

Ben-Ami, O., & Mioduser, D. (2004). The affective aspect of moderator's role conception and enactment by teachers in a-synchronous learning discussion groups. In *Proceedings of World Conference on Educational Multimedia, Hypermedia and Telecommunications (ED-MEDIA) 2004* (pp. 2831-2837). ED-MEDIA.

Berge, Z. L., & Collins, M. P. (1995). *Computer-mediated communication and the online classroom*. Cresskill, NJ: Hampton Press.

Brook, C., & Oliver, R. (2003). Designing for online learning communities. In *Proceedings of World Conference on Educational Multimedia, Hypermedia and Telecommunications (ED-MEDIA) 2003* (pp. 1494-1500). ED-MEDIA.

Cheng, Y., O'Toole, A., & Abdi, H. (2001). Classifying adults' and children's faces by sex: Computational investigations of subcategorial feature encoding. *Cognitive Science*, *25*(5), 819–838. doi:10.1207/s15516709cog2505_8.

Dyer, R., Green, R., Pitts, M., & Millward, G. (1995). What's the flaming problem? CMC - Deindividuation or disinhibiting? In Kirby, M. A. R., Dix, A. J., & Finlay, J. E. (Eds.), *People and computers X*. Cambridge, UK: Cambridge University Press.

Ekman, P. (1992). An argument for basic emotions. In Stein, N. L., & Oatley, K. (Eds.), *Basic emotions: Cognition & emotion* (pp. 169–200). Mahwah, NJ: Lawrence Erlbaum.

Garrison, D. R., & Anderson, T. (2003). *E-learning in the 21st century: A framework for research and practice*. London: Routledge Falmer. doi:10.4324/9780203166093.

Gill, A. J., Oberlander, J., & Elizabeth, A. (2006). Rating e-mail personality at zero acquaintance. *Personality and Individual Differences, 40*(3), 497–507. doi:10.1016/j.paid.2005.06.027.

Gunawardena, C. N., & Zittle, F. J. (1997). Social presence as a predictor of satisfaction within a computer-mediated conferencing environment. *American Journal of Distance Education, 11*(3), 8–26. doi:10.1080/08923649709526970.

Hancock, J. T. (2007). Digital deception: Why, when and how people lie online. In Joinson, A. N., McKenna, K., Postmes, T., & Reips, U. (Eds.), *The Oxford handbook of internet psychology* (pp. 289–301). Oxford, UK: Oxford University Press.

Izard, C. E., Libero, D. Z., Putnam, P., & Haynes, O. M. (1993). Stability of emotion experiences and their relations to traits of personality. *Journal of Personality and Social Psychology, 64*, 847–860. doi:10.1037/0022-3514.64.5.847 PMID:8505713.

Joinson, A. N. (2003). *Understanding the psychology of internet behaviour: Virtual worlds, real lives*. New York: Palgrave Macmillan.

Kang, M., Kim, S., & Park, S. (2007). Developing an emotional presence scale for measuring students' involvement during e-learning process. In *Proceedings of World Conference on Educational Multimedia, Hypermedia and Telecommunications (ED-MEDIA) 2007* (pp. 2829-2831). ED-MEDIA.

Kato, S., Kato, Y., & Scott, D. J. (2009). Relationships between emotional states and emoticons in mobile phone email communication in Japan. *International Journal on E-Learning: Corporate, Government, Healthcare, &. Higher Education, 8*(3), 385–401.

Kato, S., Kato, Y., Scott, D. J., & Sato, K. (2008). Selection of ICT in emotional communication for Japanese students: Focusing on emotional strategies and gender differences. In *Proceedings of World Conference on Educational Multimedia, Hypermedia and Telecommunications (ED-MEDIA) 2008* (pp. 1050-1057). ED-MEDIA.

Kato, Y., & Akahori, K. (2004). The accuracy of judgement of emotions experienced by partners during e-mail and face-to-face communication. In *Proceedings of International Conference on Computers in Education (ICCE) 2004* (pp. 1559-1570). ICCE.

Kato, Y., & Akahori, K. (2006). Analysis of judgment of partners' emotions during e-mail and face-to-face communication. *Journal of Science Education in Japan, 29*(5), 354–365.

Kato, Y., Kato, S., & Akahori, K. (2006a). Effects of senders' self-disclosures and styles of writing messages on recipients' emotional aspects in e-mail communication. In *Proceedings of World Conference on E-Learning in Corporate, Government, Healthcare, and Higher Education (E-Learn) 2006* (pp. 2585-2592). E-Learn.

Kato, Y., Kato, S., & Akahori, K. (2006b). Comparison of emotional aspects in e-mail communication by mobile phone with a teacher and a friend. In *Proceedings of World Conference on Educational Multimedia, Hypermedia and Telecommunications (ED-MEDIA) 2006* (pp. 425-433). ED-MEDIA.

Kato, Y., Kato, S., & Akahori, K. (2007). Effects of emotional cues transmitted in e-mail communication on the emotions experienced by senders and receivers. *Computers in Human Behavior, 23*(4), 1894–1905. doi:10.1016/j.chb.2005.11.005.

Kato, Y., Kato, S., & Chida, K. (2012). Reply timing and emotional strategy in mobile text communications of Japanese young people: Replies to messages conveying four different emotions. In Long, S. D. (Ed.), *Virtual Work and Human Interaction Research* (pp. 99–114). Hershey, PA: IGI Global. doi:10.4018/978-1-4666-0963-1.ch006.

Kato, Y., Kato, S., & Scott, D. J. (2007). Misinterpretation of emotional cues and content in Japanese email, computer conferences, and mobile text messages. In Clausen, E. I. (Ed.), *Psychology of Anger* (pp. 145–176). Hauppauge, NY: Nova Science Publishers.

Kato, Y., Kato, S., Scott, D. J., & Sato, K. (2010). Patterns of emotional transmission in Japanese young people's text-based communication in four basic emotional situations. *International Journal on E-Learning: Corporate, Government, Healthcare, &. Higher Education, 9*(2), 203–227.

Kato, Y., Kato, S., Sugimura, K., & Akahori, K. (2008). The influence of affective traits on emotional aspects of message receivers in text-based communication - Examination by the experiment using e-mail communication. *Educational Technology Review, 31*(1-2), 85–95.

Kato, Y., Scott, D. J., & Kato, S. (2011a). The influence of intimacy and gender on emotions in mobile phone email. In Gokcay, D., & Yildirim, G. (Eds.), *Affective computing and interaction: Psychological, cognitive and neuroscientific perspectives* (pp. 262–279). Hershey, PA: IGI Global.

Kato, Y., Scott, D. J., & Kato, S. (2011b). Comparing American and Japanese young people's emotional strategies in mobile phone email communication. In *Proceedings of World Conference on Educational Multimedia, Hypermedia and Telecommunications (ED-MEDIA) 2011* (pp. 170-178). ED-MEDIA.

Kato, Y., Sugimura, K., & Akahori, K. (2002). Effect of contents of e-mail messages on affections. In *Proceedings of International Conference on Computers in Education (ICCE) 2002*, (Vol. 1, pp. 428-432). ICCE.

Krauss, R. M., & Fussell, S. R. (1996). Social psychological models of interpersonal communication. In Higgins, E. T., & Kruglanski, A. W. (Eds.), *Social Psychology: Handbook of basic principles* (pp. 655–701). New York: The Guilford Press.

Kraut, R. E. (1978). Verbal and nonverbal cues in the perception of lying. *Journal of Personality and Social Psychology, 36*(4), 380–391. doi:10.1037/0022-3514.36.4.380.

Lea, M., O'Shea, T., Fung, P., & Spears, R. (1992). Flaming in computer-mediated communication: Observations, explanations, implications. In Lea, M. (Ed.), *Contexts of computer-mediated communication* (pp. 89–112). New York: Harvester Wheasheaf.

Marttunen, M., & Laurinen, L. (2001). Learning of argumentation skills in networked and face-to-face environments. *Instructional Science, 29*(2), 127–153. doi:10.1023/A:1003931514884.

Matsumoto, D. (1996). *Unmasking Japan: Myths and realities about the emotions of the Japanese.* Stanford, CA: Stanford University Press.

Matsumoto, D., & Kudoh, T. (1993). American-Japanese cultural differences in implicit theories of personality based on smile. *Journal of Nonverbal Behavior, 17*(4), 231–243. doi:10.1007/BF00987239.

Mayer, J. D. (2000). Emotion, intelligence, emotional intelligence. In Forgas, J. P. (Ed.), *The handbook of affect and social cognition* (pp. 410–431). Mahwah, NJ: Lawrence Erlbaum & Associates.

McKenna, K., & Seidman, G. (2006). Considering the interactions: The effects of the internet on self and society. In Kraut, R., Malcolm, B., & Kiesler, S. (Eds.), *Computers, phones, and the internet* (pp. 279–295). Oxford, UK: Oxford University Press.

Morahan-Martin, J. (2007). Internet use and abuse and psychological problems. In Joinson, A. N., McKenna, K., Postmes, T., & Reips, U. (Eds.), *The Oxford handbook of internet psychology* (pp. 331–345). Oxford, UK: Oxford University Press.

Patterson, M. L. (1994). Strategic functions of nonverbal exchange. In Daly, J. A., & Wiemann, J. M. (Eds.), *Strategic interpersonal communication* (pp. 273–293). Hillsdale, NJ: Erlbaum.

Rooksby, E. (2002). *E-mail and ethics: Style and ethical relations in computer-mediated communication.* New York: Routledge. doi:10.4324/9780203217177.

Salovey, P., & Mayer, J. D. (1990). Emotional intelligence. *Imagination, Cognition and Personality, 9*(3), 185–211. doi:10.2190/DUGG-P24E-52WK-6CDG.

Sato, K., Kato, Y., & Kato, S. (2008). Exploring emotional strategies in mobile phone email communication: Analysis on the impact of social presence. In *Proceedings of International Conference on Computers in Education (ICCE) 2008* (pp. 253-260). ICCE.

Scott, D. J., Coursaris, C. K., Kato, Y., & Kato, S. (2009). The exchange of emotional context in business communications: A comparison of PC and mobile email users. In Head, M. M., & Li, E. (Eds.), *Mobile and ubiquitous commerce: Advanced e-business methods* (pp. 201–219). Hershey, PA: IGI Global. doi:10.4018/978-1-60566-366-1.ch011.

Shklovski, I., Kiesler, S., & Kraut, R. (2006). The internet and social interaction: A meta-analysis and critique of studies 1995-2003. In Kraut, R., Malcolm, B., & Kiesler, S. (Eds.), *Computers, phones, and the internet* (pp. 251–264). Oxford, UK: Oxford University Press.

Siegel, J., Dubrovsky, V., Kiesler, S., & McGuire, T. W. (1986). Group processes in computer-mediated communication. *Organizational Behavior and Human Decision Processes, 37*(2), 157–187. doi:10.1016/0749-5978(86)90050-6.

Sproull, L., & Kiesler, S. (1991). *Connections: New ways of working in the networked organization.* Cambridge, MA: MIT Press.

Thompsen, P. A., & Foulger, D. A. (1996). Effects of pictographs and quoting on flaming in electronic mail. *Computers in Human Behavior, 12*(2), 225–243. doi:10.1016/0747-5632(96)00004-0.

ADDITIONAL READING

Argyle, M., & Dean, J. (1965). Eye contact, distance and affiliation. *Sociometry, 28,* 289–304. doi:10.2307/2786027 PMID:14341239.

Gunawardena, C. N. (1995). Social presence theory and implications for interaction and collaborative learning in computer conferences. *International Journal of Educational Telecommunications, 1,* 147–166.

Ito, M., Okabe, D., & Matsuda, M. (2005). *Personal, portable, pedestrian: Mobile phones in Japanese life.* Cambridge, MA: MIT Press.

Joinson, A. (2001). Self-disclosure in computer-mediated communication: The role of self-awareness and visual anonymity. *European Journal of Social Psychology*, *31*, 177–192. doi:10.1002/ejsp.36.

McGuire, T., Kiesler, S., & Siegel, J. (1987). Group and computer-mediated discussion effects in risk decision making. *Journal of Personality and Social Psychology*, *52*, 917–930. doi:10.1037/0022-3514.52.5.917.

Okabe, D., & Ito, M. (2006). Keitai in public transportation. In Ito, M., Okabe, D., & Matsuda, M. (Eds.), *Personal, portable, pedestrian: Mobile phones in Japanese life* (pp. 205–217). Cambridge, MA: MIT Press.

Reid, E. (1995). Virtual worlds: Culture and imagination. In Jones, S. G. (Ed.), *Cybersociety: Computer-mediated communication and community* (pp. 164–183). Thousand Oaks, CA: Sage.

Short, J., Williams, E., & Christie, B. (1976). *The social psychology of telecommunications*. London: John Wiley & Sons.

Sproull, L., & Kiesler, S. (1986). Reducing social context cues: electronic mail in organizational communication. *Management Science*, *32*, 1492–1512. doi:10.1287/mnsc.32.11.1492.

Sproull, L., & Kiesler, S. (1993). Computers, networks and work. In Harasim, L. (Ed.), *Global networks: Computers and international communication* (pp. 105–120). Cambridge, MA: MIT Press.

Walther, J. B., Anderson, J. F., & Park, D. W. (1994). Interpersonal effects in computer-mediated interaction. *Communication Research*, *21*, 460–487. doi:10.1177/009365094021004002.

Walther, J. B., & Burgoon, J. K. (1992). Relational communication in computer-mediated interaction. *Human Communication Research*, *19*, 50–88. doi:10.1111/j.1468-2958.1992.tb00295.x.

Chapter 2
Texted Environmental Campaign in China:
A Case Study of New Media Communication

Yuanxin Wang
Temple University, USA

ABSTRACT

This chapter examines how local residents were informed and rallied by the Internet and mobile phone messages for an unprecedented protest against the construction of a hazardous chemical plant in Xiamen, China, and how the municipal government responded by encouraging public participation in environmental decision making via the same communicational platforms. Using combined research methods including interviews and secondary data analysis, this research investigates the role of the Internet and cell phone message in mobilizing the general public to participate in the environmental protection movement in China. The role of Word Of Mouth (WOM) in the environmental movement is discovered for the first time. The unique mechanism of cellular telephones and the Internet in public participation involving multiple stakeholders in China's environmental policy-making process is also discussed.

INTRODUCTION

Mass media have been a central public arena for disseminating environmental issues and contesting claims, arguments, and opinions about our use and protection of the environment (Hansen, 2010). Media products, together with perceptions of the products by its audiences, make an impact upon political decision-makers regarding a wide scope of issues related to environmental protection issues. Over the past decade, there has been a clear transition in environment communication domain: The scope for the concept of the environment has been expanded from natural phenomenon to an anthropocentric abstraction form representing the totality of nature (Walker, 2005). Communication scholars therefore need to examine the environmental issues from racial, socio-economic, political (Hansen, 2010), and cultural perspectives (Deluca, 1999; Gibbs, 1993). In other words, mass media need to approach environmental movements and organizations as a "collection of agencies making social problems claims" (Yearley, 1991, p. 52).

DOI: 10.4018/978-1-4666-4566-0.ch002

Communication is the central means for the general public to understand the environmental issues, and mass media has been the major platform to shape the public opinion. In other words, different media systems might result in different pattern of communication and hence the social impact under the system. There is a clear discrepancy of public opinions upon environmental issues across regions or cultures. For example, surveys conducted in England and Wales on attitudes towards the environment have shown a clear increase between 1986 and 2001 in the percentages of people who were "very worried" about a broad range of environmental issue (Department for Environment, Food and Rural Affairs, 2002). Similar cases are in the wider Europe Union, Latin America, Japan, and India (Pew Global Attitudes Project, 2007). However, in China, the country with the largest population in the world (National Bureau of Statistics of China, 2013), the awareness of environmental protection remains low (Guo & Marinova, 2011), due to the limited access to and sensitivity of the information of environmental problems. Consequently, scholarly research regarding environmental communication in China remains scarce. However, the gap in environmental awareness might shrink, as the differences of nature in occidental and oriental may be subsumed under the homogenizing influences of globalization (Hansen, 2010).

Mass media also influence the pattern of their users' information-seeking behaviors. Scholars have been focusing on the use pattern of new media (the Internet and mobile phone) audience. For example, how do the interest group and stakeholders of environmental issues probe computer-mediated communication forms for environmental information and organizing campaigns. In many countries, the Internet has become an instrument for increasing public participation in environmental decision making (Scharl, 2004), as some forms of online communication, such as Bulletin Board System (BBS) Forum and Blogs, have been adopted for the discussion of environmental concerns

(Ma, Webber, & Finlayson, 2008). Additionally, some mass media also provides opportunities for environmentalist groups, rather than government sources or representatives of officialdom, to become more significant primary definers of the mass media's agenda (Abraham, 1995). However, much attention has been given to the communicational function of the Internet alone. The role of mobile phone in promoting environmental campaigns is relatively understudied.

This chapter aims to draw a dynamic map about how the environmental message was initiated and disseminated using Web-based communicational channels, and how the message tailor-made based on the natures of the Internet and cell phone mobilized the public participation in environmental protection events. To be specific, this study addresses mechanisms of mobile phone and the Internet as powerful communication channels to call for public attention on environmental issues and organize environmental protection events. The Web-based technology makes it possible for people with different social and economic backgrounds (especially marginalized grassroots) in China to communicate effectively while dealing with environmental problems and engaging in policy-making process. Besides the analysis based on mass communication frameworks, the word of mouth (WOM) communication at interpersonal level is also investigated in this study.

BACKGROUND

Key Concepts

Environment: Originally defined as "place or thing that is separate and distant from humans and their cultures" (Dawson, 2009; Hendry, 2010, p. 5). Till the early 1960s, the term environment started to be associated with a particular public conversation about problems of the relationship between human and the ecosystem they are in (Hansen, 2010, p.1). Generally, environmental issues can be sorted into three categories. One category is nature-driven environmental issues which are clearly separate from human activity, such as landslide, hurricane, earthquake, and ozone depletion. The second category is the environmental problems resulted from ongoing interactions between human and nature, such as global warming, natural resource conservation, land use management, and deforestation (Tilman & Lehman, 2001). The third category reflects human activities based on but independent of nature, such as biotechnology development, genetic modification technology, and nuclear power plants.

The emergence and prospering of *new media* (e.g., the Internet and mobile phone) reinforce and expand the capability of media in encouraging public to spontaneously participate in decision-making process with its reciprocal and instant nature. Davis and Owen (1998) suggest four approaches that *the Internet* might be used to facilitate participation: (a) providing faster and more in-depth access to news and political information, (b) linking government and citizens through e-mail, online forums, distribution lists, and political Websites, (c) providing space for discussion, (d) serving as a barometer of public opinion and offering reaction to events and decisions in real time.

Mobile Phone: Has features such as voice calls and text messaging, which has been burgeoning in the recent years (Jin & Peña, 2010). Interaction through mobile phone shares some similarities with face-to-face communication. For example, Licoppe (2004) claims that mobile technology enables people to develop a particular communication pattern in close relationships, as wireless communication facilitates "mobility, freedom, and flexibility" (Claudia & Anamaria de, 2012, p. 320) and implicit interaction (Cowan, Griswold, Barkhuus, & Hollan, 2010). Besides offering the typical features of face-to-face communication, mobile devices could also be used as pathways to anonymity, mobility, and individualism which allows greater opportunity for transgressing mor-

alized social roles (Maroon, 2006), and as tool to circumvent oppressive or intimidating situations (Gordon, 2002). During the past ten years, an improved version of mobile phone--*smart phone* presents innovative features in terms of communicational measures. A smart phone is a mobile phone with built-in applications (i.e. video player, MP3 player, television, and camera), and the ability to access the Internet (LaRue, Mitchell, Terhorst, & Karimi, 2010). These features allow people to be in constant and instant communication with their family, friends, and colleagues. The latest generation of mobile phones supports complex multi-touch input, gesture-based interaction, advanced soft keyboards, enhanced connectivity, and a great number of dedicated special-purpose applications (Bao, Pierce, Whittaker, & Zhai, 2011). Literature has been built on how the smart phone is utilized in marketing, medication, chemical, computer science, and many other fields.

Word-Of-Mouth (WOM): Is one of the most potent forms of interpersonal communication (Kiecker & Cowels, 2002). WOM has traditionally been depicted as a two-step flow of communication, which involves information being provided by an organization through mass media campaign to influence certain individuals as opinion leaders, and opinion leaders influencing others based on their knowledge and experience (Haywood, 1989). The idea of WOM echoes that hypothesis introduced by Lazarsfeld and his colleagues' (1948) "two-step flow of communication" which proposes that influences stemming from the mass media first reach "opinion leaders" who, in turn, pass on what they read and hear to those of their every-day associates for whom they are influential. Contemporarily WOM has been defined as face-to-face (or person-to-person) verbal communication (e.g., exchanges of comments, thoughts, or ideas) between two or more persons (Bone, 1995). Most existing WOM research investigates how the communication operate from the perspective of the WOM source or speaker (Reingen & Kernan, 1986; Sundaram, Kaushik, &

Webster, 1998), the effects of WOM on the listener (Bone, 1995; Herr, Kardes, & Kim, 1991), and how to generate positive WOM (Maxham, 2001). Furthermore, researchers (Maxham, 2001; Reichheld & Sasser, 1990) also suggested that positive WOM will invariably lead to action by the listener. However, scholars argue that listeners make use of WOM communications based on multiple factors (Dichter, 1966), and effective WOM usually takes places when speaker is not concerned with whether the listener engages in a specific behavior as a result of the communication (Martin & Leug, 2013). Despite the wealth of the research, few studies concerning how informants disseminate environmental information through interpersonal channels have been conducted. This study will give a first look at the communicational function of WOM in environmental movement in China.

There are three streams of theoretical and empirical work in literature on *environmental public participation* (Dietz & Stern, 2003): quality of deliberation, conflict resolution, and the lessons drawn from the practice of environmental decision-making process. Media attitudes influence public participation by making more people aware of problems associated with government (Douglas, 1995; Langton, 1978). Scholars have found that media function as an essential mediator in the relationship among individuals with diverse values and their participatory behaviors (Cohen, 1963; Dearing & Rogers, 1996; McComb & Shaw, 1972).

Mass Media and Environmental Campaigns

Many of the well-known and politically effective environment groups regard the mass media as an integral and essential part of their campaigning strategy (Hansen, 2010, p. 6). For example, stakeholders (e.g., commercial groups and environmental pressure groups) use Internet-related communicational technologies (e.g., social Website, mobile phone etc.) to seek information and organize environmental campaigns. Social groups

develop and evolve environmental issues in the media by interacting with each other in ways that define and frame stages of the developments (Hilgartner & Bosk, 1988).

Despite that environmental groups rely heavily on mass media to disseminate the messages and achieve their campaigning goals, they themselves are not the prominent source for news coverage by mainstream media (Lester, 2010; Linne & Hansen, 1999; Trumbo, 1996; Widener & Gunter, 2007). Furthermore, among the relatively limited amount of environmental news quoting environmental groups as the source, less coverage was given to human-caused issues such as such as mumps and controversy of cloning than nature-driven issues such as climate change (Hargreaves, Lewis, & Speers, 2004). Environmental news such as the news about hazardous chemical plant is less likely to be covered in mainstream media, hence the environmental groups tend to utilize alternative communicational forms such as the online blogging site and mobile phone to achieve their campaign goals. One possible factor that contributes to the under-representation of environmental groups might be the cultural concepts widely held by the audience (Gamson & Modigliani, 1989; Schudson, 1989) and political biases (Hilgartner & Bosk, 1988).

Mass media is also the major source for the general public to find major environmental issues (MORI, 2005). Hansen (2010) points out that public awareness and concern about the environment in Western countries has "waned and waxed in cycles" (p. 161), which generally echoes the fluctuations of coverage on environmental issues in media (Geiger & Eshet, 2010). Mazur (1981) further explains that there is a negative association between media coverage and the audience perception by stating that "when media coverage of a controversy increases, public opposition to the issues in question increases; when media coverage wanes, public opposition falls off" (p. 109). The rationale behind the scene might be that increased media reporting lead to increased public perceptions of risk and related negative consequences (Frewer, 2002), especially when the audiences are skeptical about the credibility of the environmental issue coverage and ready for radical action (Worcester, 1994). In this kind of scenario, downplaying environmental issues relating to hazardous consequences could be a strategy employed by the government to avoid unfavorable public attitudes towards the government. China is among the countries that choose to withhold environmental information to the general public. Consequently, the Internet has been regarded as "a potential liberator from the strictures of news" and providing new means of communication between environmental organizations and supporters (Lester, 2010, p. 111).

"New" Media and Environmental Movements

Due to the limited resources from and access to the mainstream media for certain environmental coverage, new media technologies have always been the first alternative that environmental pressure groups will turn to, for both internal and external uses (Hansen, 2010). Environmentalists started using the by-then-new media tools such as fax machines, and video cameras in the early 1980s. Over the past decade, the rapidly advancing Internet technology enables email and portable phones to become the major communicational tools for delivering and propagating information for environmental pressure groups (Hansen, 2010, p. 59). Successful examples of organizing social events by the Internet-mediated technology are not unusual. In 1998, a protest named "Hector the Forest Protector" in Tasmania was carried out using mobile phone and other Information and Communications Technologies (ICT) to connect with journalists and politicians about forestry practices. In early 2001, five days of political protests coordinated by text messages led to the resignation of Philippine President Joseph Estrada. Mobile phone has also spread widely in rural Africa and is used to improve communication and increase the effectiveness of responses to crop raids by elephants (Graham, Adams, & Kahiro, 2012). In 2003, the Global Rescue Station organized a base camp in the height of sixty-five meters above ground using online blogging sites in different languages. The purpose of those connection manners (mobile phones and online communities), besides disseminating the information among the general public, is arguably to give the mainstream media access to the story ultimately (Lester & Hutchins, 2009, p. 588).

However, the role of new media in environmental movement remains unclear and controversial. One stream of study focuses on the function of the new media in public participation. The growing body of literature on the use of new media by social movement organizations shows a "more nuanced and less sweepingly enthusiastic picture of the potential or actual role of new information and communication technologies" (Hansen, 2010, p. 61). The use of Information and Communication Technology (ICT) is more about "symbolic expressions of solidarity" (Gillan & Pickerill, 2008, p. 75) or an extension of the offline media (Kavada, 2005, p. 218), rather than a tool of organizing and mobilizing, and the movement organized by the Internet or ICTs recognize that traditional media remain an important arena for shaping public opinion and political decision making (Castells, 2007; Lester, 2010, p. 126). Hansen (2010) further argued that the impact of the Internet in campaigning activities could be cushioned if the environmental groups are not the only party employing the ICT technology into the campaigning (p. 62). Another stream of argument emphasizes that perception of environmental risks differs depending on at what level the risks are perceived (Larose & Ponton, 2000) rather than what kind of media they choose to use. In other words, people tend to minimize the gravity of the risk at individual level by disregarding or rejecting any information dissonant with their present set of attitudes, while magnify the environmental risk at collective level to affect change (Larose & Ponton, 2000). The audience's perception depends on individual's expectation and beliefs (Rotter, Chance, & Phares, 1972). Individuals who believe that events affecting their lives are controllable would be motivated to act to make the change.

New Media in China

Mediated Environmental Movement in China (PX Protest)

China's worsening environmental conditions has catalyzed a spirit of environmental civilian activism (Wang, 2010). The street protest against construction of a $1.4 billion paraxylene (PX) plant, the largest industrial project in Xiamen city, is regarded as the landmark of environmental civilian activism in history. In November 2006, the project was given the go-ahead by the government and was scheduled to go into production in 2008. The production of the chemical plant was expected to fetch RMB 80 billion (or USD 13 billion) to the city's gross annual product. Xiamen municipal government was set to basket prestige as the new plant was a world-class petro-chemical giant emerging on the west bank of the Taiwan Strait (Li, 2008).

In March 2007, Zhao Yufen, member of the Chinese People's Political Consultative Conference (CPPCC), academician at the Chinese Academy of Science, and professor at Xiamen University, raised a motion signed by 105 CPPCC members which argued that the PX plant was set to locate too close to residential areas. Any leak or explosion would put a million Xiamen residents in danger. Unfortunately the motion was not accepted by the central government and the construction of PX was on the way to start. Knowing the local government would not approve an application for protest, Xiamen residents used Internet messages and mobile phone texts to organize a "walk" on street to express their objection to the construction. On June 1st, 2007, over 10,000 people walked onto

the streets with a yellow ribbon around the wrist. Although there was no coverage of the event in the mainstream media, "citizen journalists" from all over the country flocked to Xiamen to cover the demonstration and posted the articles widely on the Internet.

Facing the pressure from the residents, local government suspended the PX project and conducted a third-party environmental appraisal of which the procedure is open to the public. A public meeting was convened on December 13th, 2007 with 90% of the 106 citizen representatives opposing the PX project. On December 19th, *People's Daily*, a national newspaper which is considered the "mouth piece" of the Central Committee of the Communist Party of China, published an article claiming that "expert opinion on the matter is tending towards unanimity, and abandonment of construction is the preferred course of action" (2009). Part of the consequence, however, is that local government introduced a by-law to prevent people from posting "damaging or unhealthy" information on the Internet.

New Media in China

Until June 2012, the ownership of mobile phone in China has reached one billion which ranks the first in the world (Reuters, 2012), and 538 million Internet users (CNNIC, 2012). The two new media forms have been widely used by young people in China, to carry out various social and political events. For example, young people in China sent text messages and chain-letter e-mails exhorting citizens to boycott Japanese merchandise and take to the streets in over ten cities in 2005 (Yardley, 2005). Short Message Service (SMS) and calls via mobile phones calling for boycotts of French supermarket Carrefour went rampant in China in 2008 in response to the disruptions of the Olympic torch relay in Paris (AFP, 2008). While mobile phone message shows great strength in immediacy, the Internet, on the other hand, provides communication medium which is "nonhierarchical, interactive, and global" (Rodan, 1998, p. 64), and hence satisfies the precondition for an environmental movement which is the availability of information about environmental conditions, regulations, and behaviors, and a space in which to discuss this (Janicke, 2006). The Internet also poses a new challenge to censorship by the government because of the breadth of online content, the rapidity with which sources of content can be moved or mirrored, and because content sources are often remote from Chinese jurisdiction (Zittrain & Edelman, 2003). Yang (2003) argues that the uses of the Internet by the general public has fostered debates about, and the articulation of, various domestic social problems, which leads to environmental democratization in cyberspace. However, the Internet is not an unbeatable liberating power for countries which comply with tight media control and censorship, such as China where the government still monitors the use of and access to the Internet, and filters out many Web sites (Ma et al., 2008). The access and availability of news could still be harnessed through strict regulations and law enforced by government and media hegemony (Roden, 1998). The media control in the Internet is still effectively carried out in China and remains a major problem inhibiting the freedom of speech and information flow in this country (Guo, 2004).

Apart from the affluent literature on the Internet communication, is the limited amount of studies of mobile communication in China which at first focused on the micro-level issues of mobile technology diffusion, adoption, and usage relating to everyday life (Ji & Li, 2009), and later on macro-level studies on telecommunication development and policy research (Jun & Hui, 2010). Although the online media has made possible active involvement, simultaneous participation for multiple users, and anti-hegemonic and anti-control information exchange, the government-imposed regulations and laws have been the critical issue for the survival of online media (Yao, 2006).

RESEARCH PROCEDURE AND FINDINGS

Research Procedure

Drawing on the personal experience by witnesses and participants in Xiamen PX protest, this chapter addresses the roles of the Internet and mobile phone in China's environmental decision-making process by analyzing the delivery channels of the environmental decision, most circulated messages in the Internet and mobile phone during the street protest period, as well as documents related to the case. Data used in this paper are retrieved from the following sources in December 2010.

Survey and Multiple Regression Analysis

Survey is among the most popular research tools to evaluate media effect. The survey was supposed to be randomly disseminated in Xiamen city. However, due to the sensitivity of the environmental topics in China, the heavy regulatory censorship over survey dissemination (as the proposal of conducting a survey needs to be previewed and approved by the local government), and the retrospective manner of the questionnaire (back to five years ago), only 52 respondents were able to return the survey with valid responses. A descriptive statistics of the variables included in the questionnaires is displayed in Table 1.

Survey questions include four sections: demographical information (sex, age, education background), time spent on mobile phone per day, receipt and relaying of the PX project message, willingness to participate the street protest. The gender breakdown of the 52 respondents was 32 females and 20 males. The statistics presented in Table 1 shows that the age range of the sample shows abnormal distribution, as most of the respondents are between 24 and 31. This limitation reflected the disadvantage or limitation of small

Table 1. Descriptive statistics of independent and dependent variables

Variable	Mean	S.D.	Skewness
Gender (Male=1)	.39	.50	-.67
Age	27.50	2.74	.80
Education (Scale of 4)	3.21	.58	.03
Time on mobile per day (in Hours)	1.61	1.08	.63
Mobile literacy (Scale of 10)	7.21	2.08	-1.29
Reception of PX text via mobile (Yes=1)	.71	.47	-1.07
Reception of PX message on the internet (Yes=1)	.86	.36	-2.30
How many people you relayed the message to	42.29	56.92	1.94
Willing to join environmental protection event (Scale of 4)	2.50	1.29	-.127
Total	52		

Source: Xiamen PX survey

sample size of this study. Roughly 70% (36) of the respondents received the text message calling for street protest, of which 5 respondents joined the demonstration crowd. Most of the respondents held a bachelor degree or higher. Most of the respondents reported a high mobile literacy (6 or above out of a scale of 10). 90% of the respondents who received the PX text message reported that they relayed the message to their friends, family members, and colleagues.

Based on the nature of the data collected in this study, a multiple regression analysis using SPSS was conducted using gender, age, education, time on mobile per day, mobile literacy, reception of PX text message, reception of PX online message, and the number of people respondents relayed the message to as the predictors, and willingness to participate environmental protection events as the criterion. The output of the analysis is presented in Table 2.

Admittedly, the estimated parameters presented in Table 2 are very likely to be biased due to small sample size. The non-probability sampling process makes the inferential statistics of the model less meaningful. In other words, it is hard to generalize the result of the analyses in this study into a larger population. Nonetheless, the outcome

of the analysis provides an opportunity for the author to have a primary look at the relationship among the variables included in the model, and identify the possible factors that have an impact upon people's willingness to participate environmental protection events. The statistics presented in Table 2 shows that age is positively associated with people's willingness to join environmental protection movements. The reason might be that when people get older, they perceive more importance of environmental issues than younger people. Surprisingly, the reception of PX text message indicates a negative and strong relationship with the willingness of environmental participation. The possible explanation to this phenomenon might be that people who received text message would either question the credibility of the message source, or believe disseminating the message is a more important and effective for heightening environmental protection awareness than protesting on the street. The number of people whom respondents relayed text message to has a weak but positive association with dependent variable. That is to say, the more people the respondents resent the message to, the more likely they will join the environmental protection events.

Table 2. Multiple regression on willingness to participate in environmental protection events

Predictor	B	S.E.	p-value
Intercept	-4.56	1.75	.048
Gender (Male=1)	-.42	.30	.212
Age	.21*	.06	.012
Education (Scale of 4)	-.19	.21	.395
Time on mobile per day (in Hours)	.16	.10	.171
Mobile literacy (Scale of 10)	.01	.06	.864
Reception of PX text via mobile (Yes=1)	-.81*	.28	.032
Reception of PX message on the internet (Yes=1)	.13	.33	.723
How many people you relayed the message to	.01***	.002	.008
Total	52		
R^2	.86		
Adjusted R^2	.628		

*p<0.05; *** p<0.01
Source: Xiamen PX survey

In-Depth Interviews

People having personal experience in Xiamen PX protest, such as protestors, environmental activists (NGO workers), and academic scholars, are interviewed to identify the special changes of the protest, the process of message dissemination, and the direct outcome from the street rally. Other factors contributing to the happening of the protest are also discussed in the interview.

The face-to-face individual interview was divided into two parts. The first part contained close-ended and semi-structured questions such as whether the interviewee agreed there were opinion leaders in this environmental campaign, whether and how the mobile and online community helped organize the street protest, and what the other factors that encouraged the public participation of the campaign were. The second part of the interview was for the interviewees to freely give comments on the whole process of PX protest. Totally eight interviews were conducted in this study including four university professors who either witnessed or experienced the PX protest, a graduate student, an activist in a local environmental group, a taxi driver, and a grocery store owner who is also a protester. Most of the interviews were conducted in Chinese, except the one with David, a university with foreign nationality In order to distinguish among different interviewees and at the same time keep the confidentiality of their personal information, every participant is given a nickname based on gender. A brief description of the interviewees is given in Table 3.

Secondary Data

News articles, scholarly research, messages circulated via the Internet and mobile phones during the protest, and other documentations relating to PX protest in Xiamen are collected to provide an insight into the studied case from multiple perspectives.

Issues and Findings

The content of the interviews and secondary data are combined and analyzed for the discussions of dynamics of the information flow in PX protest in the following section.

Table 3. Description of interviewees

Name	Gender	Age range	Background description
Cindy	Female	Over 50	Faculty in a local university in Xiamen. She has great concern about environmental issues and received PX messages during the PX protest.
Earnest	Male	Around 40	Faculty in a local university in Xiamen. He was one of the leading figures who started the PX campaign and quitted in the middle way due to the pressure from municipal government.
Simon	Male	Around 30	Faculty in a local university in Xiamen. He is Earnest's colleague. He received PX message and joined the street protest in 2007.
David	Male	Over 50	He is a university instructor with foreign nationality. He was in China in 2007 and happened to witness the street protest in a passing-by bus.
Jason	Male	24	Jason is an environmental group member in Xiamen. He went to the construction location of the PX project and told the residents the potential risk of having the chemical plant on the spot. He received and posted message of PX project through the internet and mobile phone. He did not attend the street protest.
Sunnie	Female	20	Graduate student in local university. She did not receive PX message during the protest. She was aware of the PX protest but did not attend the street event.
Shi	Male	Around 40	He received the PX message, but did not attend the event. He happened to pass the protest venue while sending a guest to the destination in 2007.
Wendy	Female	Around 30	She is an owner of grocery business. She received PX text message in 2007 and joined the street protest.

Opinion Leader

Cindy (University faculty): *Prof. Zhao was the first person who started questioning PX plant construction. She contacted the local newspaper and had the news of the toxic plant spread in Xiamen city. Zhao was deeply hurt soon after the local media coverage hinted that Zhao should take all the responsibility for the unfavorable political consequences due to the information revelation.*

Earnest (University faculty): *The PX event was indeed initiated by the scholars in Xiamen University, purely for the sake of environmental protection. After I realized that the whole issue was diverged to political direction, I quitted.*

Simon (University faculty): *Some school faculties were sued by the PX project investors, after they started the whole anti-PX campaign.*

Faculties in Xiamen University indicated a strong willingness to influence the government decision making process. And faculties can provide [scholarly] evidence to policy-makers regarding environmental protection issues.

David (University instructor with foreign nationality): *On the day of the street protest, most faculties in my school were not willing to get involved.*

Nisbet and Kotcher (2009) identified six categories of opinion leaders in environmental movement. One category of the opinion leaders boost the public's cognitive engagement with the environmental issues, increase the knowledge of the scientific and policy details, promoting mobilizing information on how to get involved, and generate greater public attention to news coverage and other available information sources (p. 331). At the early stage of the anti-PX movement, Prof. Zhao Yufen paid close attention to the issue, and considered herself more persuasive in convincing others to adopt her opinion or course of action by providing an intense involvement in objection of the construction of the PX plant, and issue-specific knowledge (Lazarsfeld, Berelson, & Gaudet, 1948). At this point, Prof. Zhao and other school faculties in Xiamen University could be identified as *issue-specific opinion leaders* (Nisbet & Kotcher, 2009). Additionally, Prof. Zhao is a prominent figure as an academician in the Chinese Academy of Sciences, and a member of the Chinese People's Political Consultative Conference (CPPCC), the country's top political advisory body (*People's Daily*, 2007). Being a professor in Department of Chemistry itself shows high level of expertise and authority in judging the hazardousness of the construction of chemical plant. Prof. Zhao later on submitted a suggestion, together with other 105 CPPCC member, during the annual session of the CPPCC in March asking for the plant to be relocated (*People's Daily*, 2007), which shows the crucial networks she possessed to create the influence on the issue. In this sense, Prof. Zhao also qualifies as *opinion leader with influencer as personality strength* (Weimann, Tustin, van Vuuren, & Joubert, 2007), which reflects confidences in leadership roles, their aptitude at shaping others' opinion and their perceived impact on social and political incomes.

The delivering and disseminating of the text message in an environmental campaign which is elaborated in the following section, could also be identified as the typical behavior of the opinion leader, as Nisbet and Kotcher (2009) argue that opinion leaders define or frame the complexities of the issue in a way that connects to the specific core values of various publics, and read the audiences with the carefully crafted message (p. 329). And the channels for the fulfilling of this task in this particular study are the Internet and mobile devices. Scholars (Boasa, Horrigan, Wellman, & Rainie, 2006) argue that the role of opinion

leaders usually performs well via face-to-face interaction, while the influence may be diminished or potentially enhance, depending on the context and nature of the campaign. The opinion leader in the PX protest functions as an enhancer was the text message are widely disseminated by the Internet and mobile phone users.

According to the two-step flow of communication (Lazarsfeld et al., 1948), the information of the polluting chemical plant is channeled to the "masses" through the leadership of the opinion leaders. Not only the people with most access to the media and higher media literacy could effectively diffuse the information to others, but also their personal influence came to illustrate the process intervening between the media's direct message and the audience's reaction to that message, and ultimately change the audience's attitudes and behaviors.

Messages on Online Community

Davis and Owen (1998) generalizes four approaches that Internet might facilitate participation: (a) providing faster and more in-depth access to news and political information, (b) linking government and citizens through e-mail, online forums, distribution lists, and political Websites, (c) providing space for discussion, (d) serving as a barometer of public opinion and offering reaction to events and decisions in real time. All the online messages quoted in this section is originally presented in Chinese on the Website and translated into English by the author.

Jason (NGO environmental group member): *During PX protest period, students [in Xiamen University] received and reposted messages in QQ[1]. They (the students) also spread the information via forums in online communities such as "Small Fish" (www. xmfish.com). "Small Fish" was banned by the local government for its allowing anonymous users to call for people to "walk* *on the street with yellow ribbon band on the wrist."* Upon the re-opening of the site, a regulation which requires user's real identity for registration was applied to all the new users. QQ was not banned. Therefore, QQ became the major platform for disseminating messages and exchanging opinions. We collected messages from the within-group discussion in QQ and reposted them in forums of other groups. That way, messages could easily reach hundreds of online users.

QQ message posted on May 29, 2007, two days before the street protest reads: *Taiwanese Youhao Chen and Xianglu Petrochemicals (Xiamen) Co. Ltd. co-invested the chemical plant to produce hyper toxic chemical products in Haicang district, Xiamen city. The consequence of this chemical product could be likened to atomic blast, and caused Leukemia and deformed babies in its neighborhood area. For the sake of our next generation, please take action to join this street protest participated by tens of thousands of other Xiamen people. Time: 8am, June 1st. [The protest] Start[s] off from your location toward the municipal building. Tie a yellow ribbon around your wrist. If you can not attend the protest, please resend this text as many times as possible. For the benefit of our living environment, please action up!*

The message presented above is the most commented and reposted message in popular Websites such as Netease and Tencent as well as local online communities such as Small Fish Forum (Lu, Shao,& Wu, 2012). Each sub-issue pertaining to the PX project was claimed to attract thousands of hits (Zhu, 2007). Core issues relating to the construction of PX project such as its toxicity are addressed in this short message. The first half of the message was delivered with a formal third person tone, which creates a neutral and authoritative context for the expertise bits in the message. The second half of the message,

started with the word "our," made the tone shift from the third person tone to first and second person tones. The tone shift gives a personal touch to the message, which makes the message more appealing to its audience.

If marginalized groups (environmental groups) wish to gain popularity among online media user, they must rhetorically re-package their claims in terms that resonate with and conform to the dominant culture and dominant interpretive packages. The message initiator had a clear knowledge about characteristics of the intended audience. The combination of the tones entertains the needs of credible online information and at the same time being addressed to as an individual person. Because the message was designed to be published on the Website where users usually do not seek in-depth information, an brief information "combo" with no missing of key words like chemical company's name, toxic products, post-impact of the chemical production, time and venue of the protest, yellow ribbon, and message resending, was packed into a short paragraph to make the message comprehensive and yet easily understood by audience at different literacy levels.

The language used, the choice of vocabulary, is the key to what we may call the ideological management of competing discourses in the public (Hansen, 2010, p. 120). The choice of vocabulary also reflects the frames that message designers tended to communicate with readers, such as why an issue might be a problem, who or what might be responsible for it, and what should be done (Nisbet, Markowitz, & Kotcher, 2012). Frames are often most effective when they appeal to morally relevant intuitions that are strongly held by an individual and segment of the public (Nisbet et al., 2012). There are at least four frames emerged in the above message, the blamed party, magnitude of the problem, relevance, and sentiment elements. The mentioning of the names of project investors and the official term of the chemical, and "hyper toxic" consequence stressed the blamed parties. The message likened the construction of the plant to "atomic blast" which is well known for its destroying power and post-traumatic impact. As the message is intended to users who lived in Xiamen, it is powerful to mention that Leukemia and deformed babies in Xiamen city which indicates a great relevancy of the project to the audiences and the wellbeing of their family and friends. Finally, as a strategy employed by most of the popular online publishers, sentiment element in the message never fails to achieve its goal of reinforcing the message and reaching maximum audience from various backgrounds. Care for "our next generation" and "our living environment" are the most fundamental hope of each individual. The passionate and emotional phrases like those had made the message appealing and well perceived by its readers. Overall, this message addresses three key tasks for claim-makers while making claims about a putative problem, commanding attention, claiming legitimacy, and invoking action (Hansen, 2010).

QQ message on June 2ⁿᵈ, 2007, one day after the street protest: This street protest has been going on for two days, which shows our attitude towards the construction of PX project. There is no need to use radical measure to express our disagreement. Instead, let's express our stance in a gentle way. If you against PX project, please place a yellow ribbon anywhere you could, your vehicle, your office table, your purse... anywhere and anytime, anti-PX, let the yellow ribbon fly across the city.

The protest held on June 1, 2007 received great attention from the local government, online media, and eventually the mainstream media. As government pledged to re-assess the environmental impact by the PX project, the main goal of the protest which is influencing the decision-making process is achieved. At this point, another message featuring the post-protest objective of the campaigners, maintaining public's environmental awareness at a high level, was tailored made and delivered to its audience. The message presented above was posted one day after the protest and delivered in first and second person tones, which again addressed message recipients as individual person with their different needs. There is no expertise information included in the message. The message calls for its audience to keep on caring for environmental protection issues. While seeing the effective outcome achieved in the environmental protection campaign, we should be aware that China government has posed heavy censorship on the online media (Harwit & Clark, 2001) during the campaign period. The government also uses online media to monitor dissent voices that are the major challenges to the Chinese central authority (Min, 2005).

Bulletin Board System (BBS) is one of the most commonly used means of online communication by Chinese Internet users (Ma et al., 2008). By using BBS, people can simply make comments after reading articles. Large amount of messages were written by the Internet users, who commented on the articles related to PX project in cyber sphere during the protest period. Most BBS message responded to PX news on the protest day found at the most popular Website in China, Sina.com (qq.com) expressed anger and concerns about possible pollution. There are still 20 percent of the replies shows support to the construction and argue that PX is not a hyper poisonous chemical, and Prof. Zhao exaggerated the impact. Very limited amount of viewers hold a neutral stance towards the PX issue.

Mobile Phone Texts

Text message: Xianglu Petrochemicals (Xiamen) Co. Ltd. has started its construction of Para-xylene chemical plant in Haicang district. The impact of the production of this hyper toxic chemical could be likened to an atomic bombing on Xiamen Island. Xiamen people's life will be full of leukemia patients and de-

formed babies. We want a good life! We want health. International organization rules that this kind of [chemical plant] project should be at least a hundred kilometers away from the city. But this project is supposed to be constructed only sixteen kilometers away from Xiamen city! For the wellbeing of our next generations, please group send this text to all your friends in Xiamen.

The first appearance of this text message is on May 20th, 2007. It was reported that over than a million Xiamen residents received the text message. 36 survey respondents claimed they received the text message, among which 30 resent the message to their friends, colleagues, and family members (also see Table 1). The message text is similar to the online message quoted in the earlier section in the chapter with slight change in wording. No clear evidence was found to claim which of the two media forms (mobile phone or the Internet) is the first to publish the message. However, the prevailing text message being identical to the one on the Internet indicates that the elements which are popular among Internet users could be equally well accepted by mobile device owners. It is reasonable to assume that compared to mobile text message, online message could reach much larger audience population for its lower cost (or literally no cost) and overcoming geographic barriers to spread the message. However, the well-established online media system also faces higher chance of being censored by the government, which makes civilian engagement in environmental protection more difficult.

On the other hand, back to 2007, the development of mobile phone technology was relatively slow-paced with many features such as group texting just starting to prosper, which make it difficult for the government to enforce timely and effective censorship over the mobile phone operating system. Unlike the online community which was monitored simultaneously by govern-

ment's filtering system, text messages containing sensitive words like "PX" and "protest" started being blocked by local government using technical measure six days after the first anti-PX text was released to public. Mobile phone communication guarantees immediacy as well as direct flow of the message from the sender to the receiver, which creates a personalized effect upon the recipients and poses stronger persuasive power to those who are affected by this particular environmental issue. Additionally, mobile phones are claimed to be less expensive than other communicational devices such as landline telephones and standard Internet (Cole-Lewis & Kershaw, 2010) and have a considerable impact in developing countries (Adler, 2007; Lasica, 2007).

David: *Text is cheaper and safer than landline.*

An excerpt of mobile text conversation between users NORTH WIND (NW) and ADDITION (A) on June 1st, 2007 (www.aboluowang.com) is presented as following:
07: 41: 39

NW: *Arrived in Xiamen city, everything appears to be normal.*
A: *What about the atmosphere on the street? Anyone wears yellow ribbon?*

07: 46: 11

NW: *No one wears yellow ribbon. All I can see is that policemen are everywhere.*

07: 51: 47

NW: *A lot of police in disguise are in this area.*

08: 27: 44

NW: *Couple of people started to curse police officer and are arrested.*

08: 28:07

NW: Now there are hundreds of people gathering on the spot, in the same number of police force.

08: 32:50

NW: Now we have over than a thousand people gathering here.

08: 42: 01

NW: The police are ready to dissolve the crowd into smaller groups. I am pushed into the police group.

08: 58: 28

NW: Now over than three thousand people gather on the street.

09: 12: 16

NW: The number of protesters exceeded 10,000!

10: 25: 55

NW: Another 10,000 people joined the crowd.

10: 35: 59

NW: We are at South Hubing road, and approaching to Fushan road.

It is not unusual for environmental campaigners to use mobile phone to organize and stay in contact with other activists. A mobile phone application "Protest4" was introduced in 2011 to help campaigners connect with each other around the world. In China, the practices of street demonstration and protest are tightly proscribed and under the auspices of maintaining "social stability" (Tao, 2011). The text conversation quoted above shows

the interactants' concern over the presence of the police force in the protest site as NW was asking whether there were policemen on the protest site and reported the policemen were separating the crowd of protestors. The purpose of the text is to warn other protestors to be cautious with the police and avoid the chaotic venue where police already took action. The conversation shows that mobile phone users were using the device to organize the street protest by asking whether icon of the event, yellow-ribbon were worn by protestors on the scene, reporting the number of participants, and informing the direction and the next stop of the "walk." In other words, mobile phone has been the only available device-on-the-scene for coordinating the mass gathering and providing timely reporting for online media, where mainstream media was not reachable or available. In this sense, mobile phone was used to balance the information asymmetry between governments and citizens, as some government officials monopolize information and completely control what information to publicize by concealing or distorting information about civic engagement in public events (Ye, 2006). In PX case, new media, mobile phone in particular, not only enhanced the communication among citizens through offering huge amount of information which is not available from other media sources on the scene, but also helped people circumvent the information control from the government and create a new platform for participants (Lu, Shao, & Wu, 2012).

Word of Mouth

Cindy (University professor): I heard that the student environmental activists went to the construction site to notify the local residents that PX plant would be hazardous to local ecosystem.

Jason: Dozens of NGO members including college students went to the area where chemical plant was supposed to be built, and knocked at the door of each household to tell the residents of the potential risk of this project. The original purpose of the action was to secure local resident's right to information, instead of to remove the plant from the area. People in this area had no knowledge about chemical pollution, nor did they care about it. All they concerned about is the sum of compensation they could get out of the re-location. Nonetheless, half month later, we found that people around us were all talking about PX project, and local government started to pay attention to the issue.

Earnest: *Communication through the Internet and mobile phone actually caused some concerns, such as credibility, and junk text message. Word Of Mouth (WOM) is rela-tively credible. To my knowledge, the effect of WOM among friends and colleagues is much bigger than mobile texts.*

David: *Xiamen is a city where news travels fast with WOM. It is actually the WOM that got the news around.*

Word of mouth has been defined as "informal, person-to-person communication between a perceived noncommercial communicator and a receiver regarding a brand, a product, an organi-zation, or a service" (Harrison-Walker, 2001, p. 63). Among the many and varied channels through which a person may receive information, it is hard to imagine any that carry the credibility and importance of interpersonal communication, or word of mouth (Godes & Mayzlin, 2004). Word of mouth is considered micro-level effects and more persuasive than mass media such as television and radio (Katz & Lazarsfeld, 1955; Walker, 1995). Given that all the literature made a distinguishable focus on persuasive effects of mobile phone text and online message, it is surprising to find that over than half of the respondents reported that they first learned about the PX project through friends, relatives, or other interpersonal channels. Couple of reasons might contribute to this phe-nomenon. First, word of mouth is a vivid form of

communication and moderated by the accessibility of other related information in memory, making the information easily accepted and remembered by its recipient. Second, word of mouth reflects a high level of relevancy between people and the issue, which reinforces its persuasive power and transmission speed. Third, word of mouth com-munication benefits from a strong interpersonal tie and added credibility to the information.

Other Factors

Shi (Taxi driver): *Most of the protestors are the residents of Haicang district where the plant was to be constructed. The construction of the chemical plant could make the property prices in the region decrease considerably.*

Sunnie (Master student): *The happening of pro-test is by large due to the local culture, as the aboriginal or non-immigrated residents cared a lot about the environmental issues of this beautiful island.*

Earnest: *The property developers in Xiamen played an important role in the street pro-test. I think the first message was actually created and disseminated by two interest groups, property developer and property owners in Haicang district. Additionally, Xiamen people could be very radical when it comes to environmental protection, so the occurrence of protest is also a cultural phenomenon.*

Jason: *There are already two chemical plants in Haicang district. The unpleasant smell from the industrial waste gas emission reminds Xiamen residents of the importance of the environmental protection issues.*

Hansen (2010) argues that people involved in an environment debates are most likely to be "claim-makers" (p. 39) including environmental pressure groups, government departments, research insti-tutions, economists, and the business industries whose operational practices are often the subjects of environmental debate and controversy. Some interviewees argue that the PX protest in Xiamen is in fact a business-related case, which involves interest of property developers, chemical plant industrialists, and other business derived from the aforementioned two. Therefore, the happening of PX protest could be jointly caused by business factors. On the other hand, Soroka's (2002) indicated that the media are less influential on issues that the public can access through direct experience or through immediate sources of information. In China's case, as environmental information has been routinely withheld by the government, and the general public has no direct access to the issue due to geographic limitations, new media could make a relatively big impact upon its readers and audiences. From this perspective, PX case reflects political concerns of the grassroots. Furthermore, Gamson and Modigliani (1989) argued that in order to gain prominence in the public sphere, an issue has to be cast in terms which resonate with existing and widely held cultural concepts. Xiamen city is known for its scenery beaches, rich history, and healthy ecosystem. Protecting natural environment has been part of the culture

rooted in local resident. From this perspective, the success of the PX protest is directly related to cultural factors.

Based on the discussion in this section, the author proposed a dynamic flow of the environmental information in PX protest period in Figure 1.

Figure 1 maps how the information regarding the polluting PX project was initiated by the opinion leader(s), processed and delivered by the online media, and finally reached the general public. The information simultaneously reached the interest group and environmental group via online platforms from opinion leaders. But the two parties delivered messages through different communicational channels to its audience, the Internet and WOM used by the environmental group and mobile text message by interest group. Based on this finding, it is not hard to conclude that the two different groups reached out to the local residents with the PX information for different purposes, despite the fact that both groups used the new media as a functional alternative for disseminating environmental information. The interest group disseminates the information to advocate or mobilize the general public to carry

Figure 1. Dynamic flow of the environmental information in PX protest

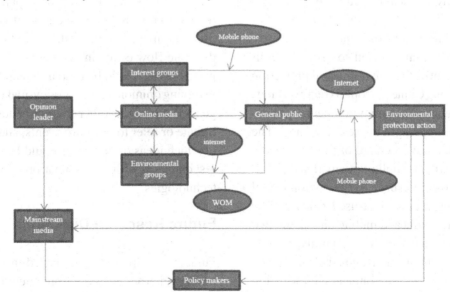

out a street demonstration, as the mobile device could keep the participants connected on the spot with its immediacy and interactivity. The environmental group, on the other hand, focused on spreading the information of pollution fast and widely. To address this particular need, the Internet could be regarded as the most effective channel to reach maximum audience, and WOM would be a powerful complementary to reach those who are not active or sufficient new media user (e.g., people with limited access to the Internet or low new media literacy). The mainstream media did not respond to the request by the opinion leaders about propagating the hazardous consequence of the PX project at the very beginning. It was until the large-scale street protest being carried out by the general public, did the mainstream media start to cover this environmental problem and ultimately function as an influencer on the policy-making process.

CONCLUSION AND FUTURE RESEARCH DIRECTIONS

Conclusion

The drastically worsening natural environment in China has been routinely underrepresented or ignored in traditional media, due to its sensitive nature and potential threaten to "social stability." Consequently, the environmental protection awareness among Chinese people is relatively low, and civic engagement in environmental policy-making is not encouraged by the government. The appearance and advancement of the new media technology has made public participation in political domain possible, especially the environmental policy-making process which used to deny public access. Online media and mobile phone, the two major members in the new media family, provide alternative communicational channels for grass-roots in China to seek environmental information and organize environmental protection campaigns. Based on an anti-pollution campaign boosted by

the use of online media and mobile phone, this chapter assisted readers in understanding the strength and weakness of new media that helped achieve a participatory goal in modern Chinese context. The role of word of mouth, as a powerful complementary communicational tool for propagating the hazardous consequence of PX project to those who are not active new technology users, and other factors which might contribute to the happening of the environmental campaign were also discussed in the chapter.

Weaving the classical communication theories such as framing and two-step flow communication into the phenomenon of the new media and unique political and social context in China, the author believes the study could serve as a map for communication scholars to understand the functional roles of opinion leaders, the Internet, and mobile phone in facilitating the grassroots or general public to participate in environmental protection events in a society where environmental issues are generally underrepresented and public convention is not supported by the government. Qualitative approaches based on secondary data and interviews are the major methods used in this chapter. Quantitative analysis based on a small-sized sample is to conducted to bridge the relationship between people's use pattern of new media devices and their likelihood to participate in environmental movement. Figure 1 presents the dynamic flow of the information in Xiamen PX protest which could be used as a tentative model involving opinion leaders, policy-makers, and the general public, that other environmentalists could imitate or refer to in future events, and a process in which ideas or behaviors could be spread and responded to with a combination of Web-based technologies.

Future Research Directions

Future research could be conducted on whether and how the Internet and mobile phone could facilitate cooperative activities in environmental campaigns across the globe, and how the pressure group's message could be tailor-made to address the trend of globalization in dealing with environmental issues and compete for mainstream media attention to the greatest extent. The study on how opinion leaders utilize new technology in environmental protection events could be furthered to their capability of influencing or shaping grassroots' opinion, and their perception of the effectiveness of the completed environmental campaign.

The scarcity of scholarly work in media and environmental issues in oriental culture suggests a meta-analysis of literature over public opinion towards environmental issues across eastern countries, as well as the factors contributing to the fickleness of the public opinion over time in one country or region could be worthy inquiry for future research.

Last but not the least, it would be important for researchers to examine the magnitude of impacts by different medium forms (television, newspaper, Internet, mobile phone, etc.) in participatory events, and how to utilize multiple propagation tools to mobilize the population with different demographic backgrounds (children, seniors, etc.) to take part in the environmental protection campaign which benefits every single living being on this beautiful planet.

REFERENCES

Abraham, J. (1995). Review of the book The mass media and environmental issues by Anders Hansen. *Media Culture & Society, 17*(3), 524–526. doi:10.1177/016344395017003012.

Adler, R. (2007). *Health care unplugged: The evolving role of wireless technology*. Oakland, CA: California Health Care Foundation.

AFP. (2008, April 23). *China hit by fresh anti-Western protests*. Retrieved from http://afp.google.com/article/ALeqM5gOTrqDV_ua80tqOwJHJb-PBOLoUjA

Bao, P., Pierce, J., Whittaker, S., & Zhai, S. (2011). *Smart phone use by non-mobile business users*. Paper presented at MobileHCI. Stockholm, Sweden.

Boase, J., Horrigan, J. B., Wellman, B., & Rainie, L. (2006). The strength of internet ties. *Pew Internet and Public Life Project*. Retrieved from http://ww.pewInternet.org/PPF/r/172/report_display.asp

Bone, P. F. (1995). Word-of-mouth effects on short-term and long-term product judgments. *Journal of Business Research, 32*(2), 213–223. doi:10.1016/0148-2963(94)00047-I.

Castells, M. (2007). Communication, power and counter-power in the network society. *International Journal of Communication, 1*(1), 238-266. doi: 1932-8036/20070238

CNNIC. (2012). 30th statistical report on Internet development in China. Retrieved from http://www1.cnnic.cn/IDR/ReportDownloads/201209/t20120928_36586.htm

Cohen, B. C. (1963). *The press and foreign policy*. Princeton, NJ: Princeton University Press.

Cole-Lewis, H., & Kershaw, T. (2010). Text messaging as a tool for behavior change in disease prevention and management. *Epidemiologic Reviews, 32*(1), 56–59. doi:10.1093/epirev/mxq004 PMID:20354039.

Davis, R., & Owen, D. (1998). *New media and American politics*. New York: Oxford University Press.

Dawson, B. (2009). The beat: Top universities rethink how to prepare e-beat journalists. *SEJ Journal, 19*(4), 20–22.

Dearing, J. W., & Rogers, E. M. (1996). *Agenda-setting*. Thousand Oaks, CA: Sage Publications.

DeLuca, K. (1999). *Image politics: The new rhetoric of environmental activism*. New York: Guilford.

Department for Environment. Food and Rural Affairs. (2002). Survey of public attitudes to quality of life and to the environment–2001. London: Crown.

Dichter, E. (1966). How word-of-mouth advertising works. *Harvard Business Review*, *44*, 147–157.

Dietz, T. (2003). What is a good decision? Criteria for environmental decision making. *Human Ecology Review*, *10*(1), 60–67.

Douglas, K. (1995). *Media culture*. New York: Routledge.

Fangchao, L. (2007, May 30). Public opposes Xiamen chemical plant. People's Daily..

Frewer, L. J. (2002). The media and genetically modified food: Evidence in support of social amplification of risk. *Risk Analysis*, *22*(4), 701–711. doi:10.1111/0272-4332.00062 PMID:12224744.

Gamson, W. A., & Modigliani, A. (1989). Media discourse and public opinion on nuclear power: A constructionist approach. *American Journal of Sociology*, *95*(1), 1–37. doi:10.1086/229213.

Geiger, B., & Eshet, Y. (2010). Two worlds of assessment of environmental health issues: The case of contaminated water wells in Ramat ha-Sharon. *Journal of Risk Research*, *14*(1). doi: doi:10.1080/13669877.2010.505688.

Gibbs, L. (1993). Celebrating ten years of triumph. *Everyone's Backyard*, *11*(1), 2–3.

Gillan, K., Pickerill, J., & Webster, F. (2008). *Anti-war activism: New media and protest in the information age*. Basingstoke, UK: Palgrave Macmillan. doi:10.1057/9780230596382.

Gordon, J. (2002). The mobile phone, an artifact of popular culture and a tool of the public sphere. *Convergence*, *8*(3), 15–26. doi:10.1177/135485650200800303.

Graham, M. D., Adams, W. M., & Kahiro, G. N. (2012). Mobile phone communication in effective human-elephant conflict management in Laikipia County, Kenya. *Oryx*, *46*(1), 137–144. doi:10.1017/S0030605311001104.

Guo, X., & Marinova, D. (2011). Environmental awareness in China: Facilitating the greening of the economy. In F. Chan, D. Marinova, & R. S. Anderssen (Eds.), *MODSIM2011: 19th International Congress on Modelling and Simulation*, (pp. 1673-1679). Perth, Australia: The Modelling and Simulation Society of Australia and New Zealand.

Hansen, A. (2010). *Environment, media and communication*. New York: Routledge.

Hargreaves, I., & Ferguson, G. (2000). *Who's misunderstanding whom? Bridging the gulf of understanding between the public, the media and science*. Swindon, UK: ESRC.

Harwit, E., & Clark, D. (2001). Shaping the internet in China. *Asian Survey*, *41*(3), 377–408. doi:10.1525/as.2001.41.3.377.

Haywood, K. M. (1989). Managing word of mouth communication. *Journal of Services Marketing*, *3*(2), 55–67. doi:10.1108/EUM0000000002486.

Herr, P. M., Kardes, F. R., & Kim, J. (1991). Effects of word-of-mouth and product attribute information on persuasion: An accessibility-diagnosticity perspective. *The Journal of Consumer Research*, *17*, 454–462. doi:10.1086/208570.

Hilgartner, S., & Bosk, C. L. (1988). The rise and fall of social problems: A public arenas model. *American Journal of Sociology*, *94*(1), 53–78. doi:10.1086/228951.

Janicke, M. (2006). The environmental state and environmental flows: The need to reinvent the nation-state. In Spaargaren, G., Mol, A. P. J., & Buttel, F. H. (Eds.), *Governing environmental flows: Global challenges to social theory*. Cambridge, UK: The MIT Press.

Jin, B., & Peña, J. F. (2010). Mobile communication in romantic relationships: Mobile phone use, relational uncertainty, love, commitment, and attachment styles. *Communication Reports*, *23*(1), 39–51. doi:10.1080/08934211003598742.

Kavada, A. (2005). Civic society organizations and the internet: The case of Amnesty International, Oxfam and the World Development Movement. In Jong, W. D., Shaw, M., & Stammers, N. (Eds.), *Global activism, global media* (pp. 208–222). London: Pluto.

Kiecker, P., & Cowles, D. (2002). Interpersonal communication and personal influence on the internet: A framework for examining online word-o-mouth. *Journal of Euromarketing*, *11*(2), 71–88. doi:10.1300/J037v11n02_04.

Langton, S. (1978). Citizen participation in America: Current reflections on the state of the art. In Langton, S. (Ed.), *Citizen participation in America*. Lexington, MA: Lexington Books.

Laros, F., & Ponton, M. (2000). Locus of control and perceptions of environmental risk factor: Inhabitants of slums facing domestic garbage. *Swiss Journal of Psychology*, *59*(3), 137–149. doi:10.1024//1421-0185.59.3.137.

LaRue, E. M., Mitchell, A. M., Terhorst, L., & Karimi, H. A. (2010). Assessing mobile phone communication utility preferences in a social support network. *Telematics and Informatics*, *27*(4), 363–369. doi:10.1016/j.tele.2010.03.002.

Lasica, J. D. (2007). *The mobile generation*. Washington, DC: Aspen Institute Communication and Society Program.

Lazarsfeld, P. F., Berelson, B., & Gaudet, H. (1948). *The people's choice* (2nd ed.). New York: Columbia University Press.

Lester, L. (2010). *Media & environment*. Cambridge, UK: Polity.

Lester, L., & Hutchins, B. (2009). Power games: Environmental protest, news media and the internet. *Media Culture & Society*, *31*(4), 579–595. doi:10.1177/0163443709335201.

Licoppe, C. (2004). 'Connected' presence: The emergence of a new repertoire for managing social relationships in a changing communication technoscape. *Environment and Planning. D, Society & Space*, *22*, 135–156. doi:10.1068/d323t.

Linne, O., & Hansen, A. (1990). *News coverage of the environment: A comparative study of journalistic practices and television presentation in Danmarks Radio and BBC*. Copenhagen, Denmark: Danmarks Radio Forlaget.

Lu, J., Shao, G., & Wu, J. (2012). New media and civic engagement in China: The case of the Xiamen PX event. *China Media Research*, *8*(2), 76–82.

Ma, J., Webber, M., & Finlayson, B. L. (2008). On sealing a lakebed: Mass media and environmental democratization in China. *Environmental Science & Policy*, *12*(1), 71–83. doi:10.1016/j.envsci.2008.09.001.

Maroon, B. (2006). Mobile sociality in urban Morocco. In Kavoori, A., & Arceneaux, N. (Eds.), *The cell phone reader: Essays in social transformation*. New York: Peter Lang.

Martin, W. C., & Leug, J. E. (2013). Modeling word-of-mouth usage. *Journal of Business Research*, *66*, 801–808. doi:10.1016/j.jbusres.2011.06.004.

Maxham, J. G. (2001). Service recover's influence on consumer satisfaction, positive word-of-mouth, and purchase intentions. *Journal of Business Research*, *54*(1), 11–24. doi:10.1016/S0148-2963(00)00114-4.

Mazur, A. (1981). Media coverage and public opinion on scientific controversies. *The Journal of Communication*, *31*(2), 106–115. doi:10.1111/j.1460-2466.1981.tb01234.x PMID:7204618.

McCombs, M. E., & Shaw, D. L. (1972). The agenda-setting function of the mass media. *Public Opinion Quarterly*, *36*, 176–187. doi:10.1086/267990.

MORI. (2005). *Information about science and technology*. Retrieved from www.opsos-mori.com/polls/2005/nesta.shtml

National Bureau of Statistics of China. (2013). *China's economy achieved a stabilized and accelerated development in the year of 2012*. Retrieved from www.stats.gov.cn/english/pressrelease/t20130118_402867147.htm

Nisbet, M. C., & Kotcher, J. E. (2009). A two-step flow of influence? Opinion-leader campaigns on climate change. *Science Communication*, *30*(3), 328–354. doi:10.1177/1075547008328797.

Nisbet, M. C., Markowitz, E. M., & Kotcher, J. E. (2012). Winning the conversation: Framing and moral messaging in environmental campaigns. In L. Ahern & D. S. Bortree (Eds.), Talking green: Exploring contemporary issues in environmental communications. New York: Peter Lang.

Reichheld, F. F., & Sasser, W. E. Jr. (1990). Zero defection: Quality comes to services. *Harvard Business Review*, 105–111. PMID:10107082.

Reingen, P. H., & Kernan, J. B. (1986). Analysis of referral networks in marketing: Methods and illustration. *JMR, Journal of Marketing Research*, *23*, 370–378. doi:10.2307/3151813.

Reuters. (2012, July 20). *China mobile subscribers up 1.1 percent in June to 1.05 billion*. Retrieved from http://www.reuters.com/article/2012/07/20/us-china-mobile-idUSBRE86J0D920120720

Rodan, G. (1998). The internet and political control in Singapore. *Political Science Quarterly*, *113*(1), 63–89. doi:10.2307/2657651.

Rotter, J. B., Chance, J. E., & Phares, E. J. (1972). *Applications of a social learning theory of personality*. New York: Holt, Rinehart & Winston.

Scharl, A. (2004). *Envirnomental online communication*. London: Springer. doi:10.1007/978-1-4471-3798-6.

Schudson, M. (1989). The sociology of news production. *Media Culture & Society*, *11*(3), 263–282. doi:10.1177/016344389011003002.

Smith, A. (2012). The best (and worst) of mobile connectivity. *Pew Internet*. Retrieved from http://pwerInternet.org/Reports/2012/Best-Worst-Mobile/Part-III/Impacts.aspx

Soroka, S. (2002). Issue attributes and agenda-setting: Media, the public, and policymakers in Canada. *International Journal of Public Opinion Research*, *14*(3), 264–285. doi:10.1093/ijpor/14.3.264.

Stamato, C., & de Moraes, A. (2012). Mobile phones and elderly people: A noisy communication. Work: A Journal of Prevention. *Assessment and Rehabilitation*, *41*, 320–327. doi: doi:10.3233/WOR-2012-1003-320.

Sundaram, D. S., Kaushik, M., & Webster, C. (1998). Word-of-mouth communications: A motivational analysis. *Advances in Consumer Research. Association for Consumer Research (U. S.)*, *25*(1), 527–531.

Tao, R. (2011, December 16). China's land grab is undermining grassroots democracy. *The Guardian*. Retrieved from http://www.guardian.co.uk/commentisfree/2011/dec/16/china-land-grab-undermining-democracy

The Pew Global Attitudes Project. (2007). *Rising environmental concern in 47-nation survey*. Pew Research Center. Retrieved from http://www.pew-global.org/files/pdf/2007%20Pew%20Global%20Attitudes%20Report%20-%20June%2027.pdf

Tilman, D., & Lehman, C. (2001). Human-caused environmental change: Impacts on plant diversity and evolution. *Proceedings of the National Academy of Sciences of the United States of America*, *98*(10), 5433–5440. doi:10.1073/pnas.091093198 PMID:11344290.

Trumbo, C. (1996). Constructing climate change: Claims and frames in US news coverage of an environmental issue. *Public Understanding of Science (Bristol, England), 5*(3), 269–283. doi:10.1088/0963-6625/5/3/006.

Walker, G. (2005). Sociological theory and the natural environment. *History of the Human Sciences, 18*(1), 77–106. doi:10.1177/0952695105051127.

Wang, Q. (2010). China's environmental civilian activism. *Science, 328*(5980), 824. doi:10.1126/science.328.5980.824-a PMID:20466902.

Weimann, G., Tustin, D. H., van Vuuren, D., & Joubert, J. P. R. (2007). Looking for opinion leaders: Traditional vs. modern measures in traditional societies. *International Journal of Public Opinion Research, 19*(2), 173–190. doi:10.1093/ijpor/edm005.

Widener, P., & Gunter, V. J. (2007). Oil spill recovery in the media: Missing an Alaska native perspective. *Society & Natural Resources, 20,* 767–783. doi:10.1080/08941920701460325.

Worcester, R. M. (1994). *Sustainable development: Who cares?* London: MORI and WBMG.

Yang, G. B. (2003). Weaving a green web: The internet and environmental activism in China. *China Environment Series, 6,* 89–93.

Yardley, J. (2005, April 25). A hundred cellphones bloom, and Chinese take to the streets. *The New York Times.* Retrieved from http://www.nytimes.com/2005/04/25/international/asia/25china.html?_r=0

Yearley, S. (1991). *The green case.* London: Harper Collins.

Zhu, H. J. (2007, May 31). Xiamen government announced to postpone the billions RMB PX project due to a rumor on its toxicity. *Southern Weekly.* Retrieved from http://www.suothcn.como/weekend/commend/200705310002.htm

Zittrain, J., & Edelman, B. (2003). Internet filtering in China. *IEEE Internet Computing, 7*(2), 70–77. doi:10.1109/MIC.2003.1189191.

ADDITIONAL READING

Ahern, L., & Bortree, D. S. (2012). *Talking green: Exploring contempory issues in environmental communications.* New York: Peter Lang.

Andreasen, A. R. (1995). *Marketing social change: Changing behavior to promote health, social development, and the environment.* New York: Jossey-Bass.

Bakhtavar, S. (2009). *Iran: The green movement.* Irving, TX: Parsa Enterprises, LLC.

Blanchard, O. (2011). *Social media ROI: Managing and measuring social media efforts in your organization.* Boston: Pearson Education.

Boykoff, J. (2006). *The suppression of dissent: How the state and mass media squelch USAmerican social movements.* New York: Routledge.

Camacho, D. E. (1998). *Environmental injustices, political struggles: Race, class and the environment.* Durham, NC: Duke University Press.

Downing, J. D. H. (2011). *Encyclopedia of social movement media.* Thousand Oaks, CA: SAGE.

Fryer, W. A., & Fryer, R. C. (2011). *Playing with media: Simple ideas for powerful sharing.* Speed of Creativity Learning LLC.

Goodstein, E. S. (2010). *Economics and the environment* (6th ed.). Danvers, MA: Wiley.

Haidt, J. (2012). *The righteous mind: Why good people are divided by politics and religion.* New York: Paththeon Books.

Hawken, P. (2008). *Blessed unrest: How the largest social movement in history is restoring grace, justice, and beauty to the world.* New York: Penguin Group.

Hendry, J. (2010). *Communication and the natural world. State College.* PA: Strata Publishing.

Hinrichs, R. A., & Kleinbach, M. H. (2012). *Energy: Its use and the environment.* Boston: Brooks/Cole.

Hjorth, L., Burgess, J., & Richardson, I. (Eds.). (2012). *Studying mobile media: Cultural technologies, mobile communication, and the iPhone.* New York, NY: Routledge.

Jenkins, H., Purushotma, R., Weigel, M., Clinton, K., & Robison, A. J. (2009). *Confronting the challenges of participatory culture: Media education for the 21st century.* Cambridge, MA: Massachusetts Institute of Technology.

Lievrouw, L. (2011). *Alternative and activist new media.* Malden, MA: Polity Press.

Lin, C. A., & Atkin, D. J. (2009). *Communication technology and social change: Theory and implications.* Mahwah, NJ: Lawrence Erlbaum Associates.

Ling, R., & Donner, J. (2009). *Mobile phones and mobile communication.* Malden, MA: Polity Press.

Mason, P. (2012). *Why it's kicking off everywhere: The new global revolutions.* Brooklyn, NY: Verso.

McAdam, D., McCarthy, J. D., & Zald, M. N. (1996). *Comparative perspectives on social movements: Political opportunities, mobilizing structures, and cultural framings.* New York: Cambridge University Press. doi:10.1017/CBO9780511803987.

Neuzil, M., & Train, R. E. (2008). *The environment and the press from adventure writing to advocacy.* Medill School of Journalism Visions of the American Press.

Porta, D. D., & Diani, M. (2006). *Social movements: An introduction* (2nd ed.). Oxford, UK: Blackwell.

Raven, P. H., Berg, L. R., & Hassenzahl, D. M. (2009). *Environment* (7th ed.). New York: Wiley.

Sandler, R., & Pezzullo, P. C. (2007). *Environmental justices and environmentalism: The social justice challenge to the environmental movement (urban and industrial environments).* Cambridge, MA: MIT Press.

Sparks, G. G. (2012). *Media effects research: A basic overview.* Boston: Wadsworth.

Stewart, C. J., Smith, C. A., & Denton, R. E. Jr. (2006). *Persuasion and social movement* (5th ed.). Waveland Press.

van de Donk, W., Loader, B. D., Nixon, P. G., & Rucht, D. (2004). *Cyberprotest: New media, citizens and social movements.* New York: Routledge.

Verba, S., Schlozman, K. L., & Brady, H. E. (1995). *Voice and equality: Civic volunteerism in American politics.* Cambridge, MA: Harvard University Press.

Wardrip-Fruin, N., & Montfort, N. (2003). *The new media reader.* Cambridge, MA: The MIT Press.

Withgott, J. H., & Laposata, M. (2011). *Essential environment: The science behind the stories plus mastering environmental science with eText* (4th ed.). New York: Benjamin Cummings.

Wyss, R. L. (2008). *Covering the environment: How journalists work the green beat.* New York: Routledge.

KEY TERMS AND DEFINITIONS

Authentic Participation: The term is used to describe effective public involvement in administrative process to have an effect on the situation.

Bulletin Board System (BBS): The abbreviation for Bulletin Board System, a computer system which provides software for log into the system and conduct a range of online activities, such as uploading and downloading software and data, browsing news sites, and exchanging opinions or information with others through email, public message boards, and instant message.

Campaign: A collective event organized by a strongly motivated group to influence the decision making process.

Decision-Making: A cognitive process of purposeful selection among given options.

Effectiveness: The capability of accomplishing a purpose and producing the intended result.

Environment: A term which means the sum of all living and non-living things that surrounded an organism or group of organisms. Social scientists tend to redefine the term by inspecting its relation to race, class, and rural issues.

Grassroots: Ordinary people at a local level who are not active in or the center of a political party.

Mobile Phone: A type of communicational device which connect to a wireless communications network through radio waves or satellite transmissions.

New Media: A group of medium which conduct interactive communication through digital devices or technology. Examples of new media include the Internet, mobile phone, computer media etc.

Public: A group of people who will be affected by certain decision, which might include stakeholders, affected public, observing public, and general public.

Public Participation: A series of procedures through which citizens are consulted, involved, and informed to have an input in decision-making process. Traditional participation mechanisms include public hearing, citizen forums, community meetings, community outreaches, citizen advisory groups etc. Novel public participation added new modes such as voting, lobbying, protesting, filing lawsuit, and physical interfering.

Public Opinion: A single opinion or a collection of opinions which are shared by the general public or a collection of opinions.

Short Message Service (SMS): A text messaging service integrated in mobile phone and Website, to exchange short messages between fixed line or mobile phone devices.

Smartphone: A type of device that combines the features of handheld computer and regular mobile phone. A smartphone allows users to store information, send e-mail, install programs etc.

The Internet: A communicational network which links smaller networks worldwide through globally shared Internet protocol suite and provides platforms such as world wide Web and data archive to exchange information and messages.

Web 2.0: A combination of different Web applications that facilitates participatory information sharing and collaborating in a social media dialogue (such as social networking sites, blogs sites) in a virtual community.

ENDNOTES

1   * QQ is an abbreviation of Tencent QQ, a social networking site in China, which provides customers with a variety of services, including instant messages, online social games, music, shopping, micro blogging, and group and voice chat.

Chapter 3

Ubiquitous Computing in the Cloud:
User Empowerment vs. User Obsequity

Primavera De Filippi
Université Paris II, France

ABSTRACT

This chapter analyses the evolution of the Internet, shifting from a decentralized architecture designed around the end-to-end principle with powerful mainframe/personal computers at each end, to a more centralized network designed according to the mainframe model, with increasingly weaker user's devices that no longer have the ability to run a server nor to process any consistent amount of data or information. The advantages of ubiquitous computing (allowing data to become available from anywhere and at any time regardless of the device) should thus be counterbalanced with the costs it entails (loss of users' autonomy, concerns as regards privacy, and freedom of expression, etc.).

1. INTRODUCTION

The advent of Internet and digital technology drastically changed the way people act and interact in everyday's life, in both personal and professional settings. Indeed, with the Internet, work, family and social life are becoming increasingly intertwined, sometimes even blurring into each other. The office does not longer consist exclusively of a place for work, but is increasingly used by people dealing with personal matters, via e-mails, instant messaging or social media. Conversely, professional activities extend throughout the day - either at home or at the office during lunch break, while traveling, or in the evening after a long day of work, people do not hesitate to check their e-mails and, if necessary, to complete their work. This naturally implies that people must be able to access their personal or professional files from anywhere and at any time, without direct access to their computer. Thus, in most developed countries, the Internet has become a necessity.

Ubiquitous computing is an attempt to answer emerging users' need for ubiquity. Without trying to resolve any specific business or technical problem, it represents an effort to elaborate new opportunities based on pervasive computing and connectivity (Bell & Dourish, 2007).

Nowadays, computing has become an integral part of everyday life – yet, it is much less visible than before. Technological advances in the computing industry are such that electronic devices

DOI: 10.4018/978-1-4666-4566-0.ch003

can be embedded in the environment in a way that is almost transparent to end-users (Weiser, 1991). Recent developments in Information and Communication Technologies (ICT) encouraged the deployment of compact users devices that communicate with powerful servers and distributed data-centers in order to mediate and support many daily activities (Lyytinen & Yoo, 2002). Personal computers, laptops, tablets or even mobile phones are turned into "intelligent devices" able to provide innovative services and applications to satisfy emerging users' needs in ways that could hardly be foreseen even just a few years earlier. Indeed, thanks to the Internet, any device - with limited computing resources - can potentially provide access to a world of information that was previously only available to a limited number of people connected to a given network.

This chapter analyzes the social, technical and legal implications of ubiquitous computing in the framework of *cloud computing* - distributed network architectures designed to provide computing resources as a service. After providing analysing the pro and cons of these new technologies, the chapter will address the implications that cloud computing might have on the interests of Internet users, whose autonomy is being increasingly impaired by the regulatory policy of large cloud operators.

2. BACKGROUND AND LITERATURE REVIEW

Definition of Cloud Computing

Cloud computing constitutes a new delivery model for IT resources based on the concept of *utility computing* – a model whereby computing resources are no longer sold *as a product*, but rather provided to consumers *as a service*. Although the term is nowadays used to refer to a large variety of online platforms, regardless of their technical attributes (Plummer, et al., 2008), *cloud computing* specifically refers to distributed online platforms

that provides configurable computing resources, dynamically, according to actual needs (Vaquero, et al., 2008). The National Institute for Standards and Technology (NIST) defines cloud computing as any online platform that relies on *ubiquity* (broad network access), *virtualisation* (resource pooling), *scalability* and *elasticity* (automatic reconfiguration of resources) to provide *on-demand* (user-centric) *metered services* (pay-as-you-go).[1]

Depending on the type of resources they provide, cloud computing platforms can be subdivided into three distinct categories: *Infrastructure as a Service* (IaaS) is a model whereby hardware resources (such as processing power, storage capacity, or network bandwidth) are provided for consumers to decide how to best put them to us; *Platform as a Service* (PaaS) is a model whereby users are provided with a specific framework or programming interface on which they can deploy their own applications; whereas *Software as a Service* (SaaS) is a model whereby consumers are only given the possibility to use particular software or online applications through an online interface which is generally accessible through a Web browser.

While cloud computing technologies are designed to allow users to access their resources from anywhere and at anytime, the actual degree of accessibility ultimately depends on type of cloud that one refers to. Namely, it is useful to distinguish between four different deployment models: *public clouds,* which are generally operated by one specific organisation that makes the infrastructure or the services it provides available to the general public, *private clouds* which are generally meant solely for the purpose of providing an infrastructure or a service to one specific organisation; *community clouds* which are intended to provide an infrastructure or services shared amongst several organisations that share similar goals or concerns, and, finally, *hybrid clouds* which combine two or more clouds (be them public, private or community clouds) into an aggregated structure.

For the purposes of this paper, we are mainly concerned with the impact of cloud computing on the online behaviour of users - whose interests are the most likely to be affected (both positively and negatively) by the latter category of clouds services. Throughout the paper, we will thus allude to *cloud computing* as referring to public clouds providing Software as a Service.

The Opportunities of the Cloud

More and more users are brought to interact with the cloud during their everyday life, in new and dynamic ways. Computing resources such as processing power, online storage and network bandwidth are progressively turning into a commodity which has become essential to most (Buyya, et al., 2008). Yet, just like water, gas, electricity and telephony, computing resources no longer needs to be purchased by the users needing them, they can now be consumed (and paid for) on a daily basis according to actual needs (Banerjee, et al., 2011). Users can thus immensely benefit from cloud computing technologies. Advantages relate not only to the benefits derived from the growing accessibility and flexibility of resources – including the comfort derived from their ubiquitous availability and ease of use, but also to the new opportunities for anyone to experiment with new business models and to provide innovative services and applications without having to undertake any substantial investment beforehand.

Indeed, cloud computing technologies, based on virtualisation, enable users to acquire only the resources they need: this is the principle of the electric grid, where users only pay for the amount of resources they effectively use (Foster, et al., 2008). This allows for a larger degree of flexibility in terms of both access and use. Given the ubiquitous character of cloud computing, in fact, data exported in the cloud become immediately accessible from anywhere and at any time, regardless of the user's device. The cloud also enhance and facilitate the deployment of these resources,

by allowing users to employ sophisticated applications without having to install or configure them onto their own devices.

Besides, with the advent of cloud computing, new business opportunities have emerged online - attracting a large number of users and start-ups, experimenting with new business models without the need to plan ahead for provisioning (Zhang, et al., 2010). This led to the emergence of a new value network operated by innovative market players that do not abide to the traditional value chain of service provision (Leimeister, et al., 2010). Thus, the cloud industry eventually paved the way for the establishment of a new commercial paradigm (so-called *u-commerce*) extending traditional commerce to an environment characterised by *network ubiquity, universality, uniqueness,* and *unison* (Watson, et al., 2002) through a series of online applications that users can access from anywhere and at anytime to enjoy unique and personalised services (Junglas & Watson, 2003).

The Dangers of the Cloud

These opportunities come, however, at a potential cost. As user interaction with the cloud increases in both frequency and intensity, individuals also become much more vulnerable to it. Such vulnerability can be largely classed into two sets of concerns. The first category revolves around users' freedoms and the potential consequences of the cloud to users' fundamental rights. The second category revolves around the increased users' dependency on the structure of the cloud itself, and the potential disempowerment that might derive from the the manner in which users interact with it.

The cloud as an online repository of computing resources posits great challenges for the maintenance and respect of users' fundamental rights. In terms of freedom of speech, the potential exists for cloud providers to access, monitor, censor, filter, block and otherwise control communications on the Internet (Karhula, 2010; Gervais,

2012; Ramachadran, et al., 2011; Lessig, 1997; Kshetri, 2010). Coupled with the general attitude of many users that do not hesitate to export personal information on the cloud, this makes for a great deal of personal data placed under the control of cloud-based service providers beyond the reach of users. Moreover, legal structures – contracts and copyright in particular – contribute to weakening users' ability to access information that should be freely available to all (De Filippi & Vieira, 2013).

The potential for user disempowerment (or *user obsequity*) is facilitated by the structure of the cloud itself. The Internet began—indeed was deliberately conceived—as a decentralized network with few control points and designed around the end-to-end principle (Frischmann, 2012). Robust interaction with the Internet infrastructure mainly due to the open character of the network, and to the fact that users were, for the most part, connected through relatively powerful computing devices (Zittrain, 2008; Lametti, 2012). The emerging cloud architecture manifests a more centralized hierarchical structure, which, along with users interacting with less powerful devices (such as tablets or smartphone), allows for a much greater degree of control from the part of cloud service providers. As opposed to their former role of contributors to the network, under the cloud paradigm, user become passive service takers.

3. ISSUES

From "Smart Phones" to "Dumb-Terminals": The End of the End-to-End Principle

The original infrastructure of the Internet was designed around the end-to-end principle and essentially made up of intelligent terminals that communicate with each other through the network. Fidelity to the decentralized architecture of the Internet was vastly assisted by the nonhierarchical,

if not almost anarchical, structure of the network - which expands as users continually add to it (Lessig, 2006). Given the open-ended protocols upon which the network was created, the intelligence or intellectual drive of the Internet was originally highly diffuse and decentralized, yet anchored in individual users from around the globe contributing to the infrastructure by either providing their own computing resources or generating new content through individual computer devices.

Over the past 20 years, users have become more and more demanding: they constantly expect new services and innovative applications that cannot be easily provided on the limited architecture of most mobile devices. Most of these applications are thus increasingly provided on remote servers accessible through the Internet. Hence, with the advent of cloud computing, we are progressively moving away from the original structure of the Internet - based on a horizontal and decentralized architecture - towards a more verticalized and centralized architecture based on increasingly less sophisticated terminals communicating through centralized online applications. On the one hand, cloud operators are creating a series of centralized platforms by aggregating an humongous amount of computing resources into large data centers distributed around the world. On the other hand, users' devices are devolving from personal computers and laptops, to less relatively powerful tablets, smart-phones or any other device whose sole function is to access a particular online application – the so-called "*thin clients*" (Zittrain, 2009). Thus, as the opportunities of ubiquitous computing are drawing users away from the decentralized architecture of the Internet and up onto the cloud, network intelligence is progressively moving from the terminals to the core of the network, with the risk of bringing the end-to-end principle of the Internet to an end.

In this regard, it is useful to analyse the implications of the use of thin client devices on the way users interact and communicate according to at least four intertwined aspects: (a) the devices themselves, (b) the software they employ, (c) the services provided on these devices, and (d) the greater system into which they connect.

To begin with, while thin clients are certainly powerful compared to older desktops and laptops, they are *relatively* less powerful compared to other component parts of the current system. Indeed, most of these devices are simply not meant to do general purpose computing, they are merely meant to connect, through the Internet, to a centralized server on which all user data is stored and most of the processing is performed. The technological platform is no longer part of the device, but is ultimately dictated by the cloud provider.

Besides, as opposed to the open Internet, where users can chose the software they use as long as they comply with the protocol, users of these thin clients are often forced to be running the software applications dictated or sanctioned by specific (often proprietary) systems. As such, thin client devices are an effective means of restricting users to only those functions deemed appropriate or necessary by the cloud operator. Indeed, average users are generally unable to write new applications or add any other kind of functionality to enhance their devices, as such addition can only be accomplished with great difficulty. As they cannot easily get access to the underlying software or code of their own devices, and given that the software is not meant to be directly altered by them, users can only rely on the capacities of the device as determined (either at the outset or through a series of remote patches and continuous updates) by the device or service provider (Zittrain, 1990). No doubt, users are generally more concerned with the user interface than with the programming potential of their devices. Thus, although internally complex, these devices are programmed to be as simple as possible, user interaction with the device is conceived to be easy, comfortable and efficient. Yet, for the sake of comfort and simplicity, much user power is lost. While many users enjoy the limited but easy

functionality offered by online cloud applications, in doing so, they are conferring more power to the service providers who actually control the communication infrastructure. The open protocols of the decentralized Internet are shunted aside in the push to enhance user mobility. These devices are "tethered" to their central core, the types of functions that the devices can perform and the applications that they run are either pre-set or controlled by the "mother" system, often remotely.[2]

Moreover, given that the cloud is—by definition—predicated on a service-oriented architecture (Yoo, 2011) most user interactions with the cloud revolve around the purchasing of *online services*. That is, rather than obtaining copies to be stored on a local hard drive, either by purchasing copies or by downloading them, users simply purchase ephemeral services on a current needs basis – through a *pay-per-view* or *pay-as-you-go* model. Under this model, users are turned into passive service-consumers and information-takers, as opposed to being pro-active information-creators or information-sharers (Lametti, 2012). Indeed, as users with less computational capacity can only interact with the cloud in the manner envisaged by the service-provider, they passively consume content and other services as opposed to generating content themselves. Access to services becomes the norm, and streaming takes over as the dominant descriptor of user behaviour (Lametti, 2012). Obviously, increased reliance on online services puts users at great risk to the extent that they might eventually lose access to these services.

Finally, most of these devices interact within proprietary systems (*walled gardens*), so that users are often required to opt for one particular system while purchasing a device. The vertical integration model of the cloud is based on providing a wide variety of convenient and easy integrated services. This is intended to entice users to a system and to subsequently keep them on that system (*user lock-in*). The situation is further exacerbated by the lack of interoperability among the competing clouds systems available to the public (Dillon, et al., 2010). While they appear comfortable and convenient for most users, once they buy in, users become bound—in the long term in most cases—to a specific, requisite technology or platform (Chow, et al., 2009). Technological incompatibilities constitute indeed an effective and dominant business model for the creation of "walled garden" – closed non-interoperable systems whose content can only be accessed according to the terms and conditions established by the online operator, by means of either contracts or technology (Boone, 2008). Besides, due to the lack of interoperability between systems, once they have been exported into the cloud, personal information and user-generated content will be difficult to transfer from one system to another – thereby allowing for the service provider to dictate terms of engagement in a manner that was heretofore impossible on an open Internet.

To conclude, in order to communicate on the Internet, users increasingly rely on technological platforms provided by third parties to access services which are themselves defined and provided by third parties. The result is that, today, most of the means of production (in terms of hardware resources, software, content or data) are concentrated in the hands of fewer, large Internet service providers. Just as in the early days of network computing, whose systems often revolved around a powerful central "mainframe" and local "dumb terminals," it is perhaps ironic that, today—in spite of the new opportunities provided by recent technological advances—we may be moving towards an analogous model of centralized computing, albeit on a global scale.

From "User Comfort" to "User Obsequity"

With the advent of cloud computing, more and more hardware, software, and informational resources are exported into the "cloud" – where they are often controlled by large corporations mainly interested in the maximization of profits (Zhang, et al., 2010). Data is no longer stored on individual users' devices, but rather in large data centers consisting of thousands of servers linked together into one large virtual machine. Applications are no longer run by end-users on their own devices, but are merely made available to the public through a Web-interface, to which users can connect at any time and from anywhere (Miller, 2008). With more reliance on cloud computing and centralized architectures, user devices become less powerful, less generative, and less capable of interacting with anything but the central server to which it is tethered (Giurgiu, et al., 2009). Thus, while ubiquitous computing definitely provides users with a greater degree of quality and comfort (Erdogmus, 2009), it is also likely to hinder users' autonomy and jeopardize their freedoms – a situation that could be described as the *tyranny of comfort*.

In spite of the growing choice of services that are nowadays available to the public, and despite the new opportunities provided by ubiquitous mobile applications, control over these applications remains ultimately centralized (Jaeger, et al., 2009). Thus, to the extent that the underlying technology of online applications determines the way people communicate with each other, users' freedoms may potentially be limited by the constraints imposed (either voluntarily or not) at the level of the user interface (Voas & Zhang, 2009). This is further aggravated by the fact that we are witnessing today a progressive rise of private ordering through the use of contractual arrangements and technological means, acting either as a complement or a supplement to the law (De Filippi & Belli, 2012). The problem is that there is, at the moment, no guarantee that regulation by the private sector remains compatible with the fundamental rights of users - especially with regard to the rights of privacy and freedom of expression (Kushida, et al., 2011). Hence, perhaps ironically, the comfort and new opportunities of ubiquitous online services are likely to impinge upon the freedom of users (De Filippi & McCarthy, 2010) and ultimately reduce their autonomy (Lametti, 2012).

Most critical in this regard is the strong level of centralization that characterizes many cloud computing platforms - allowing cloud operators to control users' communications and possibly censor them (Karhula, 2010), with obvious negative repercussions on user's rights. Today, many operators already filter or block certain types of contents they do not consider suitable to their platforms (such as offensive or pornographic content, for example).[3] Yet, cloud operators may also arbitrarily decide to censor online communications that could prejudice they own private interests (commercial or not) without taking into account the implications on users' freedom of expression and freedom to access information (Lessig, 1997). This is especially true in the case of countries with repressive governments or censorship regimes (Harwit & Clark, 2001; Kshetri, 2010).

On a different (but related) note, centralized control over the means of communication can significantly distort the type of content that users are exposed to. Driven by economic interests, many cloud operators are indeed more likely to promote the dissemination of popular content, which attracts a greater number of users and thus generates higher advertising revenues (Redden & Witschge, 2010), at the detriment of less popular, but not necessarily less important content which receives less visibility.

Thus, in the realm of cloud computing, user ubiquity and connectivity ultimately lead to user obsequity. And such obsequity relates to content as well. As resources move away from users to increasingly centralized architectures with large processing power and virtually unlimited storage capacity, users gradually lose control not only over the means of communication, but also over the content of communication (Chow, et al., 2009). Data stored in the cloud can be exploited by third parties without having to request authorisation from users, nor even to inform them of the matter (Jaeger, et al., 2008). Besides, exporting data into the cloud is likely to prevent right holders from exercising their rights. If *"code is law"* (Lessig,

2006), the user interface represents a series of technological rules that precisely determine the manner in which users can access or use their data (Kaczmarczyk, 2010). This means that, in practice, cloud operators (as data holders) have more control over the data than the actual rights holders (Wallis, et al., 2011): on the one hand, they can ignore the license of works licensed under liberal licences - such as Creative Commons - given that these works are merely made available to the public over an online interface (Mowbray, 2009); on the other hand, cloud operators can implement (either voluntarily or not) the user interface with additional restrictions that extend beyond the standard level of protection granted by the copyright regime (Jiang, 2010) – potentially even constraining the access and reuse of works that are in the public domain (De Filippi & Vieira, 2013).

Privacy, confidentiality and data protection laws have also been severely impaired by the advent of cloud computing (Takabi, et al., 2010), as much of the information that end-users would have normally stored on their computers is increasingly exported into foreign data centers (Dikaiakos, et al., 2009) whose whereabouts cannot easily be established in advance (Svantesson & Clarke, 2010). Since cloud operators can monitor most of the communications and activities taking place on their platform (Lanois, 2010), they can potentially collect a variety of personal data, provided either intentionally or unintentionally by users. This information can subsequently be exploited, either directly by the cloud operators, or indirectly by selling it to third parties (Davis & Sedsman, 2010). Hence, while many cloud services are provided to users apparently for free, users actually pay for these services with their own data (Robinson, 2010). Yet, given that no money is being transferred, such transaction is often invisible to users, who have no opportunity to negotiate the terms of the agreement (Pater, et al., 2009). Oftentimes, the privacy policies of cloud operators are neither read nor properly understood by end-users (Bezzi & Trabelsi, 2011), and many stipulate that the terms and conditions may actually change over time without further notice (Bradshaw, et al., 2011). Finally, although users are often willing to disclose personal information in exchange of a more personalized service (Guo, et al., 2009), such information is often aggregated into large databases in order to extract or infer additional information (Bollier & Firestone, 2010), whose processing has never been explicitly authorized by users.

While users could theoretically chose to avoid services that impinge upon their fundamental rights, the higher is the level of centralization, the smaller is the number of alternatives that users can choose from (Haraszti, 2010). Moreover, although users could theoretically bring proceedings against online operators violating their rights, most cloud services are delivered by a multitude of actors (subcontractors) whose identity is generally unknown to end-users (Mowbray, 2009). This makes it difficult to determine in advance what would the applicable law be in case proceedings were brought (Ward & Sipior, 2010).[4] Moreover, many of these operators do not have a direct contractual relationship with users, so that users cannot seek recourse against them without passing through a long chain of intermediaries connected through a complex chain of contractual relationships.

4. SOLUTIONS AND RECOMMENDATIONS

User-Driven Grass-Root Solutions

After an initial period of euphoria on the part of users who enjoy the benefits of ubiquitous access to a growing number of online services, the dangers of ubiquitous computing and mobile applications are becoming more apparent. Indeed, most of these benefits come along with variety of threats, security concerns (Stajano & Anderson, 2002), privacy and consumers risks (Svantesson & Clarke, 2010), as well as several social, economic and ethical implications (Bohn, et al., 2005). Users have become increasingly aware that more and more online applications are governed by centralized entities controlled by private companies and governments, with the ability to monitor, manage and control network communications (Andrejevic, 2007).

While many users willingly submit to this incremental loss of autonomy, the most savvy of them are developing alternative platforms based on decentralized architectures. Unlike the majority of cloud services relying on the use of dumb terminals specifically designed to control and monitor user activities and communications, decentralized platforms are meant to encourage users to reacquire ownership and control over the resources that had been previously exported onto the cloud (Mosch, 2011).

Theses platforms generally rely on peer-to-peer technologies, allowing for computing resources (such as memory, storage, or processing power) to be shared by direct exchange amongst the peers in the network, without requiring the intermediation of any centralized server or associated authority (Androutsellis-Theotokis & Spinellis, 2004). At first, considerable attention was put on developing peer-to-peer applications for improving content distribution on the Internet. This is illustrated by the growing number of file-sharing networks that emerged over the past few years - such as Gnutella, eDonkey and BitTorrent, to name a few - which are nowadays considered to induce the largest amount of network traffic on the Internet. Popular peer-to-peer applications also includes online streaming (such as P2PTV or DPTP for audiovisual works, Freecast for music), online file storage (such as Wuala or Buddy Backup), and collaborative tools for content production (such as Kune). Peer-to-peer technologies have been subsequently deployed in many other fields and activities, such as social media (e.g. Diaspora), distributed search engines (e.g. YaCy, Faroo). Anonymous browsing and Internet communication designed to bypass censorship and control (e.g. FreeNET, i2p, TOR), or even digital currency (e.g. BitCoin).

More recently, Eben Moglen's extensive research concerning the dangers of ubiquitous online applications in the context of cloud computing (Moglen, 2011) has led to the development of the "Freedom Box" – a device designed to facilitate the creation of a decentralized architecture enabling users to exchange information and communicate securely, away from any corporate or governmental control. Technically, the Freedom Box consists of a small plug server that relies on free software and peer-to-peer technologies to establish a decentralized network of peers (where every peer contributes with a small amount of resources to the network) allowing users to communicate more freely and autonomously on the Internet.[5]

Decentralisation has recently gone one step further, moving from the mere application or logical layer to the actual infrastructure of the network through the development of wireless ad-hoc networks ("mesh networks") connecting users to one another in a peer-to-peer fashion. By using user devices (such as mobile phones, WiFi routers, etc.) simultaneously as an access point and a relay node for other users (Akyildiz, et al., 2005; Hassna, et al., 2006) mesh networking allow people to communicate within a local community without having to pass through any centralized ISP (Dibbell, 2012).

Decentralized peer-to-peer architectures provide a series of benefits that might eventually restore the autonomy of Internet users. In terms of ubiquity and connectivity, they are such as to improve scalability and network performance by accommodating transient populations of users (Androutsellis-Theotokis & Spinellis, 2004); they can increase the resiliency of the network by avoiding dependency on centralized servers ("single points of failure"); they help preserving proper connectivity while eliminating the need for costly infrastructure by aggregating resources and providing direct communication among peers (Milojici, et al., 2002).

Moreover, by means of peer-to-peer technologies, these platforms can reestablish the original architecture of the Internet, designed as a decentralized system characterized by a network of peers interacting together with no hierarchical structure nor imbalance of power. Although it is sometimes possible to identify one or more entities in charge of administering or coordinating these networks, the regulation thereof is generally based on a decentralized system of governance. Thus, as opposed to the top-down approach to regulation adopted by many cloud operators, decentralized alternatives rely on bottom-up regulation, whereby the members of the community establish themselves the rules to which they want to abide (De Filippi & Belli, 2012).

Finally, the decentralized architecture of peer-to-peer networks is likely to provide users with a means to preserve anonymous communications, while resisting online surveillance and censorship. Anonymity is guaranteed as anyone can join and leave the network at any moment without having to ascertain their identity - although identification might nonetheless be required for accessing private or personal files (Ozhahata, et al., 2005). Besides, given that packets travel from one peer to another in a decentralized fashion, there is no central authority responsible for routing communications throughout the network. This, in conjunction with sophisticated cryptographic techniques, makes it impossible for anyone to autonomously monitor, filter and/or censor online communications without involving the overall network of peers (Endsuleit & Mie, 2006).

However, in spite of their benefits, decentralized systems are often difficult to use and not as comfortable as many cloud-based services. They nonetheless play an important role insofar as they can protect users against potential abuses by online intermediaries. Indeed, to the extent that these networks operate autonomously and independently from the infrastructure of large operators, users do not have to abide to the terms and conditions imposed by cloud providers. As such, they represent a potential alternative to the commercial offers of dominant cloud providers (De Filippi & Belli, 2012).

Users often chose to surrender some degree of privacy or autonomy in exchange of a service whose benefits are perceived to be worth the costs. Yet, the harsher the terms of use and the weaker the respect for privacy and user rights are, the less willing users will be to trade-off freedom and autonomy for more comfort and accessibility (Dinev & Hart, 2003). The deployment of decentralized networks can therefore be regarded as an effective counter-power capable of indirectly regulating the operations of large cloud service providers, by preserving the ability for users to shift towards more decentralized alternatives, in the eventually that these services would become too "foggy" or "nefarious."

While these networks needs to reach a critical mass of users in order to be viable and function properly, they do not have to be as big, nor as good as most of the cloud services they compete with. As long as such networks exist, Internet users will enjoy the possibility of becoming more independent from large cloud operators. Their mere existence constitutes therefore a safeguard for users eager to regain greater autonomy and freedom of communication, or who are no longer satisfied with the growing encroachments on privacy and civil liberties implemented by cloud operators.

And certainly there will always be a role for persons versed in the technology – the so-called hackers and geeks. As the pioneers of the digital realm, they test limits, probe technologies, identify the dangers, the vulnerabilities, the unethical or inappropriate business behaviors of cloud operators – ultimately serving as technological "watchdogs" in the cyberspace (Thomas, 2003).

Government Intervention and Collective User-Oriented Solutions

In addition to the user-driven responses described above, governmental intervention, combined with collective user-oriented solutions could be devised in order to address the twin challenges of ubiquity and autonomy in the cyberspace. The nature and viability of these solutions depend, to a large extent, on the social and political context in which they operate – which will ultimately determine the success or failure of various typologies of collective action. In particular, governmental intervention and formal government-driven solutions will be successful only where such intervention is seen as legitimate and to some extent desirable by the public. Community-based solutions, either formal or informal, will best succeed when driven by strongly committed actors whose actions are regarded as both credible and legitimate. In societies where the private sector is predominant and individual rights such as freedom of contract are cherished, instead, both formal and informal collective action might be better achieved by civil society organisations that operate beneath governmental administrations.

Regardless of the typology of actors behind these initiatives, different mechanisms might be employed as an attempt to resolve the growing challenges of cloud computing (as regards user privacy and autonomy) by focusing either on regulation or on the provision of alternative online platforms designed to better comply with users' rights and freedoms.

As for the former approach, it is our view that both government and inter-government solutions are needed. With regard to privacy, in particular, in spite of the international scope of cloud computing, domestic data protection laws could act as a baseline of protection to counterbalance the lack of bargaining power on the part of users and preserve the nature of privacy as a fundamental right (Rubenfeld, 1989). While users may by agreement or action either formally or effectively waive such protections,[6] the baseline should be set such that the cloud architecture is constructed and maintained with privacy at the forefront. Yet, governments need to cooperate in order to apply these principles around the world. Indeed, divergences amongst national regimes—most notably between strong data protection regulations in Europe and weaker privacy laws in the U.S., where most cloud computing operators are based—could *de facto* annihilate the legal protection granted to the citizens of one country insofar as the data is exported into a foreign data center (De Filippi & Porcedda, 2012).

States could also assume—either directly or indirectly—an educational function so as to make users more aware of their rights in the Internet context. Only in this manner will users be able to protect and enforce their rights whenever they choose to, taking steps to put dubious practices under scrutiny and bring violators to justice. In addition, and perhaps equally important in practice, increased awareness will allow users to waive their rights in a more informed fashion – whenever they actually can and choose to do so.

As regards users' autonomy and freedoms, a number of formal government solutions might be advanced to help protect users. Using regulatory norms and instruments, governments might attempt to create normative standards to regulate publicly-available cloud and Internet services provided by the private sector. Thus, consumer protection standards might be used to regulate contracts in this context, especially contracts of adhesion, in which users purchase Internet services but have little bargaining equality (Kessler, 1943). The rights of freedom of expression and freedom to obtain information can be relied upon in order to preclude online intermediaries from arbitrarily filtering or censoring online communications without any legitimate grounds (Cohen-Almagor, 2012). Competition and antitrust laws might also be used to ensure that major service providers compete in an open and meaningful manner, discouraging practices that would tend to greatly diminish either the number of providers or the variety of services offered to users (Sluijs, 2010). For instance, governments could mandate minimum standards of interoperability and portability, preventing large cloud operators from locking users into any one service. This might be implemented, in Europe, through an obligation for online operators to allow users to switch across services by transferring content from one to another with no technical or legal impediment.[7]

Alternatively, or as a complement to regulation, governments, public institutions (such as quangos, public research institutions or universities) and community organizations might respond by providing their own cloud-based solutions and providing their services to certain communities, segments of the population or indeed the population at large. Such responses would enable users to interact on the cloud, taking advantage of its ubiquity, without giving up their privacy or autonomy. As is the case for user-driven alternatives, collective solutions need not be as comprehensive as the cloud solutions offered by the private sector; they merely have to be a viable alternative that stands in effect as an insurance policy against the concentration of cloud power in the hands of a few.

From a governmental perspective, this can be done either indirectly, by setting up industry standards as regards accessibility, costs, interoperability and privacy rules (such as to positively direct the operations of the private sector), or directly, by providing such services themselves. The latter option can be achieved either through the creation of specific government agency or quango, or in the form of public-private partnership. For example, a government (or a group of governments acting in concert) might wish to provide cloud computing services to the general public at no or low cost, in order to ensure that all citizen-users have access and can benefit from the cloud computing potential. The implementation choice will depend on the administrative governance models particular to any given country or group of countries, and on the computing capacity at the government's disposal. Thus, in countries with a broad system of public universities or quangos with excess computing capacity,[8] governments may use this option to provide Internet services to a wide segment of the community. They may do so either by subsidizing these actors for providing such services or by providing a series of more indirect incentives. Alternatively, in countries with an under-developed framework of computing, private universities or private computing entities might be able to work with government to provide services respecting privacy and autonomy standards determined by the domestic law. Indeed, several private entities providing public cloud services may be willing to enter into agreements with governments to re-allocate some of their excess capacities in order to provide public services on their own platforms.

Finally, beyond the government and the private sector, specific communities might intervene by providing community clouds services and commons-based initiatives – some of which have already become an integral part of the Internet landscape.[9] By providing direct services to their communities, these initiatives are extremely responsive to user needs, and thereby provide a useful barometer for the kinds of services users most need. As they might with public or private entities, governments might thus partner also with community groups by providing specific resources (such as facilities or hardware infrastructures), financial grants or subventions, and so forth.

To conclude, it bears repeating that the extent of governmental or community-driven initiatives in providing ubiquitous online services need not be as extensive as those services provided to the general public by the private sector. They need only be extensive enough to provide a meaningful alternative, so as to encourage private actors to adopt equivalent or better standards.

5. CONCLUSION AND FUTURE RESEARCH DIRECTIONS

This chapter has provided an overview of the various advantages and drawbacks of ubiquitous computing, with particular focus on the most recent developments in cloud computing and the impact these developments might have on the exercise of fundamental users rights and freedoms. Attention has been drawn to the growing trend towards centralization that characterizes many online platforms, and the dangers that such centralized platforms present as regards the inherent loss of user autonomy and the potential violation of privacy rights and freedom of expression.

The objective of the chapter was not merely to describe the current state of affairs, but also—and mainly—to provide a prospective analysis of emerging trends in the context of cloud computing so as to identify the major challenges that will have to be addressed in the coming years. Most of the concerns identified above are, at the moment, still at an early stage of development. While they might eventually come true, as users seem to become more and more willing to trade-off their rights in the name of comfort and accessibility, this trend can nonetheless be reversed—or at least obstructed—by properly informing users of what their rights are and how they could effectively be limited by large online operators abusing their dominant position in the market for cloud services.

Thus far, limited research has been done to understand the relationship between ubiquitous computing and user autonomy.[10] While the present analysis present valuable insights with a view to generate awareness on this emerging issue, more research is needed to determine the extent to which our fears are actually coming true. Most critical in this regard is the need to monitor and to understand how cloud providers' policies and terms of use can actually affect user's preferences and behaviors in ubiquitous online platforms such as cloud computing. For instance, it is worth noting that increasingly intrusive privacy policies ultimately had divergent effects on user's behaviors: while many users simply submitted to the idea that "online privacy is dead" (Rauhofer, 2008), others actually decided to react by implementing alternatives solutions based on decentralized technologies that could eventually compete with the services currently offered by major cloud operators. In this last regard, more research should be undertaken in assessing the role of user- and community-driven initiatives acting as a counter-power to established commercial offers, as well as to investigate the affectivity of governmental regulation and public initiatives in counteracting the emerging trends in cloud computing.

REFERENCES

Akyildiz, I. F., Wang, X., & Wang, W. (2005). Wireless mesh networks: A survey in computer networks. Elsevier Science, 47.

Andrejevic, M. (2007). Surveillance in the digital enclosure. *Communication Review, 10*(4), 295–317. doi:10.1080/10714420701715365.

Androutsellis-Theotokis, S., & Spinellis, D. (2004). A survey of peer-to-peer content distribution technologies. *ACM Computing Surveys, 36*(4), 335–371. doi:10.1145/1041680.1041681.

Banerjee, P., Friedrich, R., Bash, C., Goldsack, P., Huberman, B. A., Manley, J., & Veitch, A. (2011). Everything as a service: Powering the new information economy. *Computer, 44*(3), 36–43. doi:10.1109/MC.2011.67.

Barkhuus, L., & Dey, A. (2003). Is context-aware computing taking control away from the user? Three levels of interactivity examined. In *Proceedings of UbiComp 2003: Ubiquitous Computing* (pp. 149–156). Berlin: Springer. doi:10.1007/978-3-540-39653-6_12.

Bell, G., & Dourish, P. (2007). Yesterday's tomorrows: Notes on ubiquitous computing's dominant vision. *Personal and Ubiquitous Computing, 11*(2), 133–143. doi:10.1007/s00779-006-0071-x.

Bergkamp, L. (2002). EU data protection policy: The privacy fallacy: Adverse effects of Europe's data protection policy in an information-driven economy. *Computer Law & Security Report, 18*(1), 31–47. doi:10.1016/S0267-3649(02)00106-1.

Bezzi, M., & Trabelsi, S. (2011). Data usage control in the future Internet cloud. *The Future Internet*, 223-231.

Bohn, J., Coroama, V., Langheinrich, M., Mattern, F., & Rohs, M. (2005). Social, economic, and ethical implications of ambient intelligence and ubiquitous computing. *Ambient Intelligence*, 5-29.

Bollier, D., & Firestone, C. M. (2010). *The promise and peril of big data.* Aspen Institute, Communications and Society Program.

Boone, M. S. (2008). The past, present, and future of computing and its impact on digital rights management. *Michigan State Law Review, 413.*

Bradshaw, S., Millard, C., & Walden, I. (2011). Contracts for clouds: Comparison and analysis of the terms and conditions of cloud computing services. *International Journal of Law and Information Technology, 19*(3), 187–223. doi:10.1093/ijlit/ear005.

Brey, P. (2005). Freedom and privacy in ambient intelligence. *Ethics and Information Technology, 7*(3), 157–166. doi:10.1007/s10676-006-0005-3.

Buyya, R., Yeo, C. S., & Venugopal, S. (2008). Market-oriented cloud computing: Vision, hype, and reality for delivering it services as computing utilities. [IEEE.]. *Proceedings of High Performance Computing and Communications, 2008,* 5–13.

Chow, R., Golle, P., Jakobsson, M., Shi, E., Staddon, J., Masuoka, R., & Molina, J. (2009). Controlling data in the cloud: Outsourcing computation without outsourcing control. In *Proceedings of the 2009 ACM Workshop on Cloud Computing Security* (pp. 85-90). ACM.

Cohen-Almagor, R. (2012). *Internet architecture, freedom of expression and social responsibility: Critical realism and proposals for a better future.*

Davis, M., & Sedsman, A. (2010). Grey areas: The legal dimensions of cloud computing. *International Journal of Digital Crime and Forensics, 2*(1), 30–39. doi:10.4018/jdcf.2010010103.

De Filippi, P., & Belli, L. (2012). The law of the cloud v the law of the land: Challenges and opportunities for innovation. *European Journal of Law and Technology, 3*(2).

de Filippi, P., & McCarthy, S. (2011). Cloud computing: Legal issues in centralized architectures. In *Proceedings of the VII International Conference on Internet, Law and Politics*. IEEE.

de Filippi, P., & McCarthy, S. (2012). Cloud computing: Centralization and data sovereignty. *European Journal of Law and Technology, 3*(2).

de Filippi, P., & Porcedda, M. G. (2012). Privacy belts on the innovation highway. In *Proceedings of Internet, Politics, Policy 2012: Big Data, Big Challenges?* Oxford Internet Institute.

de Filippi, P., & Vieira, M. (2013). The commodification of information commons. *International Journal of the Commons*.

de Schutter, O. (2000). Waiver of rights and state paternalism under the European convention on human rights. *The Northern Ireland Legal Quarterly, 51*, 487.

Dibbell, J. (2012). The shadow web. *Scientific American, 306*(3), 60–65. doi:10.1038/scientificamerican0312-60 PMID:22375324.

Dikaiakos, M. D., Katsaros, D., Mehra, P., Pallis, G., & Vakali, A. (2009). Cloud computing: Distributed internet computing for IT and scientific research. *IEEE Internet Computing, 13*(5), 10–13. doi:10.1109/MIC.2009.103.

Dillon, T., Wu, C., & Chang, E. (2010). Cloud computing: Issues and challenges. In Proceedings of Advanced Information Networking and Applications (AINA), (pp. 27-33). IEEE.

Dinev, T., & Hart, P. (2003). Privacy concerns and internet use–A model of trade-off factors. In *Proceedings of Annual Academy of Management Meeting*. Seattle, WA: IEEE.

Endsuleit, R., & Mie, T. (2006). Censorship-resistant and anonymous P2P filesharing. In Proceedings of Availability, Reliability and Security, 2006. IEEE.

Erdogmus, H. (2009). Cloud computing: Does nirvana hide behind the nebula? *IEEE Software, 26*(2), 4–6. doi:10.1109/MS.2009.31.

Foster, I., Zhao, Y., Raicu, I., & Lu, S. (2008). Cloud computing and grid computing 360-degree compared. In *Proceedings of the Grid Computing Environments Workshop, 2008*, (pp. 1-10). IEEE.

Gellman, R. (2012). Privacy in the clouds: Risks to privacy and confidentiality from cloud computing. In *Proceedings of the World Privacy Forum*. IEEE.

Giurgiu, I., Riva, O., Juric, D., Krivulev, I., & Alonso, G. (2009). Calling the cloud: Enabling mobile phones as interfaces to cloud applications. [Middleware.]. *Proceedings of Middleware, 2009*, 83–102.

Greenfield, A. (2006). *Everyware: The dawning age of ubiquitous computing*. Peachpit Press.

Guo, H., Chen, J., Wu, W., & Wang, W. (2009). Personalization as a service: The architecture and a case study. In *Proceedings of the First International Workshop on Cloud Data Management* (pp. 1-8). ACM.

Haraszti, M. (2010). Foreword. In Deibert, R. J., Palfrey, J. G., Rohozinski, R., & Zittrain, J. (Eds.), *Access controlled: The shaping of power, rights, and rule in cyberspace* (pp. xv–xvi). Cambridge, MA: MIT Press.

Hardian, B., Indulska, J., & Henricksen, K. (2006). Balancing autonomy and user control in context-aware systems-a survey. In *Proceedings of Pervasive Computing and Communications Workshops, 2006*. IEEE. doi:10.1109/PERCOMW.2006.26.

Harwit, E., & Clark, D. (2001). Shaping the internet in China: Evolution of political control over network infrastructure and content. *Asian Survey, 41*(3), 377–408. doi:10.1525/as.2001.41.3.377.

Hassnaa, M., Usman, J., Tinku, R., & Djamal-Eddine, M. (2006). A panorama on wireless mesh networks: Architectures, applications and technical challenges. In *Proceedings of the International Workshop on Wireless Mesh: Moving towards Applications (Wimeshnets 06)*. Waterloo, Canada: Wimeshnets.

Jaeger, P. T., Lin, J., & Grimes, J. M. (2008). Cloud computing and information policy: Computing in a policy cloud? *Journal of Information Technology & Politics*, *5*(3), 269–283. doi:10.1080/19331680802425479.

Jaeger, P. T., Lin, J., Grimes, J. M., & Simmons, S. N. (2009). Where is the cloud? Geography, economics, environment, and jurisdiction in cloud computing. *First Monday*, *14*(5), 1–12. doi:10.5210/fm.v14i5.2456.

Jiang, G. (2010). Rain or shine: Fair and other non-infringing uses in the context of cloud computing. *Journal of Legislature*, *36*, 395.

Junglas, I., & Watson, R. (2003). *U-commerce: A conceptual extension of e-commerce and m-commerce.*

Kaczmarczyk, K. (2010). *Predicting the future of the anti-circumvention laws in the cloud-computing world.*

Karhula, P. (2012). Internet censorship takes new forms. *Signum, 3.*

Kessler, F. (1943). Contracts of adhesion--Some thoughts about freedom of contract. *Columbia Law Review*, *43*, 629. doi:10.2307/1117230.

Kshetri, N. (2010). Cloud computing in developing economies. *Computer*, *43*(10), 47–55. doi:10.1109/MC.2010.212.

Kushida, K. E., Murray, J., & Zysman, J. (2011). Diffusing the cloud: Cloud computing and implications for public policy. *Journal of Industry, Competition and Trade*, *11*(3), 209–237. doi:10.1007/s10842-011-0106-5.

Lametti, D. (2012). *The cloud: Boundless digital potential or enclosure 3.0?.*

Lanois, P. (2010). Caught in the clouds: The web 2.0, cloud computing, and privacy. *Northwestern Journal of Technology and Intellectual Property*, *9*, 29.

Leimeister, S., Böhm, M., Riedl, C., & Krcmar, H. (2010). *The business perspective of cloud computing: Actors, roles and value networks.*

Lessig, L. (1997, July). Tyranny in the infrastructure. *Wired.*

Lessig, L. (2006). *Code: And other laws of cyberspace, version 2.0.* New York: Basic Books.

Lyytinen, K., & Yoo, Y. (2002). Ubiquitous computing. *Communications of the ACM*, *45*(12), 63.

Mell, P., & Grance, T. (2011). The NIST definition of cloud computing (draft). *NIST Special Publication*, *800*, 145.

Miller, M. (2008). *Cloud computing: Web-based applications that change the way you work and collaborate online.* Que Publishing.

Milojicic, D. S., Kalogeraki, V., Lukose, R., Nagaraja, K., Pruyne, J., Richard, B.,... Xu, Z. (2002). *Peer-to-peer computing.*

Moglen, E. (2011). *Why political liberty depends on software freedom more than ever.* Paper presented at FOSDEM Conference. Brussels, Belgium.

Mosch, M. (2011). User-controlled data sovereignty in the cloud. In *Proceedings of the PhD Symposium at the 9th IEEE European Conference on Web Services (ECOWS 2011)*. Lugano, Switzerland: IEEE.

Mowbray, M. (2009). The fog over the grimpen mire: Cloud computing and the law. *Scripted Journal of Law. Technology and Society*, *6*(1).

Ohzahata, S., Hagiwara, Y., Terada, M., & Kawashima, K. (2005). A traffic identification method and evaluations for a pure P2P application. *Passive and Active Network Measurement*, 55-68.

Patel, P., Ranabahu, A., & Sheth, A. (2009). Service level agreement in cloud computing. In *Proceedings of Cloud Workshops at OOPSLA*. OOPSLA.

Plummer, D. C., Bittman, T. J., Austin, T., Cearley, D. W., & Smith, D. M. (2008, 17 June). Cloud computing: Defining and describing an emerging phenomenon. *Gartner*.

Purtova, N. (2010). Private law solutions in European data protection: Relationship to privacy, and waiver of data protection rights. *Netherlands Quarterly of Human Rights*, 28(2), 179–198.

Rauhofer, J. (2008). Privacy is dead, get over it! 1 Information privacy and the dream of a risk-free society. *Information & Communications Technology Law*, 17(3), 185–197. doi:10.1080/13600830802472990.

Redden, J., & Witschge, T. (2010). A new news order? Online news content examined. In Fenton, N. (Ed.), *New media, old news: Journalism and democracy in the digital age*. Thousand Oaks, CA: SAGE.

Robison, W. (2010). Free at what cost? Cloud computing privacy under the stored communications act. *The Georgetown Law Journal*, 98(4).

Rubenfeld, J. (1989). The right of privacy. *Harvard Law Review*, 737–807. doi:10.2307/1341305.

Spiekermann, S., & Pallas, F. (2006). Technology paternalism–Wider implications of ubiquitous computing. *Poiesis & Praxis: International Journal of Technology Assessment and Ethics of Science*, 4(1), 6–18.

Stajano, F., & Anderson, R. (2002). The resurrecting duckling: security issues for ubiquitous computing. *Computer*, 35(4), 22–26. doi:10.1109/MC.2002.1012427.

Svantesson, D., & Clarke, R. (2010). Privacy and consumer risks in cloud computing. *Computer Law & Security Report*, 26(4), 391–397. doi:10.1016/j.clsr.2010.05.005.

Takabi, H., Joshi, J. B., & Ahn, G. J. (2010). Security and privacy challenges in cloud computing environments. *IEEE Security & Privacy*, 8(6), 24–31. doi:10.1109/MSP.2010.186.

Thomas, D. (2003). *Hacker culture*. Minneapolis, MN: University of Minnesota Press.

Vaquero, L. M., Rodero-Merino, L., Caceres, J., & Lindner, M. (2008). A break in the clouds: Towards a cloud definition. *ACM SIGCOMM Computer Communication Review*, 39(1), 50–55. doi:10.1145/1496091.1496100.

Voas, J., & Zhang, J. (2009). Cloud computing: New wine or just a new bottle? *IT Professional*, 11(2), 15–17. doi:10.1109/MITP.2009.23.

Wallis, M., Henskens, F., & Hannaford, M. (2011). Web 2.0 data: Decoupling ownership from provision. *International Journal on Advances in Internet Technology*, 4(1-2), 47–59.

Ward, B. T., & Sipior, J. C. (2010). The internet jurisdiction risk of cloud computing. *Information Systems Management*, 27(4), 334–339. doi:10.1080/10580530.2010.514248.

Watson, R. T., Pitt, L. F., Berthon, P., & Zinkhan, G. M. (2002). U-commerce: Expanding the universe of marketing. *Journal of the Academy of Marketing Science*, 30(4), 333–347. doi:10.1177/009207002236909.

Zhang, Q., Cheng, L., & Boutaba, R. (2010). Cloud computing: State-of-the-art and research challenges. *Journal of Internet Services and Applications*, 1(1), 7–18. doi:10.1007/s13174-010-0007-6.

Zittrain, J. (2003). Internet points of control. In 44 B. C. L. Rev 653..

Zittrain, J. (2006). A history of online gatekeeping. *Harvard Journal of Law & Technology, 19*, 253.

Zittrain, J. (2009). *The future of the internet--And how to stop it*. New Haven, CT: Yale University Press.

ADDITIONAL READING

Andrejevic, M. (2007). Surveillance in the digital enclosure. *Communication Review, 10*(4). doi:10.1080/10714420701715365.

Balkin, J. M. (2008). Media access: A question of design. *The George Washington Law Review, 76*(4).

Bendrath, R., & Mueller, M. (2011). The end of the net as we know it? Deep packet inspection and internet governance. *New Media & Society, 13*(7), 1142–1160. doi:10.1177/1461444811398031.

Benkler, Y. (1997). *Overcoming agoraphobia: Building the commons of the digitally networked environment.*

Benkler, Y. (2006). *The wealth of networks: How social production transforms markets and freedom.*

Bettig, R. (1997). The enclosure of cyberspace. *Critical Studies in Mass Communication, 14*(2). doi:10.1080/15295039709367004.

Boyle, J. (2008). *The public domain: Enclosing the commons of the mind.*

Burri, M. (2011). Controlling new media (without the law). M. Price & S. Verhulst (Eds.), Handbook of media law and policy. London: Routledge.

Clark, D. D. (2010). The end-to-end argument and application design: The role of trust. In 63 Fed. Comm. L.J. 357 (2010-2011).

Doctorow, C. (2012, January 13). Lockdown: The coming war on general-purpose computing. *BOING BOING*. Retrieved from http://boingboing.net/2012/01/10/lockdown.html

Dyer-Witheford, N. (2009). *Cyber-Marx: Cycles and circuits of struggle in high technology capitalism*. Urbana, IL: University of Illinois Press.

Etro, F. (2012). The economics of cloud computing. *The IUP Journal of Managerial Economics, 9*(2), 7–22.

Frischmann, B. (2009). Spillovers theory and its conceptual boundaries. *William and Mary Law Review, 51*, 801.

Frischmann, B. (2012). *Infrastructure: The social value of shared resources*. Oxford, UK: Oxford University Press. doi:10.1093/acprof:oso/9780199895656.001.0001.

Galuba, W. (2008). *Friend-to-friend computing: Building the social web at the internet edges* (Working Paper). Ecole Polytechnique Fédérale de Lausanne (EPFL).

Gervais, D. J., & Hyndman, D. (2012). Cloud control: Copyright, global memes and privacy. *Journal on Telecommunications & High Technology Law, 10*, 53.

Granstrand, O. (2000). The shift towards intellectual capitalism -- The role of infocom technologies. *Research Policy, 9*(29).

Hintz, A., & Milan, S. (2009). At the margins of Internet governance: Grassroots tech groups and communication policy. *International Journal of Media & Cultural Politics, 5*(1-2), 23–38. doi:10.1386/macp.5.1-2.23_1.

Hood, C. C., & Margetts, H. Z. (2007). *The tools of government in the digital age* (2nd ed.). New York: Palgrave Macmillan.

Karlekar, K., & Cook, S. G. (2008). Access and control: A growing diversity of threats to internet freedom. In *Freedom on the Web*. Freedom House.

Klang, M. (2006). *Disruptive technology: Effects of technology regulation on democracy*. Göteborg University.

Kushida, K., Murray, J., & Zysman, J. (2011). Diffusing the cloud: Cloud computing and implications for public policy. *Journal of Industry, Competition and Trade, 11*(3), 209–237. doi:10.1007/s10842-011-0106-5.

Lametti, D. (2005). Coming to terms with copyright. In Geist, M. (Ed.), *In the public interest: The future of Canadian copyright law* (pp. 480–516). Toronto, Canada: Irwin Law.

Lametti, D. (2010a). The objects of virtue. In Alexander, G., & Peñalver, E. (Eds.), *Property and Community* (pp. 1–37). New York: Oxford University Press.

Lametti, D. (2010b). How virtue ethics might help erase C-32's conceptual incoherence. In Geist, M. (Ed.), *From radical extremism to balanced copyright: Canadian copyright and the digital agenda* (pp. 309–340). Toronto, Canada: Irwin Law.

Lametti, D. (2011a). On creativity, copying and intellectual property. In Caso, R. (Ed.), *Plagio e creatività: Un dialogo tra diritto e altri saperi* (pp. 171–189). Trento: Università di Trento.

Lametti, D. (2011b). The virtuous p(eer): Reflections on the ethics of file sharing. In Lever, A. (Ed.), *New frontiers in the philosophy of intellectual property* (pp. 284–306). Cambridge, UK: Cambridge University Press.

Lemley, M. A., & Lessig, L. (2000). The end of end-to-end: Preserving the architecture of the internet in the broadband era. *UCLA Law Review. University of California, Los Angeles. School of Law, 48,* 925.

Lucas, M. (2007). *Decentralizing digital social networking applications* (Working Paper). Urbana, IL: University of Illinois at Urbana-Champaign.

Madison, M. J. (2003). Rights of access and the shape of the internet. *Boston College Law Review. Boston College. Law School, 44,* 433.

Mell, P., & Grance, T. (2011). National institute of standards & technology. *NIST Special Publication, 800*–145.

Moglen. (2010). *Freedom in the cloud: Software freedom, privacy, and security for web 2.0 and cloud computing*.

Mukherji, A. (2002). The evolution of information systems: Their impact on organizations and structures. *Management Decision, 40*(5), 497–507. doi:10.1108/00251740210430498.

Murray, A., & Scott, C. (2002). Controlling the new media: Hybrid responses to new forms of power. *The Modern Law Review, 65*(4), 491–516. doi:10.1111/1468-2230.00392.

Oram, A. (2001). *Peer to peer: Harnessing the power of disruptive technologies*.

Polanyi, K. (1944). *The great transformation: The political and economic origins of our time*.

Reidenberg, J. R. (1998). Lex informatica: The formulation of information policy rules through technology. *Texas Law Review, 76,* 553.

Sartor, G., & Cunha, M. V. de A. (2010). The Italian Google-case: Privacy, freedom of speech and responsibility of providers for user-generated contents. *International Journal of Law and Information Technology, 18*(4), 356–378. doi:10.1093/ijlit/eaq010.

Sinnreicha, A., Grahama, N., & Trammella, A. (2011). Weaving a new net: A mesh-based solution for democratizing networked communications. *The Information Society: An International Journal, 27*(5).

Slujis, J., Larouche, P., & Sauterr, W. (2011). *Cloud computing in the EU policy sphere*. Tilburg Law and Economics Center.

Sørensen, C., & Gibson, D. (2004). Ubiquitous visions and opaque realities: Professionals talking about mobile technologies. *Info*, *6*(3), 188–196. doi:10.1108/14636690410549516.

Walker, J. (2003). The digital imprimatur: How big brother and big media can put the Internet genie back in the bottle. *Knowledge, Technology & Policy*, *16*(3), 24–77. doi:10.1007/s12130-003-1032-6.

Weiser, M. (1991, September). The computer for the 21st century. *Scientific American*, 94–104. doi:10.1038/scientificamerican0991-94 PMID:1675486.

Whitaker, R. (2000). *The end of privacy*. The New Press.

Willey, D., & Edwards, E. K. (2002). Online self-organising social system. *Quarterly Review of Distance Education*, *3*(1).

Yoo, C. S. (2011). Cloud computing: Architectural and policy implications. *Review of Industrial Organization*, *36*, 405. doi:10.1007/s11151-011-9295-7.

Ziccardi, G. (2009). Resistance, liberation technology and human rights in the digital age. *Law. Governance and Technology Series*, *7*, 27–71.

ENDNOTES

[1] According to the National Institute for Standards and Technology (NIST), cloud computing is *"a model for enabling ubiquitous, convenient, on-demand network access to a shared pool of configurable computing resources (e.g., networks, servers, storage, applications, and services) that can be rapidly provisioned and released with minimal management effort or service provider interaction"* (Mell & Grance 2011).

[2] See e.g. the issue of remote content removal from Amazon who removed certain Kindle titles from sale—such as *Animal Farm* and *Nineteen Eighty-Four* by George Orwell—and remotely deleted these titles from purchasers' devices after discovering that the publisher lacked the rights to publish them.

[3] See e.g. the case of Facebook, which has been accused several times of political and religious censorship for suspending the accounts of hundreds of users accused of a "terms of service" violation for posting political statements or religious views. In addition, Facebook's Terms of Service prohibits 'obscene' and 'sexually explicit' material – where the assessment of such material is unilaterally carried out by Facebook's staff itself without passing through a judicial review. For more details, see De Filippi and Belli (2012).

[4] As Gellman (2012) points out, "[t]he user may be unaware of the existence of a second-degree provider or the actual location of the user's data [and] it may be impossible for a casual user to know in advance or with certainty which jurisdiction's law actually applies to information entrusted to a cloud provider."

[5] More info available at http://freedombox-foundation.org/.

[6] In certain countries, privacy is a fundamental right, which cannot be contracted around nor waived freely. In Europe, for instance, any agreement by an individual to waive some or all of the rights granted under the Data Protection Directive is both void and unenforceable - even if such agreement would actually further the interests of the data subject (Bergcamp, 2002). Yet, EC case-law and doctrine suggest that the "ban on waiver of data protection rights means not a ban of voluntary exchange of personal information for money, goods, or services,

but prohibition of giving away for remuneration of, among others, the right to consent. Therefore, commercial exchange of personal data is not, in principle, outlawed" (Purtova, 2010). For more details on the case-law of the European Court of Human Rights as regards the waiver of rights, see De Schutter (2000) referring to e.g. *Bulut v. Austria*, Application No. 17358/90, Judgement of 22 February 1996, para. 30; *Deewer v. Belgium*, Judgement of 27 February 1980 published in Ser. A, Vol. 35, p. 56.

[7] See Article 18 of the proposal for the new Data Protection Regulation in Europe, which introduced provisions for data portability imposing that users are given the opportunity to retrieve their data in a 'structured and commonly used' electronic format.

[8] Excess computing capacity in private entities like Amazon and Apple is, in fact, what led to the development of cloud computing technologies in the first place.

[9] Most popular examples community-driven online services based on cloud computing include, *inter alia*: Wikipedia.org; OpenStreetMap.org, a collaborative project to create a free editable map of the world; Sourceforge.net, a Web-based source code repository for open source software development.

[10] See, in this regards, Barkhuus and Dey (2003), Zittrain (2003, 2006, 2009), Bohn et al. (2005), Brey (2005), Greenfield (2006), Spiekermann and Pallas (2006), Hardian et al. (2006), Moglen (2010, 2011), De Filippi and McCarthy (2011, 2012), Lametti (2012).

Chapter 4
How to Design a Virtualized Platform?
A Socio-Technical Study about the Current Practices of Teleworking

Valérie Fernandez
TélécomParis Tech, France

Laurie Marrauld
TélécomParis Tech, France

ABSTRACT

In this chapter, the authors present the project "WITE 2.0." This project is at the crossroads of various issues related to mobility (Urry, 2007) and use of Information and Communication Technologies. WITE 2.0 is a part of the designing process of a collaborative communication tool: "a virtualized and unified platform." The authors define scenarios of teleworking practices, "equipped" by ICTs, and use these scenarios to better specify the platform. The project started at the end of 2010 and continued for a period of 18 months. The analysis is based on several complementary methodologies: a qualitative study (47 semi-structured interviews) and an experimentation of the platform. They present the main results of the interview survey through the following themes: remote management, skills, articulation of private and professional spheres, and the maturity of technologies. The authors also describe how these elements help the understanding of the evolution of workers' practices.

INTRODUCTION

The project WITE 2.0 (Work IT Easy) is a research and innovation program supported by public funds as well as being a multi-partner project (academic and industrial actors).

The aim of this project is to create a virtual platform. This platform represents a unified work environment, based on virtualization, instant communication and system interoperability. Furthermore, it allows individuals to work anywhere (and possibly at anytime).

The platform is a software solution that centralizes the access to a set of functionalities, originally offered by several applications: this being the principle of unified communications. Unified Communications (UC) is the integration of real-time communication services such as instant messaging (chat), presence information,

DOI: 10.4018/978-1-4666-4566-0.ch004

telephony (including IP telephony), video conferencing, data sharing (including Web connected electronic whiteboards aka IWB's or Interactive White Boards), call control and speech recognition with non-real-time communication services such as unified messaging (integrated voicemail, e-mail, SMS, and fax).

This platform is accessible from any connected terminal, either fixed or mobile (desktop, laptop, tablet, smartphone, etc.). The WITE 2.0 platform will provide a wide range of communication tools that can be activated on demand in different situations, and depending on user needs (VoIP, discussion groups, instant messaging, email, etc.).

The project has four main stages, divided into several subsections each. It is supported by a socio-technical analysis. Telecom ParisTech has assumed leadership in the scientific study of the needs and uses by administrating semi-structured interviews with individuals regularly working "remotely." We wanted to better characterize these work situations: at home, on the premises of the employer but in geographically dispersed locations: in telecentres/co-working spaces/business centers, with geo-distributed teams working together.

DESCRIPTION OF THE WITE 2.0 PROJECT

The Project Issues

Mobility at work is spreading in the context of the mobility paradigm evolution (Thomsin, 2002). The project WITE 2.0 intends to address the urgent need for solutions in the field of remote collaborative work. These needs include ways of collaborating, communicating and socializing, as well as accessing these features regardless of location, and from any workstation. It will provide a unified interface integrating all features, and have a wide range of communication tools selectable on demand.

The Project Phases

The WITE2.0 project is divided into four major phases. The first concerns the study of employee needs and uses, for remote collaborative work. In order to capture the needs and uses, we conducted a qualitative study based on 47 semi-structured interviews. The object of this phase was to highlight the varying kinds of remote collaboration in order to make recommendations related to the design of the platform. The results are published in the report "Work, socialize and collaborate remotely" (Fernandez *et al.*, 2011). The main results of this report focus on ways of socializing in a teleworking context, the question of remote management, and on the technical skills needed for the use of ICT. The recommendations focus on the access to digital resources, business information systems, and on issues related to security.

The second phase of the project focuses on the technology. It is divided into two parts. The first part consists of the writing of functional and technical specifications of the WITE2.0 platform. This document contains descriptions of service needs, and a comparison of various existing virtualization solutions. We have noticed that, since the launch of the WITE 2.0 project, some other virtualization solutions have appeared on the market (Citrix, etc.) (Wang *et al.*, 2011). Through the comparison of different solutions, we highlight the distinguishing features and the technological services of the WITE 2.0 platform. The second part of phase 2 includes the implementation of all the technical elements necessary for the platform WITE 2.0. These technical elements include the virtualization, the development of a socialization software solution, the service integration, the development of a unified software application, and undertaking a beta test of the platform.

In the third phase, the project partners have introduced new technological elements for the components and voice applications, the mobile profiles, and the SIP recorder.

The Virtualized Workstation

The major technical element of this platform is based on the virtualization of information systems (IS). The virtualization solution of workstation we are interested in is also called "PC on demand." The virtual workstation displays a virtual image on the user's workstation that is executed on a remote server (not virtualized). This technology has several advantages like:

- **Centralizing Logical Components:** operating systems (like Windows© or Macintosh©) + softwares (like Powerpoint©, Skype©, etc.).
- **Control of Workstation Lifecycles:** In general, workstation lifecycles are extended since they are used less, to launch software applications for example.
- **Manage Storage Resources:** According to Gardarin (1999), the company can exploit data resources through knowledge management; it must have the associated technical possibilities and must be able to organize data storage through virtualization IS (servers and storage elements).
- **Access to a Virtual Portal:** to offer a choice selection of applications whenever the PC is recreated. This virtual portal is customized for each company.
- **Access to a Virtual Workstation:** the employee gets to an individual virtual workstation guaranteeing them better mobility management (because they can create and destroy the virtual workstation on demand).

Virtualization simulates the installation and operation of several system components on one physical machine and allows the management services simultaneous and centralized intervention. There are several categories of virtualization technologies classified according to their objectives. The most common are:

- Full virtualization, which emulates the entire operating system and its operation on a physical machine (architecture), but it is "aware" of the emulation that hosts it.
- The paravirtualization, which emulates an operating system "aware" of its emulation in a virtual machine.
- The hardware-assisted virtualization is an extension of paravirtualization but without direct hardware access to the operating system. The technique uses a supervisor, a kind of mediator between the hardware and the operating system associated with the services.
- The partitioning is used to isolate any service originally incremented in the same operating system and therefore dependent on the latter.

The virtual workstations address a number of challenges compared to "ordinary" workstations (especially for administrative, security and deployment of machines). Virtual machines, for example, can decrease functional costs (maintenance, etc.), and technical problems such as obsolescence of the workstation. With VDI architecture, the ISD no longer has constraints related to maintenance and administration of its fleet of workstations. The user is no longer dependent on a single physical computer and can connect to their "own PC" from different physical devices, even from terminals like thin clients.

Hence, virtualization is an previously existing technology. The value of the WITE 2.0 platform is to combine this exiting technology with a collaborative tool (unified communication). The aim is in fact double: to reduce (or eliminate) data security problems, and on the other hand, improve the level of collaboration between employees.

A SOCIO-TECHNICAL STUDY

Teleworking and "Remote Collaborative Work"

In a context of managerial culture based on "face to face," the new paradigm of mobile work does not seem to be established in French companies. Some forms of work organization are deeply rooted. Some managers and IT system directors are still reluctant to introduce new technologies in their company because of security problems associated to data circulation. Our bias is to say that the paradigm shift can take place now if we take into account the issues of teleworking in "sociological" and "technical" terms: hence, the importance of analyzing the work practice organization and use of ICT, and also the experimentation of the virtual platform.

In our analysis, we are interested in a key notion: the concept of "teleworking" that we have considered in its most classic form (homeworking), but also in the most diverse realities that it could be today: either, all forms of "remote working," i.e., forms of organization and/or performing work outside the classical unity of time and place. Indeed, many studies emphasize that the unity of time and place that characterized the traditional organization of work, will tend to disappear (Davis, 2002; Cocula & Fredy-Planchot, 2003; Lallement, 2003; Chen & Nath, 2005; Jeddi & Karoui Zouaoui, 2011).

Thus, the definition of teleworking that we have selected is based on:

- The fixed place of work or alternating between several workplaces, provided they are removed from the hierarchy and/or colleagues.
- The relationship to the employer and colleagues, remotely and by electronic links, thus justifying the name teleworking (Rosanvallon, 2006).

Methodology

The first results that we will present in this chapter are based on a qualitative analysis approach. We have particularly studied the practices of coordination and cooperation in various configurations of remote work, more specifically in management practices supported by different communication technologies (fixed or mobile devices). We believe this kind of qualitative study is the most relevant in order to describe the practices of teleworkers. In the design project phase, we had little knowledge about practices of current technologies. The classic typology of the four kinds of teleworkers (homeworkers, mobile workers, the telecenter worker and the virtual team worker (Boboc et al., 2007)) needed in-depth study. We have decided to study the practices of teleworkers to understand the work organization evolution and the links with specific uses of technology. During the operational phase of the study, from May 2011 to July 2011, 47 interviews were conducted face to face with workers performing work remotely. Our sample of interviewees was compiled from information relays (managers and human resources departments in companies). These interviews, lasting for an average of 90 minutes each, were the subject of subsequent detailed accounts.

The sample is constituted with different profiles of employees. In our analysis, we define three kinds of profiles, regarding the level of responsibility and autonomy in work:

- **The Business Leaders:** They are very autonomous in their work, some have their own company.
- **The Executives and Intellectual Professions:** Graduate employees (engineers, etc.), that manage employees. Relatively autonomous, they sometimes are obliged to report their activity.
- **The Associate Professionals and Employees:** They are managed by executives. They have technical activities (see Table 1).

Table 1. Sample

	Homeworking	Alternating Homeworking	Mobile Worker
Business leaders	2	2	2
Executives and intellectual professions	1	17	14
Associate professionals – Employees	2	4	3
Total	**5**	**23**	**19**
Women	3	8	4
Men	2	15	15

RESULTS

The results of the analysis cover various aspects of the remote work of the surveyed employees:

The Articulation of Private and Professional Life: The working activity outside official hours seems to become widespread. This form of tele-working consists in regular work done outside of the official working hours, most often at home. These activities are mostly related to checking and replying to emails. People build tactics to separate their private and professional spheres. These tactics are based, for example, on partial *reachability* over the mobile phone. People choose to disconnect and not to check their mobile phones after a defined period. This strategy is the most intuitive. But, some people choose to disconnect their mobile phone to work at home without being disturbed each time. Some of the interviewed said that it is difficult to concentrate on doing a task when:

- They are at the office (colleagues interrupt them all the time, or there is lot of noise, etc.).
- They are at home when the mobile phone is switched on (or even when just the Internet is connected).

Forms of Remote "Socialization": Social networking tools seem to be effective. This proximity can develop communicative relationships of trust, explaining in part the stability of the worker community (Rosanvallon, 2005). For example, the unified communication and the social media, that employees use, seem to be very convenient. They use it to talk to each other through *chatrooms* without ever seeing each other in real life. They become friends in other social media (Facebook, etc.) and develop a real relationship of complicity and friendship. It's difficult to say if this relation is also based on trust.

New Forms of Remote Management: Traditionally, managerial control consists in direct supervision in a context of employee visibility (the manager wants to observe the worker: working hours, work process, etc.) and the physical presence of the employee (the manager wants to interact with his employees) (Felstead et al., 2003; Taskin, 2010). The remote worker has other ways of communicating and collaborating with their hierarchy and their colleagues. How do employees declare their working activities? How do managers check the working activity of their subordinates?

In our results, we noted that employees and managers develop special and varied skills, tactics, in order to manage these activities in the scope of remote working. ICT, for certain categories of workers, act as a digital control infrastructure, replacing the physical presence of the manager (control of connection time, obligation of permanent reachability via mail or instant messaging).

The current technology controls the activity of the employees very well. The managers can hear the phone calls between employees and clients without the employees' knowledge. In this case, the status of presence and the chat activity are essential when proving that the employee is working. In other cases, some managers construct "motivation" tactics by using ICTs as a lever of the collective dynamics (Chat between colleagues).

Skills Development: It appears that many people working remotely learn to use ICT more or less on a "self-taught" mode, "on the job." Some of them practice forms of computer "tinkering" as the diversion of scripts uses some business applications, etc.

Analysis of Current Technology: current technology does not allow the maintenance of conditions comparable to those offered on the premises of the employer. Sometimes, these conditions are not reproducible. In this case, the employee is forced to limit their work activity and favor some tasks. For example, he will assign specific tasks to places where he works according to the possibilities offered by their work environment. Furthermore, this segmentation may come from the desire to choose a specific work environment, one that is quieter and less disruptive than in the enterprise to perform tasks requiring more concentration.

We will now develop these elements.

The Articulation of Private and Professional Life

Spontaneously, the question of the articulation of private and professional life refers to the main advantage of remote working: to enable workers (most of the time, women) to coordinate professional activity with personal activities (like caring for children) (Laffite & Trégouet, 2002; CAS 2009).

Our study shows that others reasons explain this choice. Furthermore, remote working encourages people to develop tactics to manage the professional and personal spheres (Belton & De Coninck, 2006). Indeed, people who demanded remote working were looking for flexibility at work. However, they realized that the flexibility in remote working can be negative. During the interviews we learnt that the greatest difficulty when remote working was the fragmentation of activities (Couclelis, 2004). Children often disturb the remote workers but not only. Colleagues can be a source of disturbance, remotely via the technologies. The tactics that people develop to cope with these disturbances are actually skills. The behavior of the remote worker must be adapted to the situation of teleworking (Rey & Sitnikoff, 2004). However, these skills are not the same for all remote workers and some have more difficulty than others to manage their private and professional spheres.

To work at home, workers need to master space and time. In our sample, a lot of people have considerable autonomy in the organization of their work hours. Yet, these persons will reproduce the standard work hours when they work one day or more per week at home. This is an implicit injunction of synchronization with their colleagues and their clients. On the other hand, work at home means being present at home. The family and relatives of the family do not understand why people are present but not available. Remote workers must often make a kind of discourse of legitimacy to explain their work obligations. The remote worker must be able to isolate themselves and not answer to demands of their physical environment.

In our sample, the teleoperators in homeshoring do not need to build boundaries between private and professional lives. Compared to others employees, these people (women as it happens) do not have autonomy in the organization of their work hours. On the contrary, for the teleoperators who work exclusively at home, worked hours are fixed (even if it is shifted in the morning and the evening). The managers can control the activity of teleoperators via ICT; the employees cannot be late or missed. For instance, when the teleoperator is logged on the platform to begin their work, the manager is informed about it.

Otherwise, when the employee works remotely, he can never stop working. Sometimes, he is submitted to a never-ending "remote availibility." Thus, stopping working is becoming a skill for building boundaries between private and professional lives. For a lot of people, it is difficult to have limits because the ICTs and mobile ICTs have created a kind of dependence (Fernandez & Marrauld, 2012), sometimes compared to addiction (Orlikowski, 2010). Bernard (57 years old, purchase manager): *"Of course, the BlackBerry pushes us to work all the time. There is the little red light that flashes each time I've received an email or a call. At the end of a teleworking day and when I'm on the couch with my family, it's difficult to resist and not to check."* And the tacit injunction to answer phone calls or e-mail is stronger when the employees have spent their working hours outside of the company buildings; that's why some people compel themselves to not check their e-mails after a precise hour. Other people interviewed have decided to check their e-mails in specific slots. Of course, this strategy is not as easy for some employees who must be reachable all the time. In our opinion, all these tactics concern the "right to disconnect oneself" (Ray, 2001). It also concerns the rules of teleworking and the inequalities between those who still manage their working hours and those who can no longer do it (Jauréguiberry, 2003).

As we have seen, this strategy of being connected or not is used to stop working. But it is also used to begin working. The home can be a disrupting place but, on the contrary, it can be a quieter and calmer place than the office in company buildings. Indeed, at home people are not disturbed by colleagues asking for them all the time or by different noises in the "open spaces": *"People come in the office all the time. And if I close the door, people will think I'm being antisocial."* Some people interviewed told to us that working at home helps fight against the fragmentation of work activities and focuses on complex activities that require concentration: *"at 8.30am,*

the computer turns on, my wife and my kid are gone, and so I'm gonna be more efficient than in my office. It's calm. No phonecalls [on the fixed line]." The home becomes a "shelter," for some of them compared with the constant stress due to the presence of colleagues in the company buildings.

Therefore, the employees introduce some practices or tactics of "partial reachability, " or "disconnection." Thomas is an engineer in computational sciences. He is a "nomad worker" and works in different places. He chose not to have an Internet connection at home, because, even if *"it is a constraint to not have Internet at home … it's also a good idea.; it leads to having work schedules."*

He also explained that this is the solution he has found to avoid "permanent distraction." their "reachability" or their non-reachability was decided with their colleagues and their managers: in case of emergency, they can communicate via their mobile phone. He decided the same thing with their clients: if they want to contact them, they send them an SMS and Thomas calls back immediately, even if he is in a meeting. In the same way, if he works from others places than their home (in a co-working space, for instance) he will disconnect their NIC to work in disconnected mode and thus, he can focus on their work. Daily, Thomas finds solutions to eliminate the majority of alerts that he could receive from their mobile phone. He decided to gather all RSS in only one tab of their e-mail box. Thus, when he is not working on their computer, he is not disturbed because the alerts do not appear and they do not make noise.

"Remote" Management: How to Control and Motivate

Remote management modes concern the employee and the manager (Taskin & Tremblay, 2010). It is part of managerial culture where face-to-face is still seen as essential in establishing a social and relational context conducive to collective work and the insertion of employees (Nardi &

Whittaker, 2002). Our results show different remote management modes where some managers substitute face-to-face with another management modes while others managers use more traditional methods.

When trust is present between manager and employees, the manager can choose to evaluate their employees "on results," compared with the initial objectives. This observation is in accordance with the analysis of Dambrin (2004). However, this trust can take a time to settle, the concerned employees admit that it is rarely the method of remote management chosen for a person just starting out in business in teleworking (see Table 2).

However, other employees are "controlled" from activity reports, sometimes very frequently: weekly in some cases, meetings with their superiors fortnightly, notifications of actions for each day spent teleworking. In some virtual teams, some have to produce a notification action daily and have to report on their production directly on a wiki (Frederick, technical engineer, 31 years).

Thus, in some cases, managers use ICT as real infrastructures of control of the employee's activity. Especially for teleoperators: the manager "tracks" the teleoperator through the digital platform (hours worked as connected, number of calls). It is undoubtedly the statistic that is most often controlled concerning the teleworker in their activity (see Table 3).

Arianne (marketing manager in an IT company, 45 years old, alternating between two modes of teleworking: home working and works in customer sites): she touches base with her supervisor weekly by telephone and also writes reports.

Table 2. Process of building trust

"Flying Supervisor" [1] (David) Teleworking from home Frequency: 3 days per week at the time of the interview	**Engineer** (Fabrice) Teleworking from home, in a specific room, and from "third places" Frequency: Full Time	**Sales engineer** (Baptiste) Teleworking from home, Frequency: 1 day a week
"When I do a mission, I track hours (I inform statistics), I report and I make a point a week with my superiors ... today, I no longer do it, because they trust me." David explains that reporting of their working hours is always systematically done for the client. *"But not all tasks at home.... If I was reporting every hour, they would see how many times I had a break ... In fact, teleworking requires self-discipline."*	Fabrice explains that he is less controlled in its activity of teleworking. Their boss expects the final result from them; there are just monthly meetings. *"Part of the work is not on the screen. That activity, cannot really be controlled. "*	Baptiste explains that *"my manager was initially sent copies of all e-mails. After a time, only the important emails have been sent in copy."*

Table 3. ICT: infrastructures of control

Teleoperator (Estelle)
Estelle, 27 years old, works from home (homeshoring). Her work activity consists in calling people and proposing that they participate in donation campaigns. Her managers give her a directory of names and assigned objectives: a number of donations (preferably made by direct bank debit) to perform per hour. She operates these phone calls via a computing platform (a specific software phone, a chat tool, etc.). She communicates her presence at the workstation via the platform by a visible light that her manager can see, as well as her possible activity on the chat group in which her manager has access. She contacts her supervisor exclusively via the platform (voice, email, videoconferencing) to define or redefine the objectives and action plans as well as collective team debriefings. Estelle does not see the control by her supervisors as an intrusion or rigidity.

In our study, we encountered few situations of time stamped work. However, it appears that regular reporting systems don't seem be perceived as binding for many of the employees surveyed who say they are "*very autonomous vis-à-vis the hierarchy*" (Marie, engineer alternating office/work at home one day a week, 40 years old). Moreover, in the interviews, respondents report a genuine feeling of gratitude and loyalty to companies that "tolerate" teleworking.

Some managers are cautious of teleworking practices and choose some days in the week that they allow for teleworking. Marie (idem) explains to us: " *Not Mondays because it is the day of shopping and not Fridays because it is the day of housework. And if you are a mother, not Wednesdays because it is the day of children .*" This observation is in line with a statistical reality: teleworkers are mostly men, whereas women are more likely to use a computer professional at their place of work, factor analyzed as a lever to telework (CAS, 2009).

Managers also build tactics to dynamize their virtual team in teleworking. They use ICTs as a lever of the collective dynamics: managers use this tool to lead their subordinates who are "remote." The chat, for example, is a tool for dynamizing teams. Indeed, this type of technology supports decentralized and collaborative tools, especially social network software; they allow patterns of spontaneous interactions, potentially independent of hierarchical links (McAfee, 2009) while participating in a performative practice of team animation (see Table 4).

Finally, in light of our results, we find that the patterns of teleworkers refer to different modes of management, from directional to delegative (Hersey and Blanchard, 1971). The teleoperators seem to be the most controlled actor; mobile managers benefit from greater flexibility. However, it appears that the implementation of activities seems very constrained by the technological limitations of the equipment used, more autonomous in the case of the employees.

What ICT Skills? Between Autonomous Learning, Mastery of Technological Tools, and Variety of Use

Through the analysis of our interviews, it appears that the use of ICT as a "teleworking" medium is a challenge whatever the competencies of an individual in the field of computing. It is part of a specific skillset to be built. This learning can happen in different ways. It can refer to many original dynamics of ICT appropriation.

Learning "remote" is different depending on the configuration. Telework at home can create situations of isolation regarding technology. The home is the place that crystallizes the tensions related to learning. From a distance, it is more difficult for the employee to call a technician of the company or ask their colleagues to explain and show how "it" works. Sophie, 47 years old, expresses this point by explaining that "*we sometimes feel alone in front of the machine.*" Others explain that "*we must sometimes use a DIY – Do-*

Table 4. ICT: tools for managing geo-dispersed teams

Anatole, 22 years old, a consultant in a structure of fifteen employees, uses a collaborative platform like "Facebook." This platform comes a support of the stated policy of the company "*no mail, no PowerPoint, no meetings*" in this case; this policy participate in the strategy of "breaking" the hierarchical logic considered too "top-down."
Fabrice, 40 years old, engineer, talks about new practices of geo-dispersed team management: in his company, the tasks performed "remote" are now grouped in autonomous batches assigned to a single person. Everyone is assigned a "reference" who has previously worked on a similar project for the same client or even with whom he has strong affinities. Exchanges with the reference can be made by mail or phone. Prior to these exchanges mediated by ICTs, a meeting was organized IRL in order to create sufficient cognitive proximity.
Ariane, 37 years old, marketing manager, talks about the use of microblogging for instant communication, a practice not always in action compared to email which is more formal and allows traceability of exchanges.

It-Yourself system" (Fabrice, Technical Engineer 40 years old). Being *"alone"* encourages people to be less passive in the face of technology (Lamb & Kling, 2003).

Many interviewees had to learn to train themselves *"on the job."* *"On the job"* means, for some, taking time to use the tools available but can also bring "function creep." One of our interviewees with the other members of their project team has put in place, software of management "problems" without the agreement of the ISD.[2] She and her colleagues use this software for project management in context of geo-dispersed teams. The ergonomics and functionality are considered more attractive than the software provided by the ISD, "too rigid" from the project team point of view. This strategy of "function creep" can also be implemented to overcome some limitations of ICT, pending better: *"When I'm in Webconf [erence], I sometimes double it with a phone for better listening"* (Bernard, purchasing production director, 57 years).

Let us talk finally of Skype, whose use is not validated by ISD (of all surveyed employees). Arianne mentions the use of an opensource solution (Pingin) which is authorized but less friendly.

For the employee, access to information resources remotely, from a network external to the company confronts the rules of confidentiality and security. Indeed, companies afraid to let data escape which is considered confidential. Therefore, at home, one cannot do, in general, the same activity because of "immaturity" of the ICT available to one: no access or restricted access to one's business applications, in particular for safety reasons (even with access devices type RSA[3] key, authentication tools, etc.). The limits refer to connection times for the data storage tools or document sharing (Sharepoint, for example), and load time for heavy files containing graphics.

Are ICTs Too Immature to Allow Remote Working?

It seems crucial for the teleworker to be able to contact their manager and their team, but also their customers and suppliers. It appears from the interviews that the communication made "remotely" occurs primarily by email and phone. Therefore, it is a basic use of ICTs. Face-to-face is still important for many professionals, particularly in the case of negotiation (Fernandez & Marrauld, 2011).

However, the videophone is raised as essential equipment, provided there is a reliable and professional quality of communication. Limits to the optimal use of the videophone can be related to multiple applications that require the learning of new interfaces and features. Negative points can also be linked to the need to switch between content, the nature of the communication and application.

The multiplicity of telephone terminals (smartphones, individual landlines, phone lines via the IP box, etc.) may also complicate the process of communication. In a situation of nomadism, even if the equipment is available, you must find a system for call forwarding and activate it either remotely or do it manually.

The 3G key allows employees to move more freely and access the Internet connection from any location (with a faster or slower speed). But internationally, the costs of the 3G key connection is high, sometimes raising real problems for employees who do not pay attention to their consumption. The 3G key is a tool for mobility inside France; it still has no economic proposal that reflects the internationalization of the market for employees.

Thus, according to the respondents, the ICTs have limitations for distant data connections: some of them are related to the technologies themselves, other are related to security measures of organizations for access to their information systems.

Access to the information resources of an enterprise from an environment (hardware/network) outside the company involves some specific working configurations regarding privacy rules, security, and tools. These settings will be different depending on the situation of teleworkers, whether they are in a situation of "nomadism" or in an identified local (home or third place).

Computer station security is a major challenge in an environment where the Internet connection can be made from external networks. For now, the safety devices go through a more or less robust identification that is based on a technical infrastructure controllable by the information system. Access to services is completely regulated and controlled. In some cases of high confidentiality, applications can simply be excluded from any remote access. To date, few ICTs offer a feature facilitating mobility situations, with automatic and customizable configuration of the working environment according the location declared by the user.

For some professions, the "business applications" must be accessible in teleworking situation. This is possible only if there is a Web application (on a Website) or if the application can be "virtualized"; this is not current. Moreover, many respondents emphasize interoperability problems of operating systems. The software installed on the professional computer are not yet compatible with MAC and Linux.

The employee sometimes feels too distracted or disturbed by the continuous flow of information that reaches them; they try to disconnect. But it (offline mode) "contradicts" the logic of a system designed to maximize the responsiveness of employees as Thomas says (30 years, distributed systems engineer): *"equipment is not made for that, [...] it seems that everything is done to be connected all the time."* The user could become an "addict," as noted Orlikowski (2007) in her analysis of the uses of BlackBerry. Some technological devices consistently show the reachability of an individual. One of the interviewees

also highlights that some filtering features have disappeared, including on phones. For example, a few years ago, some operators offered services for screening calls. These features were used as a wall between private and professional spheres.

The user, in a situation of physical remoteness of their company, has specific needs (equipment and services). But they cannot take everything and must make choices concerning the devices (in particular among peripherals -printers, etc.). The multiplicity of devices installed in the different places of teleworking require drivers on each computer terminal. But there are two main obstacles to the multiplication of these driver installations: the first is related to the memory capacity and power of the technological tools: the laptop is most often less powerful than a desktop computer, a mobile phone doesn't include the same applications or the same document formats as a computer. The second barrier refers to the policies of IT departments in companies; they often limit the professional equipment used in mobility or those connected to the network of the company.

The enterprise must be sure that the responsibility of the employee will not be in question in case of an incident in the computer system. The teleworking employees need secure equipment, in order to secure the data contained in the equipment. Data hosted locally represents a risk in case of destruction or theft of equipment.

Recommendations

Based on the results of the qualitative study, we suggest some recommandations for the WITE 2.0 platform design:

Concerning the Technical Aspects: The WITE 2.0 platform must be integrated in the IS of the companies. The virtualisation makes remote connection more secure. The solution, which is based on architecture virtualization workstation Citrix offers administrators and users the features of a Thin Client. Centralization of virtualized services enables the information system directors to control their life cycle and manage security access to the resources of the organization regardless of the material used and the workplace of the individual. Indeed, the information is systematically destroyed on the host machine after use; the user's digital profile limits access to what the user needs for their work. The virtual desktop allows the user to find their regular work environment and applications that are made available by the organization. In addition, the solution guarantees the performance of the service operation as, because the component is installed on the host machine, it runs only display tasks, network management and user interface tasks. The access applications from remote and virtual environments are on a server that optimizes the allocation of resources necessary for their proper functioning. Thus, the conditions of use of digital services are not altered despite the diversity of devices used and the workplace. Among the tools needed to work remotely, other than business applications and electronic communication, telephony remains an essential service. We recommend the enrichment of the client with a component using the UDP protocol that allows the exchange of data between computer networks and telephone networks; it allows IP telephony (VoIP), in the manner of a virtualized softphone. Some useful features to call platforms are added to this, namely the ability to record and monitor telephone conversations.

Concerning the Socio-Organizational Aspects: We suggest adding some filters to specify the time of reachability and the time of availability. A lot of workers are often disturbed by their colleagues during their activity; because the colleagues do not check to see if they are busy or not (at the office and, also, at home by ICT). These filters could be used for teleworking and for the in-office working ("*I check if my colleague is available before disturbing them in their office*").

Finally, we suggest labeling the information flows received every day. We propose to label these flows in function of the urgency of the data,

the nature of the data, the work group which is concerned, and the person who sends the data, etc. For example, email boxes could be integrated with social media as a secondary function and people could juggle with different media (chat, email, timelines, etc.) subject to their needs.

CONCLUSION

Several configurations of "remote working" that we observed, contribute to a change in the usual representations of the "teleworker."

We propose here three "stereotypes."

First, the figure of the teleworker, exclusively at home, whose teleoperator is an ideal-typical figure. He uses a desk in a corner of the room or the bedroom, not in a room dedicated solely for homeworking. However, the boundaries between private and professional life are maintained due to strong control of their activity by the ICT. In fact, ICT is, for him, a "control infrastructure." Despite the physical distance, the hierarchy is near: the worked hours are controllable via the use of ICT: for instance, instant messaging allows the verification that the teleoperator is indeed behind their computer. The remote control via ICT is a substitute of direct managerial control.

Second, the figure of the mobile worker who sometimes works at home. The ICTs allows one to contact them at any time even if he is not available. For the executives, ICTs act more as a way of disrupting their work space in confusing the virtual presence status (reachable/available). Unless he defined formally beforehand their moments of when he can be contacted

Third, the figure of the worker in a co-working space or in a telecenter: he has a high degree of autonomy in organizing their work, the worker uses the telecenter to "frame" their activity (immersing themselves in a group is a way to put boundaries between the private and professional spheres), but also to densify their socioprofessional network

IRL (In Real Life). The worker in a co-working space will tend to regulate their working hours, helping them to build boundaries between private and professional spheres.

The precise definition of teleworkers is difficult to establish, as the profiles are varied and the situations diverse (new working configurations including practices of re-sedentarization activity). Embedded in a double paradigm (technological and organizational), teleworkers seem to evolve in unexpected, even paradoxical ways. In order to understand the realities of working remotely, we need to investigate the tools for teleworking in their collective aspect of interaction management, the security of sharing data and the practices of social networking tools. The technical characteristics of these tools are revealed only through the collective dynamics of remote work and vice versa.

REFERENCES

Belton, L., & de Coninck, F. (2006). Des frontières et des liens: Les topologies du privé et du professionnel pour les travailleurs mobiles. *Reseaux*, *24*(140), 67–100.

Blanchard, K. H., & Hersey, P. (1969). *Management of organizational behavior: Utilizing human resources*. Englewood Cliffs, NJ: Prentice Hall.

Boboc, A., Dalheine, L., & Mallard, A. (2007). Travailler, se déplacer et communiquer: Premiers résultats d'enquête. *Reseaux*, *24*(140), 133–158.

Centre d'Analyse Stratégique. (2009, November 25). *Le développement du télétravail dans la société numérique de demain, rapport remis au ministre de l'économie numérique*.

Chen, L., & Nath, R. (2005, Fall). Nomadic culture: Cultural support for working anytime, anywhere. *Information Systems Management*, 56–64. doi:10.1201/1078.10580530/45520.22.4 .20050901/90030.6.

Cocula, F., & Fredy-Planchot, A. (2003). Pratiquer le management à distance. *Gestion*, *2000*(1), 43–63.

Couclelis, H. (2004). Pizza over the internet: E-commerce, the fragmentation of activity, and the tyranny of the region. *Entrepreneurship and Regional Development*, *16*, 41–54. doi:10.1080/0898562042000205027.

Davis, G. B. (2002). Anytime/anyplace computing and the future of knowledge work. *Communications of the ACM*, *45*(12), 67–73. doi:10.1145/585597.585617.

Felstead, A., Jewson, N., & Walters, S. (2003). Managerial control of employees working at home. *British Journal of Industrial Relations*, *41*(2), 241–264. doi:10.1111/1467-8543.00271.

Fernandez, V., Guillot, C., & Marrauld, L. (2011). Travailler, collaborer et se sociabiliser à distance. *Rapport de recherche du projet Wite 2.0*. Retrieved from http://www.telecentres.fr/wp-content/uploads/2011/10/Rapport-etude-qualitative-WITE20-oct-2011.pdf

Fernandez, V., & Marrauld, L. (2012). Usage des téléphones portables et pratiques de la mobilité: L'analyse de journaux de bord de salariés mobiles. *Revue Française de Gestion*, *38*(226), 137–149. doi:10.3166/rfg.226.137-149.

Gardarin, G. (1999). *Intranet & bases de données: Data web, data warehouse, data mining*. Eyrolles.

Jeddi, S., & Karoui Zouaoui, S. (2011). Réflexions sur l'impact du travail mobile sur l'apprentissage individuel. In *Proceedings of the 16th seminar of AIM*. St Denis de la Réunion, France: AIM.

Laffitte, P., & Trégouet, R. (2002). *Les conséquences de l'évolution scientifique et technique dans le secteur des telecommunications: Rapport d'information 159*. Paris, France: Sénat, Office parlementaire d'évaluation des choix scientifiques et technologiques.

Lallement, M. (2003). *Temps, travail et modes de vie*. Paris, France: PUF.

Orlikowski, W. J. (2010). The sociomateriality of organizational life: Considering technology in management research. *Cambridge Journal of Economics, 34*(1), 125–141. doi:10.1093/cje/bep058.

Ray, J.-E. (2001). *Droit du travail à l'épreuve des NTIC*. Deuxième édition, décembre, éditions Liaisons, collection Droit vivant.

Rey, C., & Sitnikoff, F. (2006). Télétravail à domicile et nouveaux rapports au travail. *Revue Interventions économiques, 34*. Retrieved from http://interventionseconomiques.revues.org/697

Rosanvallon, J. (2006). Travail à distance et représentations du collectif de travail. *Revue Interventions économiques, 34*. Retrieved from: http://interventionseconomiques.revues.org/697

Taskin, L. (2010). La déspatialisation, enjeu de gestion. *Revue Française de Gestion, 202*, 53–76.

Thomsin, L. (2002). Télétravail et mobilités. Les Ed.s de l'Université de Liège, Coll. Synopsis.

Urry, J. (2007). *Mobilities*. Cambridge, UK: Polity.

Wang, J., Yang, L., Yu, M., & Wang, S. (2011). Application of server virtualization technology based on Citrix XenServer in the information center of the public security bureau and fire service department. In *Proceedings of the Computer Science and Society (ISCCS), International Symposium*. ISCCS.

ADDITIONAL READING

Lyytinen, K., & Yoo, Y. (2002). Issues and challenges in ubiquitous computing. *Communications of the ACM, 45*(12), 63–65.

Metzger, J.-L., & Cléach, O. (2004). Le télétravail des cadres: Entre suractivité et apprentissages de nouvelles temporalités. *Sociologie du Travail, 46*, 433–450. doi:10.1016/j.soctra.2004.09.001.

Prasard, P. (1993). Symbolic processes in the implementation of the technological change: A symbolic interactionist study of work computerization. *Academy of Management Journal, 36*, 1400–1429. doi:10.2307/256817 PMID:10145944.

Robey, D., Lyytinen, K., Varshney, U., Davis, G., Ackerman, M. S., & Avital, M. et al. (2004). Surfing the next wave: Design and implementation challenges of ubiquitous computing environments. *Communications of the Association for Information Systems, 13*, 697–716.

KEY TERMS AND DEFINITIONS

BYOD: A BYOD policy, or bring-your-own-device policy, is a set of rules governing a corporate IT department's level of support for employee-owned PCs, smartphones and tablets. A BYOD policy can take many different forms. Some organizations cut back on corporate-issued PCs and laptops, instead giving employees a stipend to purchase and maintain technology equipment of their choosing. More commonly, however, organizations will agree to support personal mobile devices—at least to some degree—in addition to corporate-issued equipment. The rules in a BYOD policy often vary depending on a user's role in the organization, his or her specific device, application requirements and other factors.

Function Creep: The function creep is the way of using a technology which not corresponding to the initial function of this tool. The function creep goes against the teleological function because the user finds new ways of using systems and participates to create new structural properties. The user produces function creep when he uses technology on a DIY mode (do-it-yourself), when he tinkers with the technology.

Homeshoring: Homeshoring is one of the latest developments in the field of call centers. It implies a home-based call center which provides all the services of an actual call centre. Now-a-days many companies all across the world prefer to hire home-based call center employees. This provides a career opportunity for stay-at-home parents, people with disabilities or senior citizens who cannot go out to work because of various reasons.

Mobility Turn: Described by Urry (2000) in his book *Sociology beyond Societies: Mobilities for the Twenty First Century*, "mobility turn" is the change in mobility patterns made with the introduction of ICT. In the new paradigm of mobility, the classic markers—distance and speed—are no more characteristic of free mobility and without coercion. In 2008, Kaufmann put forward three new markers that are the range of possibilities, motility and movement. The field of possibilities is all available resources in the environment of the individual who will potentially serve him to move (physically or virtually). Motility is the ability of the individual to know how to use field of possibilities to move. Finally, the movement corresponds to new forms of travel, physical or virtual, operated in geographical areas or cyberspaces connected.

Social Media: A term used to describe a variety of Web-based platforms, applications and technologies that enable people to socially interact with one another online. Some examples of social media sites and applications include Facebook, YouTube, Del.icio.us, Twitter, Digg, blogs and other sites that have content based on user participation and User-Generated Content (UGC).

Teleworking: The concept of "teleworking" can be considered in its most classic form (homeworking), but also in the most diverse realities that it could be today: either, all forms of "remote working," i.e., forms of organization and/or performing work outside the classical unity of time and place. Four kinds of teleworkers can be distinguished: homeworkers, mobile workers, the telecenter worker, and the virtual team worker. A telecenter is a work location usually in a different place than the organization's main office that provides convenient occasional access for telecommuting to work equipment that they don't have at home or on the road. A virtual team (also known as a geographically dispersed team or distributed team) is a group of individuals who work across time, space and organizational boundaries with links strengthened by ICTs. Thus, the definition of teleworking that we have selected is based on: 1) the fixed place of work or alternating between several workplaces, provided they are removed from the hierarchy and/or colleagues; 2) the relationship to the employer and colleagues, remotely and by electronic links, thus justifying the name teleworking.

Virtual Workstation: A virtual workstation uses both virtualization hardware and software technologies that, when combined, provides end users with an uncompromised workstation experience. It gives engineers and IT user's concurrent access to key workstation hardware functions previously not available with traditional virtualization technologies. You specially need to use a virtual workstation if you have a need to run applications in different OSes, diverse OS levels or types, or you need to visualize in different OSes.

ENDNOTES

1. The supervisor's role is to listen to the tele-operator agent, to help get the most suitable speech (a good argument, appropriate tone of voice, etc.) and to motivate the team.

2. Information System Direction.

3. A key RSA (Rivest-Shamir-Adleman) is an encryption algorithm of securing data exchanges with the use of two key figures. The principle is based on the use of two keys, one public, or the digital signature, the other private, the first to encode the message, the other to decode.

APPENDIX

TO GO FURTHER

This document constitutes the experimental protocol of the first prototype of the WITE 2.0 platform (now used in updated versions in companies). This protocol informs the reader about the particular nature of the elements of the platform that have been observed and evaluated before the end of the project.

WITE 2.0 – Framing elements of the experimental protocol. The implementation of the platform in an experiment is the last phase (SP4) of WITE 2.0 project. This document consists of a framing elements proposed by Telecom ParisTech and completed in consultation with members of the steering committee.

The purpose of the experiment is mainly to further one or more assumptions from the qualitative and quantitative phase analyses and is also to complete them from the field of research (experimentation).

ISSUES AND STAKEHOLDERS OF THE EXPERIMENTATION

1. Issues

This phase is to test the functionality of the platform in order to analyze the developments and services offered by the WITE 2.0 prototype. This test phase follows the qualitative (47 semi-structured interviews) and quantitative previously made studies (SP1). Consideration of these elements of analysis has led to do a number of recommendations on identified needs.

As part of the experiment, the usual features of the platform will be faced with in vivo "experiments" of different users involved in this process of experimentation.

An experiment report will be produced on the basis of the analysis of these "experiments" for the three levels of innovation brought the project:

- Technical Innovation.
- Service Innovation.
- Usage Innovation.

2. Stakeholders

Project governance experimentation should be consistent with the issues of different stakeholders thereof.

Researchers-Observers

The collection and analysis of data from the experiment will be based on user-experimenters placed in a position to use the platform. What (s) method (s) of observation? Collectively define a protocol

For example, a process ethnomethodology "equipped" to extract elements of analysis, an ex-ante and maintenance of the workplace experimenters users...

The involvement and training of players to the platform users is an important issue of the experiment. *What (s) method (s) of involvement/training?*

The introduction of technological tool requires a partner to provide the necessary use of the platform applications, such as OCS licenses. The goal is to make and keep the information in system operating conditions.

The experiment will take place in rooms equipped with Internet connection and furnished or not the closest situations and working conditions of actors users. In the first case, the goal is to reproduce the work environments of everyone taking into account elements that characterize it. For example, analyze and reproduce a minimum the type of equipment, network configuration workspace and organization of work in the office and/or in situations of "teleworking. However, the reproduction of the working conditions are not always feasible, it will consider these elements in the analysis. (For example, the profile of an employee in office isolated on a desktop PC business will hardly be integrated in the context of an experiment in open space with a BYOC system)

A relay of information to local economic actors should be established to facilitate the recruitment of players users.

The other project partners will have to decide on further actions relating to governance of the experiment.

Actors-Users Testing

- **Users:** They must be voluntary and in accordance with the conditions of the experiment.
- **Employers and Technical Services (ISD, HR):** The IT governance of the company is often a hindrance to develop activities remotely. In addition, the implementation of a new tool should be discussed with the various technical services of the employer.
- **Managers:** Steeped in particular managerial culture, managers are among the keystones of the development of teleworking. In addition, they must approve the recruitment of users, experimenters.

The Selection Process

It will take place at three levels:

1. **Technique:** It concerns the compatibility of IS employers. Company with OCS or no Web client.
2. **Managerial:** In accordance with the managerial policy of the company
3. **Professional:** On the remote activities achieved through ICT occupations.

ANALYSIS OF CONTEXT

The point is to describe the physical, technological, and organizational existing experimentation. The elements of the initial context (operational variables) must be known to observe the effects of the introduction of one or more interfering variables. We are talking here as the introduction of the WITE2.0 platform that changes induced by this teleworking. In this context the study serves as a basis of analysis the socio-technical change wrought by the introduction and use of the platform.

Variables to Take into Account

1. Work environments
   a. Locals of workers
   b. The layout of the work area (open space, isolated office, etc.)
2. The technological conditions (equipment)
   a. The hardware (computer, mobile phone, tablet, printer, copier, scanner, USB key, etc.)
   b. Generic applications used or simply available (Office, etc.)
   c. Specific business applications (CMS, ERP, etc.)
3. The organizational conditions (contexts)
   a. The face-management (How are employees supervised?)
   b. Communication and transmission of information (how employees communicate among themselves, with customers, suppliers, and their hierarchy?)
   c. Collaboration (By what means and what uses employees work with each other? Modes and forms of remote collaboration are now illustrated by a number of collaborative tools. However, their effectiveness is often challenged and observation is made largely as remote collaboration is more akin to forms of coordination that forms of co-design. Given these recent researches, which opportunities for collaborative work can then provide the platform?).

THE PROTOCOL OF THE EXPERIMENT

1. Proposal Planning

Phase 1: The Exploratory Phase

Beginning January 2012 -> End February 2012

The pilot team test internally the various features of the WITE2.0 platform of professional practices (related to the nature of its activities and its working practices "remote") and customary uses of ICT that equip their activities. The diversity of user profiles in the group will permit, at first, to scan a large number of situations of use. The partners are from different sectors of activity, level of mastery (or expertise) technological tools is varied. There is also a generational diversity. Finally, they are already working to physical distance from each other (Paris, Toulouse, etc.).

Empirical evidence should emerge following the grip of the platform. Advanced remarks will help advance the discussion of storylines evolution of features and usability proposed by WITE 2.0 platform.

In parallel with this phase of internal testing, it will finalize the framing of testing ground. Its implementation requires a prior provision of material resources (management of premises, equipment, furniture, etc.). And high-speed network connection type. The local has a capacity of 6 workstations.

Finally, the third part of this exploratory phase is the ethnographic observation of actors users in their normal work environment. The observer will refer to practices and working conditions of a typical user-experimenters selected for Phase 2 of the Rueil-Malmaison day.

Phase 2: Field Testing

Mid-February 2012 -> End April 2012

The testing phase will target different figures emerging from teleworkers elements of the qualitative survey if they are previously used, including:

- The figure of techic workcr.
- The teleworker home.
- The employee call center.
- The employee in a situation of high mobility.

Phase 3: Analysis

May 2012 - July 2012.

Comparison and analysis of the results between the different partners, both technically and on the part of the study uses.

2. Usage Scenarios

A usage scenario is described in the form of exchange events between the actor and the system.
Scenarios are classified as:

- A nominal scenario (the one place where there is no error, the one that is mainly achieved in 90% of cases).
- Alternative scenarios are variants of the nominal scenario.
- The emergency scenarios that describe the case of errors.

The usage scenario is a sequence of sequences of activities to interact with the information system for the purpose of an action.

We conduct suggestions usage scenarios based on the experiences recounted in the semi-structured interviews and the results of the quantitative survey.

Theme of the Site

What sequence of activities actor-user sets it up to go to Rueil?

Consult its mobile transport applications or other applications, choose a kind of transport, prepare an itinerary, program steps, equip in a certain way, etc.

Theme of Private/Pro Articulation

How to accept the use of a personal computer in job? What are the mechanisms of partitioning of personal and professional activity? What sequence of activities actor-user sets it up to master the joint between private and professional life? Information filtering based on source, hide icons, hide alerts, organize a schedule based on private and pro spheres (for example, I look at my personal mail at a certain time), archive folders based on the nature of the activity, etc.

Theme of Isolation and Socialization

What sequence of activities actor-user puts it up to master his work environment and manage its exposure (people, information, the interference)?

Physical or acoustic isolation in face-to-face (e.g., put the headphones to indicate its non-availability) appear on unavailable mode on chats or social networks, decrease or increase the RSS, alerts, inform fixed schedules, etc.

What sequence of activities actor-user puts it in place to communicate, collaborate, to socialize, etc.?

Use of social networks, professional networks, networks provided by the employer, communication and social media (email/video/confcall/fixed and mobile), sharing elements of privacy (vacation photos ...), organize physical meetings, etc.

Theme of Management and Control

What sequence of activities actor-user puts it in place to account for its work activity to his superiors?

Make reports of activities by various means of communication, meetings firsthand, virtual meetings, making rapid advancements points, get contacted (permanently, almost constantly, for hours), become visible (send emails, etc.), etc.

What sequence of activities the manager put it in place to monitor the activity of the remote employee?

Report request, control its presence on the working platform, wiretapping of his pro communications, frequent interactions by email/by other means of communication, use of a collaborative work platform, etc.

Theme of Skills

What sequence of activities actor-user puts it in place to develop their skills to work "remotely"? What sequence of activities actor-user puts it in place to form the ICT man working "remote"?

Function creep, DIY, asking for help to a friend, a colleague, a family member, use online training or organizations (standard ICC), using social networks, recovering from a training document on paper/ digital format of his company, to training supported by the company, etc.

Chapter 5

Explaining Mobile Services Adoption between China and Developed Countries from a Cultural Perspective

Shang Gao
Zhongnan University of Economics and Law, China

ABSTRACT

Little research has been done to explore the adoption of mobile information services from a cultural perspective. This research is designed to study mobile information services adoption from a cultural perspective. Based on the two cultural dimensions (individualism/collectivism, uncertainty avoidance), two research hypotheses are presented. To examine these hypotheses, an exploratory study is carried out with a mobile information service called Mobile Tourist Service Recommender (MTSR) system with both respondents from developed countries and China. According to the results, one research hypothesis is supported, while the other research hypothesis (H1) is not supported in this exploratory study. The findings indicate that the cultural dimensions play important roles in how mobile information services are used and adopted in two different cultural settings: culture in developed countries and the Chinese culture. The results also highlight the relevance of the cultural dimensions (individualism/collectivism, uncertainty avoidance) as the factors affecting the adoption of mobile information services.

INTRODUCTION

The rapid growth of mobile communication and usage of mobile devices in recent years has provided a great opportunity for creating a variety of mobile services. Despite this growth, there is a big difference in terms of the mobile service penetration rate among various countries. For example, although the mobile communication infrastructure is quite advanced in Europe, the European mobile commerce market is frequently presented as less advanced compared to markets in east-Asia, such as South Korea and Japan (Constantiou, Papazafeiropoulou, & Vendelø, 2009; Choi, Lee, & Kim, 2006). This highlights the need for research for cultural influence on mobile services adoption.

The advanced mobile devices enable users to try out new mobile services, but the adoption of mobile services often do not progress as expected (Carlsson, Carlsson, Hyvonen, Puhakainen, &

DOI: 10.4018/978-1-4666-4566-0.ch005

Walden, 2006). On one hand, unlike some old technology-based products (e.g., landline phones), some users are not aware of some of the mobile services which mobile devices are able to offer. On the other hand, some users are afraid to use some mobile services because of the lack of technological knowledge. Therefore, it is necessary to consider non-technical factors which might impact mobile services diffusion. The cultural perspective is one of the important concepts in the information systems research (e.g., Straub, 1994). In this study, we would like to study the adoption of mobile information services from the cultural perspective.

As cultural characteristics have a fundamental effect on how users perceive mobile services, the appropriateness of a mobile service for one culture may not be appropriate for others. Despite the importance of these cultural characteristics, little research has been performed on the effect of cultural issues on mobile services diffusion. Therefore, the objective of this research work is to investigate how the different cultural dimensions influence users' adoption of mobile services. In order to address this, we carry out an experiment to examine the adoption of some advanced mobile services with people from both China and developed countries from a cultural perspective.

The remainder of this chapter is organized as follows. In section 2, we review relevant literature on culture and mobile services adoption. The research hypotheses are presented in section 3. In section 4, we describe the mobile commerce in developed countries and China. Section 5 explores the different cultural dimensions on mobile information services adoption by an exploratory study with a mobile information service called MTSR. This is followed by a discussion of the findings and limitations of the study in section 6. Section 7 concludes this research work and points out some directions for future research.

LITERATURE REVIEW

This section presents some literature relevant to this research.

Cultural Dimensions

Culture has been defined in a number of ways because of its multi-dimensional characteristics. In (Hall, 1977), Hall distinguished cultures along two dimensions: contextuality and time perception.

Hofstede defined culture as mental programming (Hofstede, 1980), which refers to patterns of thinking, feeling, and potential acting, which were learned throughout people's lifetimes. Hofstede's study with a survey of IBM employees in 40 different countries found that the values of employees differed more based on their nationality, age, and education than their membership in organizations (Hofstede, 1980). From the study (Hofstede, 1980), four dimensions have been identified to distinguish among different cultures: uncertainty avoidance, power distance, individualism-collectivism, and masculinity-femininity. In (Hofstede & Bond, 1988), Hofstede and Bond subsequently added the fifth dimension: long-term versus short-term orientation.

In (Schwartz, Divitini, & Brasethvik, 2000), Schwartz, surveyed 56 value preferences in 25 countries and found 10 motivationally distinct value types: power, achievement, tradition, hedonism, self-direction, universalism, security, stimulation, benevolence, and conformity types. In (Schwartz & Sagiv, 1995), Schwartz identified two fundamental dimensions of cultural variables: openness to change (includes self-direction and stimulation value types) versus conservation (includes security, conformity, and traditional value types), and self-enhancement (includes hedonism, power, and achievement value types) versus self-transcendence (includes universalism and benevolence value types). Moreover, Bond's Chinese Culture Connection (CCC) study revealed four factors derived from the Chinese culture: integration, Confucian work dynamism, human-heartedness, and moral discipline (Bond, 1988).

Trompenaars and Hampden-Turner classified national culture into three dimensions: how people relate to each other, people's attitudes toward time, and people's attitudes toward their environment (Thompenaars & Hampden-Turner, 1998). He defined five dimensions of how people relate to each other: universalism-particularism (obligation to an individual versus obligation to the society), achievement-ascription (status determined by achievements or ascriptions), individualism-collectivism (degree of orientation to the self), affectivity-neutrality (express/show or control/hide feelings), and specificity-diffuseness (degree of engaging others in specific areas or in multiple areas). Compared to Hofstede's research, the strength of Trompenaars's research is that it addresses detailed insights of relationships among people.

An examination of the current literature reveals that few studies have directly addressed the adoption of mobile services from the cultural perspective. An exploratory investigation is necessary to study and understand cultural impact on the adoption of advanced mobile services. We believe this research will contribute to the current mobile services diffusion literature. An understanding of the impact of culture on mobile service adoption will help in designing better mobile services in the business market.

In Table 1, we summarize the most commonly cited cultural dimensions.

Technology Adoption

An important and long-standing research question in information systems research is how to accurately explain user adoption of information systems (DeLone & McLean, 1992). Several models have been developed to test the users' attitude and intention to adopt new technologies or information systems. These models include the

Table 1. Cultural dimensions

Cultural Dimensions	Description	Citations
Uncertainty Avoidance	The extent to which members of a culture feel threatened by uncertain or unknown situations.	(Hofstede, 1980)
Power Distance	The extent to which members of a culture expect and accept that power is distributed unequally.	(Hofstede, 1980)
Individualism versus collectivism	Degree to which people in a culture to act as individuals rather than as members of groups.	(Hofstede, 1980)
Masculinity versus femininity	Masculinity describes cultures in which social gender roles are distinct, whereas femininity describes cultures in which social genders roles overlap.	(Hofstede, 1980)
Long-term versus Short-term orientation	Short-term orientation culture focuses on the present moment, long-term orientation culture are orientated toward future rewards.	(Hofstede & Bond, 1988)
Openness to change versus conversation	The extent to which people preserve the status quo and the certainty it provides to relationships with close others, institutions and traditions, versus the extent to which people are inclined to follow their own intellectual and emotional interests in unpredictable and uncertain directions.	(Schwartz & Sagiv, 1995)
Self-enhancement versus Self-transcendence	People's tendency to transcend selfish concerns and promote the welfare of others, close and distant, and of nature, versus their tendency to enhance their personal interests.	(Schwartz & Sagiv, 1995)
Contextuality	In a high-context culture, one prefers implicit messages and indirect communications. Low-context cultures are characterized by explicit messages and direct communications.	(Hall, 1977)
Time Perception	People in monochromic cultures focus on and perform one task at a time. People in polychromic cultures can act in a parallel model.	(Hall, 1977)

Technology Acceptance Model (TAM) (Davis, 1989), Theory of Planned Behavior (TPB) (Ajzen, 1991), Innovation Diffusion Theory (IDT) (Rogers, 1995), Unified Theory of Acceptance and Use of Technology (UTAUT) (Venkatesh, Morris, Davis, & Davis, 2003).

We give an overview of the existing technology acceptance models and theories in this section.

Theory of Reasoned Action (TRA)

Technology diffusion research stems from the information systems adoption science. The earliest model attempting to explain the adoption of technologies is the Theory of Reasoned Action (Fishbein & Ajzen, 1975). The Theory of Reasoned Action (Fishbein & Ajzen, 1975) is derived from the field of social psychology and is based on the individual's attitude towards the action itself and subjective norm of the action. This theory posits that a person's volitional behavior is a function of an individual's attitude towards the behavior and subjective norms surrounding the performance of the behavior.

Technology Acceptance Model (TAM)

A number of models have been developed to test consumers' attitude and intention to adopt new technologies in the realm of information systems. Among the different models that have been proposed are the Technology Acceptance Model (TAM) (Davis, 1989; Davis, Bagozzi, & Warshaw, 1989), which is an extension of the Theory of Reasoned Action (TRA) (Fishbein & Ajzen, 1975) and appears to be one of the most widely accepted models. TAM constitutes a solid framework to examine issues that may affect user acceptance of new technologies. TAM has been tested in some domains of E-business and proved to be quite reliable to predict user acceptance of some new information technologies, such as World Wide Web (Lederer, Maupin, Sena, & Zhuang, 2000), online shopping (Gefen, 2003), etc.

TAM (see Figure 1) suggests two primary factors: Perceived Usefulness (PU) and Perceived Ease of Use (PEOU), to be of particular importance to determine user intention to use a new technology or information systems. PU (Davis, 1989) is defined as the degree to which a person believes that using a particular system would enhance his or her performance. On the other hand, PEOU (Davis, 1989) is defined as the extent to which a person believes that using a particular system would be free from effort.

TAM has been designed to study user acceptance of new information technologies and improve understanding of user adoption behavior. The model provides a means to measure the impact of external variables on users' attitudes and intentions to use new technologies. The instruments used in connection with TAM are surveys, which contain measurement items in terms of questions to measure each construct of TAM.

Using TAM as the starting point, Venkatesh and Davis (Venkatesh & Davis, 2000) have extended it to TAM2 to test user acceptance of information technology in four longitudinal field studies. The extended model, TAM2, incorporates additional theoretical constructs spanning social influence processes (subjective norm, voluntariness, and image) and cognitive instrumental processes (job relevance, output quality, result demonstrability, and perceived ease of use). The results indicated that both social influence processes and cognitive instrument processes significantly influenced user acceptance (Venkatesh & Davis, 2000).

Figure 1. Technology acceptance model (Davis, 1989)

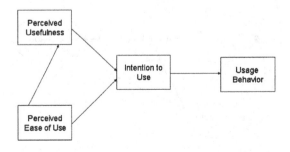

Theory of Planned Behavior (TPB)

Ajzen proposed the Theory of Planned Behavior (TPB) (Ajzen, 1991) which helps to understand how we can change the behavior of people. The TPB (see Figure 2) is a theory, which predicts deliberate behavior, because behavior can be deliberate and planned. According to TPB, human action is guided by three kinds of consideration: behavioral beliefs, normative beliefs and control beliefs. An individual's behavior can be explained by his or her behavioral intention, which is jointly influenced by attitude, subjective norms and perceived behavior control. Attitude refers to an individual's positive or negative evaluation of the performance effect of a particular behavior. Subjective norms refer to an individual's perceptions of other peoples' opinions on whether or not he or she should perform a particular behavior, while perceived behavioral control refers to an individual's perception of the presence or absence of the requisite resources or opportunities necessary for performing a behavior (Ajzen & Madden, 1986).

Innovation Diffusion Theory (IDT)

Innovation Diffusion Theory (IDT) is another well-known theory proposed by Rogers (Rogers, 1995). In recent decades, IDT has been widely used in IT and IS research (Karahanna, Straub,

Figure 2. Theory of planned behavior (Ajzen, 1991)

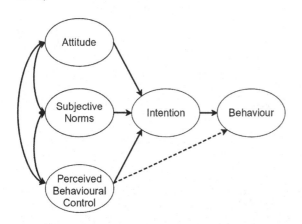

& Chervany, 1999). IDT includes five significant innovation characteristics: relative advantage, compatibility, complexity, trial ability, and observables. These characteristics are used to explain the user adoption and decision making process. They are also used to predict the implementation of new technological innovations and clarify how these variables interact with one another. The central concept of innovation diffusion is: the process in which an innovation is communicated through certain channels, over time, among the members of a social system.

The theory explains the process of the innovation decision process, the determinants of the rate of adoption, and various categories of adopters. The theory aims at predicting the likelihood and the rate of an innovation being adopted by different adopter categories.

Rogers defined the constructs of IDT as follows (Rogers, 1995):

- **Relative Advantage:** The degree to which the innovation is perceived as being better than the practice it supersedes
- **Compatibility:** Defined as the degree to which an innovation is perceived as consistent with the existing values, past experiences, and needs of potential adopters
- **Complexity:** The degree to which an innovation is perceived as relatively difficult to understand and use
- **Trial ability:** The degree to which an innovation may be experimented with before making the adoption or rejection decision
- **Observable:** The degree to which the results of an innovation are visible to others

Rogers also defined five adopter categories: innovators, early adopters, early majority, late majority and laggards (Rogers, 1995).

- Innovators are eager to try new ideas, to the point where their venturesomeness almost becomes an obsession. Innovators' interest in new ideas leads them out of a local circle of peers and into social relationships more cosmopolite than normal.

- Early adopters tend to be integrated into the local social system more than innovators. The early adopters are considered to be localites, versus the cosmopolite innovators.

- Members of the early majority category will adopt new ideas just before the average member of a social system. They interact frequently with peers, but are not often found holding leadership positions.

- The late majority are a skeptical group, adopting new ideas just after the average member of a social system. Their adoption may be borne out of economic necessity and in response to increasing social pressure.

- Laggards are traditionalists and the last to adopt an innovation. Possessing almost no opinion leadership, laggards are localite to the point of being isolates compared to the other adopter categories.

Furthermore, it is interesting to note that most research on technology diffusion focuses on the usage of new technologies of early users (e.g., innovators and early adopters). When studying new technology usage, data are often collected from the specific group of users who actually use the technologies. The usage ratio might be high since the user base is quite limited and most of the users are interested in using the new technology. However, the usage ratio might be decreasing as the user base expands to other groups of users.

Unified Theory of Acceptance and Use of Technology (UTAUT)

The aim of UTAUT (Venkatesh, et al., 2003) is to explain user intentions to use an IS and subsequent usage behavior. As illustrated in Figure 3, this unified theory holds four key constructs (performance expectancy, effort expectancy, social

influence, and facilitating conditions) which are direct determinants of usage intention and behavior. Gender, age, experience, and voluntariness of use are posited to mediate the impact of the four key constructs on usage intention and behavior. The theory was developed through a review and consolidation of the constructs of eight models that earlier research had employed to explain IS usage behavior (Theory of Reasoned Action, Technology Acceptance Model, Motivational Model, Theory of Planned Behavior, a combined Theory of Planned Behavior/Technology Acceptance Model, Model of PC Utilization, Innovation Diffusion Theory, and Social Cognitive Theory). Subsequent validation of UTAUT in a longitudinal study found it to account for 70% of the variance in usage intention (Venkatesh, et al., 2003).

Among the different models that have been proposed, TAM, which is an extension of the Theory of Reasoned Action (TRA) (Fishbein & Ajzen, 1975), appears to be the most widely adopted model. TAM focuses on the Perceived Usefulness (PU) and perceived Ease Of Use (EOU) of a system and has been tested in some domains of E-business and proved to be quite reliable to predict user acceptance of some new information technologies, such as intranet (Horton, Buck, Waterson, & Clegg, 2001), World Wide Web (Lederer, et al., 2000), electronic commerce (Pavlou, 2003), and online shopping (Gefen, 2003).

Figure 3. Unified theory of acceptance and use of technology (Venkatesh, et al., 2003)

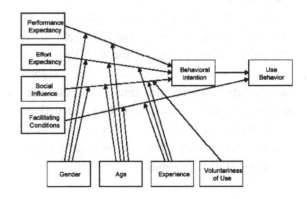

In contrast to TPB and IDT, TAM has substantial theoretical and empirical support, and it is well known for its parsimony. TAM has proven to be a parsimonious model with high explanatory power of the variance in users' behavioral intention related to IT adoption and usage across a wide variety of contexts (Taylor & Todd, 1995). TAM explains and predicts user intention and usage using two main constructs, perceived usefulness and perceived ease of use. These two factors are easy to understand and to test in practice. Hong et al. (Hong, Thong, & Tam, 2006) argue that the flexibility of TAM makes it suitable for various diverse technologies. TAM can be conceived as a fundamental model to study the adoption of mobile services.

However, TAM's limitations relative to extensibility and explanation power have been noted (Benbasat & Barki, 2007). Many researchers have suggested that TAM needs to be extended with additional variables to provide a stronger model (Legris, Ingham, & Collerette, 2003). Some argued that the constructs of TAM do not provide sufficient implications to practitioners (Benbasat & Zmud, 1999). Further, others mentioned that TAM is too generic to provide a realistic understanding with regard to the adoption of advanced mobile services and technologies (Bouwman & van de Wijngaert, 2009). Therefore, PU and EOU may not fully explain people's intention to adopt mobile services. We believe that TAM has limitations when investigating user adoption of mobile services, which is also confirmed by prior research (Wu & Wang, 2005).

Although UTAUT includes more constructs into the model, it has its own limitation. In (Bagozzi, 2007), Bagozzi criticize UTAUT for its lack of parsimony. Since UTAUT unifies more factors and consolidates the functions of the technology acceptance model with the constructs of other prominent models in IS adoption research, it increases the complexity and it is more complicated to test its applicability.

As the context in which consumers use mobile services may be more influential than the mobile services, PU and PEOU may not be adequate to cover all the factors which can explain users' adoption of mobile services. Therefore, we believe it might be helpful to integrate some factors with TAM to study the adoption of mobile services, which can in turn deepen our understanding of factors that contribute to the diffusion of mobile services. This research is based on TAM. Three additional factors, Trust, Context, Personal Initiative and Characteristics, are added to TAM to examine students' perception of mobile information services at a Norwegian university.

Mobile Services Adoption

Without certain technologies mobile services are impossible. Mobile networks need to deal with large amounts of traffic at high speed. Availability of technologies is vital to the success of mobile commerce. Over the last couple of years, wireless and mobile networks have experienced exponential growth in terms of capabilities of mobile devices, standards and network implementation, and user acceptance (Varshney & Vetter, 2000). In (Siau, Lim, & Shen, 2001), Siau et al. looked at several mobile commerce technology issues from both the device and infrastructure perspectives. The major technologies that enable connections between mobile devices and Internet are: a) Wireless Application Protocol (WAP), b) Bluetooth, c) Third-Generation (3G) network, d) Mobile WiMAX, e) Wi-Fi, f) LTE.

Over the past 10 years, mobile devices have changed the way that we work and live. Many people consider mobile devices as extensions and attachments of themselves. As technology advances, mobile devices can be used to do things and fulfill needs in a more efficient and effective manner.

Today, mobile devices are equipped with advanced technologies with the potential to be more powerful. Mobile devices are becoming the place where new technologies meet to create useful services for various users. The major characteristics of mobile devices are as follows: a communicative device, which can enable communications among users; a connective device which enable users to connect to other sources of data regardless of time and location; and a transactional device which can be used for transactions and payments.

Along with the development and utilization of wireless applications, mobile work is more and more common in the business world. Mobile work can be described as a mobile worker accomplishing mobile tasks within various location and time frames by using mobile technologics, such as mobile devices, mobile communication infrastructure and application (Zheng & Yuan, 2007). Main job categories of mobile workers include field work, sales, executives/managers, transportation/delivery, home care, emergency service workers and mobile professional (Yuan, Archer, Connelly, & Zheng, 2010). Home care is an example of typical mobile work. The task of home care work is usually started by getting assignments from the central administration office. Then, the home care work is carried out in the homes of the patients. This work is considered as highly mobile since workers need to move between patients' homes by various means of transportation (e.g., car, bus, and bike).

Compared to the rapid development of mobile technology, the research on mobile services adoption, particularly on newly developed advanced mobile information services, is still in the infancy stage. Widely accepted mobile services are still limited. According to Hosbond et al. review on the literature on mobile system development (Hosbond & Nielsen, 2005), the previous research tends to have a strong focus on the technology perspective, which focuses on how the related technologies contribute to the development of mobile systems. There are not too many studies focusing on mobile services adoption.

There are a number of issues that need to be addressed before there can be widespread diffusion of mobile services. It is believed that increased user comfort and satisfaction and more stable responses provided by high-speed network connection would encourage more advanced mobile services usage on mobile devices.

Some studies based on TAM and the other theories presented above have explored factors affecting consumer adoption of mobile services. Some of these studies are summarized in Table 1. For instance, Lu et al. (Lu, Yu, Liu, & E., 2003) studied the acceptance of Wireless Internet via Mobile Technology (WIMT) in China and indicated that the acceptance of WIMT is related to perceived usefulness, ease of use, social influence, trust, and facilitating conditions. Luarn et al. (Luarn & Lin, 2005) extended the applicability of TAM to the context of mobile banking, by adding perceived credibility, perceived self-efficacy and perceived financial cost to the model. Their findings strongly support the extended TAM in predicting users' intentions to adopt mobile banking. Yang (2005) extended TAM to study factors affecting Singaporeans' attitudes toward mobile commerce. Evidence to support the extended TAM was found in this study. By expanding TAM and IDT, Chen (2008) proposed a research model that examined the factors which determine consumer acceptance of mobile payment. Significant support for the model was found in the data collected from a survey of 299 potential mobile payment users. By expanding TAM, Gao et al. (Gao, Moe, & Krogstie, 2010) proposed the mobile services acceptance model that examined the factors which determine consumer acceptance of mobile services. Significant support for the model was found in the data collected from a survey of potential mobile information service users.

The literature on mobile services adoption is summarized in Table 2.

Table 2. Literature review on mobile services adoption

Literature	Research Purpose	Theory Used	Findings
Chen 2008 (Chen, 2008)	Explore the issues of consumer acceptance of m-payment	TAM and IDT	The findings show that consumer acceptance of m-payment were determined by four factors: Perceived Usefulness (PU), Perceived Ease of Use (PEOU), Perceived Risk (PR) and Compatibility.
(Lu, et al., 2003)	Develop the technology acceptance model for Wireless Internet via Mobile Devices (WIMD)	TAM and some additional factors, such as technology complexity, social influences, trust, etc	A framework for explaining factors that influence individual acceptance of WIMD
(Luarn & Lin, 2005)	Explore the factors determining users' acceptance of mobile banking	Extend TAM with three additional factors: Perceived Credibility, perceived self-efficacy, and perceived financial cost	The findings strongly support the appropriateness of using this extended TAM to understand the intentions of people towards the use of mobile banking services.
(Hong & Tam, 2006)	Study individual adoption of mobile data services that are used beyond conventional work settings	General technology perceptions, technology-specific perceptions, user psychographics, social influence, and demographics	The findings show that the determinants of the adoption of mobile data service are not only different from those in the work place, but are also dependent on the nature of the target technology and its usage context.
(Nysveen, Pedersen, & Thorbjørnsen, 2005)	Explore consumers' intention to use mobile services	Motivational influences, Attitudinal influences, Normative pressure, and Perceived control	The empirical results show strong support for the effects of motivational influences, attitudinal influences, normative pressure, and perceived control on consumers' intentions to use mobile services
(Kuo & Yen, 2009)	Explore consumer's perception of 3G mobile value-added services, and their behavioral intention to use these services.	TAM, Personal Innovativeness, Perceived Cost	Consumer usage rate of current 3G value-added services remains low. Consumers with higher personal innovativeness perceive a higher ease of use of value-added services.
(Mao, Srite, Thatcher, & Yaprak, 2005)	Explore key factors that influence the usefulness, ease of use, and intentions to use mobile services, such as Email, payment	TAM, Price, Accessibility, Efficacy, and Personal Innovativeness	The findings provide support for the technology acceptance model across both groups and for the importance of variables such as efficacy and personal innovativeness.
(Yang, 2005)	Explore factors affecting the adoption of mobile commerce in Singapore	TAM, Past adoption behavior, Demographic variables	The findings show that TAM was capable of providing an adequate explanation of consumer adoption decision-making process to use the M-commerce.
(Chang & Pan, 2011)	Explore factors affecting the adoption of multimedia messaging service (MMS)	TAM	The findings show that relative advantage and ease of use are important factors significantly influencing mobile users' adoption of MMS.

Culture and Mobile Services Adoption

Although it has been recognized that cultural dimensions play important roles in mobile services diffusion, not too much research work had been done to explore the influence of cultural characteristics on mobile services adoption. We

exemplify some studies here. In (Harris, Rettie, & Kwan, 2005), Harris et al. compared mobile commerce usage in the UK and Hong Kong. They found significant differences between the UK and Hong Kong in attitudes to mobile commerce services. They attributed these differences to the levels of collectivism and power distance in the cultures and to structural differences between the two markets. In (Marcus & Gould, 2000), Marcus and Gould found that cultural elements are embedded in user interfaces as a set of contextual and social cues that enable effective use by applying the cultural dimensions proposed by Hofstede (1980) to Web site design. In (Lee, Choi, Kim, & Hong, 2007), Lee et al. constructed and verified a research model, based on interaction theory and the cultural lens model, that focuses on the relationship between users' cultural profiles and post-adoption beliefs in the context of the mobile Internet.

An examination of the current literature reveals that few studies have addressed the effect of cultural characteristics on the adoption of mobile information services. An exploratory study to investigate cultural impact on mobile information services diffusion is necessary. We believe that this research will contribute to current mobile services adoption literature, as well as provide some insights for service providers within the mobile information services community. Awareness of cultural differences will also help marketing personnel promote their mobile information services in various regions all over the world.

RESEARCH HYPOTHESES

This research addresses a gap in the literature about mobile services adoption, using cultural dimensions as a primary explanatory vehicle. To our knowledge, most previous studies used TAM based research model to explore mobile services adoption. In this research, we try to understand users' attitude to adopt mobile information services from a cultural perspectives. Two of cultural dimensions proposed by Hofstede were selected to explore the adoption of mobile services. Based on our literature review on the cultural dimensions, we have developed the following two research hypotheses.

Individualism vs. Collectivism

People in high individualism cultures are self-centered, emphasize individual objectives, and attach a great importance to be treated as individuals (Furrer, Liu, & Sudharshan, 2000; Hofstede, 1980). The cultural characteristics in individualistic societies support individual achievement and self-serving behavior. Prior studies have found that this cultural characteristic has a significant impact on the usage of information systems. For example, Lee et al. (Lee, Kim, Choi, & Hong, 2010) found that mobile users in South Korea exhibit a high level of individualism, whereas mobile users in Greece exhibit a lower level of individualism.

It is believed that individualism versus collectivism is one cultural dimension that affects the adoption of mobile services. In an individualist society, people tend to use online media as a primary platform to exchange information. In a collectivist society, people often get together to exchange information or collect information in an official or formal way (e.g., physical meetings). In (Doney, Cannon, & Mullen, 1998), Doney et al. argued that people in individualism cultures attempt to maximize the gains from any opportunity that presents itself. Thus, we believe that individualists are more likely than collectivists to adopt mobile information services. Therefore, we hypothesize the following:

H1: People from high individualism cultures will be more likely to adopt mobile information services than people from low individualism cultures.

Uncertainty Avoidance

In (Straub, 1994), Straub identified uncertainty avoidance as having the most direct bearing on preference for and use of communication media. For countries in high uncertainty avoidance cultures, people are uncomfortable with uncertainty and show a low tolerance for risk. They want to avoid ambiguous situations by believing in truths and having formal rules and guidance. People in high uncertainty avoidance cultures are more likely to communication methods that were socially present (e.g., face to face communication). In a contrast, people in low uncertainty avoidance cultures often would like to take risk. In the other words, people are more willing to try out new innovations.

Several studies revealed that uncertainty avoidance influences IT system usage. In (Png, Tan, & Khai-Ling, 2001), Png et al. demonstrated that enterprises in high uncertainty avoidance countries were less likely to adopt IT infrastructure. In (Singh, Xhao, & Hu, 2003), based on content analysis of the 80 U.S. domestic and Chinese Websites, Singh et al. showed that high uncertainty avoidance cultures in China led Chinese Websites to have some localized diffusion strategies, such as free trials.

Innovative products are often associated with uncertainty. Compared to traditional information services, mobile information services can be seen as an innovative product. People from high uncertainty avoidance cultures might be anxious about being in an unfamiliar situation when using mobile information services. Therefore, we make the following hypothesis:

H2: People from high uncertainty avoidance cultures will be less likely to adopt mobile information services than people from low uncertainty avoidance cultures.

MOBILE COMMERCE IN CHINA AND DEVELOPED COUNTRIES

China and the Developed countries represent two distinct cultures. The developed countries can be seen as a representation of western culture while China represents the epitome of eastern culture. The cultural values are meant to be different in the developed countries and China. These facts provide us with a good basis to analyze mobile information services adoption between these two distinct cultures.

Mobile Commerce in the Developed Countries

In the developed countries, the usage of advanced mobile services is more popular than China. The emergence of advanced mobile devices with touch screen has attracted many people to try out advanced mobile services. While advanced mobile services are available and most users own advanced mobile devices in the developed countries, the adoption of mobile services is not progressed as expected. An exploratory study from the cultural perspective would help us understand the barriers of mobile services adoption.

Mobile Commerce in China

According to the report from the Chinese Ministry of Information Industry, the number of mobile phone subscribers in China exceeded 1 billion in March 2012 as more Chinese people began to consider mobile phones as an everyday necessity. However, the mainstream usage of mobile phones in China focuses on phone calls, SMS, instant messaging services, contact services, and purchasing ring tongs. SMS has been the number one value added mobile service in Chinese mobile commerce market. The ratio of advanced mobile phone users is still quite low. Therefore, when it comes to advanced mobile services, not many users start trying them.

Unlike the developed countries, mobile commerce can hardly reach low-income earner that constitute a majority of the population in China. But many from the young generations are comfortable with using some existing basic mobile services on mobile devices. This may help them attempt to try some advanced mobile services. As mobile communication technology is developing very fast and the mobile commerce market in China is growing, more and more advanced mobile services will be available on the business market. And it is believed that mobile commerce has a potentially exceptional future in China given that China has the largest number of mobile phone subscribers in the world.

AN EXPLORATORY STUDY WITH MTSR

To study the impact of the cultural dimensions on the adoption of mobile information services in terms of the research hypotheses proposed in the last section, an exploratory study with a mobile information service called Mobile Tourist Service Recommender system (MTSR) with both respondents from develop countries and China were carried out.

Mobile Tourist Service Recommender System (MTSR)

Mobile Tourist Service Recommender system (MTSR) is a mobile service which was developed at a Norwegian university. Some screenshots of parts of MTSR are shown in Figure 4.

The Mobile Tourist Service Recommender system is intended to help tourists find points of Interest (POI) such as hotels and restaurants in order to let them schedule their time more efficiently and increase the probability that they will visit places that they will actually enjoy. By taking location, among other things, into the consideration, the system aims to provide better information to users.

The MTSR application has many features that will help the users in their search for POIs that they will like. To provide a clear and simple interface, the MTSR client uses a standard Google Map which can be panned and zoomed. In order to separate different functionality, a tab bar with three elements is used where each tab has its own purpose.

- 'Find' is the first tab, where users may search for POIs, get information about them or the route. Several facts may be stored, namely title, address, photo, description, phone number, opening hours, category, type (e.g., Italian restaurant, Chinese restaurant, pub) and rating. However, what information that is available depends on what have been entered into the system.

Figure 4. Screenshots of mobile tourist service recommender system (MTSR)

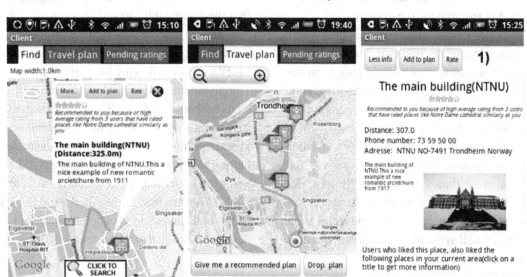

- 'Travel plan' is the second tab and is used whenever the user wants to obtain a complete itinerary. The complete itinerary will find restaurants and activities recommended for the user, and will do so by taking time as a factor.
- The last tab, the 'Pending ratings' tab, is used to display places the user have or may have visited and has yet to rate. This feature ensures that the user is reminded to rate places. There are two ways a place may be rated, either by the user explicitly selecting the place and rate it, or by pending ratings received.

The MTSR utilizes the widespread client-server model and consists of two servers, a client and the Google Maps information service. The backbone is the MTSR-server where the main functionality is handled and where the service requests are handled. This server is depended on the second server, namely the Postgis server, which is the database where information about users, POIs, geographical data, and so on is stored.

A Graphical User Interface (GUI) that collects information entered by the user or administrators is introduced to MTSR. This data will go through a three step process in order to ensure that all needed data is provided, that the information is validated and that the information is presented in a way that is suitable for the system.

We have developed a three-step process where a user is needed for the first two. The first step is entering information into a form. This form has been carefully constructed and provides some good features. Most of the fill in spots are regular text, but we do have some drop down menus where the possible values is limited to a predetermined number of choices, and to make sure that the geographical attributes are correct we have developed a JavaScript that devolves geographical points (in terms of latitude and longitude) from addresses, as well as devolving them from marked spots in the map.

The second step is an overview over all the values that have been entered. This is the validation-process, and has been constructed to let the user verify that the entered information is correct. A map is also provided so it is more convenient to verify the map data if a spot were used to represent the position of the point of interest in the last step instead of an address.

For the last step, the system will make appropriate transformations of the data. Data from the form is gathered and inserted into a database query after refinements. Refinements include giving geographical data proper Spatial Reference System Identifier (SRID) and calculating area based on the location (represented as a polygon). The step is finalized by executing the query.

Sample

We recruited the experiment subjects by posting announcements to a number of student mailing lists. Students from several departments, studying for an undergraduate program or a graduate program, were invited to participate in the experiment of using the MTSR running on an Android mobile device. Our postings explained who we are, what they are supposed to do during the MTSR experiment, and the purpose of this experiment. The participants have also been informed that the results would be reported only in aggregate and that their anonymity would be assured.

The recruitment resulted in 46 testers with some variety in major, age and experience with mobile services. Among the participants, we had 1 non-student and 46 students where 4 of these were bachelor students, 33 master students, and 6 doctoral students. 40 of these students studied at a department of science or engineering. 42 participants were between 20-30 years old, while two were under the age of 20 and two were over 30. Males were best represented with 35 participants, and the number of females was 11. The demographical data can be found in Table 3.

Table 3. Demographic information of the subjects

	Participants from Developed Countries	Participants from China
Number of Participants	36	10
Age Less than 20 20-29 30 or Over	2 34 0	0 8 2
Department Science or Engineering Others	30 6	10 0
Experience in **Mobile Services** 0-1 Year 2-5 Years More than 5 Years	2 26 8	1 6 3

Survey Instrument

The validated instrument measure in (Gao, Krogstie, & Siau, 2011) was used as the foundation to create survey items for this study. Based on our understanding on the cultural dimensions, we put the relevant validated items to the correspondent cultural dimension. As a result, 6 survey items (see Appendix 1) were included in this survey. A seven-point Likert scale, with 1 being the negative end of the scale (strongly disagree) and 7 being the positive end of the scale (strongly agree), was used to examine participants' responses to all items in the survey.

Data Collection Procedure

A paper based survey questionnaire was created to enable rapid onsite distribution during the experiment. Prior to completing the questionnaire, all participants were provided with an information sheet describing the mobile tourism service – MTSR and a mobile device having MTSR installed. In this manner, all participants got some basic ideas about the mobile service. After using the MTSR system in three defined

scenarios (see Appendix 2) for approximately 75 minutes, the questionnaire was distributed to all participants. The first scenario refers to find a restaurant. The second scenario refers to find a recommended hotel in Oslo. The third one refers to the handling of complete travel plans. After filling out the questionnaire, the participants returned the completed survey to us.

Results

The reliability of the survey items was tested by using Cronbach's Alpha coefficient. The coefficients of all dimension except power distance exceeded 0.6. According to previous research work [27], a reliability coefficient of 0.6 is marked as a lowest acceptable limit for Cronbach's Alpha for exploratory research.

Other findings are summarized as follows:

Individualism vs. Collectivism

The country effects on individualism vs. collectivism are shown in Figure 5. We found that other users' intention to use MTSR does affect individual's decision to use MTSR. Our finding on this aspect is not in line with H1. Participants' from developed countries intention to use MTSR is more likely to be influenced by the behavior of their fellows. According to the result, respondents from China are more interested to be the first one to use MTSR. In addition, respondents from China are more likely to believe the statement that using the system gives them an advantage over those who don't. It seems that young generation in China started to use online media as a main source of getting information instead of getting together to share information and expect their fellow to have the same goal or objective. This might explain why some Chinese students do not consider collecting information via mobile devices as an advantage. All in all, these three findings on Individualism vs. Collectivism do not support H1.

Figure 5. Results on individualism vs. collectivism

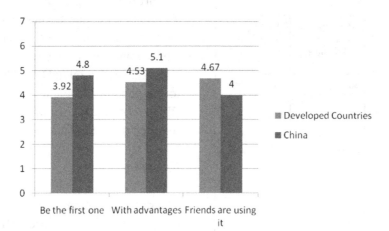

Uncertainty Avoidance

Figure 6 shows the cultural differences in terms of uncertainty avoidance dimension in this exploratory study between respondents from developed countries and China. According to the results, most respondents agreed that the data provided by the system is reliable and it is risk-free to use the system. This can be partially attributed to that the system provider of MTSR is the university. Concerning the question about the confidence in keeping MTSR system under control, it seems that some respondents from China do not want to be

a risk-taker, so that they presented a low level of confidence in using MTSR. This is also confirmed by one of the observations during the experiment. Some Chinese had some problems with completing the assigned tasks and asked some help from the instructors, because they would like to avoid ambiguous and uncomfortable situations during the experiment. As for respondents from developed countries, we found that most of them were able to finish the assigned tasks quite quickly without asking any help from the instructors, even though they might have some uncertainty about MTSR. Overall, participants from developed countries

Figure 6. Results on uncertainty avoidance

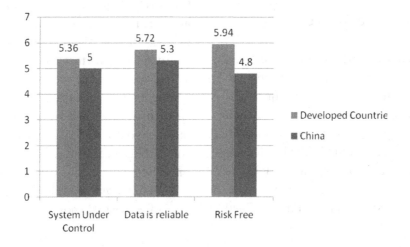

exhibit a slightly lower level of uncertainty avoidance than participants from China. These findings support H2.

Discussion and Limitations

Little research has been done to explore the adoption of mobile services in different cultural settings. This study can provide some insights for understanding the effect of the cultural dimensions on the adoption of mobile services. This research illustrates the importance of investigating the impact of cultural influence on mobile services adoption.

On one hand, from an academic perspective, this study contributes to the literature on mobile services adoption and diffusion by examining the importance of the cultural dimensions to mobile information services adoption. On the other hand, from a business perspective, the results also provided some implications for practitioners. Overall, one research hypothesis (H2) was supported in this exploratory study, the other research hypothesis (H1) was not supported in this study.

Limitations

We are also aware of some limitations of this work. To better confirm the results with greater validity, the number of participants and countries should be increased. For instance, in this study, most participants were experienced users of mobile services and mobile devices, and oversea students from China in a Norwegian university might be influenced by western culture. Secondly, there might be other factors which influence the adoption of mobile services. Future research is needed to further explore the role that other factors might play in mobile services diffusion. Third, since most participants are male, we did not study the impact of the cultural dimension (Masculinity/Femininity) on mobile information services adoption in this study. Fourth, the reliability and validity of the survey items needed to be examined in

further research. Last but not least, Likert scales are subject to three well-known biases: 1). acquiescence response bias: agreeing with statements as presented, 2). central tendency bias: avoiding the use of extreme response categories, and 3). social desirability bias: trying to portray them in a more favorable light. We tried to eliminate the problem of these biases in this study.

CONCLUSION AND FUTURE RESEARCH

This research was designed to study mobile information services adoption from the cultural perspective. The research question which drives this study is: how do the cultural dimensions influence the adoption of mobile information services? This study addresses this question by exploring the effect of the cultural dimensions in terms of individualism/collectivism, and uncertainty avoidances, on the adoption of a mobile information service at a university campus setting. The results indicate that the cultural dimensions play important roles in how mobile information services are used and adopted in two different cultural settings: the culture in developed countries and the Chinese culture. The research findings provide support for one of two research hypotheses. We believe this research contributes to both the literature and research on mobile services adoption.

As presented in our findings, the most striking finding was non-support of H1. We believe that some possible reasons exist for this finding. Firstly, the sample size of this pilot study was quite small. Most participants were experienced users of mobile devices and mobile services. They might expect to experience different kinds of new mobile services. In addition, oversea students from China might be influenced by western culture. As a result, it leads them to be the first one to try new services. Furthermore, some Chinese participants are well-educated in IT. They might be addicted to advanced mobile services.

There exist several opportunities for future research. First, the research hypotheses on the cultural dimensions can be tested in other empirical context, such as mobile banking, mobile game, mobile healthcare, mobile advertisement, and so on. Second, we plan to conduct another cross-culture study with people from other countries. Third, in this research, the respondents only used the system for a short amount of time (i.e., about 75 minutes) and that the location used was simulated. It would be interesting to see what users' thought of the system are after using it over an extended period of time as they would have gained more knowledge about the features available and the real life usefulness. We also plan to carry out research on this in the future.

ACKNOWLEDGMENT

The author would like to thank the anonymous reviewers for their helpful and constructive comments that greatly contributed to improving the final version of this chapter. The author also likes to thank the editors for their generous comments and support during the review process. Finally, the author would like to acknowledge the financial support by the Fundamental Research Funds for the Central Universities, China (Project No. ZNUFE. 2012065).

REFERENCES

Ajzen, I. (1991). The theory of planned behavior. *Organizational Behavior and Human Decision Processes*, *50*(2), 179–211. doi:10.1016/0749-5978(91)90020-T.

Ajzen, I., & Madden, T. J. (1986). Prediction of goal-directed behavior: Attitudes, intentions, and perceived behavioral control. *Journal of Experimental Social Psychology*, *22*(5), 453–474. doi:10.1016/0022-1031(86)90045-4.

Bagozzi, R. (2007). The legacy of the technology acceptance model and a proposal for a paradigm shift. *Journal of the Association for Information Systems*, *8*(4), 244–254.

Benbasat, I., & Barki, H. (2007). Quo vadis TAM. *Journal of the Association for Information Systems*, *8*(4), 211–218.

Benbasat, I., & Zmud, R. W. (1999). Empirical research in information systems: The practice of relevance. *Management Information Systems Quarterly*, *23*(1), 3–16. doi:10.2307/249403.

Bond, M. H. (1988). Finding universal dimensions of individual variation in multicultural studies of values: The rokeach and Chinese value surveys. *Journal of Personality and Social Psychology*, *55*(6), 1009. doi:10.1037/0022-3514.55.6.1009.

Bouwman, H., & van de Wijngaert, L. (2009). Coppers context, and conjoints: A reassessment of TAM. *Journal of Information Technology*, *24*, 186–201. doi:10.1057/jit.2008.36.

Carlsson, C., Carlsson, J., Hyvonen, K., Puhakainen, J., & Walden, P. (2006). Adoption of mobile devices/services—Searching for answers with the UTAUT. In *Proceedings of the 39th Annual Hawaii International Conference on System Sciences*. IEEE.

Chang, S. E., & Pan, Y.-H. V. (2011). Exploring factors influencing mobile users' intention to adopt multimedia messaging service. *Behaviour & Information Technology*, *30*(5), 659–672. doi:10.1080/01449290903377095.

Chen, L. (2008). A model of consumer acceptance of mobile payment. *International Journal of Mobile Communications*, *6*(1), 32–52. doi:10.1504/IJMC.2008.015997.

Choi, B., Lee, I., & Kim, J. (2006). Culturability in mobile data services: A qualitative study of the relationship between cultural characteristics and user-experience attributes. *International Journal of Human-Computer Interaction*, *20*(3), 171–203. doi:10.1207/s15327590ijhc2003_2.

Constantiou, I. D., Papazafeiropoulou, A., & Vendelø, M. T. (2009). Does culture affect the adoption of advanced mobile services? A comparative study of young adults' perceptions in Denmark and the UK. *SIGMIS Database, 40*(4), 132–147. doi:10.1145/1644953.1644962.

Davis, F. D. (1989). Perceived usefulness, perceived ease of use and user acceptance of information technology. *Management Information Systems Quarterly, 13*, 319–340. doi:10.2307/249008.

Davis, F. D., Bagozzi, R. P., & Warshaw, P. R. (1989). User acceptance of computer technology: A comparison of two theoretical models. *Management Science, 35*(8), 982–1003. doi:10.1287/mnsc.35.8.982.

DeLone, W., & McLean, E. (1992). Information systems success: The quest for the dependent variable. *Information Systems Research, 3*(1). doi:10.1287/isre.3.1.60.

Doney, P. M., Cannon, J. P., & Mullen, M. R. (1998). Understanding the influence of national culture on the development of trust. *Academy of Management Review, 23*(3).

Fishbein, M., & Ajzen, I. (1975). *Belief, attitude, intention and behavior: An introduction to theory and research*. Boston: Addison-Wesley.

Furrer, O., Liu, B. S.-C., & Sudharshan, D. (2000). The relationships between culture and service quality perceptions. *Journal of Service Research, 2*(4), 355–371. doi:10.1177/109467050024004.

Gao, S., Krogstie, J., & Siau, K. (2011). Developing an instrument to measure the adoption of mobile services. *Mobile Information Systems Journal, 7*(1), 45–67.

Gao, S., Moe, S. P., & Krogstie, J. (2010). An empirical test of the mobile services acceptance model. In *Proceedings of the 2010 Ninth International Conference on Mobile Business and 2010 Ninth Global Mobility Roundtable (ICMB-GMR)*. ICMB-GMR.

Gefen, D. (2003). TAM or just plain habit: A look at experienced online shoppers. *Journal of End User Computing, 15*(3), 1–13. doi:10.4018/joeuc.2003070101.

Hall, E. (1977). *Beyond culture*. New York: Anchor.

Harris, P., Rettie, R., & Kwan, C. C. (2005). Adoption and usage of m-commerce: A cross-cultural comparison of Hong Kong and United Kingdom. *Journal of Electronic Commerce Research, 6*(3), 210–224.

Hofstede, G., & Bond, M. H. (1988). The Confucius connection: From cultural roots to economic growth. *Organizational Dynamics, 16*(4), 5–21. doi:10.1016/0090-2616(88)90009-5.

Hofstede, G. H. (1980). *Culture's consequences: International differences in work-related values*. Beverly Hills, CA: Sage Publications, Inc..

Hong, S.-J., & Tam, K. Y. (2006). Understanding the adoption of multipurpose information sppliances: The case of mobile data services. *Information Systems Research, 17*(2), 162–179. doi:10.1287/isre.1060.0088.

Hong, S.-J., Thong, J. Y. L., & Tam, K. Y. (2006). Understanding continued information technology usage behavior: A comparison of three models in the context of mobile Internet. *Decision Support Systems, 42*(3), 1819–1834. doi:10.1016/j.dss.2006.03.009.

Horton, R. P., Buck, T., Waterson, P. E., & Clegg, C. W. (2001). Explaining intranet use with the technology acceptance model. *Journal of Information Technology, 16*, 237–249. doi:10.1080/02683960110102407.

Hosbond, J., & Nielsen, P. (2005). Mobile systems development: A literature review. In Sørensen, C., Yoo, Y., Lyytinen, K., & DeGross, J. (Eds.), *Designing ubiquitous information environments: Socio-technical issues and challenges (Vol. 185*, pp. 215–232). Boston: Springer. doi:10.1007/0-387-28918-6_17.

Karahanna, E., Straub, D. W., & Chervany, N. L. (1999). Information technology adoption across time: A cross-sectional comparison of pre-adoption and post-adoption beliefs. *Management Information Systems Quarterly*, *23*(2), 183–213. doi:10.2307/249751.

Kuo, Y.-F., & Yen, S.-N. (2009). Towards an understanding of the behavioral intention to use 3G mobile value-added services. *Computers in Human Behavior*, *25*(1), 103–110. doi:10.1016/j.chb.2008.07.007.

Lederer, A. L., Maupin, D. J., Sena, M. P., & Zhuang, Y. (2000). The technology acceptance model and the world wide web. *Decision Support Systems*, *29*(3), 269–282. doi:10.1016/S0167-9236(00)00076-2.

Lee, I., Choi, B., Kim, J., & Hong, S.-J. (2007). Culture-technology fit: Effects of cultural characteristics on the post-adoption beliefs of mobile Internet users. *International Journal of Electronic Commerce*, *11*(4), 11–51. doi:10.2753/JEC1086-4415110401.

Lee, I., Kim, J., Choi, B., & Hong, S.-J. (2010). Measurement development for cultural characteristics of mobile internet users at the individual level. *Computers in Human Behavior*, *26*(6), 1355–1368. doi:10.1016/j.chb.2010.04.009.

Legris, P., Ingham, J., & Collerette, P. (2003). Why do people use information technology? A critical review of the technology acceptance model. *Information & Management*, *40*(3), 191–204. doi:10.1016/S0378-7206(01)00143-4.

Lu, J., Yu, C.-S., & Liu, C. Y., & E., J. (2003). Technology acceptance model for wireless Internet. *Internet Research*, *13*(3), 206–222. doi:10.1108/10662240310478222.

Luarn, P., & Lin, H.-H. (2005). Toward an understanding of the behavioral intention to use mobile banking. *Computers in Human Behavior*, *21*(6), 873–891. doi:10.1016/j.chb.2004.03.003.

Mao, E., Srite, M., Thatcher, J. B., & Yaprak, O. (2005). A research model for mobile phone service behaviors: Empirical validation in the US and Turkey. *Journal of Global Information Technology Management*, *8*(4), 7–28.

Marcus, A., & Gould, E. W. (2000). Crosscurrents: Cultural dimensions and global web user-interface design. *Interaction*, *7*(4), 32–46. doi:10.1145/345190.345238.

Nysveen, H., Pedersen, P., & Thorbjørnsen, H. (2005). Intentions to use mobile services: Antecedents and cross-service comparisons. *Journal of the Academy of Marketing Science*, *33*(3), 330–346. doi:10.1177/0092070305276149.

Pavlou, P. A. (2003). Consumer acceptance of electronic commerce: Integrating trust and risk with the technology acceptance model. *International Journal of Electronic Commerce*, *7*(3), 101–134.

Png, I. P. L., Tan, B. C. Y., & Khai-Ling, W. (2001). Dimensions of national culture and corporate adoption of IT infrastructure. *IEEE Transactions on Engineering Management*, *48*(1), 36–45. doi:10.1109/17.913164.

Rogers, E. M. (1995). *The diffusion of innovations*. New York: Free Press.

Schwartz, D. G., Divitini, M., & Brasethvik, T. (2000). *Internet-based organizational memory and knowledge management*. Hershey, PA: IGI Global.

Schwartz, S., & Sagiv, L. (1995). Identifying culture-specifics in the content and structure of values. *Journal of Cross-Cultural Psychology*, *26*(1), 92–116. doi:10.1177/0022022195261007.

Siau, K., Lim, E.-P., & Shen, Z. (2001). Mobile commerce–Promises, challenges, and research agenda. *Journal of Database Management*, *12*(3), 4–13. doi:10.4018/jdm.2001070101.

Singh, N., Xhao, H., & Hu, X. (2003). Cultural adaptation on the web: A study of American companies' domestic and Chinese websites. *Journal of Global Information Management*, *11*(3), 63. doi:10.4018/jgim.2003070104.

Straub, D. W. (1994). The effect of culture on IT diffusion: E-mail and FAX in Japan and the U.S. *Information Systems Research*, *5*(1), 23–47. doi:10.1287/isre.5.1.23.

Taylor, S., & Todd, P. A. (1995). Understanding information technology usage: A test of competing models. *Information Systems Research*, *6*(2), 144–176. doi:10.1287/isre.6.2.144.

Thompenaars, F., & Hampden-Turner, C. (1998). *Riding the waves of culture: Understanding cultural diversity in global business*. New York: McGraw-Hill.

Varshney, U., & Vetter, R. (2000). Emerging mobile and wireless networks. *Communications of the ACM*, *43*(6), 73–81. doi:10.1145/336460.336478.

Venkatesh, V., & Davis, F. D. (2000). A theoretical extension of the technology acceptance model: Four longitudinal field studies. *Management Science*, *46*(2), 186–204. doi:10.1287/mnsc.46.2.186.11926.

Venkatesh, V., Morris, M. G., Davis, G. B., & Davis, F. D. (2003). User acceptance of information technology: Toward a unified view. *Management Information Systems Quarterly*, *27*(3), 425–478.

Wu, J.-H., & Wang, S.-C. (2005). What drives mobile commerce? An empirical evaluation of the revised technology acceptance model. *Information & Management*, *42*(5), 719–729. doi:10.1016/j.im.2004.07.001.

Yang, K. C. C. (2005). Exploring factors affecting the adoption of mobile commerce in Singapore. *Telematics and Informatics*, *22*(3), 257–277. doi:10.1016/j.tele.2004.11.003.

Yuan, Y., Archer, N., Connelly, C. E., & Zheng, W. (2010). Identifying the ideal fit between mobile work and mobile work support. *Information & Management*, *47*(3), 125–137. doi:10.1016/j.im.2009.12.004.

Zheng, W., & Yuan, Y. (2007). Identifying the differences between stationary office support and mobile work support: A conceptual framework. *International Journal of Mobile Communications*, *5*(1), 107–122. doi:10.1504/IJMC.2007.011492.

APPENDIX 1:

Table 4. Survey instrument

Cultural Dimensions	Item Number	Survey Items
Individualism vs. Collectivism	IC1	I prefer to be the first one using the mobile service.
	IC2	Using the mobile service gives me an advantage over those who don't.
	IC3	I could use the mobile service, if most friends are using the mobile services.
Uncertainty Avoidance	UA1	I could use the mobile service, if I feel confident that I can keep the service under control.
	UA2	I could use the mobile service, if I feel confident that the data returned by the service is reliable.
	UA3	I could use the mobile service, if I believe it is risk-free to use the service.

APPENDIX 2: SCENARIOS

Scenario 1

In the first scenario the testers were asked to find points of interest and information about them. In this part we wanted to investigate how easy it would be for each of the users to find places and the information associated with them. Some information, such as address, is not readily available when pressing a place on the map and we wanted to make sure the users were able to find.

For the first part they had to find a restaurant and write down the name and address of the restaurant they chose. This included finding a place and the extended information dialog in order to obtain the name and address of that particular place.

As for the second part, the testers would have to use the information about the place they found and use that to find a new place in their current area that were recommended by users who also liked the current place. This task may not be as intuitive as it was designed to be, so we included this to investigate how intuitive this task really is.

Scenario 2

The system may filter points of interest on whether or not they are recommended for the particular user. The user has to make one additional step to get the recommended points. The motivation for the first task is to investigate how easy this is to deal with. The task at hand is finding a hotel that is recommended to the user. As the system is meant to provide points of interest proximal to the user, it only searches for places that are within the field of interest (the map currently being displayed). This makes the task of finding places far away from the user's current location cumbersome as the user will have to pan the map until it is over the desired area. The second task is therefore to find a restaurant in Oslo.

The second task also explores another interesting case: If the user selects to only find recommended places, as in the prior task, and all places within the current area of the map is not recommended, the system will display a dialog that it could not find any places and that the user could try to uncheck the "Only stuff recommended for me"-option and/or zoom out. We intentionally let all restaurants in Oslo have low ratings so that they were not recommended in order to see if they realized that they had to turn the "Only stuff recommended for me"-option off to get any result.

Scenario 3

The final scenario explores the handling of complete travel plans. This feature is meant to provide several sights, such as museums and landmarks, and a couple of places to eat so that the whole day is planned by the system. All of these points of interest are recommended for the user.

As the initial task for this scenario, the user is asked to acquire a travel plan and write down the name of one of the places. The second task is to add a place to the travel plan which cannot be done from the "Travel plan"-view. The user has to enter the "Find"-view, search for a place and then add it to the plan which may or may not be intuitive to the users.

Chapter 6
Ubiquitous Game–Based Learning in Higher Education:
A Framework towards the Effective Integration of Game–Based Learning in Higher Education using Emerging Ubiquitous Technologies

Anna Kasimati
University of Piraeus, Athens

Sofia Mysirlaki
University of Piraeus, Athens

Hara Bouta
University of Piraeus, Athens

Fotini Paraskeva
University of Piraeus, Athens

ABSTRACT

The rise of mobile broadband devices and services has significantly changed the role of mobile devices in people's daily lives by enabling the provision of innovative applications and services anywhere, anytime. Despite the fact that new ideas and innovation mainly occur within Higher Education Institutions (HEIs), the adoption of mobile and ubiquitous technologies by HEIs is still in its early stages. This chapter attempts to provide a framework to support Higher Education Institutions towards implementing mobile and ubiquitous, game-based learning activities. Aligned with the objective of this book, this chapter presents some examples and best practices of implementing this framework towards achieving the learning goals of future professionals in the fields of electronic and ubiquitous commerce.

DOI: 10.4018/978-1-4666-4566-0.ch006

INTRODUCTION

This chapter presents a methodological framework towards the effective implementation of Game-Based Learning (GBL) in Higher Education Institutions (HEIs) using ubiquitous and mobile devices. The proliferation of digital games along with the effectiveness of game play on cognitive development have sparked a fascination for their integration in the learning process and educational curricula at an international level. A great number of research efforts and applications have been carried out, mainly focusing on the integration of GBL at early educational levels, specifically K-12 education (Johnson, Adams, & Cummins, 2012). However, showing consideration for the fact that the population of gamers is continuously increasing, amounting to approximately 70 million people in 2011, 40% of which are aged between 20 and 34 years old, and the fact that all 21st century learners have grown up in a world where digital games have always been an important part of their lives (Johnson, Adams, & Cummins, 2012), it is a great opportunity and a need for HEIs to focus on GBL so as to achieve their goals as regards their students' collaboration, problem solving, critical thinking, creativity and digital literacy skills. Notwithstanding the great number of HEIs including courses for game design and development in their curricula, only few of them apply basic gaming principles to enhance their educational services. GBL practices and methodologies can provide HEI with new forms of learning content, interaction and collaboration, while providing potential for constant evaluation and provision of direct feedback (Derryberry, 2012). Of paramount importance is the proliferation of mobile devices (smartphones and tablets) to further support HEIs towards adopting GBL practices. Specifically, students' ever-increasing use of ubiquitous online applications, when scrutinized within a learning-centered context, provides HEIs with a unique opportunity to easily engage students into game-based learning activities employing their mobile devices as an educational tool.

As a result, HEIs are offered the opportunity to combine two equally popular and effective learning practices (GBL and mobile) and properly integrate them into their curricula in order to enhance students' motivation and engagement, and also achieve demanding learning goals. When successfully applied, this can provide HEIs with a competitive advantage against other globally or nationally recognized HEIs due to the provision of innovative and high-quality learning services to their students.

Conclusively, GBL is expected to become a common practice in HEIs at an international level in two to three years time from now (2014-2015) (Johnson, Adams, & Cummins, 2012). However, in order for digital games to be effectively integrated in Higher Education, proper methodology and instructional design should be followed during the preparation, delivery and the evaluation phase of GBL activities. To this end, this chapter provides a robust literature review and combines GBL principles and methodologies into a framework for their proper integration in HEIs and their alignment with technological specifications of mobile and ubiquitous technologies. In more detailed, this chapter focuses on enhancing HEIs' ability to adopt and apply mobile/ubiquitous and game-based learning practices, providing significant insight and guidance throughout all development phases (design, development, implementation, assessment).

The chapter is organized in two parts where Part A investigates the basic principles towards the effective implementation of GBL (focusing on digital games) in HEIs; it further delineates the way mobile and ubiquitous technologies can support the smoothest integration of GBL in those specific organisations and its fastest adoption by relevant stakeholders (teaching staff, administrative staff, middle-level management employees, students). Part B presents best practices and examples of GBL in Higher Education using mobile/ubiquitous devices. The provision of such best practices and examples on specific relevant activities using mobile devices can guide academics and instructors realize the impact of these innovative educational practices thus leading to their fastest and smoothest adoption in HEIs' curricula.

DIGITAL AND MOBILE GAME BASED LEARNING IN HIGHER EDUCATION

Theoretical Background

Using games is identified in the literature as a good practice towards raising motivation and engagement in learning processes. They have proven to be highly effective, especially in interdisciplinary areas where students are required to combine knowledge from different fields and apply critical thinking and problem solving skills towards achieving their learning goals (Shabalina, Vorobkalov, Kataev, & Tarasenko, 2008). This suggests that they can be effectively applied within Business Schools and HEIs, for the purpose of teaching interdisciplinary courses, such as e-Business, where students need to combine their technological, management and strategic planning knowledge and skills in order to develop and provide a successful service to current or potential customers.

The term "Digital Game-based Learning" was first introduced by Prensky (Prensky, 2001) and it refers to the combination of fun and engagement with serious learning and interactive entertainment into a highly exciting medium, that of Digital Learning Games. According to this definition, Digital Games should be described by clearly defined rules and should set specific expected learning objectives goals and outcomes in order to be effectively used within a learning context. Moreover, current literature and research in the field have proven that it is essential for Digital Games (when applied within a learning context) to describe a clear story, offer interaction possibilities to users, and provide challenges and direct feedback to learners.

In order to provide a complete and robust methodology and framework for the integration of ubiquitous/mobile GBL in Higher Education, it is essential to make a short reference to the learning theories and methodologies that have been selected to support this research effort.

At first the development of the proposed framework has to be aligned with Din's recommendations for successful educational games (Din, 2006) who states that games should:

- Be immersive.
- Have elevated playability.
- Be attractive, challenging and competitive.
- Offer a goal or several goals.
- Allow players to track and manage their progress.

Further to the game-based approach, the proposed methodology has also been based on the problem-solving and experiential learning approach. Problem solving concepts and practices have been included in order to enhance students' potential to acquire both theoretical knowledge and the skills to orchestrate the obtained knowledge into practice. In order to be successfully implemented, this approach should involve students in carefully designed game tasks, which should be completed only when students manage to successfully implement a set of personal goals. Problem based learning has been identified as highly effective for the instruction of courses that combine interdisciplinary skills, as for example developing a software aimed at solving complex problems in the business sector (Davies, 1993). At this point, it needs to be mentioned that HEIs are by default aimed at providing learners with knowledge and skills in more than one disciplines. Indicative examples, fully relevant to the subject matter of this book, are courses such as "Management Science and Technology" or "e-Business" which include the instruction and delivery of both technological and management skills to learners.

With regards to experiential learning, the proposed framework adopts the relevant model proposed by Kiili (Kiili, 2005), referring to the design of educational games. In accordance with this model, the major challenge that HEIs and their instructors are faced with during the process of designing educational games, is linking gameplay (Rollings & Adams, 2003) to experiential learning in order to facilitate the flow experience, produce positive user experience for the players and maximize the impact of the game-based educational activities (Csikszentmihalyi, 1975). Experiential learning, based on the work of Dewey (1938), Piaget (1970/72) and Lewin (1951) as presented in Kolb (1984), stresses the importance of direct experience and reflective observation (Nielsen-Englyst, 2003) in order to maximize students' learning outcomes and skills. Kolb (Kolb, 1984) has proposed a methodology for experiential learning, which has been proven to be highly effective in terms of students' motivation and performance. This methodology suggests that experiential learning should include four stages: a) active experimentation, b) concrete experience, c) reflective observation of the experiments and d) abstract conceptualization and hypotheses testing.

The final learning concept included in the proposed framework refers to the term "zone of proximal development" (Vygotskiĭ, 1962). This concept is taken into account during the design of game based learning activities and suggests that the tasks to be performed should become more demanding once a student's skill level increases. This is closely related to the student's motivation and engagement. Towards increasing student's motivation and engagement, the concept of flow (Csikszentmihalyi 1975) is also included in the proposed framework. More specifically, this concept refers to an experience of intense concentration or absolute absorption (Csikszentmihalyi, 1990) that can be observed when an individual is voluntarily involved in an activity and can lead to increased cognitive processing and intellectual capacity. Aligned with the scope of this chapter, the concept of flow is investigated under the mobile learning perspective in order to allow for the maximum student's engagement and motivation during a mobile learning activity. Specifically, the inclusion of the concept of flow in educational context, has proven to promote optimal learning experiences (Csikszentmihalyi, Rathunde, and Whalen, 1993) by making students feel more pleasure and successful while attending the mobile game based learning activities, and motivate them into maximizing their effort (Nakamura & Csikszentmihalyi, 2002). As a result, and aligned with the "zone of proximal development" the proposed framework identifies the provision of immediate feedback as a critical factor towards the provision of flow experiences to students, since it can make GBL activities more interesting and enjoyable. Specifically, the theory of flow identifies interest as a vital aspect towards achieving flow experiences and thus allowing for motivation, engagement and learning (Deci & Ryan, 1987). As a result, the provision of feedback in mobile game based learning activities can ensure a balance between the student's intrinsic interest and the difficulty of tasks, and thus lead to increased students' engagement while learning activities become always more complex. Moreover, the provision of feedback can make learning more enjoyable by enhancing students' satisfaction during actual engagement in the learning tasks (Csikszentmihalyi, 1990). Aiming to maximize the benefits of the proposed mobile game based learning framework, the concept of flow (focusing on students motivation and engagement) should be incorporated in the design of mobile learning content and activities since it has been proven to have a positive impact on the effectiveness of such learning experiences (Hoffman and Novak, 1996).

Table 1 presents the major game based learning concepts of the abovementioned models and definitions incorporated in the proposed framework.

Table 1. Game-based learning concepts included in the proposed framework

Concepts included in the Proposed Framework:	Digital Game-Based Learning (Prensky, 2001)	Educational Games (Din, 2006)	Problem-Solving (Davies, 2003)	Experiential Learning (Kiili, 2005)	Experiential Learning (Kolb, 1984)
Clearly defined Rules	x				
Objectives & Goals	x	x	x		
Immersive		x			
Elevated Playability (Zone of Proximal Development"		x			
Attractive-engaging-positive user experience		x		x	
Allow players to track and manage their progress		x			
Turn theory into practice/reflective observation			x	x	x

Mobile Game-Based Learning

The term mobile learning is considered as "an extension of e-learning" (Brown, 2005) and is used to describe any learning activity that is taking place through or on a mobile device. Typical examples of mobile devices can be smartphones, tablets, PDAs, mobile phones or personal media players (Kukulska-Hulme & Traxler, 2005). The technological advances brought about in the course of the past decade have been followed by rapid evolution and penetration of mobile devices, mobile telecommunications and mobile broadband services. Devices such as smart phones and tablets have entered the mobile market and have been highly adopted, especially by the younger generation. Usage patterns of mobile devices have significantly changed. As shown in the "Top mobile Internet trends Report" (Murphy & Meeker 2011) only 32% of the total use of mobile devices refers to telephony related activity, while the rest activity includes new types of activity such as access to mail and Web applications (18%), mobile gaming, mobile social networking, etc (47%). This fact is highly indicative of the rapid explosion and growth of mobile gaming at an international level. Any digital game that can be played on any mobile device is considered to be a mobile game.

The proliferation of mobile technology and mobile gaming further expands opportunities of game based learning, providing increased potential for students' motivation and engagement any time from any place. In addition, due to their advanced features (touch screens, sensors, microphones, social networking opportunities, access to the Internet) digital games can be identified as highly pervasive and ubiquitous, and thus suitable and effective for educational purposes allowing for innovation in the learning sector.

In order to effectively combine mobile and digital game principles, it is necessary to first distinguish the features that render mobile learning different from other types of technology-enhanced learning and the way these features can be aligned to the GBL principles earlier mentioned.

Mobile learning is a flexible learning model that supports the direct provision of personalized learning content, at any time and place (Brown, 2005). According to Van't Hooft, Swan, Lin and Cook (2007) ubiquitous technologies support learning in an environment where a number of devices enable the connection to the Internet any time from any place. Research in the field has focused on the investigation of mobile learning not only as a method that allows learning on the move, but also as a context-specific and context-sensitive learning approach (Walker, 2006). Furthermore, mobile learning is acknowledged to be a form of technology-enhanced learning allowing student-content interaction in an inherently social manner (Moran & Dourish, 2001). At this point, it is worth pointing out the characteristics and features that differentiate mobile devices from other forms of digital devices. These features include: (Clarke, 2001)

- **Ubiquity:** It refers to the potential of having access to information and content available on the Web, any time and from any place. When this feature is viewed under a learning and educational perspective, it is of great value since it allows reading at any time and context, formal and informal learning, studying on the move (eg on the bus), hence increasing students' productivity and ultimately, supports the provision of context specific information and material to students as well as the provision of direct feedback.

- **Localization:** Mobile devices can identify users' specific geographic location and provide customized information and content. This feature can provide a number of benefits in learning processes as for example the provision of context specific information to students (such being the case of monuments and nearby historical sites). This can prove useful to the instructors as well, given that they can have access to information regarding students' activity, such as the exact students' location at the time of accessing the educational material. Once collected and analysed, this information can lead to the extraction of useful correlations and conclusions concerning the student's profile or studying patterns to be then incorporated into the design phase of future courses.

- **Interactivity (Kakihara, & Sørensen, 2001):** This refers to multiple types of interaction that can be observed when some-

one uses a mobile device. Specifically, within the learning context, mobile devices allow for the following forms of interactivity: student-content, student-student, student-device, and student-instructor. This enhances students' communication and collaboration skills (communication between students), as well as their decision-making skills (communication in order to solve a problem or take a decision).

- **Personalization (Abowd & Mynatt, 2000; Lyytinen & Yoo, 2002; Rao & Minakakis, 2003):** mobile devices provide content based on users' preferences and profile. This allows for the provision of customized services based on students' personal learning goals and achievements.

Via the aforementioned analysis, it is evident that mobile devices have the potential of significantly improving and changing the way the learning process is currently taking place. Mobile/ubiquitous learning provides a number of opportunities, which once carefully integrated into the learning process, can lead to the provision of improved and totally innovative educational services.

In the subsections to follow major opportunities that mobile/ubiquitous learning can offer towards improving the educational and learning sectors are outlined:

Learning can take place everywhere, at any time (Shuler, 2009): Almost all 21st century students own a mobile device they always bring with them. The fact that mobile devices can access broadband services renders the mobile device an ideal means of the dissemination of learning material when students are on the move or any place away from the class environment.

Support individuality (Shuler, 2009 and Klopfer & Squire, 2008): Advanced mobile devices (such as smartphones and tablets) can support the provision of personalized, ubiquitous and location specific learning content. These devices are aware of their owner preferences, friends, favorite places to visit, favorite Websites to access, type of applications used to download, calendar, exact geographic location at any time. The proper collection and analysis of this information enables the provision of totally personalised content to the users. With reference to learning processes, these features support the better monitoring of students, the provision of game specific information, the collection of data and information needed from the Web, and thus support the provision of personalized learning.

Portability (Pea & Maldonado, 2006): Mobile devices are characterized by their small volume and screen, a fact that makes them easily transferable. Despite their small size, mobile devices

are characterized by advanced computing power, sophisticated software and improved technological features.

Can support both formal and informal learning (Peters, 2007): Mobile devices support learning in formal and informal settings by allowing learning and studying anywhere, thus enabling changes in the learning environment and context.

In Table 2 the basic features of mobile/ubiquitous devices, their alignment with GBL principles, and the key literature review findings in terms of mobile-game based learning are summarized. As illustrated in Table 2, characteristics of mobile/ubiquitous devices are highly correlated with GBL principles. When these characteristics are

Table 2. Alignment of indicative mobile/ubiquitous devices features with GBL principles

Mobile/Ubiquitous Characteristics	Description	GBL Principle
Ubiquity	• The attribute of somebody being available and connected at any location and any given time. • Supports Continuous information exchange.	• Allows the provision of both Formal & informal learning. • Allows access to GBL from everywhere at any time. • Allows the provision of immediate feedback in response to student mistakes. • Enhances student's critical thinking and decision-making ability.
Localization	• Precise localization of a connected mobile device (when allowed by the user) • Precise information on the location of a person or a product.	• Provision of Context-specific learning content. • Customized learning content

Interactivity	• High level of interaction between
	  • User-device
	  • User-content
	  • User-other users
		• Supports social learning, collaboration, and collaborative decision-making.
		• Supports increased interaction between students and students and learning content.

Identification/ Personalization	• Users can be uniquely identified through their mobile device • Allows the monitoring and provision of data with regards to user's personal interaction with the mobile device	• Allows the provision of personalized learning content.
Users have control over their devices	• Users are familiar with their mobile devices • Feel safe when using the devices • Can decide when, whether and why they would use the device	• The game needs to allow players to track and manage their progress • Learner-centered learning • Learner is actively engaged • Minimization of technological barriers and technology adoption issues
Provides an immersive graphical interface	• The provision of a camera, combined with online broadband supports the provision of 2D graphics and even Virtual Reality & Augmented reality applications	• The game must be immersive

investigated and aligned with GBL principles, learning outcomes can be highly innovative and improved. HEIs can apply those practices although attention should be directed to their proper integration. The final deliverable of the chapter combines current GBL practices and provides a methodological framework towards the proper integration of GBL in HEIs, and their alignment with technological specifications of mobile and ubiquitous technologies.

Game-Based Learning in Higher Education

As mentioned earlier, Higher Education at a global level is and will face significant challenges in terms of the quality of the education offered to students. The need for organizational change has been obvious during the last years where a number of efforts toward the provision of innovative forms of learning are being implemented. However, the adoption of GBL by HEIs is still in very early stages, mainly due to the lack of experience and skills with regards to the preparation, design and delivery of GBL courses.

What differentiates Higher Education from K-12 Education (where GBL has been mostly applied and investigated) is its special features and the difference of learning processes that take place within HEIs as compared to those of children's education. These special features were identified by Whitton (2010) and organised in two categories: a) the characteristics of Higher Education Learners, b) the characteristics of Higher Education as illustrated in Table 3.

Mobile and Ubiquitous Learning: A Roadmap towards Its Effective Application in Higher Education

In the light of preparing a GBL framework within the Higher Education context, the aforementioned characteristics should be taken into consideration. Similarly to every learning design process, instructors should include the preparation, the design, the implementation and the evaluation phase.

Table 3. Higher education special features

A. Higher Education Learners' characteristics	
Acceptability	It refers to the concepts of play and fun, which are fully acceptable and appropriate in children's learning, and which are not easily acceptable in Higher Education. As a result, emphasis should be placed on their appropriate and purposeful integration into learning processes.
Applicability in the real world	It refers to the need of Higher Education Learners to have a clear reflection of what they learn in authentic contexts.
Motivation	Adults, and thus Higher Education students, usually have decided and voluntarily chosen to participate in the learning process in the specific field. As a result, they are already motivated to engage in the learning process. In other words, digital games in Higher Education should not be used merely to engage and motivate students, but further enhance effectiveness of the learning process.
Orientation to study	Higher Education students have a more mature and self-organised attitudes to learning. In other words, they need to understand the reasons for participating in the game, and the connection of the learning outcomes with real skills, in order to persuade them and engage them in the learning process.
B. Higher Education special characteristics	
Assessment	Despite the fact that Higher Education allows more flexibility in the use and combination of effective assessment methods, there should be described a framework based on which instructors should set the criteria and select the most effective assessment method based on their specific learning context.
Cognitive level of learning outcomes	Higher Education is usually focused on the development of high cognitive skills such as problem solving and critical thinking. This should be considered for the selection or the design of digital game aimed to be applied to the needs of Higher Education.

Preparation Phase

During the preparation phase, instructors should identify and clearly describe the learning ecosystem. This includes the identification of learners' characteristic, previous knowledge and if possible attitude towards the under instruction science and GBL practices. Learners' characteristics are crucial for the design of the learning process and activities, since they can provide input regarding their acceptability and can (positively or negatively) impact their progress, their motivation and engagement in the learning processes. Besides, during the preparation phase, technological and technical limitations (such as the Internet connection) should also be identified. Specifically, instructors should investigate whether students have the potential to access the devices needed to support the course, whether the HEI provides wireless access to the Internet, whether the software or hardware needed is available and consider the necessity for supporting the staff.

Design Phase

This is the most vital phase with reference to the implementation of Mobile/Ubiquitous GBL in HEIs. During this phase instructors should select which part(s) of the course will be carried out through BGL activities and which will be the learning goals for each of these parts. During this stage instructors are advised to align each learning goal with the GBL practice and the Mobile Device characteristic that will be selected to support the achievement of the specific goal. It is also essential for instructors to provide all the technical specifications necessary both on the HEI's behalf (equipment and software needed) and on the learner's side (mobile device specifications, Internet connection, etc.). In more detail, during this phase instructors should follow the instructional design process proposed by IEEE (2001) suggesting that instructors are advised to select suitable learning methods to address the needs of a given group of learners, within a clearly defined educational context, aiming to achieve clearly described learning objectives. This process should be slightly different in this case in order to be aligned with the specific characteristics of both mobile/Ubiquitous GBL and Higher education. Towards this direction, the steps to be taken by instructors to successfully design an effective mobile/ubiquitous GBL activity for HEI students are the following:

- At first it is necessary to give a short title to the mobile/ubiquitous GBL scenario to be designed, and clearly explain the learning difficulties it aims to overcome. This will help instructors define the specific subject matter to be supported.

- Instructors should identify the learners' characteristics. Such characteristics may include data about the students' age, previous knowledge, previous experience in GBL and mobile learning environments, their technological knowledge and capacity. Instructors are advised to carry out a short survey among potential students and directly inquire about this information. By doing so, students contribute to the design of their learning process a fact that can enhance their motivation and engagement. Such information also provides invaluable insights as regards students' personal learning objectives and can support their alignment with the objectives and goals of the GBL activity. Additionally, input concerning their motivation and attitude towards GBL and mobile learning is provided, while at the same time their participation in the learning design is increased and thus their orientation towards studying is enhanced. Finally, the design should ensure the provision of flow experiences, suitable for adult learners and students, to engage their motivation and engagement in learning processes.

- Instructors should, thereafter, describe the entire GBL activity. Instructors should use the input gathered from students to initially set the learning goals of the GBL process. Each learning goal should be aligned with at least one GBL concept, Mobile/ Ubiquitous device characteristic and an HEI's characteristic. The whole game should include all four Kolb's experiential learning phases and each phase should be accompanied by specific learning objectives. The effective use of the potential of mobile and ubiquitous devices also needs to be accentuated. Instructors should, then, decide on the features of mobile/ubiquitous devices to be included in their GBL activity and justify their decision, by expounding on the way the selected feature supports both GBL concepts and the given learning goals. They should define the level of ubiquity and interactivity to be used in each phase, how and whether the content will be customized to learners' needs and whether students' locality will be taken into consideration during the game play. At this point instructors should also decide on the technology (tool) to be used for the development of the game (is this going to be a native application, a Web-based application?). During this phase of the instructional design, instructors need to describe the rules of the game and ensure that the progress and difficulty of the game increase in conjunction with the student's progress. To put it differently, the 'zone of proximal development' and the concept of flow should be considered in order to enhance the student's engagement. Attention should be drawn to the description of the learning goals, the provision of immediate and direct feedback and the methods that will be used to assess the accomplishment of these goals. Since the mobile/ubiquitous GBL is going to be applied within an HEI context, instructors should always keep in mind and incorporate the HEI's rules or directives concerning the assessment methods to be deemed valid and lead to successful participation in any course in their GBL design. Assessment should be highly reliable and ensure that the data collected represent the student's real progress. To this end, instructors should provide both quantitative and qualitative data based on which the evaluation is going to take place. Moreover, the assessment is highly important for the profile and status of the HEI as a whole, thus if effective and reliable, it can improve the HEI's status at a national and global level. With reference to the definition of the learning goals, they should be aligned to the Higher Education special characteristics, meaning that they should ensure a) the applicability of what students learn in real world and b) learning goals should be focused on the development of cognitive skills in order to address the needs of adult learners attending HEI courses. Finally, instructors should fill in Table 4, in order to ensure that their Mobile/Ubiquitous GBL practice will be carefully designed and aligned with all necessary principles mentioned earlier in this chapter.

- The next step in the game development is related to the resources and learning material to be included in the GBL practice. While in this stage, instructors should keep in mind that the gaming environment ought to be immersive. Mobile and ubiquitous devices display increased potential for the provision of a highly immersive gaming environment, with a graphical and friendly user interface. If needed, instructors may

Table 4. The mobile/ubiquitous GBL approach in HEI

The Mobile/Ubiquitous GBL Approach in HEI						
Experiential Learning Model Stage	**Learning Activity**	**Game Activity**	**Learning Goals**	**Mobile/ Ubiquitous Characteristic Used**	**GBL Concept Supported**	**Assessment**
Active Experimentation (planning, trying out gained knowledge)						
Concrete experience (Doing)						
Reflective Observation (reviewing, reflecting of the experience)						
Abstract Conceptualization (concluding, learning from the experience)						

include an augmented gaming environment, that can increase student's intrinsic interest and motivate them to explore the innovative learning environment, implying that that they may ask students to turn on the camera application on their mobile devices and then augment students' real-world environment with computer-generated learning material and information. In all cases, the learning material should be developed properly in order to be displayed on mobile and ubiquitous devices. This means that the material should be easily customized to be displayed on a smartphone with a screen of 4 inches, or a tablet with a screen of 10 inches. The role of the HEI is deemed crucial. Specifically, the HEI should encourage instructors to decide to deliver an innovative learning practice and support them while designing such practices. It is suggested that the HEI should provide useful seminars and workshops for their teaching staff (where instructors gain hands on experience in the development of a game application in a mobile and ubiquitous device) or employ technical staff to support instructors during this effort.

- As in all software and services developed in all sectors, a pilot-testing phase is also needed in a mobile/ubiquitous GBL application. Instructors should invite a number of students to implement the GBL activities described, as they would do had they actually participated in the course. Instructors should store and collect students' activities and interactions, and ask them to report on problems they might have faced and provide a complete evaluation for the application. This evaluation should not only focus on technical issues (operationalization of the application, technical problems, connectivity issues) but also on educational issues (motivation, engagement, achievement of learning goals). The evaluation, combined with the collected data regarding students' activity should be further analysed by the instructors and be taken as input for the improvement of the mobile/ubiquitous GBL practice.

Implementation Phase

After having designed, pilot tested and revised the mobile/ubiquitous GBL application, instructors will apply it in a real context. With this purpose in mind, instructors should inform students on the way the course is going to take place, the rules of the game-play activities and the method to be used for their evaluation. During the implementation phase instructors should:

- Collect all data that refer to the students' interaction with the application. This data may include details on the time students logged into the application, the material viewed, the game-play activities implemented, the progress achieved, etc.
- Provide continuous support and direct feedback to students in order to enhance their engagement and motivation, and enhance students' flow experiences.
- Encourage them to use as many features of their mobile devices as possible (for instance, by asking them to use the microphone or the camera in order to communicate with other students).
- Provide statistic information on the average use of the application by students attending the course and information regarding their average progress. This can boost students' motivation and encourage them towards improving their performance.

Evaluation Phase

This phase has a dual objective: On the one hand, to evaluate students' performance and achievement of learning goals and on the other hand to evaluate the mobile/ubiquitous GBL application. As regards students' evaluation, instructors should apply the assessment methods that have been defined during the design phase. The assessment should evaluate students' progress towards achieving the learning outcomes and cognitive objectives of the learning approach. In terms of the effectiveness of the proposed mobile/ubiquitous GBL practice, instructors are advised to randomly divide students attending the course into two groups of equal populations. The first group should participate in the mobile/ubiquitous GBL activities, while the other group should attend traditional lectures aimed at achieving the same learning goals. Instructors will, then, evaluate both groups in terms of their performance and will follow the multi-group comparison analysis approach in order to identify potential differences in the two groups' performances. Data can be collected through a specially developed research instrument (questionnaire), focused on gathering data derived from all the evaluation factors. The research instrument can be based on technology adoption and learning theories' literature, examining both utilitarian and hedonic drivers of adoption and use (e.g., TAM, UTAUT). In addition, students participating in the proposed mobile GBL approach should be asked to further evaluate the application in terms of its learning and technological features. Input collected during the evaluation phase will be used for the development and improvement of the application.

BEST PRACTICES

In order to enhance the impact and applicability of the proposed framework, this part of the chapter presents two stances of the application of mobile Game-Based Learning in Educational Institutions (not only HEIs) employing the proposed framework. Instructors can gain knowledge and insight as regards the methodology they can use to transform their courses into innovative game-based practices.

Scenario 1: e-Business

This learning scenario has been designed to support the educational needs of future professionals of the field of electronic Business.

Preparation Phase

Problems to be addressed: Students usually face difficulties in understanding the way social media may impact an online shop/business. It is exceptionally difficult to explain how advanced ubiquitous devices have enabled the immediate flow of information, resulting in social learning phenomena (crowds herd towards a decision/attitude due to the influence their social network exerts over them through their ubiquitous devices). It is important for students to realize how they can use network effects towards improving their status and profile, communicating directly with their customers, addressing the right group of potential customers and providing context specific information to them. Until recently, this part of the course was delivered in the form of lectures and was supported by a case study. However, a ubiquitous environment supported by game-based learning principles is deemed ideal for the teaching of the concept in question.

Design Phase

Title: Enhancing social media presence of your electronic business

Learner's Characteristics: Learners are MBA students, with an age range from 25-40 years of age. They have already been taught concepts of electronic and mobile commerce, online marketing strategies and strategic information systems. They are familiar with the use of smartphones and tablets (most of the learners use their tablets during the lectures) and have also participated in some e-learning activities. They have not participated in any game-based or mobile learning activity. They are very demanding in terms of the effectiveness of their MBA and have set specific skills and objectives. They demand for directly putting the theoretical knowledge they have accumulated into practice.

Description: The mobile/ubiquitous GBL will invite students to manage their own virtual company. This application includes a graphical and immersive environment where students can log into and view a virtual business environment. Their task is to plan, implement and monitor the social media strategy of their business. To achieve this purpose, students can have access to a number of real-life scenarios and information and are asked to handle them in the most effective way. Depending on their actions, they receive immediate feedback and if needed, they are advised to study a specific part of the available theoretical material. The innovation exemplified by the mobile and ubiquitous technology employed is related to the fact that students can receive input in multiple forms depending on their personal profile (e.g. they can be informed on potential nearby customers and send them some push notification regarding offers they may be interested in depending on their location). Moreover, they can use their camera to upload photos on electronic social media, use the Internet to analyze collected data, use visualization tools available in their mobile devices. The application is designed to send push notification to students in order to provide them with the necessary input they should take into account to make a decision. The sooner they respond the more credits they gain. Needless to say that the effectiveness of the response is also taken into consideration. With the application being provided through a mobile device, students can easily have an immediate and effective encounter with the "market needs" (see Table 5).

This scenario will be pilot tested with graduate students and their feedback will be collected and analysed. Afterwards, the application will be revised and updated (if needed).

Table 5. The proposed framework in the instruction of e-business

The Proposed Framework in the Instruction of E-Business						
Experiential Learning Model Stage	**Learning Activity**	**Game Activity**	**Learning Goals**	**Mobile/ Ubiquitous Characteristic Used**	**GBL Concept Supported**	**Assessment**
Active Experimentation (planning, trying out gained knowledge)	"Managers" enter their office and are searching for the input they need to incorporate towards applying their social media strategy	This step can happen a) when students decide to enter the application by themselves b) when a push notification that asks students to enter the application has been sent to students. "Managers" enter their office and try to distinguish which of the given input should be included in their strategy. The system provides insight in the most important information, but the provision of such information is reducing with the progress of the student.	Prioritize the available information, according to company's needs	• Ubiquity • Localization (a push notification may sent, based on user's locality) • Interactivity (student-content) • Immersive graphical environment	• Immersive • Objectives and goals • clearly defined rules • elevated playablity	Based on their response
Concrete experience (Doing)	Having collected the data and considering of the available literature, students should plan and implement their strategy	Students should implement the actions they think that can maximize the benefits of their social media strategy. They can use virtual online social networks, send virtual push notification to virtual customers, etc. They have a number of available tools that can support almost every single action that student have decided to take.	Learn how to use the available tools and how each of these tools can support a specific strategy	• Ubiquity • Localization (can send push notification based on customer's locality) • Interactivity (student-content & student-student) • Immersive graphical environment • users have control over their devices	• Immersive • Objectives and goals • clearly defined rules • turn theory into practice	Based on their response
Reflective Observation (reviewing, reflecting of the experience)	They can understand the impact of their strategy	The game provides virtual and direct feedback regarding students' decisions. For example, if the strategy was successful, the game informs the user that the number of satisfied customers have been increased	Gain knowledge on the effectiveness of each strategy within specific context	• Ubiquity • Interactivity (student-content) • Identification/ Personalization • Immersive graphical environment • users have control over their devices	• Immersive • Objectives and goals • clearly defined rules • turn theory into practice	Based on their response (time and effectiveness)

continued on following page

Table 5. Continued

The Proposed Framework in the Instruction of E-Business						
Experiential Learning Model Stage	**Learning Activity**	**Game Activity**	**Learning Goals**	**Mobile/ Ubiquitous Characteristic Used**	**GBL Concept Supported**	**Assessment**
Abstract Conceptualization (concluding, learning from the experience)	They should take into account the feedback and experience gained, in order to enhance their knowledge and effectiveness in dealing future cases.	The game provides new input and user is asked to deal again the new cases.	Based on their performance, students are asked to apply gained knowledge and experience to new cases	• Ubiquity • Interactivity (student-content) •Identification/ Personalization • Immersive graphical environment • users have control over their devices	• Immersive • Objectives and goals • clearly defined rules • turn theory into practice	Based on their response

Implementation Phase

This scenario will be implemented in MBA students attending the e-Business course, and its duration will be two weeks. Students will be able to access the application whenever they want. However, push notifications will only be forwarded between 18:00 pm and 21:00 pm when students will be able to directly respond to the application's input. Due to the fact that this is an MBA course addressing the needs of future leaders and professionals, it is very important to make them feel confident about the effectiveness and reliability of the learning methods employed. Towards this direction, students will not be divided into groups; instead, they will all participate in this mobile/ ubiquitous GBL attempt.

Evaluation Phase

The final evaluation of the course will shed light on students' performance in the game, but will also rely on written exams. During the written exams, students will be given a specific case study and will be requested to propose a social media strategy that will optimize the company's benefits in the given context. Despite the fact that the evaluation is not fully carried out through a mobile/ubiquitous device, students will be asked to apply their experience and knowledge gained during their interaction with the mobile application.

Scenario 2: U-Commence in 3D Environments

This learning scenario has been designed to support the instruction of u-commerce in HEIs. A similar scenario has been proposed by Bouta H, Retalis S. and Paraskeva F. (2012), which was originally designed to be used in teaching Mathematics in Primary Education. This scenario is used as a basis since it ensures the provision of personalised content based on learner's needs as well as the acquisition of high-order thinking skills such as collaboration, critical thinking, and decision-making skills. The revised scenario is delivered through mobile and ubiquitous devices that access the 3D virtual environment of Active Worlds. Except for facilitating the instruction of u-commerce, this scenario is also aimed at enhancing higher-order cognitive skills such as critical thinking and decision-making. In this case, ubiquitous technology is employed to support the provision of a context-specific learning content within an engaging and immersive learning environment.

Preparation Phase

Problems to be addressed: Students usually face difficulties in understanding the concepts of ubiquity, and the way the features of ubiquitous technology can, provide unique opportunities for digital entrepreneurs when carefully adopted. Moreover, the acquisition of hands on experience regarding u-commerce may be highly demanding in terms of cost and time. On the other hand, the virtual environment of Active Worlds provides a unique environment for practical training, using role-playing learning activities. Well-defined scenarios can be represented as complex decision trees and when programmed in Active Worlds, they enable students to handle them in a realistic fashion and receive direct feedback within a risk-free experimentation environment.

Design Phase

Title: u-commerce in 3D environments

Learners' Characteristics: Learners are second year university students at the Department of Management Science and Technology of the Athens University of Economics and Business, and have already been acquainted with concepts of business strategy, business models, and infor-

mation systems. They are familiar with the use of smartphones and tablets and they have participated in learning activities within the virtual world of Second Life (as a result, they are familiar with virtual learning environments).

Description: The mobile/ubiquitous GBL will invite students to enter the virtual environment of Active Worlds using their mobile phones. This ensures the provision of a graphical and immersive environment. Students are asked to start a new or lead an existing business using u-commerce concepts and principles. They receive immediate feedback for their actions are able to virtually view the real outcome of their decisions. Students will also have the chance to improve their collaboration, critical thinking and decision-making skills via being asked to work in groups (see Table 6).

Table 7 shows the alignment of the characteristics of mobile and ubiquitous devices with GBL practices during the implementation of this scenario. This table is an extension of Table 2.

Implementation Phase

This scenario will be implemented in second year university students, and its duration will be a month. Students participating in the course will be randomly assigned to two groups. Group

Table 6. The proposed framework in the instruction of u-commerce

The Proposed Framework in the Instruction of U-Commerce						
Experiential Learning Model Stage	**Learning Activity**	**Game Activity**	**Learning Goals**	**Mobile/Ubiquitous Characteristic Used**	**GBL Concept Supported**	**Assessment**
Active Experimentation (planning, trying out gained knowledge)	Students enter the virtual environment and are asked to form groups. Each member should have an organizational role (eg CEO, CFO, CIO, etc.)	Students enter the virtual environment. They should try to persuade their peers in creating a team with a specific objective (eg the formation of a team that will lead a fashion on line shop)	Improve their communication and leadership skills	• Interactivity (student-content, student-student) • Immersive graphical environment	• Immersive • Objectives and goals • clearly defined rules	Based on their outcome (if they had a leading or a supportive role)

continued on following page

Table 6. Continued

The Proposed Framework in the Instruction of U-Commerce						
Experiential Learning Model Stage	**Learning Activity**	**Game Activity**	**Learning Goals**	**Mobile/Ubiquitous Characteristic Used**	**GBL Concept Supported**	**Assessment**
Concrete experience (Doing)	After the formation of the groups, students should collaborate in order to "create" a successful company operating in the u-commerce sector. During this phase, they are advised to apply their theoretical knowledge in order to fully exploit ubiquitous and pervasive features in their strategy.	Students would communicate in order to decide on the company's strategy and objectives. During these efforts, they would be given virtual ubiquitous devices to practice and experiment on.	Learn how to use ubiquitous tools in order to support a specific u-commerce strategy.	• Ubiquity • Interactivity (student-content & student-student). • Immersive graphical environment. • Users have control over their devices.	• Immersive • Objectives and goals • Clearly defined rules • Turn theory into practice.	Based on their response.
Reflective Observation (reviewing, reflecting of the experience)	They can understand the impact of their strategy.	The game provides virtual and direct feedback regarding students' decisions. Students can view the result of their actions in the virtual environment.	Gain knowledge on the effectiveness of each strategy within specific context. Improve their decision making and critical thinking skills.	• Ubiquity • Interactivity (student-content & student-student). • Identification/ Personalization. • Immersive graphical environment. • users have control over their devices	• Immersive • Objectives and goals. • Turn theory into practice.	Based on their response.
Abstract Conceptualization (concluding, learning from the experience)	They should take into account the feedback and experience gained, in order to enhance their knowledge and effectiveness in dealing future cases.	The game provides new input and user is asked to deal again the new cases.	Based on their performance, students are asked to apply gained knowledge and experience in new cases.	• Interactivity (student-content & student-student). • Identification/ Personalization. • Immersive graphical environment. • Users have control over their devices.	• Immersive • Objectives and goals. • Clearly defined rules. • Turn theory into practice.	Based on their response.

A will participate in the proposed mobile GBP scenario, while group B will attend traditional courses whose aim is to achieve the same learning goals as the proposed scenario. Students of Group A will be enabled to access the application whenever they want.

Evaluation Phase

The final phase of the course will rely on written exams that will be the same for both groups. It is expected that students in Group A will outperform students in Group B in terms of achieving a better performance in u-commerce and cognitive skills. Students of Group A will be, then, encouraged to evaluate the entire venture.

Table 7. Features of mobile and ubiquitous devices and their alignment to GBL practices in the u-commerce scenario

Mobile/Ubiquitous Characteristics	Description	GBL Principle	Screenshot from the Virtual Environment of Active Worlds
Ubiquity	Students use their mobile device to access the virtual environment of Active Worlds. They can access it from anywhere ,at any time. During their stay in the Active Worlds, they are asked to communicate in real time with other students and decide on their company's strategy.	Enhances student's critical thinking and decision-making ability.	Screenshot taken from CoSy_World (Bouta &Paraskeva, 2012)
Interactivity	In this scenario we can distinguish the following levels of interaction: Student-device Student-content Student-student during their collaboration and decision making process	Supports social learning, collaboration, and collaborative decision-making.	Screenshot taken from CoSy_World (Bouta et al., 2012)
Identification/ Personalization	Students receive feedback based on their progress and profile.	Allows the provision of personalized learning content.	Screenshot taken from CoSy_World (Bouta &Paraskeva, 2012)
Users have Control Over Their Devices	Users are familiar with their mobile devices. Moreover, they are also familiar with Active Worlds. As a result, they have the potential of becoming highly engaged in this learning process.	Students are highly engaged.	Screenshot taken from CoSy_World (Bouta, 2013)
Provides an Immersive Graphical Interface	Mobile devices support the provision of Virtual Reality & Augmented reality applications	The game must be immersive.	Screenshot taken from CoSy_World (Bouta, 2013)

RESEARCH IMPLICATIONS, LIMITATIONS, AND FUTURE RESEARCH

The proposed framework aims to guide academic staff towards including the use of digital games through mobile devices and increase the effectiveness of their learning activities. Specifically, at first place, it aims to increase the level of readiness of both academic and administrative HEIs staff to adopt such innovative learning practices. Secondly, this framework aims to introduce the benefits of the proposed innovative mobile GBL learning practice to HEIs staff and stimulate them to start adopting and implementing it in real cases.

Most importantly however, the presented framework makes an important contribution in current literature since it is the first research effort aimed to align digital games principles with mobile devices features and in the same time addresses Higher Education Institution's needs, characteristics and limitations. If properly implemented, the proposed framework can minimize the risks of failing in successfully design a mobile game based course and maximize the benefits by offering a well structured, motivating and engaging course to Higher Education student and updating Higher Education as whole.

However, being a design research effort, the proposed methodology has not yet been implemented in real settings with real students. However, there have been designed in detail two implementation scenarios (presented above), which are planned to be applied in real educational environments, aimed to measure the effectiveness of the proposed approach in the field of u-commerce.

The provision of implementation scenarios allows for this framework to act as a guide towards the more effective and easier adoption of the ubiquitous GBL by academic and admin HEIs staff. This in turn, maximizes the impact of this research effort in the field of u-learning and allows for its

easier adoption. Specifically, both professionals and under-graduate students have been selected as a pilot group of HEIs students to participate in and evaluate a learning process supported by the proposed framework. It is expected that students attending learning activities designed according to the proposed methodology will achieve higher progress in terms of motivation, engagement, cognitive skills and the relevant learning goals.

Finally, acting as a good practice, this methodology may initiate the further investigation of GBL u-learning. Provided that mobile and ubiquitous technologies are ever-changing and improving, there are still plenty of things that can be further investigated from an educational or business perspective. There is the need for a coordinated effort towards raising people and professionals' knowledge in terms of the varied potential of the promising mobile and ubiquitous technologies. When it comes to their educational role, being the central issue covered within the present chapter, it all boils down to the development of a robust theoretical model for the effective implementation of ubiquitous learning.

Research efforts should not accentuate the transformation of traditional and e-learning content into a mobile environment; instead they should highlight the provision of a theoretical model as regards the manner instructors can design their learning content based on the potential of mobile and ubiquitous technologies.

Towards this objective, the provision of a reusable, valid, accurate and conclusive methodology in the field of mobile GBL is of vital importance. To this end, there is the need for additional scenarios to be designed following the presented framework, implemented and evaluated across a number of students. Moreover, the presented methodology can be easily expanded and customized to address the needs and special characteristics of different learning groups (students, adult learners, professional training) in a number of learning fields and sciences, thus further enhancing its re-usability which is considered vital in the field of mobile and GBL learning.

Focusing on the field of u-commerce and its instruction, research and implementation efforts should be focused on the development of suitable learning content that can be effectively provided through mobile GBL processes. Such efforts need to be aligned with the always-changing features of mobile devices (such as interactivity, user-device communication, social networking features) in order to ensure the provision of engaging learning content.

The further implementation of ubiquitous GBL will ensure that future entrepreneurs and professionals will a) become familiar with mobile and ubiquitous devices and their potential, and b) have both theoretical and practical knowledge and skills to be effective incorporated in a business strategy plan. What is more, the acquisition of higher-order thinking skills, such as critical thinking, decision-making ability, collaboration, comparative analysis and creativity are enhanced during learning within a gaming environment. As a result, when combined with game-based learning, mobile learning can provide prospective professionals with skills and on hands-experience that will prove useful in the business arena.

Last but certainly not the least, the abovementioned research efforts call for the existence of trained and experienced staff (teaching and technical) to take over such initiatives and shoulder responsibilities. Future efforts should, subsequently, be focused on the provision of instruction in the fields of designing and implementing mobile and ubiquitous applications to support learning and gaming activities. Mobile and ubiquitous GBL has the potential to improve HEIs', instructors' and students' performance and can, hence, contribute to a social and economic development at an international level. The time has come for their

adoption and effective use to be encouraged so that the educational and business goals set can be realized.

CONCLUSION

This chapter presented a framework towards the adoption of innovative mobile/ubiquitous game-based learning practices and methodologies by Higher Education Institutions. Taking into consideration the opportunity that mobile technologies and GBL practices provide for Higher Education Institutions, as well as the fact that 21st century learners and citizens are familiar with mobile devices and services, the chapter presents the basic principles of game-based learning and align them with the identified characteristics and technological specifications of mobile and ubiquitous devices. The central features differentiating Higher Education Institutions from any other Educational Institutions were also presented, in order to be later incorporated in the proposed framework. As discussed in this chapter, instructors should invest much of their time to prepare and design their mobile/ubiquitous activity, in order to maximize their effectiveness. During these two phases, instructors should collect available data regarding their learners' characteristics and/or Higher Education restrictions, affordances or limitations. A detailed guide is proposed towards the effective preparation of mobile/ubiquitous game-based learning activities within Higher Education Institutions. This chapter also presents two implementation stances of this framework within the context of u-commerce instruction.

Conclusively, the proposed chapter provides Higher Education Institutions with the potential of effectively applying such practices, providing significant support and guidance for their step by step development. The adoption of ubiquitous and game-based learning practices will help academics and instructors improve their innovativeness and will facilitate their being smoothly and fast incorporated in Higher Education Institutions' curricula. Last but not least, the proposed framework, when effectively applied, can enhance Higher Education Institutions innovativeness, impact and competitiveness through the provision of innovative, effective, beyond state of the art and high-quality learning services to students.

REFERENCES

Abowd, G. D., & Mynatt, E. D. (2000). Charting past, present, and future research in ubiquitous computing. *ACM Transactions on Computer-Human Interaction*, 7(1), 29–58. doi:10.1145/344949.344988.

Bouta, H. (2013). *Design, development, application and evaluation of a 3D collaborative learning virtual environment for the teaching of mathematics in primary education*. (PhD Thesis). University of Piraeus, Piraeus, Greece.

Bouta, H., & Paraskeva, P. (2012). Cognitive apprenticeship theory for the teaching of mathematics in an online 3D virtual environment. *Journal of Mathematical Education in Science and Technology*, 44(2), 159–178. doi:10.1080/0020739X.2012.703334.

Bouta, H., Retalis, S., & Paraskeva, F. (2012). Utilising a collaborative macro-script to enhance student engagement: A mixed method study in a 3D virtual environment. *Computers & Education*, 58(1), 501–517. doi:10.1016/j.compedu.2011.08.031.

Brown, T. H. (2005). Towards a model for m-learning in Africa. *International Journal on E-Learning*, 4(3), 299–315.

Clarke, I. (2001). Emerging value propositions for m-commerce. *The Journal of Business Strategy*, 18(2), 133–148.

Csikszentmihalyi, M. (1975). *Beyond boredom and anxiety*. San Francisco, CA: Jossey-Bass.

Csikszentmihalyi, M. (1990). *Flow: The psychology of optimal experience*. New York: Harper and Row.

Csikszentmihalyi, M., Rathunde, K., & Whalen, S. (1993). *Talented teenagers: The roots of success and failure*. New York: Cambridge University Press.

Davies, S. P. (1993). Models and theories of programming strategy. *International Journal of Man-Machine Studies*, 39(2), 237–267. doi:10.1006/imms.1993.1061.

Deci, E. L., & Ryan, R. M. (1987). The support of autonomy and the control of behavior. *Journal of Personality and Social Psychology*, 53, 1024–1037. doi:10.1037/0022-3514.53.6.1024 PMID:3320334.

Derryberry, A. (2012). *Game-based learning ecosystem for higher education*. Sage Road Solutions.

Dewey, J. (1938). *Experience and education*. New York: MacMillan.

Din, H. W.-H. (2006). *Play to learn: Exploring online educational games in museums*. Paper presented at the International Conference on Computer Graphics and Interactive Techniques. New York, NY.

Hoffman, D. L., & Novak, T. P. (1996). Marketing in hypermedia computer-mediated environments: Conceptual foundations. *Journal of Marketing*, 3(60), 50–68. doi:10.2307/1251841.

IEEE. (2001). *Reference guide for instructional design and development*. Retrieved November 2010, from www.ieee.org/education_careers/education/reference_guide/index.html

Johnson, L., Adams, S., & Cummins, M. (2012). The NMC horizon report: 2012 higher education ed. Austin, TX: The New Media Consortium.

Kakihara, M., & Sørensen, C. (2001). Expanding the 'mobility' concept. *ACM SIGGROUP Bulletin, 22*(3), 33–37.

Kiili, K. (2005). Digital game-based learning: Towards an experiential gaming model. *The Internet and Higher Education, 8*(1), 13–24. doi:10.1016/j.iheduc.2004.12.001.

Klopfer, E., & Squire, K. (2008). Environmental detectives: The development of an augmented reality platform for environmental simulations. *Educational Technology Research and Development, 56*(2), 203–228. doi:10.1007/s11423-007-9037-6.

Kolb, D. A. (1984). *Experiential learning: Experience as the source of learning and development*. Englewood Cliffs, NJ: Prentice-Hall.

Kukulska-Hulme, A., & Traxler, J. (2005). *Mobile learning: A handbook for educators and trainers*. London: Routledge.

Lewin, K. (1951). *Field theory in social sciences*. New York: Harper & Row.

Lyytinen, K., & Yoo, Y. (2002). Research commentary: The next wave of nomadic computing. *Information Systems Research, 13*(4), 377–388. doi:10.1287/isre.13.4.377.75.

Moran, T. P., & Dourish, P. (2001). Introduction to this special issue on context aware computing. *Human-Computer Interaction, 16*(2), 87–95. doi:10.1207/S15327051HCI16234_01.

Murphy, M., & Meeker, M. (2011). *Top mobile internet trends*. KPCB Relationship Capital.

Nakamura, J., & Csikszentmihalyi, M. (2002). The concept of flow. In Snyder, C. R., & Lopez, S. J. (Eds.), *Handbook of positive psychology* (pp. 89–105). Oxford, UK: Oxford University Press.

Nielsen-Englyst, L. (2003). Game design for imaginative conceptualisation. In *Proceedings of the International Workshop on Experimental Interactive Learning in Industrial Management* (pp. 149-164). IEEE.

Pea, R., & Maldonado, H. (2006). WILD for learning: Interacting through new computing devices anytime, anywhere. In Sawyer, R. K. (Ed.), *The Cambridge handbook of the learning sciences* (pp. 427–441). Cambridge, UK: Cambridge University Press.

Peters, K. (2007). M-Learning: Positioning educators for a mobile, connected future. *International Journal of Research in Open and Distance Learning, 8*(2), 1–17.

Piaget, J. (1972). *The principles of genetic epistemology* (Mays, W., Trans.). New York: Basic Books.

Prensky, M. (2001). *The digital game-based learning revolution*. New York: McGraw-Hill.

Rao, B., & Minakakis, L. (2003). Evolution of mobile location-based services. *Communications of the ACM, 46*(12), 61–65. doi:10.1145/953460.953490.

Rollings, A., & Adams, E. (2003). *Andrew Rollings and Ernest Adams on game design*. New Riders Games.

Shabalina, O., Vorobkalov, P., Kataev, A., & Tarasenko, A. (2008). *Educational games for learning programming languages*. Paper presented at the Third International Conference Modern e-Learning. New York, NY.

Shuler, C. (2009). *Pockets of potential: Using mobile technologies to promote children's learning*. New York: The Joan Ganz Cooney Center at Sesame Workshop.

Van't Hooft, M., Swan, K. Lin, Y-M., & Cook, D. (2007). What is ubiquitous computing?. *Ubiquitous Computing in Education*, 3-17.

Vygotskiǐ, L. S. (1962). *Thought and language*. Cambridge, MA: The MIT Press. doi:10.1037/11193-000.

Walker, K. (2006). Introduction: Mapping the landscape of mobile learning. In Sharples, M. (Ed.), *Big issues in mobile learning: Report of a workshop by the kaleidoscope network of excellence mobile learning initiative*. Nottingham, UK: University of Nottingham.

Whitton, N. (2010). *Learning with digital games: A practical guide to engaging students in higher education*. New York: Routledge.

ADDITIONAL READING

Chang, W.-C., Chou, Y.-M., & Chen, K.-C. (2011). Game-based collaborative learning system. *Journal of Convergence Information Technology*, *6*(4), 273–284. doi:10.4156/jcit.vol6.issue4.30.

Chiong, C., & Shuler, C. (2010). *Learning: Is there an app for that? Investigations of children's usage and learning with mobile devices and apps*. New York: The Joan Ganz Cooney Center at Sesame Workshop.

Csikszentmihalyi, M. (2002). *Flow: The psychology of happiness*. London: Random House.

Ebner, M., & Holzinger, A. (2007). Successful implementation of user-centered game based learning in higher education: An example from civil engineering. *Computers & Education*, *49*(3), 873–890. doi:10.1016/j.compedu.2005.11.026.

Ha, I., Yoon, Y., & Choi, M. (2007). Determinants of adoption of mobile games under mobile broadband wireless access environment. *Information & Management*, *44*(3), 276–286. doi:10.1016/j.im.2007.01.001.

Huizenga, J., Admiraal, W., Akkerman, S., & ten Dam, G. (2009). Mobile game-based learning in secondary education: Engagement, motivation and learning in a mobile city game. *Journal of Computer Assisted Learning*, *25*(4), 332–344. doi:10.1111/j.1365-2729.2009.00316.x.

Kasimati, A. E., & Zamani, E. D. (2012). Using digital games to transform computer programming courses in higher education institutions. In *Proceedings of the European Innovation Forum 2012, Learning for Open Innovation*. IEEE.

MacInnes, I., Moneta, J., Caraballo, J., & Sarni, D. (2002). Business models for mobile content: The case of m-games. *Electronic Markets*, *12*(4), 218–227. doi:10.1080/101967802762553477.

Muilenburg, L. (2012). Ubiquitous learning: Strategies for pedagogy, course design, and technology. *American Journal of Distance Education*, *26*(3), 208–211. doi:10.1080/08923647.2012.644460.

Mysirlaki, S., & Paraskeva, F. (2010). Online games for the next generation of workers. *International Journal of Advance Corporate Learning*, *3*(4), 21–25.

Papastergiou, M. (2009). Digital game-based learning in high school computer science education: Impact on educational effectiveness and student motivation. *Computers & Education*, *52*(1), 1–12. doi:10.1016/j.compedu.2008.06.004.

van Staalduinen, J. P., & de Freitas, S. (2010). A game-based learning framework: Linking game design and learning outcomes. In K. MyintSwe (Ed.), Learning to play: Exploring the future of education with video games. New York: Peter Lang Publishers.

Venkatesh, V., & Bala, H. (2008). Technology acceptance model 3 and a research agenda on interventions. *Decision Sciences*, *39*(2), 273–315. doi:10.1111/j.1540-5915.2008.00192.x.

Warburton, S. (2009). Second Life in higher education: Assessing the potential for and the barriers to deploying virtual worlds in learning and teaching. *British Journal of Educational Technology*, *40*(3), 414–426. doi:10.1111/j.1467-8535.2009.00952.x.

KEY TERMS AND DEFINITIONS

Digital Game-Based Learning: The combination of fun and engagement with serious learning and interactive entertainment into a highly exciting medium.

Experiential Learning: The process of learning through direct experience.

Flow Experience: Experience of intense concentration or absolute absorption that can be observed when an individual is voluntarily involved in an activity and can lead to increased cognitive processing and intellectual capacity.

Game-Based Learning (GBL): Refers to a type of game play designed to support specific learning outcomes.

Immersive Digital Environment: An interactive, digital-virtual environment within which a user can immerse themselves.

Ubiquitous Devices: Devices that supports continuous exchange information between user, device and environment and allows somebody being available and connected at any location and any given time.

Zone of Proximal Development: Refers to the difference in students' actual ability to carry out specific tasks with and without support.

Chapter 7
The Role of Communication in Online Trust:
The Communicative Action Theory Contribution

Latifa Chaari
Higher Institute of Management of Tunis, Tunisia

ABSTRACT

This chapter aims at better understanding the behavior of the Internet user. It suggests studying the role of communication on the trust of Internet users towards commercial Websites. In order to realize this research, the authors mobilized the Communicative Action Theory of Jürgen Habermas (1987). Therefore, they have brought a new perspective in understanding online trust following action theory. For Habermas, communication is an action that depends on contextual, cultural, and human factors, which cannot be reduced to deterministic mechanisms. He deals with three types of action, which an actor might pursue following his interests, which can be instrumental, strategic, or emancipatory. The instrumental and strategic are purposive-rational actions, which aim at achieving success and at developing a calculated trust based on calculation of the advantages and the costs of the relation, whereas, the communicative action is coordinated by mutual understanding that allows the development of a relational trust based on social interactions. In communicative action, mutual understanding through language allows the social integration of actors and the coordination of their plans and their different interests. In this case, trust is based on a common definition of the situation and the resolution of conflicts of interests between actors. Internet is a medium of communication that can support the three kinds of action. The instrumental and strategic actions allow the development of calculated trust, whereas the communicative action allows the development of relational trust based on social interaction and mutual comprehension.

INTRODUCTION

The literature on information systems, marketing and e-commerce highlights the critical role of trust in success of Business/Consumer relationships (Gefen et al. 2003; Chouk and Perrien, 2003, 2004, 2006; McKnight et al. 2002; Hoffman et al. 1999). According to several researchers, the lack of trust is the main reason of Internet users' reluctance towards online shopping. Kearney has concluded that 82% of online shoppers abandon shopping from the early stages of their visits to

DOI: 10.4018/978-1-4666-4566-0.ch007

the Websites (Hausman and Siekpe, 2009). Quelch and Klein argue that *'trust is a critical factor in stimulating purchases over the Internet'* (cited by Corbitt et al. 2003, p.1). Online, the consumer cannot verify the quality of the offered products / services, and he cannot control the security of his personal and financial information. Thereby, he feels that his private life is totally dominated by Internet technology which exploits his vulnerability and protects the interest of the economic system (Salter, 2005). The opportunistic behavior of firms and the colonization of consumer's life world by the Web site explain his reject and his resistance from buying online.

Considering the prominent place of trust in Business/Consumer relationships, researches have focused on studying the determining factors of this phenomenon. One stream of search is characterized by a technological determinism highlighting the role of Websites' technical characteristics as perceived by Internet users (Gefen et al, 2003). Another stream deals with individual variables related to Internet user like psychological antecedents (Lundgren and Walczuch, 2004), familiarity with an Internet vendor, (Gefen, 2000; Bhattacherjee, 2002). Another research avenue was interested in the variables related to the merchant like organizational reputation (McKnight et al. 2002) and perceived size of the organization (Jarvenpaa et al. 2000). Some researchers were concerned with the pivotal role of communication in the development of online trust. Morgan and Hunt (1994), highlight that communication is a very important factor for trust development. These authors have defined communication as the formal and informal sharing of relevant, secure, and real time information between a consumer and a vendor. Chouk and Perrien, (2004) have shown the role of third parties in influencing user's attitude and trust development towards an E-merchant. However, most researchers were focused on technical and persuasive aspects of online communication and neglect to conceive it as an action that implies all participants (users

and merchant) in a social interaction. According to Shih, (2004), the purchase of an online product implies intense information communication, and an interactive behavior between firms and Internet users.

Following an instrumental rationality, the positivist approach of communication conceives the commercial Web site as a technology that supports the egocentric needs and the utilitarian interests of the parties (Firms and Internet users), protecting the capitalism ideology as the dominant class (Salter, 2005). It is a medium used by the firms to colonize the Internet users' world and to directly change their attitudes and behaviors. Along those lines, most of commercial Websites conceive the communication as one-way directed by the firm towards the Internet user where the technical features of the Website are used as a means to manipulate the Internet users' behavior. Kozinets, (2002), assumes that the market has for a long time dominated the consumer's identity who is considered passive and devoid of expression. With the theory of communicative action of Jürgen Habermas, (1987), there has been a major paradigm shift. The conviction that technology directly influences the users' behavior gives place to a new conception according to which the Internet user is considered as an actor who can accept, refuse and even criticize the received message from the commercial Website. Indeed, the interactivity which characterizes commercial Websites support new forms of communication in two directions, exceeding the traditional and the determinist forms of communication between the firms and Internet users. Among these new communication forms, we mention e-mailing, discussion forums and chat rooms which are open for all users and which make the Website a place of exchange of rational and ethical discussions as it is promoted by the democratic project of Jürgen Habermas.

The objective of our chapter is to study the role of communicative activity in the development of consumer online trust. Trust based on social interaction, not on the calculus of utilitarian interests of the relation. In this chapter, the communication is not conceptualized as a linear process oriented toward a purpose, rather, it's an action oriented towards mutual understanding and coordination of action between participants. To address the role of communication in building online trust, this chapter focuses on the Habermas' theory of action, (1987) to highlight the importance of discourse and mutual understanding in establishing collaboration and resolving conflicts, and then the development of mutual trust based on social interaction. From this perspective, shopping online is no longer seen as a passive action, it becomes an autonomous action where consumers participate actively in purchase decision. Commercial Web sites are useful not only for control but also for effective communication between actors in a democratic manner.

BACKGROUND

Definition of Trust

The literature on trust highlights its importance in exchange relations (Lewis and Weigert, 1985; Williamson, 1981, 1993). Trust is defined as a psychological state or as a risk-taking behavior or the will to completely engage in such a behavior (Chouk and Perrian, 2004, 2006). Trust is the basis of any exchange relation. Certain researchers assert that trust is difficult to define (Mayer, Davis and Schoorman, 1995). It is a vague and complex concept (Moran and Hoy, 2000), often used in exchange with other similar concepts like cooperation, confidence and predictability (Mayer, Davis and Schoorman, 1995). Furthermore, trust is a concept of multiple facets which incorporates cognitive, emotional and behavioral dimensions (Lewis and Weigert, 1985). Trust has been widely studied in several disciplines (Murphy and Blessinger, 2003). It is a multidisciplinary concept which has been the object of study of several approaches, what makes it difficult to give a universal defini-

tion. According to the philosophic approach, trust is relevant to an ethically and morally justified behavior (Moran and Hoy, 2000). In economics, trust is the rational calculation of the costs and the profits of an exchange relation (Moran and Hoy, 2000). In sociology, researchers consider trust the basis of any relation in a social system, and not a psychological state individually taken (Lewis and Weigert, 1985). In accordance with this perspective, trust allows reducing complexity, developing group solidarity, and continuing the relation (Lewis and Weigert, 1985). The psycho-sociological approach conceives trust as the expectations and the willingness of the other part during the exchange, the risks associated to these expectations, and the contextual factors that promote or inhibit trust development (Lee and Turban, 2001). In the theories of organizations, trust concept is often related to the concepts of coordination and cooperation (Mayer, Davis and Schoorman, 1995). From the outset of its integration in Marketing, trust has been associated with cooperation in the broad sense; it is considered a determining factor of commercial exchange relations (Morgan and Hunt, 1994). Literature searches have allowed us to identify two big research models for trust: the instrumental model and the relational model.

The instrumental model of trust starts from the hypothesis according to which trust is a rational decision based on calculation and a comparison of the future gains and losses of the exchange relation. According to the economist Williamson, one of the great researchers who have defended this model, trust appears as a rational behavior against risk, based on estimations of the other's action and on his *skills* or his capacity to act in the desired manner. In this perspective, trust is based on a cognitive process which responds to a need for maximization of the utility by a rational actor. It is defined as *"the anticipation that a partner in the exchange will not engage in an opportunist behavior, even in the presence of short-term compensatory incentives and long-term incentive profits"* (Williamson, 1993).

The relational model conceives trust as a social orientation towards the other. Particular emphasis is being placed on the social and the relational aspects of trust rather than the instrumental aspects. The advocates of this model highlight the importance of the relational and social factors of trust and define it as an affection related to the nature of the social link. Trust is a phenomenon which develops over time. It is an expectation based on the interactions and the lived experiences with others (Davenport and McLaughlin, 2004). It depends on previous actions, and cooperative behavior of the other party. In other words, trust is the result of mutual understanding of goals. It is based on a specific number of variables in the context of interaction such as previous experiences, social standards, and the sense of identity drawn from the relation with others based upon the alignment of the intentions and the motivations (Davenport and McLaughlin, 2004). In accordance with this orientation, trust must not be conceived as exclusively based on calculations guided by personal motivations, but it should be mainly based on interactions and interpersonal judgments in a given social context. Social sciences have been for a long time dominated by the model of rational choice according to which individuals are led by the realization of their personal interests and motivated by the maximization of their gains and the minimization of their losses in exchange relations. According to this vision, the relationships between the individuals are explained by an instrumental perspective apart from the social context wherein these relationships are held.

Trust Typologies

A distinction is often drawn between two forms of trust. The first is named 'rational trust' that is based on interest calculation. The second form of trust is termed as 'relational trust' which is essentially based on past exchanges, reputation and the respect for the standards by the exchange partner. In the same direction, McAllister (1995)

distinguishes between two types of trust: cognitive trust which refers to a rational analysis of trust consequences, and emotional trust which is based on social interactions.

Influenced by economic sciences, social sciences have tried to determine the rational bases of trust (Gléonnec, 2004). By doing so, the expectation of the other's behavior through calculation reduces the uncertainty and allows making the best decision. Thereby, this trust refers to the rational calculation of the advantages and the risks of a relation (Williamson, 1993). Generally the choice of the partner is based on the available knowledge and on "good reasons" (McAllister, 1995). This rational, calculated or cognitive trust is essentially based on individual beliefs concerning the skills of the exchange partner in order to protect itself against opportunist behavior. In his theory of rational choice relative to trust, the sociologist Coleman has conceived trust as being *"a particular level of subjective probability that another agent or group of agents will perform a particular action. When we say somebody is reliable, we have implicitly intended the probability, that he will execute a beneficial action, that he is well brought up to engage in this form of cooperation"* (Williamson, 1993). Cognitive trust is based on a rational prediction of the partner's behavior and the relation consequences. In this type of trust, the actor tries to objectively and reflectively evaluate the skills, the reliability and the reputation of his partner (McAllister, 1995).

Trust is said relational or affective when it is grounded on emotional and affective connections (McAllister, 1995). In this situation, the exchange relation is essentially motivated by social rather than instrumental needs, such as the need for identification and group belonging. On the basis of the identity notion of symbolic interactionism of Mead, relational trust is induced by a sense of identity drawn by the established relation among the members of a social group (Habermas, 1987). In the same direction, the sociologist Luhmann asserts that trust is a function of a learning process, and a body of knowledge acquired through simple interactions in the social system (cited by Gléonnec, 2004). Trust is thereby the product of the social relationships established between the actors. The belonging to the same culture and the same social context facilitates the development of trust relationships between actors, based on shared rules. Through his structuration theory, Giddens shows, that the 'routinization' of trust relationships allows concretizing them in the social system structures, as he asserts *"relations are trust based links, this trust is not given, but worked on, and this significant work is a mutual mechanism of self-disclosure"* (Gléonnec, 2004).

Online Trust

The proliferation of researches on online trust asserts the great interest given to this concept in marketing and in information systems researches (Chervany and McKnight, 2002; Gefen et al. 2003). Several researches have shown that the success of e-commerce in the context of Business to Consumer is mainly determined by the consumers' trust towards the vendors or the products which they cannot see or touch (Chouk and Perrien, 2003). For some researchers, trust is *"the foundation of any online exchange relation"* (Chouk and Perrien, 2003; Gefen and Straub, 2004, p. 2). By doing so, the lack of trust becomes one of the main reasons explaining the Internet users' reluctance towards online shopping (Lee and Turban, 2000; Pavlou, 2003). The need for trust is very important in an electronic context regarding the complexity and the uncertainty surrounding this new context (Emurian and wang, 2005). Trust allows the Internet user to exceed the feelings of uncertainty and risk, and to engage in a behavior allowing personal information exchange and online shopping (McKnight et al. 2002).

Recognizing the role played by online trust, several researches have been interested on the study of the factors promoting its development. A literature review on online trust enables us to

observe that the majority of the researches focus on the role of factors related to the consumer such as the tendency to trust, and the familiarity with the site (Bhattacherjee, 2002; Gefen et al. 2003; Chouk and Perrien, 2003, 2006). Other researches emphasize technical variables related to the site such as the ease of use (Gefen et al., 2003), the quality of the site (McKnight et al., 2002), and its respect to the private life. Another research avenue highlights the importance of the factors related to the merchant such as his reputation (McKnight et al., 2002). A new research conducted by Chouk and Perrien (2006), highlights the importance of the role of third parties in trust development (the partner companies, the word-of-mouth). However, few researches were interested in the role of communication as an action in building trust towards a commercial Website. In order to fill the gap, this chapter tries to understand the role of communication as interaction and an action on consumer trust towards a commercial Website.

Definition of Communication

The concept of communication has attracted researchers in several domains (Mattelart, 2004). With the absence of a common paradigm, and the diversity of definitions, we are assisting at an interdisciplinary domain. This concept was the center of study of three big approaches: the positivist, the interactionism and the critical approach. Thereby, unlike the positivist approach which has defined communication as a simple message transmission between two isolated subjects independent from the context, the interactionism or the pragmatic approach conceives communication as an act of interaction between social actors. The interactionism approach of communication suggests the emergence of a new approach related to a tradition of realism criticism (Habermas, 1987), based on the interpretation and the understanding of resistance, and on the concepts of 'power' and 'ideology' of Marx. All of the three approaches appeal to images completely different from human beings.

On the one side, the positivist approach limits the conception of communication to simple symbols transmission *from the source to a passive receiver*. On the other side, the interactive approach conceives communication as an interaction process, in a shared social context. According to the social critical approach the actors are endowed with an action capacity, they are capable of judging the truth, the sincerity, and the normative correctness of the received message. Thereby the receiver plays *the role of the intelligent human being who tries to understand the message* (Lee and Ngwenyama, 1997). In the present research we are going to adopt the critical and emancipatory approach of Jürgen Habermas, (1987) which emphasizes the skills of the actor and his capacity to react to a received message. Within the context of a commercial Website, the Internet user does not longer passively receive the company's sent information. It is an actor who has a high degree of autonomy and can participle at the of message., he tries to understand the message and he has at the same time the possibility to criticize it either through accepting or refusing it.

The Positivist Model of Communication

This most dominating paradigm in communication research starts from the assumption that it is possible to anticipate media effects on the passive receiver. In this context, we can quote the works of Charcot on *hypnosis* and Le Bon on the *Psychology of Crowds* (Ravault, 1986). The researches were interested in studying the effect of communicational products on receivers while disregarding the way in which they are interpreting these products. According to this model, communication is conceived as a linear schema based on transmitter/ receiver relation. Shannon has defined communication in his information theory, as *"The transmission of a message from a place to another"* (Abric, 1999). In the same perspective, functionalist sociology of media is interested in the analysis of media

effects as it is based on the hypothesis *"who says what through which channel to whom and with which effect"* (Mattelart, 2004). In this approach, the power of media consists in changing the attitudes, the knowledge, the feelings, the values, and the behavior of the receivers (Spitulnik, 1993; Mattelart, 2004). Several studies have focused on the measuring of media effect on individuals' perception. In his *"hypodermic needle"* model and the media's direct effect, Lasswell considers *"the audience as a neutral target which blindly obeys the stimulus-response theory"* (Mattelart, 2004). Similarly, the theory of the interpersonal influence or *"two-step flux"* of Lazarsfeld conceives communication as a double stage process, where the role of *"opinion leaders"* turns to be very important (Maigret, 2003). In the first stage, we find the individuals who detain information because they pay a strong attention to media and they also distinguish themselves by their capacity to translate the political aims through communication (Maigret, 2003). Second, we find those who depend on others to obtain information because they attend less broadcast media (Mattelart, 2004).

Most of the researchers who belong to the positivist model of communication have focused on the 'broadcast' aspect of the communicational process, while the 'reception' aspect is totally discarded. The signification accorded to the 'message' as well as the interactions between both parties are totally neglected by these researchers (Ravault, 1986). It is irrelevant to know whether the message receiver correctly understands its contents, or even to know whether he agrees with what has been included. This determinist paradigm in communication research was questioned by several researchers, where the attention is turned to the interpretative practices of the receivers (Spitulnik, 1993). Thereby, this paradigm has been the object of several critics. On the one hand because it neglects the individuals' role in communication process, since they are considered actors capable of speaking and acting (Habermas, 1987). On the other hand, this technological determinism ignores the fact that communication is an interaction producing a link between actors who are widely influenced by their social context (Abric, 1999).

The Interactionism Model of Communication (Palo Alto School)

During the forties, the mechanistic model of communication was questioned by the psychosocial theories on interaction and by the followers of Palo Alto school such as Hall, Goffman, Walzlawick, etc. This is a paradigm change according to which communication is conceived as an interaction situation. According to pragmatism, interaction is a global and complicated situation impossible to be decomposed into isolated variables following a linear model. By dissolving the dichotomy between message production and reception, there is a dynamic relation between the two parties where the receivers are as much sense producers as the producers themselves.

Moreover, with linguistic pragmatics authors like Grice, Searle and Austin, communication is considered as a social act through which the speaker gets involved into a real social relationship with his interlocutor. In his speech act theory, Austin distinguishes between the descriptive sense of the sentence that is its informative content through which we present a state of affairs, and the pragmatic sense according to which speech acts assume a function and create a relation between both interlocutors. To speak is *to act* at the same time, that is to achieve an act as a request, an order, an assertion, a promise, an excuse, a thanking, etc. the purpose of which is to establish a relation with the other (Habermas, 1987). The meaning of the sentence takes into consideration the context of its utterance and the conditions of its use, and not only its informative and descriptive content. With pragmatics, we have noted a

major change in communication conception as a transmission process to a social relationship conception (Lohisse, 2001). Regardless of whether we are speaking about a communicative action or a speech act, the main interest of pragmatics is focused on the importance of the context and the subject-subject relations, and not on subject-object relations, which are considered manipulative or instrumental through means of communication.

The Critical Approach to Communication (Frankfurt School)

This involves a major paradigm change in the research on communication emanating from Neo-Marxism of Frankfurt school Germany. The advantage of this approach focuses on the problematic of the power of the media and on the way they serve the interests of the dominant class. The ideological role of media in the reproduction of society's dominant structures was widely challenged by the advocates of this approach such as Horkheimer, Adorno, Marcuse and recently Habermas (Maigret, 2003). According to a critical perspective, Adorno and Horkheimer have studied the problem of the instrumental reason. They have noticed that the instrumental reason is a teleological reason relative to a goal. In the same direction, Habermas, (1987) have criticized the instrumental reason embodied in the mechanistic conception of communication which marginalizes the individual's freedom and the role which he can play in the communication process. In his critical theory of capitalism, Jürgen Habermas (1987; 1991, 1992) relates the concept of communication to the action in universal pragmatics based on the notion of speech. This speech which is based on the validity of the claims and three reports to the world indented to guarantee an agreement or a common definition of the situation.

MAIN FOCUS OF CHAPTER: THE CONTRIBUTION OF HABERMAS'S COMMUNICATIVE ACTION THEORY TO COMMUNICATION AND TRUST IN COMMERCIAL WEBSITE

Types of Actions on a Commercial Website

The work of Habermas (1987) aims at defending and reconstructing the modernity project, through his particular Theory of Communicative Action. His significant contribution is in constructing the concept of communicative rationality which is different from the instrumental and the strategic rationality. The reason should be communicational and pragmatic, based on the interaction and "the other's attitude" as asserted by Mead (Hinkle, 1992). According to Habermas (1987), communication is a lever for a democratic society. His critical theory thus excludes all forms of rhetorical speech and interactions, which are based on power and are at the origin of a distorted communication (loss of communicative action).

The theory of communicative action outlines two types of action which an actor might pursue: goal directed action which can be instrumental or strategic, and communicative action. This classification is based on the distinction of Austin between locutionary, perlocutionary, and illocutionary act. On the one hand, the instrumental and strategic actions are purposive-rational actions that aim at achieving success. On the other hand, communicative action is an action that is oriented towards mutual understanding through the use of language, argumentation and the participation of all participants in an open discourse. Based on this duality of action, Habermas (1987) distinguishes between two types of rationality: communicative rationality and goal-directed rationality. Communicative rationality is a situation where the stakeholders in a discussion achieve the same meaning. Whereas, goal directed rationality is a situation where one party aims at achieving the success of his action. According to Habermas (1987), the life world is a cultural resource which enables the construction of common sense and mutual understanding, providing a communicative rationality. On the other hand, the systems are guided by instrumental (technical) and strategic rationality. The lack of communicative activity is explained by the colonization of the life world by instrumental and strategic rationality (Habermas, 1987; Salter, 2005). The colonization aspects of Web site are at the origin of lack of online trust and the consumer's resistance from buying online. The emancipatory interests of consumer can only be achieved through open and equal discourse that guarantees his participation in the communication process.

The commercial Web site is a medium of communication that can support the three types of action. It can be used by firms and consumers to achieve their utilitarian goals (instrumental action). It can be used also to persuade consumers through social influence (strategic action). Online, the actors may also pursue communicative action coordinated by norms of action to achieve mutual understanding. The interactivity nature of the Web makes the Web site as a support of communicative action. Indeed, the consumers are no longer defined as passive recipients, but as active participants that contribute at the criticism and production of message. This point of view breaks down the distinction between firm and audiences allowing the development and sharing of information through a democratic discourse (Salter, 2005). This democratic discourse online is constituted of communicative actions that guarantee the participation of all actors. The instrumental and strategic actions allow the systemic reproduction and the development of calculated trust. On the other hand, the communicative action allows the development of mutual comprehension, the social integration of actors and their socialization, which constituted a vector for the development of relational trust based essentially on social interaction.

Goal Directed Action on a Commercial Website

Instrumental Action on a Commercial Website

The instrumental or technical action aims at reaching success in a nonsocial context (Habermas, 1987). The execution of this action requires the rational choice of a means or instruments. In this case, we are speaking about instrumental rationality related to the choice of the effective means in order to efficiently reach certain purposes. According to Habermas (1987), *"We call instrumental an action that is directed to success, when we consider it under the aspect of the pursuit of the action's technical rules and when we estimate the degree of efficiency of an intervention in a context of states of affaires and events."* In an instrumental orientation, communication in a commercial Web site is expressed in terms of simple information transmission from the firm to the Internet user in order to change his attitude and behavior. The instrumental communication refers to the effectiveness and to the efficiency of media in the transmission of information to the Internet user to satisfy his utilitarian needs for information research (Hoffman and Novak, 2000; Hoffman et al., 1999; Hoffman and Duhachek, 2003). The behavior of the Internet user is directed towards a goal of monitoring the virtual environmental through the research of commercial and technical information on the firm's services, on the sales' contract, and especially on the offered products or services (Guizon, 2001; Hoffman et al., 1999).

The Internet has the potential to change the way in which consumers shop as well as the structure of firm's sales. It gives to consumers the opportunities to search customized information in a real time and in a low cost (Ratchford et al., 2001, p.6). According to the rational choice approach, consumers often choose the sources that convey the information he needs at a lower cost to maximize the net benefit of search (Ratchford et al., 2001, p. 4). The consumer uses the commercial Web site as a tool to reduce the uncertainty through detailed, precise and clear information which allows him to make an assessment and to achieve the best choice during his shopping activity. The features of Web site that stimulate and influence consumer's decision to shop online can be summarized in vast selection of product, screening of the large number of options to reduce the costs of search, and product comparison among alternatives to help consumer in making his purchase decision (Alba et al., 1997, p. 9).

Alba et al. (1997, p. 3) focus on the critical attributes affecting the adoption of online shopping.

- Faithful reproduction of descriptive and experiential product information.
- A greatly expanded universe of offerings relative to what can be accessed now through local or catalog shopping.
- An efficient means of screening the offerings to find the most appealing options for more detailed consideration.
- Unimpeded search across stores and brands.
- Memory for past selection, which simplifies information search and purchase decisions.

The Uses and Gratifications Theory of Katz is based on the receiver's capacity of selection of the message according to his psychological needs and his goals (Maigret, 2004). This current research supposes that the receiver's behavior is directed to goals, he chooses the messages suitable with his needs. This behavior impulses individual to choose the means of communication that satisfies him. The researchers belonging to the Uses and Gratifications Theory suppose that the message receivers are usually motivated by purposes related to costs reduction and realization of the economic, cognitive, and emotional profits. These goals constitute determiners of the persuasive effect of the message and they are used by firms as action instruments.

Strategic Action on a Commercial Website

The strategic action is a social action directed to success like the instrumental action. To realize his goals, the actor directs his actions according to the other's decisions by trying to influence them. This action is described by Habermas (1987) as the mutual influence of partners acting rationally with respect to a goal, it is defined as being, *"an action directed to success, when we consider it under the aspect of a rational choice and when we estimate the degree of efficiency of the influence on the decisions of a rational partner"* (Habermas, 1987). Since it has emerged in a social system that determines and structures the behavior of social group members, the social action is essentially based on the reciprocity and the mutual adjustment of the social relationships. In a social group, the individuals often look for the group approval; they avoid any action that contradicts the group standards. Thereby, the social influence results from a process of normative dependence according to which the individuals avoid any disagreement with the group members. A disagreement, that risks to lose the social identity and the group rejection.

In order to show the importance of the phenomenon of social influence in a given social system, Lazarsfeld and his colleagues have showed the insufficiency of the direct effect model of media on the modification of consumer attitudes. Opinion leadership is a two stages communication process where the most exposed people to media can exercise an influence on their acquaintances through the transmission of the received information (Vernette and Flores, 2004). In marketing, the leadership phenomenon was used by researchers to explain the consumers' behavior and highlight the importance of the interpersonal communication networks in the efficiency of the firm's communication policies (Ben Miled and Louarn, 1994).

Indeed, opinion leaders form a very interesting target for advertising communication (Vernette and Flores, 2004), regarding their potential in the consumers' persuasion and their opinions change. Some researchers speak about *influencers* (Vernette and Flores, 2004) rather than leaders, by valorizing the interactive process in information exchange. This interpersonal communication is strengthened by online interactive exchanges. Indeed, the emergence of online discussion groups (forum, chat) allows the development of the virtual communities based on social standards permitting the formation of a specific social identity. Within these communities, certain Internet users are considered as "engines" which influence the opinion of the other group members (Vernette and Flores, 2004).

Communicative and Emancipatory Action on a Commercial Website

Communication as a phenomenon has knew a major paradigm change, which moves from an activity directed to a goal to communicative action thanks to the theory of action of Mead which is based on intersubjectivity (Habermas, 1987). The actions of actors are not only directed to success, efficiency, and personal goals realization, but they can be similarly directed to an agreement between the participants. Guided by this approach, the actors are neither opportunist nor egocentric; however, they pursue their own goals by coordinating their actions with their partners through communicative action and the use of language. This action is defined by Habermas (1987) to be an action where *"the action plans of the participating actors are not coordinated by egocentric calculations of success, but by mutual understanding acts."* Unlike the goal directed action where language is used for persuading the other and change his attitudes, in communicative action, language is a medium of mutual understanding, it is a medium of facts, experiences and shared values, through which each participant whatever was his social status has the liberty to accept, refuse or criticize a linguistic proposal on the basis of arguments (Habermas, 1987). Thereby, each interlocutor is independent to respond with "yes" or "no" to questions of truth, normative accuracy or sincerity. His speech act can be questioned either under the truth aspect with which the speaker aspires with his statement (objective world), or under the correctness aspect with which he refers to a normative context (social context) and under the sincerity aspect when he expresses a real-life experience (subjective world). This arguments exchange resulted in an ideal speech situation, which has guaranteed the participation of all actors where the power is only assigned to the best argument. The discussion's objective is to commonly define a situation based on shared meanings of reality.

The information transfer-model of communication is becoming obsolete in electronic environments (Riva & Galimberti, 1998). This model neglects the cooperative feature of communication based on reciprocal responsibility for successful interaction among interlocutors. According to this model of communication, information exists independently of the receivers. However, with the pragmatic point of view of communication, there is a big paradigm shift in the conceptualization of Internet users. They are no longer considered as passive receivers of information. The participants in the communication "*have some common ground for shared beliefs, recognize reciprocal expectations, and accept rules for interaction which serve as necessary anchors in the development of interaction*" (Riva & Galimberti, 1998). In interaction, the participants not only act as goal-directed individuals, but they actively collaborate to achieve the same meaning.

The researches on online shopping experiences have shown that the Internet users' behavior is not limited to the realization of their instrumental goals; rather, it extends to interactions research and social relationships (Dolen et al., 2007). Thereby, in order to satisfy these relational needs and within the framework of the change of marketing paradigms from a transactional marketing to a relational and interactive marketing, several commercial Websites are endowed with commercial

communication practices through which Internet users are no longer considered as passive targets who passively receive the transmitted message by the firm or by opinion leaders. On the contrary, these practices allow the users to be active, autonomous and responsible for their shopping. In this respect, the commercial Website becomes a communicational and technical object supporting an intersubjective communication as the 'shared construction of meanings' (Habermas, 1987; Riva & Galimberti, 1998). This commercial Website is defined as "*a technical object having a 'strength' which can favor practices of interaction, exchange, and coordination between individuals and groups*" (Proulx, 2007). The interactivity supplied by the Web site is defined by Alba et al, (1997, p. 2) as "*a continuous construct capturing the quality of two-way communication between two parties.*" It is "*as an element through which customers and marketing managers interact in order to satisfy the objectives of both parties*" (Dolen et al. 2007).

In order to follow the technological changes and the market requirements, the firms have increasingly implemented commercial platforms of online communication such as e-mailing, chat and discussion forums, thereby promoting a direct contact with Internet users and moving beyond the forms of forced transactions. The technology Internet offers to firms and consumers new forms of communication like chatting online. Nowadays, chat is an important element in many commercial Web sites. According to Zinkhan and his colleagues (2003, p. 1), relationships marketing based on chat rooms can improve the recognition of products and services. These authors noted that installations of chat programs on Website can increase purchases online by 41%.

According to Dolen et al. (2007), the models of online discussion are classified in dyadic communication or in discussion groups. The dyadic communication can be introduced by the customer or by the firm. In the communication introduced by the Internet user and called *customers' discussion,* the firm's customer service answers the questions formulated by Internet users in real time, in the form of recent information on the products, delivery, and other secondary services. In the *institutional discussion*, the firm sends dialog boxes, at any time, in the form of information to its Internet users to help them and to follow them. Among discussion forums, we may quote the commercial discussion groups. These new interaction forms introduced by the firm correspond to "*scheduled online meetings, to which a restricted number of customers are invited to actively participate under the form of a written discussion about a commercial subject, and a representative of the company plays the role of the discussion moderator*" (Dolen et al., 2007). During this form of interaction, the Internet users, endowed with a critical capacity regarding the message contents, discuss controversy subjects concerning the products design, the price, the after-sale services, etc.

With this form of interaction, the relations between the firm and its Internet users move downright from the linear give-receive logic to the circular give-receive-give logic. These public spaces of communication, according to Habermas (1987), promote an open interaction between the group members which manifests itself in the active division of experiences, the free information exchange, the support and the answer to the representative's questions (Dolen et al., 2007). This form of interactional communication has the potential to increase online trust based on personalized offers.

Effect of Action on Trust towards a Commercial Website

Relation between Goal-Directed Action and Calculated Trust in a Commercial Website

The behavior of the Internet user is characterized by information research, which facilitates the shopping decision. On the other side, the firm aims through marketing communication at increasing its online turnover and thus profit seeking through its instrumental actions in order to manipulate the Internet user's decision. Generally, the firm expects the consumer's reaction regarding the transmitted message in order to control the situation (Read and Wilson, 2008). These instrumental and strategic actions of participants in the commercial Web site tend to reproduce the same order of colonization of the Internet users' public sphere by the Website (Habermas, 1987). The developed trust in this case is based on the anticipation and the participants' rational calculation of the advantages and the disadvantages of the exchange relation (Williamson, 1993). The behavior of both parties which is directed towards a goal allows trust development based on the egocentric calculation of profits and the costs of the exchange relation. This conception of trust towards a commercial Website is very reductionist; it neglects the relational aspects in communication, which allows the development of an emotional trust. Communication in the commercial Web site is an interaction, it allows weaving interpersonal relations between the participants, and thereby we are speaking about relational trust.

Relation between Communicational and Emancipatory Action and Relational Trust towards a Commercial Website

Habermas (1987) postulates that the rational and mutual agreement in discussions results in a trust based on an argumentation and discussions. In the communicational action, the participants in the interaction end in a process of cooperative and intersubjective interpretation of the situation (Habermas, 1987). This exchange process of arguments aims at actions' coordination on the basis of the other's understanding and on common conviction. Besides truth, the rationality of actions depends on other criteria like the normative correctness of the actions, and the subjective truthfulness for self-meaning representations. The shared values, the sincerity and the mutual agreement allow, beyond the calculated interest, the allocation of a relational trust based on mutual understanding rather than rational calculation of the individual interests. According to the interactionism, the online communication is no longer conceived as a simple relation of mutual influences in transmitter-receiver linearity; on the contrary, the interlocutors collaborate in a dynamic process of argumentation to commonly interpret the situation. It is a process which allows problems and conflicts resolution, questions answering and expectations alignment (Morgan and Hunt, 1994). During this go and come interaction, of disturbances and compensations, strong social relationships emerge as a vector of a relational trust developed with time.

Through language, communicational action allows the symbolic reproduction of the lived world through *cultural reproduction, the social integration of the actors,* and their *socialization.* Within the framework of communicational action in a commercial Website, the linguistic interactions opened in interactive discussions about products, about purchasing terms and about shared experiences promote mutual understanding and action coordination of the participants through the realization of online shopping based on personalized offers. The communicational interaction also permits the actors' social integration through the stabilization of group solidarity (Habermas, 1987). Within online participating members, we perceive social orders which reproduce certain characteristics of face to face reality (Proulx, 2007). The virtual communities for example, are governed by mechanisms of auto-production of rules and standards, implicit and explicit codes of conduct that adjust the community functioning and determine the behavior of the participating actors. According to Proulx (2006), the virtual community indicates the *sense of belonging* which is constituted by chat users, or a discussion forum, these participants share tastes, values, interests or common objectives, and even an authentic col-

lective project. Online communication forms a social and a symbolic environment in which the participants can develop a sense of belonging to a group and can build a collective identity. During online communication, the sharing of values, beliefs and common interests, creates relations in spite of the geographical disparity. During this type of communication, geographical closeness and elements of real mode exchange disappear as essential dimensions of community feeling (Proulx, 2006, 2007).

Within the context of the social interactions based on communication, the actor is a product of interaction process during which he is subject to a socialization process through which, he is going to interiorize standards and behavior schemas. The socialization implies the acquisition of knowledge and values, which allow the individual to interact and to live in a social system. It is a *"social process by which norms, attitudes, motivations, and behavior are transmitted from specific sources to the learner"* (Ozmete and Hira, 2011). As it has been asserted by Mead, this learning process allows reducing ambiguities for future behaviors, so that the actor will no longer need to look for information in order to evaluate the situation before acting (Habermas, 1987). The "I" is not an innate property in the actor; it is rather, the product of the interaction process and socialization. The "I" reflects the approval or the disapproval granted by the group to the individual (Habermas, 1987). According to Mead, the identity is formed through the adoption of points of view of others in a social interaction. This author has shown how the child learns from childhood (games) to adopt different roles. When he becomes mature, he understands that he should adopt certain standards of behaviors to be accepted. Mead speaks of "generalized other" that designs the norms of social group that should be respected by all the members and through which they construct their identities. Identity is made from the way the individual's action is perceived by the social system.

The subject forms his personality if the world in which he acts confers to him sense through the participation in a rational discussion (Grossein, Melot, and Schluchter, 2005).

In electronic setting, the consumers learn attitudes and purchase behaviors through written messages sent by their peers or by agents-learner as socialization agents. Consumer socialization refers to the process by which individual consumers learn skills, knowledge, and attitudes from others through communication, which then assist them in functioning as consumers in the marketplace (Ward, 1974). This socialization is a result of a process of learning acquired through interactions between the consumer and socialization agents. This process of socialization implies modeling, reinforcement, and social interaction mechanisms (Nizet, 2007). In this process, the socialization agent use written messages such as positive and negative comments, discussions, experiences, advices to alter the behavior of consumer in social interaction. Through this process, consumer becomes socialized to adopt some products and behaviors that are news to him; also he avoids punishment and looks for rewards as member of social group coordinated through communication.

CONTRIBUTION AND RECOMMENDATIONS

We proposed studying consumer behavior in online ubiquities environment from the critical paradigm. This chapter emphasizes the role of communicative activity in developing online consumer's trust. This activity that aims at the coordination of contradictory interests based on mutual understanding, social integration of consumers and their online socialization. The online discourse allows the development of shared knowledge that is based on intersubjectivity and reciprocity in a social interaction. The development online trust is not limited to the rational calculation of the relation's advantages and disadvantages in a

deterministic process of communication, but it extends to the other's knowledge and the development of a relation with consumer (Gléonnec, 2004). The communication in a Website should be studied and understood through the interaction of three factors: the cognitive, the psychological, and the social factor. The firms must consider the customer as the focus of their business activities and consider profit as a consequence of customer orientation (Corbitt et al., 2003, p.3). Currently, several researches on the behavior of online consumers have shown that the latter increasingly seek social interaction in addition to their instrumental purposes (Dolen et al., 2007). The instrumental aspect of the Website is certainly obvious, but with the competition between the already existing commercial Websites, the Internet user seeks far more than the Website utility. The control of the technical elements is essential, but not sufficient, it would be necessary to control all the elements which affect communication and the Internet users' trust in an online vendor and especially the psycho-sociologic elements. In this direction, companies are recommended to concentrate not only on the utilitarian values of their commercial Web sites, rather, they have to maintain solid relations and long-term with their consumers as vector for online trust.

Internet technology has dual aspects. On the one hand, it can be used by firms to support the utilitarian interests of consumers and to preserve the ideology of economy sphere as a dominated class. From this point view, the use of Internet contributes to systemic reproduction of life world which conserves the same structure of domination in relationships between firms and their consumers. On the other hand, the characteristics and possibilities offered by the technology Internet form an entirely new situation of communication with consumers (Fam et al., 2004, p. 2). This technology has the potential to facilitate interactions between buyers and sellers. It offers new forms of communication that enable a veritable mutual comprehension and coordination of actions based on social interaction (Habermas, 1987). Studying the consumer behavior in online ubiquities online environment from the critical paradigm allows the transition of information power from firms to the consumer. This shift is called by Anderson as "shift activeness" (Fam et al., 2004, p. 2). The consumers are no longer considered as passive. For instance, they become responsible to decide what topic should be included by the firm; they can also negotiate and participate actively in the production product and information.

The adoption of this new conception gives a new understanding to the relation between firm and consumer in online environment. This understanding must place the consumer in the center of firm's consideration as active and independent actor. The earliest models of consumer behavior in online environment (Gefen et al., 2003) that are based on the famous approach Stimulus-Organism-Response where consumer can be influenced and controlled efficiently, must fail and are no longer suitable. With the assumption that consumer communicate actively online, the information is made no only by the firm but also by consumers (Fam et al., 2004, p. 3). This why, several commercial Web sites facilitate feedback when complaints about firms can be made. The paradigm centered on one-way process of communication is incomplete and should be replaced by another paradigm that valorizes two-way process of communication based on the dynamic aspect of interaction between consumers and marketers. In the interaction process, consumers are no longer passive receiver of message. Rather, they can influence the process of communication by searching, selecting and interpreting information.

FUTURE RESEARCH DIRECTIONS

Due to time, the chapter is a review of literature; it does not include empirical findings. A further study may be necessary to include a framework, which tests the theoretical concepts of Habermas' communicative action theory. This empirical work is essential to evaluate the effect of instrumental, strategic and communicational on online consumer's trust and provide additional guidelines to improve the topic and resolve the problem of consumer reluctance from buying online.

For further studies, we propose another empirical direction that will be more appropriate to understand the consumer behavior online through a netnographic method based on the study of communicational interactions online as it is formulated by Kozinets (2009).

CONCLUSION

The theory of communicative action of Habermas (1987) provides us with a theoretical framework to understand the Internet users' trust. This theory suggests that the consumers' role changes. They become active constructors of their own experience. Online communication has to change its conception. Communicating consists in establishing an interaction relation based on a process of mutual understanding which allows establishing social relationships and expressing motivations, interests and needs of all the parties where Internet users are considered as social actors (Habermas, 1987). It is a dialogue, which promotes trust through problems resolution, questions answering and expectations alignment (Morgan and Hunt, 1994). The study carried out by Duncan and Moriarty (1998) on relational marketing shows that the more the firms engage in communicational and interactive relations with Internet users, the more they will be capable of promoting online trust. Online communication must be conceived as an attempt at coordinating actions between consumers and firms based on social interaction. This interaction result in common goals that neither party can achieve individually (Stewart and Pavlou, 2002).

REFERENCES

Abric, J. (1999). *Psychologie de la communication: Théories et méthodes.* Paris, France: Armand Colin.

Aknoun, A. (1993). La communication démocratique. *Cahiers Internationaux de Sociologie, 94,* 51–70.

Alba, J. L., Weitz, B., Janiszewski, R. L., Sawyer, A., & Wood, S. (1997). Interactive home shopping: Consumer, retailer, and manufacturer incentives to participate in electronic marketplaces. *Journal of Marketing, 61*(3), 38–53. doi:10.2307/1251788.

Ben Miled, H., & Louarn, P. (1994). Analyse comparative de deux échelles de mesure du leadershio d'opinion: Validité et interprétation. *Recherche et Applications en Marketing, 9*(4), 23–51. doi:10.1177/076737019400900402.

Bhattacherjee, A. (2002). Individual trust in online firms: Scale development and initial test. *Journal of Management Information Systems, 19*(1), 211–241.

Chervany, N., & McKnight, D. (2002). What trust means in e-commerce customer relationships: An interdisciplinary conceptual typology. *International Journal of Electronic Commerce, 6*(2), 35–59.

Chouk, I., & Perrien, J. (2003). *Les déterminants de la confiance du consommateur lors d'un achat sur un site marchand: Proposition d'un cadre de recherche préliminaire. Centre de recherche DMSP. Cahier n° 318.* Université Paris-Dauphine.

Chouk, I., & Perrien, J. (2004). Les facteurs expliquant la confiance du consommateur lors d'un achat sur un site marchand: Une étude exploratoire. *Décisions Marketing,* 75-86.

Chouk, I., & Perrien, J. (2006). Déterminants de la confiance du consommateur vis-vis d'un site marchand internet non familier: Une approche par le rôle des tiers. In *Actes du XXII Congrès AFM – 11 et 12 Mai.*

Coleman, J., & Fararo, T. (1992). *Rational choice theory advocacy and critique: Key issues in sociological theory.* London: Sage Publications.

Corbitt, B., & Thanasankit, T., & Yi. (2003). Trust and e-commerce: A study of consumer perceptions. *Electronic Commerce Research and Applications, 2,* 203–215. doi:10.1016/S1567-4223(03)00024-3.

Davenport, E., & McLaughlin, L. (2004). Interpersonal trust in online partnerships: The challenge of representation. In Iivonen, M., & Huotari, M. L. (Eds.), *Trust in knowledge management and systems in organizations.* Hershey, PA: Idea Group Publishing. doi:10.4018/978-1-59140-126-1.ch005.

Dolen, W. M., Dabholkar, P. A., & Ruyter, K. (2007). La satisfaction envers les discussions en ligne de clients: L'influence des attributs technologiques perçues, des caractéristiques du groupe de discussion et du style de communication du conseiller. *Recherche et Applications en Marketing, 22*(3), 83–111. doi:10.1177/076737010702200306.

Duncan, T., & Moriarty, S. E. (1998). A communication-based marketing. *Journal of Marketing, 62,* 1–13. doi:10.2307/1252157.

Emurian, H., & Wang, Y. (2005). An overview of online trust: Concepts, elements, and implications. *Computers in Human Behavior, 21,* 105–125. doi:10.1016/j.chb.2003.11.008.

Fam, K. S., Foscht, T., & Collins, R. D. (2004). Trust and the online relationships—An exploratory study of from New Zealand. *Tourism Management, 1*(3).

Gefen, D. (2000). E-commerce: The role of familiarity and trust. *The International Journal of Management Science, 28,* 725–737.

Gefen, D., Karahanna, E., & Straub, D. (2003). Trust and TAM in online shopping: An integrated model. *Management Information Systems Quarterly, 27*(1), 51–90.

Gefen, D., & Straub, D. (2004). Consumer trust in B2C e-commerce and the importance of social presence. *Omega, 32*, 407–424. doi:10.1016/j.omega.2004.01.006.

Gléonnec, M. (2004). Confiance et usage des technologies d'information et de communication. *Consommations et Sociétés, 4.*

Grossein, J. P., Melot, R., & Schluchter, W. (2005). Action, ordre et culture: Eléments d'un programme de recherche Wébérien. *Revue Francaise de Sociologie, 46*(4), 653–683.

Guizon, A. H. (2001). Le comportement du consommateur en ligne est-il différent de son comportement en magasin? *Recherche et Applications en Marketing, 16*(3).

Habermas, J. (1987). *Raison et légitimité: Problèmes de légitimation dans le capitalisme avancé* (Lacoste, J., Trans.). Paris, France: Payot.

Habermas, J. (1987). *Théorie de l'agir communicationnel: Rationalité de l'agir et rationalisation de la société* (*Vol. 1*). (Ferry, J.-M., Trans.). Paris, France: Fayard.

Habermas, J. (1987). *Théorie de l'agir communicationnel: Pour une critique de la raison fonctionnaliste* (*Vol. 2*). (Schlegel, J.-L., Trans.). Paris, France: Fayard.

Habermas, J. (1991). *Morale et communication: Conscience morale et activité communicationnelle.* (C. Bouchindhomme, Trans.). Paris, France: Les éditions du CERF.

Habermas, J. (1992). *De l'éthique de la discussion.* (M. Hunyadi, Trans.). Paris, France: Les éditions du CERF.

Habermas, J. (1998). *On the pragmatics of communication* (Cooke, M., Ed.). Cambridge, MA: The MIT Press.

Hausman, A. V., & Siekpe, J. S. (2009). The effect of web interface features on consumer online purchase. *Journal of Business Research, 62*, 5–13. doi:10.1016/j.jbusres.2008.01.018.

Hinkle, G. J. (1992). Habermas Mead and rationality. *Studies in Symbolic Interaction, 15*(3), 315–331. doi:10.1525/si.1992.15.3.315.

Hoffman, D. L. Novak. T. P., & Schlosser, A. (2000). *Consumer control in online environments* (Working Paper, 25). Fevrier.

Hoffman, D. L., & Duhachek, A. (2003). The influence of goal-directed and experiential activities on online flow experiences. *Journal of Consumer Psychology, 13*(1-2).

Hoffman, D. L., Novak, T. P., & Peralta, M. (1999). Building consumer trust online. *Communications of the ACM, 42*(4). doi:10.1145/299157.299175 PMID:11543550.

Jarvenpaa, S. L., Tranctinsky, N., & Vitale, M. (2000). Consumer trust in an internet store. *Information Technology Management, 1*, 45–71. doi:10.1023/A:1019104520776.

Kozinets, R. V. (2002). Can consumer escape the market? Emancipatory illumination from burning man. *The Journal of Consumer Research, 29.*

Kozinets, R. V. (2009). *Netnography: Doing ethnographic research online.* London: Sage Publications.

Lee, M., & Turban, E. (2000). A trust model for consumer internet shopping. *International Journal of Electronic Commerce, 6*(1).

Lewis, D., & Weigert, A. (1985). Trust as social reality. *Social Forces, 63*(4), 967–985.

Lohisse, J. (2001). La communication de la transmission à la relation. In Thoveron, G. (Ed.), *Culture et communication.* Brussels, Belgium: Éditions De Boeck Université.

Loilier, T., & Tellier, A. (2004). Comment peut-on se faire confiance sans se voir? Le cas du développement des logiciels libres. *AIMS Management*, *7*, 275–306.

Lu, Y., & Wilson, E. (2008). Communication goals and online persuasion: An empirical examination. *Computers in Human Behavior*, *24*, 2554–2577. doi:10.1016/j.chb.2008.02.021.

Lundgren, H., & Walczuch, R. (2004). Psychological antecedents of institution-based trust in e-retailing. *Information & Management*, *42*, 159–177. doi:10.1016/j.im.2003.12.009.

Maigret, E. (2003). *Sociologie de la communication et des médias*. Paris, France: Armand Colin.

Martin, H., Chris, J., & Marcus, N. (2006). The influence of avatars on consumer shopping behavior. *Journal of Marketing*, *70*, 19–36. doi:10.1509/jmkg.70.4.19.

Mattelart, A., & Mattelart, M. (2004). Histoire des théories de la communication. Paris, France: Ed.s de la Découverte.

Mayer, R. C., Davis, J. H., & Schoorman, F. D. (1995). An integrative model of organizational trust. *Academy of Management Review*, *20*(3), 709–734.

McAllister, D. J. (1995). Affect and cognition based trust as foundations for interpersonal cooperation in organizations. *Academy of Management Journal*, *38*(1), 24–59. doi:10.2307/256727.

McKnight, H., Choudhury, V., & Kacmar, C. (2002). The impact of initial trust on intentions to transact with a web site: A trust building model. *The Journal of Strategic Information Systems*, *11*, 297–323. doi:10.1016/S0963-8687(02)00020-3.

Meunier, J., & Peraya, D. (1993). *Introduction aux théories de la communication: Analyse sémio-pragmatique de la communication médiatique*. Brussels, Belgium: De Boeck Université.

Miled, H. B., & Louarn, P. (1994). Analyse comparative de deux échelles de mesure du leadership d'opinion: Validité et interprétation. *Recherche et Applications en Marketing*, *9*(4), 23–51. doi:10.1177/076737019400900402.

Moran, M. T., & Hoy, W. K. (2000). A multidisciplinary analysis of the nature, meaning, and measurement of trust. *Review of Educational Research*, *70*(4), 547–593. doi:10.3102/00346543070004547.

Morgan, R. M., & Hunt, S. D. (1994). The commitment-trust theory of relationship marketing. *Journal of Marketing*, *58*(3), 20–38. doi:10.2307/1252308.

Murphy, G. B., & Blessinger, A. A. (2003). Perceptions of no-name recognition business to consumer e-commerce trustworthiness: The effectiveness of potential influence tactics. *The Journal of High Technology Management Research*, *14*(1), 71–92. doi:10.1016/S1047-8310(03)00005-1.

Ngwenyama, O. K., & Lee, A. S. (1997). Communication richness in electronic mail: Critical social theory and the contextuality of meaning. *MIS Quartely*, *21*(2), 145–167. doi:10.2307/249417.

Nizet, J. (2007). *La sociologie de Anthony Giddens*. Paris, France: Éditions La Découverte.

Ozmete, E., & Hira, T. (2011). Conceptual analysis of behavioral theories/models: Application to financial behavior. *European Journal of Soil Science*, *18*(3), 386–404.

Pavlou, P. (2003). Consumer acceptance of electronic commerce: Integrating trust and risk with the technology acceptance model. *International Journal of Electronic Commerce*, *7*(3), 101–134.

Proulx, S. (2006). *Communautés virtuelles: Ce qui fait lien* (pp. 13–26). Québec: Presses de l'Université Laval.

Proulx, S. (2007). L'usage des objets communicationnels: L'inscription dans le tissu social. *La société de la connaissance à l'ère de la vie numérique*, 104-111.

Ratchford, B., Talukdar, D., & Lee, M. S. (2001). A model of consumer choice of the internet as an information source. *International Journal of Electronic Commerce*, *5*(3), 7–21.

Ravault, R. J. (1986). Défense de l'identité culturelle par les réseaux traditionnels de 'coerséduction'. *Revue Internationale de Science Politique*, *7*(3), 251–280. doi:10.1177/019251218600700304.

Riva, G., & Galimberti, C. (1998). Computermediated communication: Identity and social interaction in an electronic environment. *Genetic, Social, and General Psychology Monographs*, *124*, 434–464.

Salter, L. (2005). Colonization tendencies in the development of the world wide web. *New Media & Society*, *7*(3), 291–309. doi:10.1177/1461444805050762.

Shih, H. P. (2004). An empirical study on predicting user acceptance of e-shopping on the web. *Information & Management*, *41*.

Spitulnik, D. (1993). Anthropology and mass media. *Annual Review of Anthropology*, *22*, 293–315. doi:10.1146/annurev.an.22.100193.001453.

Stewart, D. W., & Pavlou, P. A. (2002). From consumer response to active consumer: Measuring the effectiveness of interactive media. *Journal of the Academy of Marketing Science*, *30*(376).

Vernette, E., & Flores, L. (2004). Communiquez avec les leaders d'opinion en marketing: Comment et dans quels médias? *Decisions Marketing*, *35*, 23–37.

Ward, S. (1974). Consumer socialization. *The Journal of Consumer Research*, *1*(2), 1–14. doi:10.1086/208584.

Williamson, O. E. (1981). The economics of organization: The transaction cost approach. *American Journal of Sociology*, *87*(3), 548–577. doi:10.1086/227496.

Williamson, O. E. (1993). Calculativeness, trust, and economic organization. *The Journal of Law & Economics*, *36*(1), 453–486. doi:10.1086/467284.

Zinkhan, G. M., Kwak, H., Morrison, M., & Peters, C. O. (2003). Web-based chatting: Consumer communication in cyberspace. *Journal of Consumer Psychology*, *13*(1-2), 17–27. doi:10.1207/S15327663JCP13-1&2_02.

ADDITIONAL READING

Chebat, J. C., & Grenon, M. (1979). Note sur le pouvoir publicitaire. *Revue Francaise de Sociologie*, *20*(4), 733–745. doi:10.2307/3321225.

Ghiglione, R. (1986). *L'homme communiquant*. Paris, France: Armand Collin.

Godes, D., & Mayzlen, D. (2004). Using online conversation to study word of mouth communication. *Marketing Science*, *23*(4), 545–560. doi:10.1287/mksc.1040.0071.

Mucchielli, A., Corbalan, J. A., & Ferrandez, V. (2001). *Théorie des processus de la communication*. Paris, France: Armand Collins.

Searle, J. (1976). A classification of illocutionary acts. *Language in Society*, *5*(1), 1–23. doi:10.1017/S0047404500006837.

Shalin, D. (1992). Introduction: Habermas, pragmatism, interactionism. *Symbolic Interaction*, *15*(3), 251–259. doi:10.1525/si.1992.15.3.251.

Sharma, A., & Sheth, J. N. (2004). Web-based marketing the coming revolution in marketing thought and strategy. *Journal of Business Research, 59*, 696–702. doi:10.1016/S0148-2963(02)00350-8.

Te'eni, D. (2001). A cognitive affective model of organizational communication for designing IT. *Management Information Systems Quarterly, 25*(2), 251–312. doi:10.2307/3250931.

Vernette, E. (2007). Le leadership en marketing: Une double force d'attraction et de conviction. In *6ème Congrès Tendances du Marketing, Paris, Janvier 26-27*.

KEY TERMS AND DEFINITIONS

Calculated Trust: Refers to the rational calculation of the advantages and the risks relative to a relation. It is essentially based on individual beliefs concerning the skills of the exchange partner.

Communicative Action: It is a form of communication based on interaction between all actors and that aim at achieving collective understanding.

Instrumental Action: It is an action that aims at reaching success in a nonsocial context. It refers to the choice of the effective means in order to efficiently reach desired goals.

Mutual Comprehension: It is the accord or the consensus established between actors through the use of discourse and argumentation based on universal norms the equity and the participation of all parties involved in communication.

Online Trust: Consumer's expectation that the Website will not exploit his vulnerability. It is not only based on the rational calculation of the advantages and the risks inherent to relationship. It is the product of the coordination of action and mutual understanding between actors through language in a social interaction.

Relational Trust: Relational trust is grounded on emotional and affective connections. It is the product of the shared norms and social relationships established between the actors.

Strategic Action: It is a social action oriented to success like the instrumental action. To realize his goals, the actor directs his actions according to the other's decisions by trying to influence them.

Chapter 8

Evaluation of South African Universities' Web Portal Interfaces using a Triangulation of Ubiquitous Computing Evaluation Areas and Technology Acceptance Model

Vathiswa M. Booi
Tshwane University of Technology, South Africa

George E.M. Ditsa
Tshwane University of Technology, South Africa

ABSTRACT

There are growing concerns over the user friendliness and other usability issues of South African Universities' Web Portal Interfaces (UWPIs), which obviously will negate the user acceptance of the UWPIs. The main goal of this study is to develop a framework that could be used to evaluate and provide additional guidelines to improve the Usability and User Acceptance of South African UWPIs. The study applies a triangulation of Ubiquitous computing Evaluation Areas (UEAs) and the Technology Acceptance Model (TAM) as theoretical foundations to derive the research model. Multiple regression and stepwise regression analyses are used. The results suggest that Interaction and Invisibility of UWPIs are the most important measures that have a huge impact on user acceptance and usability, respectively. The results of the study provide guidelines for the design and development of South Africa UWPIs to meet their usability and user acceptance.

DOI: 10.4018/978-1-4666-4566-0.ch008

INTRODUCTION

This study is about the usability and user acceptance of Web Portal Interfaces of South African Universities. Usability and user acceptance problems of Computer System Websites and Interfaces attracted many researchers from different domains such as psychology, human factors, human computer interaction and management because of the occurrences of problems and the growing concerns associated with them. Different methods have been identified to help solve these problems.

These growing concerns over usability of the UWPIs will obviously have a negative impact on the user acceptance of the Web portal interfaces. Human Computer Interaction (HCI) standards have three goals that must be met when designing interfaces (Battleson, 2000): (a) provide support to enable users to achieve their goals and to meet their needs; (b) provide the ease of use with minimal errors; and (c) provide a pleasant interface design. Even though Websites or Web Portal Interfaces may be highly usable and may be considered as such, there are no guarantees that they will be acceptable to the users (Davis, 1989). Davis (1989) further argues that HCI research concentrates on usability as if it is a prerequisite of acceptance and overlooked some concepts of acceptability of new technologies.

Two major methodologies for usability testing which are, laboratory studies (user participation) and field studies were identified in the work of Zhang and Adipat (2005). Interface design process involves user participation and it has been considered as the best practice in the HCI domain and it was used in this study. User participatory methodology is triangulated with field study methodology in this study; whereby users were required to evaluate UWPIs in laboratory settings while responding to the questionnaire survey for this study. Questionnaire based on the research model formulated for this study was used in conducting the evaluation of the UWPIs. A pre-test and pilot test of the questionnaire was conducted

and data collected was analyzed manually. Data collected for the main survey was analyzed using SPSS. The results indicate that invisibility, application robustness and appeal of South African UWPIs give rise to the usability of the interfaces which subsequently lead to user acceptance of the portals. They also suggest that Interaction of the UWPIs have a huge impact on user acceptance. This study provides guidelines for the development and evaluation of South African UWPIs for their usability and user acceptance.

BACKGROUND

Computer System Websites and Interfaces can only add value to institutions or individuals if the systems are usable and acceptable. In his work, Nielson (1993) defines usability as a quality characteristic that measures how easy the user interfaces are for the user to use. A well-defined definition from the International Standard Organization (ISO 9241-11, 2006) defines usability as the effectiveness, efficiency and satisfaction of user requirements. Usability is intended to provide guidance to the following types of users: interface designers, who are expected to apply it during the development process; developers, who are expected to apply it during the design and implementation of system functionalities; evaluators, who are to be responsible for ensuring that products meet their recommendations and buyers are also highlighted, as they are expected to reference it during product procurement.

In their work, Nielson (1993) and Kamarulzaman (2005) state that system acceptability describes whether the system or application satisfies all needs and requirements of all stakeholders. Dillon (2001) describes user acceptance as the demonstrable preparedness within a group of users to use information technology for the preferred task. Winkler (2001) and Manouselis & Sampson (2004) explain that Web Portal is a term that is used to refer to Internet search and navigation sites that provides the starting point for Web visitors to explore and access information on the World Wide Web (WWW). The Internet Portal or Web Portal and their interfaces are described by IBM (2000) as ubiquitous, which means being or seeming to be present anytime, anywhere.

Academic institutions depend heavily on their Web portals to provide all users and stakeholders with a wide range of services and information such as: application for admissions; online registrations; academic records; leave application systems; time tables; etc. With the growing needs for Web portals to deliver these services, it means that academic institutions must pay more attention to how effective their Web portals are, how easy they are to navigate and how efficient they are.

The Higher Education Sector in South Africa consists of 23 universities, which are categories as follows: 11 traditional universities; 6 comprehensive universities (merger between Traditional universities and Technikons); and 6 universities of technology (merger between Technikons). All these universities have one major goal, which is to provide quality information and knowledge to students, staff and the general public to sustain competitive advantage locally and globally. Web portals are provided as a means of making sure that the universities achieve this goal. With the functions and services offered by universities, the question to be asked is: are users and stakeholders happy about what they are getting in terms of portal interface usability, information content, as well as their functionalities? This question raised some concerns; hence it is justifiable to evaluate university Web portal interfaces for their usability and user acceptance to make ratings and recommendations for their improvement. In order to evaluate Web portal interfaces for their usability and user acceptance a framework is needed, which will work as a guideline for evaluation.

Different frameworks for evaluating usability of ubiquitous computing applications have been developed. To mention but are few the following:

integrated usability evaluation methods (Al-Wabil and Al-Khalifa, 2009); usability evaluation framework for ubiquitous computing devices (Kim, et al., 2008); and Ubiquitous computing Evaluation Areas (Scholtz and Consolvo, 2004). There are also a number of user acceptance models that have been developed with well-known examples which include: Triandis' Theoretical Framework by Trandis (1971), Technology Acceptance Model by Davis (1986), and Theory of Planned Behavior by Ajzen (1991).

Research Problem

Web Portal Interface users are experiencing serious usability issues due to the fact that they cannot execute or complete simple tasks online. These Web portal interfaces suffer from a number of weaknesses such as technical difficulties, user unfriendliness and other usability issues. There are increasing alarms over the technical difficulties, user friendliness and other usability issues of South African UWPIs. Some of these issues raised question whether these Web portal interfaces are evaluated for usability before being presented to the public and whether the users accept these university Web portals. These usability issues will obviously have a negative impact on the user acceptance of the UWPIs.

University Web portals and their interfaces being ubiquitous computing applications, the research problem that this study therefore sought to provide answers to is: what ubiquitous criteria are used in evaluating South African Universities Web Portal Interfaces for their usability and user acceptance?

Following from the purpose of the study and research problem, the main objective addressed in this study is to select and use appropriate usability and user acceptance criteria to evaluate South African UWPIs for their Usability and User Acceptance and to provide a framework and guidelines for the improvement of them.

Related Work

In the literature, different methods to solve the problems associated with usability and user acceptance of Computer Systems Websites and Interfaces have been suggested. Kamarulzaman (2005) states the importance of evaluating new Websites and Web portal interfaces. He further argues that evaluations are useful tools for uncovering any potential problems of usability and user acceptance.

The following section presents a review of some academic Web portal evaluations for their usability and user acceptance, followed by frameworks developed and used in evaluating Web Portal Interfaces for their usability and user acceptance.

Academic Web Portal Evaluations for Usability and User Acceptance

In 2001, Zaphiris and Ellis empirically investigated the ranking and correlation between accessibility and usability of the top USA universities Websites. Two automatic evaluation tools, Bobby and LIFT, were used to measure the accessibility and usability of the top fifty universities. They described Bobby as the most widely used automatic accessibility tool, which also recommends effective Web Page Authoring for special Web browsers (e.g. the one that reads text aloud using a speech synthesizer for blind users). LIFT provides a number of catastrophic errors, e.g., errors that disable users to complete tasks, major errors such as the ones causing major impediments, minor errors such as nuisances for the users, and also cosmetic errors with low priority. Furthermore, LIFT provides a rating in a scale of excellent, good, fair and poor.

Masrek et al. (2009) adopted and adapted an infamous information system success model by Delone and McClean (1992, 2000). The purpose was to examine the effectiveness of a library portal at the University of Technology, MARA. A total of four hundred questionnaires were distributed to students in the Faculty of Information Management. These students were chosen because of their knowledge about portals. The students rated highly all the information quality attributes, namely, completeness, comprehensiveness, accuracy, timeliness, reliability and appropriateness of format.

In their study, Du Toit and Bothma (2009) investigated usability of the Website of the Department of Marketing and Retail Management (DMRM) in the University of South Africa. The purpose was to determine best practice guidelines for the development of a new departmental Website. A more structured and student-oriented approach was identified, which include usability principles to redevelop the DMRM's Websites. The approach was initially made up of five stages, which are: (1) a heuristic evaluation; (2) questionnaire-based evaluation; (3) lab-based usability study including both students and staff who are interacting with the Website; (4) tool-based automated evaluation; and (5) focus groups with students and lecturers. They have based their study on Mustafa and Al-Zou'bi (2005) study. In their study (Mustafa and Al-Zou'bi, 2005) had a set of criteria which served as the heuristics for the evaluation.

Barnard (2007) conducted a research to determine the extent to which an online community portal could manage the information needs of alumni stakeholders in the South African Higher Education Sector (SAHES). The purpose of the research was to establish an online virtual community Web portal for the University of Johannesburg alumni in order to upkeep a tailor-made approach in terms of information content, dissemination, context and commerce. The Web portals would also encourage valuable conversation between stakeholders despite location and time. A theoretical framework was established to use as a foundation from which the empirical research was conducted. University of Johannesburg was used as a case study and questionnaires were distributed to graduates at a graduation ceremony with the aim of determining what their information needs were and the content required in an online community portal. The results indicate that an online community portal could manage the information needs of alumni in South Africa. Subsequently, a prototype was proposed for an online community portal for SAHES alumni that would have a major impact on the information and communication needs of alumni for the benefit of the alumni stakeholders and even other Higher Education Institutions in South Africa.

A group of researchers from University of Maryland conducted a research that performed usability evaluation for the Master of Information Management (MIM) program Website to determine whether their Websites meet the needs of the users (Nielson, 2001). The evaluation methods used were focused on user testing task and heuristic evaluations were performed for these tasks. Future Websites design recommendations were based on the findings from the evaluations.

Usability Evaluation Frameworks of Web Portal Interfaces

In 2009, Al-Wabil and Al-Khalifa conducted a study that presented a framework developed for effectively incorporating Usability Evaluation Methods (UEMs) in usability evaluations by matching the methods' capabilities and limitations with a classification of usability problems. The developed framework was used to evaluate the usability of Mawhiba Web Portal with the identified sample which demonstrated how better coverage of usability issues had been achieved. A heuristic evaluation of the portal was based on Nielson's (2001) heuristics together with the "think-aloud protocol" to discover usability issues and to provide insight to some of the difficulties.

In their study, Kim et al. (2008) derived Ubiquitous Evaluation Factors by collecting and integrating the current usability and ubiquitous factors. The framework was developed for a Web-based system, allowing real product evaluation and making comparison of usability and evaluation

scores to be obtained. Twenty-six usability factors were used in developing the new usability system and these factors were based on characteristics of ubiquitous computing. Evaluation scores in each evaluation area were calculated and the usability performance in each device could be compared using the standardized device's components. The use of the new usability evaluation system was expected to improve IT product's usability performance. In their conclusion, it was mentioned that the framework was applied successfully to the Mawhiba Web Portal and it was also envisioned that the adoption of the developed framework could be applied to Web application evaluation studies and provide developers with informed decision.

Scholtz and Consolvo (2004) identified the need for an evaluation framework as a way of: (1) improving comparability across research efforts; (2) creating explicit structures which can be made complete and comprehensive; (3) a framework leading to the development of ubiquitous computing specific discount evaluation techniques for rapid and less costly evaluations. They incorporated ideas of usability evaluation from different researchers such as Bellotti et al. (2002), Mankoff et al. (2003), Jameson (2003), and Freidman and Kahn (2003) to form an evaluation framework which is referred to as Ubiquitous computing Evaluation Areas (UEAs). These UEAs exhibit the Interaction, Appeal, Adoption, Application Robustness, Attention, Conceptual Model, Impact and Side Effects, Invisibility, and Trust in the application area and presented with their respective conceptual measurement and metric.

User Acceptance Frameworks

The Theory of Reasoned Action (TRA) was proposed by Ajzen and Fishbein (1975 & 1980). TRA was formulated after trying to estimate the discrepancy between attitude and behavior. TRA suggests that a person's behavior is determined by his/her intention to execute the behavior and that this intention is in turn a function of his/her attitude towards the behavior and his/her subjective norm. TRA components consists of three general constructs which are: behavioral intention (*BI*), attitude (*A*), and Subjective Norm (*SN*). They further argue that TRA suggests that a person's behavioral intention depends on the person's attitude about the behavior and subjective norms ($BI = A + SN$).

TRA has been revised and extended into Theory of Planned Behavior (TPB) by Ajzen (1985). This revised and extended model included the addition of one main predictor, perceived behavioral control. Miller (2005) explained that the addition was made to account for times when people have the aim of carrying out a behavior, but the actual behavior is dissatisfying because they lack confidence or control over behavior.

TRA has been used by some IS researchers in an attempt to explain users' behavior (Davis, 1989; Davis et al., 1989; Venkatesh & Davis, 1996; Venkatesh and Morris, 2000). TRA has been deemed useful but it also has been seen as somewhat incomplete, in that it leaves aside factors that could have influence on behavioral intentions and behavior itself (Ditsa, 2003). Triandis (1971) presented a theoretical framework, which focuses on the relationships of values, attitude, and other attained behavioral dispositions to action or behavior. He further argued that behavior is influenced by social norms: these depend on messages received from others and reflect what the individuals think they should do. Triandis (1980) stated that habits are both direct and indirect determinants of behavior as well as the facilitating conditions. The frameworks emphasis is based on the fact that the occurrence of doing or using something creates a behavior and the internalization of the probabilities and values (Ditsa, 2003). He also mentioned that the values act creates one of the factors of behavioral intentions to behave, which are important factors of behavior.

Technology Acceptance Model (TAM) (Davis, 1989) is regarded as the most noticeable model describing the acceptance computer technology.

Research had identified TAM as a cost effective tool for predicting user acceptance of systems (Dillon & Morris, 1996; Park, 2006). Perceived usefulness and perceived ease of use are described by Dillon and Morris (1996) as factors that predict user acceptance of a technology. Ondin (2007) argues that substantial theoretical and empirical support has accumulated in favor of TAM compared with alternative models such as the Theory of Reasoned Action (TRA) and the Theory of Planned Behavior.

From the literature reviewed, there is limited evidence discussing the issues of the usability evaluation and user acceptance in South African universities. Subsequently there are limited criteria for evaluating ubiquitous computer applications of South African Universities for their usability and user acceptance.

The next section presents in detail the theoretical frameworks underpinning this study leading to the research model. Hypotheses were formulated based on the research model.

THEORETICAL UNDERPINNINGS OF THE STUDY

This section first presents the details of TAM which is used as one of the theoretical foundation for this study. This is followed by a detailed discussion of the Ubiquitous Computing Evaluations Areas (UEAs) Framework which is the other theoretical framework, which is triangulated with TAM to form the research model for the study.

Technology Acceptance Model

Technology Acceptance Model (TAM) is one of the theoretical foundations underpinning this study. TAM was selected for this study based on the fact that all usability and user acceptance aspects are covered in the model. Davis (1986) developed TAM which is an adaptation of TRA. He further argues that TAM uses TRA as a theoretical basis for specifying the linkages between the two key beliefs for system acceptance measures which are: (1) perceived ease of use, and (2) perceived usefulness as well as users' attitudes, intentions and the actual computer adoption behavior. He states that according to TAM, usage of information systems is determined by users' intention to use a system, which in turn is determined by the users' beliefs about the system. TAM has been compared to other theoretical models aimed at understanding IS adoption behavior and has been found to have similar or has better explanatory power than TRA and TPB (Davis, 1986).

The key constructs of TAM as depicted in Figure 1 are: Perceived Ease of Use (PEOU); Perceived Usefulness (PU); External variables (E); Attitude towards using (A); Behavioral Intention to use (BI) and the Actual System Use (SU).

Key Constructs of TAM

Perceived Usefulness

Perceived Usefulness (PU) is defined as the users' subjective probability that using a certain application system will increase his or her job performance (Davis et al., 1989, Dillon and Morris, 1996, Ondin, 2007, Hong et al, 2002). Thong et al. (2002) propose that PU has a direct influence on adoption intention and PEOU has both a direct effect and an indirect effect on intention through PU (Davis, 1989). PU can be affected by various external factors over and above PEOU. Increased PEOU can contribute towards performance as would be expected and it would have direct effect on PU (Davis, 1986; Davis et al, 1989). Thus:

$$PU = PEOU + E$$

Perceived Ease of Use

Perceived Ease of Use (PEOU) is defined as a degree to which prospective users expect the target system to be free without effort (Davis et al., 1989, Dillon and Morris, 1996, Hong et al., 2002, Ondin, 2007). According to some theories PEOU can be determined by external variables. Thus:

$$PEOU = E$$

External Variables

External variables (E) in TAM provide the bridge between internal variables (attitudes and intentions, and other individual differences, situational constrains and managerial controllable interventions) impinging on behaviour, as depicted in Figure 1 (Davis, 1989; Davis et al., 1989).

External variables (E) are posited to have influence on both PU and PEOU (Davis, 1989). Davis (1989) further explains that using the external variables, system developers can have a better control over users' beliefs of the system, and subsequently their behavioural intentions and usage of the system.

Figure 1. Technology acceptance model (source: Davis, 1989)

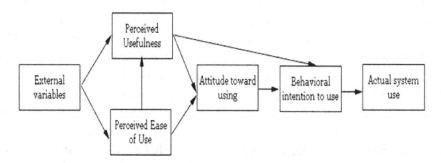

Attitude toward Using

In Ajzen and Fishbein (1980) study, attitude towards use is described as users' evaluation of the attraction of employing a certain information systems application. Davis (1989) has explained the factors that determine the use of a system as the Attitude toward using (A) by an individual and the impact which it may have on the individual's performance. According to TAM, A is jointly determined by PU and PEOU, with relative weights estimated by linear regression (Davis et al., 1989). Thus:

A= PU + PEOU

Behavioral Intention to Use

Behavioral Intention to use is sometimes described as a measure of probability a person will use a computer system. Davis (1989) insinuates that use of computer systems is determined by Behavioral Intention to use (BI). BI is also determined by the person's attitude towards the use of the system and also by his perception of its utility. Thus:

BI = A + PU

Actual System Use

Actual System Use (SU) is described as TAM's dependent variable and a measure of time or frequency of using the application (Davis, 1989). Individuals' actual system usage as theorized by TAM is determined by BI, which is in turn determined by PU and PEOU.

In their work, Davis et al. (1989) also supported a statement by Davis (1989) that BI is viewed as being jointly determined by a person's attitude toward using the system (A) and perceived usefulness (PU)(see Figure 1), with relative weights which are estimated by regression.

Modifications of TAM

TAM has been extended by Ondin (2007) by removing the attitude construct. These researchers have extended TAM in three primary ways in order to provide better understanding and its explanatory power as well as managerial control in its application. Three identified approaches are (Wixom and Todd, 2005):

1. Introducing factors from related models such as subjective norms, behavioural control and self-efficacy (Taylor and Todd, 1995; Mathieson et al., 2001).
2. Introducing additional or alternative belief factors. These factors include key related factors from the dissemination of the innovative literature such as trialability, compatibility, visibility and demonstration of results (Karahanna et al., 1999; Plouffe et al. 2001).
3. Examining backgrounds and moderators of PU and PEOU (Wixom and Todd, 2005). These include factors such as personality traits and demographics (Venkatesh, 2000; Venkatesh et al., 2000).

Davis' (1989) original study has been replicated by several researchers with the intentions of providing empirical evidence on the relationship between perceived usefulness, perceived ease of use and system use (Adams et al., 1992; Hendrickson, 1993). The main focus was on testing the validity and robustness of the questionnaire instrument developed by Davis.

A study by Adams et al. (1992) was conducted to demonstrate the validity and reliability of Davis' (1989) work. The extension included different settings and found both scales to have the validity and reliability characteristics. The internal consistency and replication reliability of the two samples were demonstrated. They further tested the relationships between perceived ease of use, perceived usefulness and system usage using structural equation modelling. The results suggest that usefulness is an important factor of system use. They also indicated the importance of both ease of use and usefulness.

In their study, Hendricks et al. (1993) explained the examination of instrument's reliability using test of internal consistency, replication with different samples and the test-retest using the same sample of the perceived usefulness and perceived ease of use scales. They argue that, to determine the stability of an instrument, a test-retest procedure must be performed. Two software packages were used as means of adding evidence concerning the reliability and stability of these scales. They further explained that the difference between test-retest method and replication method is the use of the same sample for multiple instrument administrations. Three methods were used to assess the scales' consistency and reliability. These three methods are: Cronbach's alpha; paired t-test; and correlation. The results from the study showed that while perceived usefulness and perceived ease of use of individual scale item correlation results were not high, the sub scales on the other hand were very high. Combining these results with the minimal number of important mean differences for items indicates test-retest reliability of the work performed by Davis in 1989.

Venkatesh and Davis (2000) extended TAM with the aim of explaining the perceived usefulness and system usage intentions in terms of social influence and cognitive processes. The improved model was called TAM2. TAM2 incorporated theoretical constructs covering social influence processes and cognitive instrumental processes. Social influences include constructs which are: subjective norms; voluntariness; *and* image. Cognitive instrumental processes include constructs which are: job relevance; output quality; results demonstrability; and perceived ease of use as shown in Figure 2 (Venkatesh and Davis, 2000). The voluntary and mandatory settings were utilised to test TAM2. The results from the study showed that TAM2 extends TAM by showing that subjective norms utilizes an important direct conclusion on intentions of usage over and above perceived usefulness and perceived ease of use for mandatory systems.

In 2003, Venkatesh et al. formulated the Unified Theory of Acceptance and Use of Technology (UTAUT) to integrate the main competing user acceptance models. In this model, seven constructs were considered to have significant direct factors of intention or usage in one or more of individual models. The authors theorised that four factors play an important role as direct factors of user acceptance and usage behaviour. These

Figure 2. Extension of the technology acceptance model (TAM2) (source: Venkatesh & Davis, 2000)

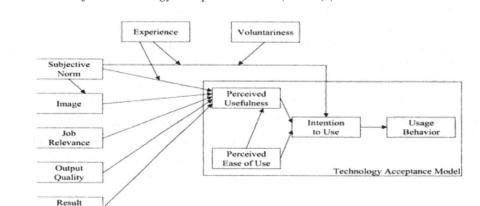

factors are: performance expectancy, effort expectancy, social influence, and facilitating conditions (see Figure 3).

It has been stated that attitude towards using technology, self-efficacy and anxiety are described as indirect factors of intention. Factors specifying the role of the key moderators are listed as gender, age, voluntariness and experience as shown in Figure 3. UTAUT was tested using the original data from four different companies and found to outperform eight individual models. The eight individual models reviewed were: TRA; TAM; the motivational model; Theory of Planned Behaviour (TPB); a model combining TAM and TPB, model of PC utilization, the innovation diffusion theory; and the social cognitive theory. The UTAUT was confirmed with data from two new organizations with similar results. They concluded by saying that UTAUT provides a useful tool for managers for assessing the probability of success for new technology introductions and help them understand the drivers of acceptance in order to proactively design intervention.

Ubiquitous Computing Evaluation Areas

Ubiquitous computing environments at times have more inflexible and constrained requirements.

This provides challenges to the design process which gives the motivation for using evaluation frameworks. Ubiquitous computing Evaluation Areas (UEAs) framework was developed by Scholtz and Conslovo (2004) for evaluating usability of University Web Portal Interfaces. The framework was developed with the hope that it will help researchers compare results, create guidelines for ubiquitous applications, reduced evaluation techniques, understanding the relevance of different evaluation techniques and a complete structure to avoid overlooking key areas of evaluation. It was highlighted that explicit structures can be made complete and comprehensive by repeated investigation over time, which supports the iterative evaluation process. The framework presents numerous metrics and conceptual measures. A conceptual measure is an observable value, whilst a metric associates meaning to the observable value by applying human judgement (Scholtz and Consolvo, 2004). For evaluators using the framework it is important to identify the direct and indirect stakeholders who are people affected by the application. They suggest that the evaluator must decide how to collect the conceptual measures.

UEAs were adopted for this study because of the conceptual measures which best complements the main objective of the study, which is

Figure 3. Unified theory of acceptance and use of technology (UTAUT) (TAM3) (source: Venkatesh, et al., 2003)

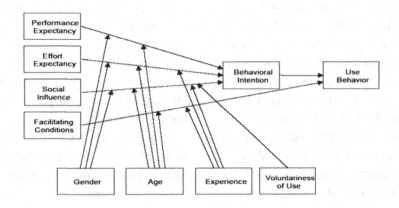

to select and use the appropriate usability and user acceptance criteria to evaluate South African Universities Web Portal Interfaces for their Usability and User Acceptance.

UEAs Constructs

The UEA constructs help in comparing the technology under evaluation to the users' normal environment (Scholtz and Consolvo, 2004). The constructs, their metrics and conceptual measures are shown in Table 1.

Applications of Utilization of the UEAs in Empirical Studies

Grudin et al. (1988) conducted a research and developed a campus tour guide application that tracked users' location and provide information about the surrounding areas of the user. The utility of the framework was assessed using case studies. The application was developed for campus visitors, mainly for prospective students. The main focus of the evaluation was on the explanatory features, the balance of attention between the device and the physical environment and the functionality of context-aware device. In their study, data was collected by means of observations, feedback from students, and the number of notes created. The results showed that the device was *distracting* because users were looking at the device instead of the surroundings. The results suggest that the users *contributed* some advice and opinions. The information posted by others was deemed useful though not all of them were accurate. Lastly the application did not always *sense user location* accurately and that users wanted *more functionality*. Scholtz and Consolvo (2004) tried to align this work with their framework by making suggestions based on Grudin et al. (1988) metrics with their UEAs metrics. They suggested appropriate UEAs construct that could be used for evaluating destruction will be attention and interaction. They also highlighted the appropriate evaluation metric for contribution adoption construct.

In another study by Moore (1991), a Personal Interaction Points (PIPs) system was developed allowing users to personalize shared devices such as fax machines, printers and copiers. The investigators studied customization of these devices using embedded displays in the environment or even portable devices. The embedded displays made use touchscreen while portable devices made use of cell-phones. The findings revealed usability, utility, trust and privacy of the two PIP methods. The findings also suggest that embedded user interface were more usable than portable interfaces and the suggested UEAs metric is Interaction. They also implied that portable interfaces had more utility compared to embedded interfaces and the suggested UEAs are Interaction and Impact and Side Effects.

Theofanos and Scholtz (2005) conducted a study to examine the utility and appropriateness of the UEAs framework developed by Scholtz and Consolvo (2004). The aim of the examination was to specifically evaluate the social aspects of ubiquitous computing. The criteria for selecting a methodology were tested by examining the utility and applicability of the framework to existing commercial ubiquitous applications. The two applications which they used are: (1) the restaurant ordering system and (2) an airport system which is using sensors in the parking lot to provide available space (Social Impacts and Side Effects). The results showed that in first evaluation the framework was good as it specified the important evaluation areas. They highlighted that in the second evaluation there was a side effect that was not considered by developers. They concluded by saying that the proposed framework did not contain appropriate metrics to assess whether good or bad design principles were achieved as well as identifying the social aspects and implications of the applications.

The next section will discuss the triangulation of the UEAs and TAM to form the research model for this study and the hypotheses formulated from the research model.

Table 1. Framework on ubiquitous computing evaluation areas (UEAs) (source: Scholtz & Consolvo, 2004)

Constructs	Metric	Conceptual Measure
Attention	Focus	Number of times a user must change focus due to technology; number of displays/actions users need to accomplish, or to check progress, of an interaction; number of events not noticed by a user in acceptable times.
	Overhead	Percent of time user spends switching among foci; workload imposed on user attributable to focus.
Adoption	Rate	New users/unit of time; user rationale for using the application over an alternative; technology usage statistics.
	Value	Changes in productivity; perceived cost/benefit; continuity for user; amount of user sacrifice.
	Cost	User willingness to purchase technology; typical time spent setting up and maintaining the technology.
	Availability	Number of actual users from each target user group; technology supply source; categories of users in post-deployment.
	Flexibility	Number of tasks user can accomplish that were not originally envisioned; user ability to modify as improvements and features are added.
Trust	Privacy	Type of information user has to divulge to obtain value from application; availability of the user's information to other users of the system or third parties.
	Awareness	Ease of coordination with others in multi-user application; number of collisions with activities of others; user understanding about how recorded data is used; user understanding inferences that can be drawn about him or her by the application.
	Control	Ability for users to manage how and by whom their data is used; types of recourse available to user in the event that his or her data is misused.
Conceptual Models	Predictability of application behavior	Degree of match between user model and behavior of application.
	Awareness of application capabilities	Degree of match between user's model and actual functionality of the application; degree of match between user's understanding of his or her responsibilities, system responsibilities, and the actual situation; degree to which user understands the application's boundary.
	Vocabulary awareness	Degree of match between user's model and the syntax used by the application
Interaction	Effectiveness	Percentage of task completion
	Efficiency	Time to complete a task
	Time to complete a task	User satisfaction User rating of performing the task
	Distraction	Time taken from the primary task; degradation of performance in primary task; level of user frustration
	Interaction transparency	Effectiveness comparisons on different sets of I/O devices
	Scalability	Effectiveness of interactions with large numbers of entities or users
	Collaborative interaction	Number of conflicts; percentage of conflicts resolved by the application; user feelings about conflicts and how they are resolved; user ability to recover from conflicts
Invisibility	Intelligibility	User's understanding of the system explanation
	Control	Effectiveness of interactions provided for user control of system initiative
	Accuracy	Match between the system's contextual model and the actual situation; appropriateness of action; match between the system action and the action the user would have requested
	Customization	Time to explicitly enter personalization information; time for the system to learn and adapt to the user's preferences

continued on following page

Table 1. Continued

Constructs	Metric	Conceptual Measure
Impact and Side Effects	Utility	Changes in productivity or performance; changes in output quality
	Behavior changes	Type, frequency, and duration; willingness to modify behavior or tasks to use application; comfort ratings of wearable system components
	Social acceptance	Requirements placed on user outside of social norms; aesthetic ratings of system components
	Environment change	Type, frequency and duration; user's willingness to modify his environment to accommodate system
Appeal	Fun	Enjoyment level when using the application; level of anticipation prior to using the application; sense of loss when the application is unavailable
	Aesthetics	Ratings of application look and feel
	Status	Pride in using and owning the application; peer pressure felt to use or own the application
Application Robustness	Robustness	Percentage of transient faults that were invisible to user
	Performance speed	Measures of time from user interaction to feedback for user
	Volatility	Measures of interruptions based on dynamic set of users, hardware, or software

Derivation of the Research Model

Actual use system has been used in this study as the acceptance of the university Web portal interfaces. Based on the definition of usability, PEOU and PU have been conceptualized as usability and therefore represented in the research model as the usability construct as indicated in Figure 4.

External variables used in this study are adopted from UEAs constructs and the selected constructs are as follows: Interaction; Appeal; Application Robustness; and Invisibility. The research model was used to empirically test the hypothesized relationship amongst the variables.

The following constructs from TAM were not used in this study because they were not applicable in this study: attitude toward using and behavioral intention.

The Adoption construct of the UEAs was not included in the research model because most of its metric evaluations variables form part of usability, which is dealt with in detail in the literature. The Attention construct are discussed and they form part of the Appeal construct. The Trust construct of the UEAs was not selected for this study because the study is mostly informational and it was only focusing on the interface of the applications.

Figure 4. The research model

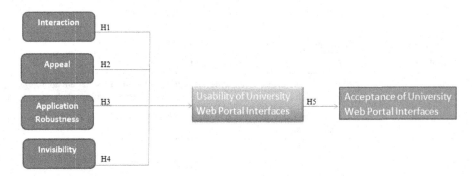

Formulation of Hypotheses towards the Study

The primary research question addressed towards the development of a framework for the evaluation of UWPIs is: What evaluation criteria do users use in evaluating South African University Web Portal Interfaces for their usability and user acceptance?

The secondary research questions addressed in the study are:

1. Which Ubiquitous computing Evaluation Areas (UEAs) impact usability of South African University Web Portal Interfaces?
2. Which UEAs impact user acceptance of South African University Web Portal Interfaces?
3. What is the relative importance of the UEAs in determining usability leading to user acceptance of South African University Web Portal Interfaces?

From the definitions of the constructs of the UEAs and TAM and the definition of usability as discussed in the Background of the study, the following hypotheses were formulated based on the research model presented in Figure 4.

H1: Interaction positively impacts usability of ubiquitous Web portal interfaces.

H2: Appeal positively impacts usability of ubiquitous Web portal interfaces.

H3: Application robustness positively impacts usability of ubiquitous Web portal interfaces.

H4: Invisibility positively impacts usability of ubiquitous Web portal interfaces.

H5: Usability of ubiquitous Web portal interfaces positively impacts user acceptance of ubiquitous Web portal interfaces.

The above hypotheses were formulated with the main purpose of answering the secondary research questions as mentioned above.

RESEARCH DESIGN AND METHODOLOGY

Research Design

The research design for this study was based on the guidelines provided by Babbie (2001) which described the important aspects of research design and methodology employed in the study.

Nature of Research

The nature of this research is exploratory and explanatory (Babbie, 2001). It is exploratory because it was generally developed to have an initial rough understanding of some of the phenomenon pertaining to usability and user acceptance, and it is explanatory because the research was conducted to discover and report some relationships among different aspects of the phenomenon under study.

Unit of Analysis

The unit of analysis for the study was individual, which comprised of existing students in South African Universities, prospective students seeking information on South African Universities, staff members, the public, employers and job seekers.

Time Dimension

There are two options in terms of time dimension for a research study: cross sectional and longitudinal (Babbie, 2001). In a cross sectional study, the unit of analysis is observed at one point in time whilst in longitudinal study, the unit study is observed over a long period of time. In this study, cross-sectional dimension is the more appropriate and feasible as it involves large scale of survey of universities in South Africa. The state of Web portal interfaces also keep on changing over time so it will not be appropriate to use longitudinal dimension, which observes the unit of analysis over a long period of time.

Research Methodology

In his work, Kim (1996) identified four methodologies for empirical information and communication technology research studies, namely: case studies; field studies; field tests (quasi-experimental); and laboratory studies (user participation). Of the four mentioned, Zhang and Adipat (2005) identified two major methodologies for usability testing which are laboratory studies (user participation) and field studies. User participation or laboratory studies have been considered to be the most appropriate methodology for this study, because the individuals such as staff, students and the general public are the ones interacting with the university portals and would be involved in the evaluation and rating of the portals. Using the user participation or laboratory studies is also considered to be very helpful to usability studies which put emphasis on comparing multiple interface designs or data input mechanism for ubiquitous computing applications. User participatory methodology is triangulated with field study methodology in this study; whereby users were required to evaluate UWPIs in laboratory settings while responding to the questionnaire survey for this study

Data Collection

Primary data was collected for this study using a self-administered questionnaire. The draft questionnaire was designed based on the constructs and variables selected from the UEAs framework and TAM using a 5-point Likert scale. A pretest of the questionnaire was carried out. A total of 5 people were given the questionnaire for evaluation. Posi-

tive feedbacks from the participants were received and the changes suggested were implemented. A pilot study using the revised questionnaire was conducted. A total of 50 participants were given the questionnaire for evaluation of the South African UWPIs in the pilot study. The data collected from the pilot study was analyzed manually and feedback from the pilot study was used to revise the main questionnaire for the study. The results of the pilot study show that South African UWPIs do not meet usability and user acceptance (Booi & Ditsa, 2012).

Validity and Reliability of Instruments

Validity and reliability of measures are important considerations in the design of questionnaires in a survey research. According to Cooper and Schindler (2008) and Babbie (2009), a measuring instrument is complete if it is valid and reliable. The reliability of the scales used in this study is presented in Table 2. As shown in Table 2, the Cronbach's Alpha for the scales is from 0.73 to 0.81, which are greater than 0.70, which indicates that the scales used for this study are reliable (Nunnally & Bernstein, 1994; Ditsa, 2003).

For the main study, a representative sample was drawn from the traditional universities, the comprehensive universities and the universities

Table 2. Reliability coefficients of scales (Cronbach's alpha) for scaled variables used in this study (N = 118, Scale 5-point Likert scale)

Variable	No. of Items	Cronbach's Alpha
Interaction	4	0.79
Appeal	4	0.78
Application Robustness	3	0.77
Invisibility	7	0.73
Usability	8	0.73
Acceptance	6	0.81

of technology in South Africa. A total of 200 questionnaires were administered and the data collected was analyzed using SPSS. The results of the main study are presented in the section below. A prototype Web portal interface will be developed to validate the results of the data analysis.

Description of Respondents

A total number of 200 questionnaires were distributed and 180 returned. Of the total 180 returned, 118 were suitable for analysis. Demographics of the 118 respondents are shown in Table 3. Forty one (34.7%) of the respondents were females and 77 (65.3%) were males. The modal age of the respondents was 18-25 (81.4%) followed by ages 26-25 (11.0%). The majority of the respondents were national certificate holders 72 (61.0%) and 32 (27.1%) of the respondents were diploma holders. Nine (7.6%) of the respondents were degree holders. Only 5 (4.2%) were post-graduate degree holders. The positions reported indicated that 95 (80.5%) of the respondents were students, 15 (12.7%) were staff members, 7 (5.9%) were both staff and students while 1 (0.8%) of the respondents were from the general public.

Table 4 shows the respondents experience with using computers and the Internet. The majority of the respondents in the study (38.1%) classified themselves as having experience with less than five years computer experience. The computer experience has a relationship with the major educational level (National Certificate) percentage which is 61% of the respondents as shown in Table 3. Because most respondents were students, the computer experience and age were expected to correlate. Sixty one (51.7%) of the respondents rated themselves as frequent Internet users who are using the Internet everyday whilst 1 (0.8%) of the respondents have never used the Internet.

Forty eight (40.7%) of the respondents rated themselves as expert casual users, whilst 46 (39.0%) of the respondents classified themselves

Table 3. Demographic data

Characteristics	Frequency	Percent (%)
Gender	41	34.7
Female	77	65.3
Male		
Age	96	81.4
18-25	13	11.0
26-35	3	2.5
36-45	5	4.2
46-55	1	0.8
above 55		
Educational Level	72	61.0
National Certificate	32	27.1
Diploma	9	7.6
Degree	4	3.4
Masters	1	0.8
Other		
Position	95	80.5
Student	15	12.7
Staff	7	5.9
Staff/Student	1	0.8
Other		

Table 4. Experience with using computers

Characteristics	Frequency	Percent (%)
Experience using Computers	45	38.1
0-4	40	33.9
5-9	20	16.9
10-14	6	5.1
15-19	7	5.9
20 or more		
How often do use the Internet?	1	0.8
never	5	4.2
rarely (once a month)	32	27.1
occasionally (once a week)	61	51.7
frequently (everyday)	19	16.1
several times a day		
Ability to use the Internet	5	4.2
novice casual	17	14.4
novice frequent	48	40.7
expert casual	46	39.0
expert frequent	2	1.7
none of the above		
Medium you often used	64	54.2
desktop (PC)	22	18.6
mobile phone	20	16.9
laptops	1	0.8
PDA's	11	9.3
Other		

as expert frequent users. The majority of the respondents 64 (54.2%) selected desktop as the medium they used to access the Internet, which correlates to the majority of the respondents which were students. Twenty two (18.6%) of the respondents selected the mobile phone as the medium they often used, 20 (16.9%) selected the laptop as medium they often used, whilst 11 (9.3%) selected the laptop, desktop and mobile phones as the medium they often used to access the Internet.

Correlation and Regression

The research model was tested using correlation and multiple regression analyses. For the preliminary analysis, Pearson's product-moment correlation coefficients (r) were computed to assess association. Multiple regression analysis (stepwise) was performed to identify the important variables that explained the usability and user acceptance of users in using UWPIs. This section presents the analyses and the identification of the important variables that explained the usability and user acceptance of UWPIs.

Tables 5 and 6 present Pearson's product-moment correlations among the variables together with their significance levels. The significance of each correlation was evaluated using two-tailed test and pairwise deletion option. As shown in

Tables 5 and 6, correlations amongst predictor variables (variables numbered 1-4) were statistically significant, with the correlation for any pair of the predictor variables not exceeding the multicollinearity criteria (0.9 and above). The correlations among the predictor variables ranged from 0.266 to 0.387. Based on these result, it was concluded that there exists no multicollinearity among the predictor variables.

The results of the Pearson's Product-moment correlations indicates that majority of correlations were statistically significant. The highest correlation reported was between Invisibility of the UWPIs and usability of UWPIs (H4, r = 0.720). The research questions which were addressed using multiple regression analysis and the stepwise regression analysis showed that *Appeal, Application Robustness* and *Invisibility* constructs from the UEAs have no significant contribution towards User Acceptance. Table 6 represents a summary of the results for research hypotheses.

In the regression analysis, the excluded variables are indicated at each stage of the regression as indicated in Table 7 and Table 8. Table 7 indicates that *interaction, appeal* and *application robustness* have been excluded in stage 1 of the regression analysis. Stage 2 indicates *that interaction* and *appeal* have been both excluded. In Stage 3 the *interaction* and *appeal* variables have been excluded. All the excluded variables have no

Table 5. Pearson's product-moment correlations among variables in research model (n = 118)

Variables	1	2	3	4	5	6
1. Interaction	1.000					
2. Appeal	.266**	1.000				
3. Application Robustness	.321**	.514**	1.000			
4. Invisibility	.387**	460**	.530**	1.000		
5. Usability	.396**	.518**	.582**	.720**	1.000	
6. Acceptance	.408**	134**	.248**	.358**	.371**	1.000
Note: Significant at **p < 0.01, *p < 0.05 (Pairwise, n = 113) Values < 0.175 are not significant at the 5% level. *p-values* for selected other values of *r* are: r = .134 .266; p = .153 .004						

Table 6. Summary of results of tests for research hypotheses

Research Hypotheses	Results
H1: Interaction positively impacts Usability of ubiquitous Web portal interfaces.	Supported
H2: Appeal positively impacts Usability of ubiquitous Web portal interfaces.	Supported
H3: Application robustness positively impacts Usability of ubiquitous Web portal interfaces.	Supported
H4: Invisibility positively impacts Usability of ubiquitous Web portal interfaces.	Supported
H5: Usability of ubiquitous Web portal interfaces positively impacts User Acceptance of ubiquitous Web portal interfaces.	Supported

Table 7. Excluded variables

Model	Estimated Beta	T	Sig.
1. Interaction	.132[a]	1.849	.067
Appeal	.256[a]	3.642	.000
Application Robustness	.281[a]	3.806	.000
2. Interaction -1.095 .276	.093[b]	1.349	.180
Appeal	.184[b]	2.523	.013
3. Interaction	.076[c]	1.126	.263

Table 8. Excluded variables

Model	Estimated Beta	t	Sig.
1. Appeal	-.004[a]	-.045	.964
Application Robustness 1.376 .172	.125[a]	1.376	.172
Invisibility	.226[a]	2.474	.015
2. Appeal	-.105[b]	-1.095	.276
Application Robustness .289 .773	.029[b]	.289	.276

significant contribution towards the usability of the UWPIs. *Invisibility* variables have an impact on the usability of the South African UWPIs. These results answer research Question 1 which is:

Which Ubiquitous computing Evaluation Areas (UEAs) impact usability of South African University Web Portal Interfaces?

Stage 1, as shown in Table 8, indicates that *appeal, application robustness* and *invisibility* have been excluded. At stage 2, the *appeal* and *application robustness* have been both been excluded. These variables have no significant contribution towards the acceptance of the UWPIs. *Interaction* variables are having an impact to user acceptance of the South African UWPIs. These results answer research Question 2 which is:

Which UEAs impact user acceptance of South African University Web Portal Interfaces?

- **Predictors in the Model:** (Constant), Invisibility.
- **Predictors in the Model:** (Constant), Invisibility, Application Robustness.
- **Predictors in the Model:** (Constant), Invisibility, Application Robustness, Appeal.
- **Dependent Variable:** Usability.
- **Predictors in the Model:** (Constant), Interaction.
- **Predictors in the Model:** (Constant), Interaction, Invisibility.
- **Dependent Variable:** Acceptance.

The stepwise regression analysis shows that *Appeal, Application Robustness* and *Invisibility* constructs from the UEAs have no significant contribution towards User Acceptance. The relative importance of the *Interaction* construct from the UEAs leading to *User Acceptance* is also indicated. These results answer research Question 3 which is:

What is the relative importance of the UEAs in determining usability leading to user acceptance of South African University Web Portal Interfaces?

Discussion of the Results

The results of the analysis indicate that all hypothesized relationships were supported. However, the results indicate that there is a low positive correlation between usability and user acceptance. This proves Dillon's (2001) explanation that there are no guarantees that the Web portals will be acceptable despite the fact that they may be highly usable. The results also show that Interaction has a huge impact when it comes to user acceptance of the UWPIs. Invisibility is rated as the most influential variable when it comes to the usability of UWPIs.

Contributions of the Study

The contributions of this study are twofold, namely theoretical and practical/managerial. Theoretically, the study confirmed that TAM together with the UEAs were appropriate reference theories to study UWPIs usability and user acceptance. The study confirmed that the developed framework was quite adequate for specifying the important evaluation areas of ubiquitous computing applications, which is in this case is the UWPIs. This study has broken a new ground in the study of South African UWPIs using TAM and the UEAs as the theoretical foundations. Further research can be done based on the results of this study.

Practically, the findings of the study have implications for the designers/developers of UWPIs. UWPIs designers/developers need to be aware of factors that contribute towards usability

leading to user acceptance. The results indicate that, *Interaction* factors have a significant influence towards Usability of UWPIs. Subsequently both *Interaction* and *Invisibility* of UWPIs have an impact on User Acceptance. This suggests that designers/developers should include all the stakeholders in developing any UWPIs. These results also suggest proper guidelines to be followed. The universities' management as well should try to monitor interface design and development processes by having a proper check on the history of the designers/developers. In summary, the results and findings of this study suggest the following actions in order to have proper criteria and to be able to evaluate any UWPIs:

- Improving the design, development and implementation of UWPIs.
- Improving the existing UWPIs towards usability leading to user acceptance.
- Further research into usability and user acceptance.

FUTURE RESEARCH DIRECTIONS

This study did not include all constructs of the UEAs framework. A further study may be necessary to include all the constructs. Also, perceived usefulness and perceived ease of use constructs of TAM were conceptualized as usability in this study. It may be necessary to treat these TAM constructs as they are in a further study.

Due to time and resource constraints, the study adopted a cross-sectional approach. The issues in this study were addressed in one point in time and some complex interrelationships between variable were not captured. A longitudinal approach may be more appropriate in helping to reveal some of these complex details. The study also focused more on one university where the study was held and very few responses from respondents from the other South African universities were captured. For further studies, it will be more appropriate if all the involved universities are evaluated with a fair sample from all of them. The general public as stakeholders in the university as mentioned earlier did not also feature much in the survey.

Based on the results of the study a prototype needs to be developed to validate the results. The results of this study can be used as guidelines for the prototype, and the prototype evaluated against the results. Future studies should therefore concentrate on the implementation of the prototype and also aim at including more variables in the research model. This may assist in explaining the variances in the usability leading to user acceptance.

This chapter addresses the theme of the book by describing the university Web portal interfaces in general including South African UWPIs as ubiquitous. This chapter also describes portals as pervading and they should be evaluated as "ubiquitous" computing artifacts, not just as stand-alone, thus widening the scope of evaluation to include factors not previously taken into account. The chapter has also broken the ground by combing the UEAs and TAM as a theoretical framework to evaluate usability and user acceptance of ubiquitous computing applications which are university Web portal interfaces.

CONCLUSION

This study reported the evaluation of South African UWPIs for usability and user acceptance. The study applied a triangulation of UEAs and TAM as a theoretical framework for the evaluation of the portal interfaces. The results suggest that invisibility, application robustness, and appeal of South African UWPIs support to the usability of South African University Web Portal Interfaces which subsequently leads to user acceptance of the UWPIs. The lowest correlation in this study is for the hypothesise relations (0.371), which is between Usability and User Acceptance of the UWPIs. This correlation implies that the basic usability requirements of UWPIs have not have been met.

REFERENCES

Adams, D. A., Nelson, R. R., & Todd, P. A. (1992). Perceived usefulness, ease of use and usage of information technology: A replication. *Management Information Systems Quarterly*, *16*, 227–247. doi:10.2307/249577.

Ajzen, I. (1991). The theory of planned behavior to leisure choice. *Journal of Leisure Research*, *24*, 207–224.

Ajzen, I., & Fishbein, M. (1980). *Understanding attitudes and predicting social behaviour*. Englewood Cliffs, NJ: Prentice-Hall.

Al-Wabil, A., & Al-Khalifa, H. (2009). A framework for integrating usability evaluations methods. *The Mawhiba Web Portal Case Study*.

Babbie, E. R. (2001). *The practice of social research*. Belmont, CA: Wadsworth Pub Co..

Babbie, E. R. (2009). *The practice of social research* (9th ed.). Belmont, CA: Wadsworth Pub Co..

Barnard, Z. (2007). *Online community portals for enhanced alumni networking*. (Doctoral Thesis). University of Johannesburg, Johannesburg, South Africa.

Battleson, B., Booth, A., & Weintrop, J. (2000). Usability testing for an academic library web site: A case study. *Journal of Librarianship*, *27*(3), 188–198.

Bellotti, V., Back, M., Edwards, W. K., Grinter, R. E., Henderson, A., & Lopes, C. (2002). Making sense of sensing systems: Five questions for designers and researchers. In *Proceedings of Conference on Human Factors in Computing Systems* (pp. 415–422). ACM Press.

Booi, V. M., & Ditsa, G. E. (2012). Evaluating South African universities web portal interfaces for usability and user acceptance: Preliminary study. In *Proceedings of IASTED International Conference on Human Computer Interaction 2012*. IASTED.

Cooper, R. C., & Schindler, P. S. (2008). *Business research methods*. New York: McGraw-Hill.

Davis, F. D. (1986). *Technology acceptance model for empirically testing new end-user information systems: Theory and results*. (PhD Thesis). MIT, Cambridge, MA.

Davis, F. D. (1989). Perceived usefulness, perceived ease of use, and user acceptance. *Management Information Systems Quarterly*, *3*(3), 319–340. doi:10.2307/249008.

Davis, F. D., Bagozzi, P. R., & Warshaw, P. R. (1989). User acceptance of computer technology: A comparison of two theoretical models. *Management Science*, *35*(8), 982–1003. doi:10.1287/mnsc.35.8.982.

Delone, W. H., & Mclean, E. R. (1992). Information systems success: The quest for the dependent variable. *Information Systems Research*, *3*(1). doi:10.1287/isre.3.1.60.

Delone, W. H., & Mclean, E. R. (2002). The Delone and McLean model of information systems success: A ten-year review. *Journal of information Systems, 19*(4).

Dillon, A. (2001). User acceptance of information technology. In Karwoski, W. (Ed.), *Encyclopedia of human factors and ergonomics*. London: Taylor and Francis.

Dillon, A., & Morris, M. G. (1996). User acceptance of information technology: Theories and models. In Williams, M. (Ed.), *Annual Review of Information Science and Technology* (*Vol. 31*, pp. 3–32). Medford, NJ: Information Today.

Ditsa, G. (2003). Executive information systems use in organisational contexts: An exploratory user behaviour testing. In *Information management: Support systems & multimedia technology*. London: IRM Press.

Du Toit, M., & Bothma, C. (2009). Evaluating the usability of an academic marketing department's website from marketing students perspective. *International Retail and Marketing Review.* Retrieved August 7, 2010, from www.computer.org/pervasive

Friedman, B., Kahn, J. R., & Borning, A. (2001). *Value sensitive design: Theory and methods* (Technology Report 02-12-01). Seattle, WA: University of Washington.

Grudin, J. (1988). Why CSCW applications fail? In *Proceedings of Computer-Supported Cooperative Work Conference*. ACM Press.

Hendrikson, A. R., Massey, P. D., & Cronan, T. P. (1993). On the test-retest reliability of perceived usefulness, perceived ease of use scales. *Management Information Systems Quarterly*, *17*, 227–230. doi:10.2307/249803.

IBM Global Education Industry. (2000). *Higher education portals: Presenting your institution to the world*. IBM.

ISO 9241-11. (1997). *Ergonomic requirements for office work with visual display terminals.*

Jameson, A. (2003). Adaptive interfaces and agents. In *The human-computer interaction handbook* (pp. 316–318). Lawrence Erlbaum Assoc..

Kamarulzaman, S. (2005). *Knowledgepoint: A study on the usability of the user interface for FTMSK'S knowledge portal*. (Bachelor Science [Hons] Information System Engineering Thesis). Faculty of Information Technology and Quantitative Science, Universiti Teknologi MARA, Shah Alam, Malaysia.

Karahanna, E., Straub, D. W., & Chervany, N. L. (1999). Information technology adoption and post adoption beliefs. *Management Information Systems Quarterly*, *23*(2). doi:10.2307/249751.

Kim, H. J., Choi, J. K., & Ji, Y. (2008). Usability evaluation framework for ubiquitous computing device. In *Proceedings of the Third 2008 International Conference on Convergence and Hybrid Information Technology*. IEEE.

Mankoff, J., Dey, A. K., Hsieh, G., Kientz, J., Lederer, S., & Ames, M. (2003). Heuristic evaluation of ambient displays. In *Proceedings of Conference on Human Factors in Computing Systems*. ACM Press.

Masrek, M. N., Jamaludin, A., & Mukhtar, S. A. (2009). Evaluating academic library portal effectiveness. *A Malaysian Case Study, 59*(3), 198-212.

Mathieson, K., Peacock, W., & Chin, W. (2001). Extending the technology acceptance model. The influence of perceived user resources. *The Data Base for Advances in Information Systems, 32*(3). doi:10.1145/506724.506730.

Moore, G. (1991). *Crossing the chasm*. New York: Harper Business.

Mustafa, S. H., & AL-Zoua'bi, L. F. (2005). *Usability of the academic websites of Jordan University: An evaluation study*.

Nielson, J. (2001). *How to conduct heuristic evaluation*. Retrieved May 7, 2010, from www.usit.com/papers/heuristic/

Nunnally, J. C., & Bernstein, I. H. (1994). *Psychometric theory* (3rd ed.). New York: McGraw-Hill.

Ondin, Z. (2007). *Usability and user acceptance of web sites of Turkish social security institutions*. (Master's Thesis). University of Bogazici, Istanbul, Turkey.

Park, S., O'Brien, M. A., Caine, K. E., Rogers, W. A., Fisk, A. D., & Van Ittersum, K. (2006). Acceptance of computer technology: Understanding the user and organizational characteristics. In *Proceeding of the Human Factors and Ergonomics Society 50th Annual Meeting*. IEEE.

Plouffe, C. R., Hulland, J., & Vandenbosch, M. (2001). Research report: Richness versus parsimony in modeling technology adoption decisions: Understanding the merchant adoption of a smart card-based payment system. *Information Systems Research, 12*(2). doi:10.1287/isre.12.2.208.9697.

Scholtz, J., & Consolvo, S. (2004). Applications: Towards a framework for evaluating ubiquitous computing applications. *Pervasive Computing*, 82-88.

Taylor, S., & Todd, P. A. (1995). Understanding information technology usage: A test of competing models. *Information Systems Resources, 6*(2).

Theofanos, M., & Scholtz, J. (2005). A framework for evaluation of ubicomp applications. In *Proceedings of CHI2005*. National Institute of Standards and Technology.

Thong, J. Y. L., Wong, W., & Tam, K. (2002). Understanding user acceptance of digital libraries: What are the roles of interface characteristics, organizational context, and individual differences? *International Journal of Human-Computer Studies, 57*, 215–242. doi:10.1016/S1071-5819(02)91024-4.

Triandis, H. C. (1971). Values, attitudes, and interpersonal behavior. In *Proceedings of the 1979 Nebraska Symposium on Motivation: Beliefs, attitudes and Values*. University of Nebraska Press.

Venkatesh, V. (2000). *Determinants of perceived ease of use: Integrating control, intrinsic motivation, and emotion into the technology acceptance model*. University of Maryland. doi:10.1287/ isre.11.4.342.11872.

Venkatesh, V., & Davis, F. D. (2000). A theoretical extension of the technology acceptance model: Four longitudinal field studies. *Management Science, 46*(2), 186–204. doi:10.1287/ mnsc.46.2.186.11926.

Venkatesh, V., Morris, M. G., Davis, G. B., & Davis, F. D. (2003). User acceptance of information technology: Toward a unified view. *Management Information Systems Quarterly, 27*, 425–478.

Winkler, R. (2001). Portals all-in-one web supersites: Features, functions, definition. In Taxonomy (3rd ed.). SAP Design Guild.

Wixom, B. H., & Todd, P. A. (2005). A theoretical integration of user satisfaction and satisfaction and technology acceptance. *Information Systems Research, 16*(1), 85–102. doi:10.1287/ isre.1050.0042.

Zaphiris, P., & Ellis, R. D. (2001). Website usability and content accessibility of the top USA universities. In *Proceedings of WebNet 2001 Conference*. Orlando, FL: WebNet.

Zhang, D., & Adipat, B. (2005). Challenges, methodologies, and issue in usability testing of mobile applications. *International Journal of Human-Computer Interaction, 18*(3). doi:10.1207/ s15327590ijhc1803_3.

KEY TERMS AND DEFINITIONS

Technology Acceptance Model: The Technology Acceptance Model (TAM) is an information systems theory that models how users come to accept and use a technology.

Triangulation: Triangulation is a powerful technique that facilitates validation of data through cross verification from more than two sources. In particular, it refers to the application and combination of several research methodologies in the study of the same phenomenon.

Ubiquitous Computing Evaluation Areas (UEAs): Framework developed with the hope that it will help researchers compare results, create guidelines for ubiquitous applications, reduced evaluation techniques, understanding the relevance of different evaluation techniques and a complete structure to avoid overlooking key areas of evaluation.

University Web Portal Interfaces (UWPIs): The Internet Portals under evaluation.

Usability: Is defined as the effectiveness, efficiency, and satisfaction of user requirements.

User Acceptance: Is the demonstrable preparedness within a group of users to use information technology for the preferred task.

Web Portals: The Internet Portal or Web Portal and their interfaces, are describe as ubiquitous-meaning being or seeming to be present anytime, anywhere.

Chapter 9
Telepresence, Flow, and Behaviour in the Virtual Retail Environment

Saïd Ettis
University of Gabes, Tunisia

ABSTRACT

Flow theory, as a basis to facilitate the development of compelling experiences, has received growing attention over the past two decades. Facing this plethora of interest, it is obvious that telepresence and flow in human-computer interactions are important issues. The objectives of this chapter is to review and empirically analyze the relationships among flow theory, the telepresence concept, and online behaviour. Particularly, this research investigates the impact of telepresence and flow on Websites visitors' visit time, perceived visit time, and number of visited pages. An online survey was conducted. The findings indicate that telepresence has a positive effect on the flow state, as measured by concentration and enjoyment. The consumers' level of concentration positively influenced their visit time, perceived visit time, and number of visited pages. Enjoyment has a positive effect on perceived visit time, but no significant effect on actual visit time and number of visited pages. Discussion and implications of these results are exhibited. Suggestions concerning future research are also presented.

INTRODUCTION

Mediated Communication Technology has undergone significant development over the past decades. They tend to utilise multiple media and richer graphical interfaces to excite and engage the user. Recently, new forms of communication and technology are emerging such as virtual reality display function, 3D graphics, video, interface avatars, online chat, and recommendation tools (Zhao & Dholakia, 2009). One key advantage of these Web 2.0 interactive technologies is that they provide users with a higher level of telepresence (or presence) within their virtual environment (Siriaraya & Ang, 2012). This heightened level of telepresence could potentially result in a more satisfying and immersive experience. This experience allows users to perceive an augmented sense of flow; a state of total concentration and enjoyment (Jahn, Drengner, & Furchheim, 2013; Koufaris, 2002; Novak, Hoffman & Yung, 2000; Wang, Baker, Wagner, & Wakefield, 2007).

Practitioners and academics alike have recognised telepresence and flow as a key attribute of the user interaction experience with new media (Mollen & Wilson, 2010; Tikkanen, Hietanen,

DOI: 10.4018/978-1-4666-4566-0.ch009

Henttonen, & Rokka, 2009; Wang, Yang, & Hsu, 2013), making these environments valuable as tools for use in purposes such as educational, entertainment, and e-commerce activity. Despite the growing importance of these new media and their adoption, the special characteristics of virtual worlds and their impact on user behaviour needs to be further explored (Domina, Lee, & MaGillivray, 2012; Kober & Neuper, 2013; Rose, Clark, Samouel, & Hair, 2012; Tikkanen et al., 2009).

The objective of this chapter is to review the flow theory, the telepresence concept and their interrelationship with the online behaviour. We apply this framework to Web stores. Hence, this research empirically investigates the impact of telepresence and flow state experienced during online shopping, on e-commerce Websites visitor's behaviour. Understanding factors that influenceuse of a virtual world for shopping will help e-retailers create compelling virtual environments and develop better marketing strategies to enhance the consumer shopping experience in the virtual stores, while positively influencing purchase and return intentions.

The chapter is organised as follows. We first review the literature on flow and telepresence and their impact on the online consumer's behaviour. Next, we summarise the theoretical foundations of relationships between the multiple conceptual models' constructs and develop our hypotheses. The empirical study's methodology is described and the results are presented on the observed relationships. The chapter concludes with a discussion of the findings and suggestions for further research.

OVERVIEW OF CONCEPTUAL FRAMEWORK

Flow Experience

Csikszentmihalyi (1975, 1990) developed a theory of flow: "the state in which people are so involved in an activity that nothing else seems to matter" (Csikszentmihalyi, 1975, p. 4). According to Csikszentmihalyi (1975, 1990), in this dynamic state, individual's attention is fully concentrated on the task at hand, elevating cognitive processing capacity beyond normal level and making intellectual performance easier and more pleasant.

This cognitive state has been characterised as an "optimal experience" that is "intrinsically enjoyable" (Csikszentmihalyi, 1997). Flow occurs when someone is participating in an activity for its own sake. The experience stands out as being exceptional compared with activities in everyday life (Csikszentmihalyi, 1997). In flow, the persons are fully absorbed in what they are doing, feel motivated, happy, and cognitively efficient (Särkelä, Takatalo, May, Laakso, & Nyman 2009), and they are intrinsically motivated to repeat the activity continually (Csikszentmihalyi & Csikszentmihalyi, 1988).

While flow does refer to a specific state, it is a continuous variable in that different levels of flow can occur, ranging from none to an intense (or complete) state (Csikszentmihalyi & Csikszentmihalyi, 1988). The components of such intrinsically rewarding flow experiences are a clear goal, balance between the challenge and the skills required to meet it, the feeling of full control over the activity, immediate and efficient feedback, concentration and focus, loss of self-consciousness, loss of a sense of time, and an activity that becomes autotelic (Csikszentmihalyi & Csikszentmihalyi, 1988; Csikszentmihalyi, 1997).

While there is still some debate, inconsistencies and discrepancies concerning the definition of flow, it is widely accepted that the balance between skills and challenges, and a sufficient level of control and playfulness, are the main antecedents of flow (Csikszentmihalyi & Csikszentmihalyi, 1988; Novak et al., 2000; Särkelä et al., 2009).

The flow is linked to behaviour. Flow experience may enhance increased learning, increased perceived behavioural control, increased exploratory and participatory behaviour, and positive subjective experiences (Hoffman & Novak, 1996).

Flow affects attitude toward e-learning (Choi, Kim, & Kim, 2007), attitude toward playing online game, intention to play online game (Hsu & Lu, 2003), positive affect (Chen, Wigand, & Nilan, 1999), and more frequent computer use (Ghani & Deshpande, 1994).

Although originally flow was applied in the analysis of such activities as rock climbing and dancing, flow has been found to be a useful construct for describing more general human-computer interactions. Human–computer interactions have such special characteristics that make them suitable to be described by using the flow construct (Csikszentmihalyi, 1990; Ghani & Deshpande, 1994; Ghani, Supnick, & Rooney 1991; Trevino & Webster, 1992; Webster, Trevino, & Rayan, 1993).

Hoffman and Novak (1996) claim that an online shopping environment can bring about a state of flow. Hoffman and Novak (1996) and Novak et al. (2000) adapted Csikszentmihalyi's theory of flow to cover consumer navigation behaviour in the Web. They defined flow as "the state occurring during network navigation which is characterised by a seamless sequence of responses facilitated by machine interactivity, intrinsically enjoyable, accompanied by a loss of self-consciousness, and self-reinforcing" (Novak et al., 2000, p. 22). Hoffman and Novak (1996) propose that creating a commercially compelling Website depends on the success of online marketers to create opportunities for consumers to experience flow. This is because the computer-mediated environment incorporates various types of interactivity and vividness that has the potential to create a sense of immersion, control, and immediate feedback making the Web open to flow experiences (Shih, 1998; Steuer, 1992).

Hoffman and Novak (1996) provided a conceptual model of flow that detailed its antecedents and consequences. According to their model, online flow is determined by high levels of skills and control, high levels of challenge and arousal, focused attention, interactivity, and telepresence, which in turn leads to more browsing and, ultimately, purchase.

Initially, Csikszentmihalyi (1975) described flow as consisting of nine dimensions. However, more recently the theory has been often measured using fewer dimensions (Domina et al., 2012). Flowing Ghani and Deshpande (1994), Ghani et al. (1991), and Koufaris (2002), in this research, the flow concept is operationalised as involving two dimensions: concentration and enjoyment. These dimensions are more directly related to the virtual world environment (Domina et al., 2012; Hooker, Wasko, & Paradice, 2009; Hua & Haughton, 2008).

For an individual to be in flow, they must concentrate on their activity. Therefore, concentration has been a significant measure of flow (Koufaris, 2002). Concentration is the extent to which the individual's attention is completely absorbed by the activity to the extent that nothing else matter (Csikszentmihalyi, 1990). It is the intensity of focus of attention given to the task at hand (Domina et al., 2012; Koufaris, 2002; Lu, Zhou, & Wang, 2009).

Enjoyment is regarded as an intrinsic motivation. Enjoyment is similar to the emotional response of pleasure from environmental psychology (Koufaris, 2002). It captures an individual's subjective gratification of the interaction with the technology (Ghani & Deshpande, 1994). Enjoyment can be defined as the degree to which using a virtual world is perceived to be enjoyable regardless of any performance consequences (Domina et al., 2012; Lu et al., 2009; Venkatesh, 2000). The flow experience itself is a pleasant experience, and hence the action where flow is attained is seen as meaningful, fluent, and efficient (Särkelä et al., 2009). In technology adoption studies, the concept of enjoyment has been defined and measured as the extent to which the activity of using a specific system is perceived to be enjoyable in its own right, aside from any performance consequences resulting from system use (Davis, Bagozzi, & Warshaw, 1992).

Telepresence

Besides skill, challenge, and interactivity, telepresence is an important antecedent of flow in virtual environment (Cauberghe, Maggie, & Patrick, 2011; Hoffman & Novak, 1996; Novak et al., 2000). The term telepresence was introduced by Minsky (1980) which is sometimes referred to as "presence".

Lombard and Ditton's (1997) review of literatures finds six conceptualizations of telepresence. (1) Presence as social richness: the extent to which a medium is perceived as sociable, warm, sensitive, personal or intimate when it is used to interact with other people; (2) presence as realism: the degree to which a medium can produce seemingly accurate representations of objects, events, and people; representations that look, sound, and/or feel like the "real" thing; (3) presence as transportation: can be identified: "You are there," in which the user is transported to another place; "It is here," in which another place and the objects within it are transported to the user; and "We are together," in which two (or more) communicators are transported together to a place that they share; (4) presence as immersion: the degree of perceptual and psychological immersion in the virtual environment; (5) presence as social actor within medium: the degree of illogically overlook the mediated or even artificial nature of an entity within a medium and attempt to interact with it; (6) presence as medium as social actor: the extent to which users ignore, in a counter-logical way, the mediated nature of a communication experience and treat the medium as a social entity.

Within these conceptualizations, researchers have proposed several definitions of telepresence. In terms of computer-mediated communication, telepresence has been widely viewed as a sense of "being there" (Reeves, Lombard, & Melwani,

1992). Telepresence is the extent to which one feels present in the mediated environment rather than in the immediate physical environment (Steuer, 1992). It's the sense of being transported to the mediated environment, rather than being in one's own physical environment (Biocca, 1997). Similarly, telepresence is the extent to which one feels present in the computer-mediated environment rather than in one's immediate physical environment (Hoffman & Novak, 1996). Fiore, Kim, and Lee (2005) viewed telepresence as an immersive response whereby consumers perceive the artificial environment to provide the necessary cognitive and sensory input equivalent to that of the more concrete real environment. More simply, telepresence has been described as a perceptual illusion of non-mediation (Lombard & Ditton, 1997, p. 2).

The definition of telepresence is still a less cohesive issue, which has led to a wide range of different operationalizations (Friedman et al., 2006; Sas & O'Hare, 2003; Schuemie, Straaten, Krijn, & Mast, 2001). While all start with Steuer's (1992) definition, the empirical studies tend to operationalise the construct of telepresence with components such as control (Fiore et al., 2005), spatial presence, involvement, interest, verisimilitude (Suh & Chang, 2006), and attention aspects (Witmer & Singer, 1998). According to Jeandrain (2001), there are two types of telepresence: physical telepresence and social telepresence. Physical telepresence occurs when customers perceive they are transported into the environment defined by the message or information on the Web. Social telepresence occurs when the Internet is so transparent that the customers perceive it as simply a conduit to interact with other persons on the Internet in the same way as in person-to-person interaction. In the same manner, IJsselsteijn, Freeman, and de Ridder (2001) divided the concept into spatial presence; the illusion of being present in a mediated room, social presence; the illusion of being present together with a mediated person, and co-presence; the combination of both illusions.

The media features and user characteristics determine Telepresence. Interactivity and vividness (richness or) are the two most significant media characteristics capable of influencing the telepresence (Hoffman & Novak, 1996; Shih, 1998; Steuer, 1992). Interactivity is viewed as the extent to which users can participate in modifying the form and content of a mediated environment in real time (Steuer, 1992). It has three basic components: speed, range, and mapping. Speed refers to the rapidity of the response of the machine to a particular action; range refers to the number of possible actions (such as hyperlinks, search engine, downloading, or product trial) available to a customer at a given time; mapping refers to the intuitiveness of how human actions are connected to actions in the mediated environment and naturalness of Web navigation that customers will experience (Steuer, 1992). Vividness is defined as the degree of the representational richness of a mediated environment as defined by its formal features (Steuer, 1992). It includes two sensory aspects of the media: the breadth and the depth. The breadth refers to the number of sensory dimensions presented. The depth refers to the resolution or the quality of the stimuli transmitted. Kim and Biocca (1997) and Klein (2003) claim that both antecedents are necessary for telepresence to occur. In other words, interactivity may generate feelings of telepresence, but only for vivid stimuli (Cauberghe et al., 2011).

Users' characteristics include their cognitive and perceptive abilities, attention level, length of exposure to and/or interaction with the product, and, finally, familiarity with the mediated environment (Debbabi, Daassi, & Baile, 2010).

Telepresence has been found to affect diverse marketing variables. In the Internet context, Hopkins, Raymond, and Mitra (2004) found that telepresence positively influence a broad range of consumer responses, such as attitudes toward the ad and attitudes toward the brand. In studying television infomercials, Kim & Biocca (1997) demonstrate that telepresence produced favorable brand preference. In addition, Li, Daugherty, and

Biocca (2002), Grigorovici and Constantin (2004), Klein, (2003), and Kim & Biocca (1997) indicate that a higher degree of telepresence results in greater perceived product knowledge and improve brand attitudes. Hopkins, et al., (2004), Jee and Lee (2002), and Fiore et al., (2005) found evidence that telepresence generate purchase intention. In contrast, Suh and Chang (2006) find no direct association between telepresence and purchase intention.

RESEARCH MODEL

While there is a body of work attempting to empirically test Hoffman and Novak's (1996) model (Novak et al., 2000; Rettie, 2001; Wang & Hsiao, 2012) and supporting a causal relationship between flow and online consumer behaviour (Mathwick & Rigdon, 2004; Richard & Chandra, 2005), the relationship of flow to anything commercially consequential remains to be not well established (Mollen & Wilson, 2010; Rose et al., 2012). The behavioural consequences of flow are not all scanned. This research contributes on empirical advancement of this experience by considering the following three flow consequences: in-store e-consumer's actual visit time, perceived visit time, and number of visited pages. These constructs are an important measure of customer retention and Website's stickiness (Lin, 2007).

The concepts of flow and telepresence have obviously several similarities such as the immersive component and intense feelings of involvement (Weibel, Wissmath, Habegger, Steiner, & Groner 2008). That is why, telepresence has been conceived of as a kind of flow experience (Draper, Kaber, & Usher, 1998; Jacobson, 2002) or as an antecedent (Hoffman & Novak, 1996; Novak et al., 2000; Skadberg & Kimmel, 2004). In this research, we followed the second perspective and studied telepresence as enhancing factor of flow.

Flow, measured by concentration and enjoyment, is assumed to be determined by telepresence. Highly concentrated and enjoyed consumers are expected to spend more time and to visit more pages. The conceptual model is depicted in Figure 1. Hypotheses related to the model's relationships will be developed and theoretically supported.

HYPOTHESES

Telepresence and Flow Experience

Previously, the two concepts have been studied interdependently. Telepresence has been assumed an experience that occurs in mediated-environments like teleoperations (Draper et al., 1998), television (Cauberghe et al., 2011; Kim & Biocca, 1997), mobile television (Jung, Begona, & Sonja, 2009) and video games (Bracken & Skalski, 2009). However, there are only few studies, in which telepresence and flow have been examined together in mediated environments (Takatalo, Nyman, & Laaksonen, 2008). Moreover, there are only a few studies in which the relationship between telepresence and flow is investigated based on empirical evidence (Nijs et al., 2012).

Hoffman and Novak (1996), Bystrom, Barfield, and Hendrix (1999), Draper et al. (1998), Reeves et al. (1992); Steuer (1992) hypothesised that

within computer mediated environments, telepresence leads to more flow. Novak et al., (2000) empirically supported this assumption. These authors conducted an online survey and found that enhanced telepresence in Web environment indeed corresponds to enhanced flow. Nijs et al. (2012) showed a significantly strong correlation between flow and telepresence in the context of interactive music systems. They reported that the scores for telepresence significantly and positively predicted the flow state. Furthermore, Weibel et al. (2008) observed a strong relation between telepresence and flow while playing online games.

More specifically, little research has examined if telepresence creates enjoyment and concentration, but some researchers have speculated about an association between these states (Yim, Drumwright, & Cicchirillo, 2012). Telepresence permits media users to immerse themselves in the world constructed within a medium, which leads to a loss of self-consciousness and a sense of escape from the real world (Heeter, 1995; Weibel et al., 2008; Yim et al,. 2012). The immersive experience causes them to forget their real word, and thus, enjoyment occurs (Hoffman & Novak, 1996; Sherry, 2004; Vorderer, Klimmt, & Ritterfeld, 2004; Yim et al,. 2012). Other researchers indicate

Figure 1. The conceptual model

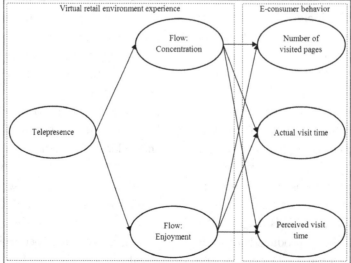

that participants who experienced telepresence reported that their media experiences were enjoyable and pleasant (Daugherty, Li, & Biocca, 2005; Lombard & Ditton, 1997; Vorderer et al., 2004; Yim et al., 2012).

Similarly, Argawal and Karahanna (2000) explain that an immersed individual feels a lower cognitive burden and demonstrate more cognitive absorption and focused attention. Finneran and Zhang (2003) argue that telepresence is an essential factor for enabling the person to remain concentrated on the computer-based task.

Due to these assumptions and findings, we hypothesise that there is a connection between telepresence and flow dimensions:

H.1. Telepresence will positively affect flow experience:
H.1.1. Telepresence will positively affect concentration.
H.1.2. Telepresence will positively affect enjoyment.

Flow Experience and E-consumer Behaviour

Hoffman and Novak (1996) originally conceptualised that flow would lead to important e-consumer behavioural consequences. Subsequent work has confirmed these hypotheses, and has further revealed that flow affects the key consumer behaviour (Hoffman & Novak, 2009). Empirical research has found that consumers who experience flow tend to be less price-sensitive, have more fun while shopping, and develop more favorable attitudes toward online stores and purchase intention (Huang, 2006; Korzaan, 2003; Koufaris, 2002; Novak et al., 2000; Richard & Chandra, 2005). A higher level of flow was positively related to affective responses and number of return visits to the Website (Fortin & Dholokia, 2005; Nel, Niekerk, Berthon, & Davies, 1999). Flow experiences appears to be a driver of positive aroused feelings, higher satisfaction levels, positive word-of-mouth (O'Cass & Carlson, 2010; Shin, 2006),

exploratory behaviour (Korzaan, 2003), more Website browsing (Smith & Sivakumar, 2004), and unplanned purchases (Koufaris, 2002) (see Hoffman & Novak, 2009).

In the flow literature, concentration and enjoyment have been found to increase the overall experience for computer users (Webster et al., 1993). As a result, consumer approach behaviour is enhanced (Koufaris, 2002; Wakefield & Baker, 1998). Enjoyment is particularly important, as when users are enjoying themselves they are more likely to have a positive attitude toward the new technology (Domina et al., 2012; Li & Huang, 2009). In addition, it has indicated that enjoyment positively influence the e-mail use (Trevino & Webster, 1992), other software use (Webster et al., 1993), and Web use (Koufaris, 2002; Novak et al., 2000). Studies on acceptance of new technologies, such as mobile phones and instant messaging, confirm the role that enjoyment plays in influencing users' attitudes and behavioural intentions (Domina et al., 2012; Kim, Ma, & Park, 2009; Lu et al., 2009). In e-commerce field, Childers, Carr, Peck, and Carson (2001) found enjoyment to be positively related to attitude towards a Website. Similarly, Heijden (2003) found enjoyment positively related to attitude toward the use of Websites and whether users intended to visit the site. Lin, Fang, and Tu (2010) found that enjoyment significantly influenced consumer satisfaction and intention to return to an online shopping environment. In addition, it has showed that enjoyment positively influences customer loyalty (Cyr, Head, & Ivanov, 2009; Koufaris, 2002).

Concentration has been found to positively influence the intention to use a system repeatedly (Webster et al., 1993). Similarly, we know that high concentration have a positive impact on Website user's intention to return and purchase intentions (Hooker et al., 2009; Koufaris, 2002; Lin et al., 2010). Furthermore, it is demonstrated that concentration has a significant influence on perceived usefulness and perceived ease of use in Web environment (Agarwal & Karahanna, 2000), of a university Website (Zhang, Li, & Sun, 2006), and of mobile TV (Jung et al., 2009). Additionally, interrupted or irritated users report a decrease in their satisfaction in an online shopping or gaming environment (Xia & Sudharshan, 2000).

While we know of no research in which enjoyment and concentration are tested related to number of visited pages and visit duration, our study is informed by the mentioned investigations. Therefore, extrapolating from the above, we expect the effects of concentration and enjoyment, as a measure of flow, on number of visited pages and actual visit time, to be positive. E-consumers in flow state were supposed to visit more pages and actually extent there Website visit duration.

In defining flow, Csikszentmihalyi (1990), refers to a condition of time distortion. Individuals who are in a state of flow are characterised as being so deeply involved in the task at hand that they lose the sense of self and track of time. Consequently, they are unaware of time passing (Csikszentmihalyi, 1997). The immersive and gratifying experience causes browsers to forget the time elapsed in the computer-mediated environment (Hoffman & Novak, 1996). While on the Web, time goes by quickly and without notice. Therefore, we hypothesise that flow experience will make consumer losses control over the amount of perceived time spent online. Then, time will seem passing faster than it really is. We, therefore, postulate that:

H.2. Flow experience influences e-consumer behaviour in the flowing way:

H.2.1. Concentration will positively affect number of visited pages.

H.2.2. Concentration will positively affect actual visit time.

H.2.3. Concentration will negatively affect perceived visit time.

H.2.4. Enjoyment will positively affect number of visited pages.

H.2.5. Enjoyment will positively affect actual visit time.

H.2.6. Enjoyment will negatively affect perceived visit time.

METHODOLOGY

Data Collection and Sample

A self-administered online survey was conducted to test the hypothesised relationships. The data were collected from a fictitious consumer electronics online retailer. The Website was created for the purpose of this research. The retailer Website was carefully created by experts with a Web content and design similar to others e-commerce Website in the net. This was to prevent the e-store from being confounded by an unnatural or strange design that is not well suited to the consumer's expectations. The homepage include the most common interactive functions and graphical interfaces. The Website was uploaded to the Internet. In this method, the content was viewed in its actual form and in a realistic setting.

Respondents received clear written instructions on how to access and surf the Website, and answer the online questionnaire. Respondents visited the Website without artificial restrictions. Consumers decide for themselves which pages they view, which functions they use, and how long they stay. They completed the online questionnaire immediately thereafter. One participant was randomly rewarded with €30 gift certificate. The sample was recruited with a convenience sampling method.

Measurements

This study involves six latent variables as indicated in the research framework. The questionnaire included items to measure telepresence, concentration and enjoyment. These variables were measured using five-point Likert scales. All measures were drawn from previous research based on their psychometric properties and adapted for the online context. Ten items adapted from

Kim and Biocca (1997) measure Telepresence. Items that measure concentration and enjoyment are adopted from Ghani and Deshpande (1994). Number of visited pages and actual visit time are measured using the clickstream data recorded in Web server log files. The log files register all the requests and information transferred between the client (the visitor's computer) and the company's commercial Website server (Bucklin & Sismeiro, 2003). Perceived visit time required subjects to report in minutes how much time did they think spend visiting the Website. Finally, demographics such as age, gender, and education were collected.

RESULTS

Sample Composition

A total of 400 consumers completed the survey. However, we followed previous research and assumed that a visit is inadequate to measure the actual time and the number of visited pages (1) if there is an idle period of at least 30 minutes, and (2) if the total of visited pages was less than three (Catledge & Pitkow, 1995; Bucklin et al., 2002). The elimination of inadequate cases reduces our sample to 318 respondents.

A total of 49.8% female and 50.2% male were questioned. The mean age of the sample is 29 years. All education groups were represented but the sample was somewhat skewed toward more educated consumers. A total of 44 percent of the sample indicated they purchase online at least one time per month with an average time spent online of 22 hours per week and length of using the Internet of 7 years. The total description of participants is reported in Table 1.

Measurement Model Evaluation

The proposed model shown in Figure 1 was tested with IBM SPSS AMOS 20.0, using the two-step model-building approach as specified by Anderson and Gerbing (1988). The Cronbach's alpha

reliability of the scales is satisfactory observing in this way the minimum of 0.60 (Nunnally, 1978). The measurement model, including the latent constructs and their respective observed variables, was analyzed to measure convergent and discriminant validity. All constructs exhibited levels of Jöreskog rhô reliability that exceeded 0.7 (Fornell & Larckers, 1981). Convergent validity is measured based on the average variance extracted from each construct. The average variance extracted for all constructs exceeded the recommended value of 0.50 (Hair, Black, Babin, & Anderson, 2010). The measurement model shows a good fit (Chi-square = 111.234; df = 58; RMSEA = 0.054; CFI = 0.949; NFI = 0.960; AGFI = 0.920; TLI = 0.973) with all the fit-indices better than the cut-off values recommended (Hair et al., 2010) (Table 2).

As shown in Table 3, the square root of the average variance extracted of each construct was greater than the correlations between the construct and any other construct in the model, satisfying Fornell and Larckers' (1981) criteria for discriminant validity.

Structural Model Evaluation and Hypotheses Testing

The initial analysis of the structural model indicated six significant relationships. However, the fit of the model was relatively poor because the root mean squared error of approximation (RMSEA) was greater than 0.08 (Bagozzi & Yi, 1988). Then, to improve the model, the paths with insignificant regression weights were dropped and another path analysis was conducted on the revised model. The results of the final model estimates are presented in Table 4.

The results show that the fit of the final model was more satisfactory. Chi-square was 164.160 with 95 degrees of freedom. The AGFI was 0.899; the NFI was 0.934; the TLI was 0.956; the CFI was 0.965; and the RMSEA was 0.057 (confidence interval 90 percent: 0.046-0.069), all of which were well within recommended guide-

Table 1. The survey sample composition (N=318)

Characteristics	Value
Gender	
- Female	49.8 %
- Male	50.2 %
Age	Mean = 29
Education	
- High school	10.4 %
- Undergraduate	06.6 %
- Graduate	83.0 %
Marital status	
- Single	51.2 %
- Married	46.7 %
- Divorced or separated	02.1 %
Annual income	
- Below 900 €/month	20.4 %
- 900-1500 €/month	17.6 %
- 1501-3000 €/month	26.0 %
- 3001-6000 €/month	14.9 %
- 6001 €/month and above	04.2 %
- Undisclosed	17.0 %
Length of using the internet	Mean = 7 years
Time spent online per week	Mean = 22 hours
Number of online purchases	
- Never	20.4 %
- Sometime	35.5 %
- 1 time per month	25.8 %
- 2 times per month	08.8 %
- 3 times a month	04.4 %
- 4 times per month	01.6 %
- More than 4 times per month	03.5 %

Table 2. Indicators of reliability and validity of measurement scales (N = 318)

Constructs	Reliability Cronbach alpha	Reliability Jöreskog rhô	Convergent Validity
Telepresence	0,90	0.89	0.57
Enjoyment	0.86	0.82	0.60
Concentration	0.90	0.86	0.62
Model Fit	Chi-square = 111.234; df = 58; GFI = 0.949 ; AGFI = 0.920 ; RMSEA = 0.054 ; NFI = 0.960 ; TLI = 0.973; CFI = 0.980		

lines. Four out of the hypothesised relationships were supported.

As expected, telepresence has a significant effect on the flow state. This effect was positive for concentration (Standardised Regression Weights $\beta = 0.442$; t-value = 7.169; p < 0.001) and for enjoyment (Standardised Regression Weights $\beta = 0.559$; t-value = 8.253; p < 0.001). These results lead us to accept the hypothesis H.1.1 and H.1.2.

Table 3. Indicators of discriminant validity of constructs (correlation coefficient matrix; N = 318)

	Telepresence	Enjoyment	Concentration
Telepresence	*0.75*		
Enjoyment	0.49**	*0.77*	
Concentration	0.44**	0.42**	*0.78*

Note: The diagonal elements show the square root of the average variance extracted; the off diagonal elements show the correlations between the constructs

** *p* < 0.01

Table 4. Results of hypotheses testing (N = 318)

Hypo.	Path	Standardized Regression Weights	Standard error	C.R t-value	Testing
H.1.1	Telepresence → Concentration	0.442	0.087	7.169***	*Accepted*
H.1.2	Telepresence → Enjoyment	0.559	0.071	8.253***	*Accepted*
H.2.1	Concentration → Number of visited pages	0.666	0.209	4.305***	*Accepted*
H.2.2	Concentration → Actual visit time	0.599	0.264	2.850**	*Accepted*
H.2.3	Concentration → Perceived visit time	0.445	0.288	2.154*	Rejected
H.2.4	Enjoyment → Number of visited pages	-0.063	0.291	-0.392	Rejected
H.2.5	Enjoyment → Actual visit time	0.121	0.369	0.546	Rejected
H.2.6	Enjoyment → Perceived visit time	0.433	0.375	2.153*	Rejected
Model Fit		Chi-square = 164.160; df = 95 GFI = 0.929 ; AGFI = 0.899 ; RMSEA = 0.057 ; NFI = 0.934 ; TLI = 0.956 ; CFI = 0.965			
Squared Multiple Correlations		Concentration = 0.195; Enjoyment = 0.312; Number of visited pages = 0.444; Actual visit time = 0.358; Perceived visit time = 0.480			

***: p < 0.001; **: p < 0.01; *: p < 0.05

Concentration had positive influences on number of visited pages (Standardised Regression Weights β = 0.666; t-value = 4.305; p < 0.001), actual visit time (Standardised Regression Weights β = 0.599; t-value = 2.850; p < 0.01), and perceived visit time (Standardised Regression Weights β = 0.445; t-value = 2.154; p < 0.05), suggesting support for Hypothesis H.2.1 and H.2.2, but not H.2.3 which suppose a negative relationship.

Further, we found that there is a significant and positive relationship between enjoyment and perceived visit time (Standardised Regression Weights β = 0.433; t-value = 2.153; p < 0.05), suggesting reject of hypothesis H.2.6. The

relationship is expected to be negative. However, enjoyment was not found to significantly influence number of visited pages and actual visit time, disconfirming H.2.4 and H.2.5. Key statistics for the final structural model evaluation are reported in Figure 2.

DISCUSSION

In this study, based on the flow theory, telepresence is considered to predict Websites visitor's experience of flow as measured by concentration and enjoyment. Flow is assumed to influences e-

Figure 2.Structural model

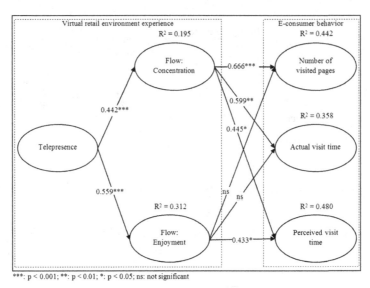

***: p < 0.001; **: p < 0.01; *: p < 0.05; ns: not significant

consumer behaviour in terms of number of visited pages, actual visit time, and perceived visit time. Among eight hypotheses, this research finds support for four. It has showed that telepresence is an important determinant of flow. The concentration dimension of flow is crucial to enhance consumer's number of visited pages and visit time. Consequently, this research gives evidence that the flow theory and the telepresence concept are valuable in the context of online shopping.

Our findings show that telepresence could enhance the flow sate. The more the Website visitors are immersed and feel present in the mediated virtual environment, the more they will tend to be concentrated and enjoyed, and then experience flow. These results are in line with previous assumption that telepresence leads to more flow (Hoffman & Novak, 1996; Reeves et al., 1992; Steuer, 1992) and support previous empirical findings on telepresence as a flow antecedent (Nijs et al., 2012; Novak et al., 2000; Park & Hwang, 2009; Weibel et al., 2008).

Moreover, these results are in line with theoretical elaborations on the relationship between telepresence and enjoyment. Our findings suggest a positive relationship between both constructs.

The "feeling of being there" and the "perceptual illusion of non-mediation" may lead consumer to find the shopping process in a e-retail store interesting, fun, and pleasant, rather than just a matter of product research and acquisition. These results are similar to those supposed by previous research (Hoffman & Novak, 1996; Lombard & Ditton, 1997; Shih, 1998; Yim et al,. 2012) and empirically obtained by others (Daugherty, Li, & Biocca, 2005; Lombard & Ditton, 1997; Weibel et al., 2008; Yim et al., 2012).

In the same way, findings from this study seem to empirically validate the relationship between the constructs of telepresence and concentration. We can affirm, as Finneran and Zhang (2003), that in a computer-mediated environment, telepresence is an essential factor for enabling the person to remain concentrated on the computer-based task. However, this is not consistent with pervious theoretically assertions that users' attention to media may affects their sense of telepresence (Kim & Biocca, 1997; Steuer, 1992; Witmer & Singer, 1998). Hence, the relationship between telepresence and concentration may have an element of reciprocity.

Our results also confirmed some prior research on the theoretically elaborated relationship between flow and consumer behaviour. Interestingly, we found that e-consumers in flow state might visit more pages and extent their Website visit duration. This effect is mainly produced by concentration. This result is consistent with previous research stated that in flow, consumer is more likely to explore the e-store Website (Ghani et al., 1991; Ghani & Deshpande, 1994; Hoffman & Novak, 1996; Korzaan, 2003; Novak et al., 2000; Webster et al., 1993). An in-store exploratory behaviour might lead to broader exposure to content and increase the urge to buy impulsively (Beatty & Ferrel, 1998; Koufaris, 2002).

Despite the lack of empirical evidence available on the relationships between concentration and consumer behaviour in the Internet context, our findings highlight the role played by concentration. There is support for the effect of concentration on the customer navigation processes depth. That is, less distraction while e-shopping (such as popups, e-mail, social networks, instant messaging, children, television, telephone, or colleagues), lead customer to spend more time and visit more e-store Website's pages, and therefore engage in more exploratory browsing in the Web store resulting perhaps in more purchases. Lin (2007) showed that Website's stickiness, the Website's ability to retain online customers and prolong the duration of each stay, is one of the key factors in influencing the online customer's intention to purchase.

Our results on enjoyment – e-behaviour relationships were surprising. We found no effect of enjoyment on number of visited pages as on actual visit time. This is opposite to the finding of the research that has argued a positive relationship between enjoyment and exploratory behaviour (Ghani & Deshpande, 1994; Hoffman & Novak, 1996; Novak, Hoffman & Yung, 2000; Richard & Chandra, 2005; Webster et al., 1993; Shen, 2012). Though the enjoyment measurement scale

exhibited acceptable levels of reliability and validity, this result casts doubt on the appropriateness of the scale developed by Ghani and Deshpande (1994) for e-shopping tasks.

This research also provided some counter-intuitive insights regarding the relationships enjoyment—perceived visit time and concentration—perceived visit time. These relationships were significant, but not in the desired direction. We supposed a negative effect of enjoyment and concentration on perceived time visit. Results revealed a positive effect. Certainly, one would expect something negative, such as flow to decrease perceived visit duration. Theoretically, this finding is not consistent with the sense of a distortion in time perception (Csikszentmihalyi, 1977), in which the consumer is unaware of time passing so that time appears to pass more quickly. A possible explanation is that, although, operationally, respondents were asked to assess the perceived visit time to the nearest minute, they estimated it in multiples of five minutes. Hence, the perceived time was mistakenly amplified. An alternative explanation is that flow dimensions (or antecedents) other than concentration and enjoyment such as curiosity, intrinsic interest, and control, had led to time distortion during respondents' e-shopping experience.

IMPLICATIONS

Based on these collective findings, it appears that telepresence plays an important role in influencing flow. Flow in turn influences e-consumer behaviour in the context of the Internet shopping. These results have a number of theoretical, methodological, and managerial implications.

From a theoretical point of view, our research demonstrates that the flow theory and telepresence concept are a suitable framework to explain e-consumer behaviour. Although telepresence and flow experiences are recognised as a decisive characteristic for a successful e-shopping Website, there are very few substantial studies, providing empirical evidence. Thus, the results presented in this chapter would shed light on this issue.

In addition, it confirms that concentration is a key element of flow experience in online shopping (Ghani & Deshpande, 1994; Ghani, Supnick, & Rooney, 1991; Haffman & Novak, 1996; Koufaris, 2002; Novak et al., 2000). This study offers an example regarding concentration as a positive outcome of telepresence and an antecedent of e-consumer behaviour. Like so, it helps to fill a gap in our understanding of the direction of causality between these constructs.

From a methodological point of view, the method using clickstream was successfully implemented to predict visit duration and number of visited pages in the context of e-shopping Websites. The ability of Websites to track the behaviour of their visitors throughout clickstream-recorded data provide researchers and practitioners with the opportunity to study how users browse or navigate Websites (Bucklin & Sismeiro, 2003; Bucklin et al., 2002). This study is a fruitful illustration of the clickstream data use to measure e-consumer behaviour.

From a practical point of view, our research shows, simply, that it is crucial to provide consumers with flow and telepresence opportunities. Higher telepresence while shopping refers to more enjoyment and concentration and thus more flow. Managers are requested to try crating commercial Websites in such a way that telepresence and flow experiences are enhanced. Factors such as good interactivity, entertainment value, attractive interface, rich content, quick download time, convenient navigational architecture, and other facets of human-computer interaction may be significant contributors.

Likewise, managers must pay close attention to how they design controllable elements of the Website in order to avoid distractions. Interfering ads, video, music, or animations may reduce user concentration and thereby inhibit flow experience. Retailers can develop marketing strategies to help consumers on these concerns and to deliver telepresence and flow experiences, which facilitate favourable consumer behaviour outcomes. E-stores who succeed in doing so may be more successful.

LIMITATIONS AND FUTURE RESEARCH DIRECTIONS

This study is prone to some limitations that require further future investigations. Although this study gave us rich insight, the results were limited by the convenience sample, which may affect the validity of results. For sure, the results would have been more relevant if a probabilistic sampling method was used. An additional limitation is that the impact of telepresence and flow was tested for only one Website. It will be desirable to replicate this research in cooperation with e-commerce retailers. Then, a larger sample and a richer clickstream log files can be obtained.

Another limitation is the exclusion of other flow dimensions. In this study, only concentration and enjoyment as flow dimensions were measured. We recommend other researchers to consider other constructs such as control, challenge and curiosity in examining flow experience in a virtual environment. Therefore, we believe that the construct of flow can be elaborated upon in depth by integrating these constructs.

The findings above suggest the importance of the telepresence for flow in virtual settings. In the literature on flow, empirical examinations of the relationships between telepresence and the components of flow experiences are scarce. For more rigorous and practical implications, further research is needed to empirically investigate the role of telepresence in enhancing the other components of flow mentioned by Csikszentmihalyi (1997).

Moreover, we know relatively little about the vividness and interactivity characteristics of Websites that encourage telepresence and flow. For instance, it would be appreciated to elucidate the role played by the collaborative Web 2.0 interactive technologies such as wiki, podcast, geographic mapping, and social sharing. Further research is needed, thus designers will be given clearer guidance as to what aspects they can alter to increase the chances of the user having an optimal experience.

In addition, it would be valuable to monitor individual antecedents of telepresence and flow experience. In e-marketing, there have been studies on a variety of individual characteristics such as motivation, knowledge, need for cognition, shopping familiarity, and innovativity. In addition, it is important to examine the role of socio-demographic characteristics (gender, age, education…), situational factors (product and Internet involvement, shopping goals...), and cultural settings. Such investigations will be valuable for our understanding of the universal phenomenon.

Further recommendation for future research is that researchers extend the scope of the e-consumer behaviours to get a more profound understanding of telepresence and flow outcomes in e-shopping. It might be valuable to test the effects of cognitive and affective dependent variables such as satisfaction, impulse buying, recall, loyalty, and brand image change. Besides, it will be worthwhile to use clickstream data to assess the role played by telepresence and flow in user's decision to continue browsing the site or to exit and how long a user views each page during a site visit.

Finally, future research could analyze several other interesting issues that remain unresolved. Future studies will be required to investigate telepresence and flow experience in other device such as smartphones, handheld computers, and PDA. It will be interesting to assess the extent to which a tiny screen may hinder telepresence and flow experiences.

CONCLUSION

In summary, the attempt in this study was to improve the understanding of users' online experience. Telepresence and flow are considered a key aspect of this experience. To this end, we examined whether telepresence predict e-store visitor's experience of flow. Flow is including two dimensions: concentration and enjoyment. Flow is assumed to be linked to e-consumer behaviour. The number of visited pages, actual visit time, and perceived visit time were measured. The study showed that telepresence and flow are valuable in the context of e-shopping. Creating opportunities that enhance these states motivate e-consumers to visit more pages and extent their Website visit duration.

This chapter may stimulate more research in this field identified as still being under-explored. The research area is potentially fruitful. Many issues remain unresolved and many questions unanswered. The literature on telepresence and flow is extensive, but there are many challenges that need to be resolved. These challenges are mostly methodological. Studies involving flow measurement assessment demonstrate that some potentially serious difficulties exist, and researchers need to think carefully about the direction of causality between flow constructs and the measurement approaches (Hoffman & Novak, 2009; Koufaris, 2002; Siekpe, 2005).

REFERENCES

Agarwal, R., & Karahanna, E. (2000). Time when you're having fun: Cognitive absorption and beliefs about information technology usage. *Management Information Systems Quarterly, 24,* 665–694. doi:10.2307/3250951.

Anderson, J. C., & Gerbing, D. W. (1988). Structural equation modeling in practice: A review and recommended two-step approach. *Psychological Bulletin, 103*(3), 411–423. doi:10.1037/0033-2909.103.3.411.

Bagozzi, R. P., & Yi, Y. (1988). On the use of structural equation models in experimental designs. *JMR, Journal of Marketing Research, 26,* 278–284.

Beatty, S. E., & Ferrell, M. E. (1998). Impulse buying: Modeling its precursors. *Journal of Retailing, 74*(2), 169–191. doi:10.1016/S0022-4359(99)80092-X.

Biocca, K. (1997). The cyber's dilemma: Progressive embodiment in virtual environments. *Journal of Computer Mediated Communication, 3*(2). Retrieved February 6, 2012, from http://jcmc.indiana.edu/vol3/issue2/biocca2.html

Bracken, C. C., & Skalski, P. (2009). Telepresence and video games: The impact of image quality. *PsychNology Journal, 7*(1), 101–112.

Bucklin, R. E., Lattin, J., Ansari, A., Bell, D., Coupey, E., & Gupta, S. et al. (2002). Choice and the internet: From clickstream to research stream. *Marketing Letters, 13*(3), 245–258. doi:10.1023/A:1020231107662.

Bucklin, R. E., & Sismeiro, C. (2003). A model of web site browsing behavior estimated on clickstream data. *JMR, Journal of Marketing Research, 40*(3), 249–267. doi:10.1509/jmkr.40.3.249.19241.

Bystrom, K., Barfield, W., & Hendrix, C. (1999). A conceptual model of the sense of presence in virtual environments. *Presence (Cambridge, Mass.), 8*(2), 241–244. doi:10.1162/105474699566107.

Catledge, L. D., & Pitkow, J. E. (1995). Characterizing browsing strategies in the world wide web. *Computer Networks and ISDN Systems, 27*(6), 1065–1073. doi:10.1016/0169-7552(95)00043-7.

Cauberghe, V., Geuens, M., & Pelsmacker, P. D. (2011). Context effects of TV programme-induced interactivity and telepresence on advertising responses. *International Journal of Advertising, 30*(4), 641–663. doi:10.2501/IJA-30-4-641-663.

Chen, H., Wigand, R. T., & Nilan, M. S. (1999). Optimal experience of web activities. *Computers in Human Behavior, 15*(5), 585–608. doi:10.1016/S0747-5632(99)00038-2.

Childers, T. L., Carr, C., Peck, J., & Carson, S. (2001). Hedonic and utilitarian motivations for online retail shopping behavior. *Journal of Retailing, 77,* 511–535. doi:10.1016/S0022-4359(01)00056-2.

Choi, D. H., Kim, J., & Kim, S. H. (2007). ERP training with a web-based electronic learning system: The flow theory perspective. *International Journal of Human-Computer Studies, 65*(3), 223–243. doi:10.1016/j.ijhcs.2006.10.002.

Csikszentmihalyi, M. (1975). *Beyond boredom and anxiety.* San Francisco, CA: Jossey-Bass.

Csikszentmihalyi, M. (1977). *Beyond boredom and anxiety* (2nd ed.). San Francisco, CA: Jossey-Bass.

Csikszentmihalyi, M. (1990). *Flow: The psychology of optimal experience.* New York: Harper and Row.

Csikszentmihalyi, M. (1997). *Finding flow: The psychology of engagement with everyday life.* New York: Basic Books.

Csikszentmihalyi, M., & Csikszentmihalyi, I. S. (1988). *Optimal experience: Psychological studies of flow in consciousness.* New York: University of Cambridge Press. doi:10.1017/CBO9780511621956.

Cyr, D., Head, M., & Ivanov, A. (2009). Perceived interactivity leading to e-loyalty: Development of a model for cognitive–affective user responses. *International Journal of Human-Computer Studies, 67,* 850–869. doi:10.1016/j.ijhcs.2009.07.004.

Daugherty, T., Li, H., & Biocca, F. (2005). Experiential ecommerce: A summary of research investigating the impact of virtual experience on consumer learning. In Haugtvedt, C. P., Machleit, K. A., & Yalch, R. F. (Eds.), *Online consumer psychology: Understanding and influencing consumer behavior in the virtual world* (pp. 457–490). Hillsdale, NJ: Lawrence Erlbaum.

Davis, F. D., Bagozzi, R. P., & Warshaw, P. R. (1992). Extrinsic and intrinsic motivation to use computers in the workplace. *Journal of Applied Social Psychology*, *22*(14), 1111–1132. doi:10.1111/j.1559-1816.1992.tb00945.x.

Debbabi, S., Daassi, M., & Baile, S. (2010). Effect of online 3D advertising on consumer responses: The mediating role of telepresence. *Journal of Marketing Management*, *26*(9-10), 967–992. doi:10.1080/02672570903498819.

Domina, T., Lee, S. E., & MacGillivray, M. (2012). Understanding factors affecting consumer intention to shop in a virtual world. *Journal of Retailing and Consumer Services*, *19*, 613–620. doi:10.1016/j.jretconser.2012.08.001.

Draper, J. V., Kaber, D. B., & Usher, J. M. (1998). Telepresence. *Human Factors*, *40*, 354–375. doi:10.1518/001872098779591386 PMID:9849099.

Finneran, C., & Zhang, P. (2003). A person-artifact-task model of flow antecedents within computer-mediated environments. *International Journal of Human-Computer Studies*, *59*(4), 475–496. doi:10.1016/S1071-5819(03)00112-5.

Fiore, A. M., Kim, J., & Lee, H. H. (2005). Effect of image interactivity technology on consumer responses toward the online retailer. *Journal of Interactive Marketing*, *19*(3), 38–53. doi:10.1002/dir.20042.

Fornell, C. D., & Larcker, F. (1981). Evaluating structural equation models with unobservable variables and measurement errors. *JMR, Journal of Marketing Research*, *18*(3), 39–50. doi:10.2307/3151312.

Fortin, D. R., & Dholakia, R. R. (2005). Interactivity and vividness effects on social presence and involvement with a web-based advertisement. *Journal of Business Research*, *58*(3), 387–396. doi:10.1016/S0148-2963(03)00106-1.

Friedman, D., Brogni, A., Guger, C., Antley, A., Steed, A., & Slater, M. (2006). Sharing and analysing data from presence experiments. *Presence (Cambridge, Mass.)*, *15*, 599–610. doi:10.1162/pres.15.5.599.

Ghani, J. A., & Deshpande, S. P. (1994). Task characteristics and the experience of optimal flow in human-computer interaction. *The Journal of Psychology*, *128*(4), 381–391. doi:10.1080/00223980.1994.9712742.

Ghani, J. A., Supnick, R., & Rooney, P. (1991). The experience of flow in computer-mediated and in face-to-face groups. In J. I. DeGross, I. Benbasat, G. DeSanctis, & C. M. Beath (Eds.), *Proceedings of the 12th International Conference on Information Systems* (pp. 16-18). New York: IEEE.

Grigorovici, D., & Constantin, C. (2004). Experiencing interactive advertising beyond rich media: Impacts of ad type and presence on brand effectiveness in 3D gaming immersive virtual environment. *Journal of Interactive Advertising*, *5*(1), 22–36. doi:10.1080/15252019.2004.10722091.

Hair, J., Black, W., Babin, B., & Anderson, R. (2010). *Multivariate data analysis* (7th ed.). Upper Saddle River, NJ: Prentice-Hall, Inc..

Heeter, C. (1995). Communication research on consumer VR. In Biocca, F., & Levy, M. R. (Eds.), *Communication in the age of virtual reality* (pp. 191–218). Hillsdale, NJ: Lawrence Erlbaum Associates.

Heijden, V. D. H. (2003). Factors influencing the usage of websites: The case of a generic portal in The Netherlands. *Information & Management, 40*(6), 541–549. doi:10.1016/S0378-7206(02)00079-4.

Hoffman, D., & Novak, T. P. (2009). Flow online: Lessons learned and future prospects. *Journal of Interactive Marketing, 23*(1), 23–34. doi:10.1016/j.intmar.2008.10.003.

Hoffman, D. L., & Novak, T. P. (1996). Marketing in hypermedia computer-mediated environments: Conceptual foundations. *Journal of Marketing, 60*(3), 50–69. doi:10.2307/1251841.

Hooker, R., Wasko, M., & Paradice, D. (2009). Linking brand attitudes and purchase intent in virtual worlds. In A. Z. Phoenix (Ed.), *ICIS Proceedings.* IEEE.

Hopkins, C. D., Raymond, M. A., & Mitra, A. (2004). Consumer responses to perceived telepresence in the online advertising environment: The moderating role of involvement. *Marketing Theory, 4*(1-2), 137–162. doi:10.1177/1470593104044090.

Hsu, C. L., & Lu, H. P. (2003). Why do people play on-line games? An extended TAM with social influences and flow experience. *Information & Management, 41*, 853–868. doi:10.1016/j.im.2003.08.014.

Hua, G., & Haughton, D. (2008). Virtual world's adoption: A research framework and empirical study. *Online Information Review, 33*(5), 889–900. doi:10.1108/14684520911001891.

Huang, M. H. (2006, May). Flow, enduring and situational involvement in the web environment: A tripartite second-order examination. *Psychology and Marketing, 23*, 383–411. doi:10.1002/mar.20118.

Ijsselsteijn, W. A., Freeman, J., & de Ridder, H. (2001). Presence: Where we are? *Cyberpsychology & Behavior, 4*(2), 179–182. doi:10.1089/109493101300117875 PMID:11710245.

Jacobson, D. (2002). On theorizing presence. *Journal of Virtual Environments, 6*(1).

Jahn, S., Drengner, J., & Furchheim, P. (2013). Flow revisited process conceptualization and extension to reactive consumption experiences. In *Proceedings of the AMA Winter Educators' Conference.* Las Vegas, NV: AMA.

Jeandrain, A. C. (2001). Essay about telepresence effects on persuasion: Three possible explanations. In *Proceedings of the Fourth Annual International Workshop on Presence,* (pp. 123-127). Philadelphia: IEEE.

Jee, J., & Lee, W. N. (2002). Antecedents and consequences of perceived interactivity: An exploratory study. *Journal of Interactive Advertising, 3*(1). Retrieved February 6, 2012, from http://www.jiad.org/

Jung, Y., Begona, P. M., & Sonja, W. P. (2009). Consumer adoption of mobile TV: Examining psychological flow and media content. *Computers in Human Behavior, 25*, 123–129. doi:10.1016/j.chb.2008.07.011.

Kim, J., Ma, Y. J., & Park, J. (2009). Are US consumers ready to adopt mobile technology for fashion goods? *Journal of Fashion Marketing and Management, 13*(2), 215–230. doi:10.1108/13612020910957725.

Kim, T., & Biocca, F. (1997). Telepresence via television: Two dimensions of telepresence may have different connections to memory and persuasion. *Journal of Computer Mediated Communication, 3*(2). Retrieved February 06, 2012, from http://jcmc.indiana.edu/vol3/issue2/kim.html

Klein, L. R. (2003). Creating virtual product experiences: The role of telepresence. *Journal of Interactive Marketing, 17*(1), 41–55. doi:10.1002/dir.10046.

Kober, S. E., & Neuper, C. (2013). Personality and presence in virtual reality: Does their relationship depend on the used presence measure? *International Journal of Human-Computer Interaction, 29*(1), 13–25. doi:10.1080/10447318.2012.668131.

Korzaan, M. L. (2003). Going with the flow: Predicting online purchase intentions. *Journal of Computer Information Systems, 43*(4), 25–31.

Koufaris, M. (2002). Applying the technology acceptance model and flow theory to online consumer behavior. *Information Systems Research, 13*(2), 205–223. doi:10.1287/isre.13.2.205.83.

Li, H., Daugherty, T., & Biocca, F. (2002). Impact of 3-D advertising on product knowledge, brand attitude, and purchase intention: The mediating role of presence. *Journal of Advertising, 31*(3), 43–57. doi:10.1080/00913367.2002.10673675.

Li, Y. H., & Huang, J. W. (2009). Applying theory of perceived risk and technology acceptance model in the online shopping channel. *World Academy of Science. Engineering and Technology, 53,* 919–925.

Lin, C. Y., Fang, K., & Tu, C. C. (2010). Predicting consumer repurchase intentions to shop online. *Journal of Computers, 5*(10), 1527–1533. doi:10.4304/jcp.5.10.1527-1533.

Lin, J. C. C. (2007). Online stickiness: Its antecedents and effect on purchasing intention. *Behaviour & Information Technology, 26*(6), 507–516. doi:10.1080/01449290600740843.

Lombard, M., & Ditton, T. (1997). At the heart of it all: The concept of presence. *Journal of Computer Mediated-Communication, 3*(2). Retrieved February 6, 2012, from http://jcmc.indiana.edu/vol3/issue2/lombard.html

Lu, Y., Zhou, T., & Wang, B. (2009). Exploring Chinese users' acceptance of instant messaging using the theory of planned behavior, the technology acceptance model, and the flow theory. *Computers in Human Behavior, 25,* 29–39. doi:10.1016/j.chb.2008.06.002.

Mathwick, C., & Rigdon, E. (2004). Play, flow, and the online search experience. *The Journal of Consumer Research, 31*(2), 324–332. doi:10.1086/422111.

Minsky, M. (1980). Telepresence. *Omni (New York, N.Y.), 21,* 45–51.

Mollen, A., & Wilson, H. (2010). Engagement, telepresence and interactivity in online consumer experience: Reconciling scholastic and managerial perspectives. *Journal of Business Research, 63,* 919–925. doi:10.1016/j.jbusres.2009.05.014.

Nel, D., Niekerk, R. V., Berthon, J. P., & Davies, T. (1999). Going with the flow: Web sites and customer involvement. *Internet Research, 9*(2), 109–116. doi:10.1108/10662249910264873.

Nijs, L., Coussement, P., Moens, B., Amelinck, D., Lesaffre, M., & Leman, M. (2012). Interacting with the music paint machine: Relating the constructs of flow experience and presence. *Interacting with Computers, 24,* 237–250. doi:10.1016/j.intcom.2012.05.002.

Novak, T. P., Hoffman, D. L., & Yung, Y. F. (2000). Measuring the flow construct in online environments: A structural modeling approach. *Marketing Science, 19*(1), 22–42. doi:10.1287/mksc.19.1.22.15184.

Nunnally, J. (1978). *Psychometric theory.* New York: McGraw-Hill.

O'Cass, A., & Carlson, J. (2010). Examining the effects of website-induced flow in professional sporting team websites. *Internet Research, 20*(2), 115–134. doi:10.1108/10662241011032209.

Park, S. B., & Hwang, H. (2009). Understanding online game addiction: Connection between presence and flet. In *Proceedings of the 13th International Conference on Human-Computer Interaction, Interacting in Various Application Domains* (pp. 378-386). IEEE.

Reeves, B., Lombard, M., & Melwani, G. (1992). *Faces on the screen: Pictures or natural experience?* Paper presented to the Mass Communication Division at the Annual Conference of the International Communication Association. Miami, FL.

Rettie, R. (2001). An exploration of flow during internet use. *Internet Research: Electronic Networking Applications and Policy, 11*(2), 103–113. doi:10.1108/10662240110695070.

Richard, M. O. (2005). Modelling the impact of Internet atmospherics on surfer behaviour. *Journal of Business Research, 58*(12), 1632–1642. doi:10.1016/j.jbusres.2004.07.009.

Rose, S., Clark, M., Samouel, P., & Hair, N. (2012). Online customer experience in e-retailing: An empirical model of antecedents and outcomes. *Journal of Retailing, 88*(2), 308–322. doi:10.1016/j.jretai.2012.03.001.

Särkelä, H., Takatalo, J., May, P., Laakso, M., & Nyman, G. (2009). The movement patterns and the experiential components of virtual environments. *International Journal of Human-Computer Studies, 67*, 787–799. doi:10.1016/j.ijhcs.2009.05.003.

Sas, C., & O'Hare, G. (2003). The presence equation: An investigation into cognitive factors underlying presence. *Presence (Cambridge, Mass.), 12*(5), 523–537. doi:10.1162/105474603322761315.

Schuemie, M., Straaten, V., Krijn, M. P., & Mast, C. V. (2001). Research on presence in VR: A survey. *Cyberpsychology & Behavior, 4*(2), 183–201. doi:10.1089/109493101300117884 PMID:11710246.

Shen, J. (2012). Social comparison, social presence, and enjoyment in the acceptance of social shopping websites. *Journal of Electronic Commerce Research, 13*(3), 198–212.

Sherry, J. L. (2004). Flow and media enjoyment. *Communication Theory, 14*(4), 328–347. doi:10.1111/j.1468-2885.2004.tb00318.x.

Shih, C. F. E. (1998). Conceptualizing consumer experiences in cyberspace. *European Journal of Marketing, 32*(7-8), 655–663. doi:10.1108/03090569810224056.

Shin, N. (2006). Online learner's flow experience: An empirical study. *British Journal of Educational Technology, 37*(5), 705–720. doi:10.1111/j.1467-8535.2006.00641.x.

Siekpe, J. S. (2005). An examination of the multidimensionality of flow construct in a computer-mediated environment. *Journal of Electronic Commerce Research, 6*(1). Retrieved February 06, 2012, from www.csulb.edu/web/journals/jecr/issues/20051/paper2.pdf

Siriaraya, P., & Ang, C. S. (2012). Age differences in the perception of social presence in the use of 3D virtual world for social interaction. *Interacting with Computers, 24*, 280–291. doi:10.1016/j.intcom.2012.03.003.

Skadberg, Y. X., & Kimmel, J. R. (2004). Visitors' flow experience while browsing a web site: Its measurement, contributing factors and consequences. *Computers in Human Behavior, 20*(4), 403–422. doi:10.1016/S0747-5632(03)00050-5.

Smith, D. N., & Sivakumar, K. (2004). Flow and internet shopping behavior: A conceptual model and research propositions. *Journal of Business Research, 1*(10), 1199–1208. doi:10.1016/S0148-2963(02)00330-2.

Steuer, J. (1992). Defining virtual reality: dimensions determining telepresence. In Biocca, F., & Levy, M. R. (Eds.), *Communication in the age of virtual reality* (pp. 33–56). Hillsdale, NJ: Lawrence Erlbaum Associates.

Suh, K. S., & Chang, S. (2006). User interfaces and consumer perceptions of online stores: The role of telepresence. *Behaviour & Information Technology*, *25*(2), 99–113. doi:10.1080/01449290500330398.

Takatalo, J., Nyman, G., & Laaksonen, L. (2008). Components of human experience in virtual environments. *Computers in Human Behavior*, *24*, 1–15. doi:10.1016/j.chb.2006.11.003.

Tikkanen, H., Hietanen, J., Henttonen, T., & Rokka, J. (2009). Exploring virtual worlds: Success factors in virtual world marketing. *Management Decision*, *47*(8), 1357–1381. doi:10.1108/00251740910984596.

Trevino, L. K., & Webster, J. (1992). Flow in computer-mediated communication. *Communication Research*, *19*(5), 539–573. doi:10.1177/009365092019005001.

Venkatesh, V. (2000). Determinants of perceived ease of use: Integrating control, intrinsic motivation, and emotion into the technology acceptance model. *Information Systems Research*, *11*(4), 342–365. doi:10.1287/isre.11.4.342.11872.

Vorderer, P., Klimmt, C., & Ritterfeld, U. (2004). Enjoyment: At the heart of media entertainment. *Communication Theory*, *14*, 388–408. doi:10.1111/j.1468-2885.2004.tb00321.x.

Wakefield, K. L., & Baker, J. (1998). Excitement at the mall: Determinants and effects on shopping reponse. *Journal of Retailing*, *74*(4), 515–539. doi:10.1016/S0022-4359(99)80106-7.

Wang, C. C., Yang, Y. H., & Hsu, M. C. (2013). *The recent development of flow theory research: A bibliometric study*. Paper presented at the 2013 International Conference on e-CASE & e-Tech. Kitakyushu, Japan.

Wang, L. C., Baker, J., Wagner, J., & Wakefield, K. (2007). Can a retail web site be social? *Journal of Marketing*, *71*, 143–157. doi:10.1509/jmkg.71.3.143.

Wang, L. C., & Hsiao, D. F. (2012). Antecedents of an in retail store shopping. *Journal of Retailing and Consumer Services*, *19*, 381–389. doi:10.1016/j.jretconser.2012.03.002.

Webster, J., Trevino, L. K., & Ryan, L. (1993). The dimensionality and correlates of flow in human computer interactions. *Computers in Human Behavior*, *9*(4), 411–426. doi:10.1016/0747-5632(93)90032-N.

Weibel, D., Wissmath, B., Habegger, S., Steiner, Y., & Groner, R. (2008). Playing online games against computer- vs. human-controlled opponents: Effects on presence and enjoyment. *Computers in Human Behavior*, *24*, 2274–2291. doi:10.1016/j.chb.2007.11.002.

Witmer, B. G., & Singer, M. J. (1998). Measuring presence in virtual environments: A presence questionnaire. *Presence (Cambridge, Mass.)*, *7*, 225–240. doi:10.1162/105474698565686.

Xia, L., & Sudharshan, D. (2002). Effects of interruptions on consumer online decision processes. *Journal of Consumer Psychology*, *12*(3), 265–280. doi:10.1207/S15327663JCP1203_08.

Yim, M. Y., Cicchirillo, V. J., & Drumwright, M. E. (2012). The impact of stereoscopic three-dimensional (3-d) advertising: The role of presence in enhancing advertising effectiveness. *Journal of Advertising*, *41*(2), 113–112. doi:10.2753/JOA0091-3367410208.

Zhang, P., Li, N., & Sun, H. (2006). Affective quality and cognitive absorption: Extending technology acceptance research. In *Proceedings of the Hawaii International Conference on System Sciences* (HICSS). IEEE.

Zhao, M., & Dholakia, R. R. (2009). A multi-attribute model of website interactivity and customer satisfaction: An application of the Kano model. *Managing Service Quality*, *19*(3), 286–307. doi:10.1108/09604520910955311.

ADDITIONAL READING

Ariely, D. (2000). Controlling the information flow: Effects on consumers' decision-making and preferences. *The Journal of Consumer Research, 27*(2), 233–248. doi:10.1086/314322.

Bolton, R., & Saxena-Iyer, S. (2009). Interactive services: A framework, synthesis and research directions. *Journal of Interactive Marketing, 23*(1), 91–104. doi:10.1016/j.intmar.2008.11.002.

Bridges, E., & Florsheim, R. (2008). Hedonic and utilitarian shopping goals: The online experience. *Journal of Business Research, 61*, 309–314. doi:10.1016/j.jbusres.2007.06.017.

Cai, S., & Xu, Y. (2006). Effects of outcome, process and shopping enjoyment on online consumer behavior. *Electronic Commerce Research and Applications, 5*(4), 272–281. doi:10.1016/j.elerap.2006.04.004.

Coyle, J. R., & Thorson, E. (2001). The effects of progressive levels of interactivity and vividness in web marketing sites. *Journal of Advertising, 30*(3), 65–77. doi:10.1080/00913367.2001.10673646.

Csikszentmihalyi, M., & LeFevre, J. A. (1989). Optimal experience in work and leisure. *Journal of Personality and Social Psychology, 56*, 815–822. doi:10.1037/0022-3514.56.5.815 PMID:2724069.

Ellis, G. D., Voelkl, J. E., & Morris, C. (1994). Measurement and analysis issues with explanation of variance in daily experience using the flow model. *Journal of Leisure Research, 26*(4), 337–356.

Forsythe, S., & Bailey, A. (1996). Shopping enjoyment, perceived time poverty, and time spent shopping. *Clothing & Textiles Research Journal, 14*(3), 185–191. doi:10.1177/0887302X9601400303.

Guo, Y., & Poole, M. (2009). Antecedents of flow in online shopping: A test of alternative models. *Information Systems Journal, 19*(4), 369–390. doi:10.1111/j.1365-2575.2007.00292.x.

Henrikki, T., Hietanen, J., Henttonen, T., & Rokka, J. (2009). Exploring virtual worlds: Success factors in virtual world marketing. *Management Decision, 47*(8), 1357–1381. doi:10.1108/00251740910984596.

Jackson, S. A. (1996). Toward a conceptual understanding to the flow experience in elite athletes. *Research Quarterly for Exercise and Sport, 67*(1), 76–90. doi:10.1080/02701367.1996.10607928 PMID:8735997.

Jackson, S. A., & Marsh, H. W. (1996). Development and validation of a scale to measure optimal experience: The flow state scale. *Journal of Sport & Exercise Psychology, 18*(1), 17–35.

Keng, C. J., & Lin, H. Y. (2006). Impact of telepresence levels on internet advertising effects. *Cyberpsychology & Behavior, 9*(1), 82–94. doi:10.1089/cpb.2006.9.82 PMID:16497121.

Massimini, F., & Carli, M. (1988). The systematic assessment of flow in daily experience. In Csikszenhmihalyi, M., & Csikszentmihalyi, I. (Eds.), *Optimal experience: Psychological studies of flow in consciousness* (pp. 266–287). New York: Cambridge University Press. doi:10.1017/CBO9780511621956.016.

Mehrabian, A., & Russell, J. A. (1974). *An approach to environmental psychology.* Cambridge, MA: MIT Press.

Novak, T. P., Hoffman, D. L., & Duhachek, A. (2003). The influence of goal-directed and experiential activities on online flow experiences. *Journal of Consumer Psychology, 13*(1-2), 3–16. doi:10.1207/S15327663JCP13-1&2_01.

Pace, S. (2004). Grounded theory of the flow experiences of web users. *International Journal of Human-Computer Studies, 60*(3), 327–363. doi:10.1016/j.ijhcs.2003.08.005.

Pearce, J., Ainley, M., & Howard, S. (2005). The ebb and flow of online learning. *Journal of Computers and Human Behaviour, 21*(5), 745–771.

Pelet, J. É., & Lecat, B. (2011). Enhancing learning and cooperation through digital virtual worlds. *International Journal of Virtual and Personal Learning Environments*, 3(2), 59–76. doi:10.4018/jvple.2012040104.

Privette, G. (1983). Peak experience, peak performance and flow: A comparative analysis of positive human experiences. *Journal of Personality and Social Psychology*, 45(6), 1361–1368. doi:10.1037/0022-3514.45.6.1361.

Privette, G., & Bundrick, C. (1987). Measurement of experience: Constructs and content validity of the experience questionnaire. *Perceptual and Motor Skills*, 65(1), 315–332. doi:10.2466/pms.1987.65.1.315.

Privette, G., & Bundrick, C. (1991). Peak experience, peak performance and flow: Correspondence of personal descriptions and theoretical constructs. *Journal of Social Behavior and Personality*, 6(5), 169–188.

Reeves, B., & Nass, C. (1996). *The media equation: How people treat computers, television and new media like real people and places*. Stanford, CA: CSLI Publications and Cambridge University Press.

Sénécal, S., Gharbi, J. E., & Nantel, J. (2002). The influence of flow on hedonic and utilitarian shopping values. In Broniarczyk, S., & Nakamoto, K. (Eds.), *Advances in consumer research* (*Vol. 29*, pp. 483–484). Provo, UT: Association for Consumer Research.

Voelkl, J. E., & Ellis, G. D. (1998). Measuring experiences in daily life: An examination of the items used to measure challenge and skill. *Journal of Leisure Research*, 30(3), 380–389.

Young, C. E. (2004). Capturing the flow of emotion in television commercials: A new approach. *Journal of Advertising Research*, 44(2), 202–209. doi:10.1017/S0021849904040103.

KEY TERMS AND DEFINITIONS

Challenge: Level of perceived complexity and the number of possibilities for action in the virtual environment.

Clickstream: The path a visitor takes through one or more Web sites reflecting a series of choices made both within a Website (e.g., which pages to visit, how long to stay, whether or not to make an online purchase) and across Web sites (e.g., which sites to visit). Clickstream data are captured in server log files.

Concentration: The extent to which the individual's attention is completely absorbed by the activity to the extent that nothing else matter.

Control: The individual's perception of exercising control and dominating the interaction with the technology.

Curiosity: An individual's sensory or cognitive desire to attain competence with the technology and explore the interaction possibilities available.

Enjoyment: Individual's subjective gratification of the interaction with the technology, so the using of the virtual world is perceived to be enjoyable regardless of any performance consequences.

Exploratory Behaviour: It is a curiosity-motivated, variety-seeking, risk-taking, and innovative behaviour.

Flow: The state in which people are so involved in an activity that nothing else seems to matter, so in this dynamic state, individual's attention is fully concentrated on the task at hand, elevating cognitive processing capacity beyond normal level, and making intellectual performance easier and more pleasant.

Telepresence: Extent to which one feels present and immersed in the mediated virtual environment, rather than in one's immediate physical environment.

Chapter 10
"From Clicks to Taps and Swipes":
Translating User Needs to a Mobile Knowledge Management Experience

Madhavi M. Chakrabarty
Verizon Wireless, USA

ABSTRACT

Organizations constantly strive to improve the richness and reach of their knowledge resources to ensure optimal performance of their employees in their job functions. Some of the techniques that organizations have used in the past have included state-of-the-art search engines, creating a directed navigation by mapping content to employee transactions, and incorporating user experience design heuristics. Search engine improvement is reputed to be the most used technique, even though its effectiveness in organizational knowledge management systems has not been confirmed. With more and more organizations now having a mobile employee base, there is now a need to provide employees access to organizational resources anytime and anywhere. This chapter provides insight into some of the challenges in organizational knowledge management systems and the implications of designing a mobile system. It proposes some heuristics on designing a knowledge management system for mobile systems and proposes a framework to validate it against available user acceptance models.

INTRODUCTION

Knowledge management systems can be defined as systems that support creation, transfer and application of knowledge in organizations (Alavi & Leidner, 2001). To make a knowledge management system effective, it has to be easy to access, and provide accurate information in a timely manner. For a long time, organizations have depended on a good knowledge management system for the learning and training needs of their employees. In the context of an organizational knowledge management system, knowledge resources include reference content and learning content that employees use to maintain and improve their explicit knowledge (Collins, 2012). A good knowledge management system also helps to capture the tacit knowledge of its user base. The success of an organizational knowledge management system depends on how effectively it can be used by its user base at the time of need.

DOI: 10.4018/978-1-4666-4566-0.ch010

The improvements over time in knowledge management systems were geared towards improving ease of access, time to access information and the accuracy of information accessed from the knowledge management systems (Becerra-Fernandez, Gonzalez, & Sabherwal, 2004). These three parameters are the major driving factors for all the research related to the design, implementation and management of knowledge management systems in general and organizational knowledge management systems in particular. Improving ease of access in design of knowledge management systems have been based on principles and guidelines of usability and user experience design (Karner & Droschl, 2002). The design of the navigation and menus reflect guidelines from user experience handbooks and experts and the influence of these experts on the design of organizational knowledge management systems. Search engine integration to existing knowledge management systems helped to improve time to access information in large knowledge bases (Becerra-Fernandez et al., 2004; Robertson, 2006). The search engines varied from a basic keyword only search engine to more intelligent and smarter search engines (Bughin et al., July 2011). Directed navigation was another attempt to design the system so that it mimicked the behavior of the users and presented the right information at the time of need, thereby attempting to improve the accuracy as well as ease of access of information. Directed navigation required the knowledge managers to understand the different transactions and inquiries that were performed by the users of the system and then design a system that categorized the content based on the type of transactions and where the user was in the transaction. All the above improvements resulted in a progressive and steady improvement in the design, development, implementation and performance of the knowledge management systems over time.

One important factor that enabled the evolution of knowledge management systems was the evolution in the areas of system hardware, software, and other performance driving measures. These factors have impacted the development of IT systems in general. Even as knowledge management systems were becoming more efficient with the right hardware choices, another change that was happening was in the organizational landscapes. More and more organizations were incorporating faster computing resources to handle their IT needs (Chase, 2008). Many organizations were going global and their organizational knowledge needs were growing exponentially with it. Currently, organizations are also becoming mobile, and along with the organizations, the workforce is also becoming mobile (Antill, 2013; Citrix White paper, Oct 2012). Overall, over the last decade, the improving computational resources resulted in the organizations ability to implement more robust and efficient systems and mobilization of the organizations has generated the need for these organizations to create a knowledge management system that can be accessed anywhere and anytime by the user base so that the users can continue being effective in their job requirements.

Many organizations are seeking the solution for a mobile knowledge management system by using traditional usability and user feedback techniques to gather requirements. But preliminary implementations and results have shown that while users know what they want, they sometimes do not know what they need (Churchville, 2008). Many organizations have reported that in going back to the users, the top feedback received was the need for a "Google" search engine. While Google works perfectly in the chaotic Internet world, a search engine implementation does not solve all the issues and requirements of a mobile knowledge management system. Therefore, the need arises to discover the needs of the mobile employees and how they can be resolved when designing a tool that helps them perform their job responsibilities in a mobile environment.

This chapter discusses the progressive improvement of organizational knowledge management systems and the drivers that prompted these changes. The background section discusses the different efforts and the impact of these efforts in the development of the literature in knowledge management systems. Search and directed navigation have been the biggest change agents in improving the effectiveness (ease of access, timeliness and accuracy of information) of the knowledge management systems. The background section of the chapter discusses the influence and limitations of the inclusion of enterprise search engines and directed navigation on creating effective knowledge management systems. The background section also discusses the often ignored topic of user experience in the domain of knowledge management. The contribution of this chapter is in extending the knowledge management systems in a mobile environment. To design a successful knowledge management system for the mobile world, there is a need to go beyond traditional user experience approaches to understand the specific needs of the user base. Organizations are facing specific challenges and roadblocks in mobilizing their workforce while ensuring that the workforce does not suffer in terms of developing their explicit and tacit knowledge. Providing an effective knowledge management system with the introduction of mobile work environments has become a catalyst that many knowledge managers are using to reinvent how the knowledge management systems are designed. An approach and heuristic is provided as an option for knowledge managers to recreate their knowledge management systems in the refined ecosystem of hardware, software and communication technologies now available to the knowledge managers.

BACKGROUND

Knowledge management systems have been used by organizations to keep its work force updated with the knowledge and information they need to perform business, and complete transactions that are a part of their job responsibilities. Organizational knowledge management resources

include both reference content and learning content. Employees may refer to their organization's knowledge resources to undergo training that improves their knowledge of the business subject matter or they may refer to it during a business process when they are looking for answers to specific questions. For example, the customer service representatives in an organization may refer to their organizational knowledge bases to answer a customer's question or help them troubleshoot any issue they may be facing with the product, system or service provided by the organization. Similarly, a sales representative may use the knowledge base to create a proposal to a prospective client in order to earn a new business. When an employee is hired into an organization or moves into a new role within the same organization, the organization may require the employee to complete certain training programs that prepares the employees in their new roles. Also, as employees are working in their roles, they end up creating best practices that may help others in the role to learn and perform better. All these information that is used to train an employee or help an employee perform their duties are encompassed in the organizational knowledge management system (Wang, 1995).

The design and implementation of knowledge management systems have changed significantly over the past 20 or so years. The amount of knowledge created and served by organizations has grown exponentially over this time (Rosenbaum, 2011). This in turn has resulted in a never ending quest for knowledge managers have been to design faster systems which serve accurate information at the time of need. The development of knowledge management systems for organizational learning has lead to improved business knowledge of its employees. The employees keep themselves updated with the business knowledge, the organizational policies and other content to better serve their client base. The success of a knowledge management system depends on how fast and how accurately it can serve information at the time of need to the employees. If an employee is tenured or has been performing the same job over a period of time, they may not need to refer to the knowledge resources to answer the most common questions. For example, a sales rep will not need to refer to the shipping and return policy each time he or she is completing the sales process. Therefore, while organizational knowledge encompasses the whole universe of information required in the business of the organization, a knowledge management system has to be designed such that only the relevant information is available to the user at the time of the need. This makes the job of knowledge managers a never ending quest of being able to provide the most robust systems in the hands of its users so that they can maximize the resources available to them (Sharmin, Bailey, Coats, & Hamilton., 2009).

Introduction of Search Engines in Knowledge Management Systems

One major milestone in development of organizational knowledge management system has been the inclusion of "enterprise search engines." Search engines return a set of listings in response to a search query. Search provides the users with a way to circumvent the navigation and access information directly from the listings in the search results. Google has in many ways made the access of information on the Internet very easy (Barroso, Dean, & Micro, 2003; Cho & Roy, 2004). It is sometimes the only access point for users to surf the huge repository of information on the Internet. Users who use Google within or outside the organization as a way to surf the Web look for the same ease of access to information in organizational knowledge management systems.

Enterprise search engines work the same way except that the search result are limited to the information available in the knowledge resources within the organization. It may be restricted to only the internal documents in the organizations knowledgebase or may include external content from specific online resources. The reaction of the users to the inclusion of search engines has been very positive as it has proved to be a handy tool when the navigation is either not optimal or cognitively does not align to the activity that the employee is performing. It also extends the cognitive model of information searching that users are used to outside of their work schedule.

Directed Navigation in Knowledge Management System

Another methodology that has improved information access in organizational knowledge management systems is the methodology of "directed navigation" (Oberbeck, 2004). Organizational process and procedures can be bucketed into specific queries. For example, a pricing query, a sales query, a trouble shooting query etc. The foundation of directed navigation is based on the assumption that organizational content can be categorized in the same structure as the organizational query (Choo, 1998; Grant, 1996). Therefore, in the design of directed navigation, the attempt is to classify and tag the content based on the query it helps answer. The system then directs users to certain pieces of content in a pre-organized sequence so that it mimics the transaction being performed by the user. When the user is in the system, the system guides them to the next logical piece of content as per a rules engine that is built into it. The directed navigation approach works very well when the user is performing a transaction that is available in the rules engine of the system. But contrary to the user's expectation, the system fails when users have to complete a transaction that does not fall into the classifications defined in the rules engine and or is an exception.

While directed navigation improves the time and accuracy to information access in the most common user query scenario, it fails when the inbuilt rules engine does not account for a certain user query. It also fails when the rules engine does not account for the users thought process. Also, as mentioned earlier, users do not refer to knowledge resources and content for the most common queries and tasks because the frequency and repetitive nature of these queries result in the knowledge in these scenarios to become the "tacit knowledge" of the user (Nonaka, 1994). Also, very often in the organizations, it is hard to find two inquiries are exactly alike. Most user queries have some level of uniqueness. Therefore, directed navigation does not work for all types of organizational queries and knowledge requirements.

The Impact of User Experience in Development of Knowledge Management

Enterprise search and directed navigation were introduced into knowledge management systems as a result of studies that showed the ease of information access attributed to these methodologies. The success of these methodologies was validated by reaching back to the user to understand their perceived satisfaction in using these systems. Various user experience guidelines and heuristics were introduced to make the knowledge management systems easy to use. Over time, it became a practice in many organizations to run periodic user testing sessions to gather inputs regarding the existing knowledge management systems, and the user inputs were used to refine or redefine organizational knowledge management systems. Most of the user testing used in these scenarios are in the form of focus groups, user surveys, one-on-one semi-structured interviews and wireframe walkthroughs (Ben Shneiderman & Plaisant, 1997). The details of the user-testing as applied in the domain of organizational knowledge management system are as follows.

In focus groups, groups of 10 – 15 users are scheduled for a session where a facilitator helps them to discuss the current issues they are facing with their knowledge management systems. The focus group facilitator may have a set of directed questions based on the particular aspects of the systems they are targeting for improvement. The facilitator uses these questions to make sure the conversation remain in the scope that the team can influence.

User Surveys are a set of questions that can be sent out to the users to gather responses or satisfaction levels on specific aspects of the current knowledge management system or prospective features on the next generation knowledge management system. User surveys can either target the entire population if the user base is relatively small, or can be targeted to stratified segments of the population representing different user types in different user roles from different part of the organization.

In one-on-one semi-structured interviews, facilitators ask directed questions to a user on how they use the existing systems, what issues they face and any other feedback they may have. Semi-structured interviews are used to complement focus groups, as in focus groups the discussion may get channelized on one specific aspect depending on whom the user group represents and who has the strongest voice.

Wireframe walkthroughs are used later in the development cycle when the knowledge managers are more certain about the improvements they are proposing in the next phase. They draw out detailed screens and interaction in a mock interface and take it back to the user base to understand the ease of use, and find any issues with the new design before the system is implemented. It helps the developers to design a system that is more user-centric and a higher chance of success.

These user experience perspectives have helped understand the specific issues that users are facing and the can lead to the requirements for the next iteration of improvements to the knowledge management systems. This section illustrated the improvements and changes that have shaped the design of knowledge management systems by large. However, over this time, there were other changes that have impacted the organizational environment, one of which is the mobilization of the work force. Mobile devices and systems have infiltrated the organizational landscape as organizations became virtual and employees became more mobile. With the advent of mobile devices, there is a need to equip the employees with a mobile device to conduct business. And subsequently, there is a need to provide knowledge resources to the employees so that the employees are able to access the knowledge management content anywhere and anytime (Borg, 27 July 2011).

Past Studies in Mobile Knowledge Management Systems

The literature on the use and evaluation of knowledge management systems in mobile environments is very limited. While mobile devices have been available in many forms since the early 2000s, the technology became more widespread and accepted within the enterprises after the launch of the iPads in 2010. Earlier, the mobile technologies that were used in organizations were not targeted for any enterprise applications including knowledge management usage. The introduction of the 10" tablet, specifically with the Apple Ipad can be considered the catalyst that made many organizations think about inclusion of mobile devices into their business processes.

Claimed as the first study in the area of mobile knowledge management systems, the study on user acceptance of mobile knowledge management systems (Chen and Huang, 2010) focuses on the ability of performance on users using mobile phones and PDAs as compared to laptops. The authors claim that this paper is the first study that encourages learners to acquire, store, share, apply and create knowledge. However, the study or the authors do not mention the system design to be a function of the mobility of the system.

There are other studies on mobile interfaces and the implementation in knowledge management system. These studies (Kumar, Dey and Rao, 2011; Balfanz, Grimm and Tazari, 2005) are focused on the architecture of the enterprise environment, deployment, security and restriction

issues rather than the users perspective and usage behavior. The studies make no mention of the design of the interfaces and factors influencing the system interface design.

Other researchers have addressed only specific aspects of the design of mobile applications. For example, there are research studies that focus on the challenges of organizations to move to mobile technologies (Antill, 2013; Peskin, 2011), the impact of ergonomics in mobile system design (Rauch, 2011), the ability of accessing information anywhere and anytime, in terms of location and time (Borg, 2011; Zakaria, Melinckx, & Wilemon, 2004), the strategy of engaging the X-gen users in teaching and learning environments (Duffy, 2007). There are some studies that address design considerations (Grimm, Tazari and Balfanz, 2005) but were published much before the first tablets (10" screens) were introduced as a viable option in the enterprise market. Therefore, these resources cannot be claimed as a prior work in the design of knowledge management system in organizations.

Based on the background and the past research on the evolution of knowledge management systems and the changing organizational technological landscape, the next section discusses the challenges in design of mobile knowledge management systems and a heuristic based approach to solve for the challenges and design a mobile knowledge management system. It ends with a section that discusses a modified TAM (Technology Acceptance Model) to understand the user acceptance of the system that is designed.

MAIN FOCUS OF THE CHAPTER

Success and Limitations of Search Engines and Directed Navigation in Knowledge Management Systems

As mentioned earlier, organizational knowledge managers have a never ending challenge of providing the latest and accurate information to the employees at the time of need. Organizations change over time. These changes can be in their business model, the products and services they provide or their business processes and goals. Knowledge management systems have to keep evolving with every change in the organization to maintain the relevance of the workforce in the changing business world. This helps to improve the tacit and explicit knowledge of the employees and gives them timely access to information.

As discussed in the previous section, the developments in search engine and the methodology of directed navigation were two significant developments that impacted the way organizational knowledge management systems are developed (Cho & Roy, 2004; Oberbeck, 2004). Search engines could range from a simple keyword search to a more intelligent natural language search feature. Depending on the size of the organization and the allocated budget for the knowledge management initiatives, the return-on-investment did not justify improving the search engines. On the other hand, the initiatives in directed navigation provided a solution against information overloading. When the directed navigation was designed right, the users were only presented with the relevant pieces of content at any point in time depending on what transaction they were addressing and where in the transaction they were (Grant, 1996). The challenge with directed navigation was that the needs and usage of content by the employees were very unique and it was hard to create a transaction level navigation for all content. Content could seldom be bucketed into inquiry types and transactions that users were completing during the day. Users were forced to re-navigate the content from the start in order to be able to answer queries, leading to user frustration and dissatisfaction (Presentations, October 17-19, 2012).

In the discussion on the challenges of refining the knowledge management systems, it might be argued that it would be easy to dynamically address these issues with appropriate logging, reporting and analytic tools. While many organizations use

the latest and most robust logging techniques for their client facing system, the same is lacking for their internal knowledge management system (Human Factors International, Presentations, October 17-19, 2012). It is hard for many organizations to prove the return-on-investment on an initiative that is potentially a cost cutting mechanism for the organization. Therefore, even though the knowledge management systems may have logging and reporting capabilities, it is unlikely to be captured and integrated to the rules engines or search capabilities of the tools used by the knowledge management systems.

This section presented the success and the challenges faced in development of knowledge management systems that can be attributed to search and directed navigation. The next section presents the more detailed challenge of the impact of user experience.

Success and Limitations of User Experience in Knowledge Management Systems

User experience heuristics and guidelines have been used to improve the ease of use of organizational knowledge management systems. Improving the ease of use improves the user acceptance and thereby the usage of the systems. Many organizations incorporate certain levels of user experience and usability perspective when it comes to improving their organization's knowledge management systems (Martin, 2013). Some of the recommendations are incorporated from the prescribed guidelines and heuristics as recommended by the subject matter experts (Human Factors International; Nielson, 1992). Many organizations organize user testing sessions and data gathering sessions to understand what the users were looking for and if there are gaps in the existing system that needs to be addressed in the next generation of knowledge management systems. Some of these user testing and data gathering techniques include focus groups, survey feedback and user feedback of the current systems (Kuhn, 2000; Oppenheim, 1992). To understand how the user base uses the systems, knowledge managers sometimes use a technique called user base shadowing. Here the experts spend time with the users of the system as they complete their daily job requirements. This way, the experts are able to document real issues and challenges faced by the users as they access and use the information provided by the knowledge systems. While users provide feedback during focus group session and one-on-one semi-structured interviews, they may fail to elucidate certain issues because they are so used to working around them while performing their jobs.

While user-experience feedbacks help to understand many concerns that the users are facing, it sometimes fails to get any feedback on what additional enhancement would make the system easier to use. Most of the feedbacks from user are a reflection of their usage of the Internet outside of their work schedules. As a result, organizations are discovering that when they reach out to the users for feedback on what needs to be done to improve the knowledge management systems, the general feedback is to provide them with a "Google" for their systems, so that they can just get to the information they are looking for (Voorhees, 2002).Several organizations have compiled their responses from their users. Some of the anecdotal responses include: "…just give us a blank page with a Google search button," and "Give us Google and we can figure out the information we are looking for" (Several Presentations, October 17-19, 2012). If this user need is translated into an actionable item, it would result in investing in a more robust search engine.

However, ineffectiveness of a knowledge management system is not necessarily as the result of an inadequate search engine. A Internet search engine like Google works better in chaotic data because chaotic data accounts for different vocabularies, user description of the problem and the ambiguity of search terms used by the users (Kleinberg,

1999; Song, Luo, Wen, Yu, & Hon, 2007). An organizational knowledge management system on the other hand is very structured and consistent when it comes to using terms and definitions. When employees look for information based on user queries, their language may not always reflect the language used by the subject matter experts of the organization. Therefore, understanding the specific needs might not always be in asking the user what they want and the knowledge managers need to investigate beyond user feedback to look for answers.

Introduction of Mobile Interfaces

Apart from the challenges mentioned above, a more recent challenge has been the changing ecosystem in the organizations. Of special interest in this chapter is the introduction of mobile devices and interfaces into the organizational ecosystem (Cearley, 2012; Peskin, 2011). Organizational information technology assets have changed from desktops and laptops to include cell phones, tablets and mobile hotspots (Dimensional Research, 2011). Organizations allow their employees to use mobile devices like cell phones and tablets to organize and perform their business responsibilities. This change was the result of businesses becoming more mobile as they are expanding their client bases and operations across the globe (Zakaria, Melinckx, & Wilemon, 2004). Business clients are spread all across the globe and business provide 24/7 support to their clients. Sales representatives travel around the globe to sell products and services to potential clients. A major enabling factor that has supported this change in the way organizations has been the improvement of wireless and mobile technologies that have resulted in a wide spectrum of devices and connectivity technologies to become available for business of all size and shapes (Dimensional Research, 2011).

With the mobilization of organizations, the employees and their workplace, there was a need to mobilize the learning and reference content that the employees needed to keep up with the organizations needs and to help them complete their job responsibilities with access to the right information at the right time. Therefore, the challenge for the knowledge managers was to enable mobile organizational knowledge resources to its employees at any time or at any place. Many organizations were willing to invest in new technologies and infrastructure to support the growing needs of the business and its employees. This new requirement came as a boon to the knowledge managers who saw this new option as a chance to revamp the existing knowledge management systems rather than go for a progressive update or facelift on an existing system.

The mobile knowledge management systems have to be designed to account for portability and around the paradigm of a mobile interface design. Because the domain of mobile user interfaces is very new, the existing studies and references are not sufficient to support a particular design strategy as compared to another. However, some characteristics of mobile interfaces need to be taken into account as the systems are designed and deployed. For example, in designing a system for mobile interfaces, ergonomics plays a major role in designing the interface (Rauch, 2011). Users use their mobile devices while doing another activity – like walking, talking or using another device. Users were also most likely to carrying the device in their hands as they use it, which means they are able to use the interface with at most one hand. Information in mobile devices is accessed by tapping rather than clicking. While Web based applications provide a top or a left menu for navigation, in mobile devices, a left or top navigation may not necessarily provide the best navigation experience or ease of use. To take advantage of the tapping feature and the availability of the entire surface area to design the menu, the system can be designed as a function of the surface area of the device.

Since the mobile device will be used by the employee while on the move, the second factor to consider is that they will not be single tasking. So it is very unlikely of them to be focused on the single task of looking for content at any moment of need. Therefore, providing an interface that they can navigate beyond the virtue of eye movement and navigation will make the interface more acceptable. For example, when users use a television remote control or a telephone handset, they know the relative location of the different buttons and use their muscle memory to navigate through the different buttons and menu items. They can operate the remote while staring at the television set. The same holds true for other interfaces like gaming systems and car dashboard. While the user can very easily navigate on these systems owing to their muscle memory, they will become more frustrated when the remotes are replaced with another from a different make and model. It is easy to visualize the frustration of a driver using the different controls in a rental car and trying to figure out what each knob, switch and icon means. The same can be translated into the mobile interface of knowledge management systems. The advantages of navigation using muscle memory need to be translated to the mobile interfaces as well. For example, the "bottom right" of the screen can always link to "current industry news" or the top left of every page can have the feature to let the user share the page with coworkers. The users could tap the bottom right without having to look at the screen and be directed to the current industry news section. Another way to enable hands free navigation would be to include a voice interface to navigate and retrieve information made the device and system (Mocherman, 2012). Voice navigation makes the system accessible to visually challenged users as well as provides an alternate navigation for the sighted users (Mocherman, 2012). The location and voice commands in this case have to be carefully decided and designed because once users get comfortable using the system, it will be very hard to make any changes and not get the user frustrated while using the modified interface.

Given the challenges and new features provided by the mobile interfaces, the next section provides a workable approach to design the navigation and layout of the knowledge management systems.

A Workable Solution to Navigation Design

Given the challenges of the existing knowledge management systems, the limitations of traditional feedback gathering sessions and the changing landscape of the organizational structures and expectations, it is necessary to device a combination of intrusive and non-intrusive mechanisms to design a system that would truly meet the needs of the users while helping the bottom line of the organization.

As mentioned in the section on "Success and limitations of user experience in knowledge management systems," user experience methodologies might not yield the right feedback when designing the navigation of a mobile knowledge management system. When user feedback techniques like focus groups and user surveys do not yield any actionable items, it becomes necessary to find alternate mechanisms to understand user behavior in knowledge management systems and how the behavior would be impacted when the system is mobilized. In other words, the challenge is to understand what the users need and not what the users want. One aspect to consider is the amount of information that needs to be provided to the user in the mobile interface. Too little information will not be result in a usable tool, and too much information will lead to information overload for the user, but will also tax the mobile bandwidth of the mobile devices. For mobile systems it also translates into understanding what resources needs to be included in the system and how it can be accessed in the system. The "what" can be answered using a combination of existing log files and interactive sessions like card-sorting.

The "how" can be answered by understanding the system characteristics that can or cannot be used on the mobile device.

Before going into details regarding the "what" and "how," a brief description of card sorting is presented. In card-sorting, a facilitator hands out a set of cards to the users (Nielsen, 1995; Spencer & Warfel, 2004). Each card in the set of cards is prewritten with words or phrases in a particular domain. The users are asked to group the different words and phrases so that like ones are in one group. The users are also asked to rank the different words and phrases in one group according to their relative importance. There are different variations of the card-sorting activity that can be included on a need basis like, users can be asked to note down important words and phrases missing from the set, or users can be asked to note down alternate words or synonyms that are more widely used as compared to the word on the card (Nielsen, 1995). There are computer based card-sorting tools that are now available to enable the facilitator to conduct multiple card sorting sessions in parallel and remotely (Nielsen, 1995; Spencer & Warfel, 2004). Card sorting exercises help to understand the way users perceive the relative importance of the different terms and the location of similar terms together when designing navigation in an online system. The technique of card-sorting in answering "what" and "how" of organizational knowledge management system design are discussed next.

Answering the "what" requires tracing content footprint of the users in the existing systems. Users use reference and learning content during their work routine in a pull or push manner. Pull means when the user comes across something during a work day and wants to know more about it (Duffy, 2007). Push means when training or other content gets pushed to the user for him or her to complete (Duffy, 2007). Understanding when the users choose one type of content over the other and how users navigate through the content helps to identify the different content types, the relative importance and usage frequency. The information can be collected from the basic usage logs of the systems or a page view reporting if available. In case these logs are not available, knowledge workers can be creative in trying to get this information from indirect sources such as update history on each content page, feedback received in each content page or even a user-shadowing exercise. In any case, attention needs to be paid to seasonal and yearly variations of usage logs for the different content pieces.

A very important view of the users' footprint can be analyzed using search logs on a system. This log not only provides information on usage and relative importance of different types of content, it can also provide an insight into the vocabulary of the employees and the customers being served by the employees. Since the employees search the knowledge base in response to a customer's query, most often they repeat the same words or phrase as used by the customers in the search engine. As discussed earlier, this may not always return the right result, because the customer's terminology may be different from the one used by the organization internally. A correlation between the search term and search rating of the content piece accessed can be done to remove language ambiguity and wording inconsistencies. The search log also helps in aligning the vocabulary of the content closer to the vocabulary of the employees and the customers.

The approach here presents the use of the usage log and search log to understand the pattern of content navigation by the users. Matching up the search log data with the content usage data helps to resolve ambiguity in the organization's vocabulary. Therefore, a key point in analyzing the content usage pattern by the users depends on being able to analyze one set of logs in context of other log files. In the same way, having access to the transactions of the users and being able to understand the frequency of content access in context of the transaction either through navigation or search will provide valuable and a complete picture of user and his/her intent of using a specific piece of content.

After analyzing the usage logs and the search logs, a card-sorting exercise can be done using the top search terms key phrases from the top used content over the past few months or years depending on how far the knowledge managers find the data to be relevant. The navigation elements can be designed based on the results of the card-sorting data. The card sorting exercise can be repeated with different user groups with various job responsibilities to understand how content was perceived and used differently by different user groups. This can help to personalize the navigation elements for the different user groups.

Once the navigation elements are decided, the next step is to answer how to place these navigational elements on the mobile interface? As discussed previously, the navigation of the system can be designed as a function of the display surface of the mobile device. Depending on the output of the card-sorting exercise, the navigation can be designed as a matrix, a radial or a treemap (Shneiderman, 2002) as suited for that particular dataset. For example, if the analysis shows that the content can be structured as categories with similar subcategories, the interface can be designed as a matrix layout as shown in Figure 1. If the card-sorting analysis shows that the content can be grouped under a few categories that are very distinct and non-overlapping, the interface can be designed as a radial screen with a pie section of the screen devoted to a particular content type as shown in Figure 2. If the analysis results in a dataset of hierarchical data with a limited number of top categories, the interface can be designed as a treemap as shown in Figure 3. Knowledge managers can be creative when it comes to creating this interface because the end goal is to create an interface that requires very little cognitive processing when users are accessing the system. It also makes the interface exciting and less overbearing leading to increased usage of the system. Care has to be taken in deciding on the navigation, because once users are accustomed to one particular layout, changing it will lead to the users getting frustrated or losing confidence in the system.

Figure 1. A matrix layout for the mobile knowledge management system

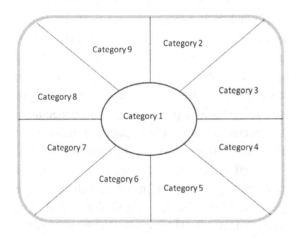

Figure 3. A treemap layout for the mobile knowledge management system

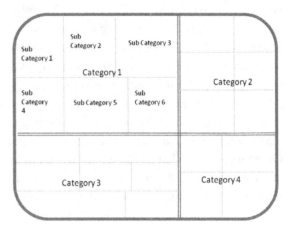

Figure 2. A radial layout for the mobile knowledge management system

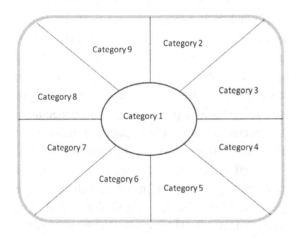

If designed effectively, the navigation layout will be an abstracted version of the directed navigation. In addition to all the advantages that directed navigation provides, this navigation lets the users start the directed approach from any point. Apart from the navigation, it is always recommended to include a search feature in the navigation. If the interface is designed effectively, navigation will overtake the use of search engine. However, the occasional user query, or while including a new type of content or new user type, the search feature can provide a neat navigation element for users to circumvent the layout on the screen.

Validating against User Acceptance

The success of the system and its adoption by the user base can be best described by how well the users have accepted the system. One of the most established methodologies for defining system acceptance is the TAM (Technology Acceptance Model) (Venkatesh, 2000). The original TAM model defines two constructs as determinants of user acceptance (Davis, 1989). These two constructs are perceived usefulness and perceived ease of use, where perceived usefulness is a measure of the degree to which an individual believes that the developed system will enhance their job performance and the perceived ease of use is the degree to which the system would be intuitive or free of effort. Other variants of the TAM model were developed when the original model either could not describe a system acceptance behavior or the original model had to be expanded to define new constructs that in turn encapsulated the constructs in the original TAM model. Some variants of the TAM model focused on the attitudes of users on the

Internet and modified the TAM model to explain how attitudes determine system usage (Davis, Bagozzi, & Warshaw, 1992; Lederer, Maupin, Sena, & Zhuang, 2000; Porter & Donthu, 2006). Other researchers describe the role of factors such as age, education, income and race as factors that impact perceived ease of use, perceived usefulness which in turn impact the attitude and usage of the system (Agarwal & Prasad, 1997; Venkatesh, 2000; Venkatesh, Morris, & Ackerman, 2000). Over time, the TAM model has evolved to include and categorize the different constructs and their impact on the intention to use any new system. The roadmap of the TAM model development included the influence of TAM on the world wide Web acceptance model (Lederer, Maupin, Sena, & Zhuang, 2000), task technology fit constructs (Goodhue & Thompson, 1995; Goodhue, 1995) and the role of user characteristics (Compeau & Higgins, 1995), and many more.

While most of these models specify the motivation for selecting the specific criteria, and each of the constructs amplify or reduce the impact of the parameters that define the behavioral intention to use, the UTAUT (Unified Theory of Acceptance and Use of Technology) of Venkatesh and Davis encompasses all the previous work into one umbrella model (Venkatesh, Morris, Davis, & Davis, 2003). The constructs used in the UTAUT model are being used as a baseline for this chapter because the constructs of UTAUT can be closely associated with the different aspects of mobile technology, knowledge management system and organizational knowledge that are being discussed in this chapter.

The four main drivers of UTAUT are performance expectancy, effort expectancy, social influence and facilitating conditions. Performance expectancy is the degree to which an individual believes that using the system will help them perform their job responsibilities more effectively (Venkatesh, Morris, Davis, & Davis, 2003). Venkatesh et. al. also identify performance expectancy to be the construct that encapsulates all constructs related to perceived usefulness and is the strongest predictor of intention of use for the users. For mobile knowledge management systems designed using the heuristics proposed in this chapter, the constructs related to performance expectancy are assumed to rate higher because one of the drivers of this technology is in aiding the users to have access to all their knowledge resources even if the user is at a remote location and is not connected to the organization's corporate domain. The use of mobile technologies help the user by providing an anywhere, anytime access to the knowledge resources using an interface that helps to connect by getting the client's attention and admiration for the organizations' technological capabilities.

Effort expectancy is defined as the perceived degree of ease in using the system by the users (Venkatesh, Morris, Davis, & Davis, 2003). While there may be initial resistance by users in accepting newer systems and technologies, mobile devices with touch based interactions have been touted for their ease of use, very short learning curves and ease of expansion to users with accessibility needs. Since the design of the system is based on the ability to use the system while multitasking or with less cognitive processing, effort expectancy is expected to positively impact the intention to use for mobile knowledge management solutions.

Social influence is defined as the degree of user's perception of how important others believe they should use the system (Venkatesh, Morris, Davis, & Davis, 2003). Social influence is expected to be very high on the impact of using mobile knowledge management systems. Employees typically will use the mobile knowledge resources in communicating with potential clients to complete a proposal or as a support functionality to improve the customer experience. In either capacity, staying updated on the latest devices, and technologies improve the trust of potential and existing clients in the technological efficiencies of the organization that is their product/ service provider.

Facilitating conditions is the degree to which individuals believe that the organization has the infrastructure and know how to support the new system (Venkatesh, Morris, Davis, & Davis,

2003). For mobile knowledge management systems, facilitating conditions can be main reason for acceptance or rejection of the system. Mobile technologies come with two very serious concerns for organizations in terms of information security and bandwidth restrictions. Organizations have an ongoing challenge to make sure that the information in their knowledge resources is only reaching the intended employees and users. In designing a mobile system, organizations have to plan for loss and theft of devices and the issues related to the access of the devices by unauthorized users. Similarly, on the question of bandwidth, organizations have to work with limitations of speed and data transfer over mobile/ WI-FI networks. Some organizations may limit access to video content on the networks while other organizations may decide to preload larger information chunks onto the device hardware. The choice, flexibility and process of organizations will ultimately drive the experience and the facilitating condition of the organization.

While a detailed analysis of the user acceptance model is out of scope of this chapter and has be undertaken by the implementer of the system, the framework provided in this section can be used by knowledge managers to understand the level of acceptance of mobile organizational knowledge systems.

FUTURE RESEARCH DIRECTIONS

The above sections present an approach to recreate knowledge management systems for organizational learning. A future research direction in this area can focus on making the organizational knowledge management systems more robust by including feedbacks from the current and intended implementation of the systems; and incorporate the feedbacks to make the system more effective. For example, tracing the user's footprint in the redesigned navigation on the mobile interface can help to tailor the mobile user interface for the next

generation of knowledge management systems. While a discussion is included in this chapter on the UTAUT model (Venkatesh, Morris, Davis, & Davis, 2003) and its implication on a system design or redesign, a future work in this area could focus on validating a stable implementation of the system against the UTAUT model.

Another future research could focus on including organizational knowledge as an integrated aspect of another system so that the knowledge systems are no longer a discrete solution. Organizational knowledge management systems become integrated as a part of the business process or other tools, systems and processes used by the users. Integrated knowledge management systems do not refer to help files and other support systems that users would typically refer to in order to complete the process. Rather, it refers to unobtrusively incorporating organizational knowledge and learning resources into other systems and business processes so that users consider these resources as another aspect of the workflow in their jobs. Resources would need to be created and delivered in different ways in order to achieve this state. However, since users would not have to go to a different location each time he/she is looking for information; it would make the system more intuitive, effective and usable. Incorporating techniques such as "nuggets" or "Did you knows" at appropriate parts of the business process would make it more interactive, interesting and directed leading to better tacit knowledge and retention of the knowledge by the users. Usage and effectiveness of integrated knowledge resources are not well known in literature and needs better analysis to evaluate the cost-benefit analysis of such an implementation.

Another direction for future research could be the inclusion of collaborative techniques into the mobile knowledge management systems. Systems based on user created data like forums, communities-of-practice and intra-organization wikis are used in many organizations to supplement organizational knowledge resources. There is a potential to use these knowledge resources as a feedback mechanism to drive some of the techniques used in this chapter. For example, rather than device a card-sorting technique to create organizational vocabulary, a text mining tool may be able to accomplish the same task by analyzing user posted content from the intra-organizational systems. Again, the improvement in effectiveness as a result of this technique needs to be studied and the return on investment justified. Moreover, the practicality of creating a text mining utility for this purpose needs to be validated in an organizational setting.

CONCLUSION

When traditional methods of data collection fail to provide the requirements for developing the next generation of organizational knowledge management systems, it is necessary to collect data in novice ways and analyze them in innovative ways to understand how the current systems are used, what are the main issues of the users and what are the drivers of the new development. This chapter provides an approach to developing and designing a knowledge management system based on system usage metrics collected from current knowledge management systems already in use by an organization. The requirements of the new system are formalized based on the users' content footprint in the current knowledge management systems in the organization. The drivers in this approach were the introduction of mobile devices into the workforce as a vehicle of change.

While this chapter presents the use case for an organizational knowledge management system and the inclusion of mobile devices as the change agent, the same paradigm could be extended for other system in different domain. To develop a system that will improve effectiveness and efficiency, it is necessary to understand the dynamics of the current system, the process where it works and where it fails. It is also necessary to understand the

dynamics for the evolving ecosystem and change agents of the organization and other aspects of the organization to ensure a successful implementation of the next generation of the systems. And as it has been presented in this chapter, certain change agents provide a platform for the system developers to rethink and re-envision the development of a system from scratch rather than to develop a system that is incrementally an improved version from the system already in use.

REFERENCES

Agarwal, R., & Prasad, J. (1997). The role of innovation characteristics and perceived voluntariness in the acceptance of information technologies. *Decision Sciences*, *28*(3), 557–582. doi:10.1111/j.1540-5915.1997.tb01322.x.

Alavi, M., & Leidner, D. E. (2001). Review: Knowledge management and knowledge management systems: Conceptual foundations and research issues. *Management Information Systems Quarterly*, *25*(1), 107–136. doi:10.2307/3250961.

Antill, D. (2013). *Effective workspace management 2013, part 1-4.* Paper presented at the Cloud Computing, Executive insights and Mobile Management at AppSense. New York, NY.

Balfanz, D., Grimm, M., & Tazari, M.-R. (2005). *A reference architecture for mobile knowledge management.* Paper presented at the Dagstuhl Seminar Proceedings. Mobile Computing and Ambient Intelligence: The Challenge of Multimedia. New York, NY.

Barroso, L., Dean, J., & Micro, U. H. (2003). Web search for a planet: The Google cluster architecture. *IEEE Computer*, *23*(2), 22–28.

Becerra-Fernandez, I., Gonzalez, A., & Sabherwal, R. (2004). *Knowledge management: Challenges, solutions and technologies.* Englewood Cliffs, NJ: Pearson Prentice Hall.

Borg, A. (2011). *Enterprise mobility management goes global: Mobility becomes core IT*. Retrieved August 24, 2011, from http://www.aberdeen.com/Aberdeen-Library/7282/RB-enterprise-mobility-management.aspx

Bughin, J., Corb, L., Manyika, J., Nottebohms, O., Chui, M., Barbat, B. D. M., & Said, R. (2011). *The impact of internet technologies: Search*. Mckinsey & Company.

Cearley, D. (2012). *Gartner identifies the top 10 strategic technology trends for 2013*. Orlando, FL: Gartner.

Chase, N. (2008). An exploration of the culture of information technology: Focus on unrelenting change. *Journal of Information, Information Technology, and Organizations, 3*.

Chen, H.-R., & Huang, H.-L. (2010). User acceptance of mobile knowledge management learning system: Design and analysis. *Journal of Educational Technology & Society, 13*(3), 70–77.

Cho, J., & Roy, S. (2004). Impact of search engines on page popularity. In *Proceedings of the 13th International Conference on World Wide Web*. ACM.

Choo, C. W. (1998). *The knowing organization: How organizations use information to construct meaning, create knowledge and make decisions*. New York: Oxford University Press.

Churchville, D. (2008). *Agile thinking: Leading successful software projects and teams*.

Citrix. (2012). *Workplace of the future* (White paper). Citrix.

Collins, H. (2012). *Tacit and explicit knowledge*. Chicago: University Of Chicago Press.

Compeau, D. R., & Higgins, C. A. (1995). Computer self-efficacy: Development of a measure and initial test. *Management Information Systems Quarterly, 19*(2), 189–211. doi:10.2307/249688.

Davis, F. D. (1989). Perceived usefulness, perceived ease of use and user acceptance of information technology. *Management Information Systems Quarterly, 13*(3), 319–339. doi:10.2307/249008.

Davis, F. D., Bagozzi, R. P., & Warshaw, P. R. (1992). Extrinsic and intrinsic motivation to use computers in the workplace. *Journal of Applied Social Psychology, 22*(14), 1111–1132. doi:10.1111/j.1559-1816.1992.tb00945.x.

Dimensional Research. (2011). *Enterprise iPad and tablet adoption: A survey*. Dimensional Research.

Duffy, P. (2007). *Engaging the YouTube Google-eyed generation: Strategies for using web 2.0 in teaching and learning*. Paper presented at the European Conference on ELearning, ECEL. London, UK.

Goodhue, D. L. (1995). Understanding user evaluations of information systems. *Management Science, 41*(12), 1827–1844. doi:10.1287/mnsc.41.12.1827.

Goodhue, D. L., & Thompson, R. L. (1995). Task-technology fit and individual performance. *Management Information Systems Quarterly, 19*(2), 213–236. doi:10.2307/249689.

Grant, R. M. (1996). Prospering in dynamically-competetive environments: Organizational capability as knowledge Integration. *Organization Science, 7*(4), 375–387. doi:10.1287/orsc.7.4.375.

Grimm, M., Tazari, M.-R., & Balfanz, D. (2005). A reference model for mobile knowledge management. In *Proceedings of I-KNOW '05*. Graz, Austria: I-KNOW.

Human Factors International. (n.d.). *Case studies*. Retrieved from http://www.humanfactors.com/about/casestudies-applications.asp

Karner, H., & Droschl, G. (2002). Usage-centered interface design for knowledge management software. *Journal of Universal Computer Science*, 8(6).

Kleinberg, J. M. (1999). Authoritative sources in a hyperlinked environment. *Journal of the ACM*, 46(5), 604–632. doi:10.1145/324133.324140.

KMWorld. (2012, October 17-19). *KMWorld Conference 2012*. Washington, DC: KM World.

Kuhn, K. (2000). Problems and benefits of requirements gathering with focus groups: A case-study. *International Journal of Human-Computer Interaction*, 12(3-4), 309–325. doi:10.1080/10447318.2000.9669061.

Kumar, R., Dey, S., & Rao, G. K. (2011). Investigation of mobile knowledge management: Developing and integrating enterprise app. store with existing knowledge management system. In *Proceedings of the International Journal of Computer Applications® (IJCA) Third Annual Global Business, IT and Management for Economic Development Conference (BITMED)*. BITMED.

Lederer, A. L., Maupin, D. J., Sena, M. P., & Zhuang, Y. (2000). The technology acceptance model and the world wide web. *Decision Support Systems*, 29(3), 269–282. doi:10.1016/S0167-9236(00)00076-2.

Martin, E. J. (2013, January 18). Responsive web design vs. user experience. *eContent Magazine*.

Mocherman, A. (2012). Why speech is key for a great mobile customer service experience. *Nuance - Insights from the Customer Experience Experts, 2012*.

Nielsen, J. (1995). *Card sorting to discover the users' model of the information space*. Retrieved from http://www.useit.com/papers/sun/cardsort.html

Nielson, J. (1992, March). The usability engineering life cycle. *IEEE Computer*, 12-22.

Nonaka, I. (1994). A dynamic theory of organizational knowledge creation. *Organization Science*, 5(1), 14–37. doi:10.1287/orsc.5.1.14.

Oberbeck, H. (2004). *Learning with hypermedia: The impact of content design and learner characteristics on navigation and the knowledge acquisition process*. Brunswick, Germany: Technischen Universität Carolo-Wilhelmina zu.

Oppenheim, A. N. (1992). *Questionaire design: Interviewing and attiture measurement*. New York: Pinter Publishers.

Peskin, D. (2011, September 27). *News on the go: How mobile devices are changing the world's information ecosystem*.

Porter, C. E., & Donthu, N. (2006). Using the technology acceptance model to explain how attitudes determine Internet usage: The role of perceived access barriers and demographics. *Journal of Business Research*, 59(9), 999–1007. doi:10.1016/j.jbusres.2006.06.003.

Rauch, M. (2011). *Mobile documentation: Usability guidelines, and considerations for providing documentation on Kindle, tablets, and smartphones*. Paper presented at the Professional Communication Conference (IPCC). New York, NY.

Robertson, J. (2006). *Good search is knowledge management*. Retrieved from www.steptwo.com.au

Rosenbaum, S. (2011). *Curation nation: How to win in a world where consumers are creators*. New York: McGraw-Hill.

Sharmin, M., Bailey, B. P., Coats, C., & Hamilton, K. (2009). *Understanding knowledge management practices for early design activity and its implication for reuse*. Paper presented at the CHI 2009. Boston, MA.

Shneiderman, B. (2002). The eyes have it: A task by data type taxonomy for information visualization. In *Proceedings IEEE Visual Languages*. Boulder, CO: IEEE.

Shneiderman, B., & Plaisant, C. (1997). *Evaluating interface designs in designing the user interface: Strategies for effective human-computer interaction* (3rd ed.). Boston, MA: Addison-Wesley Longman Publishing Co., Inc..

Song, R., Luo, Z., Wen, J.-R., Yu, Y., & Hon, H.-W. (2007). Identifying ambiguous queries in web search. In *Proceeding of WWW '07 Proceedings of the 16th International Conference on World Wide Web*. New York, NY: IEEE.

Spencer, D., & Warfel, T. (2004). *Card sorting: A definitive guide*. Retrieved from http://boxesandarrows.com/card-sorting-a-definitive-guide/

Venkatesh, V. (2000). Determinants of perceived ease of use: Integrating perceived behavioral control, computer anxiety and enjoyment into the technology acceptance model. *Information Systems Research*, *11*(4), 342–365. doi:10.1287/isre.11.4.342.11872.

Venkatesh, V., Morris, M. G., & Ackerman, P. L. (2000). A longitudinal field investigation of gender differences in individual technology adoption decision making processes. *Organizational Behavior and Human Decision Processes*, *83*(1), 33–60. doi:10.1006/obhd.2000.2896 PMID:10973782.

Venkatesh, V., Morris, M. G., Davis, G. B., & Davis, F. D. (2003). User acceptance of information technology: Toward a unified view. *Management Information Systems Quarterly*, *27*(3), 425–478.

Voorhees, E. M. (2002). *Overview of TREC*. Paper presented at The Eleventh Text Retrieval Conference. New York, NY.

Wang, X. (1995). *Learning by observation and practice: An incremental approach for planning operator acquisition*. Paper presented at the 2nd International Conference on Machine Learning. San Francisco, CA.

Zakaria, N., Melinckx, A. A., & Wilemon, D. (2004). Working together apart? Building a knowledge-sharing culture for global virtual teams. *Creativity and Innovation Management*, *13*, 15–29. doi:10.1111/j.1467-8691.2004.00290.x.

ADDITIONAL READING

Barakova, E. I., Spink, A. S., & Ruyter, B. d. (2013, January). Trends in measuring human behavior and interaction. *Personal and Ubiquitous Computing*. doi:10.1007/s00779-011-0478-x.

Becerra-Fernandez, I., Gonzalez, A., & Sabherwal, R. (2004). *Knowledge management: Challenges, solutions and technologies*. Englewood Cliffs, NJ: Pearson Prentice Hall.

Blankson, S. (2008). *Search Engine optimization (SEO): How to optimize your website for internet search engines (Google, Yahoo! MSN Live, AOL, Ask, AltaVista, FAST, GigaBlast, Snap, LookSmart and more)*. Blankson Enterprises Limited.

Card, S. K., Mackinlay, J., & Shneiderman, B. (1999). *Readings in information visualization: Using vision to think*. Morgan Kauffman.

Charan, R. (2001). *What the CEO wants you to know*. Crown Business.

Fleischner, M. M. H. (2011). *SEO made simple: Strategies for dominating the world's largest search engine CreateSpace* (2nd ed.). Independent Publishing Platform.

Hedden, H. (2010, May 3). *The accidental taxonomist*. Information Today, Inc.

Katz, J. (2012). *Designing information: Human factors and common sense in information design.* New York: Wiley.

Larkin, J., & Simon, H. A. (1987). Why a diagram is (sometimes) worth ten thousand words. *Cognitive Science, 11*(1), 65–69. doi:10.1111/j.1551-6708.1987.tb00863.x.

Media Lab, M. I. T. (2007). *Things that think consortium.* Retrieved November 2, 2007., from http://ttt.media.mit.edu

Norman, D. A. (1988). *The design of everyday things.* New York: Basic Books.

Pirolli, P., & Card, S. K. (1995). Information foraging in information access environments. In *Proceedings of the Conference on Human Factors in Computing - CHI'95.* Denver, CO: ACM.

Sommerville, I. (2001). *Software engineering* (6th ed.). Boston: Pearson Education Limited.

Strigl, D., & Swiatek, F. (2011). *Managers, can you hear me now? Hard-hitting lessons on how to get real results.* New York: McGraw-Hill.

Sutcliffe, A. (2003). Multimedia user interface design. In *Proceedings of the Human-Computer Interaction Handbook: Fundamentals, Evolving Technologies and Emerging Applications* (pp. 245-262). Lawrence Erlbaum Associates, Inc.

Tufte, E. R. (2001). *The visual display of quantitative information* (2nd ed.). Graphics Press.

Vandenbosch, B., & Huff, S. (1997, March). Searching and scanning: How executives obtain information from executive information systems. *Management Information Systems Quarterly,* 81–105. doi:10.2307/249743.

Ware, C. (2000). *Information visualization: Perception for design.* San Francisco, CA: Morgan Kaufmann Publishers.

Weiser, M. (1991, September). The computer for the twenty-first century. *Scientific American,* 94–100. doi:10.1038/scientificamerican0991-94 PMID:1675486.

York, J., & Pendharkar, P. C. (2004). Human-computer interaction issues for mobile computing in a variable work context. *International Journal of Human-Computer Studies, 60,* 771–797. doi:10.1016/j.ijhcs.2003.07.004.

KEY TERMS AND DEFINITIONS

Card Sorting: Card sorting is a user experience technique where a facilitator presents a user with a set of terms pertaining to the user's domain and the user is asked to sort and rank the terms into groups and categories. This exercise helps the facilitating group to understand the categorization of the different terms, the relative importance of the terms and any cognitive relationship between the different terms in the set. This exercise is commonly used by user experience professionals in knowledge management and taxonomy projects.

Content Footprint: Content footprint is the navigation pattern of the users as they traverse through the different pieces of content over a period of time or while completing a business transaction.

Directed Navigation: In the domain of knowledge management, directed navigation refers to creating a knowledge management system based on the mental model of understanding when and how the user will need to access the content. It assumes a certain number of business inquiries and attempts to create a knowledge management system that organizes the organizational information according to the transactional flow in the business inquiries.

Knowledge Managers: Knowledge managers are individuals or teams in an organization whose primary job responsibility is to provide the best in class knowledge management system to its user base.

Mobile Knowledge Management Systems: Mobile Knowledge Management Systems are knowledge management systems that are available to the users through a mobile interface. Such systems are available anywhere and anytime no matter if the user is on the corporate network or not.

Muscle Memory: Muscle memory is the term given to the fact that after a period of usage of a system or interface, users tend to use the most accessed part of the navigation without having to process it as an action actively. For example, users using a QWERTY keyboard have developed the knowledge of the relative location of the keys so that they can use the keyboard without having to look explicitly at the keyboard. Similarly, users using a TV remote can switch on and off the TV using the remote without having to explicitly look at the remote control panel.

Organizational Knowledge Management: Organizational Knowledge Management refers to the organizational process through which organizations and corporate offices create, update and maintain their business processes, procedures, workflows and other documents that guide their employees through their job responsibilities.

Reference Content: The information regarding an organization, its business processes, policies and procedures available to its employees for the purpose of customer support and conducting other business processes.

Technology Acceptance Model (TAM Model): A well defined framework for understanding user acceptance of any system based on perceived usefulness and perceived ease of use. Several authors have published researches based on the TAM model and have improved upon it with time to understand the different constructs impacting system acceptance by users.

User Base Shadowing: In order to understand the usage of existing systems by users, user experience practitioners spend their time with the users as they are completing their job responsibilities. This helps the practitioner to understand the needs and requirements of the user as it pertains to the existing system. User base shadowing helps to elicit user needs and requirements that users may fail to articulate in a focus group setting because users get used to the system and fail to recognize specific steps or issues.

User Experience: User Experience refers to the study of the ease of use of a system or product by its intended audience. The acceptance and usage of any system or product is directly proportional to a better user experience of the system or product.

Chapter 11
Understanding Brand Implication and Engagement on Facebook

Marie Haikel-Elsabeh
University Paris X, France

ABSTRACT

What are the drivers for Brand engagement and implication on Facebook? In order to explore the impact of motivations on content and information sharing on Facebook brand pages, this study proposes an analysis focused on a reduced number of motivations and a proposal of a statistical model attempting to link the frequency of posting and liking on Facebook in general and Brand engagement to motivations. The aim of the study is to assess the impact of motivations on brand implication and frequency of posting on Facebook. The authors use the concept of brand implication measure a deep interest toward brands on Facebook. The concept of frequency of posting and liking focuses on the tendency to post or like frequently each time the user connects to Facebook. The motivations the authors introduced are based on the literature for sharing on social networks.

1. INTRODUCTION

Increasingly marketers are interested by social network and virtual community analysis. Firms want to understand their Facebook, Twitter, Pinterest fans. Yet, researchers want to understand why individuals post online by studying the context of professional virtual communities for instance (Wasko and Faraj 2005). Also, why do they adopt certain types of behaviors online as in travel related Websites for example (Kyung Hyan, Gretzel, 2008). The authors are also interested by their relations to virtual communities (Dholakia et al. 2004). Indeed, researchers have employed various theories regarding social network analysis (Wellman & Gulia, 1999), motivational theory (Bagozzi & Dholakia, 2002), and brand engagement (Sprott, Czellar & Spangenberg, 2009). We chose the social network Facebook because brands are increasingly developing their strategy to target their fans on their brand pages.

The Facebook is a social network that was launched in 2004 for college and high school communities. Facebook was funded by Mark Zuckerberg and his college friends in Harvard. In September 2012, Facebook attained a billion of active users worldwide. Half of Facebook users connect to Facebook by using a cellphone.

DOI: 10.4018/978-1-4666-4566-0.ch011

Among online social networks, Facebook stands out for three reasons: its success for university users, the quality of the personal information displayed on platform, and the fact that individuals are not anonymous. Facebook is of interest to researchers for two reasons: 1) as a mass social phenomenon in itself; 2) as a unique window of observation on the privacy attitudes and the patterns of information revelation among individuals.

Facebook is a real opportunity for marketers. There are 18 million users in France and 10 million spend 55 minutes per day on the platform. The aim of the study conducted by a communication Web agency called DDB is to understand why brand fans in France like their favorite brands on Facebook. The majority of users that answered the survey were women (55%) the average age was 31 years old. The fans that are heavy likers are called "Hard core users." They connect to Facebook several times a day. They use the platform to have fun (49%), talk to their families and friends (32%), and to search for new information (16%).

Why Facebook users become brand fans? For 75% of users they liked a brand because they received an invitation or email. They also liked a brand because of the Word of Mouth of their friends on Facebook (59%). The other reason why they liked a brand is because they conducted an active search on Facebook to find a specific brand or product (49%).

Fans have specific expectations toward their favorite brands: they want to gain the attention of their favorite brands when they become fans (53%). When they are attached to the brand, they become ambassadors (48%) and recommend the brand to their friends.

Fans want the brands to have on their pages: promotions (41%), news regarding the brand (35%). Yet, not all fans are ready to comment or like: only 50% of the fans are ready to contribute on the brand page. Nonetheless, 76% have already liked a brand post on a brand page.

Being a fan impacts the intentions of buying the brands' products and services (36%). Brand

fans are also 92% to recommend the brand to their friends. The hard users give a very high grade (between 8 and 10) to their favorite brands on Facebook.

Nonetheless, brand fans can be quick to unlike a brand on Facebook, specifically when the brand posts too much information (82%). This phenomenon should be carefully studied and taken into account by both researchers and marketers alike.

What are Brand pages users on Facebook interested by? According to the study, Facebook users tend to be interested by media (55%), important causes (51%), and fashion and luxury brands (46%).

The DDB study was focused on a reduced number of users. Yet when we go on Social bakers Website we can clearly see the favorite brands worldwide on Facebook with regards to the total number of likes. If we look at the top ten, 7 out of 10 brands provide food and/or beverages to the masses: Coca cola, Red Bull, Starbucks, Oreo, McDonald's, WalMart. Thus food related brand appear to dominated worldwide on Facebook.

Thus it is essential to study the literature on Brand communities to comprehend more deeply why users engage in brand engagement behavior and why do users contribute to brand communities on Facebook. Brand communities are defined by Muniz and O'Guinn (2001) as a "specialized, non-geographically bound community, based on a structured set of social relations among admirers of a brand." The members of brand community share in common their interest for a brand but also consume the brand's products or services. These individuals share knowledge about the brand's news, share information about their interest for the brand. According to McAlexander et al. (2002) brand communities enable the "creation and negotiation of meaning." The social structure and the exchange of information foster brand engagement and loyalty Muniz and O'Guinn (2001). Individuals have several motivations to engage in communities according to Sarason (1974) they do it to feel socially connected, thus in joining social media they feel connected (Gangadharbhatla, 2008; Tardini & Cantoni, 2005). Indeed, according to Dholakia et al. (2004) there are individual as well as group motivations for participating in brand communities in social networks. The individual drivers are that social network users that engage in virtual communities seek to share and learn information and to engage in social relations in the community.

The aim of this paper is to propose a new scale of motivations for online posting on brand Facebook pages. Our objective is to assess whether the motives for posting on a brand page on Facebook have an impact on brand interest behavior (brand engagement) with regards to the general frequency of posting on Facebook.

2. BACKGROUND

Three axes were explored to comprehend the drivers for brand engagement on Facebook. First we studied the literature on the eWOM on Facebook to comprehend why users recommend and like to share information about brands with others. Second, we studied the motivations for brand engagement behavior: what are users motivations to contribute to brand communities. Third, we analyzed the literature on brand implication in order to explain the phenomenon of brand interest on Facebook.

Indeed, users were first going on Facebook to exchange with their friends, to express their daily lives and observe that of others, to strengthen their personal networks, to keep in touch with long distance relationships. Yet, now, brands are increasingly using Facebook to develop new relationships with their users and hopefully consumers. They invested massively social networks like Facebook because it is both cost effective compared to traditional campaigns, and because it enables brands to observe their fans/consumers and to analyze their needs to develop marketing strategies. The other reason is that they are also interested by

the possibilities in terms of co-creation and the development of new initiatives with their consumers. Indeed, brands invest massively to analyze the discussions on their Facebook pages in order to understand their fans and their specific needs.

2.1. Understanding eWOM as a New Brand Engagement Behavior on Facebook

The Internet has opened the path to new interactions between brands and consumers. Indeed, consumers have new platforms to gain further knowledge about new products and services. They also have the possibility to have new and more interactions with other consumers and to benefit from their experiences. These interactions are conducted by emails, forums, online communities, newsgroups, chats, social networks, Websites, blogs. As such, interpersonal influence extends to the Internet and can be called electronic word-of-mouth (eWOM). This phenomena can be initiated by both firms and individuals.

Yet, before defining eWOM it is important to define WOM. The Word of Mouth Marketing Association proposes a definition of the concept of WOM:

"Word of mouth marketing encompasses dozens of marketing techniques that are geared toward encouraging and helping people to talk to each other about products" (WOMMA 2005) (http://www.womma.org).

The concept of WOM was discovered and analysed in the fifties. One of the first analyst and researcher of WOM, William H. Whyte studied in 1954 a WOM phenomenon in Philadelphia. He analyzed the spreading of air conditioners in Philadelphia's suburbs. He described in the study a a communication network between neighbours in a suburb in Philadelphia. He discovered this cluster of air conditionners from the same brand by studying aerial shots of a specific neighborood. The reason for this, he found later, were small WOM networks among the neighbours (Whyte

1954). Indeed, classic WOM is purely product oriented; consumers were telling their private networks composed of friends, family, neighbors and colleagues about their favorite products. The earliest researchers on WOM as Katz and Lazarfeld (1955) discovered that WOM is more effective in influencing costumer purchase than advertising. Other researchers like Engel et al. (1969) established a distinction between good WOM and bad WOM and the impact of both on product purchase. Brown and Reingen (1987) used Granovetter's (1973) theory on weak and strong ties to measure the impact of WOM. They discovered that the information that ist he most influential comes from strong ties. According to Bone (1995) WOM has an impact on immediate or delayed product choice. The source of the WOM is essential: when the WOM comes from a perceived expert it has an impact on the purchase decision of the consumer. Thus WOM is not unidimensional, indeed, various criterias impact WOM: ties between individuals, type and category of products, tonality of the message, etc.

Nonetheless, now eWOM is more multidimensional; consumers can share information regarding a game initiated by the brand on the Facebook as much as they can share information about the brand's products. Thus, the concept has evovlved and the type of information shared are more numerous. Also, the impact on sales of the Facebook eWOM is more indirect and it is unclear, regardless of some studies, what is the actual impact on sales.

For Bickart and Schindler (2001) show in their study that product related information on a forum has more impact and credibility than information on a professional Website. Hennig-Thurau et al (2004) analyzed the factors that explain the motivation to engage in online WOM and discovered that they are the same as traditional WOM.

2.2. The Motivations for Brand Engagement on Facebook

The concept of motivation is a recent conceptualization that emerged with the theory of hedonism. The concept of hedonism states that individuals search to maximize their pleasure and that of others through their behaviors. Thus their motivations are to maximize their pleasure and to avoid pain or discomfort (Fabien Fenouillet 2012). For Doron and Paron (1991) the definition of motivation is simple: "The motivations are provoked by needs and are the frameworks and conceptualization of actions." Thus, motivations are the drivers behind behavior. As such, it was essential to study the drivers behind brand engagement on Facebook by analyzing the motivations to share content on Facebook brand pages. In Table 1, we analyze the literature on the motivations for sharing content on social networks.

We studied different motivations and concepts from Dholakia et al. (2004). Yet we found that what Dholakia calls "purposive value" is the same as the motivation we identified in the literature that is called "knowledge sharing." The social status motivation we identified in the literature is similar to Dholakia's concept of "Maintaining interpersonal interconnectivity," "Mutual accommodation" and "Evaluative social identity. These two motivations explains in our model very strongly why individuals share often content on Facebook and why they are engaged toward the brand. We tested a new scale of motivation in a first study on 238 students in engineering, business management, sociology, and economics. As we can see in Table 1, we first built a scale. We used the scale in the questionnaire for the first study, we adapted this motivations from the book of Henry Murray (1938) "Explorations in personality" and from various authors who wrote articles

Table 1. Factor analysis of the motivation scale

Items	Social status	Knowledge sharing	Cocreation	Power	Recognition-affiliation	Norm of reciprocity-altruism
I share knowledge to transmit my knowledge to other Facebook users		,890				
I share specific knowledge on Facebook		,854				
I share content on Facebook to learn in return.		,675				
I share content on Facebook to show my expertise.		,516				
I share content on Facebook to be part of a community					,593	
I share content on Facebook to enhance my reputation	,804					
I share content on Facebook to enhance my reputation in the community	,906					
I share content on Facebook to earn the respect of other users	,893					
I share content on Facebook to earn a public recognition	,781					
I share content on Facebook to be recognized for my contributions	,679					
I share content on Facebook to take part in a community					,616	
I share content on Facebook for others to approve of me	,749					
I share content on Facebook because I want others to share my opinion.	,582					
I share content on Facebook to attract attention.	,890					
I share content on Facebook to differentiate myself from other users	,621					
I share content on Facebook to provoke other users				,638		
I share content on Facebook to influence other users				,562		
I share content on Facebook to dominate other users.				,553		
I share content on Facebook concerning a product I already tested.						
I share content on Facebook to participate to an innovative project with the firm.			,901			
I share content with the firm to take create a new product with the firm.			,710			
I share content on Facebook to have an answer to what I posted.						,557
I share content on Facebook to receive answers from other users.						,682

about motivations for online posting in forums, blogs, and social networks in different contexts (Sports communities, IPhone fans, professional communities) (Wu and Sukoco, 2010; Marett and Joshi, 2009; Wasko and Faraj, 2005; Yoo and Gretzel, 2008). These motivations were selected specifically from the literature on online communities because they are essentially focused on the users' motivations to have position in a social group and to contribute to the group by building an exchange of information. Thus, these motivations can be used for both communities on Facebook in general but also for the specific case of brand communities. The main motivations of the scale are:

- Status in the community.
- Co-creation.
- Norm of reciprocity.

All of the motivations of the scale in the study were found to be significant with an Cronbach

Alpha above 0.85 (Peterson, 1995). Indeed, that proves that these motivations explain why we post online content, why we post frequently and why we are engaged toward the brands.

2.3. Brand Implication: a General Interest to Brands on Facebook

There are very few scales regarding brand engagement: the most renowned scale is Brand Engagement in Self-concept (Sprott, Czellar & Spangenberg, 2009). The concept of this scale is that individuals acquire brand products not because they are purely materialist but because these products also shape their self-concept. Sprott, Czellar, and Spangenberg (2009) test the validity of their scale in five distinct studies. They found that consumers that have a high BESC score have clearer memories of their favorite brands. These individuals also have a stronger personal relation to those brands and stronger loyalty than the average consumer. We readapted three items from the BESC scale to measure brand engagement.

Nonetheless, in order to understand how and why the fans of a specific brand page were engaged to the brand we had to assess their level of implication. Gilles Laurent and Jean-Noël Kapferer (1985) measured the consumers involvement profiles they created a scale to measure the level of importance of certain categories of products for the consumers. We readapted to the specific context of the Facebook brand pages these items by focusing on the importance for the consumer to consult the pages news, to use the pages services in order to measure brand engagement. Thus, we combined two different scales in order to measure brand engagement.

3. CREATION AND DEVELOPMENT OF THE MOTIVATION SCALE

The aim of this study was to develop and create a new scale of motivations for posting on Facebook brand pages. By analyzing the literature on motiva-tions we discovered that there are 3 main theories of motivations to share information:

1. The cognitive motivation theory relates to desire of the individual to share his knowledge and to receive knowledge with and from others. Indeed, the cognitive motivations enables us to comprehend the drivers of information sharing on Facebook. People share their knowledge to obtain more recognition for their contributions and to exchange information with other people (Bock et al. 2005). For Bock et al. (2005) there is an anticipation of reciprocity for the people who share their knowledge. They hope that the people will respond to their knowledge sharing and possibly share knowledge too. Also, according to Ellahi and Mushtaq (2011) the motivations of bloggers to share knowledge, for instance, has a positive impact on intentions to share knowledge on their blogs. Indeed, people who share knowledge on Facebook have a motivation for knowledge sharing. Knowledge sharing is a display of one's accumulation of information and capacity to learn specialist knowledge regarding a brand's product and services. This knowledge sharing is also linked to the desire to build relationships:

   a. **Knowledge Sharing:** The motivation of knowledge sharing concerns the desire to share knowledge with other contributors to a brand community on Facebook (Henning et Thennau 2010). The members of brand community want to have an expert status and gain recognition because they shared knowledge with the brand community members and showed the brand that they know its products. Indeed, the person who shares knowledge with a brand community on Facebook will seek both the attention of the members and the brand.

2. The altruistic motivation theory is based on the drive that leads an individual to help his peers and to inform them in order to help them. This theory is extremely important in the literature of motivations because it is opposed to the concept of hedonistic motivations. Hedonist motivations are linked to the desire of people to act in order to gain more pleasure and/or immediate satisfaction of their inner needs. Yet these two motivational theories are complementary; according to Kant (Jean Lacroix, 1966) the act of doing good is linked to the fulfilling of a natural inclination. For Kant true morality would be to obey a higher moral law and not to obey our natural inclination to help other. Thus, helping other would be seen as a moral action in the Kantian perspective. Yet, in our perspective the hedonist and altruistic motivations both differ in the sense that the main aim of the altruistic motivations is to help another party while the aim of the hedonist motivations is to satisfy oneself. This desire to help other is also linked to another important theory, the theory of social identity (Dholakia et al. 2004). Individual can feel empathy and have altruistic motivations because they build their identity with regards to a human group or community. The individual builds an auto-concept of his relationship and place with and within the community. He also defines his sense of community based on the relationship he has with the community. For Doowhang Lee et al. (2011) it's the concept of social identity which defines the sense of belonging to a community. Several motivations embody this concept of altruistic motivations:

   a. **Norm of Reciprocity:** The motivation of help is linked to desire to accomplish a good and fulfilling action by aiding other users (Henning & Thennau, 2010). The brand fans on Facebook tend to contribute to help other members of the community with their insights.

   b. **Help:** The motivation to help is related to the wish to help other members on Facebook (Wu and Sukoco 2010).

   c. **Revenge:** The motivation of revenge is related to the desire to adopt a vengeful stance toward the brand or the brand community members, but it is also linked to the will to inform other of the misdeeds of a brand or of other individuals (Yoo and Gretzel 2011).

3. The motivation of sense of community theory is based on the fact that individuals want to build their individuality in relation to a community and find a specific position within that community in order to fit in and to belong. Indeed, according to Muniz and O'Guinn (2001) individuals need to have a sense of community in order to relate to a community and to also consider more specifically what is their position and how they are perceived by the other community members:

   a. **Status in the Community:** The motivation of status in the community is related to the concept of social status. Individuals with this motive want to have a special status within a virtual community on Facebook. They want to exist for the fans and the brand and have a specific and distinct status.

   b. **Co-Creation:** The motivation of co-creation is in line with the creative impulse of Facebook users who want to go beyond simple contributions and to create new and innovative products with the brands (Wu and Sukoco 2010).

   c. **Power:** The motivation of power is the intention to control events and people. Individuals with these motives tend to try to dominate others within a Facebook brand community (Wu and Sukoco 2010).

   d. **Affiliation:** The motivation of affiliation is linked to desire to identify oneself to a brand community (Wu and Sukoco 2010).

e. **Recognition:** The motivation of recognition is related to the desire to be recognized for one's contributions to the brand community (Wu and Sukoco 2010).

f. **Self-Protection:** The motivation of self-protection is related to the desire to protect oneself against the attacks of other community members by posting content (Murray 1938).

g. **Perseveration:** The motivation of perseveration is related to the desire to keep on posting content despite a gradual loss of interest (Murray 1938). This motivation is linked to the fact that to be like other and to exist in a community individual keep on posting on Facebook.

These three theories overlap in the sense that they relate to the fact that individuals base their knowledge and information sharing on their relation to a community (like a brand community, or a group of friends on Facebook) or a defined entity or individual (like a brand, or a friend on Facebook). Thus, it appears clearly that knowledge sharing is a definite strategy to build a relationship and to exist within the sphere of Facebook.

We analyzed the literature on motivations and developed a scale composed of the 10 motivations cited above:

1. **Status in the Community:** The motivation of status in the community is related to the concept of social status. Individuals with this motive want to have a special status within a virtual community on Facebook. They want to exist for the fans and the brand and have a specific and distinct status.

2. **Co-Creation:** The motivation of co-creation is in line with the creative impulse of Facebook users who want to go beyond simple contributions and to create new and innovative products with the brands (Wu and Sukoco 2010).

3. **Power:** The motivation of power is the intention to control events and people. Individuals with these motives tend to try to dominate others within a Facebook brand community (Wu and Sukoco 2010).

4. **Norm of Reciprocity:** The motivation of help is linked to desire to accomplish a good and fulfilling action by aiding other users (Henning et Thennau 2010). The brand fans on Facebook tend to contribute to help other members of the community with their insights.

5. **Knowledge Sharing:** The motivation of knowledge sharing concerns the desire to share knowledge with other contributors to a brand community on Facebook (Henning et Thennau 2010).

6. **Affiliation:** The motivation of affiliation is linked to desire to identify oneself to a brand community (Wu and Sukoco 2010).

7. **Recognition:** The motivation of recognition is related to the desire to be recognized for one's contributions to the brand community (Wu and Sukoco 2010).

8. **Altruism:** The motivation of altruism is linked to the desire to help other and to feel empathy toward them in brand community (Wu and Sukoco 2010).

9. **Revenge:** The motivation of revenge is related to the desire to adopt a vengeful stance toward the brand or the brand community members (Yoo and Gretzel 2011).

10. **Self-Protection:** The motivation of self-protection is related to the desire to protect oneself against the attacks of other community members by posting content (Murray 1938).

11. **Perseveration:** The motivation of perseveration is related to the desire to keep on posting content despite a gradual loss of interest (Murray 1938).

12. **Help:** The motivation to help is related to the wish to help other members on Facebook (Wu and Sukoco 2010).

We then reduced the scale by factorizing with Maximum Likelihood with SPSS 21. Certain motivations were reunited like recognition and affiliation and norm of reciprocity and altruism. We eliminated the items that were beneath 0.5 (Nunally 1978).

Tables 1 and 2 show how the scale was reduced and then introduced in the model. After the reduction of the scale we calculated the Cronbach Alpha's of all motivations and found that there were all above 0, 85 (Nunally 1978) (Table 2).

Table 3 summarizes the different stages of the scale reduction, then it shows the final motivations that were kept in the model. Indeed, these motivations were the only ones that explained posting frequency on Facebook. We eliminated the motivations that did not explain frequency of posting on Facebook. We renamed the meta-motivation that was created with the motivations of altruism and norm of reciprocity: "norm of reciprocity." We renamed it because the altruistic motivations were linked to expectations of reciprocity: When I help other, I expect them to help me too.

The motivations that we kept in the model were mainly linked to one's position within the community (Status and Power that are combined in the meta-motivation influence). Yet, they were also linked to the desire to contribute to the community and to the brand by building an interactive and productive relationship (Co-creation and Norm of reciprocity that are combined in the meta-motivation of coproduction). The motivations that explain the most the frequency of sharing (posting or liking) are linked to one's desire to exist by acting. The desire to act often in order to get others attention is a defining trait of Facebook users and of brand community members.

4. CREATION AND DEVELOPMENT OF THE BRAND ENGAGEMENT SCALE

Brand engagement is the process of building a bond with a brand. The BESC scale (Sprott, Czellar, & Spangenberg, 2009) is related to the tendency of consumers to include important brands as a part of their self-concept. The scale has a predictive ability of the consumer preferences regarding brands, and how they memorize and integrate those brands in their lives. Yet, the BESC scale did not include items on the general interest to a certain category of products, thus we adapted items from the article of Jean Noel Kapferer (1985) on brand implication which measures the interest to a specific products categories. We measured the internal consistency of this new scale by doing a factor analysis. We found that items represented a single factor. Thus we calculated the Cronbach Alpha in order to measure the internal consistency of this new brand engagement indicator (see Table 4).

Table 2. Cronbach alpha of the motivation scale

	Social Status	Knowledge sharing	Co-creation	Power	Recognition and affiliation	Norm of reciprocity and Altruism
Cronbach Alpha	0, 854	0, 867	0, 900	0, 888	0, 890	0, 852

Table 3. Reduction of motivations scale

Motivations first study	The reduced scale of motivations	The meta-motivations in the frequency model	The meta-motivations in the frequency model
Status in the communitiy	Status in the community	Status in the community	Influence
Recognition	Recognition and affiliation		
Affiliation	Affiliation		
Exhibition	Exhibition		
Altruism	Altruism and norm of reciprocity	Altruism and norm of reciprocity renamed "norm of reciprocity"	Coproduction
Revenge			
Co-creation	Co-creation	Co-creation	Coproduction
Power	Power	Power	Influence
Knowledge sharing	Knowledge sharing		
Self-protection			
Perseveration			
Norm of reciprocity			
Help			

5. HYPOTHESES

Our hypotheses were focused on our study of literature. We discovered that there were no articles linking effectively motivations and frequency of sharing on Facebook. As such, we developed first a motivation scale, and then a frequency of sharing scale to measure whether motivations has an impact on frequency of sharing. To measure frequency of sharing we focused on liking and posting two important behaviors on Facebook.

We also introduced a brand engagement variable to measure whether users who were active on Facebook were also more brand implicated. By brand implication, we measured the general interest for brands on Facebook.

The aim of the study is to provide a framework to explain whether the motivations explain users' activity on Facebook: frequency of likes and posts. The second aim of this study is to assess whether motivations explain why individuals are implicated with brands on Facebook.

Table 4. Factor analysis and Cronbach alpha of brand engagement

Brand engagement items	Factor analysis	Cronbach Alpha
When I share content on social networks it is brand related content	0,823	0,821
The brands that I like resemble my lifestyle	0,810	0,812
My favourite brands are part of my life	0,802	0,804
I often go on brand's Facebook pages	0,890	0,900

For Ulusu Yesim (2011) time spent and frequency of posting on Facebook has a positive impact on brand community motivations and behavior on Facebook. Thus we hypothesize that social motivations have an impact on the frequency of posting and liking:

Hypotheses 1: The meta-motivation of coproduction has a positive impact on users' frequency of liking on Facebook.

Hypotheses 2: The meta-motivation of influence has a positive impact on users' frequency of liking on Facebook.

Hypotheses 3: The meta-motivation of influence has a positive impact on users' frequency of posting on Facebook.

Hypotheses 4: The meta-motivation of coproduction has a positive impact on users' frequency of posting on Facebook.

According to Rifon et al. (2010) and Lee, Kim, and Kim (2011), altruistic and social motivations explain why individuals adopt brand engagement behavior. Thus, we could hypothesize that social and altruistic behavior engage in brand engagement.

Hypotheses 5: The frequency of posting has a positive impact on Brand engagement on Facebook.

Hypotheses 6: The frequency of liking has a positive impact on Brand engagement on Facebook.

Our hypotheses (from 1 to 4) are focused on the impact of motivations on the general frequency of sharing of sharing on Facebook. The second set hypotheses are focused on the Brand engagement.

6. DATA COLLECTION

The study we conducted aimed at building new scales of motivation and brand behavior for engaging in brand interest behavior on Facebook brand pages. The survey was posted to students from three universities on the blog of marketing students, and by email over a period of three months. Our aim was to collect the answers of students between the age of 20 to 30 years old because we also targeted PHD students that can be older than Master degree students. We chose students in humanities and engineer: students in marketing, students in sociology, and students in computer science.

A first version of the questionnaire was tested in February 2012. The questionnaire was sent to 5 experts (teachers and PHD students) that are specialized in e-marketing. After this first pre-test, several modifications were introduced. The questionnaire was launched in March 2012 over a period of three months.

The survey was completed by 240 respondents. Overall 51.5% of the respondents were women while 48.5% were men. Most of the respondents were students of the age of 18-25: 68%. The other respondents were 22% to be aged of 25 to 35. The rest of the respondents were PHD candidates that were older between from 35 to 40: 10%.

Our decision to target students on Facebook to measure and understand the drivers of brand implication was based on the assessment of the statistics proposed by the Website Socialbaker.com. The biggest age group is between 18 to 24 years old and 25 to 34 years old in France (http://www.socialbakers.com/facebook-statistics/france). The other significant similarity was that there were more female respondents than male, in France there are 51% female users and 49% male users on Facebook.

7. MEASURE

All the items of the study were adapted from the literature on motivation for sharing and engaging on brand related behavior on social networks and more specifically on Facebook. The original six motivations and meta-motivations were used to create a measurement instrument of the motivations for brand interest. The brand engagement concept was measured with items explaining users' implication and interest to brands on Facebook. A five point Likert scale was used to assess the degree of agreement with the statements proposed. Several items were included in the survey to assess the profile of respondents: age, sex, professional activity, liking and posting frequency on Facebook. The frequency of posting and liking was measured with a ten point frequency scale. The scale was built on the fact that users when they go on Facebook will adopt certain behavior with regards to posting and liking the question was when they would log on Facebook how many times would they like and post.

For this study, we used both SPSS Statistics to reduce the scale of motivations, and SPSS 21 and AMOS 21 to create a structural equation model. Principal component factorial analysis with Maximum Likelihood estimate was used to reduce the motivation scale and the brand engagement scale. For each study, the Cronbach Alpha of the scale of motivation was computed and was above 0, 8 which attests of the scale's reliability (Peterson 1995).

8. RESULTS

Overall the model fit is acceptable with a RMSEA of 0,040 and a NFI and CFI close to 1. These results show that there are no misspecifications in this model and that the data fits the model. All hypotheses were supported except number 6. Indeed, it appears that the frequency of liking in general doesn't explain brand implication on Facebook but that it's the frequency of posting that is more explanatory of users' Brand engagement (H5).

The results were overall surprising it appears that the meta-motivation of influence is more important than the meta-motivation of coproduction to explain why users are active on Facebook (H1,

H2, H3, H4). The main explanation is that one's social position within a Facebook community explains why he will tend to contribute more often on Facebook. He will first contribute to exist within the community and secondly to be seen as different and more important than his peers in the community. That's why it is more important for them to post frequently, in order to express their opinions than to like (eventhough he does both actively). The motivation of coproduction also has impact on Facebook frequency of liking and posting. Yet, oddly, it will explain more the frequency of liking than posting. The fact is that individuals that want to share content are more keen on liking to show an existing content than to post. Thus although both meta-motivations are important to explain the frequency of sharing on Facebook some meta-motivations are more important than others to explain the frequency of posting rather than liking (see Figure 1 and Table 5).

Overall, there are clear links between motivations and frequency of posting and liking, but also between frequency of posting and liking and brand implication. There is a causal chain in the model that can be explained by the fact that users that have strong influence and coproduction motivations and that are active on Facebook will tend to be more interested and implicated toward brands and brand pages on Facebook.

This scale can be used for brands as tool to cluster their users and to target specific users by focusing on their need to be influential and to coproduce products with the brand. They could also target the other users by trying to provoke the same type of motivations in them.

9. ISSUES, CONTROVERSIES, PROBLEMS

The limitations of this scale are that they should be introduced in models with other variables to measure the contextual variations and also they

Figure 1. Structural equation model

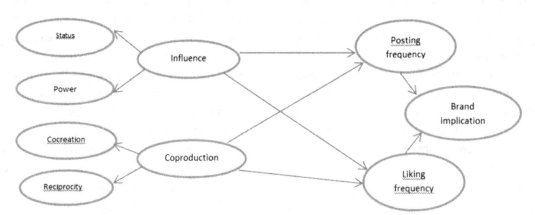

Table 5. Results of the structural equation model

Structural model results							
Model fit indices	X²	X²/df		RMSEA	NFI		CFI
Values	2213	2213/989		0,040	0,930		0, 950
Hypotheses		Paths	Estimate	S.E.	C.R.	P	Results
H1	Frequency of liking <--- Coproduction		.740	.065	11.329	***	H1 validated
H2	Frequency of liking <--- Influence		.798	.063	12.750	***	H2 validated
H3	Frequency of posting <--- Influence		.914	.059	15.438	***	H3 validated
H4	Frequency of posting <--- Coproduction		.504	.064	7.876	***	H4 validated
H5	Brand implication <--- Frequency of Posting		.860	.155	5.554	***	H6 validated
H6	Brand implication <--- Frequency of Likes		-.229	.138	-1.654	.098	H7 not validated

should be adapted for each context. Nonetheless, these limitations can be anticipated and the scale can be developed and adapted for specific contexts. Also, we did not integrate in the study the type and subject of content and we did not test what would be the impact of motivations on the tendency to share certain content.

10. SOLUTIONS AND RECOMMENDATIONS

New types of motivations could be studied in order to enrich the scale but also other type of behavior. An interesting study could take into consideration the contextual aspect by observing different type of posts on different brand pages in order to create a new classification of brand pages motivations and content sharing behavior. This classification would then enable us to observe frequency of posting with regard to the content posted.

Other motivations can also be studied like the exhibitionist and voyeuristic motivations to engage in posting, commenting, and liking behavior on Facebook (Bumgarner 2007). Bumgarner explains in his study that users tend to share content because they have strong exhibitionist and voyeuristic motivations. Thus new types of motivations based on the potential behavior of users could be integrated and studied with respect to Facebook specificities. This new area of study could open the path to a richer scale that would not only be aimed at measuring the frequency of sharing but also the very link between contextual motivations and contextual behavior.

11. FUTURE RESEARCH DIRECTIONS

Overall, this base scale can be enriched and further developed for case studies. Future researchers can also exploit the scale to enrich their studies in order to comprehend why users will adopt certain behaviors on Facebook. A potential study could be focused on the impact of motivations on intentions and on real behavior. Also the motivations can be used to define psychological traits and to categorize types of consumers and of brand community members. Indeed, cluster analysis could be used to define new consumer profiles and brand community members and to compare these different profiles.

12. CONCLUSION

Facebookers use Facebook to engage in a social activity and to communicate with their friends, family, colleagues. Typical Facebook users will talk to their friends, look at other people's photos, read their profiles, talk about the new updates from their friends. Facebook users have a gossiping activity on Facebook and enjoy observing others news. They also tend to appreciate and like the content posted by their friends. As such, they are sensitive to content promoted by their friends regarding brands.

Overall, the motivations were found to have a significant impact on the activity on Facebook. The meta-motivation of influence explains why individuals post frequently on Facebook. Users post because they want to exist within their own Facebook community first, even when they post on Facebook brand pages. This motivation explains also why individuals will tend to like more frequently on Facebook. Liking is not simple phenomena, it means that the user is selecting content for their community. It is a Facebook ritual that enables the user to express his preferences in terms of content to his community and to show that he's active for his community. The meta-motivation of coproduction is also important, and explains why individuals posts and likes frequently on Facebook. Users that are active on Facebook enjoy contributing and helping the brand and the brand community. They also want to build relationship and create new products and services with the brand and brand community members.

Users that contribute to Facebook brand pages have different motivational profiles and involvement with the brand communities. These users also tend to have a stronger activity on Facebook in general.

We validated the scale of motivation and the scale of brand engagement by conducting a single study, the scale should be tested further in order to be validated.

REFERENCES

Acquisti, A., & Ralph, G. (2006). Imagined communities: Awareness, information dharing, and privacy on the Facebook. [LNCS]. *Proceedings of Privacy Enhancing Technologies*, *4258*, 36–58. doi:10.1007/11957454_3.

Allan, S., & Gilbert, P. (1997). Submissive behaviour and psychopathology. *The British Journal of Clinical Psychology, 36*, 467–488. doi:10.1111/j.2044-8260.1997.tb01255.x PMID:9403141.

Allan, S., & Gilbert, P. (1997). Submissive behaviour and psychopathology. *The British Journal of Clinical Psychology, 36*, 467–488. doi:10.1111/j.2044-8260.1997.tb01255.x PMID:9403141.

Allport, F. H. (1962). A structuronomic conception of behavior: Individual and collective. *Journal of Abnormal and Social Psychology, 64*, 3–30. doi:10.1037/h0043563 PMID:13860640.

Anderson, C. (2006). *La longue traîne: Une nouvelle économie est là!* Paris, France: Pearson Education France.

Anderson, E. W. (1998). Customer satisfaction and word of mouth. *Journal of Service Research, 1*(1), 5–17. doi:10.1177/109467059800100102.

Aral, S. (2010, June 7). Identifying social influence: A comment on opinion leadership and social contagion in new product diffusion. *SSRN eLibrary*.

Baek, K., Holton, A., Harp, D., & Yaschur, C. (2011). The links that bind: Uncovering novel motivations for linking on Facebook. *Computers in Human Behavior, 27*(6), 2243–2248. doi:10.1016/j.chb.2011.07.003.

Bakshy, E., Rosenn, I., Marlow, C., & Adamic, L. (2012, January 19). *The role of social networks in information diffusion*. Retrieved from http://arxiv.org/abs/1201.4145

Bandura, A. (2003). *Auto-efficacité: Le sentiment d'efficacité personnelle*. Paris: De Boeck.

Bass, F. (1969). A new product growth model for consumer durables. *Management Science, 15*(5), 215–227. doi:10.1287/mnsc.15.5.215.

Beauvisage, T., Beuscart, J.-S., Couronné, T., & Mellet, K. (2011). *Le succès sur internet repose-t-il sur la contagion? Une analyse critique de la littérature sur la viralité*. Sous presse.

Berger, J., & Milkman, K. L. (2009). Social transmission and viral culture. *Operations and Information Management*. Retrieved from http://opimWeb.wharton.upenn.edu/people/faculty.cfm

Berger, J., & Milkman, K. L. (2012). What makes online content viral? *JMR, Journal of Marketing Research, 49*(2), 192–205. doi:10.1509/jmr.10.0353.

Berger, J., & Schwartz, E. M. (2011). What drivers immediate and ongoing word of mouth. *JMR, Journal of Marketing Research, 48*, 869–880. doi:10.1509/jmkr.48.5.869.

Berger, J. A., & Iyengar, R. (2012, February 29). *How interest shapes word-of-mouth over different channels*. Retrieved from http://ssrn.com/abstract=2013141

Bickart, B., & Schindler, R. M. (2001). Internet forums as influential sources of consumer information. *Journal of Interactive Marketing, 15*, 31–52. doi:10.1002/dir.1014.

Blomström, R., Lind, E., & Persson, F. (2012). *Triggering factors for word-of-mouth: A case study of Tipp-Ex's viral marketing campaign*. Retrieved from http://hj.diva-portal.org/smash/record.jsf?pid=diva2:529823

Blondel, V. D., Guillaume, J. L., Lambiotte, R., & Lefebvre, E. (2008). Fast unfolding of communities in large networks. *Journal of Statistical Mechanics*, 10.

Bock, G. W., & Kim, Y. (2002). Breaking the myths of rewards: An exploratory study of attitudes about knowledge sharing. *Information Resources Management Journal, 15*(2), 14–21. doi:10.4018/irmj.2002040102.

Bock, G. W., Zmud, R. W., Kim, Y.-G., & Lee, J.-N. (2005). Behavioral intention formulation in knowledge sharing: Examining the roles of extrinsic motivators, social–psychological forces, and organizational climate. *Management Information Systems Quarterly*, *29*(1), 87–111.

Bone, P. F. (1995). Word-of-mouth effects on short-term and long-term product judgements. *Journal of Business Research*, *32*, 213–224. doi:10.1016/0148-2963(94)00047-I.

Bone, P. F. (1995). Word-of-mouth effects on short-term and long-term product judgements. *Journal of Business Research*, *32*, 213–224. doi:10.1016/0148-2963(94)00047-I.

Brodie, R. J., Ilic, A., Juric, B., & Hollebeek, L. (2011). Consumer engagement in a virtual brand community: An exploratory analysis. *Journal of Business Research*.

Brooks, R. C. Jr. (1957). Word-of-mouth advertising in selling new products. *Journal of Marketing*, *22*(2), 154–161. doi:10.2307/1247212.

Brown, J. J., & Reingen, P. H. (1987). Social ties and word-of-mouth referral behavior. *The Journal of Consumer Research*, *14*, 350–362. doi:10.1086/209118.

Brown, J. J., & Reingen, P. H. (1987). Social ties and word-of-mouth referral behavior. *The Journal of Consumer Research*, *14*, 350–362. doi:10.1086/209118.

Bulik, B. S. (2007). This frog speaks volumes about word-of-mouth. *Advertising Age*, *78*(4), 4–23.

Bumgarner, B. A. (2007). Exploring the uses and gratifications of Facebook among emerging adults. *First Monday*, *12*(11). Retrieved from http://firstmonday.org/htbin/cgiwrap/bin/ojs/index.php/fm/article/viewArticle/2026/1897 doi:10.5210/fm.v12i11.2026.

Casaló, L., Flavián, C., & Guinalíu, M. (2011). Understanding the intention to follow the advice obtained in an online travel community. *Computers in Human Behavior*, *27*, 622–633. doi:10.1016/j.chb.2010.04.013.

Centola, D. (2010). The spread of behavior in an online social network experiment. *Science*, *329*(5996), 1194–1197. doi:10.1126/science.1185231 PMID:20813952.

Cha, M., Haddadi, H., Benevenuto, F., & Gummadi, K. P. (2010). Measuring user influence in Twitter: The million follower fallacy. In *Proceedings of the 4th International AAAI Conference on Weblogs and Social Media (ICWSM)*. AAAI.

Cha, M., Mislove, A., Adams, B., & Gummadi, K. P. (2008). Characterizing social cascades in Flickr. In *Proceedings of the First Workshop on Online Social Networks*, (pp. 13–18). New York, NY: ACM.

Cha, M., Pérez, J. A. N., & Haddadi, H. (2012). The spread of media content through blogs. *Social Network Analysis and Mining*, *2*(3), 249–264. doi:10.1007/s13278-011-0040-x.

Chan, D. K.-S., & Cheng, G. H.-L. (2004). A comparison of offline and online friendship qualities at different stages of relationship development. *Journal of Social and Personal Relationships*, *21*(3), 305–320. doi:10.1177/0265407504042834.

Chaudhuri, A., & Holbrook, M. B. (2001). The chain of rffects from brand trust and brand affect to brand performance: The role of brand loyalty. *Journal of Marketing*, *65*(2), 81–93. doi:10.1509/jmkg.65.2.81.18255.

Cheema, A., & Kaikati, A. M. (2010). The effect of need for uniqueness on word of mouth. *JMR, Journal of Marketing Research*, *47*(3), 553–563. doi:10.1509/jmkr.47.3.553.

Chelminski, P., & Coulter, R. A. (2011). An examination of consumer advocacy and complaining behavior in the context of service failure. *Journal of Services Marketing*, *25*(5), 361–370. doi:10.1108/08876041111149711.

Cheung, C., Lee, M., & Jin, X. (2011). Customer engagement in an online social platform: A conceptual model and scale development. In *Proceedings of ICIS*. ICIS.

Chevalier, J., & Mayzlin, D. (2006). The effect of word of mouth on sales: Online book reviews. *JMR, Journal of Marketing Research*, *43*(3), 345–354. doi:10.1509/jmkr.43.3.345.

Chu, S. C., & Kim, Y. (2011). Determinants of consumer engagement in electronic word-of-mouth (eWOM) in social networking sites. *International Journal of Advertising*, *30*, 47–75. doi:10.2501/IJA-30-1-047-075.

Chung, C., & Darke, P. (2006). The consumer as advocate: Self-relevance, culture, and word-of mouth. *Marketing Letters*, *17*(4), 269–279. doi:10.1007/s11002-006-8426-7.

Churchill, G. A. (1979). A paradigm for developing better measures of marketing constructs. *JMR, Journal of Marketing Research*, *16*, 64–73. doi:10.2307/3150876.

Cova, B. (1997). Community and consumption: Towards a definition of the linking value of products and services. *European Journal of Marketing*, *31*(3-4).

Crandall, L. J. (1980). Adler's concept of social interest: Theory, measurement, and implications for adjustment. *Journal of Personality and Social Psychology*, *39*, 481–495. doi:10.1037/0022-3514.39.3.481.

Creamer, M. (2012). *Study: Only 1% of Facebook 'fans' engage with brands*. Retrieved from http://adage.com/article/digital/study-1-facebook-fansengage-brands/232351/

Cross, S. E., Bacon, P. L., & Morris, M. L. (2000). The relational-interdependent self-construal and relationships. *Journal of Personality and Social Psychology*, *78*, 791–808. doi:10.1037/0022-3514.78.4.791 PMID:10794381.

Cross, S. E., & Madson, L. (1997). Models of the self: Self-construals and gender. *Psychological Bulletin*, *122*, 5–37. doi:10.1037/0033-2909.122.1.5 PMID:9204777.

Czepiel, J. A. (1974). Word-of-mouth processes in the diffusion of a major technological innovation. *JMR, Journal of Marketing Research*, *11*(2), 172–180. doi:10.2307/3150555.

Davenport, T. H., & Prusak, L. (1997). *Working knowledge: How organizations manage what they know*. Project Management Institute.

Davenport, T. H., & Prusak, L. (1998). *Working knowledge: How organizations manage what they know*. Boston: Harvard Business School Press.

Debos, F. (2007). Les relations numériques individu-marque. *Document Numérique, 10*(3), 63-73. Retrieved from www.cairn.info/revue-document-numerique-2007-3-page-63.htm

Deci, E. L., & Ryan, R. M. (1985). *Intrinsic motivation and self-determination in human behavior*. New York: Plenum Publishing Co. doi:10.1007/978-1-4899-2271-7.

Deci, E. L., & Ryan, R. M. (1987). The support of autonomy and the control of behavior. *Journal of Personality and Social Psychology*, *53*, 1024–1037. doi:10.1037/0022-3514.53.6.1024 PMID:3320334.

Dholakia, U. M., Bagozzi, R. P., & Pearo, L. K. (2004). A social influence model of consumer participation in network- and small-group-based virtual communities. *International Journal of Research in Marketing*, *21*(3), 241–263. doi:10.1016/j.ijresmar.2003.12.004.

Dholakia, U. M., Bagozzi, R. P., & Pearo, L. K. (2004). A social influence model of consumer participation in network- and small-group-based virtual communities. *International Journal of Research in Marketing, 21*(3), 241–263. doi:10.1016/j.ijresmar.2003.12.004.

Dichter, E. (1966). How word-of-mouth advertising works. *Harvard Business Review, 16,* 147–166.

DiMicco, J. M., & Millen, D. R. (2007). Identity management: Multiple presentations of self in Facebook. In *Proceedings of the 2007 International ACM Conference on Supporting Group Work* (pp. 383-386). New York: ACM.

Dobele, A., Lindgreen, A., Beverland, M., Vanhamme, J., & van Wijk, R. (2007, July). Why pass on viral messages? Because they connect emotionally. *Business Horizons, 50*(4), 291–304. doi:10.1016/j.bushor.2007.01.004.

Dobele, A., Toleman, D., & Beverland, M. (2005). Controlled infection! Spreading the brand message through viral marketing. *Business Horizons, 48*(2), 143–149. doi:10.1016/j.bushor.2004.10.011.

Dodson, J. A., & Muller, E. (1978). Models of new product diffusion through advertising and word-of-mouth. *Management Science, 24*(15), 1568–1578. doi:10.1287/mnsc.24.15.1568.

Doron, P. (1991). *Le dictionnaire de psychologie.* PUF.

Dubach-Spiegler, E., Hildebrand, C., & Michahelles, F. (2011). Social networks in pervasive advertising and shopping. In *Pervasive advertising* (pp. 208–225). New York: Springer. doi:10.1007/978-0-85729-352-7_10.

Duhan, D. F., Johnson, S. D., Wilcox, J. B., & Harrell, G. D. (1997). Influences on consumer use of word-of-mouth recommendation sources. *Journal of the Academy of Marketing Science, 25*(4), 283–295. doi:10.1177/0092070397254001.

Engel, J. E., Blackwell, R. D., & Kegerreis, R. J. (1969). How information is used to adopt an innovation. *Journal of Advertising Research, 9,* 3–8.

Feick, L. F., & Price, L. L. (1987). The market maven: A diffuser of marketplace information. *Journal of Marketing, 51*(1), 83–97. doi:10.2307/1251146.

Fenouillet, F. (2012). *La motivation.* Paris, France: Dunod.

Fogg, B. J., & Eckles, D. (2007). The behavior chain for online participation: How successful web services structure persuasion. [IEEE.]. *Proceedings of Persuasive, 2007,* 199–209. doi:10.1007/978-3-540-77006-0_25.

Golder, S. A., Wilkinson, D., & Huberman, B. A. (2007). Rhythms of social interaction: Messaging within a massive online network. In *Proceedings of the Third International Conference on Communities and Technologies* (pp. 41–66). London: Springer.

Gustafsson, A., Johnson, M. D., & Roos, I. (2005). The effects of customer satisfaction, relationship commitment dimensions, and triggers on customer retention. *Journal of Marketing, 69*(4). doi:10.1509/jmkg.2005.69.4.210.

Hargittai, E. (2007). Whose space? Differences among users and non-users of social network sites. *Journal of Computer-Mediated Communication, 13*(1). doi:10.1111/j.1083-6101.2007.00396.x.

Hau, Y. S., & Kim, Y.-G. (2011). Why would online gamers share their innovation-conducive knowledge in the online game user community? Integrating individual motivations and social capital perspectives. *Computers in Human Behavior, 27*(2), 956–970. doi:10.1016/j.chb.2010.11.022.

Hennig-Thurau, T., Malthouse, E. C., Friege, C., Gensler, S., Lobschat, L., Rangaswamy, A., & Skiera, B. (2010). The impact of new media on customer relationships. *Journal of Service Research, 75*(3), 311–330. doi:10.1177/1094670510375460.

Hennig-Thurau, T., Malthouse, E. C., Friege, C., Gensler, S., Lobschat, L., Rangaswamy, A., & Skiera, B. (2010). The impact of new media on customer relationships. *Journal of Service Research*, *75*(3), 311–330. doi:10.1177/1094670510375460.

Hinz, O., Skiera, B., Barrot, C., & Becker, J. U. (2011). Seeding strategies for viral marketing: An empirical comparison. *Journal of Marketing*, *75*, 55–71. doi:10.1509/jm.10.0088.

Hollebeek, L. (2011). Exploring customer brand engagement: Definition and themes. *Journal of Strategic Marketing*, *19*(7), 555–573. doi:10.1080/0965254X.2011.599493.

Hollebeek, L. D. (2011). Demystifying customer brand engagement: Exploring the loyalty nexus. *Journal of Marketing Management*, *27*(7-8), 785–807. doi:10.1080/0267257X.2010.500132.

Huang, C.-C. (2009). Knowledge sharing and group cohesiveness on performance: An empirical study of technology R&D teams in Taiwan. *Technovation*, *29*(11), 786–797. doi:10.1016/j.technovation.2009.04.003.

Hung, S.-Y., Durcikova, A., Lai, H.-M., & Lin, W.-M. (2011). The influence of intrinsic and extrinsic motivation on individuals' knowledge sharing behavior. *International Journal of Human-Computer Studies*, *69*(6), 415–427. doi:10.1016/j.ijhcs.2011.02.004.

Katz, E., & Lazarfeld, P. F. (1955). *Personal influence*. Glencoe, IL: Free Press.

Kyung Hyan, Y., & Gretzel, U. (2008). What motivates consumers to write online travel reviews? *Information Technology & Tourism*, *10*, 283–295. doi:10.3727/109830508788403114.

Lacroix, J. (1966). *Kant et le kantisme*. Paris, France: Ed. Presses Universitaires de France.

Landers, R. N., & Lounsbury, J. W. (2006). An investigation of big five and narrow personality traits in relation to internet usage. *Computers in Human Behavior*, *22*, 283–293. doi:10.1016/j.chb.2004.06.001.

Laroche, M., Habibi, M. R., & Richard, M.-O. (2012). To be or not to be in social media: How brand loyalty is affected by social media? *International Journal of Information Management*.

Laroche, M., Habibi, M. R., Richard, M.-O., & Sankaranarayanan, R. (2012). The effects of social media based brand communities on brand community markers, value creation practices, brand trust and brand loyalty. *Computers in Human Behavior*, *28*(5), 1755–1767. doi:10.1016/j.chb.2012.04.016.

Laurent, G., & Kapferer, J.-N. (1985). Consumer involvement profiles: A new and practical approach to consumer involvement. *JMR, Journal of Marketing Research*, *22*(1), 41–53. doi:10.2307/3151549.

Lee, D., Kim, H. S., & Kim, J. K. (2011). The impact of online brand community type on consumer's community engagement behaviors: Consumer-created vs. marketer-created online brand community in online social-networking Web sites. *Cyberpsychology, Behavior, and Social Networking*, *14*, 1–2. doi:10.1089/cyber.2009.0397.

Levin, M.-J. (2013). Facebook: Les fans de marque à la loupe. *Emarketing.fr*. Retrieved from http://www.e-marketing.fr/Marketing-Magazine/Article/Facebook-les-fans-de-marque-a-la-loupe-38380-1.htm

Lin, M.-J. J., Hung, S.-W., & Chen, C.-J. (2009). Fostering the determinants of knowledge sharing in professional virtual summer. *Journal of Computer Information Systems*, *25*(4), 929–939.

McAlexander, J. H., Schouten, J. W., & Koenig, H. F. (2002). Building brand community. *Journal of Marketing*, *66*(1), 38–54. doi:10.1509/jmkg.66.1.38.18451.

Muniz, A., & O'Guinn, T. (2001). Brand community. *The Journal of Consumer Research*, *27*, 412–432. doi:10.1086/319618.

Murray, H. A. (1938). *Explorations in personality*. New York: Oxford University Press.

Nunnally, J. (1978). *Psychometric theory*. New York: McGraw-Hill.

Porter, C., Donthu, N., MacElroy, W., & Wydra, D. (2011). How to foster and sustain engagement in virtual communities. *California Management Review*, *53*(4), 80–110. doi:10.1525/cmr.2011.53.4.80.

Rifon, N. J., Choi, S. M., Trimble, C. S., & Li, H. (2004). Congruence effects in sponsorship: The mediating role of sponsor credibility and consumer attributions of sponsor motive. *Journal of Advertising*, *33*, 29–42. doi:10.1080/00913367.2004.10639151.

Sprott, D., Czellar, S., & Spangenberg, E. (2009). The importance of a general measure of brand engagement on market behavior: Development and validation of a scale. *JMR, Journal of Marketing Research*, *46*(1), 92–104. doi:10.1509/jmkr.46.1.92.

The New York Times Insight Group. (n.d.). *The psychology of sharing*. Retrieved from http://nytmarketing.whsites.net/mediakit/pos/

Ulusu, Y. (2010). Determinant factors of time spent on Facebook: Brand community engagement and usages types. *Journal of Yasar University*, *5*(18), 2949–2957.

WARC. (2012). *Brands seeking ROI metrics for Facebook*. Retrieved August 17, 2012, from http://www.warc.com/LatestNews/News/EmailNews.news?ID=30250&Origin=WARCNewsEmail

Wasko, M. M., & Faraj, S. (2005). Why should I share? Examining social capital and knowledge contribution in electronic networks of practice. *Management Information Systems Quarterly*, *29*, 35–57.

Whyte, W. H. Jr. (1954). The web of word of mouth. *Fortune*, *50*, 140–143.

Yoo, K.-H., & Gretzel, U. (2011). Influence of personality on travel-related consumer-generated media creation. *Computers in Human Behavior*, *27*(2), 609–621. doi:10.1016/j.chb.2010.05.002.

Yoo, K.-H., & Gretzel, U. (2011). Influence of personality on travel-related consumer-generated media creation. *Computers in Human Behavior*, *27*(2), 609–662. doi:10.1016/j.chb.2010.05.002.

ADDITIONAL READING

Aaker, J. (1992). The negative attraction effect? A study of the attraction effect under judgment and choice. *Advances in Consumer Research. Association for Consumer Research (U. S.)*, *18*, 462–469.

Aaker, J., Fournier, S., & Brasel, S. A. (2008). *When good brands do bad*. Working Paper Series. Berkeley, CA: Center for Responsible Business, UC Berkeley.

Aaker, J., & Smith, A. (2010). *The dragonfly effect: Quick, effective, and powerful ways to use social media to drive social change*. New York: John Wiley and Sons.

Aalbers, R., & Dolfsma, W. (2011). *Individual positioning in innovation networks: On the role of individual motivation*. Druid Society.

Arndt, J. (1968). Selective processes in word of mouth. *Journal of Advertising Research*, *8*(3), 19–22.

Backstrom, L., Huttenlocher, D., Kleinberg, J., & Lan, X. (2006). Group formation in large social networks: Membership, growth, and evolution. In *Proceedings of the 12th ACM SIGKDD International Conference on Knowledge Discovery and Data Mining* (pp. 44-54). New York: ACM.

Bagozzi, R. P. (1995). Reflections on relationship marketing in consumer markets. *Journal of the Academy of Marketing Science, 23*(4), 272–277. doi:10.1177/009207039502300406.

Bagozzi, R. P., & Dholakia, U. M. (2002). Intentional social action in virtual communities. *Journal of Interactive Marketing, 16*(2), 2–21. doi:10.1002/dir.10006.

Balter, D., & Butman, J. (2005). *Grapevine: The new art of word-of-mouth marketing*. New York: Portfolio Books.

Bampo, M., Ewing, M. T., Mather, D. R., Stewart, D., & Wallace, M. (2008). The effects of the social structure of digital networks on viral marketing performance. *Information Systems Research, 19*(3), 273–290. doi:10.1287/isre.1070.0152.

Bayus, B. L. (1985). Word of mouth: The indirect effects of marketing efforts. *Journal of Advertising Research, 25*(3), 31–39.

Bryant, J., & Zillmann, D. (2002). *Media effects: Advances in theory and research* (2nd ed.). Mahwah, NJ: Lawrence Erlbaum Associates.

Ellison, N. B., Steinfield, C., & Lampe, C. (2007). The benefits of Facebook friends: Social capital and college students' use of online social network sites. *Journal of Computer-Mediated Communication, 12*(4), 1143–1168. doi:10.1111/j.1083-6101.2007.00367.x.

Lampe, C., Ellison, N. B., & Steinfeld, C. (2007). A familiar Face(book): Profile elements as signals in an online social network. In *Proceedings of CHI '07* (pp. 435–444). New York: ACM Press.

Lampe, C., Ellison, N. B., & Steinfield, C. (2006). A Face(book) in the crowd: Social searching vs. social browsing. [New York: ACM.]. *Proceedings of CSCW, 06*, 167–170. doi:10.1145/1180875.1180901.

Lampe, C., Ellison, N. B., & Steinfield, C. (2008). Changes in use and perception of Facebook. [New York: ACM.]. *Proceedings of CSCW, 08*, 721–730. doi:10.1145/1460563.1460675.

Lewis, C., & Fabos, B. (2005). Instant messaging, literacies, and social identities. *Reading Research Quarterly, 40*(4), 470–501. doi:10.1598/RRQ.40.4.5.

Lewis, K., Kaufman, J., Gonzalez, M., Wimmer, A., & Christakis, N. (2008). Tastes, ties and time: A new social network dataset using Facebook.com. *Social Networks, 30*, 330–342. doi:10.1016/j.socnet.2008.07.002.

Lichtlé, M. C., & Plichlon, V. (2008). Mieux comprendre la fidélité des consommateurs. *Recherche et Applications en Marketing, 23*(4). doi:10.1177/076737010802300405.

McKenna, K. Y. A., Green, A. S., & Glenson, M. E. J. (2002). Relationship formation on the internet: What's the big attraction? *The Journal of Social Issues, 58*(1), 9–31. doi:10.1111/1540-4560.00246.

Sawhney, M., Verona, G., & Prandelli, E. (2005). Collaborating to create: The internet as a platform for customer engagement in product innovation. *Journal of Interactive Marketing, 19*(4). doi:10.1002/dir.20046.

Tirunillai, S., & Tellis, G. J. (2011). Does chatter really matter? The impact of online consumer generated content on a firm's financial performance. *Journal of Marine Science, 31*(2), 198–215. doi:10.1287/mksc.1110.0682.

Veltkamp, M., Custers, R., & Aarts, H. (2011). Motivating consumer behavior by subliminal conditioning in the absence of basic needs. *Journal of Consumer Psychology*, *21*, 49–56. doi:10.1016/j.jcps.2010.09.011.

Wolfradt, U., & Doll, J. (2001). Motives of adolescents to use the internet as a function of personality traits, personal and social factors. *Journal of Educational Computing Research*, *24*(1), 13–27. doi:10.2190/ANPM-LN97-AUT2-D2EJ.

Xiang, Z., & Gretzel, U. (2010). Role of social media in online travel information search. *Tourism Management*, *31*(2), 179–188. doi:10.1016/j.tourman.2009.02.016.

KEY TERMS AND DEFINITIONS

Brand Engagement: Brand engagement is how the consumer considers a specific brand and relates it to his lifestyle and self-concept.

Brand Implication: Brand implication is the level of involvement and interest of a consumer toward a specific brand.

Facebook Brand Pages: Facebook brand pages are Facebook pages that are dedicated to specific brands. These pages aim to attract Facebook users that are fans of the brands in order to build brand capital, and/or to provide certain services.

Frequency of Sharing: The concept of frequency of sharing in the article relates to how many times an individual will an individual post, like, comment, share, tag, when he connects to Facebook.

Motivations: Motivations are the drivers to actions. They are the pre-requisites to goal accomplishment.

Social Network: A social network is by definition a social structure made of social actors. A social network on the Internet is composed of several agents: individuals, brands, organisations, and firms who connect to specific platforms to interact with other agents.

Word of Mouth Marketing: Word of mouth marketing encompasses dozens of marketing techniques that are geared toward encouraging and helping people to talk to each other about products.

Conclusion

Even if the virtual shop we described in the preface, based on a pair of goggles enabling customers to shop while swimming is not available yet, we are approaching it at the speed of a galloping horse. Competing in an oversaturated online market is hard, and simply setting up a powerful e-commerce Website is sometimes not enough to draw the sales a company wants. Using social media strategies to promote an online store or creating a community in order to turn an e-commerce Website into something more than just a place to buy products can help increase sales. This is why companies are more and more using Instagram (http://instagram.com/) or Pinterest (https://pinterest.com/) as ways to promote themselves, but it is not enough, and on top of interface concerns, making the consumer even more concentrated on a product, in reference to Ettis's chapter, can help. Indeed, the device can become a key factor of success, and therefore, its connectivity can enhance the e-commerce Website capabilities.

Consumers who write about products and services in online forums offer a goldmine of marketing insights. A lot of consumers write about products and services in online forums and social media, and they create a body of opinions and reflections that has the potential to give companies insights that market research cannot generate.

As customers, we are being watched. Every detail from our location via mobile phone, purchases via credit cards, transactions via online banking, interests via Web-surfing, basically everything excluding our innermost thoughts, is being recorded since the advent of Web and mobile devices. We are part of a collection where our information is being documented, down to the very communications we have on the phone. Recently, the alarming level of government involvement in our personal lives has been brought to public attention with the unveiling of the biggest government telephone surveillance operation in history. Does the idea of privacy no longer exist?

In a recent article, Pelet, Diallo, and Papadopoulou presented the results of a confirmatory study with 698 respondents. The study questioned respondents about their use of smart phone and Social Networks Systems (SNS) in the context of mobile commerce Website interfaces as well as security and privacy issues. The objective was to facilitate the understanding of the rapidly evolving and expanding technology of smart phones and SNS and explore its potential for m-commerce purposes. Results show that trust and ease-of-use were important and could enable m-commerce Websites and SNS to leverage their benefits and appeal in this promising market that is m-commerce. The same remains with u-commerce, as bounds simply go a little further, expanding the possibilities of devices: after mobiles and tablets, goggles, knives, cars, and clothes will enable anyone to shop online.

In their study, Kato, Kato, and Chida focused on mobile text messages, which are considered to be a form of synchronous communication, whereas conventional computer-based email is an asynchronous communication form in which delays between sending and replying are common. For this reason, some people are happy to wait several days for an email reply before perceiving that a reply is late. However, even in cases in which the reply takes a long time, rather than have an emotional awareness as seen experimentally in this study, in most cases recipients begin to self-question whether they have done something wrong. In other words, personal computer email and mobile phone email communications are seen as very different despite both being forms of email communication. For this reason, there is merit in this study considering the response timing for communication via mobile text messages. The findings indicate that the reply timing for mobile text messages serves as an emotional clue in the interaction between senders and receivers of these communications.

This study focused on how recipients felt with regard to the timing of replies to mobile text messages, especially toward the act of senders who intentionally waiting before replying. A comparison with the results of their previous study on how senders feel in this case (Kato, Kato, & Chida, 2012), especially the mindset of senders that wait before responding, revealed differences between the emotional strategic intent of senders for waiting before replying (Kato, Kato, & Chida, 2012) and how they were actually perceived by the recipients. Based on this, there is thought to be a perpetual gap between senders and recipients in the intentional manipulation of reply timing (especially waiting before replying). Senders who intentionally manipulate the timing for negative or hostile emotions such as sadness, anger, or guilt actually run the risk of creating the opposite feelings in the recipient. Specifically, when the sender intentionally delays replying with the intent of lessening these negative or hostile feelings, this may actually increase the recipient's feelings of these emotions.

The participants of this survey were Japanese people in Japan. Therefore, surveys should be administered in other countries and intercultural comparative studies should be performed. Obtaining quantitative trends in reply timing could be useful in the educational arena, such as choosing the most effective time in e-learning to send messages. There is therefore merit in working on an experimental design to measure actual reply timing.

In her chapter, Wang shows that the drastically worsening natural environment in China has been routinely underrepresented or ignored in traditional media, due to its sensitive nature and potential threat to "social stability." Consequently, the environmental protection awareness among Chinese people is relatively low, and civic engagement in environmental policy-making is not encouraged by the government. The appearance and advancement of the new media technology has made public participation in political domain possible, especially the environmental policy-making process that used to deny public access. Online media and mobile phones, the two major members in the new media family, provide alternative communicational channels for grassroots in China to seek environmental information and organize environmental protection campaigns. Based on an anti-pollution campaign boosted by the use of online media and mobile phone, this chapter assisted readers in understanding the strength and weakness of new media that helped achieve a participatory goal in modern Chinese context. The role of word of mouth, as a powerful complementary communicational tool for propagating the hazardous consequence of PX project to those who are not active new technology users, and other factors which might contribute to the happening of the environmental campaign were also discussed in the chapter.

Weaving the classical communication theories such as framing and two-step flow communication into the phenomenon of the new media and unique political and social context in China, the author believes the study could serve as a map for communication scholars to understand the functional roles of opinion leaders, the Internet, and mobile phones in facilitating the grassroots or general public to participate in environmental protection events in a society where environmental issues are generally underrepresented and public convention is not supported by the government. Qualitative approaches based on secondary

240

data and interviews are the major methods used in this chapter. Quantitative analysis based on a small-sized sample is conducted to bridge the relationship between people's use pattern of new media devices and their likelihood to participate in environmental movement. Graph 1 presents the dynamic flow of the information in Xiamen PX protest which could be used as a tentative model involving opinion leaders, policy-makers, and the general public, which other environmentalists could imitate or refer to in future events, and a process in which ideas or behaviors could be spread and responded to with a combination of Web-based technologies.

Future research could be conducted on whether and how the Internet and mobile phone could facilitate cooperative activities in environmental campaigns across the globe, and how the pressure group's message could be tailor-made to address the trend of globalization in dealing with environmental issues and compete for mainstream media attention to the greatest extent. The study on how opinion leaders utilize new technology in environmental protection events could be furthered to their capability of influencing or shaping grassroots' opinion, and their perception of the effectiveness of the completed environmental campaign.

The scarcity of scholarly work in media and environmental issues in oriental culture suggests a meta-analysis of literature over public opinion towards environmental issues across eastern countries, as well as the factors contributing to the fickleness of the public opinion over time in one country or region, could be worthy inquiry for future research. Last but not the least, it would be important for researchers to examine the magnitude of impacts by different medium forms (television, newspaper, Internet, mobile phone, etc.) in participatory events, and how to utilize multiple propagation tools to mobilize the population with different demographic backgrounds (children, seniors, etc.) to take part in the environmental protection campaign that benefits every single living being on this beautiful planet.

De Filippi has provided in her chapter an overview of the various advantages and drawbacks of ubiquitous computing, with particular focus on the most recent developments in cloud computing and the impact these developments might have on the exercise of fundamental users rights and freedoms. Attention has been drawn to the growing trend towards centralization that characterizes many online platforms and the dangers that such centralized platforms present as regards the inherent loss of user autonomy and the potential violation of privacy rights and freedom of expression.

The objective of the chapter was not merely to describe the current state of affairs, but also—and mainly—to provide a prospective analysis of emerging trends in the context of cloud computing so as to identify the major challenges that will have to be addressed in the coming years. Most of the concerns identified above are, at the moment, still at an early stage of development. While they might eventually come true, as users seem to become more and more willing to trade-off their rights in the name of comfort and accessibility, this trend can nonetheless be reversed—or to the least obstructed—by properly informing users of what their rights are and how they could effectively be limited by large online operators abusing their dominant position in the market for cloud services.

Thus far, limited research has been done to understand the relationship between ubiquitous computing (See Barkhuus & Dey, 2003; Zittrain, 2003, 2006, 2009; Bohn et al., 2005; Brey, 2005; Greenfield, 2006; Spiekermann & Pallas, 2006; Hardian et al., 2006; Moglen, 2011; De Filippi & McCarthy, 2011, 2012; Lametti, 2012). While the analysis presents valuable insights with a view to generate awareness on this emerging issue, more research is needed to determine the extent to which our fears are actually coming true. Most critical in this regard is the need to monitor and to understand how cloud providers' policies and terms of use can actually affect user's preferences and behaviors in ubiquitous online platforms such as cloud computing. For instance, it is worth noting that increasingly intrusive privacy policies ultimately had divergent effects on user's behaviors: while many users simply submitted to the idea that "online privacy is dead" (Rauhofer, 2008), others actually decided to react by implementing alternatives solutions based on decentralized technologies that could eventually compete with the services currently offered by major cloud operators. In this last regard, more research should be undertaken in assessing the role of user- and community-driven initiatives acting as a counter-power to established commercial offers, as well as to investigate the effectiveness of governmental regulation and public initiatives in counteracting the emerging trends in cloud computing.

Fernandez and Marrauld have shown several configurations of "remote working" that they observed which contribute to a change in the usual representations of the "teleworker." They propose here three "stereotypes." First, it is the figure of the teleworker, exclusively at home, whose tele-operator is an ideal-typical figure. He uses a desk in a corner of the room or the bedroom, not in a room dedicated solely for homework. However, the boundaries between private and professional life are maintained due to strong control of their activity by the ICT. In fact, ICT is, for him, a "control infrastructure." Despite the physical distance, the hierarchy is near: the worked hours are controllable via the use of ICT: for instance, instant messaging allows the verification that the tele-operator is indeed behind their computer. The remote control via ICT is a substitute of direct managerial control.

Second, it is the figure of the mobile worker who sometimes works at home. The ICTs allows one to contact them at any time even if he is not available. For the executives, ICTs act more as a way of disrupting their work space in confusing the virtual presence status (reachable/available). Unless he defined formally beforehand their moments of when he can be contacted.

Third, the figure of the worker in a co-working space or in a telecenter: he has a high degree of autonomy in organizing their work, the worker uses the telecenter to "frame" their activity (immersing himself in a group is a way to put boundaries between the private and professional spheres), but also to densify their socioprofessional network IRL (In Real Life). The worker in a co-working space will tend to regulate their working hours, helping them to build boundaries between private and professional spheres.

The precise definition of teleworkers is difficult to establish, as the profiles are varied and the situations diverse (new working configurations including practices of re-sedentarization activity). Embedded in a double paradigm (technological and organizational), teleworkers seem to evolve in unexpected, even paradoxical ways. In order to understand the realities of working remotely, we need to investigate the tools for teleworking in their collective aspect of interaction management, the security of sharing data and the practices of social networking tools. The technical characteristics of these tools are revealed only through the collective dynamics of remote work and vice versa.

Gao presents a study on mobile information services adoption from the culture perspective. The research question which drives this study is: how do the cultural dimensions influence the adoption of mobile information services? This study addresses this question by exploring the effect of the cultural dimensions in terms of individualism/collectivism, and uncertainty avoidances, on the adoption of a mobile information service at a university campus setting. The results indicate that the cultural dimensions play important roles in how mobile information services are used and adopted in two different cultural settings: the culture in developed countries and the Chinese culture. The research findings provide support for one of two research hypotheses. We believe this research contributes to both the literature and research on mobile services adoption. As presented in their findings, the most striking finding was non-support of H1. They believe that some possible reasons exist for this finding. Firstly, the sample size of this pilot study was quite small. Most participants were experienced users of mobile devices and mobile services. They might expect to experience different kinds of new mobile services. In addition, overseas students from China might be influenced by western culture. As a result, it leads them to be the first one to try new services. Furthermore, some Chinese participants are well educated in IT. They might be addicted to advanced mobile services.

There exist several opportunities for future research. First, the research hypotheses on the cultural dimensions can be tested in other empirical context, such as mobile banking, mobile game, mobile healthcare, mobile advertisement, and so on. Second, we plan to conduct another cross-culture study with people from other countries. Third, in this research, the respondents only used the system for a short amount of time (i.e., about 75 minutes) and that the location used was simulated. It would be interesting to see what users' thought of the system are after using it over an extended period of time as they would have gained more knowledge about the features available and the real life usefulness. We also plan to carry out research on this in the future.

Kasimati *et al.*'s chapter presented a framework towards the adoption of innovative mobile/ubiquitous game-based learning practices and methodologies by Higher Education Institutions. Taking into consideration the opportunity that mobile technologies and GBL practices provide for Higher Education Institutions, as well as the fact that 21st century learners and citizens are familiar with mobile devices and services, the chapter presents the basic principles of game-based learning and align them with the identified characteristics and technological specifications of mobile and ubiquitous devices. The central features differentiating Higher Education Institutions from any other Educational Institutions were also presented, in order to be later incorporated in the proposed framework. As discussed in this chapter, instructors should invest much of their time to prepare and design their mobile/ubiquitous activity in order to maximize their effectiveness. During these two phases, instructors should collect available data regarding their learners' characteristics and/or Higher Education restrictions, affordances, or limitations. A detailed guide is proposed towards the effective preparation of mobile/ubiquitous game-based learning activities within Higher Education Institutions. This chapter also presents two implementation stances of this framework within the context of u-commerce instruction.

Conclusively, the chapter provides Higher Education Institutions with the potential of effectively applying such practices, providing significant support and guidance for their step by step development. The adoption of ubiquitous and game-based learning practices will help academics and instructors improve their innovativeness and will facilitate their being smoothly and fast incorporated in Higher Education Institutions' curricula. Last but not least, the proposed framework, when effectively applied, can enhance Higher Education Institutions innovativeness, impact and competitiveness through the provision of innovative, effective, beyond state of the art and high-quality learning services to students.

Chaari's chapter shows that the theory of communicative action of Habermas (1987) provides us with a theoretical framework to understand the Internet users' trust. This theory suggests that the consumers' role changes. They become active constructors of their own experience. Online communication has to change its conception. Communicating consists in establishing an interaction relation based on a process of mutual understanding which allows establishing social relationships and expressing motivations, interests, and needs of all the parties where Internet users are considered as social actors (Habermas, 1987). It is a dialogue that promotes trust through problems resolution, question answering, and expectation alignment (Morgan and Hunt, 1994). The study carried out by Duncan and Moriarty (1998) on relational marketing shows that the more the firms engage in communicational and interactive relations with Internet users, the more they will be capable of promote online trust. Online communication must be conceived as an attempt at coordinating actions between consumers and firms based on social interaction. This interaction result in common goals that neither party can achieve individually (Stewart and Pavlou, 2002).

Booi and Ditsa have reported in their study the evaluation of South African UWPIs for usability and user acceptance. The study applied a triangulation of UEAs and TAM as a theoretical framework for the evaluation of the portal interfaces. The results suggest that invisibility, application robustness, and appeal of South African UWPIs support to the usability of South African University Web Portal Interfaces which subsequently leads to user acceptance of the UWPIs. The lowest correlation in this study is for the hypothesized relations (0.371), which is between Usability and User Acceptance of the UWPIs. This correlation implies that the basic usability requirements of UWPIs have not been met.

Ettis has shown in his study which attempt was to improve the understanding of users' online experience. Telepresence and flow are considered a key aspect of this experience. To this end, we examined whether telepresence predicts e-store visitors' experience of flow. Flow is including two dimensions: concentration and enjoyment. Flow is assumed to be linked to e-consumer behaviour. The number of visited pages, actual visit time, and perceived visit time were measured. The study showed that telepresence and flow are valuable in the context of e-shopping. Creating opportunities that enhance these states motivate e-consumers to visit more pages and extent their Website visit duration.

This chapter may stimulate more research in this field identified as still being under-explored. The research area is potentially fruitful. Many issues remain unresolved and many questions unanswered. The literature on telepresence and flow is extensive, but there are many challenges that need to be resolved. These challenges are mostly methodological. Studies involving flow measurement assessment demonstrate that some potentially serious difficulties exist, and researchers need to think carefully about the direction of causality between flow constructs and the measurement approaches (Hoffman & Novak, 2009; Koufaris, 2002; Siekpe, 2005).

Chakrabarty shows that when traditional methods of data collection fail to provide the requirements for developing the next generation of organizational knowledge management systems, it is necessary to collect data in novice ways and analyze them in innovative ways to understand how the current systems are used, what are the main issues of the users and what are the drivers of the new development. This chapter provides an approach to developing and designing a knowledge management system based on system usage metrics collected from current knowledge management systems already in use by an organization. The requirements of the new system are formalized based on the users' content footprint in the current knowledge management systems in the organization. The drivers in this approach were the introduction of mobile devices into the workforce as a vehicle of change.

While this chapter presents the use case for an organizational knowledge management system and the inclusion of mobile devices as the change agent, the same paradigm could be extended for other system in different domain. To develop a system that will improve effectiveness and efficiency, it is necessary to understand the dynamics of the current system, the process where it works and where it fails. It is also necessary to understand the dynamics for the evolving ecosystem and change agents of the organization and other aspects of the organization to ensure a successful implementation of the next generation of the systems. And as it has been presented in this chapter, certain change agents provide a platform for the system developers to rethink and re-envision the development of a system from scratch rather than to develop a system that is incrementally an improved version from the system already in use.

To conclude, Haikel-Elsabeh has shown Facebookers use Facebook to engage in a social activity and to communicate with their friends, family, colleagues. Typical Facebook users will talk to their friends, look at other people's photos, read their profiles, and talk about the new updates from their friends. Facebook users have a gossiping activity on Facebook and enjoy observing others' news. They also tend to appreciate and like the content posted by their friends. As such, they are sensitive to content promoted by their friends regarding brands. Overall, the motivations were found to have a significant impact on the activity on Facebook. The meta-motivation of influence explains why individuals post frequently on Facebook. Users post because they want to exist within their own Facebook community first, even when they post on Facebook brand pages. This motivation explains also why individuals will tend to like more frequently on Facebook. Liking is not a simple phenomena; it means that the user is selecting content for their community. It is a Facebook ritual that enables the user to express his preferences in terms of content to his community and to show that he's active for his community. The meta-motivation of coproduction is also important and explains why individuals posts and likes frequently on Facebook. Users who are active on Facebook enjoy contributing and helping the brand and the brand community. They also want to build relationships and create new products and services with the brand and brand community members. Users that contribute to Facebook brand pages have different motivational profiles and involvement with the brand communities. These users also tend to have a stronger activity on Facebook in general. They validated the scale of motivation and the scale of brand engagement by conducting a single study; the scale should be tested further in order to be validated.

Taking into account all the contributions discussed in the previous paragraphs, we hope this book will serve as an inspiring springboard for initiating activity in u-commerce for both researchers and practitioners.

Jean-Eric Pelet
Université de Nantes, France

Panagiota Papadopoulou
University of Athens, Greece

REFERENCES

Barkhuus, L., & Dey, A. (2003). Is context-aware computing taking control away from the user? Three levels of interactivity examined. In *Proceedings of UbiComp 2003: Ubiquitous Computing* (pp. 149–156). Berlin: Springer. doi:10.1007/978-3-540-39653-6_12.

Bohn, J., Coroama, V., Langheinrich, M., Mattern, F., & Rohs, M. (2005). Social, economic, and ethical implications of ambient intelligence and ubiquitous computing. *Ambient Intelligence*, 5-29.

Bonazzi, R., Liu, Z., Ganière, S., & Pigneur, Y. (2013). A dynamic privacy manager for compliance in pervasive computing. In *Data Mining*. Concepts, Methodologies, Tools, and Applications.

Brey, P. (2005). Freedom and privacy in ambient intelligence. *Ethics and Information Technology*, 7(3), 157–166. doi:10.1007/s10676-006-0005-3.

De Filippi, P., & McCarthy, S. (2011). Cloud computing: Legal issues in centralized architectures. In *Proceedings of the VII International Conference on Internet, Law and Politics*. IEEE.

De Filippi, P., & McCarthy, S. (2012). Cloud computing: Centralization and data sovereignty. *European Journal of Law and Technology, 3*(2).

Duncan, T., & Moriarty, S. E. (1998). A communication-based marketing. *Journal of Marketing, 62,* 1–13. doi:10.2307/1252157.

Greenfield, A. (2006). *Everyware: The dawning age of ubiquitous computing.* Peachpit Press.

Habermas, J. (1987). *Raison et légitimité: Problèmes de légitimation dans le capitalisme avancé. Traduit de l'allemand par Jean Lacoste.* Paris: Payot.

Habermas, J. (1987). Théorie de l'agir communicationnel: Rationalité de l'agir et rationalisation de la société. Tome 1, traduit de l'allemand par Jean-Marc Ferry. Fayard.

Habermas, J. (1987). Théorie de l'agir communicationnel: Pour une critique de la raison fonctionnaliste. Tome 2, traduit de l'allemand par Jean-Louis Schlegel. Fayard.

Hardian, B., Indulska, J., & Henricksen, K. (2006). Balancing autonomy and user control in context-aware systems-A survey. In *Proceedings of Pervasive Computing and Communications Workshops, 2006.* IEEE. doi:10.1109/PERCOMW.2006.26.

Hoffman, D. L., & Novak, T. P. (1996). Marketing in hypermedia computer-mediated environments: Conceptual foundations. *Journal of Marketing, 60*(3), 50–69. doi:10.2307/1251841.

Kato, Y., Kato, S., & Chida, K. (2012). Reply timing and emotional strategy in mobile text communications of Japanese young people: Replies to messages conveying four different emotions. In Long, S. D. (Ed.), *Virtual Work and Human Interaction Research* (pp. 99–114). Hershey, PA: IGI Global. doi:10.4018/978-1-4666-0963-1.ch006.

Koufaris, M. (2002). Applying the technology acceptance model and flow theory to online consumer behavior. *Information Systems Research, 13*(2), 205–223. doi:10.1287/isre.13.2.205.83.

Lametti, D. (2012). *The cloud: Boundless digital potential or enclosure 3.0?* Moglen, E. (2011). *Why political liberty depends on software freedom more than ever.* Paper presented at the FOSDEM Conference. Brussels, Belgium.

Morgan, R. M., & Hunt, S. D. (1994). The commitment-trust theory of relationship marketing. *Journal of Marketing, 58*(3), 20–38. doi:10.2307/1252308.

Pelet, J.-É., Diallo, M. F., & Papadopoulou, P. (2013). *How can social networks systems be an m-commerce strategic weapon? Privacy concerns based on consumer satisfaction.* Paper presented at Congrès Européen de Marketing EMAC. Istanbul, Turkey.

Rauhofer, J. (2008). Privacy is dead, get over it! 1 Information privacy and the dream of a risk-free society. *Information & Communications Technology Law, 17*(3), 185–197. doi:10.1080/13600830802472990.

Siekpe, J. S. (2005). An examination of the multidimensionality of flow construct in a computer-mediated environment. *Journal of Electronic Commerce Research, 6*(1). Retrieved February 6, 2012, from www.csulb.edu/Web/journals/jecr/issues/20051/paper2.pdf

Spiekermann, S., & Pallas, F. (2006). Technology paternalism–Wider implications of ubiquitous computing. *Poiesis & Praxis: International Journal of Technology Assessment and Ethics of Science, 4*(1), 6–18.

Stewart, D. W., & Pavlou, P. A. (2002). From consumer response to active consumer: Measuring the effectiveness of interactive media. *Journal of the Academy of Marketing Science, 30*(376).

Zittrain, J. (2003). Internet points of control. In 44 B. C. L. Rev 653..

Zittrain, J. (2006). A history of online gatekeeping. *Harvard Journal of Law & Technology, 19*(253).

Zittrain, J. (2009). *The future of the internet--And how to stop it*. New Haven, CT: Yale University Press.

Compilation of References

Abowd, G. D., & Mynatt, E. D. (2000). Charting past, present, and future research in ubiquitous computing. *ACM Transactions on Computer-Human Interaction, 7*(1), 29–58. doi:10.1145/344949.344988.

Abraham, J. (1995). Review of the book The mass media and environmental issues by Anders Hansen. *Media Culture & Society, 17*(3), 524–526. doi:10.1177/016344395017003012.

Abric, J. (1999). *Psychologie de la communication: Théories et méthodes.* Paris, France: Armand Colin.

Acquisti, A., & Ralph, G. (2006). Imagined communities: Awareness, information dharing, and privacy on the Facebook.[LNCS]. *Proceedings of Privacy Enhancing Technologies, 4258*, 36–58. doi:10.1007/11957454_3.

Adams, D. A., Nelson, R. R., & Todd, P. A. (1992). Perceived usefulness, ease of use and usage of information technology: A replication. *Management Information Systems Quarterly, 16*, 227–247. doi:10.2307/249577.

Adler, R. (2007). *Health care unplugged: The evolving role of wireless technology.* Oakland, CA: California Health Care Foundation.

AFP. (2008, April 23). *China hit by fresh anti-Western protests.* Retrieved from http://afp.google.com/article/ALeqM5gOTrqDV_ua80tqOwJHJbPBOLoUjA

Agarwal, R., & Karahanna, E. (2000). Time when you're having fun: Cognitive absorption and beliefs about information technology usage. *Management Information Systems Quarterly, 24*, 665–694. doi:10.2307/3250951.

Agarwal, R., & Prasad, J. (1997). The role of innovation characteristics and perceived voluntariness in the acceptance of information technologies. *Decision Sciences, 28*(3), 557–582. doi:10.1111/j.1540-5915.1997.tb01322.x.

Ajzen, I. (1991). The theory of planned behavior to leisure choice. *Journal of Leisure Research, 24*, 207–224.

Ajzen, I. (1991). The theory of planned behavior. *Organizational Behavior and Human Decision Processes, 50*(2), 179–211. doi:10.1016/0749-5978(91)90020-T.

Ajzen, I., & Fishbein, M. (1980). *Understanding attitudes and predicting social behaviour.* Englewood Cliffs, NJ: Prentice-Hall.

Ajzen, I., & Madden, T. J. (1986). Prediction of goal-directed behavior: Attitudes, intentions, and perceived behavioral control. *Journal of Experimental Social Psychology, 22*(5), 453–474. doi:10.1016/0022-1031(86)90045-4.

Aknoun, A. (1993). La communication démocratique. *Cahiers Internationaux de Sociologie, 94*, 51–70.

Akyildiz, I. F., Wang, X., & Wang, W. (2005). Wireless mesh networks: A survey in computer networks. Elsevier Science, 47.

Alavi, M., & Leidner, D. E. (2001). Review: Knowledge management and knowledge management systems: Conceptual foundations and research issues. *Management Information Systems Quarterly, 25*(1), 107–136. doi:10.2307/3250961.

Alba, J. L., Weitz, B., Janiszewski, R. L., Sawyer, A., & Wood, S. (1997). Interactive home shopping: Consumer, retailer, and manufacturer incentives to participate in electronic marketplaces. *Journal of Marketing, 61*(3), 38–53. doi:10.2307/1251788.

Allan, S., & Gilbert, P. (1997). Submissive behaviour and psychopathology. *The British Journal of Clinical Psychology, 36,* 467–488. doi:10.1111/j.2044-8260.1997. tb01255.x PMID:9403141.

Allport, F. H. (1962). A structuronomic conception of behavior: Individual and collective. *Journal of Abnormal and Social Psychology, 64,* 3–30. doi:10.1037/h0043563 PMID:13860640.

Al-Wabil, A., & Al-Khalifa, H. (2009). A framework for integrating usability evaluations methods. *The Mawhiba Web Portal Case Study.*

Anderson, C. (2006). *La longue traîne: Une nouvelle économie est là!* Paris, France: Pearson Education France.

Anderson, E. W. (1998). Customer satisfaction and word of mouth. *Journal of Service Research, 1*(1), 5–17. doi:1 0.1177/109467059800100102.

Anderson, J. C., & Gerbing, D. W. (1988). Structural equation modeling in practice: A review and recommended two-step approach. *Psychological Bulletin, 103*(3), 411–423. doi:10.1037/0033-2909.103.3.411.

Andrejevic, M. (2007). Surveillance in the digital enclosure. *Communication Review, 10*(4), 295–317. doi:10.1080/10714420701715365.

Androutsellis-Theotokis, S., & Spinellis, D. (2004). A survey of peer-to-peer content distribution technologies. *ACM Computing Surveys, 36*(4), 335–371. doi:10.1145/1041680.1041681.

Antill, D. (2013). *Effective workspace management 2013, part 1-4.* Paper presented at the Cloud Computing, Executive insights and Mobile Management at AppSense. New York, NY.

Aral, S. (2010, June 7). Identifying social influence: A comment on opinion leadership and social contagion in new product diffusion. *SSRN eLibrary.*

Babbie, E. R. (2001). *The practice of social research.* Belmont, CA: Wadsworth Pub Co..

Babbie, E. R. (2009). *The practice of social research* (9th ed.). Belmont, CA: Wadsworth Pub Co..

Baek, K., Holton, A., Harp, D., & Yaschur, C. (2011). The links that bind: Uncovering novel motivations for linking on Facebook. *Computers in Human Behavior, 27*(6), 2243–2248. doi:10.1016/j.chb.2011.07.003.

Bagozzi, R. (2007). The legacy of the technology acceptance model and a proposal for a paradigm shift. *Journal of the Association for Information Systems, 8*(4), 244–254.

Bagozzi, R. P., & Yi, Y. (1988). On the use of structural equation models in experimental designs. *JMR, Journal of Marketing Research, 26,* 278–284.

Bakshy, E., Rosenn, I., Marlow, C., & Adamic, L. (2012, January 19). *The role of social networks in information diffusion.* Retrieved from http://arxiv.org/abs/1201.4145

Balfanz, D., Grimm, M., & Tazari, M.-R. (2005). *A reference architecture for mobile knowledge management.* Paper presented at the Dagstuhl Seminar Proceedings. Mobile Computing and Ambient Intelligence: The Challenge of Multimedia. New York, NY.

Bandura, A. (2003). *Auto-efficacité: Le sentiment d'efficacité personnelle.* Paris: De Boeck.

Banerjee, P., Friedrich, R., Bash, C., Goldsack, P., Huberman, B. A., Manley, J., & Veitch, A. (2011). Everything as a service: Powering the new information economy. *Computer, 44*(3), 36–43. doi:10.1109/MC.2011.67.

Bao, P., Pierce, J., Whittaker, S., & Zhai, S. (2011). *Smart phone use by non-mobile business users.* Paper presented at MobileHCI. Stockholm, Sweden.

Barkhuus, L., & Dey, A. (2003). Is context-aware computing taking control away from the user? Three levels of interactivity examined. In *Proceedings of UbiComp 2003: Ubiquitous Computing* (pp. 149–156). Berlin: Springer. doi:10.1007/978-3-540-39653-6_12.

Barnard, Z. (2007). *Online community portals for enhanced alumni networking.* (Doctoral Thesis). University of Johannesburg, Johannesburg, South Africa.

Barroso, L., Dean, J., & Micro, U. H. (2003). Web search for a planet: The Google cluster architecture. *IEEE Computer, 23*(2), 22–28.

Bass, F. (1969). A new product growth model for consumer durables. *Management Science, 15*(5), 215–227. doi:10.1287/mnsc.15.5.215.

Battleson, B., Booth, A., & Weintrop, J. (2000). Usability testing for an academic library web site: A case study. *Journal of Librarianship, 27*(3), 188–198.

Beatty, S. E., & Ferrell, M. E. (1998). Impulse buying: Modeling its precursors. *Journal of Retailing, 74*(2), 169–191. doi:10.1016/S0022-4359(99)80092-X.

Beauvisage, T., Beuscart, J.-S., Couronné, T., & Mellet, K. (2011). *Le succès sur internet repose-t-il sur la contagion? Une analyse critique de la littérature sur la viralité*. Sous presse.

Becerra-Fernandez, I., Gonzalez, A., & Sabherwal, R. (2004). *Knowledge management: Challenges, solutions and technologies*. Englewood Cliffs, NJ: Pearson Prentice Hall.

Bell, G., & Dourish, P. (2007). Yesterday's tomorrows: Notes on ubiquitous computing's dominant vision. *Personal and Ubiquitous Computing, 11*(2), 133–143. doi:10.1007/s00779-006-0071-x.

Bellotti, V., Back, M., Edwards, W. K., Grinter, R. E., Henderson, A., & Lopes, C. (2002). Making sense of sensing systems: Five questions for designers and researchers. In *Proceedings of Conference on Human Factors in Computing Systems* (pp. 415–422). ACM Press.

Belton, L., & de Coninck, F. (2006). Des frontières et des liens: Les topologies du privé et du professionnel pour les travailleurs mobiles. *Reseaux, 24*(140), 67–100.

Ben Miled, H., & Louarn, P. (1994). Analyse comparative de deux échelles de mesure du leadership d'opinion: Validité et interprétation. *Recherche et Applications en Marketing, 9*(4), 23–51. doi:10.1177/076737019400900402.

Ben-Ami, O., & Mioduser, D. (2004). The affective aspect of moderator's role conception and enactment by teachers in a-synchronous learning discussion groups. In *Proceedings of World Conference on Educational Multimedia, Hypermedia and Telecommunications (ED-MEDIA) 2004* (pp. 2831-2837). ED-MEDIA.

Benbasat, I., & Barki, H. (2007). Quo vadis TAM. *Journal of the Association for Information Systems, 8*(4), 211–218.

Benbasat, I., & Zmud, R. W. (1999). Empirical research in information systems: The practice of relevance. *Management Information Systems Quarterly, 23*(1), 3–16. doi:10.2307/249403.

Berger, J. A., & Iyengar, R. (2012, February 29). *How interest shapes word-of-mouth over different channels*. Retrieved from http://ssrn.com/abstract=2013141

Berger, J., & Milkman, K. L. (2009). Social transmission and viral culture. *Operations and Information Management*. Retrieved from http://opimWeb.wharton.upenn.edu/people/faculty.cfm

Berger, J., & Milkman, K. L. (2012). What makes online content viral? *JMR, Journal of Marketing Research, 49*(2), 192–205. doi:10.1509/jmr.10.0353.

Berger, J., & Schwartz, E. M. (2011). What drivers immediate and ongoing word of mouth. *JMR, Journal of Marketing Research, 48*, 869–880. doi:10.1509/jmkr.48.5.869.

Berge, Z. L., & Collins, M. P. (1995). *Computer-mediated communication and the online classroom*. Cresskill, NJ: Hampton Press.

Bergkamp, L. (2002). EU data protection policy: The privacy fallacy: Adverse effects of Europe's data protection policy in an information-driven economy. *Computer Law & Security Report, 18*(1), 31–47. doi:10.1016/S0267-3649(02)00106-1.

Bezzi, M., & Trabelsi, S. (2011). Data usage control in the future Internet cloud. *The Future Internet*, 223-231.

Bhattacherjee, A. (2002). Individual trust in online firms: Scale development and initial test. *Journal of Management Information Systems, 19*(1), 211–241.

Bickart, B., & Schindler, R. M. (2001). Internet forums as influential sources of consumer information. *Journal of Interactive Marketing, 15*, 31–52. doi:10.1002/dir.1014.

Biocca, K. (1997). The cyber's dilemma: Progressive embodiment in virtual environments. *Journal of Computer Mediated Communication, 3*(2). Retrieved February 6, 2012, from http://jcmc.indiana.edu/vol3/issue2/biocca2.html

Blanchard, K. H., & Hersey, P. (1969). *Management of organizational behavior: Utilizing human resources.* Englewood Cliffs, NJ: Prentice Hall.

Blomström, R., Lind, E., & Persson, F. (2012). *Triggering factors for word-of-mouth: A case study of Tipp-Ex's viral marketing campaign.* Retrieved from http://hj.diva-portal.org/smash/record.jsf?pid=diva2:529823

Blondel, V. D., Guillaume, J. L., Lambiotte, R., & Lefebvre, E. (2008). Fast unfolding of communities in large networks. *Journal of Statistical Mechanics*, 10.

Boase, J., Horrigan, J. B., Wellman, B., & Rainie, L. (2006). The strength of internet ties. *Pew Internet and Public Life Project.* Retrieved from http://ww.pewInternet.org/PPF/r/172/report_display.asp

Boboc, A., Dalheine, L., & Mallard, A. (2007). Travailler, se déplacer et communiquer: Premiers résultats d'enquête. *Reseaux, 24*(140), 133–158.

Bock, G. W., & Kim, Y. (2002). Breaking the myths of rewards: An exploratory study of attitudes about knowledge sharing. *Information Resources Management Journal, 15*(2), 14–21. doi:10.4018/irmj.2002040102.

Bock, G. W., Zmud, R. W., Kim, Y.-G., & Lee, J.-N. (2005). Behavioral intention formulation in knowledge sharing: Examining the roles of extrinsic motivators, social–psychological forces, and organizational climate. *Management Information Systems Quarterly, 29*(1), 87–111.

Bohn, J., Coroama, V., Langheinrich, M., Mattern, F., & Rohs, M. (2005). Social, economic, and ethical implications of ambient intelligence and ubiquitous computing. *Ambient Intelligence*, 5-29.

Bollier, D., & Firestone, C. M. (2010). *The promise and peril of big data.* Aspen Institute, Communications and Society Program.

Bond, M. H. (1988). Finding universal dimensions of individual variation in multicultural studies of values: The rokeach and Chinese value surveys. *Journal of Personality and Social Psychology, 55*(6), 1009. doi:10.1037/0022-3514.55.6.1009.

Bone, P. F. (1995). Word-of-mouth effects on short-term and long-term product judgements. *Journal of Business Research, 32*, 213–224. doi:10.1016/0148-2963(94)00047-I.

Booi, V. M., & Ditsa, G. E. (2012). Evaluating South African universities web portal interfaces for usability and user acceptance: Preliminary study. In *Proceedings of IASTED International Conference on Human Computer Interaction 2012*. IASTED.

Boone, M. S. (2008). The past, present, and future of computing and its impact on digital rights management. *Michigan State Law Review, 413*.

Borg, A. (2011). *Enterprise mobility management goes global: Mobility becomes core IT.* Retrieved August 24, 2011, from http://www.aberdeen.com/Aberdeen-Library/7282/RB-enterprise-mobility-management.aspx

Bouta, H. (2013). *Design, development, application and evaluation of a 3D collaborative learning virtual environment for the teaching of mathematics in primary education.* (PhD Thesis). University of Piraeus, Piraeus, Greece.

Bouta, H., & Paraskeva, P. (2012). Cognitive apprenticeship theory for the teaching of mathematics in an online 3D virtual environment. *Journal of Mathematical Education in Science and Technology, 44*(2), 159–178. doi:10.1080/0020739X.2012.703334.

Bouta, H., Retalis, S., & Paraskeva, F. (2012). Utilising a collaborative macro-script to enhance student engagement: A mixed method study in a 3D virtual environment. *Computers & Education, 58*(1), 501–517. doi:10.1016/j.compedu.2011.08.031.

Bouwman, H., & van de Wijngaert, L. (2009). Coppers context, and conjoints: A reassessment of TAM. *Journal of Information Technology, 24*, 186–201. doi:10.1057/jit.2008.36.

Bracken, C. C., & Skalski, P. (2009). Telepresence and video games: The impact of image quality. *PsychNology Journal, 7*(1), 101–112.

Bradshaw, S., Millard, C., & Walden, I. (2011). Contracts for clouds: Comparison and analysis of the terms and conditions of cloud computing services. *International Journal of Law and Information Technology, 19*(3), 187–223. doi:10.1093/ijlit/ear005.

Brey, P. (2005). Freedom and privacy in ambient intelligence. *Ethics and Information Technology, 7*(3), 157–166. doi:10.1007/s10676-006-0005-3.

Brodie, R. J., Ilic, A., Juric, B., & Hollebeek, L. (2011). Consumer engagement in a virtual brand community: An exploratory analysis. *Journal of Business Research.*

Brook, C., & Oliver, R. (2003). Designing for online learning communities. In *Proceedings of World Conference on Educational Multimedia, Hypermedia and Telecommunications (ED-MEDIA) 2003* (pp. 1494-1500). ED-MEDIA.

Brooks, R. C. Jr. (1957). Word-of-mouth advertising in selling new products. *Journal of Marketing, 22*(2), 154–161. doi:10.2307/1247212.

Brown, J. J., & Reingen, P. H. (1987). Social ties and word-of-mouth referral behavior. *The Journal of Consumer Research, 14*, 350–362. doi:10.1086/209118.

Brown, T. H. (2005). Towards a model for m-learning in Africa. *International Journal on E-Learning, 4*(3), 299–315.

Bucklin, R. E., Lattin, J., Ansari, A., Bell, D., Coupey, E., & Gupta, S. et al. (2002). Choice and the internet: From clickstream to research stream. *Marketing Letters, 13*(3), 245–258. doi:10.1023/A:1020231107662.

Bucklin, R. E., & Sismeiro, C. (2003). A model of web site browsing behavior estimated on clickstream data. *JMR, Journal of Marketing Research, 40*(3), 249–267. doi:10.1509/jmkr.40.3.249.19241.

Bughin, J., Corb, L., Manyika, J., Nottebohms, O., Chui, M., Barbat, B. D. M., & Said, R. (2011). *The impact of internet technologies: Search.* Mckinsey & Company.

Bulik, B. S. (2007). This frog speaks volumes about word-of-mouth. *Advertising Age, 78*(4), 4–23.

Bumgarner, B. A. (2007). Exploring the uses and gratifications of Facebook among emerging adults. *First Monday, 12*(11). Retrieved from http://firstmonday.org/htbin/cgiwrap/bin/ojs/index.php/fm/article/viewArticle/2026/1897 doi:10.5210/fm.v12i11.2026.

Buyya, R., Yeo, C. S., & Venugopal, S. (2008). Market-oriented cloud computing: Vision, hype, and reality for delivering it services as computing utilities.[IEEE.]. *Proceedings of High Performance Computing and Communications, 2008*, 5–13.

Bystrom, K., Barfield, W., & Hendrix, C. (1999). A conceptual model of the sense of presence in virtual environments. *Presence (Cambridge, Mass.), 8*(2), 241–244. doi:10.1162/105474699566107.

Carlsson, C., Carlsson, J., Hyvonen, K., Puhakainen, J., & Walden, P. (2006). Adoption of mobile devices/services—Searching for answers with the UTAUT. In *Proceedings of the 39th Annual Hawaii International Conference on System Sciences.* IEEE.

Casaló, L., Flavián, C., & Guinalíu, M. (2011). Understanding the intention to follow the advice obtained in an online travel community. *Computers in Human Behavior, 27*, 622–633. doi:10.1016/j.chb.2010.04.013.

Castells, M. (2007). Communication, power and counter-power in the network society. *International Journal of Communication, 1*(1), 238-266. doi: 1932-8036/20070238

Catledge, L. D., & Pitkow, J. E. (1995). Characterizing browsing strategies in the world wide web. *Computer Networks and ISDN Systems, 27*(6), 1065–1073. doi:10.1016/0169-7552(95)00043-7.

Cauberghe, V., Geuens, M., & Pelsmacker, P. D. (2011). Context effects of TV programme-induced interactivity and telepresence on advertising responses. *International Journal of Advertising, 30*(4), 641–663. doi:10.2501/IJA-30-4-641-663.

Cearley, D. (2012). *Gartner identifies the top 10 strategic technology trends for 2013.* Orlando, FL: Gartner.

Centola, D. (2010). The spread of behavior in an online social network experiment. *Science, 329*(5996), 1194–1197. doi:10.1126/science.1185231 PMID:20813952.

Centre d'Analyse Stratégique. (2009, November 25). *Le développement du télétravail dans la société numérique de demain, rapport remis au ministre de l'économie numérique.*

Cha, M., Haddadi, H., Benevenuto, F., & Gummadi, K. P. (2010). Measuring user influence in Twitter: The million follower fallacy. In *Proceedings of the 4th International AAAI Conference on Weblogs and Social Media (ICWSM).* AAAI.

Cha, M., Mislove, A., Adams, B., & Gummadi, K. P. (2008). Characterizing social cascades in Flickr. In *Proceedings of the First Workshop on Online Social Networks*, (pp. 13–18). New York, NY: ACM.

Cha, M., Pérez, J. A. N., & Haddadi, H. (2012). The spread of media content through blogs. *Social Network Analysis and Mining, 2*(3), 249–264. doi:10.1007/s13278-011-0040-x.

Chan, D. K.-S., & Cheng, G. H.-L. (2004). A comparison of offline and online friendship qualities at different stages of relationship development. *Journal of Social and Personal Relationships, 21*(3), 305–320. doi:10.1177/0265407504042834.

Chang, S. E., & Pan, Y.-H. V. (2011). Exploring factors influencing mobile users' intention to adopt multimedia messaging service. *Behaviour & Information Technology, 30*(5), 659–672. doi:10.1080/01449290903377095.

Chase, N. (2008). An exploration of the culture of information technology: Focus on unrelenting change. *Journal of Information, Information Technology, and Organizations, 3*.

Chaudhuri, A., & Holbrook, M. B. (2001). The chain of rffects from brand trust and brand affect to brand performance: The role of brand loyalty. *Journal of Marketing, 65*(2), 81–93. doi:10.1509/jmkg.65.2.81.18255.

Cheema, A., & Kaikati, A. M. (2010). The effect of need for uniqueness on word of mouth. *JMR, Journal of Marketing Research, 47*(3), 553–563. doi:10.1509/jmkr.47.3.553.

Chelminski, P., & Coulter, R. A. (2011). An examination of consumer advocacy and complaining behavior in the context of service failure. *Journal of Services Marketing, 25*(5), 361–370. doi:10.1108/08876041111149711.

Cheng, Y., O'Toole, A., & Abdi, H. (2001). Classifying adults' and children's faces by sex: Computational investigations of subcategorial feature encoding. *Cognitive Science, 25*(5), 819–838. doi:10.1207/s15516709cog2505_8.

Chen, H.-R., & Huang, H.-L. (2010). User acceptance of mobile knowledge management learning system: Design and analysis. *Journal of Educational Technology & Society, 13*(3), 70–77.

Chen, H., Wigand, R. T., & Nilan, M. S. (1999). Optimal experience of web activities. *Computers in Human Behavior, 15*(5), 585–608. doi:10.1016/S0747-5632(99)00038-2.

Chen, L. (2008). A model of consumer acceptance of mobile payment. *International Journal of Mobile Communications, 6*(1), 32–52. doi:10.1504/IJMC.2008.015997.

Chen, L., & Nath, R. (2005, Fall). Nomadic culture: Cultural support for working anytime, anywhere. *Information Systems Management*, 56–64. doi:10.1201/1078.10580530/45520.22.4.20050901/90030.6.

Chervany, N., & McKnight, D. (2002). What trust means in e-commerce customer relationships: An interdisciplinary conceptual typology. *International Journal of Electronic Commerce, 6*(2), 35–59.

Cheung, C., Lee, M., & Jin, X. (2011). Customer engagement in an online social platform: A conceptual model and scale development. In *Proceedings of ICIS*. ICIS.

Chevalier, J., & Mayzlin, D. (2006). The effect of word of mouth on sales: Online book reviews. *JMR, Journal of Marketing Research, 43*(3), 345–354. doi:10.1509/jmkr.43.3.345.

Childers, T. L., Carr, C., Peck, J., & Carson, S. (2001). Hedonic and utilitarian motivations for online retail shopping behavior. *Journal of Retailing, 77*, 511–535. doi:10.1016/S0022-4359(01)00056-2.

Cho, J., & Roy, S. (2004). Impact of search engines on page popularity. In *Proceedings of the 13th International Conference on World Wide Web*. ACM.

Choi, B., Lee, I., & Kim, J. (2006). Culturability in mobile data services: A qualitative study of the relationship between cultural characteristics and user-experience attributes. *International Journal of Human-Computer Interaction, 20*(3), 171–203. doi:10.1207/s15327590ijhc2003_2.

Choi, D. H., Kim, J., & Kim, S. H. (2007). ERP training with a web-based electronic learning system: The flow theory perspective. *International Journal of Human-Computer Studies, 65*(3), 223–243. doi:10.1016/j.ijhcs.2006.10.002.

Choo, C. W. (1998). *The knowing organization: How organizations use information to construct meaning, create knowledge and make decisions.* New York: Oxford University Press.

Chouk, I., & Perrien, J. (2004). Les facteurs expliquant la confiance du consommateur lors d'un achat sur un site marchand: Une étude exploratoire. *Décisions Marketing,* 75-86.

Chouk, I., & Perrien, J. (2006). Déterminants de la confiance du consommateur vis-vis d'un site marchand internet non familier: Une approche par le rôle des tiers. In *Actes du XXII Congrès AFM – 11 et 12 Mai.*

Chouk, I., & Perrien, J. (2003). *Les déterminants de la confiance du consommateur lors d'un achat sur un site marchand: Proposition d'un cadre de recherche préliminaire. Centre de recherche DMSP. Cahier n° 318.* Université Paris-Dauphine.

Chow, R., Golle, P., Jakobsson, M., Shi, E., Staddon, J., Masuoka, R., & Molina, J. (2009). Controlling data in the cloud: Outsourcing computation without outsourcing control. In *Proceedings of the 2009 ACM Workshop on Cloud Computing Security* (pp. 85-90). ACM.

Chung, C., & Darke, P. (2006). The consumer as advocate: Self-relevance, culture, and word-of mouth. *Marketing Letters, 17*(4), 269–279. doi:10.1007/s11002-006-8426-7.

Churchill, G. A. (1979). A paradigm for developing better measures of marketing constructs. *JMR, Journal of Marketing Research, 16,* 64–73. doi:10.2307/3150876.

Churchville, D. (2008). *Agile thinking: Leading successful software projects and teams.*

Chu, S. C., & Kim, Y. (2011). Determinants of consumer engagement in electronic word-of-mouth (eWOM) in social networking sites. *International Journal of Advertising, 30,* 47–75. doi:10.2501/IJA-30-1-047-075.

Citrix. (2012). *Workplace of the future* (White paper). Citrix.

Clarke, I. (2001). Emerging value propositions for m-commerce. *The Journal of Business Strategy, 18*(2), 133–148.

CNNIC. (2012). 30th statistical report on Internet development in China. Retrieved from http://www1.cnnic.cn/IDR/ReportDownloads/201209/t20120928_36586.htm

Cocula, F., & Fredy-Planchot, A. (2003). Pratiquer le management à distance. *Gestion, 2000*(1), 43–63.

Cohen-Almagor, R. (2012). *Internet architecture, freedom of expression and social responsibility: Critical realism and proposals for a better future.*

Cohen, B. C. (1963). *The press and foreign policy.* Princeton, NJ: Princeton University Press.

Cole-Lewis, H., & Kershaw, T. (2010). Text messaging as a tool for behavior change in disease prevention and management. *Epidemiologic Reviews, 32*(1), 56–59. doi:10.1093/epirev/mxq004 PMID:20354039.

Coleman, J., & Fararo, T. (1992). *Rational choice theory advocacy and critique: Key issues in sociological theory.* London: Sage Publications.

Collins, H. (2012). *Tacit and explicit knowledge.* Chicago: University Of Chicago Press.

Compeau, D. R., & Higgins, C. A. (1995). Computer self-efficacy: Development of a measure and initial test. *Management Information Systems Quarterly, 19*(2), 189–211. doi:10.2307/249688.

Constantiou, I. D., Papazafeiropoulou, A., & Vendelø, M. T. (2009). Does culture affect the adoption of advanced mobile services? A comparative study of young adults' perceptions in Denmark and the UK. *SIGMIS Database, 40*(4), 132–147. doi:10.1145/1644953.1644962.

Cooper, R. C., & Schindler, P. S. (2008). *Business research methods.* New York: McGraw-Hill.

Corbitt, B., & Thanasankit, T., & Yi. (2003). Trust and e-commerce: A study of consumer perceptions. *Electronic Commerce Research and Applications, 2,* 203–215. doi:10.1016/S1567-4223(03)00024-3.

Couclelis, H. (2004). Pizza over the internet: E-commerce, the fragmentation of activity, and the tyranny of the region. *Entrepreneurship and Regional Development, 16,* 41–54. doi:10.1080/0898562042000205027.

Cova, B. (1997). Community and consumption: Towards a definition of the linking value of products and services. *European Journal of Marketing*, *31*(3-4).

Crandall, L. J. (1980). Adler's concept of social interest: Theory, measurement, and implications for adjustment. *Journal of Personality and Social Psychology*, *39*, 481–495. doi:10.1037/0022-3514.39.3.481.

Creamer, M. (2012). *Study: Only 1% of Facebook 'fans' engage with brands*. Retrieved from http://adage.com/article/digital/study-1-facebook-fansengage-brands/232351/

Cross, S. E., Bacon, P. L., & Morris, M. L. (2000). The relational-interdependent self-construal and relationships. *Journal of Personality and Social Psychology*, *78*, 791–808. doi:10.1037/0022-3514.78.4.791 PMID:10794381.

Cross, S. E., & Madson, L. (1997). Models of the self: Self-construals and gender. *Psychological Bulletin*, *122*, 5–37. doi:10.1037/0033-2909.122.1.5 PMID:9204777.

Csikszentmihalyi, M. (1975). *Beyond boredom and anxiety*. San Francisco, CA: Jossey-Bass.

Csikszentmihalyi, M. (1977). *Beyond boredom and anxiety* (2nd ed.). San Francisco, CA: Jossey-Bass.

Csikszentmihalyi, M. (1990). *Flow: The psychology of optimal experience*. New York: Harper and Row.

Csikszentmihalyi, M. (1997). *Finding flow: The psychology of engagement with everyday life*. New York: Basic Books.

Csikszentmihalyi, M., & Csikszentmihalyi, I. S. (1988). *Optimal experience: Psychological studies of flow in consciousness*. New York: University of Cambridge Press. doi:10.1017/CBO9780511621956.

Csikszentmihalyi, M., Rathunde, K., & Whalen, S. (1993). *Talented teenagers: The roots of success and failure*. New York: Cambridge University Press.

Cyr, D., Head, M., & Ivanov, A. (2009). Perceived interactivity leading to e-loyalty: Development of a model for cognitive–affective user responses. *International Journal of Human-Computer Studies*, *67*, 850–869. doi:10.1016/j.ijhcs.2009.07.004.

Czepiel, J. A. (1974). Word-of-mouth processes in the diffusion of a major technological innovation. *JMR, Journal of Marketing Research*, *11*(2), 172–180. doi:10.2307/3150555.

Daugherty, T., Li, H., & Biocca, F. (2005). Experiential ecommerce: A summary of research investigating the impact of virtual experience on consumer learning. In Haugtvedt, C. P., Machleit, K. A., & Yalch, R. F. (Eds.), *Online consumer psychology: Understanding and influencing consumer behavior in the virtual world* (pp. 457–490). Hillsdale, NJ: Lawrence Erlbaum.

Davenport, E., & McLaughlin, L. (2004). Interpersonal trust in online partnerships: The challenge of representation. In Iivonen, M., & Huotari, M. L. (Eds.), *Trust in knowledge management and systems in organizations*. Hershey, PA: Idea Group Publishing. doi:10.4018/978-1-59140-126-1.ch005.

Davenport, T. H., & Prusak, L. (1997). *Working knowledge: How organizations manage what they know*. Project Management Institute.

Davenport, T. H., & Prusak, L. (1998). *Working knowledge: How organizations manage what they know*. Boston: Harvard Business School Press.

Davies, S. P. (1993). Models and theories of programming strategy. *International Journal of Man-Machine Studies*, *39*(2), 237–267. doi:10.1006/imms.1993.1061.

Davis, F. D. (1986). *Technology acceptance model for empirically testing new end-user information systems: Theory and results*. (PhD Thesis). MIT, Cambridge, MA.

Davis, F. D. (1989). Perceived usefulness, perceived ease of use and user acceptance of information technology. *Management Information Systems Quarterly*, *13*(3), 319–339. doi:10.2307/249008.

Davis, F. D., Bagozzi, P. R., & Warshaw, P. R. (1989). User acceptance of computer technology: A comparison of two theoretical models. *Management Science*, *35*(8), 982–1003. doi:10.1287/mnsc.35.8.982.

Davis, F. D., Bagozzi, R. P., & Warshaw, P. R. (1992). Extrinsic and intrinsic motivation to use computers in the workplace. *Journal of Applied Social Psychology*, *22*(14), 1111–1132. doi:10.1111/j.1559-1816.1992.tb00945.x.

Davis, G. B. (2002). Anytime/anyplace computing and the future of knowledge work. *Communications of the ACM*, *45*(12), 67–73. doi:10.1145/585597.585617.

Davis, M., & Sedsman, A. (2010). Grey areas: The legal dimensions of cloud computing. *International Journal of Digital Crime and Forensics*, *2*(1), 30–39. doi:10.4018/jdcf.2010010103.

Davis, R., & Owen, D. (1998). *New media and American politics*. New York: Oxford University Press.

Dawson, B. (2009). The beat: Top universities rethink how to prepare e-beat journalists. *SEJ Journal*, *19*(4), 20–22.

de Filippi, P., & McCarthy, S. (2011). Cloud computing: Legal issues in centralized architectures. In *Proceedings of the VII International Conference on Internet, Law and Politics*. IEEE.

de Filippi, P., & Vieira, M. (2013). The commodification of information commons. *International Journal of the Commons*.

De Filippi, P., & Belli, L. (2012). The law of the cloud v the law of the land: Challenges and opportunities for innovation. *European Journal of Law and Technology*, *3*(2).

de Filippi, P., & McCarthy, S. (2012). Cloud computing: Centralization and data sovereignty. *European Journal of Law and Technology*, *3*(2).

de Filippi, P., & Porcedda, M. G. (2012). Privacy belts on the innovation highway. In *Proceedings of Internet, Politics, Policy 2012: Big Data, Big Challenges?* Oxford Internet Institute.

de Schutter, O. (2000). Waiver of rights and state paternalism under the European convention on human rights. *The Northern Ireland Legal Quarterly*, *51*, 487.

Dearing, J. W., & Rogers, E. M. (1996). *Agenda-setting*. Thousand Oaks, CA: Sage Publications.

Debbabi, S., Daassi, M., & Baile, S. (2010). Effect of online 3D advertising on consumer responses: The mediating role of telepresence. *Journal of Marketing Management*, *26*(9-10), 967–992. doi:10.1080/02672570903498819.

Debos, F. (2007). Les relations numériques individu-marque. *Document Numérique*, *10*(3), 63-73. Retrieved from www.cairn.info/revue-document-numerique-2007-3-page-63.htm

Deci, E. L., & Ryan, R. M. (1985). *Intrinsic motivation and self-determination in human behavior*. New York: Plenum Publishing Co. doi:10.1007/978-1-4899-2271-7.

Deci, E. L., & Ryan, R. M. (1987). The support of autonomy and the control of behavior. *Journal of Personality and Social Psychology*, *53*, 1024–1037. doi:10.1037/0022-3514.53.6.1024 PMID:3320334.

Delone, W. H., & Mclean, E. R. (2002). The Delone and McLean model of information systems success: A ten-year review. *Journal of information Systems*, *19*(4).

Delone, W. H., & Mclean, E. R. (1992). Information systems success: The quest for the dependent variable. *Information Systems Research*, *3*(1). doi:10.1287/isre.3.1.60.

DeLuca, K. (1999). *Image politics: The new rhetoric of environmental activism*. New York: Guilford.

Department for Environment. Food and Rural Affairs. (2002). Survey of public attitudes to quality of life and to the environment–2001. London: Crown.

Derryberry, A. (2012). *Game-based learning ecosystem for higher education*. Sage Road Solutions.

Dewey, J. (1938). *Experience and education*. New York: MacMillan.

Dholakia, U. M., Bagozzi, R. P., & Pearo, L. K. (2004). A social influence model of consumer participation in network- and small-group-based virtual communities. *International Journal of Research in Marketing*, *21*(3), 241–263. doi:10.1016/j.ijresmar.2003.12.004.

Dibbell, J. (2012). The shadow web. *Scientific American*, *306*(3), 60–65. doi:10.1038/scientificamerican0312-60 PMID:22375324.

Dichter, E. (1966). How word-of-mouth advertising works. *Harvard Business Review*, *16*, 147–166.

Dietz, T. (2003). What is a good decision? Criteria for environmental decision making. *Human Ecology Review*, *10*(1), 60–67.

Dikaiakos, M. D., Katsaros, D., Mehra, P., Pallis, G., & Vakali, A. (2009). Cloud computing: Distributed internet computing for IT and scientific research. *IEEE Internet Computing*, *13*(5), 10–13. doi:10.1109/MIC.2009.103.

Dillon, T., Wu, C., & Chang, E. (2010). Cloud computing: Issues and challenges. In Proceedings of Advanced Information Networking and Applications (AINA), (pp. 27-33). IEEE.

Dillon, A. (2001). User acceptance of information technology. In Karwoski, W. (Ed.), *Encyclopedia of human factors and ergonomics*. London: Taylor and Francis.

Dillon, A., & Morris, M. G. (1996). User acceptance of information technology: Theories and models. In Williams, M. (Ed.), *Annual Review of Information Science and Technology* (*Vol. 31*, pp. 3–32). Medford, NJ: Information Today.

Dimensional Research. (2011). *Enterprise iPad and tablet adoption: A survey*. Dimensional Research.

DiMicco, J. M., & Millen, D. R. (2007). Identity management: Multiple presentations of self in Facebook. In *Proceedings of the 2007 International ACM Conference on Supporting Group Work* (pp. 383-386). New York: ACM.

Din, H. W.-H. (2006). *Play to learn: Exploring online educational games in museums*. Paper presented at the International Conference on Computer Graphics and Interactive Techniques. New York, NY.

Dinev, T., & Hart, P. (2003). Privacy concerns and internet use–A model of trade-off factors. In *Proceedings of Annual Academy of Management Meeting*. Seattle, WA: IEEE.

Ditsa, G. (2003). Executive information systems use in organisational contexts: An exploratory user behaviour testing. In *Information management: Support systems & multimedia technology*. London: IRM Press.

Dobele, A., Lindgreen, A., Beverland, M., Vanhamme, J., & van Wijk, R. (2007, July). Why pass on viral messages? Because they connect emotionally. *Business Horizons*, *50*(4), 291–304. doi:10.1016/j.bushor.2007.01.004.

Dobele, A., Toleman, D., & Beverland, M. (2005). Controlled infection! Spreading the brand message through viral marketing. *Business Horizons*, *48*(2), 143–149. doi:10.1016/j.bushor.2004.10.011.

Dodson, J. A., & Muller, E. (1978). Models of new product diffusion through advertising and word-of-mouth. *Management Science*, *24*(15), 1568–1578. doi:10.1287/mnsc.24.15.1568.

Dolen, W. M., Dabholkar, P. A., & Ruyter, K. (2007). La satisfaction envers les discussions en ligne de clients: L'influence des attributs technologiques perçues, des caractéristiques du groupe de discussion et du style de communication du conseiller. *Recherche et Applications en Marketing*, *22*(3), 83–111. doi:10.1177/076737010702200306.

Domina, T., Lee, S. E., & MacGillivray, M. (2012). Understanding factors affecting consumer intention to shop in a virtual world. *Journal of Retailing and Consumer Services*, *19*, 613–620. doi:10.1016/j.jretconser.2012.08.001.

Doney, P. M., Cannon, J. P., & Mullen, M. R. (1998). Understanding the influence of national culture on the development of trust. *Academy of Management Review*, *23*(3).

Doron, P. (1991). *Le dictionnaire de psychologie*. PUF.

Douglas, K. (1995). *Media culture*. New York: Routledge.

Draper, J. V., Kaber, D. B., & Usher, J. M. (1998). Telepresence. *Human Factors*, *40*, 354–375. doi:10.1518/001872098779591386 PMID:9849099.

Du Toit, M., & Bothma, C. (2009). Evaluating the usability of an academic marketing department's website from marketing students perspective. *International Retail and Marketing Review*. Retrieved August 7, 2010, from www.computer.org/pervasive

Dubach-Spiegler, E., Hildebrand, C., & Michahelles, F. (2011). Social networks in pervasive advertising and shopping. In *Pervasive advertising* (pp. 208–225). New York: Springer. doi:10.1007/978-0-85729-352-7_10.

Duffy, P. (2007). *Engaging the YouTube Google-eyed generation: Strategies for using web 2.0 in teaching and learning.* Paper presented at the European Conference on ELearning, ECEL. London, UK.

Duhan, D. F., Johnson, S. D., Wilcox, J. B., & Harrell, G. D. (1997). Influences on consumer use of word-of-mouth recommendation sources. *Journal of the Academy of Marketing Science, 25*(4), 283–295. doi:10.1177/0092070397254001.

Duncan, T., & Moriarty, S. E. (1998). A communication-based marketing. *Journal of Marketing, 62,* 1–13. doi:10.2307/1252157.

Dyer, R., Green, R., Pitts, M., & Millward, G. (1995). What's the flaming problem? CMC - Deindividuation or disinhibiting? In Kirby, M. A. R., Dix, A. J., & Finlay, J. E. (Eds.), *People and computers X.* Cambridge, UK: Cambridge University Press.

Ekman, P. (1992). An argument for basic emotions. In Stein, N. L., & Oatley, K. (Eds.), *Basic emotions: Cognition & emotion* (pp. 169–200). Mahwah, NJ: Lawrence Erlbaum.

Emurian, H., & Wang, Y. (2005). An overview of online trust: Concepts, elements, and implications. *Computers in Human Behavior, 21,* 105–125. doi:10.1016/j.chb.2003.11.008.

Endsuleit, R., & Mie, T. (2006). Censorship-resistant and anonymous P2P filesharing. In Proceedings of Availability, Reliability and Security, 2006. IEEE.

Engel, J. E., Blackwell, R. D., & Kegerreis, R. J. (1969). How information is used to adopt an innovation. *Journal of Advertising Research, 9,* 3–8.

Erdogmus, H. (2009). Cloud computing: Does nirvana hide behind the nebula? *IEEE Software, 26*(2), 4–6. doi:10.1109/MS.2009.31.

Fam, K. S., Foscht, T., & Collins, R. D. (2004). Trust and the online relationships—An exploratory study of from New Zealand. *Tourism Management, 1*(3).

Feick, L. F., & Price, L. L. (1987). The market maven: A diffuser of marketplace information. *Journal of Marketing, 51*(1), 83–97. doi:10.2307/1251146.

Felstead, A., Jewson, N., & Walters, S. (2003). Managerial control of employees working at home. *British Journal of Industrial Relations, 41*(2), 241–264. doi:10.1111/1467-8543.00271.

Fenouillet, F. (2012). *La motivation.* Paris, France: Dunod.

Fernandez, V., Guillot, C., & Marrauld, L. (2011). Travailler, collaborer et se sociabiliser à distance. *Rapport de recherche du projet Wite 2.0.* Retrieved from http://www.telecentres.fr/wp-content/uploads/2011/10/Rapport-etude-qualitative-WITE20-oct-2011.pdf

Fernandez, V., & Marrauld, L. (2012). Usage des téléphones portables et pratiques de la mobilité: L'analyse de journaux de bord de salariés mobiles. *Revue Française de Gestion, 38*(226), 137–149. doi:10.3166/rfg.226.137-149.

Finneran, C., & Zhang, P. (2003). A person-artifact-task model of flow antecedents within computer-mediated environments. *International Journal of Human-Computer Studies, 59*(4), 475–496. doi:10.1016/S1071-5819(03)00112-5.

Fiore, A. M., Kim, J., & Lee, H. H. (2005). Effect of image interactivity technology on consumer responses toward the online retailer. *Journal of Interactive Marketing, 19*(3), 38–53. doi:10.1002/dir.20042.

Fishbein, M., & Ajzen, I. (1975). *Belief, attitude, intention and behavior: An introduction to theory and research.* Boston: Addison-Wesley.

Fogg, B. J., & Eckles, D. (2007). The behavior chain for online participation: How successful web services structure persuasion.[IEEE.]. *Proceedings of Persuasive, 2007,* 199–209. doi:10.1007/978-3-540-77006-0_25.

Fornell, C. D., & Larcker, F. (1981). Evaluating structural equation models with unobservable variables and measurement errors. *JMR, Journal of Marketing Research, 18*(3), 39–50. doi:10.2307/3151312.

Fortin, D. R., & Dholakia, R. R. (2005). Interactivity and vividness effects on social presence and involvement with a web-based advertisement. *Journal of Business Research, 58*(3), 387–396. doi:10.1016/S0148-2963(03)00106-1.

Foster, I., Zhao, Y., Raicu, I., & Lu, S. (2008). Cloud computing and grid computing 360-degree compared. In *Proceedings of the Grid Computing Environments Workshop, 2008,* (pp. 1-10). IEEE.

Frewer, L. J. (2002). The media and genetically modified food: Evidence in support of social amplification of risk. *Risk Analysis*, 22(4), 701–711. doi:10.1111/0272-4332.00062 PMID:12224744.

Friedman, B., Kahn, J. R., & Borning, A. (2001). *Value sensitive design: Theory and methods* (Technology Report 02-12-01). Seattle, WA: University of Washington.

Friedman, D., Brogni, A., Guger, C., Antley, A., Steed, A., & Slater, M. (2006). Sharing and analysing data from presence experiments. *Presence (Cambridge, Mass.)*, 15, 599–610. doi:10.1162/pres.15.5.599.

Furrer, O., Liu, B. S.-C., & Sudharshan, D. (2000). The relationships between culture and service quality perceptions. *Journal of Service Research*, 2(4), 355–371. doi:10.1177/109467050024004.

Gamson, W. A., & Modigliani, A. (1989). Media discourse and public opinion on nuclear power: A constructionist approach. *American Journal of Sociology*, 95(1), 1–37. doi:10.1086/229213.

Gao, S., Moe, S. P., & Krogstie, J. (2010). An empirical test of the mobile services acceptance model. In *Proceedings of the 2010 Ninth International Conference on Mobile Business and 2010 Ninth Global Mobility Roundtable (ICMB-GMR).* ICMB-GMR.

Gao, S., Krogstie, J., & Siau, K. (2011). Developing an instrument to measure the adoption of mobile services. *Mobile Information Systems Journal*, 7(1), 45–67.

Gardarin, G. (1999). *Intranet & bases de données: Data web, data warehouse, data mining.* Eyrolles.

Garrison, D. R., & Anderson, T. (2003). *E-learning in the 21st century: A framework for research and practice.* London: Routledge Falmer. doi:10.4324/9780203166093.

Gefen, D. (2000). E-commerce: The role of familiarity and trust. *The International Journal of Management Science*, 28, 725–737.

Gefen, D. (2003). TAM or just plain habit: A look at experienced online shoppers. *Journal of End User Computing*, 15(3), 1–13. doi:10.4018/joeuc.2003070101.

Gefen, D., Karahanna, E., & Straub, D. (2003). Trust and TAM in online shopping: An integrated model. *Management Information Systems Quarterly*, 27(1), 51–90.

Gefen, D., & Straub, D. (2004). Consumer trust in B2C e-commerce and the importance of social presence. *Omega*, 32, 407–424. doi:10.1016/j.omega.2004.01.006.

Geiger, B., & Eshet, Y. (2010). Two worlds of assessment of environmental health issues: The case of contaminated water wells in Ramat ha-Sharon. *Journal of Risk Research*, 14(1). doi: doi:10.1080/13669877.2010.505688.

Gellman, R. (2012). Privacy in the clouds: Risks to privacy and confidentiality from cloud computing. In *Proceedings of the World Privacy Forum.* IEEE.

Ghani, J. A., Supnick, R., & Rooney, P. (1991). The experience of flow in computer-mediated and in face-to-face groups. In J. I. DeGross, I. Benbasat, G. DeSanctis, & C. M. Beath (Eds.), *Proceedings of the 12th International Conference on Information Systems* (pp. 16-18). New York: IEEE.

Ghani, J. A., & Deshpande, S. P. (1994). Task characteristics and the experience of optimal flow in human-computer interaction. *The Journal of Psychology*, 128(4), 381–391. doi:10.1080/00223980.1994.9712742.

Gibbs, L. (1993). Celebrating ten years of triumph. *Everyone's Backyard*, 11(1), 2–3.

Gill, A. J., Oberlander, J., & Elizabeth, A. (2006). Rating e-mail personality at zero acquaintance. *Personality and Individual Differences*, 40(3), 497–507. doi:10.1016/j.paid.2005.06.027.

Gillan, K., Pickerill, J., & Webster, F. (2008). *Anti-war activism: New media and protest in the information age.* Basingstoke, UK: Palgrave Macmillan. doi:10.1057/9780230596382.

Giurgiu, I., Riva, O., Juric, D., Krivulev, I., & Alonso, G. (2009). Calling the cloud: Enabling mobile phones as interfaces to cloud applications.[Middleware.]. *Proceedings of Middleware, 2009*, 83–102.

Gléonnec, M. (2004). Confiance et usage des technologies d'information et de communication. *Consommations et Sociétés, 4*.

Golder, S. A., Wilkinson, D., & Huberman, B. A. (2007). Rhythms of social interaction: Messaging within a massive online network. In *Proceedings of the Third International Conference on Communities and Technologies* (pp. 41–66). London: Springer.

Goodhue, D. L. (1995). Understanding user evaluations of information systems. *Management Science, 41*(12), 1827–1844. doi:10.1287/mnsc.41.12.1827.

Goodhue, D. L., & Thompson, R. L. (1995). Task-technology fit and individual performance. *Management Information Systems Quarterly, 19*(2), 213–236. doi:10.2307/249689.

Gordon, J. (2002). The mobile phone, an artifact of popular culture and a tool of the public sphere. *Convergence, 8*(3), 15–26. doi:10.1177/135485650200800303.

Graham, M. D., Adams, W. M., & Kahiro, G. N. (2012). Mobile phone communication in effective human-elephant conflict management in Laikipia County, Kenya. *Oryx, 46*(1), 137–144. doi:10.1017/S0030605311001104.

Grant, R. M. (1996). Prospering in dynamically-competitive environments: Organizational capability as knowledge Integration. *Organization Science, 7*(4), 375–387. doi:10.1287/orsc.7.4.375.

Greenfield, A. (2006). *Everyware: The dawning age of ubiquitous computing*. Peachpit Press.

Grigorovici, D., & Constantin, C. (2004). Experiencing interactive advertising beyond rich media: Impacts of ad type and presence on brand effectiveness in 3D gaming immersive virtual environment. *Journal of Interactive Advertising, 5*(1), 22–36. doi:10.1080/15252019.2004.10722091.

Grimm, M., Tazari, M.-R., & Balfanz, D. (2005). A reference model for mobile knowledge management. In *Proceedings of I-KNOW '05*. Graz, Austria: I-KNOW.

Grossein, J. P., Melot, R., & Schluchter, W. (2005). Action, ordre et culture: Eléments d'un programme de recherche Wébérien. *Revue Francaise de Sociologie, 46*(4), 653–683.

Grudin, J. (1988). Why CSCW applications fail? In *Proceedings of Computer-Supported Cooperative Work Conference*. ACM Press.

Guizon, A. H. (2001). Le comportement du consommateur en ligne est-il différent de son comportement en magasin? *Recherche et Applications en Marketing, 16*(3).

Gunawardena, C. N., & Zittle, F. J. (1997). Social presence as a predictor of satisfaction within a computer-mediated conferencing environment. *American Journal of Distance Education, 11*(3), 8–26. doi:10.1080/08923649709526970.

Guo, H., Chen, J., Wu, W., & Wang, W. (2009). Personalization as a service: The architecture and a case study. In *Proceedings of the First International Workshop on Cloud Data Management* (pp. 1-8). ACM.

Guo, X., & Marinova, D. (2011). Environmental awareness in China: Facilitating the greening of the economy. In F. Chan, D. Marinova, & R. S. Anderssen (Eds.), *MODSIM2011: 19th International Congress on Modelling and Simulation,* (pp. 1673-1679). Perth, Australia: The Modelling and Simulation Society of Australia and New Zealand.

Gustafsson, A., Johnson, M. D., & Roos, I. (2005). The effects of customer satisfaction, relationship commitment dimensions, and triggers on customer retention. *Journal of Marketing, 69*(4). doi:10.1509/jmkg.2005.69.4.210.

Habermas, J. (1991). *Morale et communication: Conscience morale et activité communicationnelle*. (C. Bouchindhomme, Trans.). Paris, France: Les éditions du CERF.

Habermas, J. (1992). *De l'éthique de la discussion*. (M. Hunyadi, Trans.). Paris, France: Les éditions du CERF.

Habermas, J. (1987). *Raison et légitimité: Problèmes de légitimation dans le capitalisme avancé* (Lacoste, J., Trans.). Paris, France: Payot.

Habermas, J. (1987). *Théorie de l'agir communicationnel: Pour une critique de la raison fonctionnaliste (Vol. 2)*. (Schlegel, J.-L., Trans.). Paris, France: Fayard.

Habermas, J. (1998). *On the pragmatics of communication* (Cooke, M., Ed.). Cambridge, MA: The MIT Press.

Hair, J., Black, W., Babin, B., & Anderson, R. (2010). *Multivariate data analysis* (7th ed.). Upper Saddle River, NJ: Prentice-Hall, Inc..

Hall, E. (1977). *Beyond culture*. New York: Anchor.

Hancock, J. T. (2007). Digital deception: Why, when and how people lie online. In Joinson, A. N., McKenna, K., Postmes, T., & Reips, U. (Eds.), *The Oxford handbook of internet psychology* (pp. 289–301). Oxford, UK: Oxford University Press.

Hansen, A. (2010). *Environment, media and communication*. New York: Routledge.

Haraszti, M. (2010). Foreword. In Deibert, R. J., Palfrey, J. G., Rohozinski, R., & Zittrain, J. (Eds.), *Access controlled: The shaping of power, rights, and rule in cyberspace* (pp. xv–xvi). Cambridge, MA: MIT Press.

Hardian, B., Indulska, J., & Henricksen, K. (2006). Balancing autonomy and user control in context-aware systems-a survey. In *Proceedings of Pervasive Computing and Communications Workshops, 2006*. IEEE. doi:10.1109/PERCOMW.2006.26.

Hargittai, E. (2007). Whose space? Differences among users and non-users of social network sites. *Journal of Computer-Mediated Communication, 13*(1). doi:10.1111/j.1083-6101.2007.00396.x.

Hargreaves, I., & Ferguson, G. (2000). *Who's misunderstanding whom? Bridging the gulf of understanding between the public, the media and science*. Swindon, UK: ESRC.

Harris, P., Rettie, R., & Kwan, C. C. (2005). Adoption and usage of m-commerce: A cross-cultural comparison of Hong Kong and United Kingdom. *Journal of Electronic Commerce Research, 6*(3), 210–224.

Harwit, E., & Clark, D. (2001). Shaping the internet in China: Evolution of political control over network infrastructure and content. *Asian Survey, 41*(3), 377–408. doi:10.1525/as.2001.41.3.377.

Hassnaa, M., Usman, J., Tinku, R., & Djamal-Eddine, M. (2006). A panorama on wireless mesh networks: Architectures, applications and technical challenges. In *Proceedings of the International Workshop on Wireless Mesh: Moving towards Applications (Wimeshnets 06)*. Waterloo, Canada: Wimeshnets.

Hausman, A. V., & Siekpe, J. S. (2009). The effect of web interface features on consumer online purchase. *Journal of Business Research, 62*, 5–13. doi:10.1016/j.jbusres.2008.01.018.

Hau, Y. S., & Kim, Y.-G. (2011). Why would online gamers share their innovation-conducive knowledge in the online game user community? Integrating individual motivations and social capital perspectives. *Computers in Human Behavior, 27*(2), 956–970. doi:10.1016/j.chb.2010.11.022.

Haywood, K. M. (1989). Managing word of mouth communication. *Journal of Services Marketing, 3*(2), 55–67. doi:10.1108/EUM0000000002486.

Heeter, C. (1995). Communication research on consumer VR. In Biocca, F., & Levy, M. R. (Eds.), *Communication in the age of virtual reality* (pp. 191–218). Hillsdale, NJ: Lawrence Erlbaum Associates.

Heijden, V. D. H. (2003). Factors influencing the usage of websites: The case of a generic portal in The Netherlands. *Information & Management, 40*(6), 541–549. doi:10.1016/S0378-7206(02)00079-4.

Hendrikson, A. R., Massey, P. D., & Cronan, T. P. (1993). On the test-retest reliability of perceived usefulness, perceived ease of use scales. *Management Information Systems Quarterly, 17*, 227–230. doi:10.2307/249803.

Hennig-Thurau, T., Malthouse, E. C., Friege, C., Gensler, S., Lobschat, L., Rangaswamy, A., & Skiera, B. (2010). The impact of new media on customer relationships. *Journal of Service Research, 75*(3), 311–330. doi:10.1177/1094670510375460.

Herr, P. M., Kardes, F. R., & Kim, J. (1991). Effects of word-of-mouth and product attribute information on persuasion: An accessibility-diagnosticity perspective. *The Journal of Consumer Research, 17*, 454–462. doi:10.1086/208570.

Hilgartner, S., & Bosk, C. L. (1988). The rise and fall of social problems: A public arenas model. *American Journal of Sociology, 94*(1), 53–78. doi:10.1086/228951.

Hinkle, G. J. (1992). Habermas Mead and rationality. *Studies in Symbolic Interaction, 15*(3), 315–331. doi:10.1525/si.1992.15.3.315.

Hinz, O., Skiera, B., Barrot, C., & Becker, J. U. (2011). Seeding strategies for viral marketing: An empirical comparison. *Journal of Marketing*, *75*, 55–71. doi:10.1509/jm.10.0088.

Hoffman, D. L. Novak. T. P., & Schlosser, A. (2000). *Consumer control in online environments* (Working Paper, 25). Fevrier.

Hoffman, D. L., & Duhachek, A. (2003). The influence of goal-directed and experiential activities on online flow experiences. *Journal of Consumer Psychology*, *13*(1-2).

Hoffman, D. L., & Novak, T. P. (1996). Marketing in hypermedia computer-mediated environments: Conceptual foundations. *Journal of Marketing*, *3*(60), 50–68. doi:10.2307/1251841.

Hoffman, D. L., Novak, T. P., & Peralta, M. (1999). Building consumer trust online. *Communications of the ACM*, *42*(4). doi:10.1145/299157.299175 PMID:11543550.

Hoffman, D., & Novak, T. P. (2009). Flow online: Lessons learned and future prospects. *Journal of Interactive Marketing*, *23*(1), 23–34. doi:10.1016/j.intmar.2008.10.003.

Hofstede, G. H. (1980). *Culture's consequences: International differences in work-related values*. Beverly Hills, CA: Sage Publications, Inc..

Hofstede, G., & Bond, M. H. (1988). The Confucius connection: From cultural roots to economic growth. *Organizational Dynamics*, *16*(4), 5–21. doi:10.1016/0090-2616(88)90009-5.

Hollebeek, L. (2011). Exploring customer brand engagement: Definition and themes. *Journal of Strategic Marketing*, *19*(7), 555–573. doi:10.1080/0965254X.2011.599493.

Hollebeek, L. D. (2011). Demystifying customer brand engagement: Exploring the loyalty nexus. *Journal of Marketing Management*, *27*(7-8), 785–807. doi:10.1080/0267257X.2010.500132.

Hong, S.-J., & Tam, K. Y. (2006). Understanding the adoption of multipurpose information sppliances: The case of mobile data services. *Information Systems Research*, *17*(2), 162–179. doi:10.1287/isre.1060.0088.

Hong, S.-J., Thong, J. Y. L., & Tam, K. Y. (2006). Understanding continued information technology usage behavior: A comparison of three models in the context of mobile Internet. *Decision Support Systems*, *42*(3), 1819–1834. doi:10.1016/j.dss.2006.03.009.

Hooker, R., Wasko, M., & Paradice, D. (2009). Linking brand attitudes and purchase intent in virtual worlds. In A. Z. Phoenix (Ed.), *ICIS Proceedings*. IEEE.

Hopkins, C. D., Raymond, M. A., & Mitra, A. (2004). Consumer responses to perceived telepresence in the online advertising environment: The moderating role of involvement. *Marketing Theory*, *4*(1-2), 137–162. doi:10.1177/1470593104044090.

Horton, R. P., Buck, T., Waterson, P. E., & Clegg, C. W. (2001). Explaining intranet use with the technology acceptance model. *Journal of Information Technology*, *16*, 237–249. doi:10.1080/02683960110102407.

Hosbond, J., & Nielsen, P. (2005). Mobile systems development: A literature review. In Sørensen, C., Yoo, Y., Lyytinen, K., & DeGross, J. (Eds.), *Designing ubiquitous information environments: Socio-technical issues and challenges* (Vol. 185, pp. 215–232). Boston: Springer. doi:10.1007/0-387-28918-6_17.

Hsu, C. L., & Lu, H. P. (2003). Why do people play online games? An extended TAM with social influences and flow experience. *Information & Management*, *41*, 853–868. doi:10.1016/j.im.2003.08.014.

Hua, G., & Haughton, D. (2008). Virtual world's adoption: A research framework and empirical study. *Online Information Review*, *33*(5), 889–900. doi:10.1108/14684520911001891.

Huang, C.-C. (2009). Knowledge sharing and group cohesiveness on performance: An empirical study of technology R&D teams in Taiwan. *Technovation*, *29*(11), 786–797. doi:10.1016/j.technovation.2009.04.003.

Huang, M. H. (2006, May). Flow, enduring and situational involvement in the web environment: A tripartite second-order examination. *Psychology and Marketing*, *23*, 383–411. doi:10.1002/mar.20118.

Human Factors International. (n.d.). *Case studies*. Retrieved from http://www.humanfactors.com/about/casestudies-applications.asp

Hung, S.-Y., Durcikova, A., Lai, H.-M., & Lin, W.-M. (2011). The influence of intrinsic and extrinsic motivation on individuals' knowledge sharing behavior. *International Journal of Human-Computer Studies, 69*(6), 415–427. doi:10.1016/j.ijhcs.2011.02.004.

IBM Global Education Industry. (2000). *Higher education portals: Presenting your institution to the world.* IBM.

IEEE. (2001). *Reference guide for instructional design and development.* Retrieved November 2010, from www.ieee.org/education_careers/education/reference_guide/index.html

Ijsselsteijn, W. A., Freeman, J., & de Ridder, H. (2001). Presence: Where we are? *Cyberpsychology & Behavior, 4*(2), 179–182. doi:10.1089/109493101300117875 PMID:11710245.

ISO 9241-11. (1997). *Ergonomic requirements for office work with visual display terminals.*

Izard, C. E., Libero, D. Z., Putnam, P., & Haynes, O. M. (1993). Stability of emotion experiences and their relations to traits of personality. *Journal of Personality and Social Psychology, 64*, 847–860. doi:10.1037/0022-3514.64.5.847 PMID:8505713.

Jacobson, D. (2002). On theorizing presence. *Journal of Virtual Environments, 6*(1).

Jaeger, P. T., Lin, J., & Grimes, J. M. (2008). Cloud computing and information policy: Computing in a policy cloud? *Journal of Information Technology & Politics, 5*(3), 269–283. doi:10.1080/19331680802425479.

Jaeger, P. T., Lin, J., Grimes, J. M., & Simmons, S. N. (2009). Where is the cloud? Geography, economics, environment, and jurisdiction in cloud computing. *First Monday, 14*(5), 1–12. doi:10.5210/fm.v14i5.2456.

Jahn, S., Drengner, J., & Furchheim, P. (2013). Flow revisited process conceptualization and extension to reactive consumption experiences. In *Proceedings of the AMA Winter Educators' Conference.* Las Vegas, NV: AMA.

Jameson, A. (2003). Adaptive interfaces and agents. In *The human-computer interaction handbook* (pp. 316–318). Lawrence Erlbaum Assoc..

Janicke, M. (2006). The environmental state and environmental flows: The need to reinvent the nation-state. In Spaargaren, G., Mol, A. P. J., & Buttel, F. H. (Eds.), *Governing environmental flows: Global challenges to social theory.* Cambridge, UK: The MIT Press.

Jarvenpaa, S. L., Tranctinsky, N., & Vitale, M. (2000). Consumer trust in an internet store. *Information Technology Management, 1*, 45–71. doi:10.1023/A:1019104520776.

Jeandrain, A. C. (2001). Essay about telepresence effects on persuasion: Three possible explanations. In *Proceedings of the Fourth Annual International Workshop on Presence,* (pp. 123-127). Philadelphia: IEEE.

Jeddi, S., & Karoui Zouaoui, S. (2011). Réflexions sur l'impact du travail mobile sur l'apprentissage individuel. In *Proceedings of the 16th seminar of AIM.* St Denis de la Réunion, France: AIM.

Jee, J., & Lee, W. N. (2002). Antecedents and consequences of perceived interactivity: An exploratory study. *Journal of Interactive Advertising, 3*(1). Retrieved February 6, 2012, from http://www.jiad.org/

Jiang, G. (2010). Rain or shine: Fair and other non-infringing uses in the context of cloud computing. *Journal of Legislature, 36*, 395.

Jin, B., & Peña, J. F. (2010). Mobile communication in romantic relationships: Mobile phone use, relational uncertainty, love, commitment, and attachment styles. *Communication Reports, 23*(1), 39–51. doi:10.1080/08934211003598742.

Johnson, L., Adams, S., & Cummins, M. (2012). The NMC horizon report: 2012 higher education ed. Austin, TX: The New Media Consortium.

Joinson, A. N. (2003). *Understanding the psychology of internet behaviour: Virtual worlds, real lives.* New York: Palgrave Macmillan.

Junglas, I., & Watson, R. (2003). *U-commerce: A conceptual extension of e-commerce and m-commerce.*

Jung, Y., Begona, P. M., & Sonja, W. P. (2009). Consumer adoption of mobile TV: Examining psychological flow and media content. *Computers in Human Behavior, 25*, 123–129. doi:10.1016/j.chb.2008.07.011.

Kaczmarczyk, K. (2010). *Predicting the future of the anti-circumvention laws in the cloud-computing world.*

Kakihara, M., & Sørensen, C. (2001). Expanding the 'mobility' concept. *ACM SIGGROUP Bulletin, 22*(3), 33–37.

Kamarulzaman, S. (2005). *Knowledgepoint: A study on the usability of the user interface for FTMSK'S knowledge portal.* (Bachelor Science [Hons] Information System Engineering Thesis). Faculty of Information Technology and Quantitative Science, Universiti Teknologi MARA, Shah Alam, Malaysia.

Kang, M., Kim, S., & Park, S. (2007). Developing an emotional presence scale for measuring students' involvement during e-learning process. In *Proceedings of World Conference on Educational Multimedia, Hypermedia and Telecommunications (ED-MEDIA) 2007* (pp. 2829-2831). ED-MEDIA.

Karahanna, E., Straub, D. W., & Chervany, N. L. (1999). Information technology adoption across time: A cross-sectional comparison of pre-adoption and post-adoption beliefs. *Management Information Systems Quarterly, 23*(2), 183–213. doi:10.2307/249751.

Karahanna, E., Straub, D. W., & Chervany, N. L. (1999). Information technology adoption and post adoption beliefs. *Management Information Systems Quarterly, 23*(2). doi:10.2307/249751.

Karhula, P. (2012). Internet censorship takes new forms. *Signum, 3*.

Karner, H., & Droschl, G. (2002). Usage-centered interface design for knowledge management software. *Journal of Universal Computer Science, 8*(6).

Kato, S., Kato, Y., Scott, D. J., & Sato, K. (2008). Selection of ICT in emotional communication for Japanese students: Focusing on emotional strategies and gender differences. In *Proceedings of World Conference on Educational Multimedia, Hypermedia and Telecommunications (ED-MEDIA) 2008* (pp. 1050-1057). ED-MEDIA.

Kato, Y., & Akahori, K. (2004). The accuracy of judgement of emotions experienced by partners during e-mail and face-to-face communication. In *Proceedings of International Conference on Computers in Education (ICCE) 2004* (pp. 1559-1570). ICCE.

Kato, Y., Kato, S., & Akahori, K. (2006). Effects of senders' self-disclosures and styles of writing messages on recipients' emotional aspects in e-mail communication. In *Proceedings of World Conference on E-Learning in Corporate, Government, Healthcare, and Higher Education (E-Learn) 2006* (pp. 2585-2592). E-Learn.

Kato, Y., Kato, S., & Akahori, K. (2006). Comparison of emotional aspects in e-mail communication by mobile phone with a teacher and a friend. In *Proceedings of World Conference on Educational Multimedia, Hypermedia and Telecommunications (ED-MEDIA) 2006* (pp. 425-433). ED-MEDIA.

Kato, Y., Scott, D. J., & Kato, S. (2011). Comparing American and Japanese young people's emotional strategies in mobile phone email communication. In *Proceedings of World Conference on Educational Multimedia, Hypermedia and Telecommunications (ED-MEDIA) 2011* (pp. 170-178). ED-MEDIA.

Kato, Y., Sugimura, K., & Akahori, K. (2002). Effect of contents of e-mail messages on affections. In *Proceedings of International Conference on Computers in Education (ICCE) 2002*, (Vol. 1, pp. 428-432). ICCE.

Kato, S., Kato, Y., & Scott, D. J. (2009). Relationships between emotional states and emoticons in mobile phone email communication in Japan. *International Journal on E-Learning: Corporate, Government, Healthcare, &. Higher Education, 8*(3), 385–401.

Kato, Y., & Akahori, K. (2006). Analysis of judgment of partners' emotions during e-mail and face-to-face communication. *Journal of Science Education in Japan, 29*(5), 354–365.

Kato, Y., Kato, S., & Akahori, K. (2007). Effects of emotional cues transmitted in e-mail communication on the emotions experienced by senders and receivers. *Computers in Human Behavior, 23*(4), 1894–1905. doi:10.1016/j.chb.2005.11.005.

Kato, Y., Kato, S., & Chida, K. (2012). Reply timing and emotional strategy in mobile text communications of Japanese young people: Replies to messages conveying four different emotions. In Long, S. D. (Ed.), *Virtual Work and Human Interaction Research* (pp. 99–114). Hershey, PA: IGI Global. doi:10.4018/978-1-4666-0963-1.ch006.

Kato, Y., Kato, S., & Scott, D. J. (2007). Misinterpretation of emotional cues and content in Japanese email, computer conferences, and mobile text messages. In Clausen, E. I. (Ed.), *Psychology of Anger* (pp. 145–176). Hauppauge, NY: Nova Science Publishers.

Kato, Y., Kato, S., Scott, D. J., & Sato, K. (2010). Patterns of emotional transmission in Japanese young people's text-based communication in four basic emotional situations. *International Journal on E-Learning: Corporate, Government, Healthcare, &. Higher Education, 9*(2), 203–227.

Kato, Y., Kato, S., Sugimura, K., & Akahori, K. (2008). The influence of affective traits on emotional aspects of message receivers in text-based communication - Examination by the experiment using e-mail communication. *Educational Technology Review, 31*(1-2), 85–95.

Kato, Y., Scott, D. J., & Kato, S. (2011). The influence of intimacy and gender on emotions in mobile phone email. In Gokcay, D., & Yildirim, G. (Eds.), *Affective computing and interaction: Psychological, cognitive and neuroscientific perspectives* (pp. 262–279). Hershey, PA: IGI Global.

Katz, E., & Lazarfeld, P. F. (1955). *Personal influence.* Glencoe, IL: Free Press.

Kavada, A. (2005). Civic society organizations and the internet: The case of Amnesty International, Oxfam and the World Development Movement. In Jong, W. D., Shaw, M., & Stammers, N. (Eds.), *Global activism, global media* (pp. 208–222). London: Pluto.

Kessler, F. (1943). Contracts of adhesion--Some thoughts about freedom of contract. *Columbia Law Review, 43,* 629. doi:10.2307/1117230.

Kiecker, P., & Cowles, D. (2002). Interpersonal communication and personal influence on the internet: A framework for examining online word-o-mouth. *Journal of Euromarketing, 11*(2), 71–88. doi:10.1300/J037v11n02_04.

Kiili, K. (2005). Digital game-based learning: Towards an experiential gaming model. *The Internet and Higher Education, 8*(1), 13–24. doi:10.1016/j.iheduc.2004.12.001.

Kim, H. J., Choi, J. K., & Ji, Y. (2008). Usability evaluation framework for ubiquitous computing device. In *Proceedings of the Third 2008 International Conference on Convergence and Hybrid Information Technology.* IEEE.

Kim, T., & Biocca, F. (1997). Telepresence via television: Two dimensions of telepresence may have different connections to memory and persuasion. *Journal of Computer Mediated Communication, 3*(2). Retrieved February 06, 2012, from http://jcmc.indiana.edu/vol3/issue2/kim.html

Kim, J., Ma, Y. J., & Park, J. (2009). Are US consumers ready to adopt mobile technology for fashion goods? *Journal of Fashion Marketing and Management, 13*(2), 215–230. doi:10.1108/13612020910957725.

Kleinberg, J. M. (1999). Authoritative sources in a hyper-linked environment. *Journal of the ACM, 46*(5), 604–632. doi:10.1145/324133.324140.

Klein, L. R. (2003). Creating virtual product experiences: The role of telepresence. *Journal of Interactive Marketing, 17*(1), 41–55. doi:10.1002/dir.10046.

Klopfer, E., & Squire, K. (2008). Environmental detectives: The development of an augmented reality platform for environmental simulations. *Educational Technology Research and Development, 56*(2), 203–228. doi:10.1007/s11423-007-9037-6.

KMWorld. (2012, October 17-19). *KMWorld Conference 2012.* Washington, DC: KM World.

Kober, S. E., & Neuper, C. (2013). Personality and presence in virtual reality: Does their relationship depend on the used presence measure? *International Journal of Human-Computer Interaction, 29*(1), 13–25. doi:10.1080/10447318.2012.668131.

Kolb, D. A. (1984). *Experiential learning: Experience as the source of learning and development.* Englewood Cliffs, NJ: Prentice-Hall.

Korzaan, M. L. (2003). Going with the flow: Predicting online purchase intentions. *Journal of Computer Information Systems, 43*(4), 25–31.

Koufaris, M. (2002). Applying the technology acceptance model and flow theory to online consumer behavior. *Information Systems Research, 13*(2), 205–223. doi:10.1287/isre.13.2.205.83.

Kozinets, R. V. (2002). Can consumer escape the market? Emancipatory illumination from burning man. *The Journal of Consumer Research, 29.*

Kozinets, R. V. (2009). *Netnography: Doing ethnographic research online*. London: Sage Publications.

Krauss, R. M., & Fussell, S. R. (1996). Social psychological models of interpersonal communication. In Higgins, E. T., & Kruglanski, A. W. (Eds.), *Social Psychology: Handbook of basic principles* (pp. 655–701). New York: The Guilford Press.

Kraut, R. E. (1978). Verbal and nonverbal cues in the perception of lying. *Journal of Personality and Social Psychology*, *36*(4), 380–391. doi:10.1037/0022-3514.36.4.380.

Kshetri, N. (2010). Cloud computing in developing economies. *Computer*, *43*(10), 47–55. doi:10.1109/MC.2010.212.

Kuhn, K. (2000). Problems and benefits of requirements gathering with focus groups: A case-study. *International Journal of Human-Computer Interaction*, *12*(3-4), 309–325. doi:10.1080/10447318.2000.9669061.

Kukulska-Hulme, A., & Traxler, J. (2005). *Mobile learning: A handbook for educators and trainers*. London: Routledge.

Kumar, R., Dey, S., & Rao, G. K. (2011). Investigation of mobile knowledge management: Developing and integrating enterprise app. store with existing knowledge management system. In *Proceedings of the International Journal of Computer Applications® (IJCA) Third Annual Global Business, IT and Management for Economic Development Conference (BITMED)*. BITMED.

Kuo, Y.-F., & Yen, S.-N. (2009). Towards an understanding of the behavioral intention to use 3G mobile value-added services. *Computers in Human Behavior*, *25*(1), 103–110. doi:10.1016/j.chb.2008.07.007.

Kushida, K. E., Murray, J., & Zysman, J. (2011). Diffusing the cloud: Cloud computing and implications for public policy. *Journal of Industry, Competition and Trade*, *11*(3), 209–237. doi:10.1007/s10842-011-0106-5.

Kyung Hyan, Y., & Gretzel, U. (2008). What motivates consumers to write online travel reviews? *Information Technology & Tourism*, *10*, 283–295. doi:10.3727/109830508788403114.

Lacroix, J. (1966). *Kant et le kantisme*. Paris, France: Ed. Presses Universitaires de France.

Laffitte, P., & Trégouet, R. (2002). *Les conséquences de l'évolution scientifique et technique dans le secteur des telecommunications: Rapport d'information 159*. Paris, France: Sénat, Office parlementaire d'évaluation des choix scientifiques et technologiques.

Lallement, M. (2003). *Temps, travail et modes de vie*. Paris, France: PUF.

Lametti, D. (2012). *The cloud: Boundless digital potential or enclosure 3.0?*.

Landers, R. N., & Lounsbury, J. W. (2006). An investigation of big five and narrow personality traits in relation to internet usage. *Computers in Human Behavior*, *22*, 283–293. doi:10.1016/j.chb.2004.06.001.

Langton, S. (1978). Citizen participation in America: Current reflections on the state of the art. In Langton, S. (Ed.), *Citizen participation in America*. Lexington, MA: Lexington Books.

Lanois, P. (2010). Caught in the clouds: The web 2.0, cloud computing, and privacy. *Northwestern Journal of Technology and Intellectual Property*, *9*, 29.

Laroche, M., Habibi, M. R., & Richard, M.-O. (2012). To be or not to be in social media: How brand loyalty is affected by social media? *International Journal of Information Management*.

Laroche, M., Habibi, M. R., Richard, M.-O., & Sankaranarayanan, R. (2012). The effects of social media based brand communities on brand community markers, value creation practices, brand trust and brand loyalty. *Computers in Human Behavior*, *28*(5), 1755–1767. doi:10.1016/j.chb.2012.04.016.

Laros, F., & Ponton, M. (2000). Locus of control and perceptions of environmental risk factor: Inhabitants of slums facing domestic garbage. *Swiss Journal of Psychology*, *59*(3), 137–149. doi:10.1024//1421-0185.59.3.137.

LaRue, E. M., Mitchell, A. M., Terhorst, L., & Karimi, H. A. (2010). Assessing mobile phone communication utility preferences in a social support network. *Telematics and Informatics*, *27*(4), 363–369. doi:10.1016/j.tele.2010.03.002.

Lasica, J. D. (2007). *The mobile generation*. Washington, DC: Aspen Institute Communication and Society Program.

Laurent, G., & Kapferer, J.-N. (1985). Consumer involvement profiles: A new and practical approach to consumer involvement. *JMR, Journal of Marketing Research, 22*(1), 41–53. doi:10.2307/3151549.

Lazarsfeld, P. F., Berelson, B., & Gaudet, H. (1948). *The people's choice* (2nd ed.). New York: Columbia University Press.

Lea, M., O'Shea, T., Fung, P., & Spears, R. (1992). Flaming in computer-mediated communication: Observations, explanations, implications. In Lea, M. (Ed.), *Contexts of computer-mediated communication* (pp. 89–112). New York: Harvester Wheasheaf.

Lederer, A. L., Maupin, D. J., Sena, M. P., & Zhuang, Y. (2000). The technology acceptance model and the world wide web. *Decision Support Systems, 29*(3), 269–282. doi:10.1016/S0167-9236(00)00076-2.

Lee, D., Kim, H. S., & Kim, J. K. (2011). The impact of online brand community type on consumer's community engagement behaviors: Consumer-created vs. marketer-created online brand community in online social-networking Web sites. *Cyberpsychology, Behavior, and Social Networking, 14*, 1–2. doi:10.1089/cyber.2009.0397.

Lee, I., Choi, B., Kim, J., & Hong, S.-J. (2007). Culture-technology fit: Effects of cultural characteristics on the post-adoption beliefs of mobile Internet users. *International Journal of Electronic Commerce, 11*(4), 11–51. doi:10.2753/JEC1086-4415110401.

Lee, I., Kim, J., Choi, B., & Hong, S.-J. (2010). Measurement development for cultural characteristics of mobile internet users at the individual level. *Computers in Human Behavior, 26*(6), 1355–1368. doi:10.1016/j.chb.2010.04.009.

Lee, M., & Turban, E. (2000). A trust model for consumer internet shopping. *International Journal of Electronic Commerce, 6*(1).

Legris, P., Ingham, J., & Collerette, P. (2003). Why do people use information technology? A critical review of the technology acceptance model. *Information & Management, 40*(3), 191–204. doi:10.1016/S0378-7206(01)00143-4.

Leimeister, S., Böhm, M., Riedl, C., & Krcmar, H. (2010). *The business perspective of cloud computing: Actors, roles and value networks.*

Lessig, L. (1997, July). Tyranny in the infrastructure. *Wired.*

Lessig, L. (2006). *Code: And other laws of cyberspace, version 2.0.* New York: Basic Books.

Lester, L. (2010). *Media & environment*. Cambridge, UK: Polity.

Lester, L., & Hutchins, B. (2009). Power games: Environmental protest, news media and the internet. *Media Culture & Society, 31*(4), 579–595. doi:10.1177/0163443709335201.

Levin, M.-J. (2013). Facebook: Les fans de marque à la loupe. *Emarketing.fr.* Retrieved from http://www.e-marketing.fr/Marketing-Magazine/Article/Facebook-les-fans-de-marque-a-la-loupe-38380-1.htm

Lewin, K. (1951). *Field theory in social sciences*. New York: Harper & Row.

Lewis, D., & Weigert, A. (1985). Trust as social reality. *Social Forces, 63*(4), 967–985.

Licoppe, C. (2004). 'Connected' presence: The emergence of a new repertoire for managing social relationships in a changing communication technoscape. *Environment and Planning. D, Society & Space, 22*, 135–156. doi:10.1068/d323t.

Li, H., Daugherty, T., & Biocca, F. (2002). Impact of 3-D advertising on product knowledge, brand attitude, and purchase intention: The mediating role of presence. *Journal of Advertising, 31*(3), 43–57. doi:10.1080/00913367.2002.10673675.

Lin, C. Y., Fang, K., & Tu, C. C. (2010). Predicting consumer repurchase intentions to shop online. *Journal of Computers, 5*(10), 1527–1533. doi:10.4304/jcp.5.10.1527-1533.

Lin, J. C. C. (2007). Online stickiness: Its antecedents and effect on purchasing intention. *Behaviour & Information Technology, 26*(6), 507–516. doi:10.1080/01449290600740843.

Lin, M.-J. J., Hung, S.-W., & Chen, C.-J. (2009). Fostering the determinants of knowledge sharing in professional virtual summer. *Journal of Computer Information Systems, 25*(4), 929–939.

Linne, O., & Hansen, A. (1990). *News coverage of the environment: A comparative study of journalistic practices and television presentation in Danmarks Radio and BBC.* Copenhagen, Denmark: Danmarks Radio Forlaget.

Li, Y. H., & Huang, J. W. (2009). Applying theory of perceived risk and technology acceptance model in the online shopping channel. *World Academy of Science. Engineering and Technology, 53,* 919–925.

Lohisse, J. (2001). La communication de la transmission à la relation. In Thoveron, G. (Ed.), *Culture et communication.* Brussels, Belgium: Éditions De Boeck Université.

Loilier, T., & Tellier, A. (2004). Comment peut-on se faire confiance sans se voir? Le cas du développement des logiciels libres. *AIMS Management, 7,* 275–306.

Lombard, M., & Ditton, T. (1997). At the heart of it all: The concept of presence. *Journal of Computer Mediated-Communication, 3*(2). Retrieved February 6, 2012, from http://jcmc.indiana.edu/vol3/issue2/lombard.html

Luarn, P., & Lin, H.-H. (2005). Toward an understanding of the behavioral intention to use mobile banking. *Computers in Human Behavior, 21*(6), 873–891. doi:10.1016/j.chb.2004.03.003.

Lu, J., Shao, G., & Wu, J. (2012). New media and civic engagement in China: The case of the Xiamen PX event. *China Media Research, 8*(2), 76–82.

Lu, J., Yu, C.-S., & Liu, C. Y., & E., J. (2003). Technology acceptance model for wireless Internet. *Internet Research, 13*(3), 206–222. doi:10.1108/10662240310478222.

Lundgren, H., & Walczuch, R. (2004). Psychological antecedents of institution-based trust in e-retailing. *Information & Management, 42,* 159–177. doi:10.1016/j.im.2003.12.009.

Lu, Y., & Wilson, E. (2008). Communication goals and online persuasion: An empirical examination. *Computers in Human Behavior, 24,* 2554–2577. doi:10.1016/j.chb.2008.02.021.

Lu, Y., Zhou, T., & Wang, B. (2009). Exploring Chinese users' acceptance of instant messaging using the theory of planned behavior, the technology acceptance model, and the flow theory. *Computers in Human Behavior, 25,* 29–39. doi:10.1016/j.chb.2008.06.002.

Lyytinen, K., & Yoo, Y. (2002). Research commentary: The next wave of nomadic computing. *Information Systems Research, 13*(4), 377–388. doi:10.1287/isre.13.4.377.75.

Lyytinen, K., & Yoo, Y. (2002). Ubiquitous computing. *Communications of the ACM, 45*(12), 63.

Maigret, E. (2003). *Sociologie de la communication et des médias.* Paris, France: Armand Colin.

Ma, J., Webber, M., & Finlayson, B. L. (2008). On sealing a lakebed: Mass media and environmental democratization in China. *Environmental Science & Policy, 12*(1), 71–83. doi:10.1016/j.envsci.2008.09.001.

Mankoff, J., Dey, A. K., Hsieh, G., Kientz, J., Lederer, S., & Ames, M. (2003). Heuristic evaluation of ambient displays. In *Proceedings of Conference on Human Factors in Computing Systems.* ACM Press.

Mao, E., Srite, M., Thatcher, J. B., & Yaprak, O. (2005). A research model for mobile phone service behaviors: Empirical validation in the US and Turkey. *Journal of Global Information Technology Management, 8*(4), 7–28.

Marcus, A., & Gould, E. W. (2000). Crosscurrents: Cultural dimensions and global web user-interface design. *Interaction, 7*(4), 32–46. doi:10.1145/345190.345238.

Maroon, B. (2006). Mobile sociality in urban Morocco. In Kavoori, A., & Arceneaux, N. (Eds.), *The cell phone reader: Essays in social transformation.* New York: Peter Lang.

Martin, E. J. (2013, January 18). Responsive web design vs. user experience. *eContent Magazine.*

Martin, H., Chris, J., & Marcus, N. (2006). The influence of avatars on consumer shopping behavior. *Journal of Marketing, 70,* 19–36. doi:10.1509/jmkg.70.4.19.

Martin, W. C., & Leug, J. E. (2013). Modeling word-of-mouth usage. *Journal of Business Research, 66,* 801–808. doi:10.1016/j.jbusres.2011.06.004.

Marttunen, M., & Laurinen, L. (2001). Learning of argumentation skills in networked and face-to-face environments. *Instructional Science, 29*(2), 127–153. doi:10.1023/A:1003931514884.

Masrek, M. N., Jamaludin, A., & Mukhtar, S. A. (2009). Evaluating academic library portal effectiveness. *A Malaysian Case Study, 59*(3), 198-212.

Mathieson, K., Peacock, W., & Chin, W. (2001). Extending the technology acceptance model. The influence of perceived user resources. *The Data Base for Advances in Information Systems, 32*(3). doi:10.1145/506724.506730.

Mathwick, C., & Rigdon, E. (2004). Play, flow, and the online search experience. *The Journal of Consumer Research, 31*(2), 324–332. doi:10.1086/422111.

Matsumoto, D. (1996). *Unmasking Japan: Myths and realities about the emotions of the Japanese*. Stanford, CA: Stanford University Press.

Matsumoto, D., & Kudoh, T. (1993). American-Japanese cultural differences in implicit theories of personality based on smile. *Journal of Nonverbal Behavior, 17*(4), 231–243. doi:10.1007/BF00987239.

Mattelart, A., & Mattelart, M. (2004). Histoire des théories de la communication. Paris, France: Ed.s de la Découverte.

Maxham, J. G. (2001). Service recover's influence on consumer satisfaction, positive word-of-mouth, and purchase intentions. *Journal of Business Research, 54*(1), 11–24. doi:10.1016/S0148-2963(00)00114-4.

Mayer, J. D. (2000). Emotion, intelligence, emotional intelligence. In Forgas, J. P. (Ed.), *The handbook of affect and social cognition* (pp. 410–431). Mahwah, NJ: Lawrence Erlbaum & Associates.

Mayer, R. C., Davis, J. H., & Schoorman, F. D. (1995). An integrative model of organizational trust. *Academy of Management Review, 20*(3), 709–734.

Mazur, A. (1981). Media coverage and public opinion on scientific controversies. *The Journal of Communication, 31*(2), 106–115. doi:10.1111/j.1460-2466.1981.tb01234.x PMID:7204618.

McAlexander, J. H., Schouten, J. W., & Koenig, H. F. (2002). Building brand community. *Journal of Marketing, 66*(1), 38–54. doi:10.1509/jmkg.66.1.38.18451.

McAllister, D. J. (1995). Affect and cognition based trust as foundations for interpersonal cooperation in organizations. *Academy of Management Journal, 38*(1), 24–59. doi:10.2307/256727.

McCombs, M. E., & Shaw, D. L. (1972). The agenda-setting function of the mass media. *Public Opinion Quarterly, 36*, 176–187. doi:10.1086/267990.

McKenna, K., & Seidman, G. (2006). Considering the interactions: The effects of the internet on self and society. In Kraut, R., Malcolm, B., & Kiesler, S. (Eds.), *Computers, phones, and the internet* (pp. 279–295). Oxford, UK: Oxford University Press.

McKnight, H., Choudhury, V., & Kacmar, C. (2002). The impact of initial trust on intentions to transact with a web site: A trust building model. *The Journal of Strategic Information Systems, 11*, 297–323. doi:10.1016/S0963-8687(02)00020-3.

Mell, P., & Grance, T. (2011). The NIST definition of cloud computing (draft). *NIST Special Publication, 800*, 145.

Meunier, J., & Peraya, D. (1993). *Introduction aux théories de la communication: Analyse sémio-pragmatique de la communication médiatique*. Brussels, Belgium: De Boeck Université.

Miled, H. B., & Louarn, P. (1994). Analyse comparative de deux échelles de mesure du leadership d'opinion: Validité et interprétation. *Recherche et Applications en Marketing, 9*(4), 23–51. doi:10.1177/076737019400900402.

Miller, M. (2008). *Cloud computing: Web-based applications that change the way you work and collaborate online*. Que Publishing.

Milojicic, D. S., Kalogeraki, V., Lukose, R., Nagaraja, K., Pruyne, J., Richard, B.,... Xu, Z. (2002). *Peer-to-peer computing*.

Minsky, M. (1980). Telepresence. *Omni (New York, N.Y.), 21*, 45–51.

Mocherman, A. (2012). Why speech is key for a great mobile customer service experience. *Nuance - Insights from the Customer Experience Experts, 2012*.

Moglen, E. (2011). *Why political liberty depends on software freedom more than ever*. Paper presented at FOSDEM Conference. Brussels, Belgium.

Mollen, A., & Wilson, H. (2010). Engagement, telepresence and interactivity in online consumer experience: Reconciling scholastic and managerial perspectives. *Journal of Business Research, 63*, 919–925. doi:10.1016/j.jbusres.2009.05.014.

Moore, G. (1991). *Crossing the chasm*. New York: Harper Business.

Morahan-Martin, J. (2007). Internet use and abuse and psychological problems. In Joinson, A. N., McKenna, K., Postmes, T., & Reips, U. (Eds.), *The Oxford handbook of internet psychology* (pp. 331–345). Oxford, UK: Oxford University Press.

Moran, M. T., & Hoy, W. K. (2000). A multidisciplinary analysis of the nature, meaning, and measurement of trust. *Review of Educational Research, 70*(4), 547–593. doi:10.3102/00346543070004547.

Moran, T. P., & Dourish, P. (2001). Introduction to this special issue on context aware computing. *Human-Computer Interaction, 16*(2), 87–95. doi:10.1207/S15327051HCI16234_01.

Morgan, R. M., & Hunt, S. D. (1994). The commitment-trust theory of relationship marketing. *Journal of Marketing, 58*(3), 20–38. doi:10.2307/1252308.

MORI. (2005). *Information about science and technology*. Retrieved from www.opsos-mori.com/polls/2005/nesta.shtml

Mosch, M. (2011). User-controlled data sovereignty in the cloud. In *Proceedings of the PhD Symposium at the 9th IEEE European Conference on Web Services (ECOWS 2011)*. Lugano, Switzerland: IEEE.

Mowbray, M. (2009). The fog over the grimpen mire: Cloud computing and the law. *Scripted Journal of Law. Technology and Society, 6*(1).

Muniz, A., & O'Guinn, T. (2001). Brand community. *The Journal of Consumer Research, 27*, 412–432. doi:10.1086/319618.

Murphy, G. B., & Blessinger, A. A. (2003). Perceptions of no-name recognition business to consumer e-commerce trustworthiness: The effectiveness of potential influence tactics. *The Journal of High Technology Management Research, 14*(1), 71–92. doi:10.1016/S1047-8310(03)00005-1.

Murphy, M., & Meeker, M. (2011). *Top mobile internet trends*. KPCB Relationship Capital.

Murray, H. A. (1938). *Explorations in personality*. New York: Oxford University Press.

Mustafa, S. H., & AL-Zoua'bi, L. F. (2005). *Usability of the academic websites of Jordan University: An evaluation study*.

Nakamura, J., & Csikszentmihalyi, M. (2002). The concept of flow. In Snyder, C. R., & Lopez, S. J. (Eds.), *Handbook of positive psychology* (pp. 89–105). Oxford, UK: Oxford University Press.

National Bureau of Statistics of China. (2013). *China's economy achieved a stabilized and accelerated development in the year of 2012*. Retrieved from www.stats.gov.cn/english/pressrelease/t20130118_402867147.htm

Nel, D., Niekerk, R. V., Berthon, J. P., & Davies, T. (1999). Going with the flow: Web sites and customer involvement. *Internet Research, 9*(2), 109–116. doi:10.1108/10662249910264873.

Ngwenyama, O. K., & Lee, A. S. (1997). Communication richness in electronic mail: Critical social theory and the contextuality of meaning. *MIS Quarterly, 21*(2), 145–167. doi:10.2307/249417.

Nielsen, J. (1995). *Card sorting to discover the users' model of the information space*. Retrieved from http://www.useit.com/papers/sun/cardsort.html

Nielsen-Englyst, L. (2003). Game design for imaginative conceptualisation. In *Proceedings of the International Workshop on Experimental Interactive Learning in Industrial Management* (pp. 149-164). IEEE.

Nielson, J. (1992, March). The usability engineering life cycle. *IEEE Computer*, 12-22.

Nielson, J. (2001). *How to conduct heuristic evaluation*. Retrieved May 7, 2010, from www.usit.com/papers/heuristic/

Nijs, L., Coussement, P., Moens, B., Amelinck, D., Lesaffre, M., & Leman, M. (2012). Interacting with the music paint machine: Relating the constructs of flow experience and presence. *Interacting with Computers, 24*, 237–250. doi:10.1016/j.intcom.2012.05.002.

Nisbet, M. C., Markowitz, E. M., & Kotcher, J. E. (2012). Winning the conversation: Framing and moral messaging in environmental campaigns. In L. Ahern & D. S. Bortree (Eds.), Talking green: Exploring contemporary issues in environmental communications. New York: Peter Lang. Fangchao, L. (2007, May 30). Public opposes Xiamen chemical plant. People's Daily..

Nisbet, M. C., & Kotcher, J. E. (2009). A two-step flow of influence? Opinion-leader campaigns on climate change. *Science Communication*, *30*(3), 328–354. doi:10.1177/1075547008328797.

Nizet, J. (2007). *La sociologie de Anthony Giddens*. Paris, France: Éditions La Découverte.

Nonaka, I. (1994). A dynamic theory of organizational knowledge creation. *Organization Science*, *5*(1), 14–37. doi:10.1287/orsc.5.1.14.

Novak, T. P., Hoffman, D. L., & Yung, Y. F. (2000). Measuring the flow construct in online environments: A structural modeling approach. *Marketing Science*, *19*(1), 22–42. doi:10.1287/mksc.19.1.22.15184.

Nunnally, J. (1978). *Psychometric theory*. New York: McGraw-Hill.

Nunnally, J. C., & Bernstein, I. H. (1994). *Psychometric theory* (3rd ed.). New York: McGraw-Hill.

Nysveen, H., Pedersen, P., & Thorbjørnsen, H. (2005). Intentions to use mobile services: Antecedents and cross-service comparisons. *Journal of the Academy of Marketing Science*, *33*(3), 330–346. doi:10.1177/0092070305276149.

Oberbeck, H. (2004). *Learning with hypermedia: The impact of content design and learner characteristics on navigation and the knowledge acquisition process*. Brunswick, Germany: Technischen Universität Carolo-Wilhelmina zu.

O'Cass, A., & Carlson, J. (2010). Examining the effects of website-induced flow in professional sporting team websites. *Internet Research*, *20*(2), 115–134. doi:10.1108/10662241011032209.

Ohzahata, S., Hagiwara, Y., Terada, M., & Kawashima, K. (2005). A traffic identification method and evaluations for a pure P2P application. *Passive and Active Network Measurement*, 55-68.

Ondin, Z. (2007). *Usability and user acceptance of web sites of Turkish social security institutions*. (Master's Thesis). University of Bogazici, Istanbul, Turkey.

Oppenheim, A. N. (1992). *Questionaire design: Interviewing and attiture measurement*. New York: Pinter Publishers.

Orlikowski, W. J. (2010). The sociomateriality of organizational life: Considering technology in management research. *Cambridge Journal of Economics*, *34*(1), 125–141. doi:10.1093/cje/bep058.

Ozmete, E., & Hira, T. (2011). Conceptual analysis of behavioral theories/models: Application to financial behavior. *European Journal of Soil Science*, *18*(3), 386–404.

Park, S. B., & Hwang, H. (2009). Understanding online game addiction: Connection between presence and flet. In *Proceedings of the 13th International Conference on Human-Computer Interaction, Interacting in Various Application Domains* (pp. 378-386). IEEE.

Park, S., O'Brien, M. A., Caine, K. E., Rogers, W. A., Fisk, A. D., & Van Ittersum, K. (2006). Acceptance of computer technology: Understanding the user and organizational characteristics. In *Proceeding of the Human Factors and Ergonomics Society 50th Annual Meeting*. IEEE.

Patel, P., Ranabahu, A., & Sheth, A. (2009). Service level agreement in cloud computing. In *Proceedings of Cloud Workshops at OOPSLA*. OOPSLA.

Patterson, M. L. (1994). Strategic functions of nonverbal exchange. In Daly, J. A., & Wiemann, J. M. (Eds.), *Strategic interpersonal communication* (pp. 273–293). Hillsdale, NJ: Erlbaum.

Pavlou, P. (2003). Consumer acceptance of electronic commerce: Integrating trust and risk with the technology acceptance model. *International Journal of Electronic Commerce*, *7*(3), 101–134.

Pea, R., & Maldonado, H. (2006). WILD for learning: Interacting through new computing devices anytime, anywhere. In Sawyer, R. K. (Ed.), *The Cambridge handbook of the learning sciences* (pp. 427–441). Cambridge, UK: Cambridge University Press.

Peskin, D. (2011, September 27). *News on the go: How mobile devices are changing the world's information ecosystem.*

Peters, K. (2007). M-Learning: Positioning educators for a mobile, connected future. *International Journal of Research in Open and Distance Learning, 8*(2), 1–17.

Piaget, J. (1972). *The principles of genetic epistemology* (Mays, W., Trans.). New York: Basic Books.

Plouffe, C. R., Hulland, J., & Vandenbosch, M. (2001). Research report: Richness versus parsimony in modeling technology adoption decisions: Understanding the merchant adoption of a smart card-based payment system. *Information Systems Research, 12*(2). doi:10.1287/isre.12.2.208.9697.

Plummer, D. C., Bittman, T. J., Austin, T., Cearley, D. W., & Smith, D. M. (2008, 17 June). Cloud computing: Defining and describing an emerging phenomenon. *Gartner.*

Png, I. P. L., Tan, B. C. Y., & Khai-Ling, W. (2001). Dimensions of national culture and corporate adoption of IT infrastructure. *IEEE Transactions on Engineering Management, 48*(1), 36–45. doi:10.1109/17.913164.

Porter, C. E., & Donthu, N. (2006). Using the technology acceptance model to explain how attitudes determine Internet usage: The role of perceived access barriers and demographics. *Journal of Business Research, 59*(9), 999–1007. doi:10.1016/j.jbusres.2006.06.003.

Porter, C., Donthu, N., MacElroy, W., & Wydra, D. (2011). How to foster and sustain engagement in virtual communities. *California Management Review, 53*(4), 80–110. doi:10.1525/cmr.2011.53.4.80.

Prensky, M. (2001). *The digital game-based learning revolution.* New York: McGraw-Hill.

Proulx, S. (2007). L'usage des objets communicationnels: L'inscription dans le tissu social. *La société de la connaissance à l'ère de la vie numérique,* 104-111.

Proulx, S. (2006). *Communautés virtuelles: Ce qui fait lien* (pp. 13–26). Québec: Presses de l'Université Laval.

Purtova, N. (2010). Private law solutions in European data protection: Relationship to privacy, and waiver of data protection rights. *Netherlands Quarterly of Human Rights, 28*(2), 179–198.

Rao, B., & Minakakis, L. (2003). Evolution of mobile location-based services. *Communications of the ACM, 46*(12), 61–65. doi:10.1145/953460.953490.

Ratchford, B., Talukdar, D., & Lee, M. S. (2001). A model of consumer choice of the internet as an information source. *International Journal of Electronic Commerce, 5*(3), 7–21.

Rauch, M. (2011). *Mobile documentation: Usability guidelines, and considerations for providing documentation on Kindle, tablets, and smartphones.* Paper presented at the Professional Communication Conference (IPCC). New York, NY.

Rauhofer, J. (2008). Privacy is dead, get over it! 1 Information privacy and the dream of a risk-free society. *Information & Communications Technology Law, 17*(3), 185–197. doi:10.1080/13600830802472990.

Ravault, R. J. (1986). Défense de l'identité culturelle par les réseaux traditionnels de 'coerséduction'. *Revue Internationale de Science Politique, 7*(3), 251–280. doi: 10.1177/019251218600700304.

Ray, J.-E. (2001). *Droit du travail à l'épreuve des NTIC.* Deuxième édition, décembre, éditions Liaisons, collection Droit vivant.

Redden, J., & Witschge, T. (2010). A new news order? Online news content examined. In Fenton, N. (Ed.), *New media, old news: Journalism and democracy in the digital age.* Thousand Oaks, CA: SAGE.

Reeves, B., Lombard, M., & Melwani, G. (1992). *Faces on the screen: Pictures or natural experience?* Paper presented to the Mass Communication Division at the Annual Conference of the International Communication Association. Miami, FL.

Reichheld, F. F., & Sasser, W. E. Jr. (1990). Zero defection: Quality comes to services. *Harvard Business Review,* 105–111. PMID:10107082.

Reingen, P. H., & Kernan, J. B. (1986). Analysis of referral networks in marketing: Methods and illustration. *JMR, Journal of Marketing Research, 23,* 370–378. doi:10.2307/3151813.

Rettie, R. (2001). An exploration of flow during internet use. *Internet Research: Electronic Networking Applications and Policy, 11*(2), 103–113. doi:10.1108/10662240110695070.

Reuters. (2012, July 20). *China mobile subscribers up 1.1 percent in June to 1.05 billion*. Retrieved from http://www.reuters.com/article/2012/07/20/us-china-mobile-idUSBRE86J0D920120720

Rey, C., & Sitnikoff, F. (2006). Télétravail à domicile et nouveaux rapports au travail. *Revue Interventions économiques, 34*. Retrieved from http://interventionseconomiques.revues.org/697

Richard, M. O. (2005). Modelling the impact of Internet atmospherics on surfer behaviour. *Journal of Business Research, 58*(12), 1632–1642. doi:10.1016/j.jbusres.2004.07.009.

Rifon, N. J., Choi, S. M., Trimble, C. S., & Li, H. (2004). Congruence effects in sponsorship: The mediating role of sponsor credibility and consumer attributions of sponsor motive. *Journal of Advertising, 33*, 29–42. doi:10.1080/00913367.2004.10639151.

Riva, G., & Galimberti, C. (1998). Computer-mediated communication: Identity and social interaction in an electronic environment. *Genetic, Social, and General Psychology Monographs, 124*, 434–464.

Robertson, J. (2006). *Good search is knowledge management*. Retrieved from www.steptwo.com.au

Robison, W. (2010). Free at what cost? Cloud computing privacy under the stored communications act. *The Georgetown Law Journal, 98*(4).

Rodan, G. (1998). The internet and political control in Singapore. *Political Science Quarterly, 113*(1), 63–89. doi:10.2307/2657651.

Rogers, E. M. (1995). *The diffusion of innovations*. New York: Free Press.

Rollings, A., & Adams, E. (2003). *Andrew Rollings and Ernest Adams on game design*. New Riders Games.

Rooksby, E. (2002). *E-mail and ethics: Style and ethical relations in computer-mediated communication*. New York: Routledge. doi:10.4324/9780203217177.

Rosanvallon, J. (2006). Travail à distance et représentations du collectif de travail. *Revue Interventions économiques, 34*. Retrieved from: http://interventionseconomiques.revues.org/697

Rosenbaum, S. (2011). *Curation nation: How to win in a world where consumers are creators*. New York: McGraw-Hill.

Rose, S., Clark, M., Samouel, P., & Hair, N. (2012). Online customer experience in e-retailing: An empirical model of antecedents and outcomes. *Journal of Retailing, 88*(2), 308–322. doi:10.1016/j.jretai.2012.03.001.

Rotter, J. B., Chance, J. E., & Phares, E. J. (1972). *Applications of a social learning theory of personality*. New York: Holt, Rinehart & Winston.

Rubenfeld, J. (1989). The right of privacy. *Harvard Law Review*, 737–807. doi:10.2307/1341305.

Salovey, P., & Mayer, J. D. (1990). Emotional intelligence. *Imagination, Cognition and Personality, 9*(3), 185–211. doi:10.2190/DUGG-P24E-52WK-6CDG.

Salter, L. (2005). Colonization tendencies in the development of the world wide web. *New Media & Society, 7*(3), 291–309. doi:10.1177/1461444805050762.

Särkelä, H., Takatalo, J., May, P., Laakso, M., & Nyman, G. (2009). The movement patterns and the experiential components of virtual environments. *International Journal of Human-Computer Studies, 67*, 787–799. doi:10.1016/j.ijhcs.2009.05.003.

Sas, C., & O'Hare, G. (2003). The presence equation: An investigation into cognitive factors underlying presence. *Presence (Cambridge, Mass.), 12*(5), 523–537. doi:10.1162/105474603322761315.

Sato, K., Kato, Y., & Kato, S. (2008). Exploring emotional strategies in mobile phone email communication: Analysis on the impact of social presence. In *Proceedings of International Conference on Computers in Education (ICCE) 2008* (pp. 253-260). ICCE.

Scharl, A. (2004). *Envirnomental online communication*. London: Springer. doi:10.1007/978-1-4471-3798-6.

Scholtz, J., & Consolvo, S. (2004). Applications: Towards a framework for evaluating ubiquitous computing applications. *Pervasive Computing*, 82-88.

Schudson, M. (1989). The sociology of news production. *Media Culture & Society, 11*(3), 263–282. doi:10.1177/016344389011003002.

Schuemie, M., Straaten, V., Krijn, M. P., & Mast, C. V. (2001). Research on presence in VR: A survey. *Cyberpsychology & Behavior*, *4*(2), 183–201. doi:10.1089/109493101300117884 PMID:11710246.

Schwartz, D. G., Divitini, M., & Brasethvik, T. (2000). *Internet-based organizational memory and knowledge management*. Hershey, PA: IGI Global.

Schwartz, S., & Sagiv, L. (1995). Identifying culture-specifics in the content and structure of values. *Journal of Cross-Cultural Psychology*, *26*(1), 92–116. doi:10.1177/0022022195261007.

Scott, D. J., Coursaris, C. K., Kato, Y., & Kato, S. (2009). The exchange of emotional context in business communications: A comparison of PC and mobile email users. In Head, M. M., & Li, E. (Eds.), *Mobile and ubiquitous commerce: Advanced e-business methods* (pp. 201–219). Hershey, PA: IGI Global. doi:10.4018/978-1-60566-366-1.ch011.

Shabalina, O., Vorobkalov, P., Kataev, A., & Tarasenko, A. (2008). *Educational games for learning programming languages*. Paper presented at the Third International Conference Modern e-Learning. New York, NY.

Sharmin, M., Bailey, B. P., Coats, C., & Hamilton, K. (2009). *Understanding knowledge management practices for early design activity and its implication for reuse*. Paper presented at the CHI 2009. Boston, MA.

Shen, J. (2012). Social comparison, social presence, and enjoyment in the acceptance of social shopping websites. *Journal of Electronic Commerce Research*, *13*(3), 198–212.

Sherry, J. L. (2004). Flow and media enjoyment. *Communication Theory*, *14*(4), 328–347. doi:10.1111/j.1468-2885.2004.tb00318.x.

Shih, C. F. E. (1998). Conceptualizing consumer experiences in cyberspace. *European Journal of Marketing*, *32*(7-8), 655–663. doi:10.1108/03090569810224056.

Shih, H. P. (2004). An empirical study on predicting user acceptance of e-shopping on the web. *Information & Management*, 41.

Shin, N. (2006). Online learner's flow experience: An empirical study. *British Journal of Educational Technology*, *37*(5), 705–720. doi:10.1111/j.1467-8535.2006.00641.x.

Shklovski, I., Kiesler, S., & Kraut, R. (2006). The internet and social interaction: A meta-analysis and critique of studies 1995-2003. In Kraut, R., Malcolm, B., & Kiesler, S. (Eds.), *Computers, phones, and the internet* (pp. 251–264). Oxford, UK: Oxford University Press.

Shneiderman, B. (2002). The eyes have it: A task by data type taxonomy for information visualization. In *Proceedings IEEE Visual Languages*. Boulder, CO: IEEE.

Shneiderman, B., & Plaisant, C. (1997). *Evaluating interface designs in designing the user interface: Strategies for effective human-computer interaction* (3rd ed.). Boston, MA: Addison-Wesley Longman Publishing Co., Inc..

Shuler, C. (2009). *Pockets of potential: Using mobile technologies to promote children's learning*. New York: The Joan Ganz Cooney Center at Sesame Workshop.

Siau, K., Lim, E.-P., & Shen, Z. (2001). Mobile commerce–Promises, challenges, and research agenda. *Journal of Database Management*, *12*(3), 4–13. doi:10.4018/jdm.2001070101.

Siegel, J., Dubrovsky, V., Kiesler, S., & McGuire, T. W. (1986). Group processes in computer-mediated communication. *Organizational Behavior and Human Decision Processes*, *37*(2), 157–187. doi:10.1016/0749-5978(86)90050-6.

Siekpe, J. S. (2005). An examination of the multidimensionality of flow construct in a computer-mediated environment. *Journal of Electronic Commerce Research*, *6*(1). Retrieved February 06, 2012, from www.csulb.edu/web/journals/jecr/issues/20051/paper2.pdf

Singh, N., Xhao, H., & Hu, X. (2003). Cultural adaptation on the web: A study of American companies' domestic and Chinese websites. *Journal of Global Information Management*, *11*(3), 63. doi:10.4018/jgim.2003070104.

Siriaraya, P., & Ang, C. S. (2012). Age differences in the perception of social presence in the use of 3D virtual world for social interaction. *Interacting with Computers*, *24*, 280–291. doi:10.1016/j.intcom.2012.03.003.

Skadberg, Y. X., & Kimmel, J. R. (2004). Visitors' flow experience while browsing a web site: Its measurement, contributing factors and consequences. *Computers in Human Behavior, 20*(4), 403–422. doi:10.1016/S0747-5632(03)00050-5.

Smith, A. (2012). The best (and worst) of mobile connectivity. *Pew Internet*. Retrieved from http://pwerInternet.org/Reports/2012/Best-Worst-Mobile-Part-III/Impacts.aspx

Smith, D. N., & Sivakumar, K. (2004). Flow and internet shopping behavior: A conceptual model and research propositions. *Journal of Business Research, 1*(10), 1199–1208. doi:10.1016/S0148-2963(02)00330-2.

Song, R., Luo, Z., Wen, J.-R., Yu, Y., & Hon, H.-W. (2007). Identifying ambiguous queries in web search. In *Proceeding of WWW '07 Proceedings of the 16th International Conference on World Wide Web.* New York, NY: IEEE.

Soroka, S. (2002). Issue attributes and agenda-setting: Media, the public, and policymakers in Canada. *International Journal of Public Opinion Research, 14*(3), 264–285. doi:10.1093/ijpor/14.3.264.

Spencer, D., & Warfel, T. (2004). *Card sorting: A definitive guide*. Retrieved from http://boxesandarrows.com/card-sorting-a-definitive-guide/

Spiekermann, S., & Pallas, F. (2006). Technology paternalism–Wider implications of ubiquitous computing. *Poiesis & Praxis: International Journal of Technology Assessment and Ethics of Science, 4*(1), 6–18.

Spitulnik, D. (1993). Anthropology and mass media. *Annual Review of Anthropology, 22*, 293–315. doi:10.1146/annurev.an.22.100193.001453.

Sprott, D., Czellar, S., & Spangenberg, E. (2009). The importance of a general measure of brand engagement on market behavior: Development and validation of a scale. *JMR, Journal of Marketing Research, 46*(1), 92–104. doi:10.1509/jmkr.46.1.92.

Sproull, L., & Kiesler, S. (1991). *Connections: New ways of working in the networked organization*. Cambridge, MA: MIT Press.

Stajano, F., & Anderson, R. (2002). The resurrecting duckling: security issues for ubiquitous computing. *Computer, 35*(4), 22–26. doi:10.1109/MC.2002.1012427.

Stamato, C., & de Moraes, A. (2012). Mobile phones and elderly people: A noisy communication. Work: A Journal of Prevention. *Assessment and Rehabilitation, 41*, 320–327. doi: doi:10.3233/WOR-2012-1003-320.

Steuer, J. (1992). Defining virtual reality: dimensions determining telepresence. In Biocca, F., & Levy, M. R. (Eds.), *Communication in the age of virtual reality* (pp. 33–56). Hillsdale, NJ: Lawrence Erlbaum Associates.

Stewart, D. W., & Pavlou, P. A. (2002). From consumer response to active consumer: Measuring the effectiveness of interactive media. *Journal of the Academy of Marketing Science, 30*(376).

Straub, D. W. (1994). The effect of culture on IT diffusion: E-mail and FAX in Japan and the U.S. *Information Systems Research, 5*(1), 23–47. doi:10.1287/isre.5.1.23.

Suh, K. S., & Chang, S. (2006). User interfaces and consumer perceptions of online stores: The role of telepresence. *Behaviour & Information Technology, 25*(2), 99–113. doi:10.1080/01449290500330398.

Sundaram, D. S., Kaushik, M., & Webster, C. (1998). Word-of-mouth communications: A motivational analysis. *Advances in Consumer Research. Association for Consumer Research (U. S.), 25*(1), 527–531.

Svantesson, D., & Clarke, R. (2010). Privacy and consumer risks in cloud computing. *Computer Law & Security Report, 26*(4), 391–397. doi:10.1016/j.clsr.2010.05.005.

Takabi, H., Joshi, J. B., & Ahn, G. J. (2010). Security and privacy challenges in cloud computing environments. *IEEE Security & Privacy, 8*(6), 24–31. doi:10.1109/MSP.2010.186.

Takatalo, J., Nyman, G., & Laaksonen, L. (2008). Components of human experience in virtual environments. *Computers in Human Behavior, 24*, 1–15. doi:10.1016/j.chb.2006.11.003.

Tao, R. (2011, December 16). China's land grab is undermining grassroots democracy. *The Guardian*. Retrieved from http://www.guardian.co.uk/commentisfree/2011/dec/16/china-land-grab-undermining-democracy

Taskin, L. (2010). La déspatialisation, enjeu de gestion. *Revue Française de Gestion, 202*, 53–76.

Taylor, S., & Todd, P. A. (1995). Understanding information technology usage: A test of competing models. *Information Systems Resources, 6*(2).

Taylor, S., & Todd, P. A. (1995). Understanding information technology usage: A test of competing models. *Information Systems Research, 6*(2), 144–176. doi:10.1287/isre.6.2.144.

The New York Times Insight Group. (n.d.). *The psychology of sharing*. Retrieved from http://nytmarketing.whsites.net/mediakit/pos/

The Pew Global Attitudes Project. (2007). *Rising environmental concern in 47-nation survey*. Pew Research Center. Retrieved from http://www.pewglobal.org/files/pdf/2007%20Pew%20Global%20Attitudes%20Report%20-%20June%2027.pdf

Theofanos, M., & Scholtz, J. (2005). A framework for evaluation of ubicomp applications. In *Proceedings of CHI2005*. National Institute of Standards and Technology.

Thomas, D. (2003). *Hacker culture*. Minneapolis, MN: University of Minnesota Press.

Thompenaars, F., & Hampden-Turner, C. (1998). *Riding the waves of culture: Understanding cultural diversity in global business*. New York: McGraw-Hill.

Thompsen, P. A., & Foulger, D. A. (1996). Effects of pictographs and quoting on flaming in electronic mail. *Computers in Human Behavior, 12*(2), 225–243. doi:10.1016/0747-5632(96)00004-0.

Thomsin, L. (2002). Télétravail et mobilités. Les Ed.s de l'Université de Liège, Coll. Synopsis.

Thong, J. Y. L., Wong, W., & Tam, K. (2002). Understanding user acceptance of digital libraries: What are the roles of interface characteristics, organizational context, and individual differences? *International Journal of Human-Computer Studies, 57*, 215–242. doi:10.1016/S1071-5819(02)91024-4.

Tikkanen, H., Hietanen, J., Henttonen, T., & Rokka, J. (2009). Exploring virtual worlds: Success factors in virtual world marketing. *Management Decision, 47*(8), 1357–1381. doi:10.1108/00251740910984596.

Tilman, D., & Lehman, C. (2001). Human-caused environmental change: Impacts on plant diversity and evolution. *Proceedings of the National Academy of Sciences of the United States of America, 98*(10), 5433–5440. doi:10.1073/pnas.091093198 PMID:11344290.

Trevino, L. K., & Webster, J. (1992). Flow in computer-mediated communication. *Communication Research, 19*(5), 539–573. doi:10.1177/009365092019005001.

Triandis, H. C. (1971). Values, attitudes, and interpersonal behavior. In *Proceedings of the 1979 Nebraska Symposium on Motivation: Beliefs, attitudes and Values*. University of Nebraska Press.

Trumbo, C. (1996). Constructing climate change: Claims and frames in US news coverage of an environmental issue. *Public Understanding of Science (Bristol, England), 5*(3), 269–283. doi:10.1088/0963-6625/5/3/006.

Ulusu, Y. (2010). Determinant factors of time spent on Facebook: Brand community engagement and usages types. *Journal of Yasar University, 5*(18), 2949–2957.

Urry, J. (2007). *Mobilities*. Cambridge, UK: Polity.

Van't Hooft, M., Swan, K. Lin, Y-M., & Cook, D. (2007). What is ubiquitous computing?. *Ubiquitous Computing in Education*, 3-17.

Vaquero, L. M., Rodero-Merino, L., Caceres, J., & Lindner, M. (2008). A break in the clouds: Towards a cloud definition. *ACM SIGCOMM Computer Communication Review, 39*(1), 50–55. doi:10.1145/1496091.1496100.

Varshney, U., & Vetter, R. (2000). Emerging mobile and wireless networks. *Communications of the ACM, 43*(6), 73–81. doi:10.1145/336460.336478.

Venkatesh, V. (2000). *Determinants of perceived ease of use: Integrating control, intrinsic motivation, and emotion into the technology acceptance model*. University of Maryland. doi:10.1287/isre.11.4.342.11872.

Venkatesh, V., & Davis, F. D. (2000). A theoretical extension of the technology acceptance model: Four longitudinal field studies. *Management Science, 46*(2), 186–204. doi:10.1287/mnsc.46.2.186.11926.

Venkatesh, V., Morris, M. G., & Ackerman, P. L. (2000). A longitudinal field investigation of gender differences in individual technology adoption decision making processes. *Organizational Behavior and Human Decision Processes*, *83*(1), 33–60. doi:10.1006/obhd.2000.2896 PMID:10973782.

Venkatesh, V., Morris, M. G., Davis, G. B., & Davis, F. D. (2003). User acceptance of information technology: Toward a unified view. *Management Information Systems Quarterly*, *27*(3), 425–478.

Vernette, E., & Flores, L. (2004). Communiquez avec les leaders d'opinion en marketing: Comment et dans quels médias? *Decisions Marketing*, *35*, 23–37.

Voas, J., & Zhang, J. (2009). Cloud computing: New wine or just a new bottle? *IT Professional*, *11*(2), 15–17. doi:10.1109/MITP.2009.23.

Voorhees, E. M. (2002). *Overview of TREC*. Paper presented at The Eleventh Text Retrieval Conference. New York, NY.

Vorderer, P., Klimmt, C., & Ritterfeld, U. (2004). Enjoyment: At the heart of media entertainment. *Communication Theory*, *14*, 388–408. doi:10.1111/j.1468-2885.2004.tb00321.x.

Vygotskiĭ, L. S. (1962). *Thought and language*. Cambridge, MA: The MIT Press. doi:10.1037/11193-000.

Wakefield, K. L., & Baker, J. (1998). Excitement at the mall: Determinants and effects on shopping reponse. *Journal of Retailing*, *74*(4), 515–539. doi:10.1016/S0022-4359(99)80106-7.

Walker, G. (2005). Sociological theory and the natural environment. *History of the Human Sciences*, *18*(1), 77–106. doi:10.1177/0952695105051127.

Walker, K. (2006). Introduction: Mapping the landscape of mobile learning. In Sharples, M. (Ed.), *Big issues in mobile learning: Report of a workshop by the kaleidoscope network of excellence mobile learning initiative*. Nottingham, UK: University of Nottingham.

Wallis, M., Henskens, F., & Hannaford, M. (2011). Web 2.0 data: Decoupling ownership from provision. *International Journal on Advances in Internet Technology*, *4*(1-2), 47–59.

Wang, C. C., Yang, Y. H., & Hsu, M. C. (2013). *The recent development of flow theory research: A bibliometric study*. Paper presented at the 2013 International Conference on e-CASE & e-Tech. Kitakyushu, Japan.

Wang, J., Yang, L., Yu, M., & Wang, S. (2011). Application of server virtualization technology based on Citrix XenServer in the information center of the public security bureau and fire service department. In *Proceedings of the Computer Science and Society (ISCCS), International Symposium*. ISCCS.

Wang, X. (1995). *Learning by observation and practice: An incremental approach for planning operator acquisition*. Paper presented at the 2nd International Conference on Machine Learning. San Francisco, CA.

Wang, L. C., Baker, J., Wagner, J., & Wakefield, K. (2007). Can a retail web site be social? *Journal of Marketing*, *71*, 143–157. doi:10.1509/jmkg.71.3.143.

Wang, L. C., & Hsiao, D. F. (2012). Antecedents of an in retail store shopping. *Journal of Retailing and Consumer Services*, *19*, 381–389. doi:10.1016/j.jretconser.2012.03.002.

Wang, Q. (2010). China's environmental civilian activism. *Science*, *328*(5980), 824. doi:10.1126/science.328.5980.824-a PMID:20466902.

WARC. (2012). *Brands seeking ROI metrics for Facebook*. Retrieved August 17, 2012, from http://www.warc.com/LatestNews/News/EmailNews.news?ID=30250&Origin=WARCNewsEmail

Ward, B. T., & Sipior, J. C. (2010). The internet jurisdiction risk of cloud computing. *Information Systems Management*, *27*(4), 334–339. doi:10.1080/10580530.2010.514248.

Ward, S. (1974). Consumer socialization. *The Journal of Consumer Research*, *1*(2), 1–14. doi:10.1086/208584.

Wasko, M. M., & Faraj, S. (2005). Why should I share? Examining social capital and knowledge contribution in electronic networks of practice. *Management Information Systems Quarterly*, *29*, 35–57.

Watson, R. T., Pitt, L. F., Berthon, P., & Zinkhan, G. M. (2002). U-commerce: Expanding the universe of marketing. *Journal of the Academy of Marketing Science*, *30*(4), 333–347. doi:10.1177/009207002236909.

Webster, J., Trevino, L. K., & Ryan, L. (1993). The dimensionality and correlates of flow in human computer interactions. *Computers in Human Behavior*, *9*(4), 411–426. doi:10.1016/0747-5632(93)90032-N.

Weibel, D., Wissmath, B., Habegger, S., Steiner, Y., & Groner, R. (2008). Playing online games against computer- vs. human-controlled opponents: Effects on presence and enjoyment. *Computers in Human Behavior*, *24*, 2274–2291. doi:10.1016/j.chb.2007.11.002.

Weimann, G., Tustin, D. H., van Vuuren, D., & Joubert, J. P. R. (2007). Looking for opinion leaders: Traditional vs. modern measures in traditional societies. *International Journal of Public Opinion Research*, *19*(2), 173–190. doi:10.1093/ijpor/edm005.

Whitton, N. (2010). *Learning with digital games: A practical guide to engaging students in higher education*. New York: Routledge.

Whyte, W. H. Jr. (1954). The web of word of mouth. *Fortune*, *50*, 140–143.

Widener, P., & Gunter, V. J. (2007). Oil spill recovery in the media: Missing an Alaska native perspective. *Society & Natural Resources*, *20*, 767–783. doi:10.1080/08941920701460325.

Williamson, O. E. (1981). The economics of organization: The transaction cost approach. *American Journal of Sociology*, *87*(3), 548–577. doi:10.1086/227496.

Williamson, O. E. (1993). Calculativeness, trust, and economic organization. *The Journal of Law & Economics*, *36*(1), 453–486. doi:10.1086/467284.

Winkler, R. (2001). Portals all-in-one web supersites: Features, functions, definition. In Taxonomy (3rd ed.). SAP Design Guild.

Witmer, B. G., & Singer, M. J. (1998). Measuring presence in virtual environments: A presence questionnaire. *Presence (Cambridge, Mass.)*, *7*, 225–240. doi:10.1162/105474698565686.

Wixom, B. H., & Todd, P. A. (2005). A theoretical integration of user satisfaction and satisfaction and technology acceptance. *Information Systems Research*, *16*(1), 85–102. doi:10.1287/isre.1050.0042.

Worcester, R. M. (1994). *Sustainable development: Who cares?* London: MORI and WBMG.

Wu, J.-H., & Wang, S.-C. (2005). What drives mobile commerce? An empirical evaluation of the revised technology acceptance model. *Information & Management*, *42*(5), 719–729. doi:10.1016/j.im.2004.07.001.

Xia, L., & Sudharshan, D. (2002). Effects of interruptions on consumer online decision processes. *Journal of Consumer Psychology*, *12*(3), 265–280. doi:10.1207/S15327663JCP1203_08.

Yang, G. B. (2003). Weaving a green web: The internet and environmental activism in China. *China Environment Series*, *6*, 89–93.

Yang, K. C. C. (2005). Exploring factors affecting the adoption of mobile commerce in Singapore. *Telematics and Informatics*, *22*(3), 257–277. doi:10.1016/j.tele.2004.11.003.

Yardley, J. (2005, April 25). A hundred cellphones bloom, and Chinese take to the streets. *The New York Times*. Retrieved from http://www.nytimes.com/2005/04/25/international/asia/25china.html?_r=0

Yearley, S. (1991). *The green case*. London: Harper Collins.

Yim, M. Y., Cicchirillo, V. J., & Drumwright, M. E. (2012). The impact of stereoscopic three-dimensional (3-d) advertising: The role of presence in enhancing advertising effectiveness. *Journal of Advertising*, *41*(2), 113–112. doi:10.2753/JOA0091-3367410208.

Yoo, K.-H., & Gretzel, U. (2011). Influence of personality on travel-related consumer-generated media creation. *Computers in Human Behavior*, *27*(2), 609–621. doi:10.1016/j.chb.2010.05.002.

Yuan, Y., Archer, N., Connelly, C. E., & Zheng, W. (2010). Identifying the ideal fit between mobile work and mobile work support. *Information & Management*, *47*(3), 125–137. doi:10.1016/j.im.2009.12.004.

Zakaria, N., Melinckx, A. A., & Wilemon, D. (2004). Working together apart? Building a knowledge-sharing culture for global virtual teams. *Creativity and Innovation Management*, *13*, 15–29. doi:10.1111/j.1467-8691.2004.00290.x.

Zaphiris, P., & Ellis, R. D. (2001). Website usability and content accessibility of the top USA universities. In *Proceedings of WebNet 2001 Conference*. Orlando, FL: WebNet.

Zhang, P., Li, N., & Sun, H. (2006). Affective quality and cognitive absorption: Extending technology acceptance research. In *Proceedings of the Hawaii International Conference on System Sciences* (HICSS). IEEE.

Zhang, D., & Adipat, B. (2005). Challenges, methodologies, and issue in usability testing of mobile applications. *International Journal of Human-Computer Interaction*, *18*(3). doi:10.1207/s15327590ijhc1803_3.

Zhang, Q., Cheng, L., & Boutaba, R. (2010). Cloud computing: State-of-the-art and research challenges. *Journal of Internet Services and Applications*, *1*(1), 7–18. doi:10.1007/s13174-010-0007-6.

Zhao, M., & Dholakia, R. R. (2009). A multi-attribute model of website interactivity and customer satisfaction: An application of the Kano model. *Managing Service Quality*, *19*(3), 286–307. doi:10.1108/09604520910955311.

Zheng, W., & Yuan, Y. (2007). Identifying the differences between stationary office support and mobile work support: A conceptual framework. *International Journal of Mobile Communications*, *5*(1), 107–122. doi:10.1504/IJMC.2007.011492.

Zhu, H. J. (2007, May 31). Xiamen government announced to postpone the billions RMB PX project due to a rumor on its toxicity. *Southern Weekly*. Retrieved from http://www.suothcn.como/weekend/commend/200705310002.htm

Zinkhan, G. M., Kwak, H., Morrison, M., & Peters, C. O. (2003). Web-based chatting: Consumer communication in cyberspace. *Journal of Consumer Psychology*, *13*(1-2), 17–27. doi:10.1207/S15327663JCP13-1&2_02.

Zittrain, J. (2003). Internet points of control. In 44 B. C. L. Rev 653..

Zittrain, J. (2006). A history of online gatekeeping. *Harvard Journal of Law & Technology*, *19*, 253.

Zittrain, J. (2009). *The future of the internet--And how to stop it*. New Haven, CT: Yale University Press.

Zittrain, J., & Edelman, B. (2003). Internet filtering in China. *IEEE Internet Computing*, *7*(2), 70–77. doi:10.1109/MIC.2003.1189191.

About the Contributors

Jean-Eric Pelet holds a PhD in Marketing and an MBA in Information Systems and a BA (Hns) in Advertising. As an assistant professor in management, he works on problems concerning consumer behaviour when using a Website or other information system (e-learning, knowledge management, e-commerce platforms) and how the interface can change that behavior. His main interest lies in the variables that enhance navigation in order to help people to be more efficient with these systems. He works as a visiting professor both in France and abroad (England, Switzerland, Thaïland) teaching e-marketing, ergonomics, usability, and consumer behaviour at Design Schools (Nantes), Business Schools (Paris, Reims), and Universities (Paris Dauphine – Nantes). Dr. Pelet has also actively participated in a number of European Community and National research projects. His current research interests focus on social networks, interface design, and usability.

Panagiota Papadopoulou holds a BSc (Hons) in Informatics from the University of Athens, an MSc (Distinction) in Distributed and Multimedia Information Systems from Heriot-Watt University, and a PhD in Information Systems and E-Commerce from the University of Athens. She has extensive teaching experience at undergraduate and postgraduate courses, as an adjunct faculty member at the University of Athens, the University of Pireaus, the University of Peloponnese, the University of Central Greece, Harokopio University, and other tertiary education institutions. Dr. Papadopoulou has participated in a number of European Community and National research projects. She also serves as an external evaluator of research and development projects and proposals for public organizations. She has published more than 45 papers in international journals and conferences and authored a book for the Hellenic Open University. Her current research interests focus on online trust, e-commerce, interface design, and social computing.

* * *

Vathiswa Booi is currently a Lecturer at the Tshwane University Technology in Pretoria, South Africa. She holds a B.Tech. (Hons) degree in Information Technology and an M.Tech. degree in Information Networks. Her current research interests include Mobile & Pervasive Computing, Agent Based Models and Human Computer Interaction (HCI). Miss Booi has published a number of scholarly articles including a book chapter and many refereed conference papers.

Hara Bouta (PhD) has a long career as a classroom teacher and has an M.A. in teaching Mathematics. Her research interests are in the e-CSCL field and the implementation of 3D environments in K-12 education and her work on the use of 3D virtual environments in education has been published in journals and international conferences.

Latifa Chaari is a Contractual Assistant Professor at Manouba University, The Higher Institute of Accountancy and Entrepreneurial Administration, Department of Management in Tunisia. Ph D Student at the Higher Institute of Management of Tunis. His general interests include Information Systems, Management sciences, and Information and Communication Technologies. Dr Latifa Chaari is particularly interested in the Psychological aspects in Technology-mediated Communication.

Madhavi Chakrabarty is a user experience specialist at Verizon Wireless and an Adjunct Professor with Rutgers University. Her areas of expertise include information representation, cognitive processes in decision-making, visual problem solving, multi-modal communications, and cognitive design in human computer interaction. She received her Ph.D. (Jan 2010) in Information Systems from New Jersey Institute of Technology, Newark, NJ, and her Masters in Computer Applications from Indian Institute of Technology, New Delhi, India. Before earning her Ph.D, Madhavi worked as a IT professional for several years in varied roles as a developer, project manager, and consultant for organizations like IBM, AstraZeneca, TMI, Nuance, Avaya, and Motorola. As an independent researcher and writer, Madhavi's areas of interests include information representation, user and customer experience. She collaborates with different research and learning organizations in her research initiatives. She has publications in refereed peer reviewed journals and books and numerous conference presentations. Madhavi works with school and college level students in helping them understand concepts of problem solving, improvisation, and creative solutions. She currently serves as a Parent Coach for a group of elementary school students in "Odyssey of the Mind Experience."

Kunihiro Chida is a professional Japanese animation artist in Toei Animation Institute. His main work is many background pictures for internationally-renowned animations, "One Piece," "Dragon Ball," "Dr. Slump," and so on. His general research interests are applications to computer-mediated communications of "Image BG," a technique for expressing the emotional states of animated characters in background images.

George Ditsa is currently an Associate Professor at the Tshwane University Technology in Pretoria, South Africa. He holds a B.Sc. (Hons) degree in Computer Science, an MBA (IS), and PhD (IS) degrees. Dr. Ditsa worked for many years as a programmer/analyst and project team leader in various organizations before joining the academia. Dr. Ditsa currently lectures and researches in Information Systems (IS) and related disciplines. Dr. Ditsa has won a number of research grants and awards. His current research interests include Strategic IS Management, IS Project Management, Cultural Issues in IS management, Knowledge Management & Knowledge Management Systems, Mobile & Pervasive Computing, ICT for Development and Human Computer Interaction (HCI). Dr. Ditsa has supervised a number of postgraduate students in his research interest areas. Dr. is currently an Associated Editor of two journals and he is on the editorial review board of five journals. He also serves as an External Theses Examiner for some universities. Dr. Ditsa has published a number of scholarly articles including a book, book chapters, journal papers, and many refereed conference papers.

Saïd Ettis is an Assistant Professor at the University of Gabes, Higher Institute of Management (ISG), Gabes, Tunisia. He holds the Ph.D from Higher Institute of Economics and Management – IAE (IEMN-IAE), University of Nantes, France. He teaches Marketing, E-marketing, Market Research, and Management. His research interests are related to consumer behavior and Human-Computer Interactions.

Valérie Fernandez is Professor in Management Sciences at Telecom Paristech, LTCI – CNRS laboratory. She holds a PhD in Management Sciences and a qualification for PhD supervisor. She is project leader of international and national research programs (PCRD European programs, FUI Programs, CNRS, French-China collaboration programs, ...) and Head of Advanced Master's Program in Management of Technical Project with ESSEC Business School.

Primavera De Filippi is a researcher at the CERSA / CNRS / Université Paris II, where she is currently working on the legal implications of cloud computing and peer-to-peer technologies. She holds a PhD from the European University Institute in Florence, where she explored the legal challenges of copyright law in the digital environment. Primavera is also an administrator of the Communia association for the public domain, a coordinator at the Open Knowldege Foundation and legal expert for Creative Commons in France.

Shang Gao is Associate Professor at school of business administration at the Zhongnan University of Economics and Law, China. He obtained his PhD (2011) in information systems from the Norwegian University of Science and Technology (NTNU), and his MSc (2006) in Engineering and Management of Information Systems from the Royal Institute of Technology (KTH), Sweden. His research interests include mobile information systems, technology diffusion, and information systems modeling. He has published more than 20 refereed papers in journals, books, and archival proceedings since 2006.

Marie Haikel-Elsabeh is a researcher on social networks and PhD candidate in management. Her areas of interest are the study of motivations to share, the comprehension of information sharing, on social networks. She is also very active on social networks like Twitter and goes under the name @ Ghostbusterint.

Anna Kasimati is an e-business and e-learning researcher. Anna is currently a Research Associate at the ISTLab Wireless Research Center of the Athens University of Economics and Business. She holds a BSc in Management Science and Technology from the Athens University of Economics and Business, and an MSc in 'Technology Education & Digital Systems' specializing in e-learning, at the University of Piraeus. Her research interests focus in the integration of advance/mobile technologies and digital games in business and learning processes. Anna has successfully implemented a number of projects in the fields Technology Enhanced Learning and has acted as a reviewer for international conferences as well as edited books in the fields of electronic/ubiquitous business and technology enhanced learning. More information can be found at www.annakasimati.gr.

Shogo Kato is an Associate Professor in the School of Arts and Sciences, Tokyo Woman's Christian University in Japan, and a part-time instructor in the Faculty of Economics, Dokkyo University in Japan. He earned a Ph.D. from Tokyo Institute of Technology in 2005. His general research interests include educational technology, the application of behavior science, psychology, and Information and Communication Technology (ICT) to educational scenes. Dr. Kato is particularly interested in the emotional aspects in virtual community, such as Internet bullying.

Yuuki Kato is an Assistant Professor at Sagami Women's University, Faculty of Arts and Sciences, Department of Information and Media Studies in Japan. He earned a Ph.D. from Tokyo Institute of Technology in 2005. His general research interests include educational technology, the application of behavior science, psychology, and Information and Communication Technology (ICT) to educational scenes. Dr. Kato is particularly interested in the emotional aspects in technology-mediated human communications.

Laurie Marrauld is postdoctoral in Management Sciences at the CNRS Institute Mines-Telecom ParisTech, under the supervision of Valerie Fernandez. She is interested in topics related to "mobility equipped" and to emerging realities and interactions mediated by mobile ICT. Her doctoral thesis was about a research project on the development of a virtual platform of teleworking. She works on developing features to use teleworking platforms, particularly through the study of social media in business companies.

Sofia Mysirlaki is a PhD candidate in the Department of Digital Systems of University of Piraeus (Greece), in the research Area of Technology-Enhanced Learning. She holds a Master of Science (Msc) in E-learning. Her research interests include Multi User Virtual Environments (MUVEs) and Game-Based Learning (GBL), and her work on the use of digital games in education has been published in journals and international conferences. She has many years of experience in teaching and has been involved in the design and development of technology enhanced learning systems in various R & D Projects as an e-learning expert.

Fotini Paraskeva is an Assistant Professor at the Department of Digital Systems, of the University of Piraeus (Greece). She holds a Bachelor degree in Education from National and Kapodistrian University of Athens (NKUoA), Greece. She obtained her Ph.D. in Educational Psychology from NKUoA in the domain of Learning with Technology. Her research interest is broadly of study learning with media and ICT in educational settings, with particular emphasis on cognitive, emotional, and social aspects of learning. Her current work also involves specific applied research design of the use of ICT in rich training and work environments, such as professional development in IT context, based on quantitative and qualitative methodologies.

Yuanxin Wang is a doctoral student in School of Media and Communication of Temple University, USA. She holds a Master of Philosophy degree in Communication from Hong Kong Baptist University, Hong Kong, and a Master of Arts in International Journalism from University of Central Lancashire, UK. Her research interests include new media studies, environmental communication, intercultural communication, and media effects. Currently, she is interested in investigating the Internet users' behavior using advanced online data analysis techniques.

Index